Service and Repair Manual for BMW 5-Series

Martynn Randall

Models covered *(4151 - 272 - 8AX1)*

BMW 5-Series (E39) models with 6-cylinder petrol engines
520i, 523i, 525i, 528i & 530i Saloon & Estate (Touring)
2.0 litre (1991cc), 2.2 litre (2171cc), 2.5 litre (2494cc), 2.8 litre (2793cc) & 3.0 litre (2979cc) 6-cylinder petrol

Does NOT cover 535i, 540i or M5 with V8 petrol engines, or Diesel models
Does NOT cover new 5-Series range introduced September 2003

ABCDE
FGH

A book in the **Haynes Service and Repair Manual Series**

ISBN **978 1 78521 045 7**

British Library Cataloguing in Publication Data
A catalogue record for this book is available from the British Library.

Printed in Malaysia

Haynes Publishing
Sparkford, Yeovil, Somerset BA22 7JJ, England

Haynes North America, Inc
859 Lawrence Drive, Newbury Park, California 91320, USA

Printed using NORBRITE BOOK 48.8gsm (CODE: 40N6533) from NORPAC; procurement system certified under Sustainable Forestry Initiative standard. Paper produced is certified to the SFI Certified Fiber Sourcing Standard (CERT - 0094271)

Contents

LIVING WITH YOUR BMW

Contents

Advanced driving

Many people see the words 'advanced driving' and believe that it won't interest them or that it is a style of driving beyond their own abilities. Nothing could be further from the truth. Advanced driving is straightforward safe, sensible driving - the sort of driving we should all do every time we get behind the wheel.

An average of 10 people are killed every day on UK roads and 870 more are injured, some seriously. Lives are ruined daily, usually because somebody did something stupid. Something like 95% of all accidents are due to human error, mostly driver failure. Sometimes we make genuine mistakes - everyone does. Sometimes we have lapses of concentration. Sometimes we deliberately take risks.

For many people, the process of 'learning to drive' doesn't go much further than learning how to pass the driving test because of a common belief that good drivers are made by 'experience'.

Learning to drive by 'experience' teaches three driving skills:

- ☐ Quick reactions. (Whoops, that was close!)
- ☐ Good handling skills. (Horn, swerve, brake, horn).
- ☐ Reliance on vehicle technology. (Great stuff this ABS, stop in no distance even in the wet...)

Drivers whose skills are 'experience based' generally have a lot of near misses and the odd accident. The results can be seen every day in our courts and our hospital casualty departments.

Advanced drivers have learnt to control the risks by controlling the position and speed of their vehicle. They avoid accidents and near misses, even if the drivers around them make mistakes.

The key skills of advanced driving are **concentration,** effective all-round **observation, anticipation** and **planning.** When **good vehicle handling** is added to these skills, all driving situations can be approached and negotiated in a safe, methodical way, leaving nothing to chance.

Concentration means applying your mind to safe driving, completely excluding anything that's not relevant. Driving is usually the most dangerous activity that most of us undertake in our daily routines. It deserves our full attention.

Observation means not just looking, but seeing and seeking out the information found in the driving environment.

Anticipation means asking yourself what is happening, what you can reasonably expect to happen and what could happen unexpectedly. (One of the commonest words used in compiling accident reports is 'suddenly'.)

Planning is the link between seeing something and taking the appropriate action. For many drivers, planning is the missing link.

If you want to become a safer and more skilful driver and you want to enjoy your driving more, contact the Institute of Advanced Motorists at www.iam.org.uk, phone 0208 996 9600, or write to IAM House, 510 Chiswick High Road, London W4 5RG for an information pack.

Working on your car can be dangerous. This page shows just some of the potential risks and hazards, with the aim of creating a safety-conscious attitude.

General hazards

Scalding

• Don't remove the radiator or expansion tank cap while the engine is hot.
• Engine oil, automatic transmission fluid or power steering fluid may also be dangerously hot if the engine has recently been running.

Burning

• Beware of burns from the exhaust system and from any part of the engine. Brake discs and drums can also be extremely hot immediately after use.

Crushing

• When working under or near a raised vehicle, always supplement the jack with axle stands, or use drive-on ramps. ***Never venture under a car which is only supported by a jack.***

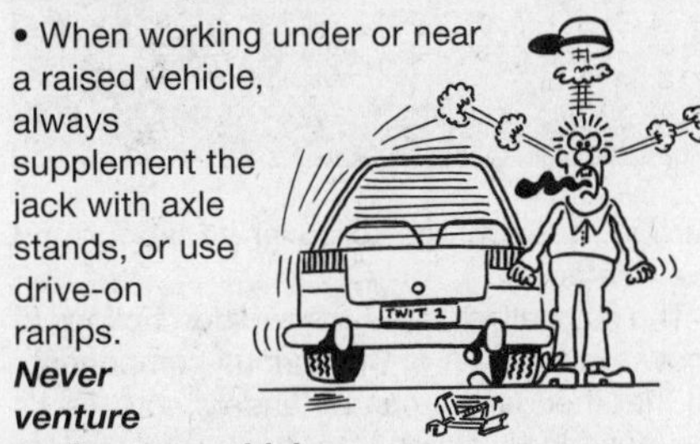

• Take care if loosening or tightening high-torque nuts when the vehicle is on stands. Initial loosening and final tightening should be done with the wheels on the ground.

Fire

• Fuel is highly flammable; fuel vapour is explosive.
• Don't let fuel spill onto a hot engine.
• Do not smoke or allow naked lights (including pilot lights) anywhere near a vehicle being worked on. Also beware of creating sparks (electrically or by use of tools).
• Fuel vapour is heavier than air, so don't work on the fuel system with the vehicle over an inspection pit.
• Another cause of fire is an electrical overload or short-circuit. Take care when repairing or modifying the vehicle wiring.
• Keep a fire extinguisher handy, of a type suitable for use on fuel and electrical fires.

Electric shock

• Ignition HT voltage can be dangerous, especially to people with heart problems or a pacemaker. Don't work on or near the ignition system with the engine running or the ignition switched on.

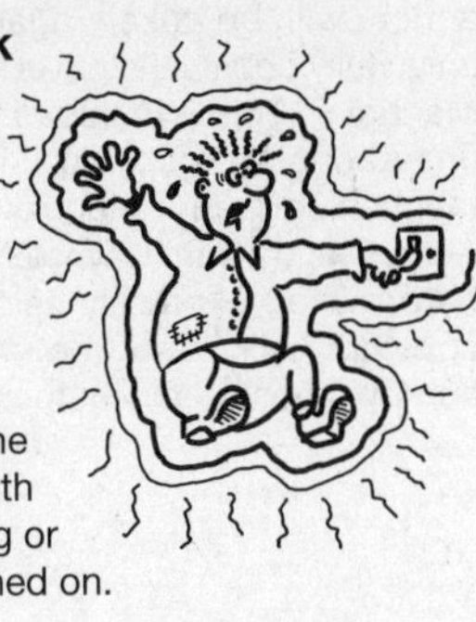

• Mains voltage is also dangerous. Make sure that any mains-operated equipment is correctly earthed. Mains power points should be protected by a residual current device (RCD) circuit breaker.

Fume or gas intoxication

• Exhaust fumes are poisonous; they often contain carbon monoxide, which is rapidly fatal if inhaled. Never run the engine in a confined space such as a garage with the doors shut.

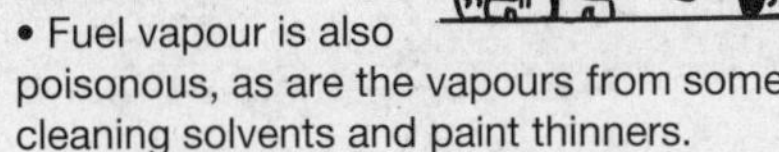

• Fuel vapour is also poisonous, as are the vapours from some cleaning solvents and paint thinners.

Poisonous or irritant substances

• Avoid skin contact with battery acid and with any fuel, fluid or lubricant, especially antifreeze, brake hydraulic fluid and Diesel fuel. Don't syphon them by mouth. If such a substance is swallowed or gets into the eyes, seek medical advice.
• Prolonged contact with used engine oil can cause skin cancer. Wear gloves or use a barrier cream if necessary. Change out of oil-soaked clothes and do not keep oily rags in your pocket.
• Air conditioning refrigerant forms a poisonous gas if exposed to a naked flame (including a cigarette). It can also cause skin burns on contact.

Asbestos

• Asbestos dust can cause cancer if inhaled or swallowed. Asbestos may be found in gaskets and in brake and clutch linings. When dealing with such components it is safest to assume that they contain asbestos.

Special hazards

Hydrofluoric acid

• This extremely corrosive acid is formed when certain types of synthetic rubber, found in some O-rings, oil seals, fuel hoses etc, are exposed to temperatures above 400°C. The rubber changes into a charred or sticky substance containing the acid. *Once formed, the acid remains dangerous for years. If it gets onto the skin, it may be necessary to amputate the limb concerned.*
• When dealing with a vehicle which has suffered a fire, or with components salvaged from such a vehicle, wear protective gloves and discard them after use.

The battery

• Batteries contain sulphuric acid, which attacks clothing, eyes and skin. Take care when topping-up or carrying the battery.
• The hydrogen gas given off by the battery is highly explosive. Never cause a spark or allow a naked light nearby. Be careful when connecting and disconnecting battery chargers or jump leads.

Air bags

• Air bags can cause injury if they go off accidentally. Take care when removing the steering wheel and/or facia. Special storage instructions may apply.

Diesel injection equipment

• Diesel injection pumps supply fuel at very high pressure. Take care when working on the fuel injectors and fuel pipes.

⚠ ***Warning: Never expose the hands, face or any other part of the body to injector spray; the fuel can penetrate the skin with potentially fatal results.***

Remember...

DO

• Do use eye protection when using power tools, and when working under the vehicle.

• Do wear gloves or use barrier cream to protect your hands when necessary.

• Do get someone to check periodically that all is well when working alone on the vehicle.

• Do keep loose clothing and long hair well out of the way of moving mechanical parts.

• Do remove rings, wristwatch etc, before working on the vehicle – especially the electrical system.

• Do ensure that any lifting or jacking equipment has a safe working load rating adequate for the job.

DON'T

• Don't attempt to lift a heavy component which may be beyond your capability – get assistance.

• Don't rush to finish a job, or take unverified short cuts.

• Don't use ill-fitting tools which may slip and cause injury.

• Don't leave tools or parts lying around where someone can trip over them. Mop up oil and fuel spills at once.

• Don't allow children or pets to play in or near a vehicle being worked on.

The new BMW 5-Series was introduced in April 1996 and was originally available with a choice of 2.0 litre (1991cc), 2.5 litre (2494cc) and 2.8 litre (2793cc) DOHC 24V engines. In September 2000 the range was 'facelifted' with minor cosmetic revisions, and the engine range was extended to include 2.2 litre (2171cc) and 3.0 litre (2979cc). At first, models were available in four-door Saloon form only, but later Touring estate models became available.

All engines are derived from the well-proven engines which have appeared in many BMW vehicles. The engines covered by this manual are of six-cylinder double-overhead camshaft design, mounted longitudinally with the transmission mounted on its rear. Both manual and automatic transmissions are available.

All models have fully-independent front and rear suspension, manufactured almost entirely from aluminium.

A wide range of standard and optional equipment is available within the BMW 5-Series range to suit most tastes, including central locking, electric windows, air conditioning, an electric sunroof, an anti-lock braking system, a traction control system, a dynamic stability control system, and numerous airbags.

Provided that regular servicing is carried out in accordance with the manufacturer's recommendations, the BMW should prove reliable and very economical. The engine compartment is well-designed, and most of the items requiring frequent attention are easily accessible.

Your BMW 5-Series manual

The aim of this manual is to help you get the best value from your vehicle. It can do so in several ways. It can help you decide what work must be done (even should you choose to get it done by a garage). It will also provide information on routine maintenance and servicing, and give a logical course of action and diagnosis when random faults occur. However, it is hoped that you will use the manual by tackling the work yourself. On simpler jobs it may even be quicker than booking the car into a garage and going there twice, to leave and collect it. Perhaps most important, a lot of money can be saved by avoiding the costs a garage must charge to cover its labour and overheads.

The manual has drawings and descriptions to show the function of the various components so that their layout can be understood. Tasks are described and photographed in a clear step-by-step sequence.

References to the 'left' and 'right' of the vehicle are in the sense of a person in the driver's seat facing forward.

Acknowledgements

Thanks are due to Draper Tools Limited, who provided some of the workshop tools, and to all those people at Sparkford who helped in the production of this manual.

We take great pride in the accuracy of information given in this manual, but vehicle manufacturers make alterations and design changes during the production run of a particular vehicle of which they do not inform us. No liability can be accepted by the authors or publishers for loss, damage or injury caused by any errors in, or omissions from, the information given.

Illegal copying

The following pages are intended to help in dealing with common roadside emergencies and breakdowns. You will find more detailed fault finding information at the back of the manual, and repair information in the main chapters.

If your car won't start and the starter motor doesn't turn

- ☐ If it's a model with automatic transmission, make sure the selector is in P or N.
- ☐ Open the right-hand storage tray in the luggage compartment and make sure that the battery terminals are clean and tight.
- ☐ Switch on the headlights and try to start the engine. If the headlights go very dim when you're trying to start, the battery is probably flat. Get out of trouble by jump starting (see next page) using a friend's car.

If your car won't start even though the starter motor turns as normal

- ☐ Is there fuel in the tank?
- ☐ Is there moisture on electrical components under the bonnet? Switch off the ignition, then wipe off any obvious dampness with a dry cloth. Spray a water-repellent aerosol product (WD-40 or equivalent) on ignition and fuel system electrical connectors like those shown in the photos.

A Check the security of the ignition coil harness connector.

B Check the airflow meter wiring connector with the ignition switched off.

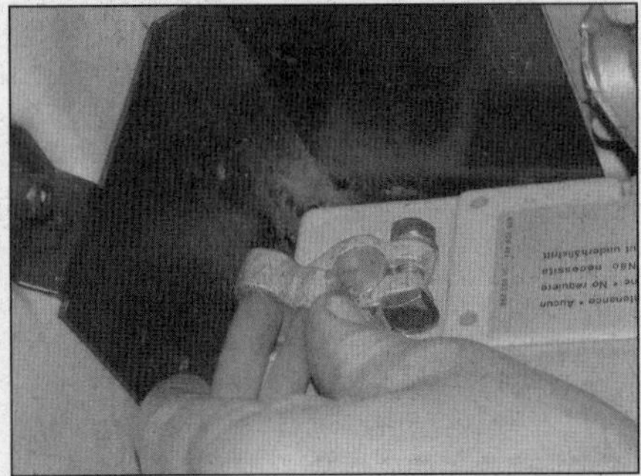

C Check the security and condition of the battery terminals (located in the luggage compartment).

Check that electrical connections are secure (with the ignition switched off) and spray them with a water dispersant spray like WD40 if you suspect a problem due to damp.

Jump starting

When jump-starting a car using a booster battery, observe the following precautions:

- ✔ Before connecting the booster battery, make sure that the ignition is switched off.
- ✔ Ensure that all electrical equipment (lights, heater, wipers, etc) is switched off.
- ✔ Take note of any special precautions printed on the battery case.
- ✔ Make sure that the booster battery is the same voltage as the discharged one in the vehicle.
- ✔ If the battery is being jump-started from the battery in another vehicle, the two vehicles MUST NOT TOUCH each other.
- ✔ Make sure that the transmission is in neutral (or PARK, in the case of automatic transmission).

Jump starting will get you out of trouble, but you must correct whatever made the battery go flat in the first place. There are three possibilities:

1 The battery has been drained by repeated attempts to start, or by leaving the lights on.

2 The charging system is not working properly (alternator drivebelt slack or broken, alternator wiring fault or alternator itself faulty).

3 The battery itself is at fault (electrolyte low, or battery worn out).

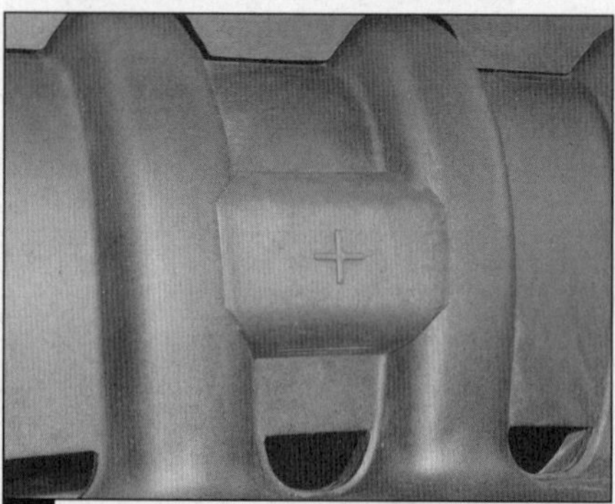

1 Unclip the plastic cover from the jump-start terminal (+) on the top of the inlet manifold, and connect the red jump lead to the terminal.

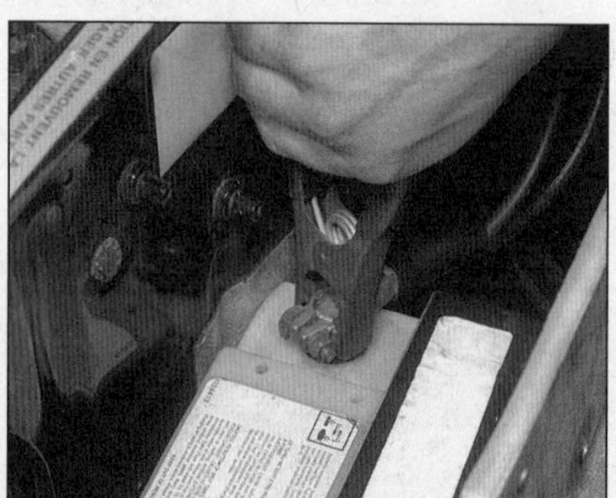

2 Connect the other end of the red lead to the positive (+) terminal of the booster battery.

3 Connect one end of the black jump lead to the negative (-) terminal of the booster battery.

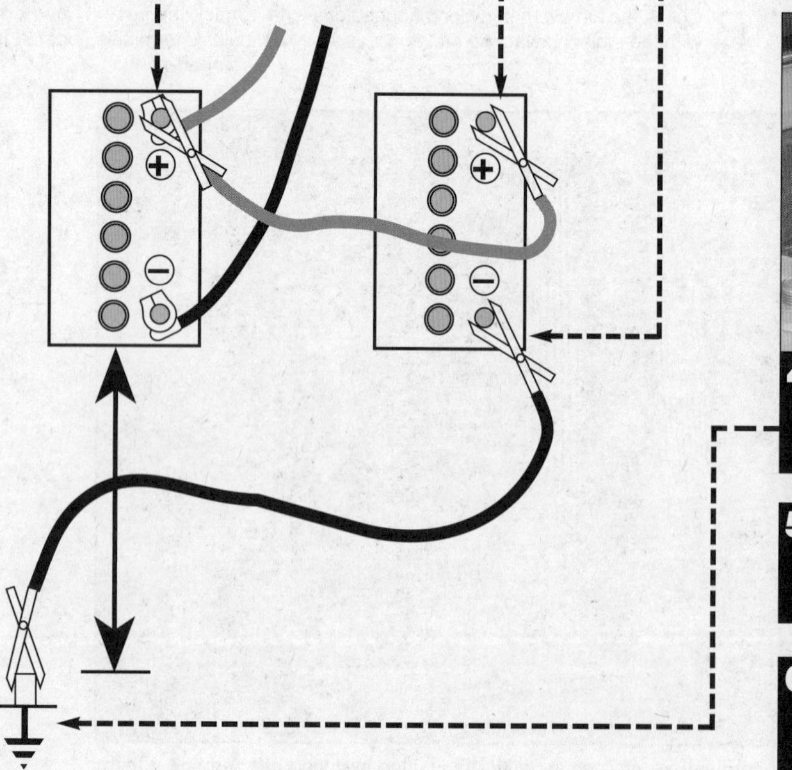

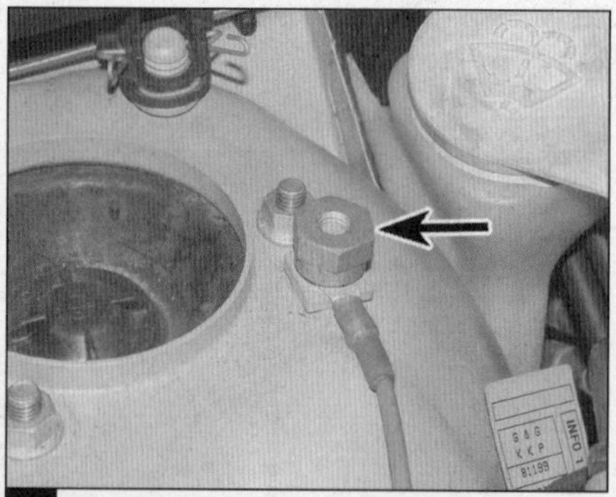

4 Connect the other end of the black jump lead to jump start negative terminal located on the right-hand suspension turret in the engine compartment.

5 Make sure that the jump leads will not come into contact with the cooling fan drivebelts or other moving parts on the engine.

6 Start the engine, then with the engine running at fast idle speed, disconnect the jump leads in the reverse order of connection, ie, negative (black) lead first. Securely refit the plastic cover to the jump start positive terminal.

Wheel changing

Warning: Do not change a wheel in a situation where you risk being hit by another vehicle. On busy roads, try to stop in a lay-by or a gateway. Be wary of passing traffic while changing the wheel – it is easy to become distracted by the job in hand.

Preparation

- ☐ When a puncture occurs, stop as soon as it is safe to do so.
- ☐ Park on firm level ground, if possible, and well out of the way of other traffic.
- ☐ Use hazard warning lights if necessary.
- ☐ If you have one, use a warning triangle to alert other drivers of your presence.
- ☐ Apply the handbrake and engage first or reverse gear (or Park on models with automatic transmission).
- ☐ Chock the wheel diagonally opposite the one being removed – a chock is located beneath the jack under the luggage compartment lid.
- ☐ If the ground is soft, use a flat piece of wood to spread the load under the foot of the jack.

The spare wheel is stored in the floor of the luggage compartment. The tools are also stored in the luggage compartment floor on Touring models, and to the underside of the boot lid on Saloon models.

Changing the wheel

1 On all models, lift the luggage compartment floor and the cover over the spare wheel. Undo the wingnuts (arrowed) and remove the jack and wheel chock.

2 Place the chock behind or in front (as applicable) of the wheel diagonally opposite to the one to be removed.

3 Undo the wing nut and lift the spare wheel from the luggage compartment.

4 Remove the wheelbrace from the boot lid (Saloon) or floor (Touring).

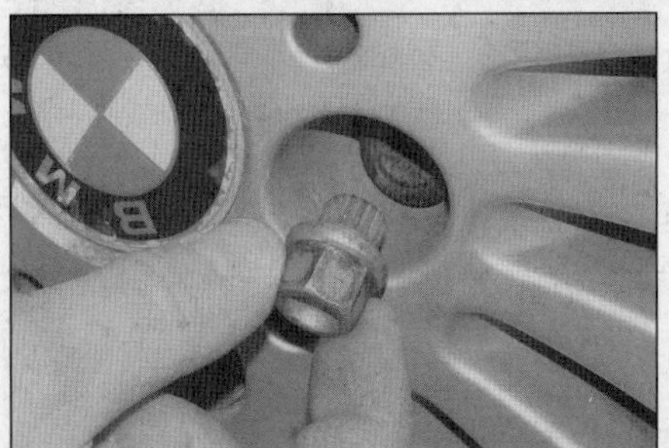

5 Pulling by hand or using a screwdriver, remove the wheel trim/hub cap (as applicable) then slacken each wheel bolt by a half turn. If anti-theft wheel bolts are fitted, pull the plastic cover from the bolt, then slacken them using the adapter supplied in the tool kit.

6 Locate the jack head under the jacking point nearest to the wheel that is to be removed. As the jack is raised, the head must enter the rectangular recess in the jacking point.

7 Make sure the jack is located on firm ground then turn the jack handle clockwise until the wheel is raised clear of the ground. Unscrew the wheel bolts and remove the wheel. Fit the spare wheel and screw in the wheel bolts. Lightly tighten the bolts with the wheelbrace then lower the vehicle to the ground.

8 Securely tighten the wheel bolts in the sequence shown then refit the wheel trim/hub cap (as applicable). Stow the punctured wheel and tools back in the luggage compartment and secure them in position. Note that the wheel bolts should be slackened and retightened to the specified torque at the earliest possible opportunity.

Finally...

- ☐ Remove the wheel chocks.
- ☐ Stow the jack, chock and tools in the correct locations in the car.
- ☐ Check the tyre pressure on the wheel just fitted. If it is low, or if you don't have a pressure gauge with you, drive slowly to the next garage and inflate the tyre to the correct pressure.
- ☐ Have the damaged tyre or wheel repaired as soon as possible, or another puncture will leave you stranded.

Identifying leaks

Puddles on the garage floor or drive, or obvious wetness under the bonnet or underneath the car, suggest a leak that needs investigating. It can sometimes be difficult to decide where the leak is coming from, especially if the engine bay is very dirty already. Leaking oil or fluid can also be blown rearwards by the passage of air under the car, giving a false impression of where the problem lies.

Warning: Most automotive oils and fluids are poisonous. Wash them off skin, and change out of contaminated clothing, without delay.

The smell of a fluid leaking from the car may provide a clue to what's leaking. Some fluids are distinctively coloured. It may help to clean the car carefully and to park it over some clean paper overnight as an aid to locating the source of the leak. Remember that some leaks may only occur while the engine is running.

Sump oil

Engine oil may leak from the drain plug...

Oil from filter

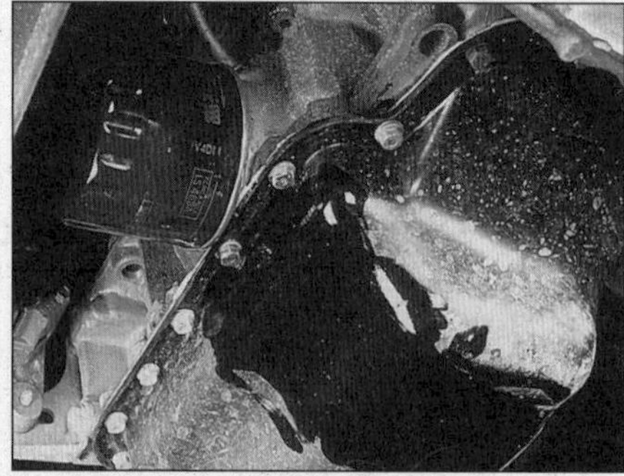

...or from the base of the oil filter.

Gearbox oil

Gearbox oil can leak from the seals at the inboard ends of the driveshafts.

Antifreeze

Leaking antifreeze often leaves a crystalline deposit like this.

Brake fluid

A leak occurring at a wheel is almost certainly brake fluid.

Power steering fluid

Power steering fluid may leak from the pipe connectors on the steering rack.

Towing

When all else fails, you may find yourself having to get a tow home – or of course you may be helping somebody else. Long-distance recovery should only be done by a garage or breakdown service. For shorter distances, DIY towing using another car is easy enough, but observe the following points:

☐ Use a proper tow-rope – they are not expensive. The vehicle being towed must display an ON TOW sign in its rear window.

☐ Always turn the ignition key to the 'on' position when the vehicle is being towed, so that the steering lock is released, and that the direction indicator and brake lights work.

☐ Only attach the tow-rope to the towing eyes provided. The towing eye is supplied as part of the tool kit which is fitted under the luggage compartment lid or floor. To fit the eye, press the arrow symbol and swing out the access cover from the front/rear bumper (as applicable). Screw the eye into position and tighten it securely.

☐ Before being towed, release the handbrake and select neutral on the transmission. On models with automatic transmission, set the selector lever to position N. Maximum towing speed is 43 mph, and maximum distance is 90 miles.

☐ Note that greater-than-usual pedal pressure will be required to operate the brakes, since the vacuum servo unit is only operational with the engine running.

☐ Greater-than-usual steering effort will be required.

☐ The driver of the car being towed must keep the tow-rope taut at all times to avoid snatching.

☐ Make sure that both drivers know the route before setting off.

☐ Only drive at moderate speeds and keep the distance towed to a minimum. Drive smoothly and allow plenty of time for slowing down at junctions.

Introduction

There are some very simple checks which need only take a few minutes to carry out, but which could save you a lot of inconvenience and expense.

These *Weekly checks* require no great skill or special tools, and the small amount of time they take to Keeping an eye on tyre condition and pressures, will not only help to stop them wearing out prematurely, but could also save your life.

☐ Many breakdowns are caused by electrical problems. Battery-related faults are particularly common, and a quick check on a regular basis will often prevent the majority of these.

☐ If your car develops a brake fluid leak, the first time you might know about it is when your brakes don't work properly. Checking the level regularly will give advance warning of this kind of problem.

☐ If the oil or coolant levels run low, the cost of repairing any engine damage will be far greater than fixing the leak, for example.

Underbonnet check points

◀ **2.0 litre M52 engine**

A *Engine oil level dipstick*
B *Engine oil filler cap*
C *Coolant expansion tank*
D *Brake and clutch fluid reservoir (under the pollen filter housing)*
E *Screen washer fluid reservoir*

◀ **2.5 litre M54 engine**

A *Engine oil level dipstick*
B *Engine oil filler cap*
C *Coolant expansion tank*
D *Brake and clutch fluid reservoir*
E *Screen washer fluid reservoir*

Engine oil level

Before you start

✔ Make sure that your car is on level ground.
✔ Check the oil level before the car is driven, or at least 5 minutes after the engine has been switched off.

If the oil is checked immediately after driving the vehicle, some of the oil will remain in the upper engine components, resulting in an inaccurate reading on the dipstick.

The correct oil

Modern engines place great demands on their oil. It is very important that the correct oil for your car is used (See *Lubricants and fluids*).

Car Care

- If you have to add oil frequently, you should check whether you have any oil leaks. Place some clean paper under the car overnight, and check for stains in the morning. If there are no leaks, the engine may be burning oil, or the oil may only be leaking when the engine is running.

- Always maintain the level between the upper and lower dipstick marks (see photo 3). If the level is too low severe engine damage may occur. Oil seal failure may result if the engine is overfilled by adding too much oil.

1 The dipstick top is often brightly coloured for easy identification (see *Underbonnet check points* for exact location). Withdraw the dipstick.

2 Using a clean rag or paper towel remove all oil from the dipstick. Insert the clean dipstick into the tube as far as it will go, then withdraw it again.

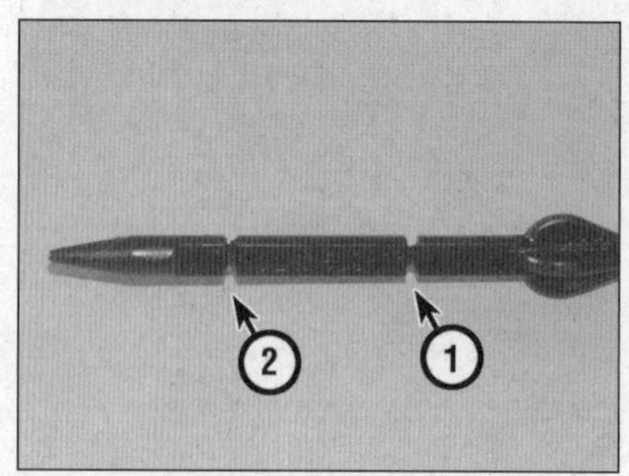

3 Note the oil level on the end of the dipstick, which should be between the upper maximum mark (1) and lower minimum mark (2). Approximately 1.0 litre of oil will raise the level from the lower mark to the upper mark.

4 Oil is added through the filler cap. Unscrew the cap and top-up the level; a funnel may help to reduce spillage. Add the oil slowly, checking the level on the dipstick often. Don't overfill (see *Car Care*).

Power steering fluid level

Before you start

✔ Park the vehicle on level ground.
✔ Set the steering wheel straight-ahead. For the check to be accurate, the steering must not be turned while the level is being checked.
✔ The engine should be turned off.

Safety First!

- The need for frequent topping-up indicates a leak, which should be investigated immediately.

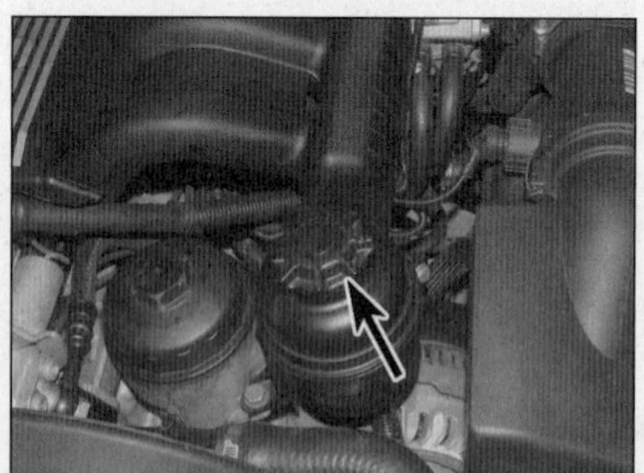

1 The reservoir is located near the front of the engine compartment. Wipe clean the area around the reservoir filler neck and unscrew the filler cap/dipstick from the reservoir.

2 Insert the dipstick into the reservoir (without screwing on the cap), then remove it. The fluid level should be between MIN and MAX.

3 When topping-up, use the specified type of fluid and do not overfill the reservoir. When the level is correct, securely refit the cap.

Coolant level

Warning: DO NOT attempt to remove the expansion tank pressure cap when the engine is hot, as there is a very great risk of scalding. Do not leave open containers of coolant about, as it is poisonous.

Car Care

- With a sealed-type cooling system, adding coolant should not be necessary on a regular basis. If frequent topping-up is required, it is likely there is a leak. Check the radiator, all hoses and joint faces for signs of staining or wetness, and rectify as necessary.

- It is important that antifreeze is used in the cooling system all year round, not just during the winter months. Don't top-up with water alone, as the antifreeze will become too diluted.

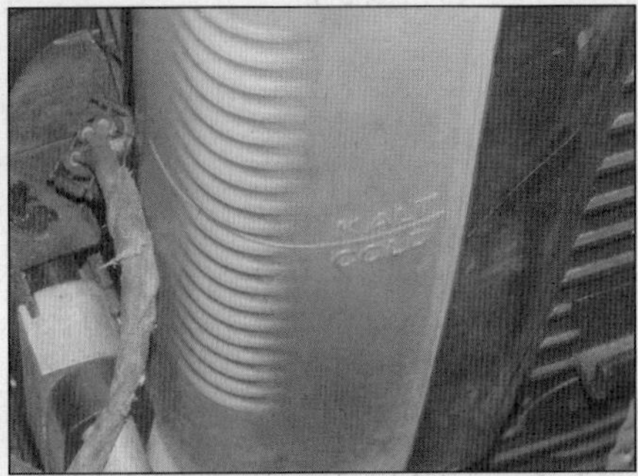

1 One some models, the translucent coolant expansion tank incorporated into the left-hand side of the radiator, is marked with the correct level when the coolant is cold (20°C).

2 One other models, the coolant expansion tank incorporates a float device which indicates the level of coolant. When the upper end of the float protrudes no more than 20 mm above the filler neck, the level is correct. See the information adjacent to the filler neck.

3 If topping-up is necessary, **wait until the engine is cold**. Slowly unscrew the expansion tank cap, to release any pressure present in the cooling system, and remove it.

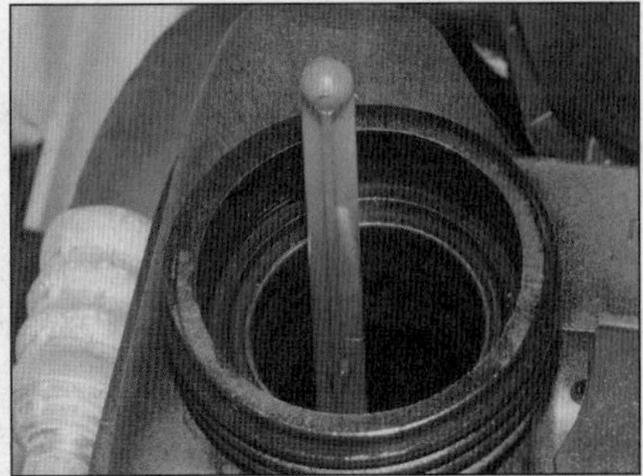

4 Add a mixture of water and antifreeze to the expansion tank until the level of the coolant is just below the 'Kalt/Cold' mark on the expansion tank, or until the top of the indicator float protrudes no more than 20 mm above the filler neck. Refit the cap and tighten it securely.

Screen washer fluid level*

**On models with a headlight washer system, the screen wash is also used to clean the headlights.*

Screenwash additives not only keep the windscreen clean during foul weather, they also prevent the washer system freezing in cold weather – which is when you are likely to need it most. Don't top-up using plain water as the screenwash will become too diluted, and will freeze during cold weather.

Caution: On no account use coolant antifreeze in the washer system – this could discolour or damage paintwork.

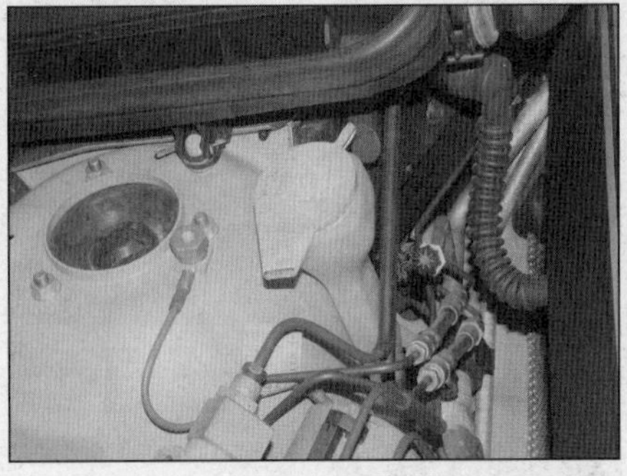

1 The screen washer fluid reservoir is located in the front right-hand corner of the engine compartment. The level is indicated by a 'check-tube' located in front of the right-hand suspension tower in the engine compartment.

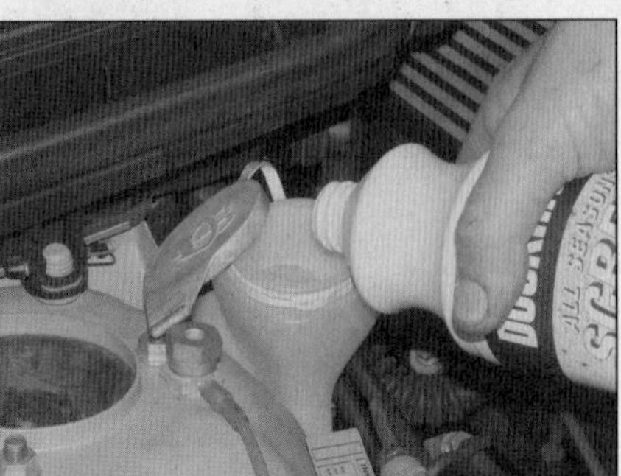

2 When topping-up, add a screenwash additive in the quantities recommended by the manufacturer.

Brake and clutch fluid level

Warning:
● Brake fluid can harm your eyes and damage painted surfaces, so use extreme caution when handling and pouring it.
● Do not use fluid that has been standing open for some time, as it absorbs moisture from the air, which can cause a dangerous loss of braking effectiveness..

Before you start

● Make sure that your car is on level ground.

The fluid level in the reservoir will drop slightly as the brake pads wear down, but the fluid level must never be allowed to drop below the MIN mark.

Safety First!

● If the reservoir requires repeated topping-up this is an indication of a fluid leak somewhere in the system, which should be investigated immediately.

● If a leak is suspected, the car should not be driven until the braking system has been checked. Never take any risks where brakes are concerned.

1 Release the clip and remove the lid from the driver's side pollen filter housing.

2 Release the clip and pull the air duct from the filter housing, then rotate it upwards and remove it from the bulkhead.

3 Release the clip and lift the pollen filter housing away.

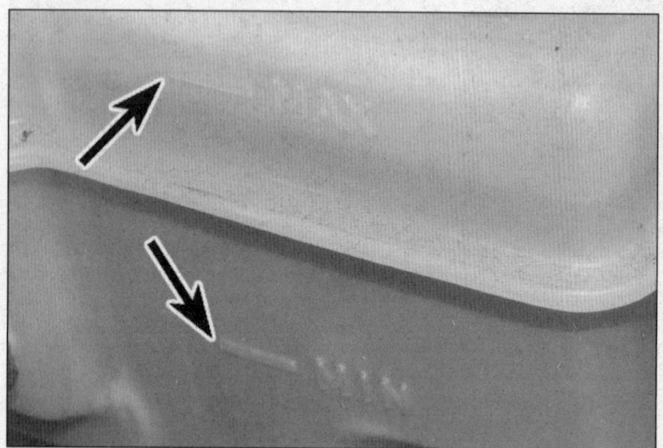

4 The MAX and MIN marks are indicated on the side of the reservoir. The fluid level must be kept between the marks at all times.

5 If topping-up is necessary, first wipe clean the area around the filler cap to prevent dirt entering the hydraulic system.

6 Unscrew the reservoir cap and carefully lift it out of position, taking care not to damage the level switch float. Inspect the reservoir, if the fluid is dirty the hydraulic system should be drained and refilled (see Chapter 1).

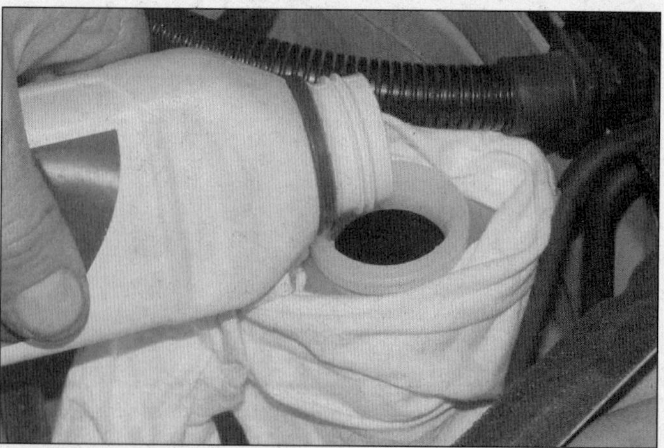

7 Carefully add fluid taking care not to spill it onto the surrounding components. Use only the specified fluid; mixing different types can cause damage to the system. After topping-up to the correct level, securely refit the cap and wipe off any spilt fluid.

Tyre condition and pressure

It is very important that tyres are in good condition, and at the correct pressure - having a tyre failure at any speed is highly dangerous. Tyre wear is influenced by driving style - harsh braking and acceleration, or fast cornering, will all produce more rapid tyre wear. As a general rule, the front tyres wear out faster than the rears. Interchanging the tyres from front to rear ("rotating" the tyres) may result in more even wear. However, if this is completely effective, you may have the expense of replacing all four tyres at once!

Remove any nails or stones embedded in the tread before they penetrate the tyre to cause deflation. If removal of a nail does reveal that the tyre has been punctured, refit the nail so that its point of penetration is marked. Then immediately change the wheel, and have the tyre repaired by a tyre dealer.

Regularly check the tyres for damage in the form of cuts or bulges, especially in the sidewalls. Periodically remove the wheels, and clean any dirt or mud from the inside and outside surfaces. Examine the wheel rims for signs of rusting, corrosion or other damage. Light alloy wheels are easily damaged by "kerbing" whilst parking; steel wheels may also become dented or buckled. A new wheel is very often the only way to overcome severe damage.

New tyres should be balanced when they are fitted, but it may become necessary to re-balance them as they wear, or if the balance weights fitted to the wheel rim should fall off. Unbalanced tyres will wear more quickly, as will the steering and suspension components. Wheel imbalance is normally signified by vibration, particularly at a certain speed (typically around 50 mph). If this vibration is felt only through the steering, then it is likely that just the front wheels need balancing. If, however, the vibration is felt through the whole car, the rear wheels could be out of balance. Wheel balancing should be carried out by a tyre dealer or garage.

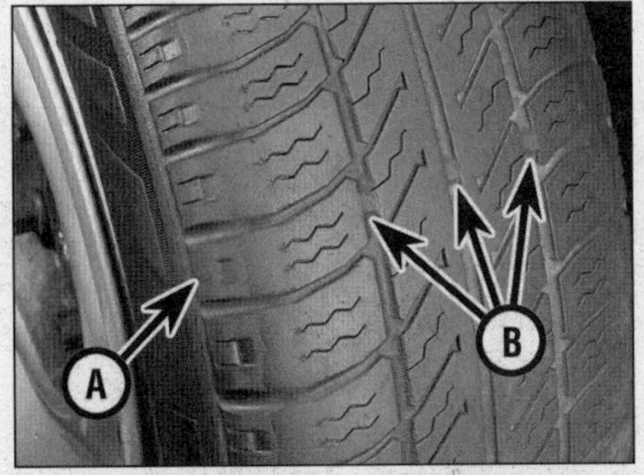

1 *Tread Depth - visual check*
The original tyres have tread wear safety bands (B), which will appear when the tread depth reaches approximately 1.6 mm. The band positions are indicated by a triangular mark on the tyre sidewall (A).

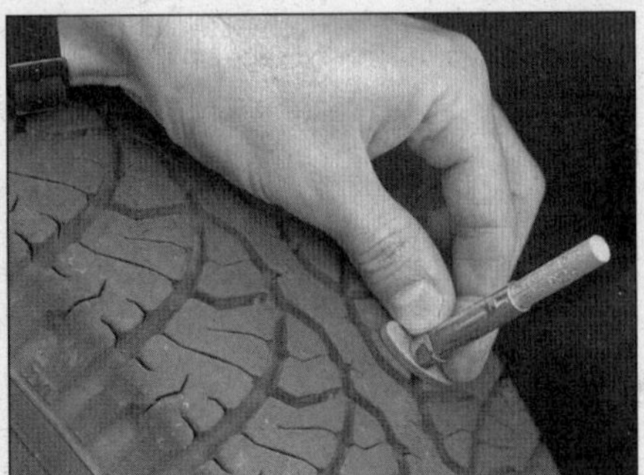

2 *Tread Depth - manual check*
Alternatively, tread wear can be monitored with a simple, inexpensive device known as a tread depth indicator gauge.

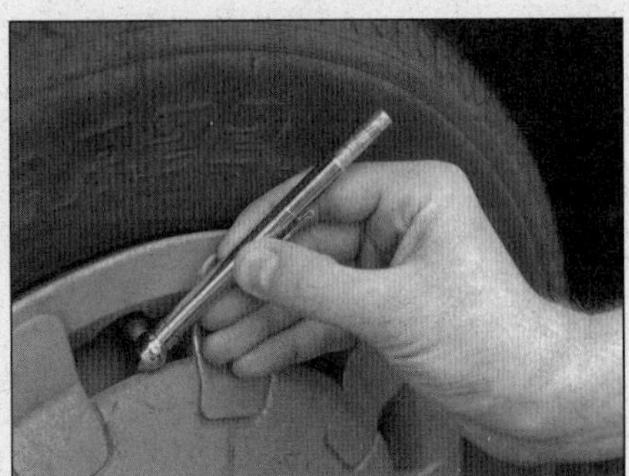

3 *Tyre Pressure Check*
Check the tyre pressures regularly with the tyres cold. Do not adjust the tyre pressures immediately after the vehicle has been used, or an inaccurate setting will result.

Tyre tread wear patterns

Shoulder Wear

Underinflation (wear on both sides)
Under-inflation will cause overheating of the tyre, because the tyre will flex too much, and the tread will not sit correctly on the road surface. This will cause a loss of grip and excessive wear, not to mention the danger of sudden tyre failure due to heat build-up.
Check and adjust pressures
Incorrect wheel camber (wear on one side)
Repair or renew suspension parts
Hard cornering
Reduce speed!

Centre Wear

Overinflation
Over-inflation will cause rapid wear of the centre part of the tyre tread, coupled with reduced grip, harsher ride, and the danger of shock damage occurring in the tyre casing.
Check and adjust pressures

If you sometimes have to inflate your car's tyres to the higher pressures specified for maximum load or sustained high speed, don't forget to reduce the pressures to normal afterwards.

Uneven Wear

Front tyres may wear unevenly as a result of wheel misalignment. Most tyre dealers and garages can check and adjust the wheel alignment (or "tracking") for a modest charge.
Incorrect camber or castor
Repair or renew suspension parts
Malfunctioning suspension
Repair or renew suspension parts
Unbalanced wheel
Balance tyres
Incorrect toe setting
Adjust front wheel alignment
Note: *The feathered edge of the tread which typifies toe wear is best checked by feel.*

Battery

Caution: Before carrying out any work on the vehicle battery, read the precautions given in 'Safety first!' at the start of this manual.

✔ Make sure that the battery tray is in good condition, and that the clamp is tight. Corrosion on the tray, retaining clamp and the battery itself can be removed with a solution of water and baking soda. Thoroughly rinse all cleaned areas with water. Any metal parts damaged by corrosion should be covered with a zinc-based primer, then painted.

✔ Periodically (approximately every three months), check the charge condition of the battery, as described in Chapter 5A.

✔ If the battery is flat, and you need to jump start your vehicle, see *Roadside Repairs*.

HAYNES HiNT

Battery corrosion can be kept to a minimum by applying a layer of petroleum jelly to the clamps and terminals after they are reconnected.

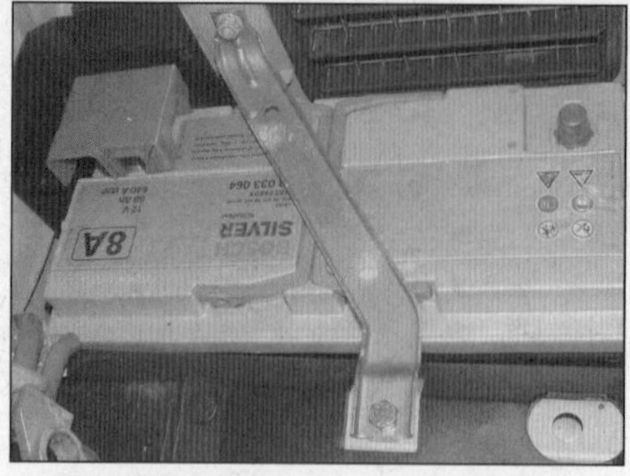

1 The battery is located in the right-hand rear corner of the luggage compartment. On Saloon models, release the clip and open the right-hand storage tray. On Touring models, rotate the fastener 90° anti-clockwise, and remove the right-hand side luggage compartment storage tray.

2 Check the tightness of battery clamps (A) to ensure good electrical connections. You should not be able to move them. Also check each cable (B) for cracks and frayed conductors.

3 If corrosion (white, fluffy deposits) is evident, remove the cables from the battery terminals, clean them with a small wire brush, then refit them. Automotive stores sell a tool for cleaning the battery post . . .

4 . . . as well as the battery cable clamps

Electrical systems

✔ Check all external lights and the horn. Refer to the appropriate Sections of Chapter 12 for details if any of the circuits are found to be inoperative.

✔ Visually check all accessible wiring connectors, harnesses and retaining clips for security, and for signs of chafing or damage.

HAYNES HiNT *If you need to check your brake lights and indicators unaided, back up to a wall or garage door and operate the lights. The reflected light should show if they are working properly.*

1 If a single indicator light, stop-light or headlight has failed, it is likely that a bulb has blown and will need to be renewed. Refer to Chapter 12 for details. If both stop-lights have failed, it is possible that the switch has failed (see Chapter 9).

2 If more than one indicator light or tail light has failed check that a fuse has not blown or that there is a fault in the circuit (see Chapter 12). The fuses are located in the fusebox in the passenger side glovebox. Details of the circuits protected by the fuses are shown on the card in the fusebox. Open the glovebox, rotate the fasteners 90° anti-clockwise and lower the fusebox cover from the roof of the glovebox.

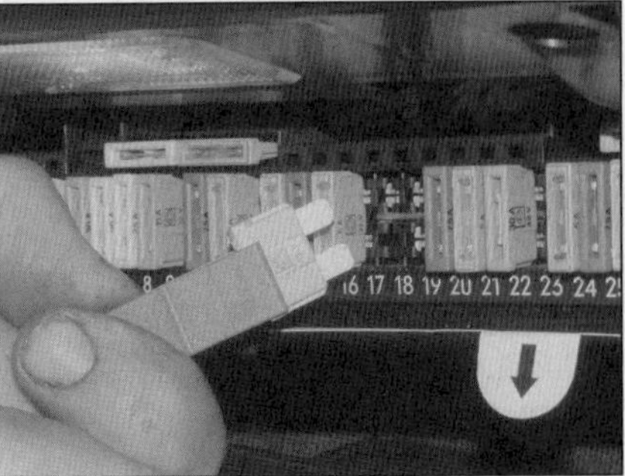

3 To renew a blown fuse, simply pull it out and fit a new fuse of the correct rating (see Chapter 12). If the fuse blows again, it is important that you find out why – a complete checking procedure is given in Chapter 12.

Wiper blades

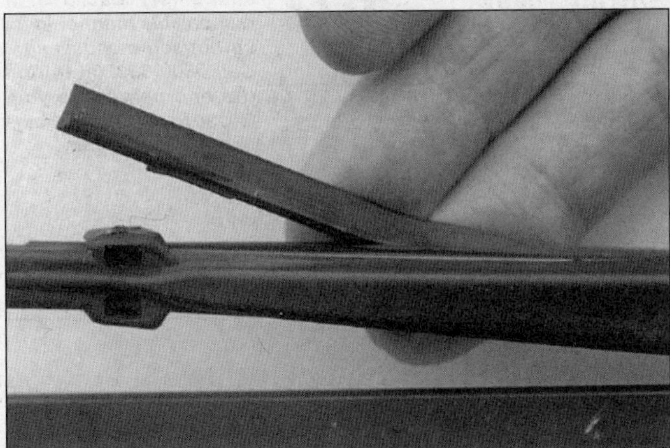

1 Check the condition of the wiper blades; if they are cracked or show any signs of deterioration, or if the glass swept area is smeared, renew them. Wiper blades should be renewed annually.

2 To remove a wiper blade, pull the arm away from the screen until it locks. Use a screwdriver to slide the clip to the unlocked position. Disengage the blade from the arm.

Lubricants and fluids

Engine	
All engines (excluding M54 engines from 09/01)	BMW Long-life 98 SAE 0W-40 or SAE 5W-30 (fully synthetic) to ACEA A3 may be used for topping-up **only** (eg, Castrol Syntec)
M54 engines from 09/01	BMW Long-life 01 SAE 0W-40 or SAE 5W-30 (fully synthetic) to ACEA A3 may be used for topping-up **only** (eg, Castrol Syntec)
Cooling system	Long-life ethylene glycol based antifreeze*
Manual transmission	
Transmissions with an orange 'ATF' label adjacent to the filler plug (up to 09/1997)	ATF D (eg, Duckhams Unimatic)
Transmissions from 09/1997	BMW Lifetime transmission oil MTF-LT-1
Automatic transmission	BMW Lifetime transmission oil*
Final drive unit	SAE 75W/90 EP*
Braking system	Hydraulic fluid to DOT 4
Power steering	Dexron II* or Pentosin CHF (marked as ATF or CHF on the reservoir filler cap)

**Refer to your BMW dealer for brand name and type recommendations*

Choosing your engine oil

Engines need oil, not only to lubricate moving parts and minimise wear, but also to maximise power output and to improve fuel economy.

HOW ENGINE OIL WORKS

• *Beating friction*

Without oil, the moving surfaces inside your engine will rub together, heat up and melt, quickly causing the engine to seize. Engine oil creates a film which separates these moving parts, preventing wear and heat build-up.

• *Cooling hot-spots*

Temperatures inside the engine can exceed 1000° C. The engine oil circulates and acts as a coolant, transferring heat from the hot-spots to the sump.

• *Cleaning the engine internally*

Good quality engine oils clean the inside of your engine, collecting and dispersing combustion deposits and controlling them until they are trapped by the oil filter or flushed out at oil change.

OIL CARE - FOLLOW THE CODE

To handle and dispose of used engine oil safely, always:

- ***Avoid skin contact with used engine oil. Repeated or prolonged contact can be harmful.***
- ***Dispose of used oil and empty packs in a responsible manner in an authorised disposal site. Call 0800 663366 to find the one nearest to you. Never tip oil down drains or onto the ground.***

Tyre pressures

The tyre pressures are given on a label affixed to the driver's door aperture.

Chapter 1
Routine maintenance and servicing

Contents

Degrees of difficulty

Easy, suitable for novice with little experience 	**Fairly easy,** suitable for beginner with some experience 	**Fairly difficult,** suitable for competent DIY mechanic	**Difficult,** suitable for experienced DIY mechanic 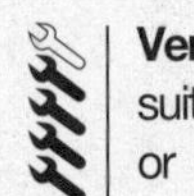	**Very difficult,** suitable for expert DIY or professional

Lubricants and fluids

Refer to *Weekly checks* on page 0•18

Capacities

Engine oil (including filter)

All engines	6.5 litres

Cooling system

All engines	10.5 litres

Transmission

Manual transmission (approximate)	1.1 litres
Automatic transmission (approximate)	3.3 litres

Final drive unit

All models	1.1 litres

Power-assisted steering

All models (approximate)	1.2 litres

Fuel tank

All models (approximate)	78 litres

Cooling system

Antifreeze mixture:	
50% antifreeze	Protection down to -30°C (-22°F)

Note: *Refer to antifreeze manufacturer for latest recommendations.*

Ignition system

Spark plugs:	Type	Electrode gap
M52 engines	Bosch F7 LDCR	0.9 mm
M52TU engines	NGK BKR 6E QYP	0.9 mm
M54 engines	Bosch FGR 7 DQP	1.6 mm

Brakes

Brake pad friction material minimum thickness	3.0 mm
Handbrake shoe friction material minimum thickness	1.5 mm

Torque wrench settings

	Nm	lbf ft
Cylinder block coolant drain plug	25	18
Engine sump oil drain plug:		
M12 plug	25	18
M18 plug	35	26
M22 plug	60	44
Roadwheel bolts	110	81
Spark plugs:		
M12 thread	23	17
M14 thread	30	22

All E39 5-Series models are equipped with a service display in the centre of the instrument panel, which shows the type of service next due, and the distance remaining until the service is required. Once that distance is reduced to zero, the display then shows the distance since the service was due. Two types of service are specified, an 'Oil Service' and an 'Inspection Service'. For more details, refer to the Owner's Handbook supplied with the vehicle.

There are two different inspection services, Inspection I and Inspection II, these should be carried out alternately with some additional items to be included every second Inspection II. If you are unclear as to which inspection schedule was carried out last time start with Inspection II (including the additional items).

To reset the service interval display indicator on models up to 09/2000, a BMW service tool is required which plugs into the diagnostic plug in the engine compartment. Aftermarket alternatives to the BMW tool are produced by several leading tool manufacturers and should be available from larger car accessory shops. On models produced after 09/2000, the indicator can be reset using the trip reset button in the instrument cluster.

Every 250 miles (400 km) or weekly

- ☐ Refer to *Weekly checks*

Oil service

- ☐ Renew the engine oil and filter (Section 3)*
- ☐ Reset the service interval display (Section 4)
- ☐ Check the front brake pad thickness (Section 5)
- ☐ Check the rear brake pad thickness (Section 6)
- ☐ Check the operation of the handbrake (Section 7)
- ☐ Renew the pollen filters (Section 8)

* **Note:** *Frequent oil and filter changes are good for the engine. We recommend changing the oil at least once a year.*

Inspection I

Carry out all the operations listed under Oil service, along with the following:

- ☐ Check all underbonnet components and hoses for fluid leaks (Section 9)
- ☐ Check the condition of the auxiliary drivebelt(s), and renew if necessary (Section 10)
- ☐ Check the steering and suspension components for condition and security (Section 11)

Inspection I (continued)

- ☐ Check the exhaust system and mountings (Section 12)
- ☐ Check the condition and operation of the seat belts (Section 13)
- ☐ Lubricate all hinges and locks (Section 14)
- ☐ Check the headlight beam alignment (Section 15)
- ☐ Check the operation of the windscreen/headlight washer system(s) (as applicable) (Section 16)
- ☐ Check the engine management system (Section 17)
- ☐ Carry out a road test (Section 18)
- ☐ Check the water drain under the brake servo (Section 19)

Inspection II

Carry out all the operations listed under Inspection I, along with the following:

- ☐ Renew the spark plugs (Section 20)
- ☐ Renew the air filter element (Section 21)
- ☐ Check the condition of the driveshaft gaiters (Section 22)
- ☐ Check the condition of the handbrake shoe linings (Section 23)

Every second Inspection II

- ☐ Renew the fuel filter (Section 24)

Every 2 years

Note: *BMW specify that the following should be carried out regardless of mileage:*

- ☐ Renew the brake fluid (Section 25)

Every 3 years

Note: *BMW specify that the following should be carried out regardless of mileage:*

- ☐ Renew the coolant (Section 26)

Underbonnet view of a 2.0 litre (M52 engine) model

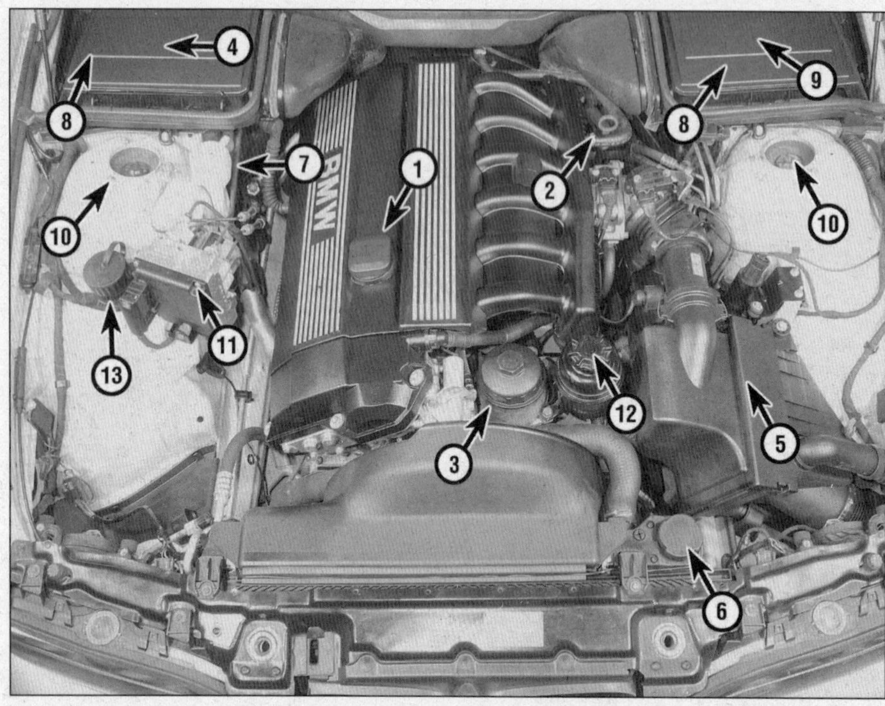

1. *Engine oil filler cap*
2. *Engine oil level dipstick*
3. *Oil filter cover*
4. *Brake and clutch fluid reservoir (under pollen filter housing)*
5. *Air cleaner housing*
6. *Coolant expansion tank*
7. *Washer fluid reservoir*
8. *Pollen filter covers*
9. *Engine electrical box (under pollen filter housing)*
10. *Suspension strut upper mounting*
11. *ABS unit*
12. *Power steering reservoir*
13. *Diagnostic plug*

Underbonnet view of a 2.5 litre (M54 engine) model

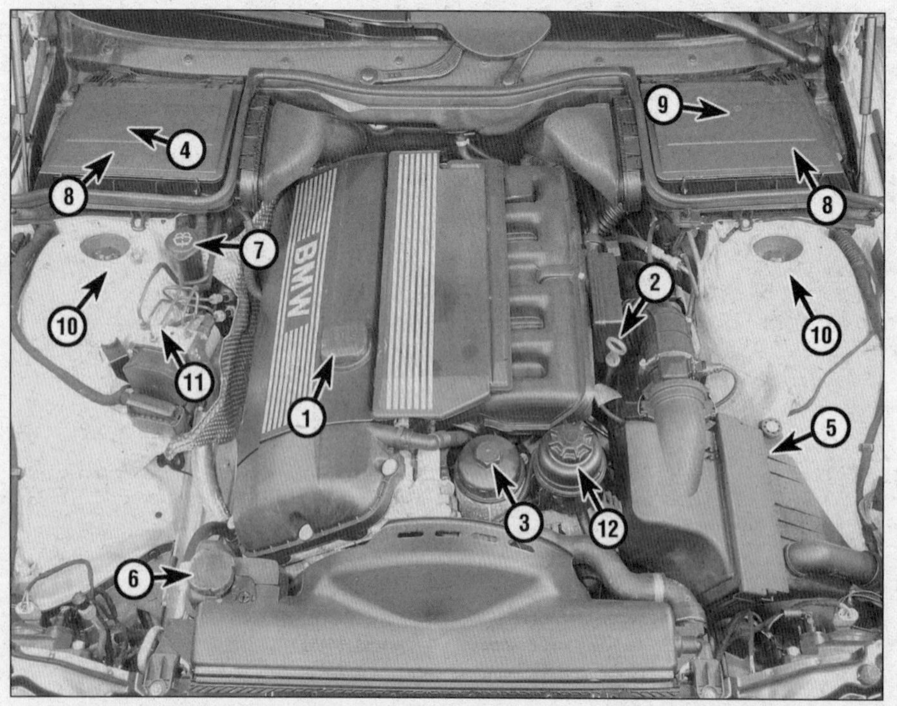

1. *Engine oil filler cap*
2. *Engine oil level dipstick*
3. *Oil filter cover*
4. *Brake and clutch fluid reservoir (under pollen filter housing)*
5. *Air cleaner housing*
6. *Coolant expansion tank*
7. *Washer fluid reservoir*
8. *Pollen filter covers*
9. *Engine electrical box (under pollen filter housing)*
10. *Suspension strut upper mounting*
11. *ABS unit*
12. *Power steering reservoir*

Front underbody view (2.0 litre model – others similar)

1 *Engine oil (sump) drain plug*
2 *Front subframe*
3 *Radiator*
4 *Front exhaust pipes*
5 *Front suspension control arm*
6 *Front brake caliper*
7 *Steering rack*
8 *Anti-roll bar*
9 *Coolant drain plug*
10 *Front suspension tension arm*

Rear underbody view (2.0 litre model – other models similar)

1 *Fuel tank*
2 *Exhaust tail box*
3 *Final drive unit*
4 *Suspension swinging arm*
5 *Suspension subframe*
6 *Handbrake cable*
7 *Driveshaft*
8 *Anti-roll bar*
9 *Propeller shaft*

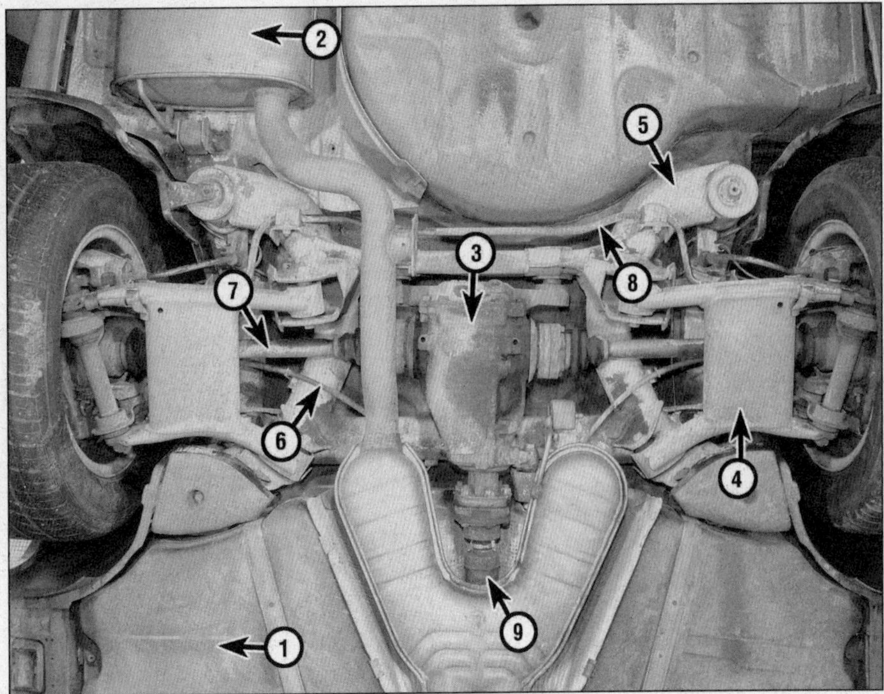

1 Introduction

1 This Chapter is designed to help the home mechanic maintain his/her vehicle for safety, economy, long life and peak performance.

2 The Chapter contains a master maintenance schedule, followed by Sections dealing specifically with each task in the schedule. Visual checks, adjustments, component renewal and other helpful items are included. Refer to the accompanying illustrations of the engine compartment and the underside of the vehicle for the locations of the various components.

3 Servicing your vehicle in accordance with the service indicator display and the following Sections will provide a planned maintenance programme, which should result in a long and reliable service life. This is a comprehensive plan, so maintaining some items but not others at the specified service intervals will not produce the same results.

4 As you service your vehicle, you will discover that many of the procedures can – and should – be grouped together, because of the particular procedure being performed, or because of the proximity of two otherwise-unrelated components to one another. For example, if the vehicle is raised for any reason, the exhaust can be inspected at the same time as the suspension and steering components.

5 The first step in this maintenance programme is to prepare yourself before the actual work begins. Read through all the Sections relevant to the work to be carried out, then make a list and gather all the parts and tools required. If a problem is encountered, seek advice from a parts specialist, or a dealer service department.

2 Regular maintenance

1 If, from the time the vehicle is new, the routine maintenance schedule is followed closely, and frequent checks are made of fluid levels and high-wear items, as suggested throughout this manual, the engine will be kept in relatively good running condition, and the need for additional work will be minimised.

2 It is possible that there will be times when the engine is running poorly due to the lack of regular maintenance. This is even more likely if a used vehicle, which has not received regular and frequent maintenance checks, is purchased. In such cases, additional work may need to be carried out, outside of the regular maintenance intervals.

3 If engine wear is suspected, a compression test (refer to Chapter 2A) will provide valuable information regarding the overall performance of the main internal components. Such a test can be used as a basis to decide on the extent of the work to be carried out. If, for example, a compression test indicates serious internal engine wear, conventional maintenance as described in this Chapter will not greatly improve the performance of the engine, and may prove a waste of time and money, unless extensive overhaul work is carried out first.

4 The following series of operations are those most often required to improve the performance of a generally poor-running engine:

Primary operations

a) Clean, inspect and test the battery (See 'Weekly checks').
b) Check all the engine-related fluids (See 'Weekly checks').
c) Check the condition and tension of the auxiliary drivebelt (Section 10).
d) Renew the spark plugs (Section 20).
e) Check the condition of the air filter, and renew if necessary (Section 21).
f) Check the fuel filter (Section 24).
g) Check the condition of all hoses, and check for fluid leaks (Section 9).

5 If the above operations do not prove fully effective, carry out the following secondary operations:

Secondary operations

All items listed under *Primary operations*, plus the following:

a) Check the charging system (see Chapter 5A).
b) Check the ignition system (see Chapter 5B).
c) Check the fuel system (see relevant Part of Chapter 4).

Oil service

3 Engine oil and filter renewal

1 Frequent oil and filter changes are the most important preventative maintenance work which can be undertaken by the DIY owner. As engine oil ages, it becomes diluted and contaminated, which leads to premature engine wear.

2 Before starting this procedure, gather together all the necessary tools and materials. Also make sure you have plenty of clean rags and newspapers handy, to mop-up any spills. Ideally, the engine oil should be warm, as it will drain better, and more built-up sludge will be removed with it. Take care, however, not to touch the exhaust or any other hot parts of the engine when working under the car. To avoid any possibility of scalding, and to protect yourself from possible skin irritants and other harmful contaminants in used engine oils, it is advisable to wear gloves. Access to the underside of the car will be improved if it can be raised on a lift, driven onto ramps, or jacked up and supported on axle stands (see *Jacking and vehicle support*). Whichever method is chosen, make sure the car remains level, or if it is at an angle, so that the drain plug is at the lowest point. The sump drain plug is accessed via a removable flap in the engine undershield **(see illustration)**

3 Working in the engine compartment, locate the oil filter housing on the left-hand side of the engine, in front of the intake manifold.

4 Place a wad of rag around the bottom of the housing to absorb any spilt oil.

5 Using a special oil filter removal tool or socket (36 mm), unscrew and remove the cover, and lift the filter cartridge out. It is possible to unscrew the cover using a strap wench **(see illustrations)**. The oil will drain

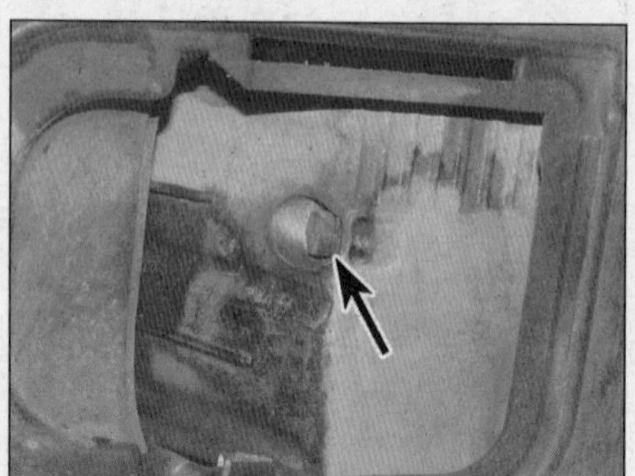

3.2 Access to the sump oil drain plug (arrowed) is via a flap in the engine undershield

3.5a Use a 36 mm socket to unscrew the filter cap . . .

3.5b . . . or a strap wrench

3.8 Fit a new O-ring seal to the oil filter cap

3.9 Fit the new oil filter element to the cap

from the housing back into the sump as the cover is removed. **Note:** *Some early models may be equipped with a filter which has a central bolt. Undo the bolt to remove the cover.*

6 Remove the old filter and O-ring seal from the cover.

7 Using a clean rag, wipe the mating faces of the housing and cover.

8 Fit new O-ring to the cover **(see illustration)**.

9 Fit the new filter cartridge to the cover **(see illustration)**.

10 Smear a little clean engine oil on the O-ring, refit the cover (and bolt – where applicable) and tighten it to 25 Nm (18 lbf ft) if using the special filter removal tool, or securely if using a strap wrench.

11 Working under the car, slacken the sump drain plug about half a turn **(see illustration 3.2)**. Position the draining container under the drain plug, then remove the plug completely. If possible, try to keep the plug pressed into the sump while unscrewing it by hand the last couple of turns.

12 Recover the drain plug sealing ring.

13 Allow some time for the old oil to drain, noting that it may be necessary to reposition the container as the oil flow slows to a trickle.

14 After all the oil has drained, wipe off the drain plug with a clean rag. Check the sealing washer condition, and renew it if necessary. Clean the area around the drain plug opening, then refit and tighten the plug **(see illustration)**.

15 Remove the old oil and all tools from under the car, close the sump plug access flap, then lower the car to the ground (if applicable).

16 Remove the dipstick then unscrew the oil filler cap from the cylinder head cover. Fill the engine, using the correct grade and type of oil (see *Weekly checks*). An oil can spout or funnel may help to reduce spillage. Pour in half the specified quantity of oil first, then wait a few minutes for the oil to fall to the sump. Continue adding oil a small quantity at a time until the level is up to the lower mark on the dipstick. Finally, bring the level up to the upper mark on the dipstick. Insert the dipstick, and refit the filler cap.

17 Start the engine and run it for a few minutes; check for leaks around the oil filter seal and the sump drain plug. Note that there may be a delay of a few seconds before the oil pressure warning light goes out when the engine is first started, as the oil circulates through the engine oil galleries and the new oil filter, before the pressure builds-up.

18 Switch off the engine, and wait a few minutes for the oil to settle in the sump once more. With the new oil circulated and the filter completely full, recheck the level on the dipstick, and add more oil as necessary.

19 Dispose of the used filter and engine oil safely, with reference to *General repair procedures* in the *Reference* section of this manual.

4 Resetting the service interval display

Models up to 09/2000

Note: *The following is for use with the special BMW service tool and adapter. If an aftermarket tool is being used, refer to the instructions supplied by its manufacturer.*

1 Turn the ignition off, unscrew the cap, then plug BMW service interval resetting tool 62 1 110 (or equivalent) and into the engine compartment diagnostic socket **(see illustration)**.

2 Ensure that all electrical items are switched off then turn on the ignition switch. **Note:** *Do not start the engine.*

3 To reset an Oil Service, press and hold the yellow button; the green light will illuminate. After about 3 seconds the yellow light will illuminate for about 12 seconds, and then go out.

4 To reset an Inspection Service, press and hold the red Inspection button; the green (function check) light will illuminate. After about 3 seconds the red lamp should also light, remain on for about 12 seconds, and then go out. Release the Inspection button and the green (function check) light will go out.

5 If the clock (annual service) symbol was

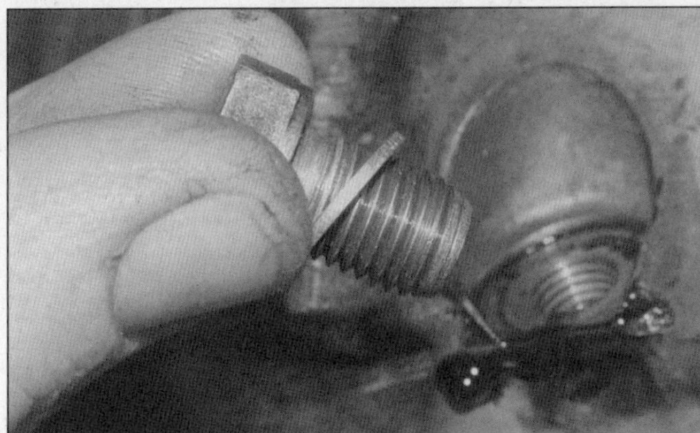
3.14 Renew the sealing washer if necessary, and refit the drain plug

4.1 Plug the service reset tool into the diagnostic plug in the engine compartment (models up to 09/2000)

illuminated at the same time as the Oil Service or Inspection indicator, wait 20 seconds then repeat the operation in paragraph 4.

6 Turn off the ignition switch and disconnect the resetting tool and adapter from the diagnostic connector.

7 Turn the ignition switch on and check that the Service Interval Display has been reset.

Models from 09/2000

Reset oil/inspection service and brake fluid renewal

8 Insert the ignition key and turn it to position 0.

9 Press and hold the trip meter button, then turn the ignition key to position 1.

10 Keep the button pressed for approximately 5 seconds until the display shows either 'Oil service' or 'Inspection' along with 'Reset' or 'Re', then release the button.

11 Press the trip button again, and hold it for approximately 5 seconds until the display flashes 'Reset' or 'Re', then release it.

12 After briefly showing the new interval, it will then show the 'Brake fluid renewal' interval. The following will appear in the display: 'Clock symbol' and 'Reset' or 'Re'. Press and hold the trip button again for approximately 5 seconds until the display flashes 'Reset' or 'Re', then release it.

13 Whilst the display is flashing, momentarily press the trip button to reset the brake fluid renewal interval.

14 After briefly showing the new interval, it displays 'End SIA' for approximately 2 seconds. This indicates that the Service Interval Adjustment has been completed. Turn the ignition off to complete the procedure.

Reset oil/inspection service only

15 Insert the ignition key and turn it to position 0.

16 Press and hold the trip meter button, then turn the ignition key to position 1.

17 Keep the button pressed for approximately 5 seconds until the display shows either 'Oil service' or 'Inspection' along with 'Reset' or 'Re', then release the button.

18 Press the trip button again, and hold it for approximately 5 seconds until the display flashes 'Reset' or 'Re', then release it.

19 Whilst the display is flashing, press the trip button momentarily to reset the service interval.

20 After briefly showing the new interval, it will then show the 'Brake fluid renewal' interval. The following will appear in the display: 'Clock symbol' and 'Reset' or 'Re'. Press the trip button momentarily to skip the brake fluid renewal interval reset option. The display will change to 'End SIA' This indicates that the Service Interval Adjustment has been completed. Turn the ignition off to complete the procedure.

Reset brake fluid renewal only

21 Insert the ignition key and turn it to position 0.

22 Press and hold the trip meter button, then turn the ignition key to position 1.

23 Keep the button pressed for approximately 5 seconds until the display shows either 'Oil service' or 'Inspection' along with 'Reset' or 'Re', then release the button.

24 Momentarily press the trip button to skip the Oil Service or Inspection Service internal reset option.

25 The display will show the clock symbol and 'Reset' or 'Re'. Press the button again for approximately 5 seconds, until the display flashes 'Reset' or 'Re'.

26 Whilst the display is flashing, press the trip button momentarily to reset the brake fluid renewal interval.

27 After briefly showing the new interval, it displays 'End SIA' for approximately 2 seconds. This indicates that the Service Interval Adjustment has been completed. Turn the ignition off to complete the procedure.

5 Front brake pad check

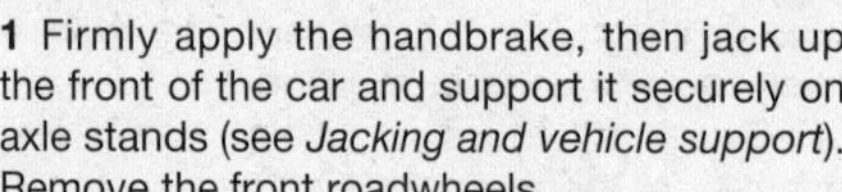

1 Firmly apply the handbrake, then jack up the front of the car and support it securely on axle stands (see *Jacking and vehicle support*). Remove the front roadwheels.

2 For a comprehensive check, the brake pads should be removed and cleaned. The operation of the caliper can then also be checked, and the condition of the brake disc itself can be fully examined on both sides. Refer to Chapter 9 for further information.

3 If any pad's friction material is worn to the specified thickness or less, *all four pads must be renewed as a set.*

6 Rear brake pad check

1 Chock the front wheels, then jack up the rear of the car and support it on axle stands (see *Jacking and vehicle support*). Remove the rear roadwheels.

2 For a quick check, the thickness of friction material remaining on each brake pad can be measured through the top of the caliper body. If any pad's friction material is worn to the specified thickness or less, *all four pads must be renewed as a set*.

3 For a comprehensive check, the brake pads should be removed and cleaned. This will permit the operation of the caliper to be checked, and the condition of the brake disc itself to be fully examined on both sides. Refer to Chapter 9 for further information.

7 Handbrake check

Check and, if necessary, adjust the handbrake as described in Chapter 9. Check that the handbrake cables are free to move easily and lubricate all exposed linkages/cable pivots.

8 Pollen filters renewal

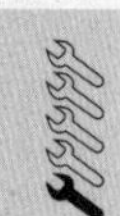

1 Working at the rear of the engine compartment, fold forward the retaining clip and remove the filter cover **(see illustrations)**. Note that two pollen filters are fitted – one in the left-hand corner of the engine compartment, and one in the right-hand corner.

2 Manoeuvre the filter housing from the housing **(see illustration)**.

3 Install the new filter element into the housing, ensuring that it's fitted the correct way up.

4 Refit the filter cover, and secure it in place with the retaining clip.

8.1a Pull the pollen filter cover clip forwards . . .

8.1b . . . and remove the cover . . .

8.2 . . . followed by the filter element

Inspection I

9 Hose and fluid leak check

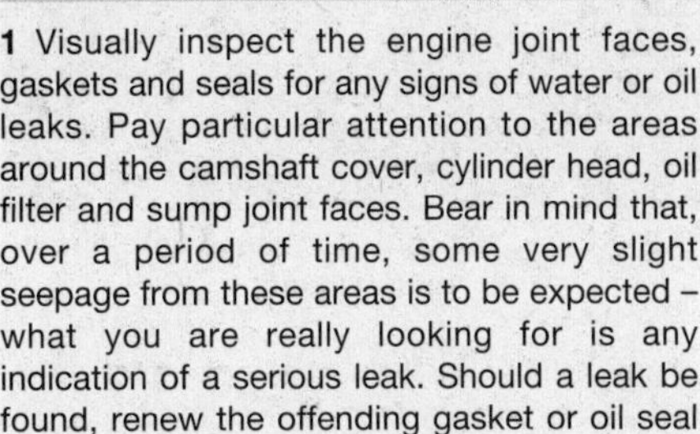

1 Visually inspect the engine joint faces, gaskets and seals for any signs of water or oil leaks. Pay particular attention to the areas around the camshaft cover, cylinder head, oil filter and sump joint faces. Bear in mind that, over a period of time, some very slight seepage from these areas is to be expected – what you are really looking for is any indication of a serious leak. Should a leak be found, renew the offending gasket or oil seal by referring to the appropriate Chapters in this manual.

2 Also check the security and condition of all the engine-related pipes and hoses. Ensure that all cable-ties or securing clips are in place and in good condition. Clips which are broken or missing can lead to chafing of the hoses, pipes or wiring, which could cause more serious problems in the future.

3 Carefully check the radiator hoses and heater hoses along their entire length. Renew any hose which is cracked, swollen or deteriorated. Cracks will show up better if the hose is squeezed. Pay close attention to the hose clips that secure the hoses to the cooling system components. Hose clips can pinch and puncture hoses, resulting in cooling system leaks.

4 Inspect all the cooling system components (hoses, joint faces, etc) for leaks **(see Haynes Hint)**. Where any problems of this nature are found on system components, renew the component or gasket with reference to Chapter 3.

5 Where applicable, inspect the automatic transmission fluid cooler hoses for leaks or deterioration.

6 With the car raised, inspect the petrol tank and filler neck for punctures, cracks and other damage. The connection between the filler neck and tank is especially critical. Sometimes a rubber filler neck or connecting hose will leak due to loose retaining clamps or deteriorated rubber.

A leak in the cooling system will usually show up as white- or rust-coloured deposits on the area adjoining the leak.

7 Carefully check all rubber hoses and metal fuel lines leading away from the petrol tank. Check for loose connections, deteriorated hoses, crimped lines, and other damage. Pay particular attention to the vent pipes and hoses, which often loop up around the filler neck and can become blocked or crimped. Follow the lines to the front of the car, carefully inspecting them all the way. Renew damaged sections as necessary.

8 Closely inspect the metal brake pipes which run along the car underbody. If they show signs of excessive corrosion or damage they must be renewed.

9 From within the engine compartment, check the security of all fuel hose attachments and pipe unions, and inspect the fuel hoses and vacuum hoses for kinks, chafing and deterioration.

10 Check the condition of the power steering fluid hoses and pipes.

10 Auxiliary drivebelt(s) check and renewal

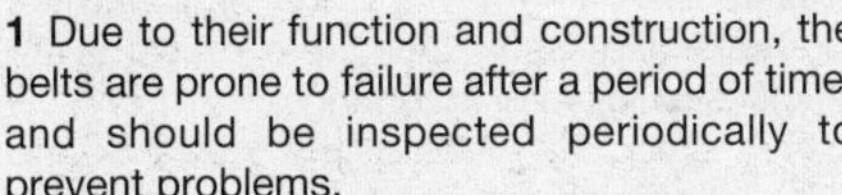

Check

1 Due to their function and construction, the belts are prone to failure after a period of time, and should be inspected periodically to prevent problems.

2 The number of belts used on a particular car depends on the accessories fitted. Drivebelts are used to drive the coolant pump, alternator, power steering pump and air conditioning compressor.

3 To improve access for belt inspection, if desired, remove the viscous cooling fan and cowl as described in Chapter 3.

4 With the engine stopped, using your fingers (and an electric torch if necessary), move along the belts, checking for cracks and separation of the belt plies. Also check for fraying and glazing, which gives the belt a shiny appearance. Both sides of the belts should be inspected, which means the belt will have to be twisted to check the underside. If necessary turn the engine using a spanner or socket on the crankshaft pulley bolt to that the whole of the belt can be inspected.

Renewal

Air conditioning compressor

5 Access is most easily obtained from under the car. If desired, jack up the front of the car and support securely on (see *Jacking and vehicle support*). Undo the screws and remove the engine undershield.

6 On models with a hydraulic tensioner, prise the cover from the centre of the tensioner pulley. Engage a hexagon bit and extension bar with the tensioner bolt, and lever the tensioner clockwise **(see illustration)**. Slide the belt from the pulleys.

7 On models with a mechanical tensioner, using a spanner on the hexagon section of the pulley arm, rotate the tensioner clockwise, and remove the belt from the pulleys **(see illustration)**.

8 On all models, lever the tensioner until the drivebelt can be fitted around the pulleys, then release the tensioner. Ensure that the belt is engaged with the grooves in the pulleys.

9 Refit the pulley cover (where applicable) and lower the car to the ground.

Coolant pump/ alternator/power steering pump

10 Where applicable, remove the air conditioning compressor drivebelt as described previously in this Section.

11 If the drivebelt is to be re-used, mark the running direction of the belt before removal.

12 Remove the viscous cooling fan and shroud as described in Chapter 3.

13 Make a careful note of the routing of the drivebelt before removal.

14 Prise the cover from the centre of the tensioner pulley. Engage a socket with the tensioner bolt or hexagonal section, and rotate the pulley arm clockwise until the

10.6 Prise off the plastic cover, and rotate the tensioner clockwise

10.7 Rotate the pulley arm clockwise

10.14a Prise the plastic cap from the pulley . . .

10.14b . . . rotate the tensioner clockwise . . .

10.14c . . . and lock it in place with a drill bit (arrowed)

locking holes in the arm and housing align. Insert a suitable rod or drill bit into the holes to lock it in place **(see illustrations)**. Remove the belt from the pulleys.

15 If the original belt is being refitted, observe the running direction mark made before removal.

16 Engage the belt with the pulleys, ensuring that it is routed as noted before removal. Make sure that the belt engages correctly with the grooves in the pulleys **(see illustration)**. Compress the tensioner, remove the locking rod/drill and slowly allow the tensioner to tension the belt.

17 Refit the viscous cooling fan and shroud with reference to Chapter 3.

18 Where applicable, refit the air conditioning compressor drivebelt as described previously in this Section.

11 Steering and suspension check

Front suspension and steering

1 Raise the front of the car, and securely support it on axle stands (see *Jacking and vehicle support*).

2 Visually inspect the balljoint dust covers and the steering rack-and-pinion gaiters for splits, chafing or deterioration. Any wear of these components will cause loss of lubricant, then dirt and water entry, resulting in rapid deterioration of the balljoints or steering gear.

3 Check the power steering fluid hoses for chafing or deterioration, and the pipe and hose unions for fluid leaks. Also check for signs of fluid leakage under pressure from the steering gear rubber gaiters, which would indicate failed fluid seals within the steering gear.

4 Grasp the roadwheel at the 12 o'clock and 6 o'clock positions, and try to rock it **(see illustration)**. Very slight free play may be felt, but if the movement is appreciable, further investigation is necessary to determine the source. Continue rocking the wheel while an assistant depresses the footbrake. If the movement is now eliminated or significantly reduced, it is likely that the hub bearings are at fault. If the free play is still evident with the footbrake depressed, then there is wear in the suspension joints or mountings.

5 Now grasp the wheel at the 9 o'clock and 3 o'clock positions, and try to rock it as before. Any movement felt now may again be caused by wear in the hub bearings or the steering track rod balljoints. If the inner or outer balljoint is worn, the visual movement will be obvious.

6 Using a large screwdriver or flat bar, check for wear in the suspension mounting bushes by levering between the relevant suspension component and its attachment point. Some movement is to be expected as the mountings are made of rubber, but excessive wear should be obvious. Also check the condition of any visible rubber bushes, looking for splits, cracks or contamination of the rubber.

7 With the car standing on its wheels, have an assistant turn the steering wheel back-and-forth about an eighth of a turn each way. There should be very little, if any, lost movement between the steering wheel and roadwheels. If this is not the case, closely observe the joints and mountings previously described, but in addition, check the steering column universal joints for wear, and the rack-and-pinion steering gear itself.

Strut/shock absorber

8 Check for any signs of fluid leakage around the suspension strut/shock absorber body, or from the rubber gaiter around the piston rod. Should any fluid be noticed, the suspension strut/shock absorber is defective internally, and should be renewed. **Note:** *Suspension struts/shock absorbers should always be renewed in pairs on the same axle.*

9 The efficiency of the suspension strut/shock absorber may be checked by bouncing the car at each corner. Generally speaking, the body will return to its normal position and stop after being depressed. If it rises and returns on a rebound, the suspension strut/shock absorber is probably suspect. Examine also the suspension strut/shock absorber upper and lower mountings for any signs of wear.

10 On models with self-levelling electro-pneumatic system, check the rubber bellows of the air spring units for deterioration or damage.

10.16 Note the auxiliary belt's routing

11.4 Check for wear in the hub bearings/suspension joints by grasping the wheel and trying to rock it

12 Exhaust system check

1 With the engine cold (at least an hour after the car has been driven), check the complete exhaust system from the engine to the end of the tailpipe. The exhaust system is most easily checked with the car raised on a hoist, or suitably supported on axle stands, so that the exhaust components are readily visible and accessible.

2 Check the exhaust pipes and connections for evidence of leaks, severe corrosion and

12.2 Check the condition of the exhaust mountings

damage. Make sure that all brackets and mountings are in good condition, and that all relevant nuts and bolts are tight **(see illustration)**. Leakage at any of the joints or in other parts of the system will usually show up as a black sooty stain in the vicinity of the leak.

3 Rattles and other noises can often be traced to the exhaust system, especially the brackets and mountings. Try to move the pipes and silencers. If the components are able to come into contact with the body or suspension parts, secure the system with new mountings. Otherwise separate the joints (if possible) and twist the pipes as necessary to provide additional clearance.

13 Seat belt check

1 Carefully examine the seat belt webbing for cuts or any signs of serious fraying or deterioration. If the seat belt is of the retractable type, pull the belt all the way out, and examine the full extent of the webbing.

2 Fasten and unfasten the belt, ensuring that the locking mechanism holds securely and releases properly when intended. If the belt is of the retractable type, check also that the retracting mechanism operates correctly when the belt is released.

3 Check the security of all seat belt mountings and attachments which are accessible from inside the car, without removing any trim or other components.

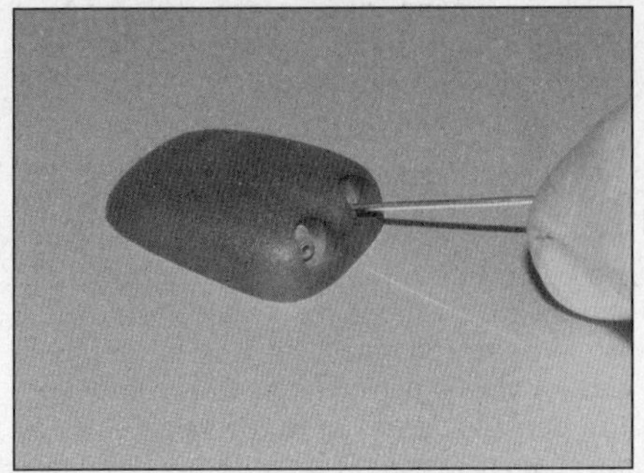

16.1 Use a fine pin or length of wire to adjust the washer jet aim

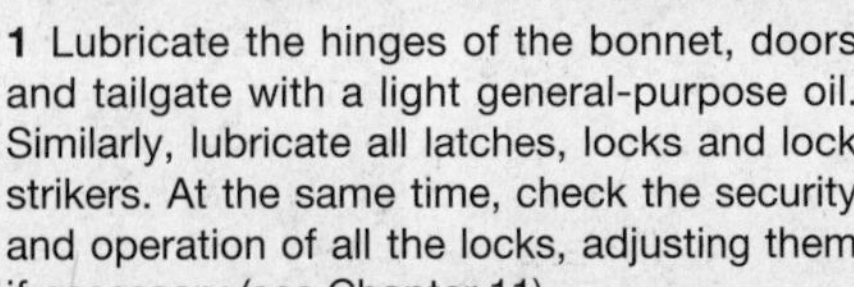

14 Hinge and lock lubrication

1 Lubricate the hinges of the bonnet, doors and tailgate with a light general-purpose oil. Similarly, lubricate all latches, locks and lock strikers. At the same time, check the security and operation of all the locks, adjusting them if necessary (see Chapter 11).

2 Lightly lubricate the bonnet release mechanism and cable with a suitable grease.

15 Headlight beam alignment check

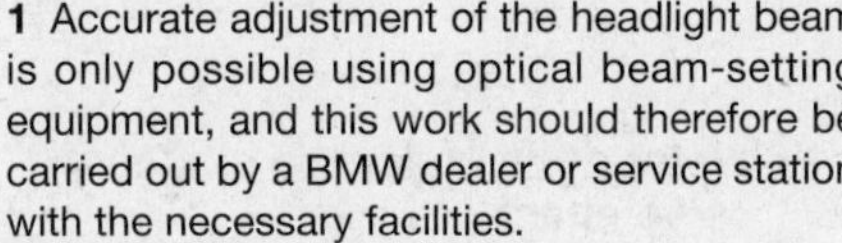

1 Accurate adjustment of the headlight beam is only possible using optical beam-setting equipment, and this work should therefore be carried out by a BMW dealer or service station with the necessary facilities.

2 Basic adjustments can be carried out in an emergency, and further details are given in Chapter 12.

16 Windscreen/headlight washer system(s) check

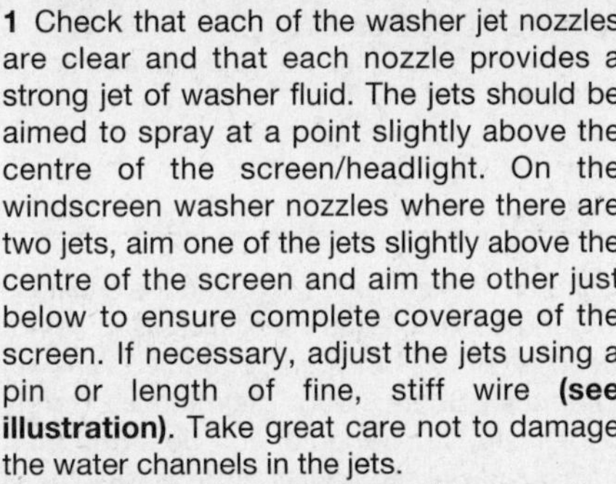

1 Check that each of the washer jet nozzles are clear and that each nozzle provides a strong jet of washer fluid. The jets should be aimed to spray at a point slightly above the centre of the screen/headlight. On the windscreen washer nozzles where there are two jets, aim one of the jets slightly above the centre of the screen and aim the other just below to ensure complete coverage of the screen. If necessary, adjust the jets using a pin or length of fine, stiff wire **(see illustration)**. Take great care not to damage the water channels in the jets.

2 Adjustment of the headlight washer jets requires the use of BMW special tool 00 9 100.

17 Engine management system check

1 This check is part of the manufacturer's maintenance schedule, and involves testing the engine management system using special dedicated test equipment. Such testing will allow the test equipment to read any fault codes stored in the electronic control unit memory.

2 Unless a fault is suspected, this test is not essential, although it should be noted that it is recommended by the manufacturers.

3 If access to suitable test equipment is not possible, make a thorough check of all ignition, fuel and emission control system components, hoses, and wiring, for security and obvious signs of damage. Further details of the fuel system, emission control system and ignition system can be found in Chapters 4 and 5.

18 Road test

Instruments and electrical equipment

1 Check the operation of all instruments and electrical equipment.

2 Make sure that all instruments read correctly, and switch on all electrical equipment in turn, to check that it functions properly.

Steering and suspension

3 Check for any abnormalities in the steering, suspension, handling or road 'feel'.

4 Drive the car, and check that there are no unusual vibrations or noises.

5 Check that the steering feels positive, with no excessive 'sloppiness', or roughness, and check for any suspension noises when cornering and driving over bumps.

Drivetrain

6 Check the performance of the engine, clutch (where applicable), gearbox/transmission and driveshafts.

7 Listen for any unusual noises from the engine, clutch and gearbox/transmission.

8 Make sure that the engine runs smoothly when idling, and that there is no hesitation when accelerating.

9 Check that, where applicable, the clutch action is smooth and progressive, that the drive is taken up smoothly, and that the pedal travel is not excessive. Also listen for any noises when the clutch pedal is depressed.

10 On manual gearbox models, check that all gears can be engaged smoothly without noise, and that the gear lever action is smooth and not abnormally vague or 'notchy'.

11 On automatic transmission models, make sure that all gearchanges occur smoothly, without snatching, and without an increase in engine speed between changes. Check that all the gear positions can be selected with the car at rest. If any problems are found, they should be referred to a BMW dealer or suitably-equipped specialist.

Braking system

12 Make sure that the car does not pull to one side when braking, and that the wheels do not lock when braking hard.

13 Check that there is no vibration through the steering when braking.

14 Check that the handbrake operates correctly without excessive movement of the lever, and that it holds the car stationary on a slope.

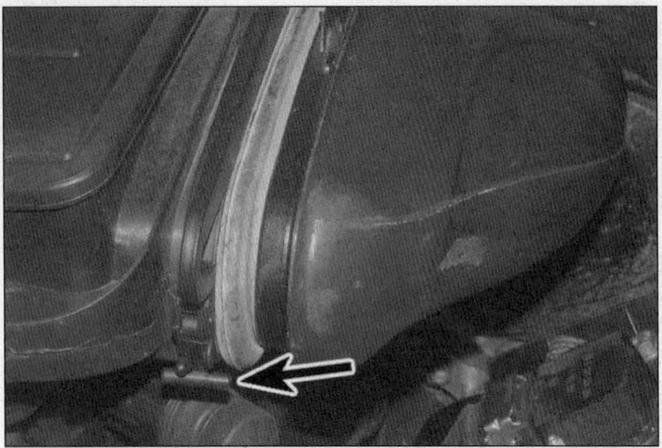

19.1a Release the clip (arrowed), and disconnect the air duct . . .

19.1b . . . then remove the cover, release the clip (arrowed) and remove the pollen filter housing

15 Test the operation of the brake servo unit as follows. With the engine off, depress the footbrake four or five times to exhaust the vacuum. Hold the brake pedal depressed, then start the engine. As the engine starts, there should be a noticeable 'give' in the brake pedal as vacuum builds-up. Allow the engine to run for at least two minutes, and then switch it off. If the brake pedal is depressed now, it should be possible to detect a hiss from the servo as the pedal is depressed. After about four or five applications, no further hissing should be heard, and the pedal should feel much harder.

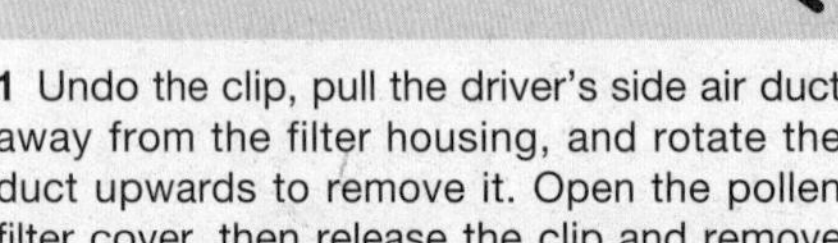

19 Water drain under the brake servo check

1 Undo the clip, pull the driver's side air duct away from the filter housing, and rotate the duct upwards to remove it. Open the pollen filter cover, then release the clip and remove the pollen filter housing **(see illustrations)**.
2 Check the brake servo drain channel for blockage from debris, etc, and clean it if necessary **(see illustration)**.
3 Refit the pollen filter housing and air duct.

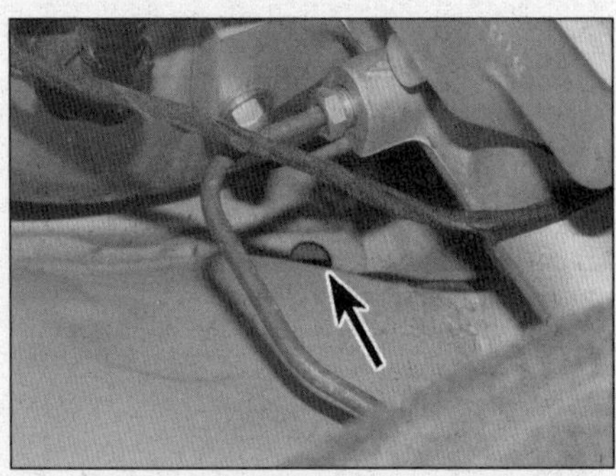

19.2 Ensure the water drain channel (arrowed) under the servo is free from debris

Inspection II

20 Spark plug renewal

General

1 The correct functioning of the spark plugs is vital for the correct running and efficiency of the engine. It is essential that the plugs fitted are appropriate for the engine (the suitable type is specified at the beginning of this Chapter). If this type is used, and the engine is in good condition, the spark plugs should not need attention between scheduled renewal intervals. Spark plug cleaning is rarely necessary, and should not be attempted unless specialised equipment is available, as damage can easily be caused to the firing ends.

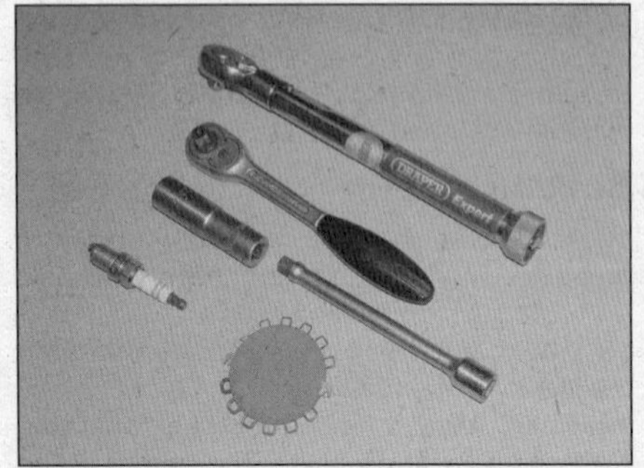

20.5 Tools required for spark plug removal, gap adjustment and refitting

2 The spark plugs are fitted under the ignition coils in the centre of the cylinder head.
3 Remove the ignition coils (Chapter 5B).
4 It is advisable to remove any dirt from the spark plug recesses, using a clean brush, vacuum cleaner or compressed air before removing the plugs, to prevent dirt dropping into the cylinders.
5 Unscrew the plugs using a spark plug spanner, suitable box spanner, or a deep socket and extension bar **(see illustration)**. Keep the socket aligned with the spark plug – if it is forcibly moved to one side, the ceramic insulator may be broken off.
6 Examination of the spark plugs will give a good indication of the condition of the engine. If the insulator nose of the spark plug is clean and white, with no deposits, this is indicative of a weak mixture or too hot a plug (a hot plug transfers heat away from the electrode slowly, a cold plug transfers heat away quickly).
7 If the tip and insulator nose are covered with hard black-looking deposits, then this is indicative that the mixture is too rich. Should the plug be black and oily, then it is likely that the engine is fairly worn, as well as the mixture being too rich.
8 If the insulator nose is covered with light tan to greyish-brown deposits, then the mixture is correct, and it is likely that the engine is in good condition.
9 When buying new spark plugs, it is important to obtain the correct plugs for your engine (see Specifications).
10 If the spark plugs are of the multi-electrode type, the gap between the centre electrode and the earth electrodes cannot be adjusted. However, if single electrode plugs are being fitted, the gap between the earth and centre electrode must be correct. If it is too large or too small, the size of the spark and its efficiency will be seriously impaired. The gap should be set to the value given by the spark plug manufacturer.
11 To set the gap on single electrode plugs, measure it with a feeler blade or wire gauge,

20.11a Measure the spark plug gap with a wire gauge . . .

then bend the outer plug electrode until the correct gap is achieved **(see illustrations)**. The centre electrode should never be bent, as this may crack the insulator and cause plug failure, if nothing worse. If using feeler blades, the gap is correct when the appropriate-size blade is a firm sliding fit.

12 Special spark plug electrode gap adjusting tools are available from most motor accessory shops, or from some spark plug manufacturers.

13 Before fitting the spark plugs, check that the threaded connector sleeves (on top of the plug) are tight, and that the plug exterior surfaces and threads are clean. It is very often difficult to insert spark plugs into their holes without cross-threading them. To avoid this possibility, fit a short length of hose over the end of the spark plug **(see Haynes Hint)**.

14 Remove the rubber hose (if used), and

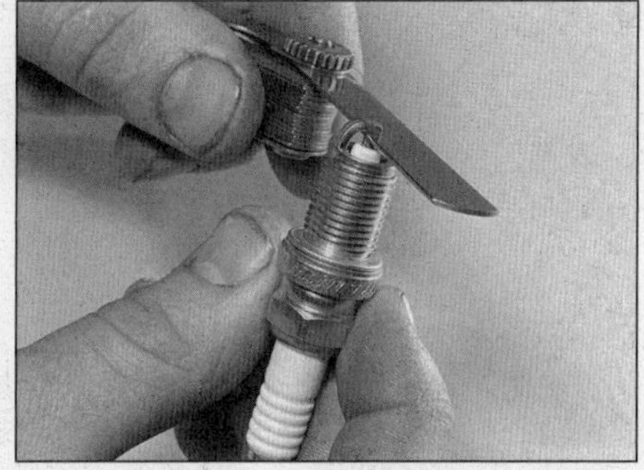

20.11b . . . or feeler gauge

tighten the plug to the specified torque (see Specifications) using the spark plug socket and a torque wrench. Fit the remaining plugs in the same way.

15 Refit the ignition coils (see Chapter 5B).

21 Air filter element renewal

1 The air cleaner assembly is located at the front left-hand corner of the engine compartment.

2 Release the securing clips, and slide the filter element tray up from the housing **(see illustrations)**.

3 Lift out the filter element **(see illustration)**.

4 Wipe out the air cleaner housing and the tray.

21.2a Press in the retaining clips . . .

21.2b . . . slide up the air filter element tray . . .

21.3 . . . and lift out the filter element

22.1 Check the condition of the driveshaft gaiters

It is often difficult to insert spark plugs into their holes without cross-threading them. To avoid this possibility, fit a short length of 8 mm internal diameter rubber/plastic hose over the end of the spark plug. The flexible hose acts as a universal joint to help align the plug with the plug hole. Should the plug begin to cross-thread, then the hose will slip on the spark plug, preventing thread damage to the cylinder head.

5 Lay the new filter element in position, then slide the tray into the housing until it locks in position.

6 Secure the retaining clips.

22 Driveshaft gaiter check

1 With the car raised and securely supported on stands, slowly rotate the rear roadwheel. Inspect the condition of the outer constant velocity (CV) joint rubber gaiters, squeezing the gaiters to open out the folds **(see illustration)**. Check for signs of cracking, splits or deterioration of the rubber, which may allow the grease to escape, and lead to water and grit entry into the joint. Also check the security and condition of the retaining clips. Repeat these checks on the inner CV joints. If any damage is found, the gaiters should be renewed (see Chapter 8).

2 At the same time, check the general condition of the CV joints themselves by first holding the driveshaft and attempting to rotate the wheel. Repeat this check by holding the inner joint and attempting to rotate the driveshaft. Any appreciable movement indicates wear in the joints, wear in the driveshaft splines, or a loose driveshaft retaining nut.

23 Handbrake shoe check

Referring to Chapter 9, remove the rear brake discs and inspect the handbrake shoes for signs of wear or contamination. Renew the shoes if necessary.

24.2 The fuel filter is located on a bracket bolted to the left-hand chassis member adjacent to the transmission

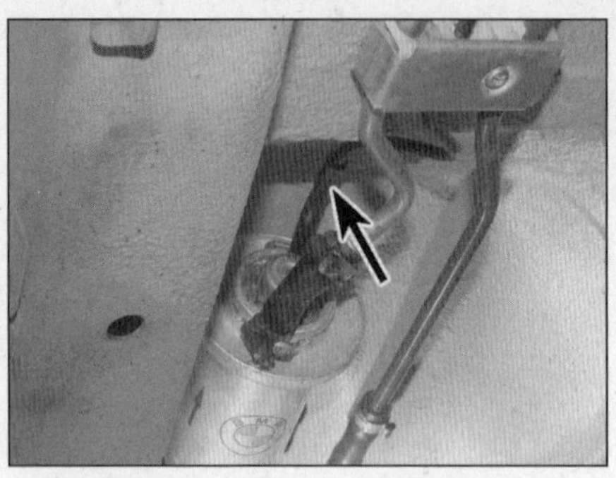

24.6 On M54 engined models, disconnect the fuel regulator vacuum hose (arrowed)

24.8 The arrow on the filter body points in the direction of fuel flow (towards the engine)

Every second Inspection II

24 Fuel filter renewal

1 Depressurise the fuel system (Chapter 4A).
2 The fuel filter is located on a bracket bolted to the left-hand chassis member adjacent to the transmission **(see illustration)**.
3 Jack up the car and support on axle stands (see *Jacking and vehicle support*).
4 Undo the screws/nuts, prise up the centre pins and lever out the 5 plastic expansion rivets at its outer edge, then remove the cover from the fuel filter/regulator assembly.
5 On all models, note their fitted locations, and clamp the hoses to and from the fuel filter. Slacken the retaining clips and disconnect the hoses from the filter. Be prepared for fluid spillage.
6 On M54 engined models, disconnect the vacuum pipe from the regulator **(see illustration)**.
7 On all models, slacken the filter clamp bolt or nut, and slide the filter down from under the car. Where necessary, transfer the mounting bracket from the old filter to the new one.
8 Refitting is a reversal of removal, but make sure that the flow direction arrow on the filter points in the direction of fuel flow (ie, towards the engine) **(see illustration)**. If the arrow is not visible, the front end of the filter is stamped OUT.

Every 2 years

25 Brake fluid renewal

Warning: Brake hydraulic fluid can harm your eyes and damage painted surfaces, so use extreme caution when handling and pouring it. Do not use fluid that has been standing open for some time, as it absorbs moisture from the air. Excess moisture can cause a dangerous loss of braking effectiveness.

1 The procedure is similar to that for the bleeding of the hydraulic system as described in Chapter 9, except that the brake fluid reservoir should be emptied using a clean poultry baster or similar before starting, and allowance should be made for the old fluid to be expelled when bleeding a section of the circuit.
2 Working as described in Chapter 9, open the first bleed screw in the sequence, and pump the brake pedal gently until nearly all the old fluid has been emptied from the master cylinder reservoir.
3 Top-up to the MAX level with new fluid, and continue pumping until only the new fluid remains in the reservoir, and new fluid can be seen emerging from the bleed screw. Tighten the screw, and top the reservoir level up to the MAX level line.
4 Work through all remaining bleed screws in the sequence until new fluid can be seen at all of them. Be careful to keep the master cylinder reservoir topped-up to above the MIN level at all times, or air may enter the system and increase the length of the task.

Old hydraulic fluid is usually much darker in colour than the new, making it easy to distinguish the two.

5 When the operation is complete, check that all bleed screws are securely tightened, and that their dust caps are refitted. Wash off all traces of spilt fluid, and recheck the master cylinder reservoir fluid level.
6 Check the operation of the brakes before taking the car on the road.

Every 3 years

26 Coolant renewal

Cooling system draining

Warning: Wait until the engine is cold before starting this procedure. Do not allow antifreeze to come in contact with your skin, or with the painted surfaces of the car. Rinse off spills immediately with plenty of water. Never leave antifreeze lying around in an open container, or in a puddle in the driveway or on the garage floor. Children and pets are attracted by its sweet smell, but antifreeze can be fatal if ingested.

1 With the engine completely cold, cover the expansion tank cap with a wad of rag, and slowly turn the cap anti-clockwise to relieve the pressure in the cooling system (a hissing sound may be heard). Wait until any pressure in the system is released, then continue to turn the cap until it can be removed.
2 Unscrew the bleed screw from the top of the hose junction above the expansion tank. Some models are equipped with an additional

bleed screw adjacent to the oil filter cap **(see illustrations).**

3 Undo the retaining screws/clips and remove the undershield from beneath the engine.

4 Position a suitable container beneath the drain plug(s) on the base of the radiator, and on some models, the expansion tank. Unscrew the drain plugs and allow the coolant to drain into the container **(see illustrations).**

5 To fully drain the system, also unscrew the coolant drain plug from the right-hand side of the cylinder block and allow the remainder of the coolant to drain into the container **(see illustration).** On M52 engines the drain plug is adjacent to the No 5 cylinder, and on M52TU and M54 engines, the drain plug is adjacent to No 2 cylinder.

6 If the coolant has been drained for a reason other than renewal, then provided it is clean and less than two years old, it can be re-used, though this is not recommended.

7 Once all the coolant has drained, refit the bleed screw to the hose junction. Fit a new sealing washer to the block drain plug and tighten it to the specified torque.

Cooling system flushing

8 If coolant renewal has been neglected, or if the antifreeze mixture has become diluted, then in time, the cooling system may gradually lose efficiency, as the coolant passages become restricted due to rust, scale deposits, and other sediment. The cooling system efficiency can be restored by flushing the system clean.

9 The radiator should be flushed independently of the engine, to avoid unnecessary contamination.

Radiator flushing

10 To flush the radiator, disconnect the top and bottom hoses and any other relevant hoses from the radiator, with reference to Chapter 3.

11 Insert a garden hose into the radiator top inlet. Direct a flow of clean water through the radiator, and continue flushing until clean water emerges from the radiator bottom outlet.

12 If after a reasonable period, the water still does not run clear, the radiator can be flushed with a good proprietary cooling system cleaning agent. It is important that their manufacturer's instructions are followed carefully. If the contamination is particularly bad, insert the hose in the radiator bottom outlet, and reverse-flush the radiator.

26.2a Open the bleed screw (arrowed) at the top of the expansion tank

26.2b and (on some models) by the oil filter housing

Engine flushing

13 To flush the engine, remove the thermostat as described in Chapter 3, then temporarily refit the thermostat cover.

14 With the top and bottom hoses disconnected from the radiator, insert a garden hose into the radiator top hose. Direct a clean flow of water through the engine, and continue flushing until clean water emerges from the radiator bottom hose.

15 On completion of flushing, refit the thermostat and reconnect the hoses with reference to Chapter 3.

Cooling system filling

Note: *Some models are equipped with a 'latent heat accumulator'. This is a system whereby heat from the coolant system is stored in a facia-mounted insulated reservoir. The reservoir contains a salt mixture, which is converted from a solid state to a liquid state by the hot engine coolant. This system is capable of retaining heat for several days, even at very low outside temperatures. When the engine is restarted, the liquid salt mixture converts back to a solid state – the latent heat released is available for immediate use to defrost the windows, heat the passenger cabin, and reduce the engine warm-up time.*

Models without Latent Heat Store

16 Before attempting to fill the cooling system, make sure that all hoses and clips are in good condition, and that the clips are tight and the radiator and cylinder block drain plugs are securely tightened. Note that an antifreeze mixture must be used all year round, to prevent corrosion of the engine components (see following sub-Section).

17 Slacken the bleed screw(s) **(see illustrations 25.2a and 25.2b).**

18 Turn on the ignition, and set the heater control to maximum temperature, with the fan speed set to 'low'. This opens the heating valves.

19 Remove the expansion tank filler cap. Fill the system by slowly pouring the coolant into the expansion tank to prevent airlocks from forming.

20 If the coolant is being renewed, begin by pouring in a couple of litres of water, followed by the correct quantity of antifreeze, then top-up with more water.

21 As soon as coolant free from air bubbles emerges from the radiator bleed screw(s), tighten the screw(s) securely.

22 Once the level in the expansion tank starts to rise, squeeze the radiator top and bottom hoses to help expel any trapped air in the system. Once all the air is expelled, top-up the coolant level to the MAX mark and refit the expansion tank cap.

23 Start the engine and run it until it reaches normal operating temperature, then stop the engine and allow it to cool.

24 Check for leaks, particularly around disturbed components. Check the coolant level in the expansion tank, and top-up if necessary. Note that the system must be cold

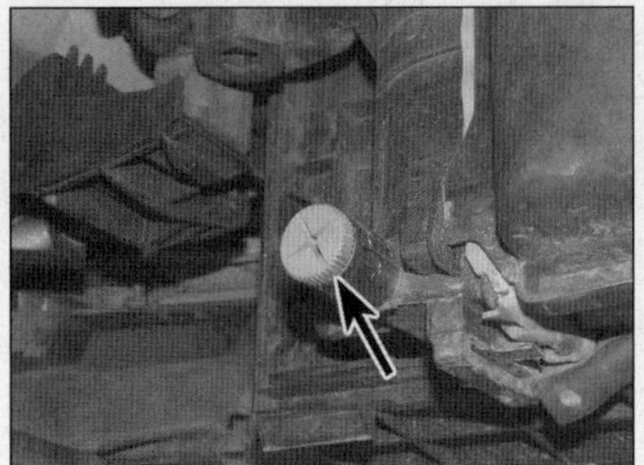

26.4a Radiator drain plug (arrowed) – M52 engine

26.4b Radiator drain plug (arrowed) – M54 engine

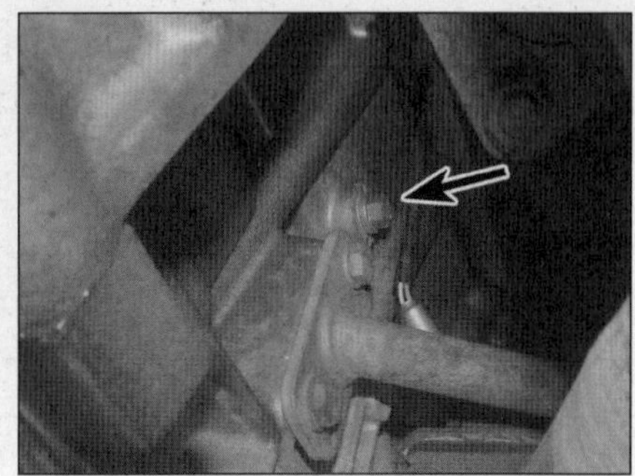

26.5 Cylinder block drain plug (arrowed) – M52 engine

before an accurate level is indicated in the expansion tank. If the expansion tank cap is removed while the engine is still warm, cover the cap with a thick cloth, and unscrew the cap slowly to gradually relieve the system pressure (a hissing sound will normally be heard). Wait until any pressure remaining in the system is released, then continue to turn the cap until it can be removed.

Models with Latent Heat Store

25 On these models, the coolant refilling procedure is identical to that previously described, but there are three additional requirements,

1) *After filling the expansion tank to the Max mark, the system must be pressurised to 1.5 bar, using the type of cooling system pressure tester that fits onto the expansion tank neck.*
2) *Whilst the system is pressurised, remove the pollen filter and housing, open the bleed screw in the hose to the latent heat store. Once air bubbles cease to emerge from the bleed screw, tighten it securely.*
3) *Now specialist BMW test equipment must be connected to the diagnostic plug, to activate the auxiliary water pump and latent heat store valve unit for approximately 5 minutes. After this, re-open the bleed screw and vent any air bubbles. Disconnect the test equipment, and relieve the pressure in the system.*

26 In the absence of the special BMW test equipment, Bleed the system as described for models without latent heat store and then, should the vehicle show the slightest sign of overheating (keep an eye on the temperature gauge) or a reduction in heater performance, drive the vehicle to a BMW dealer or suitably-equipped specialist and have the above procedure carried out.

Antifreeze mixture

27 The antifreeze should always be renewed at the specified intervals. This is necessary not only to maintain the antifreeze properties, but also to prevent corrosion which would otherwise occur as the corrosion inhibitors become progressively less effective.

28 Always use an ethylene-glycol based antifreeze which is suitable for use in mixed-metal cooling systems. The quantity of antifreeze and levels of protection are indicated in the Specifications.

29 Before adding antifreeze, the cooling system should be completely drained, preferably flushed, and all hoses checked for condition and security.

30 After filling with antifreeze, a label should be attached to the expansion tank, stating the type and concentration of antifreeze used, and the date installed. Any subsequent topping-up should be made with the same type and concentration of antifreeze.

31 Do not use engine antifreeze in the windscreen/tailgate washer system, as it will damage the vehicle paintwork. A screenwash additive should be added to the washer system in the quantities stated on the bottle.

Chapter 2 Part A:
Engine in-car repair procedures

Contents

Degrees of difficulty

Easy, suitable for novice with little experience 	**Fairly easy,** suitable for beginner with some experience 	**Fairly difficult,** suitable for competent DIY mechanic	**Difficult,** suitable for experienced DIY mechanic	**Very difficult,** suitable for expert DIY or professional

Specifications

General

Engine code:	
1991 cc engine up to 09/98	M52 B20
1991 cc engine from 09/98	M52TU B20
2171 cc engine	M54 B22
2494 cc engine up to 09/98	M52 B25
2494 cc engine from 09/98 to 09/00	M52TU B25
2494 cc engine from 09/00	M54 B25
2793 cc engine up to 09/98	M52 B28
2793 cc engine from 09/98	M52TU B28
2979 cc engine	M54 B30
Bore:	
M52 B20 engine	80.00 mm
M52TU B20 engine	80.00 mm
M54 B22 engine	80.00 mm
All other engines	84.00 mm
Stroke:	
M52 B20 engine	66.00 mm
M52TU B20 engine	66.00 mm
M54 B22 engine	72.00 mm
M52 B25 engine	75.00 mm
M52TU B25 engine	75.00 mm
M54 B25 engine	75.00 mm
M52 B28 engine	84.00 mm
M52TU B28 engine	84.00 mm
M54 B30 engine	89.60 mm
Maximum engine power:	
M52 B20 engine	110 kW at 5900 rpm
M52TU B20 engine	110 kW at 5900 rpm
M54 B22 engine	125 kW at 6250 rpm
M52 B25 engine	125 kW at 5500 rpm
M52TU B25 engine	125 kW at 5500 rpm
M54 B25 engine	141 kW at 6000 rpm
M52 B28 engine	142 kW at 5300 rpm
M52TU B28 engine	142 kW at 5500 rpm
M54 B30 engine	170 kW at 5900 rpm

General (continued)

Maximum engine torque:	
M52 B20 engine	190 Nm at 4200 rpm
M52TU B20 engine	190 Nm at 3500 rpm
M54 B22 engine	210 Nm at 3500 rpm
M52 B25 engine	245 Nm at 3950 rpm
M52TU B25 engine	245 Nm at 3500 rpm
M54 B25 engine	245 Nm at 3500 rpm
M52 B28 engine	280 Nm at 3950 rpm
M52TU B28 engine	280 Nm at 3500 rpm
M54 B30 engine	300 Nm at 3500 rpm
Direction of engine rotation	Clockwise (viewed from front of vehicle)
No 1 cylinder location	Timing chain end
Firing order	1-5-3-6-2-4
Compression ratio:	
M52 B20 engine	11.0 : 1
M52TU B20 engine	11.0 : 1
M54 B22 engine	10.7 : 1
M52 B25 engine	10.5 : 1
M52TU B25 engine	10.5 : 1
M54 B25 engine	10.5 : 1
M52 B28 engine	10.2 : 1
M52TU B28 engine	10.2 : 1
M54 B30 engine	10.2 : 1
Minimum compression pressure	10.0 to 11.0 bar

Camshafts

Endfloat	0.150 to 0.330 mm

Lubrication system

Minimum oil pressure at idle speed	0.5 bar
Regulated oil pressure	4.0 bar
Oil pump rotor clearances:	
Outer rotor to pump body	0.100 to 0.176 mm
Inner rotor endfloat	0.030 to 0.080 mm
Outer rotor endfloat	0.040 to 0.090 mm

Torque wrench settings

	Nm	lbf ft
Automatic transmission-to-engine bolts:		
Hexagon bolts:		
M8 bolts	24	18
M10 bolts	45	33
M12 bolts	82	61
Torx bolts:		
M8 bolts	21	15
M10 bolts	42	31
M12 bolts	72	53
Big-end bearing cap bolts*:		
Stage 1	5	4
Stage 2	20	15
Stage 3	Angle-tighten a further 70°	
Camshaft bearing cap nuts:		
M6 nuts	10	7
M7 nuts	15	11
M8 nuts	20	15
Camshaft screw-in pin	20	15
Camshaft screw-in pin nut:		
Stage 1	5	4
Stage 2	10	7
Camshaft setscrew **(left-hand thread)**	10	7
Camshaft sprocket:		
Stage 1	5	4
Stage 2:		
Screws	20	15
Nuts	10	7
Chain tensioner cover plug	40	30
Chain tensioner plunger cylinder	70	52
Crankshaft position sensor (M52 engine)	10	7

Torque wrench settings (continued)	**Nm**	**lbf ft**
Crankshaft pulley hub bolt*	410	303
Crankshaft rear oil seal housing bolts:		
M6 bolts	10	7
M8 bolts	22	16
Crankshaft vibration damper/pulley-to-hub bolts	22	16
Cylinder head bolts*:		
M52 engines:		
Stage 1	30	22
Stage 2	Angle-tighten a further 90°	
Stage 3	Angle-tighten a further 90°	
M52TU and M54 engines:		
Stage 1	40	30
Stage 2	Angle-tighten a further 90°	
Stage 3	Angle-tighten a further 90°	
Cylinder head cover bolts:		
M6 bolts	10	7
M7 bolts	15	11
Driveplate bolts*	120	89
Flywheel bolts*	105	77
Front crossmember bolts:*		
M10	47	35
M12	105	77
Ignition coil bolts	5	4
Main bearing cap bolts*:		
M52 engine with cast iron cylinder block:		
Stage 1	20	15
Stage 2	Angle-tighten a further 50°	
M52 engine with aluminium cylinder block, M52TU and M54 engines:		
Stage 1	20	15
Stage 2	Angle-tighten a further 70°	
Manual transmission-to-engine bolts:		
Hexagon head bolts:		
M8 bolts	25	18
M10 bolts	49	36
M12 bolts	74	55
Torx head bolts:		
M8 bolts	22	16
M10 bolts	43	32
M12 bolts	72	53
Oil feed pipe to VANOS adjustment unit	32	24
Oil filter housing and pipes on crankcase:		
M8	22	16
M20	40	30
Oil pipe to camshaft bearings	10	7
Oil pressure switch	27	20
Oil pump bolts (M8 bolts)	22	16
Oil pump cover	10	7
Oil pump sprocket nut **(left-hand thread)**:		
M6 thread	10	7
M10 x 1.00 mm thread	25	18
M10	47	35
Oil spray nozzles	10	7
Oil temperature switch	27	20
Sump oil drain plug:		
M12 plug	25	18
M22 plug	60	44
Sump to block:		
M6	10	7
M8	22	16
Sump lower section to upper section	10	7
Timing cover to crankcase:		
M6	10	7
M8	22	16
M10:		
Stage 1	20	15
Stage 2	Angle-tighten a further 70°	

Torque wrench settings (continued)

	Nm	lbf ft
Upper and lower timing chain cover nuts and bolts:		
M6 nuts/bolts	10	7
M7 nuts/bolts	15	11
M8 nuts/bolts	20	15
M10 nuts/bolts	47	35
VANOS solenoid valve	30	22
VANOS oil feed pipe to oil filter housing	32	24
VANOS adjustment unit cover screw plugs	50	37

** Do not re-use*

1 General information

How to use this Chapter

This Part of Chapter 2 describes the repair procedures that can reasonably be carried out on the engine while it remains in the vehicle. If the engine has been removed from the vehicle and is being dismantled as described in Part B, any preliminary dismantling procedures can be ignored.

Note that, while it may be possible physically to overhaul items such as the piston/connecting rod assemblies while the engine is in the car, such tasks are not usually carried out as separate operations. Usually, several additional procedures are required (not to mention the cleaning of components and oilways); for this reason, all such tasks are classed as major overhaul procedures, and are described in Part B of this Chapter.

Part B describes the removal of the engine/transmission from the car, and the full overhaul procedures that can then be carried out.

Engine description

General

The M52, M52TU and M54 engines are of 6-cylinder double overhead camshaft design, mounted in-line, with the transmission bolted to the rear end. The main differences between the engines are that the M52 engine is equipped with variable position control (VANOS) on the intake camshaft only, whilst the M52TU and M54 engines are equipped with VANOS on both camshafts. M54 unit is equipped with fully electronic throttle control (no throttle cable).

A timing chain drives the exhaust camshaft, and the intake camshaft is driven by a second chain from the end of the exhaust camshaft. Hydraulic cam followers are fitted between the camshafts and the valves. Each camshaft is supported by seven bearings incorporated in bearing castings fitted to the cylinder head.

The crankshaft runs in seven main bearings of the usual shell-type. Endfloat is controlled by thrust bearing shells on No 6 main bearing.

The pistons are selected to be of matching weight, and incorporate fully-floating gudgeon pins retained by circlips.

The oil pump is chain-driven from the front of the crankshaft.

Variable camshaft timing control

On all models, a variable camshaft timing control system, known as VANOS, is fitted. The VANOS system uses data supplied by the DME engine management system (see Chapter 4A), to adjust the timing of the camshafts independently via a hydraulic control system (using engine oil as the hydraulic fluid). On the M52 engine only the intake camshaft is fitted with VANOS, whereas on the M52TU and M54 engines VANOS is fitted to both camshafts. The camshaft timings are varied according to engine speed, retarding the timing (opening the valves later) at low and high engine speeds to improve low-speed driveability and maximum power respectively. At medium engine speeds, the camshaft timings are advanced (opening the valves earlier) to increase mid-range torque and to improve exhaust emissions.

Repairs with engine in place

The following operations can be carried out without having to remove the engine from the vehicle:

a) Removal and refitting of the cylinder head.
b) Removal and refitting of the timing chain and sprockets.
c) Removal and refitting of the camshafts.
d) Removal and refitting of the sump.
e) Removal and refitting of the big-end bearings, connecting rods, and pistons.*
f) Removal and refitting of the oil pump.
g) Renewal of the engine/transmission mountings.
h) Removal and refitting of the flywheel/driveplate.

** Although it is possible to remove these components with the engine in place, for reasons of access and cleanliness it is recommended that the engine is removed.*

2 Compression test – description and interpretation

1 When engine performance is down, or if misfiring occurs which cannot be attributed to the ignition or fuel systems, a compression test can provide diagnostic clues as to the engine's condition. If the test is performed regularly, it can give warning of trouble before any other symptoms become apparent.

2 The engine must be fully warmed-up to normal operating temperature, the battery must be fully-charged, and all the spark plugs must be removed (Chapter 1). The aid of an assistant will also be required.

3 Remove the fuel pump fuse (located in the passenger compartment fusebox), and if possible, start the engine and allow it to run until the residual fuel in the system is exhausted. Failure to do so could result in damage to the catalytic converter.

4 Fit a compression tester to the No 1 cylinder spark plug hole – the type of tester which screws into the plug thread is to be preferred.

5 Have the assistant hold the throttle wide open, and crank the engine on the starter motor. After one or two revolutions, the compression pressure should build-up to a maximum figure, and then stabilise. Record the highest reading obtained.

6 Repeat the test on the remaining cylinders, recording the pressure in each.

7 All cylinders should produce very similar pressures; a difference of more than 2 bars between any two cylinders indicates a fault. Note that the compression should build-up quickly in a healthy engine; low compression on the first stroke, followed by gradually-increasing pressure on successive strokes, indicates worn piston rings. A low compression reading on the first stroke, which does not build-up during successive strokes, indicates leaking valves or a blown head gasket (a cracked head could also be the cause). Deposits on the undersides of the valve heads can also cause low compression.

8 BMW minimum values for compression pressures are given in the Specifications.

9 If the pressure in any cylinder is low, carry out the following test to isolate the cause. Introduce a teaspoonful of clean oil into that cylinder through its spark plug hole, and repeat the test.

10 If the addition of oil temporarily improves the compression pressure, this indicates that bore or piston wear is responsible for the pressure loss. No improvement suggests that leaking or burnt valves, or a blown head gasket, may be to blame.

11 A low reading from two adjacent cylinders is almost certainly due to the head gasket

3.4 Unclip the plastic cover (arrowed) from the intake camshaft

3.5 Fit the special tool to the VANOS oil port

3.8a With the No 1 piston at TDC, the tips of the front cam lobes face each other

having blown between them; the presence of coolant in the engine oil will confirm this.

12 If one cylinder is about 20 percent lower than the others and the engine has a slightly rough idle, a worn camshaft lobe could be the cause.

13 If the compression reading is unusually high, the combustion chambers are probably coated with carbon deposits. If this is the case, the cylinder head should be removed and decarbonised.

14 On completion of the test, refit the spark plugs (see Chapter 1) and refit the fuel pump fuse.

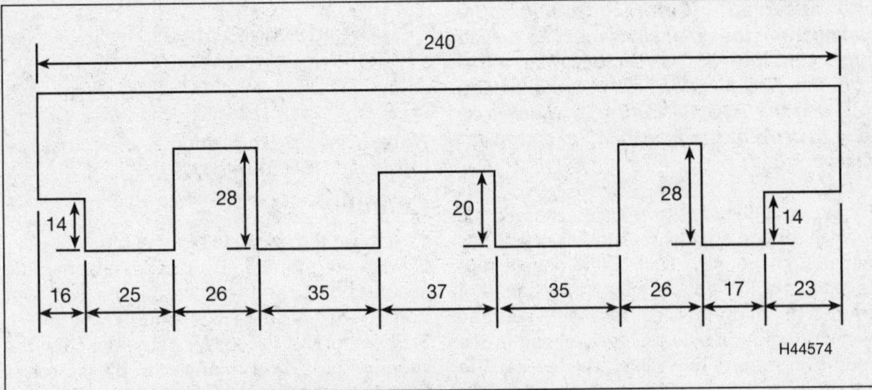

3.8b Make up a template from sheet metal

All dimensions in mm

3 Top Dead Centre (TDC) for No 1 piston – locating

Note: *To lock the engine in the TDC position, reset the VANOS units, and to check the position of the camshafts, special tools will be required. Some of these tools can easily be improvised. Read through the text prior to attempting the procedure.*

1 Top Dead Centre (TDC) is the highest point in the cylinder that each piston reaches as it travels up and down when the crankshaft turns. Each piston reaches TDC at the end of the compression stroke and again at the end of the exhaust stroke, but TDC generally refers to piston position on the compression stroke. No 1 piston is at the timing chain end of the engine.

2 Positioning No 1 piston at TDC is an essential part of many procedures, such as timing chain removal and camshaft removal.

3 Remove the cylinder head cover as described in Section 4.

4 Unclip the plastic cover from the intake camshaft **(see illustration)**.

M52TU and M54 engines

5 In order to accurately set the camshaft positions, the VANOS units must be set as follows. Unscrew the VANOS unit oil pressure pipe from the intake camshaft VANOS unit, and fit special BMW tool 11 3 450 to the port on the VANOS unit **(see illustration)**.

6 Using a clean cloth, cover the top of the VANOS unit as, when compressed air is applied, some oil will be sprayed out.

7 Connect a compressed air line to the union of the special tool, and apply a pressure of 2.0 to 8.0 bar. This pressure will reset the VANOS units as the engine is rotated.

All engines

8 Using a socket or spanner on the crankshaft pulley bolt, turn the engine clockwise at least two complete revolutions until the tips of the front cam lobes on the exhaust and intake camshafts face one another. Note that the square flanges on the rear of the camshafts should be positioned with the sides of the flanges exactly at right-angles to the top surface of the cylinder head. BMW special tools 11 3 240 are available to lock the camshafts in this position. The tools slide over the square flanges of the camshafts and hold them at 90° to the cylinder head upper surface, once the two outer cylinder head cover studs have been removed. If the tools are not available, an alternative can be fabricated from steel or aluminium plate **(see illustrations)**.

9 Pull the blanking plug from the timing hole in the left-hand rear corner flange of the cylinder block (access is much improved if the starter motor is removed – see Chapter 5A).

10 To 'lock' the crankshaft in position, a special tool will now be required. BMW tool 11 2 300 can be used, but one can be made up by machining a length of steel rod **(see illustration)**.

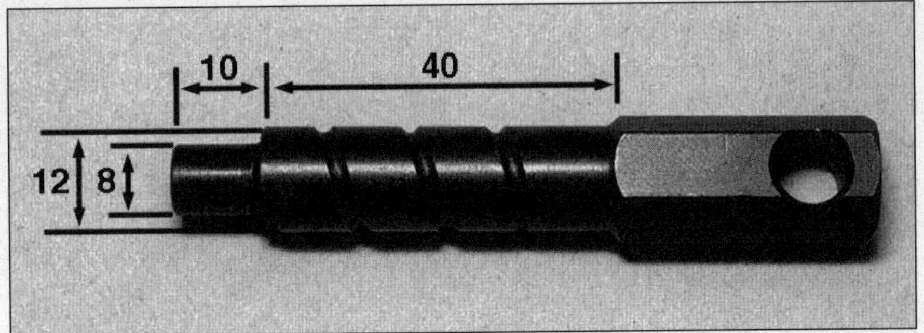

3.10 Flywheel locking tool

All dimensions in mm

11 Insert the rod through the timing hole. If necessary, turn the crankshaft slightly until the rod enters the TDC hole in the flywheel **(see illustrations)**.

12 The crankshaft is now 'locked' in position with No 1 piston at TDC. On M52TU and M54 engines, disconnect the compressed air from the VANOS oil port.

Warning: If, for any reason, it is necessary to turn either or both of the camshafts with No 1 piston positioned at TDC, and either of the timing chain tensioners are slackened or removed (or the timing chains removed), the following precaution must be observed. Before turning the camshaft(s), the crankshaft must be turned approximately 30° anti-clockwise away from the TDC position (remove the locking rod from the TDC hole in the flywheel to do this) to prevent the possibility of piston-to-valve contact.

13 **Do not** attempt to turn the engine with the flywheel or camshaft(s) locked in position, as engine damage may result. If the engine is to be left in the 'locked' state for a long period of time, it is a good idea to place suitable warning notices inside the vehicle, and in the engine compartment. This will reduce the possibility of the engine being cranked on the starter motor.

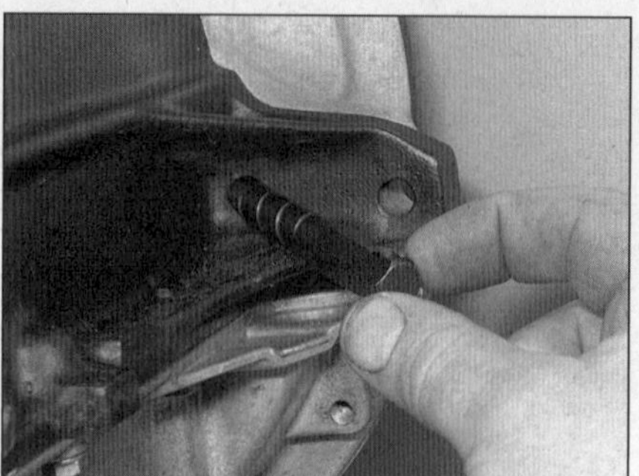

3.11a Insert the rod through the timing hole . . .

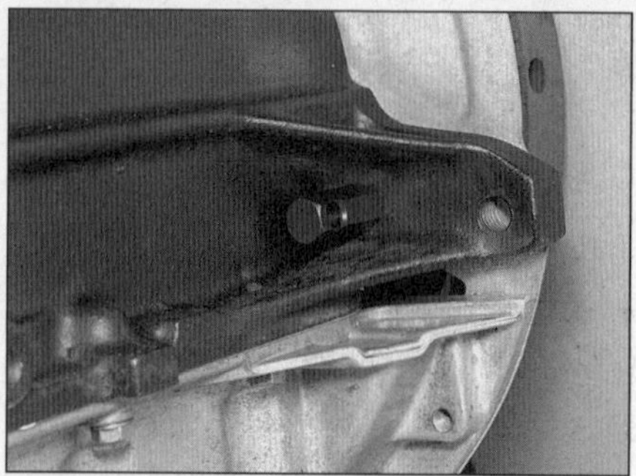

3.11b . . . until it enters the TDC hole in the flywheel – engine removed for clarity

4 Cylinder head cover – removal and refitting

Note: *New gaskets and/or seals may be required on refitting – see text.*

Removal

1 Remove the engine oil filler cap.

2 Prise out the two cover caps, unscrew the securing nuts, and remove the plastic cover from the fuel rail **(see illustration)**.

3 Prise out the two cover caps, unscrew the securing nuts, and remove the plastic cover from the ignition coils, then manipulate the cover over the oil filler neck.

4 Note their fitted positions, then unbolt the earth leads from cylinder head cover **(see illustration)**.

5 Slide up the locking elements and unplug the wiring connectors from the ignition coils. Note there are two different types of wiring connector locking elements used **(see illustrations)**.

6 Release the wiring from the clips on the cylinder head cover, then move the complete ducting/wiring assembly to one side, clear of the cylinder head cover.

7 Unscrew the ignition coil securing nuts/screws (single-spark coils only), then carefully pull the coils from the spark plugs **(see illustrations)**. Note the locations of the earth leads and the coil wiring brackets.

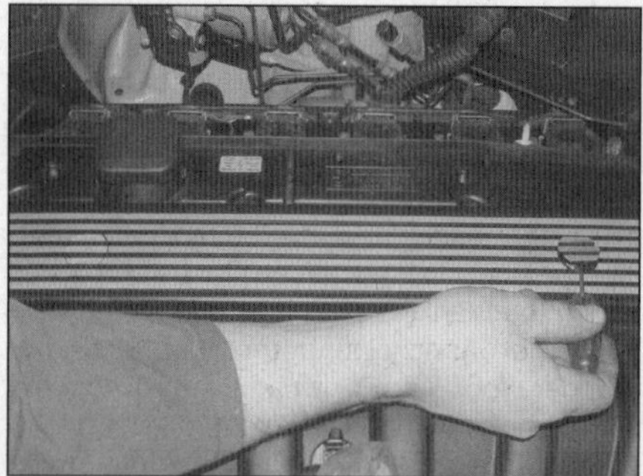

4.2 Prise out the cover caps

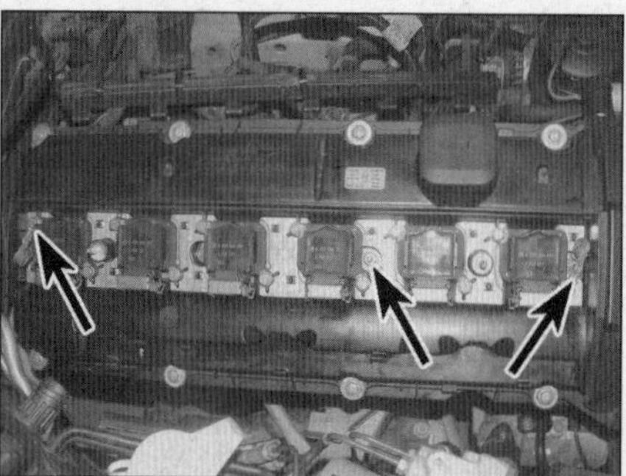

4.4 Note their positions, then unbolt the earth leads (arrowed) from the cylinder head cover – M52 engine

4.5a Slide up the catch and disconnect the wiring plug (single-spark coils) . . .

4.5b . . . or lift the lever and disconnect the wiring plug (rod-type coils)

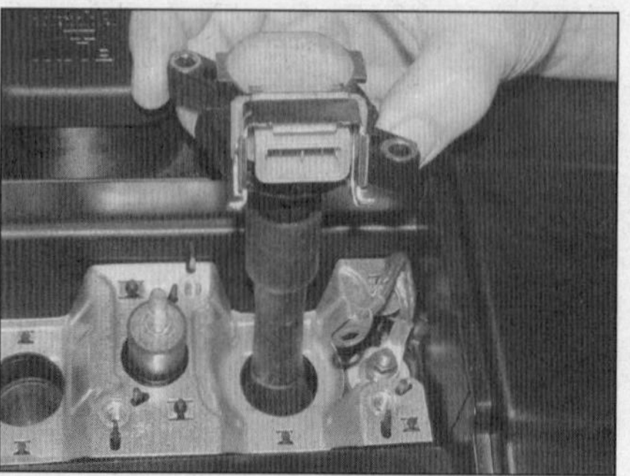

4.7a Undo the bolts and pull the single-spark coils from place

4.7b Rod-type coils simply pull up from position

4.8 Squeeze the collar and disconnect the breather hose from the cylinder head cover

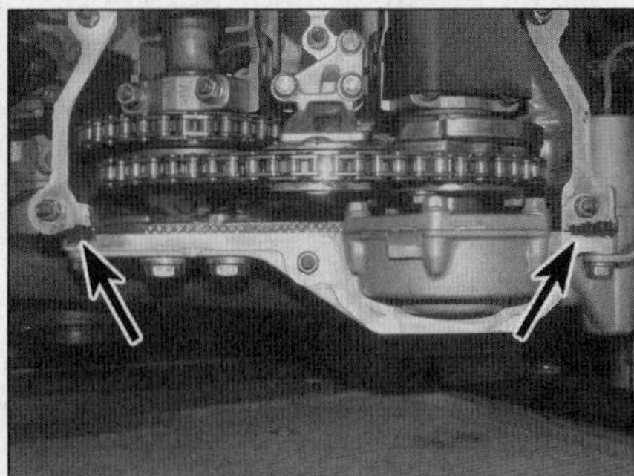

4.11a Apply sealant to the area where the VANOS unit meets the cylinder head (arrowed) . . .

4.11b . . . and the corners of the semi-circular cut-outs at the rear of the cylinder head (arrowed)

4.11c Don't forget to fit the spark plug hole gaskets

8 Squeeze together the two sides of the retaining collar and disconnect the breather hose from the side of the cylinder head cover **(see illustration)**.

9 Unscrew the securing bolts/nuts (including the ones in the centre of the cover) and lift off the cylinder head cover. Note the locations of all washers, seals and gaskets, and recover any which are loose.

Refitting

10 Commence refitting by checking the condition of all seals and gaskets. Renew any which are perished or damaged.

11 Clean the gasket/sealing faces of the cylinder head and the cylinder head cover, then apply a bead of Drei Bond 1209 (available from BMW dealers and automotive parts retailers) to the area where the VANOS unit/timing chain cover meets the cylinder head, and the corners of the semi-circular cut-out sections at the rear of the cylinder head and (on M52TU and M54 engines) the VANOS unit. Lay the main (outer) gasket and the spark plug hole (centre) gaskets in position on the cylinder head cover **(see illustrations)**.

12 Lay the cylinder head cover in position, taking care not to disturb the gaskets. Check that the tabs on the rear of the main gasket are correctly positioned in the cut-outs in the rear of the cylinder head.

5.5 Undo the bolts and remove the damper/pulley from the hub

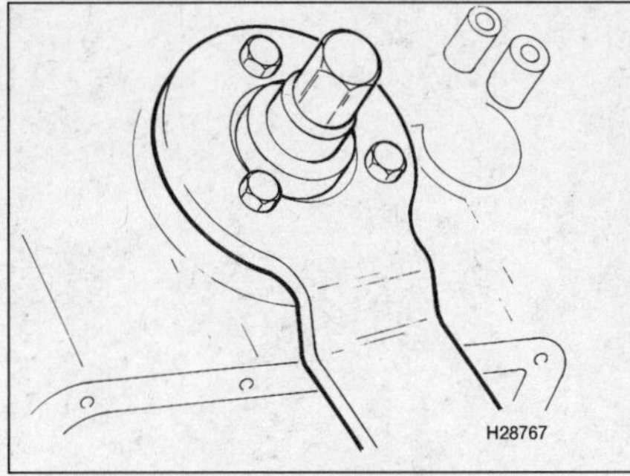

5.7 BMW special tools used to hold the crankshaft pulley hub

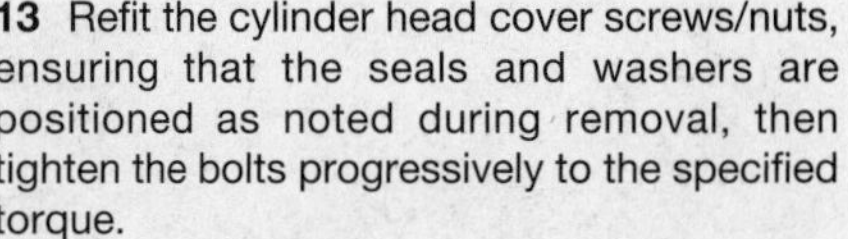

13 Refit the cylinder head cover screws/nuts, ensuring that the seals and washers are positioned as noted during removal, then tighten the bolts progressively to the specified torque.

14 Further refitting is a reversal of the removal procedure, bearing in mind the following points.

a) Check that the ignition coil earth leads are correctly positioned as noted before removal.

b) Tighten the coil securing nuts/screws to the specified torque.

c) Check that the rubber seals are in place when reconnecting the HT lead plugs to the coils.

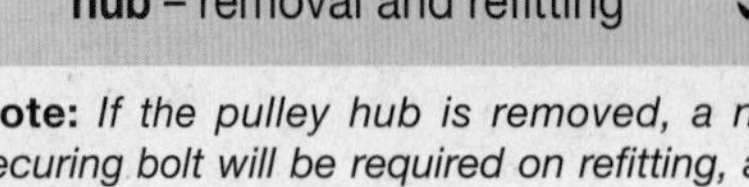

5 Crankshaft vibration damper/pulley and pulley hub – removal and refitting

Note: *If the pulley hub is removed, a new securing bolt will be required on refitting, and a torque wrench capable of measuring very high torque will be required.*

Removal

1 Remove the clips/screws and remove the engine undershield.

2 Remove the viscous cooling fan and cowl assembly as described in Chapter 3.

3 Remove the auxiliary drivebelts as described in Chapter 1.

4 Two different designs of damper/pulley and hub may be fitted. On some models the pulley/damper is bolted to the hub (two piece), and on others the hub is integral with the damper/pulley (one piece).

Two piece damper/pulley and hub

5 Unscrew the securing bolts, and remove the vibration damper/pulley from the hub **(see illustration)**. If necessary, counterhold the hub using a socket or spanner on the hub securing bolt.

6 To remove the hub, the securing bolt must be unscrewed.

Warning: The crankshaft pulley hub securing bolt is very tight. A tool will be required to counterhold the hub as the bolt is unscrewed. Do not attempt the job using inferior or poorly-improvised tools, as injury or damage may result.

7 Make up a tool to hold the pulley hub. A suitable tool can be fabricated using two lengths of steel bar, joined by a large pivot bolt. Bolt the holding tool to the pulley hub using the pulley-to-hub bolts **(see illustration)**. Alternatively use special tools 11 2 150 and 11 2 410 available from BMW dealers or automotive tool specialists.

8 Using a socket and a long swing-bar, loosen the pulley hub bolt. Note that the bolt is very tight.

9 Unscrew the pulley hub bolt, and remove

5.9 Unscrew the hub bolt and remove the washer . . .

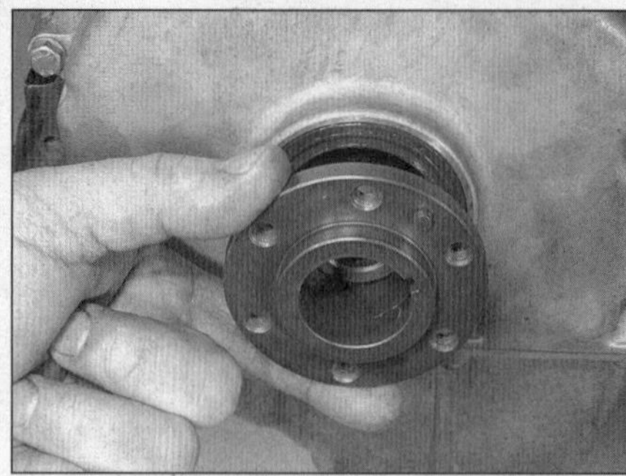

5.10 . . . then withdraw the hub

5.12a Using BMW special tools to counterhold the pulley/hub . . .

5.12b . . . or use a strap wrench to hold it

the washer **(see illustration)**. Discard the bolt, a new one must be used on refitting.

10 Withdraw the hub from the end of the crankshaft **(see illustration)**. If the hub is tight, use a puller to draw it off.

11 Recover the Woodruff key from the end of the crankshaft if it is loose.

One piece damper/pulley and hub

12 In order to prevent the hub from rotating whilst undoing the central bolt, BMW specify the use of tools 11 8 190 and 11 8 200, which engage in the holes between the webs of the pulley hub. In the absence of these tools, it may be possible to prevent the hub from rotating by using a strap wrench around the pulley **(see illustrations)**. The bolt is very tight, and assistance will be required.

13 Undo the hub bolt, and remove the washer. Discard the bolt, a new one must be fitted.

14 Withdraw the hub from the end of the crankshaft. If the hub is tight, use a puller to draw it off.

15 Recover the Woodruff key from the end of the crankshaft if it is loose.

Refitting

16 If the pulley hub has been removed, it is advisable to take the opportunity to renew the oil seal in the lower timing chain cover, with reference to Section 6.

17 If the pulley hub has been removed, proceed as follows, otherwise proceed to paragraph 21 (two piece damper/pulley and hub).

18 Where applicable, refit the Woodruff key to the end of the crankshaft, then align the groove in the pulley hub with the key, and slide the hub onto the end of the crankshaft.

19 Refit the washer, noting that the shoulder on the washer must face the hub, and fit a **new** hub securing bolt.

Two piece damper/pulley and hub

20 Bolt the holding tool to the pulley hub, as during removal, then tighten the hub bolt to the specified torque. Take care to avoid injury and/or damage.

21 Where applicable, unbolt the holding tool, and refit the vibration damper/pulley, ensuring that the locating dowel on the hub engages with the corresponding hole in the damper/pulley.

22 Refit the damper/pulley securing bolts, and tighten to the specified torque. Again, counterhold the pulley if necessary when tightening the bolts.

One piece damper/pulley and hub

23 Counterhold the hub using the method employed during removal, and tighten the bolt to the specified torque.

All models

24 Refit the auxiliary drivebelts as described in Chapter 1.

25 Refit the viscous cooling fan and cowl as described in Chapter 3.

26 Where applicable, refit the splash guard to the engine underside.

6 Timing chain cover – removal and refitting

Note: *New timing cover gaskets and a new crankshaft front oil seal will be required on refitting. RTV sealant will be required to coat the cylinder head/cylinder block joint – see text.*

Removal

1 Drain the cooling system as described in Chapter 1.

2 Remove the cylinder head cover as described in Section 4.

3 Remove the auxiliary drivebelts as described in Chapter 1.

4 Remove the thermostat as described in Chapter 3.

5 Remove the crankshaft pulley/damper and hub as described in Section 5.

6 Remove the sump as described in Section 12.

7 Undo the two bolts and remove the auxiliary drivebelt tensioner **(see illustration)**.

8 The coolant pump pulley must now be removed. Counterhold the pulley by wrapping an old drivebelt around it and clamping tightly, then unscrew the securing bolts and withdraw the pulley.

9 On M52 engines, unbolt the crankshaft position sensor from above the crankshaft pulley position, and move it to one side.

10 On all engines, working at the top of the timing chain cover, drive out the two cover dowels. Drive out the dowels towards the rear of the engine, using a pin-punch (less than 5.0 mm diameter) **(see illustration)**.

11 It is now necessary to remove the VANOS

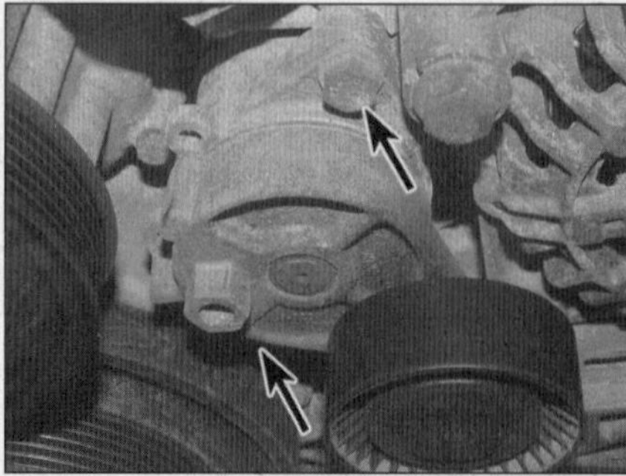

6.7 Unscrew the tensioner bolts (arrowed)

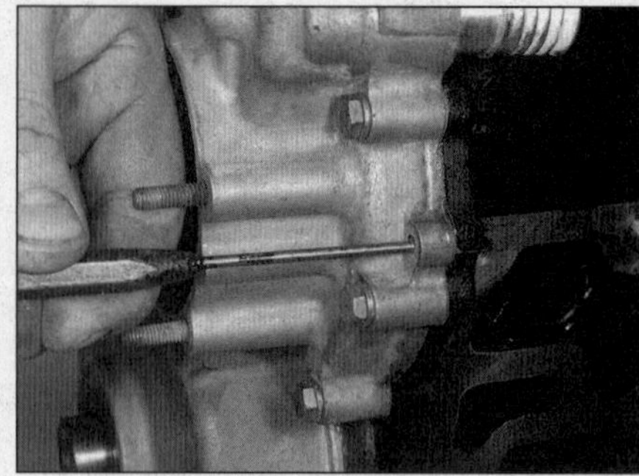

6.10 Drive the locating dowels from the timing chain cover

6.12 Remove the timing chain cover-to-cylinder head bolts (arrowed)

6.13a Unscrew the securing bolts (arrowed) . . .

adjustment unit (see Section 9), for access to the timing chain cover-to-cylinder head bolts.

12 Unscrew the three timing chain cover-to-cylinder head bolts, and lift the bolts from the cylinder head. Note that one of the bolts also secures the secondary timing chain guide **(see illustration)**.

13 Unscrew the timing chain cover-to-cylinder block bolts, then withdraw the cover from the front of the engine **(see illustrations)**. Recover the gaskets.

Refitting

14 Commence refitting by levering out the oil seal from the timing chain cover.

15 Thoroughly clean the mating faces of the cover, cylinder block and cylinder head.

16 Fit a new oil seal to the timing chain cover, using a large socket or tube, or a block of wood to drive the seal into position **(see illustration)**.

17 Drive the cover dowels into position in the top of the cover so that they protrude from the rear (cylinder block mating) face of the cover by approximately 2.0 to 3.0 mm.

18 Position new gaskets on the cover, and hold them in position using a little grease.

19 Apply a little Drei Bond 1209 (available from BMW dealers and automotive parts retailers) to the cylinder head/cylinder block joint at the two points where the timing chain cover contacts the cylinder head gasket **(see illustration)**.

20 Offer the cover into position, ensuring that the gaskets stay in place. Make sure that the dowels engage with the cylinder block, and fit the cover securing bolts. Tighten the bolts finger-tight only at this stage.

21 Drive in the cover dowels until they are flush with the outer face of the cover.

22 Progressively tighten the cover securing bolts to the specified torque (do not forget the three cover-to-cylinder head bolts).

23 Refit the VANOS adjustment unit as described in Section 9.

24 Refit the crankshaft damper/pulley hub and damper/pulley as described in Section 5.

25 On M52 engines, refit the crankshaft position sensor and tighten the bolt to the specified torque.

26 The remainder of refitting is a reversal of removal, bearing in mind the following points.

a) Ensure the auxiliary drivebelt hydraulic tensioner strut is fitted correctly. The TOP/OBEN arrow must point upwards.

b) Refit the auxiliary drivebelts with reference to Chapter 1.

c) Refit the thermostat and housing with reference to Chapter 3.

d) Refit the cylinder head cover (Section 4).

e) Refit the sump as described in Section 12.

f) On completion, refill the cooling system and check the coolant level, as described in Chapter 1 and 'Weekly Checks' respectively.

7 Timing chains – removal, inspection and refitting

Secondary chain removal

1 Remove the VANOS adjustment unit as described in Section 9.

M52 engine

2 Remove the four exhaust sprocket retaining screws previously slackened during the VANOS removal procedure, along with the thrustwasher.

3 Slacken and remove the nuts securing the sprocket to the intake camshaft. Note that some engines are fitted with just a single thrustwasher over the intake camshaft

6.13b . . . and remove the timing chain cover (shown with the cylinder head removed)

6.16 Drive the new oil seal into position

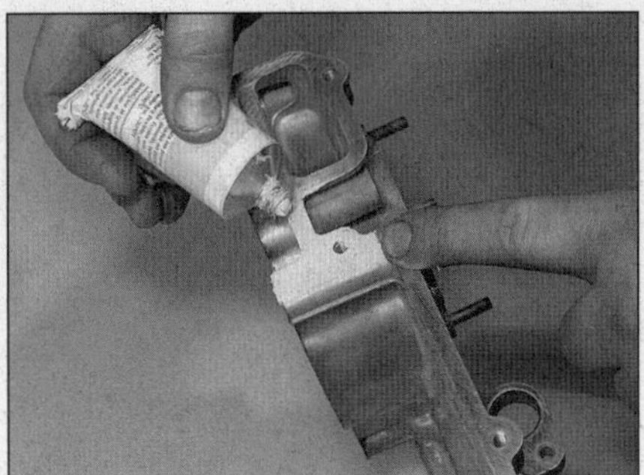
6.19 Apply sealant to the areas where the timing chain cover contacts the cylinder head gasket

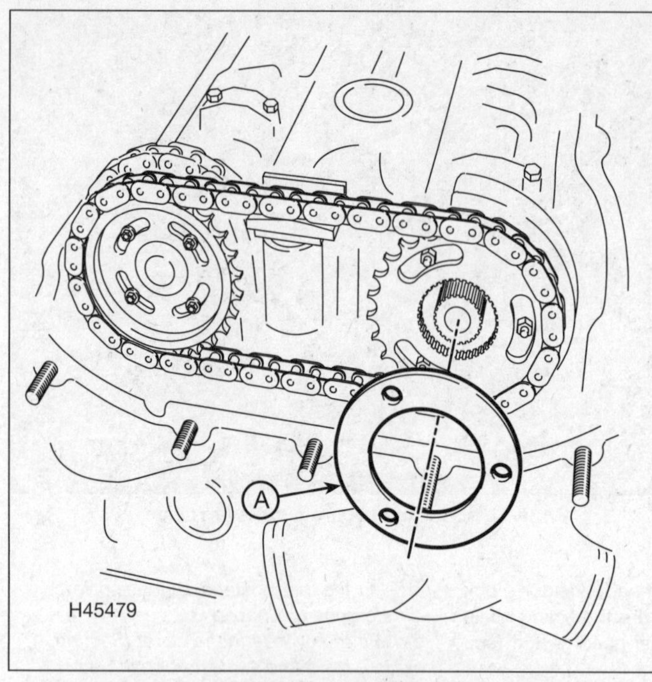

7.3a Some M52 engines are fitted with a single thrustwasher (A) . . .

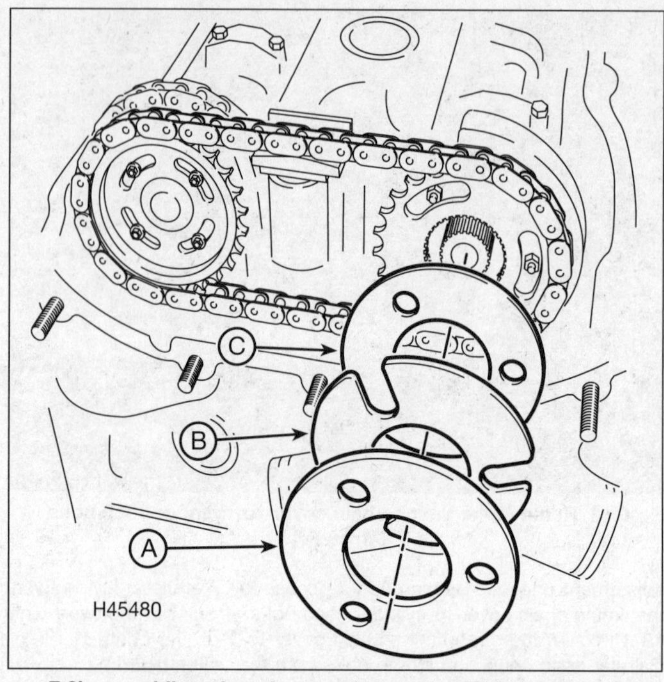

7.3b . . . whilst others have a plate spring (B) in between a 4.0 mm (A) and a 2.0 mm thick thrustwasher (C)

sprocket, whilst some are fitted with two thrustwashers and a plate spring **(see illustrations)**. Remove the thrustwasher(s) and plate spring as appropriate.

4 Remove the exhaust and intake camshaft sprockets together with the secondary chain.

7.5 Unscrew the timing chain tensioner from the right-hand side of the engine

7.8 Remove the sensor gear and plate spring from the exhaust camshaft sprocket

M52TU and M54 engines

5 Unscrew the timing chain tensioner plunger from the right-hand side of the engine **(see illustration)**. Discard the sealing ring, a new one must be fitted.

7.7 Use a drill bit (arrowed) to lock down the secondary timing chain tensioner

7.9 Undo the three nuts and remove the corrugated washer from the sprocket

Warning: The chain tensioner plunger has a strong spring. Take care when unscrewing the cover plug.

6 If the tensioner is to be re-used, compress and release the tensioner plunger a few times, to evacuate any oil inside.

7 Press down the secondary chain tensioner plunger and lock it in place by inserting a suitable drill bit **(see illustration)**.

8 Undo the nuts and remove the camshaft position sensor gear from the exhaust camshaft sprocket, then remove the plate spring **(see illustration)**.

9 Undo the three intake camshaft sprocket nuts and remove the corrugated washer **(see illustration)**.

10 Unscrew the three screws from the exhaust camshaft sprocket and lift away the secondary chain together with the sprockets, friction washer and intake camshaft toothed shaft **(see illustration)**. If these items are to

7.10 Remove the exhaust sprocket with the chain, friction washer, intake sprocket and the intake camshaft toothed shaft

7.15 The sprocket securing bolt holes/studs must be aligned in the centre of the sprocket holes

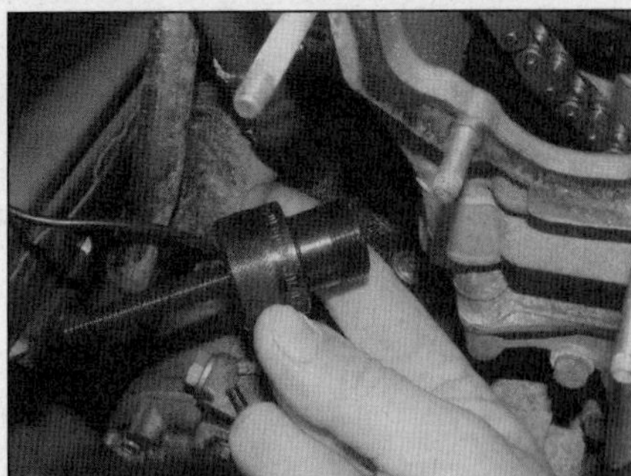

7.19 Fit the BMW tool into the tensioner aperture

7.20 Insert the chain into the special tool. If the tool is not available, arrange them so there are 16 pins between the positions indicated

be re-used, store them together in order that they are refitted to their original locations.

Secondary chain inspection

11 The chain should be renewed if the sprockets are worn or if the chain is worn (indicated by excessive lateral play between the links, and excessive noise in operation). It is wise to renew the chain in any case if the engine is dismantled for overhaul. Note that the rollers on a very badly worn chain may be slightly grooved. To avoid future problems, if there is any doubt at all about the condition of the chain, renew it.

12 Examine the teeth on the sprockets for wear. Each tooth forms an inverted V. If worn, the side of each tooth under tension will be slightly concave in shape when compared with the other side of the tooth (ie, the teeth will have a hooked appearance). If the teeth appear worn the sprockets must be renewed. Also check the chain guide and tensioner contact surfaces for wear, and renew any worn components as necessary.

Secondary chain refitting

13 Ensure that No 1 piston is still positioned at TDC, with the crankshaft locked in position. Check the position of the camshafts using the template.

M52 Engine

14 Lay the chain over the sprockets, noting that when the sprockets are refitted, the securing bolt holes/studs on the camshafts must be centred in the elongated holes in the sprockets. Note that the intake camshaft sprocket fits with the flat side facing the VANOS adjustment unit, and the raised collar facing the camshaft.

15 Fit the sprockets to the camshafts, ensuring that the securing bolts holes/studs are aligned with the centre of the elongated sprocket holes **(see illustration)**.

16 Refit the thrustwasher(s) and plate spring to the intake camshaft sprocket as applicable. On engines with the two thrustwashers and plate spring, the 2.0 mm thick thrustwasher is fitted first, followed by the plate spring (concave side towards the sprocket) and 4.0 mm thick thrustwasher. Tighten the retaining nuts to the specified torque.

17 Refit the thrustwasher to the exhaust camshaft, but only finger-tighten the retaining nuts at this stage. The sprocket must be able to rotate independently of the camshaft.

18 Refit the VANOS unit as described in Section 9.

M52TU and M54 engines

19 Check that the primary chain and sprocket on the exhaust camshaft is still in place. Fit special tool 11 4 220 into the primary tensioner aperture, then turn the adjuster screw on the tool until the end of the screw just touches the tensioning rail **(see illustration)**.

20 In order to establish the correct relationship between the two sprockets and the chain, access to BMW special tool 11 6 180 is necessary. Insert the two sprockets into the chain and lay the assembly in the special tool. In the absence of the special tool, arrange the sprockets so that there are 16 chain pins between the positions on the sprockets **(see illustration)**.

21 Fit the chain and sprockets over the end of the camshafts so that the 'master' tooth gap on the inner diameter of the intake sprocket exactly aligns with the 'master' tooth gap on the shaft protruding from the end of the camshaft **(see illustration)**.

22 Refit the toothed shaft into the end of the intake camshaft, and insert the locking pin or 'master' spline so that it fits into the 'master' tooth gap in both the camshaft and sprocket **(see illustration)**. Push the toothed shaft into the intake sprocket until approximately 1 mm of the splines can still be seen.

23 Refit the corrugated washer onto the intake sprocket with the FRONT marking forward. Refit the securing nuts, but only hand-tighten them at this stage.

24 Refit the screws to the exhaust sprocket, tighten them to 5 Nm (4 lbf ft), then undo them 180°.

25 Fit the friction washer and plate spring to the exhaust sprocket. Note that the spring

7.21 The gaps in the intake sprocket and camshaft must align (arrowed)

7.22 Insert the toothed shaft locking pin or 'master' spline into the tooth gaps

7.25 Fit the plate spring with the F at the front

7.26 Fit the sensor gear so that the arrow aligns with the upper gasket face (arrowed)

7.30 Use the special BMW tool to centre the toothed shafts and sprockets

must be fitted with the F mark facing forward. If the mark is no longer visible, fit the spring with the convex side to the front **(see illustration)**.

26 Refit the exhaust camshaft position sensor gear with the raised section to the right-hand side of the engine and the arrow aligned with the cylinder head upper gasket face **(see illustration)**. Hand-tighten the nuts only at this stage

27 Pull out the exhaust toothed shaft from the centre of the sprocket as far as it will go.

28 Compress the secondary chain tensioner plunger and remove the locking pin/drill bit.

29 Using a torque wrench, apply a torque of 0.7 Nm (0.5 lbf ft) to the adjusting screw on the special tool fitted to the primary chain tensioner aperture. In the absence of a suitable torque wrench, turn the adjusting screw by hand just enough to remove any play in the chain. Check that all play has been removed by attempting to turn the primary chain sprocket on the exhaust camshaft by hand.

30 To ensure that the toothed shafts in the sprockets, and the sprockets themselves are correctly centred, BMW tool 11 6 150 must be fitted in place of the VANOS unit. Position the tool over the VANOS unit mounting studs (without the gasket), and evenly tighten the nuts until the tool is in full contact with the cylinder head. This tool positions the toothed shafts, and holds them in place whilst the sprocket bolts/nuts are tightened **(see illustration)**. This tool is critical to the timing of the camshafts, and its use is essential.

31 Evenly and progressively tighten the sprockets nuts/bolts to the specified Stage 1 torque, beginning with the Torx screws of the exhaust sprocket, followed by the exhaust sprocket nuts, and then the intake sprocket nuts. Repeat the sequence tightening the screws to the Stage 2 torque and then the nuts. With the sprockets nuts/screws tightened and the BMW tool 11 6 150 still in place, remove the locking pin from the crankshaft, and the locking tools/template from the rear ends of the camshafts. Using a spanner or socket on the crankshaft pulley bolt, rotate the crankshaft two complete revolutions clockwise until the crankshaft locking pin can be re-inserted.

32 Check the position of the camshafts with the locking tools/template, and ensure the camshaft timing is correct. **Note:** *Due to the rubberised sprocket(s), tolerance in the VANOS unit and the toothed shafts running clearance, the tool locking the intake camshaft may misalign by up to 1.0 mm with the square flange, but the timing would still be considered correct.*

33 Remove the toothed shaft/sprocket centring/positioning tool, and refit the VANOS adjustment unit as described in Section 9.

Primary chain removal

34 Remove the secondary timing chain as described previously in this Section.

M52 engine

35 Remove the drill locking the secondary chain tensioner plunger in position, then lift out the plunger and spring, unscrew the securing bolts, and withdraw the secondary chain tensioner from the cylinder head **(see illustrations)**.

36 Unscrew the securing bolts and withdraw the secondary chain guide **(see illustrations)**.

7.35a Lift out the plunger and spring . . .

7.35b . . . then unscrew the securing bolts . . .

7.35c . . . and withdraw the secondary chain tensioner

7.36a Unscrew the securing bolts (arrowed) . . .

7.36b . . . and withdraw the secondary chain guide

7.40 Withdraw the exhaust sprocket complete with chain

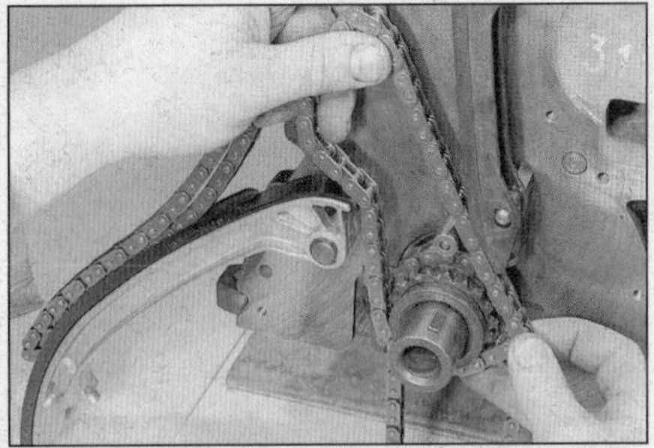
7.42 Manipulate the tensioner rail and unhook the chain from the crankshaft sprocket – viewed with the engine removed

7.43 Remove the clip from the lower pivot to remove the tensioner rail – viewed with the engine removed

7.44 Release the retaining clips to remove the chain guide

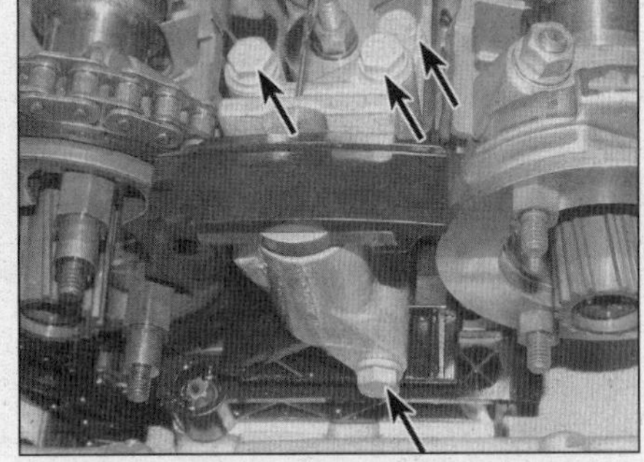
7.46 Remove the secondary chain tensioner bolts (arrowed)

7.47 Undo the three screw-in pins from the exhaust sprocket

37 Unscrew the timing chain tensioner plunger cover plug from the right-hand side of the engine. Recover the sealing ring.

Caution: The chain tensioner plunger has a strong spring. Take care when unscrewing the cover plug.

38 Recover the spring and withdraw the tensioner plunger.

39 Remove the timing chain cover as described in Section 6.

40 Withdraw the primary chain sprocket from the exhaust camshaft, complete with the chain **(see illustration)**. Remove the sprocket. Note which way the sprocket faces to ensure correct installation.

41 Note the routing of the chain in relation to the tensioner rail and the chain guide.

42 Manipulate the tensioner rail as necessary to enable the chain to be unhooked from the crankshaft sprocket and lifted from the engine **(see illustration)**.

Warning: Once the primary timing chain has been removed, do not turn the crankshaft or camshafts, as there is a danger of the valves hitting the pistons.

43 If desired, the tensioner rail can now be removed after removing the clip from the lower pivot **(see illustration)**.

44 Similarly, the chain guide can be removed after releasing the upper and lower retaining clips. Take care when releasing the retaining clips, as the clips are easily broken **(see illustration)**.

M52TU and M54 engines

45 Remove the toothed shaft and sleeve from the centre of the exhaust camshaft sprocket.

46 Undo the four bolts and remove the secondary chain tensioner **(see illustration)**.

47 Undo the three 'screw-in' pins from the exhaust sprocket, lift the chain and remove the sprocket from the end of the camshaft **(see illustration)**. Note which way round the sprocket is fitted.

48 Remove the timing chain cover as described in Section 6.

49 Note the routing of the chain in relation to the tensioner rail and the chain guide.

50 Manipulate the tensioner rail as necessary to enable the chain to be unhooked from the crankshaft sprocket and lifted from the engine **(see illustration 7.42)**.

Warning: Once the primary timing chain has been removed, do not turn the crankshaft or the camshafts, as there is a danger of the valves hitting the pistons.

51 If desired, the tensioner rail can now be removed after removing the clip from the lower pivot **(see illustration 7.43)**.

52 Similarly, the chain guide can be removed after releasing the upper and lower retaining clips. Take care when releasing the retaining clips, as the clips are easily broken **(see illustration 7.44)**.

Primary chain refitting

53 Ensure No 1 piston is still at TDC, with the crankshaft locked in position. Check the position of the camshafts using the template.

54 Commence refitting by engaging the chain with the crankshaft sprocket.

55 Where applicable, refit the chain guide and the tensioner rail, ensuring that the chain is correctly routed in relation to the guide and tensioner rail, as noted before removal. Take care when refitting the chain guide, as the clips are easily broken.

M52 engine

56 Manipulate the exhaust camshaft primary chain sprocket until the timing arrow is pointing vertically (12 o'clock position in relation to the engine block), then engage the chain with the sprocket. Fit the sprocket the to exhaust camshaft, aligning the sprocket so that the tapped holes in the camshaft flange are positioned at the ends of the elongated slots in the sprocket **(see illustration)**. Ensure the sprocket is facing the correct way as noted before removal.

7.56 The tapped holes in the camshaft flange should be positioned at the ends of the elongated slots in the sprocket

7.61 Align the arrow on the sprocket with the upper edge of the cylinder head (arrowed)

7.66 The toothed shaft master spline must engage with the corresponding tooth gap in the camshaft and sleeve

7.67 The holes in the sprocket must be central in the oval holes in the toothed sleeve (arrowed)

57 Install the secondary chain guide and the secondary chain tensioner. Note that the tensioner plunger must be installed with the cut-out in the plunger pad positioned on the right-hand side of the engine.
58 Fit special tool 11 4 220 into the tensioner aperture (see Section 9), then turn the adjuster screw on the tool until the end of the screw just touches the tensioning rail. Note that the exhaust camshaft sprocket should now have moved anti-clockwise so that the tapped holes in the camshaft flange are centred in the elongated holes in the sprocket.
59 Refit the timing chain cover as described in Section 6.
60 Install the secondary timing chain as previously described in this Section.

M52TU and M54 engines

61 Manipulate the exhaust camshaft primary chain sprocket until the timing arrow on the sprocket is aligned with the upper edge of the cylinder head, then engage the chain with the sprocket **(see illustration)**. Fit the sprocket to the exhaust camshaft. Ensure that the sprocket is fitted the correct way round as noted before removal, and that the timing arrow is still in alignment with the upper edge of the cylinder head.
62 Refit the timing chain cover as described in Section 6.
63 Fit special tool 11 4 220 into the tensioner aperture (see Section 9), then turn the adjuster screw on the tool until the end of the screw just touches the tensioning rail. Note that the exhaust camshaft sprocket may now have moved anti-clockwise – if necessary reposition the sprocket in the chain so that the timing arrow re-aligns with the upper surface of the cylinder head.
64 Insert the three 'screw-in' pins through the exhaust sprocket, and tighten them to the specified torque.
65 Refit the secondary timing chain tensioner and tighten the bolts securely.
66 Refit the toothed shaft and sleeve to the exhaust camshaft sprocket so that the 'master' tooth gap in the sleeve aligns exactly with the corresponding tooth gap in the end of the camshaft. Note that the toothed shaft incorporates a pin or 'master' spline which must engage in both tooth gaps **(see illustration)**.
67 Push the exhaust camshaft tooth shaft in until the threaded holes in the camshaft sprocket are central with respect to the oval holes in the tooth sleeve **(see illustration)**.
68 Refit the secondary timing chain as described in this Section.

8 Timing chain sprockets and tensioners – removal, inspection and refitting

Camshaft sprockets

1 Removal, inspection and refitting of the sprockets is described as part of the secondary timing chain removal and refitting procedure in Section 7.

Crankshaft sprocket

Removal

2 The sprocket is combined with the oil pump drive sprocket. On some engines, the sprocket may be a press-fit on the end of the crankshaft.
3 Remove the primary timing chain as described in Section 7.
4 Slide the sprocket from the front of the crankshaft. If the sprocket is a press-fit, use a three-legged puller to pull the sprocket from the crankshaft. Protect the threaded bore in the front of the crankshaft by refitting the pulley hub bolt, or by using a metal spacer between the puller and the end of the crankshaft. Note which way round the sprocket is fitted to ensure correct refitting.
5 Once the sprocket has been removed, recover the Woodruff key from the slot in the crankshaft if it is loose.

Inspection

6 Inspection is described with the timing chain inspection procedure in Section 7.

Refitting

7 Where applicable, refit the Woodruff key to the slot in the crankshaft.
8 Slide the sprocket into position on the crankshaft. Ensure that the sprocket is fitted the correct way round as noted before removal. If a press-fit sprocket is to be refitted, before refitting, the sprocket must be heated to a temperature of 150°C. **Do not** exceed this temperature, as damage to the sprocket may result.
9 Once the sprocket has been heated to the given temperature, align the slot in the sprocket with the Woodruff key, then tap the sprocket into place with a socket or metal tube.

Warning: When the sprocket is heated, take precautions against burns – the metal will stay hot for some time.

10 Refit the primary timing chain as described in Section 7.

Secondary chain tensioner

Removal

11 Remove the secondary timing chain as described in Section 7.
12 Remove the tool locking the secondary timing chain tensioner in position, then withdraw the plunger, spring and plunger housing **(see illustrations)**.

8.12a Withdraw the secondary timing chain plunger . . .

8.12b . . . spring . . .

8.12c . . . and plunger housing

8.13 Withdraw the secondary timing chain tensioner housing

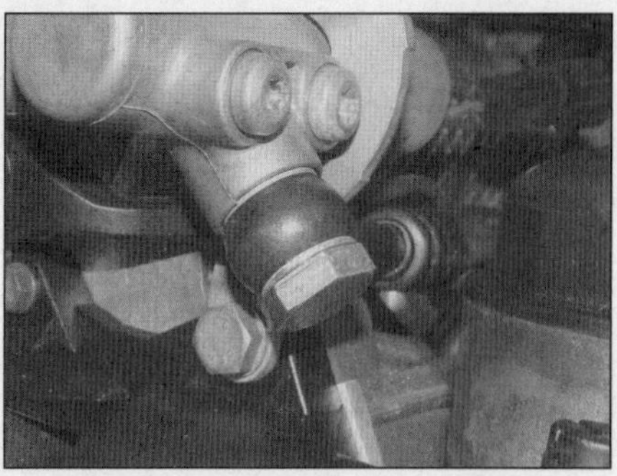

9.3 Unscrew the VANOS union bolt

13 Unscrew the securing bolts and withdraw the chain tensioner housing from the cylinder head **(see illustration)**.

Inspection

14 Inspect the tensioner, and renew if necessary. Check the plunger and the plunger housing for wear and damage. Inspect the chain contact face of the plunger slipper for wear, and check the condition of the spring. Renew any components which are worn or damaged.
15 When refitting the plunger to the tensioner, note that the cut-out in the plunger should be positioned on the right-hand side of the engine when the assembly is refitted.

Refitting

16 Refit the chain tensioner and tighten the bolts securely.
17 Refit the tool to lock the tensioner in position.
18 Refit the secondary timing chain as described in Section 7.

Primary chain tensioner

19 Removal and refitting is described as part of the primary timing chain removal procedure in Section 7.

9 Variable valve timing system (VANOS) components – removal, inspection and refitting

Adjustment unit – removal

1 Remove the viscous cooling fan and fan cowl assembly as described in Chapter 3.
2 Remove the cylinder head cover as described in Section 4.

M52 engine

3 Unscrew the union bolt, and disconnect the oil feed pipe from the front of the VANOS adjustment unit **(see illustration)**. Recover the sealing rings.
4 Disconnect the VANOS solenoid valve wiring plug.
5 Unscrew the securing nut and bolt, and remove the engine lifting bracket from the front of the engine.
6 Trace the wiring back from the crank angle sensor and disconnect the wiring plug, then

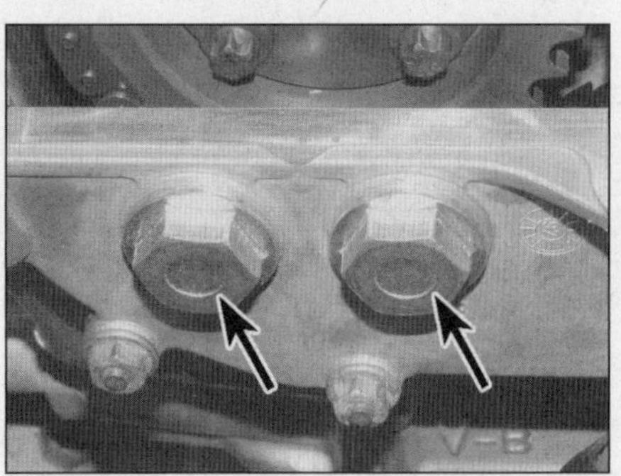

9.9 Undo the two cover plugs (arrowed)

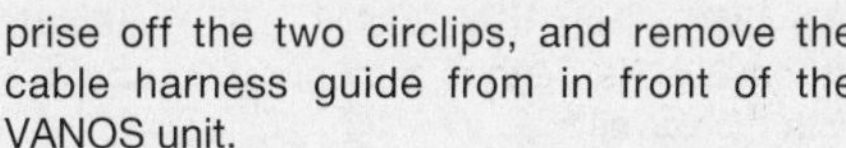

prise off the two circlips, and remove the cable harness guide from in front of the VANOS unit.
7 Unclip the plastic cover from the intake camshaft.
8 Position the crankshaft and camshafts at TDC on No 1 piston, as described in Section 3.
9 Unscrew the two cover plugs from the front of the VANOS adjustment unit to expose the lower exhaust camshaft sprocket securing bolts **(see illustration)**. Recover the sealing rings.
10 Slacken all four exhaust camshaft sprocket securing bolts.
11 Press the secondary timing chain tensioner pad down, and lock it in position using a tool made up from a length of welding rod or similar material. Insert the tool through the holes in the top of the tensioner to hold the tensioner plunger down **(see illustration 7.7)**.
12 Unscrew the nuts securing the VANOS

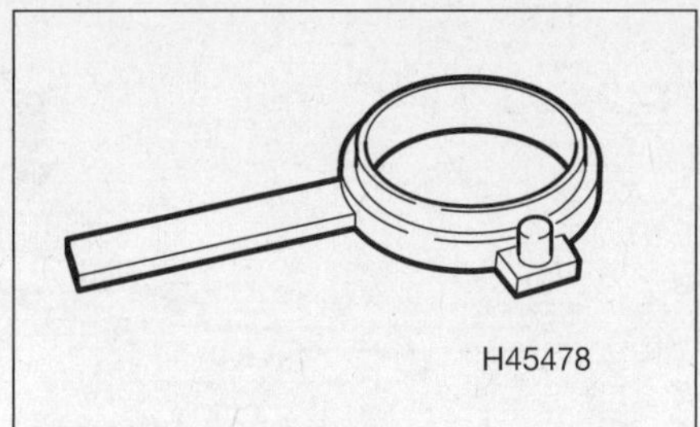

9.13a A special BMW tool (11 5 490) is available to rotate the exhaust camshaft sprocket and secondary chain as the VANOS unit is withdrawn

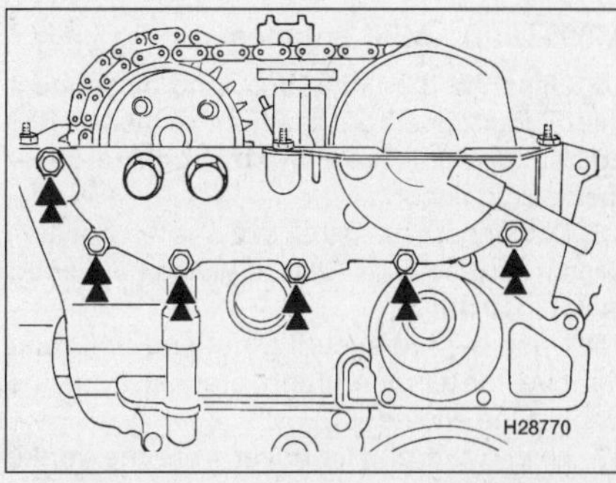

9.12 Unscrew the securing nuts (arrowed) and remove the VANOS adjustment unit

adjustment unit to the timing cover **(see illustration)**.
13 Two different intake camshaft sprockets may be fitted. The first type has just one thrustwasher fitted, and the second type has two thrustwashers either side of a plate spring (see paragraph 3 of Section 7). If your engine has just the one thrustwasher, the VANOS adjustment unit can be simply pulled from place. If your engine has two thrustwashers and a plate spring, the exhaust camshaft sprocket must be rotated clockwise (without moving the camshaft) as the VANOS adjustment unit is withdraw. A special BMW tool (No 11 5 490) is available to rotate the sprocket, although it may be possible to construct a home-made equivalent **(see illustration)**. With great care, it is possible to rotate the exhaust camshaft using a large screwdriver **(see illustration)**. Recover the gasket.

9.13b With care, the exhaust sprocket can be turned with a large flat-bladed screwdriver

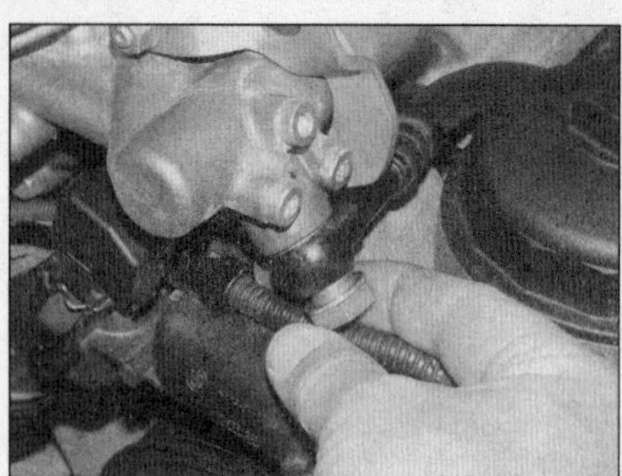
9.14 Disconnect the oil feed pipe from the VANOS unit

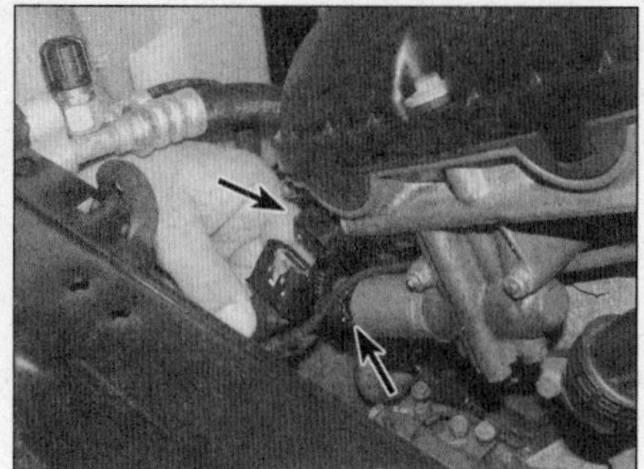
9.15 Disconnect the camshaft position sensor and the solenoid valve (arrowed)

9.19 Undo the cover plugs from the VANOS unit (arrowed)

M52TU and M54 engines

14 Unscrew the union bolt, and disconnect the oil feed pipe from the front of the VANOS adjustment unit **(see illustration).** Recover the sealing rings.

15 Disconnect the exhaust camshaft position sensor and solenoid valves wiring connector **(see illustration).**

16 Unscrew the securing nut and bolt, and remove the engine lifting bracket from the front of the engine.

17 Unclip the plastic cover from the intake camshaft.

18 Position the crankshaft and camshafts at TDC on No 1 piston, as described in Section 3.

19 Unscrew the two cover plugs from the front of the VANOS adjustment unit **(see illustration).** Be prepared for oil spillage and discard the sealing rings, new ones must be fitted.

20 Using a pair of thin-nose pliers pull the sealing caps from the end of the camshafts **(see illustration).**

21 Using a Torx bit, unscrew the setscrews from the end of the camshafts. Note that the setscrews are **left-hand thread** and unscrew clockwise **(see illustration).**

22 Undo the retaining nuts and remove the VANOS adjustment unit from the front of the engine. Recover the gasket.

23 Do not rotate the crankshaft, camshafts or move the toothed shaft in the end of the camshafts with the VANOS unit removed, otherwise the pistons may come in contact with the valves.

Adjustment unit – inspection

24 To test the operation of the VANOS adjustment unit, special equipment is required. Testing must therefore be entrusted to a BMW dealer.

Adjustment unit – refitting

25 Ensure that the crankshaft and camshafts are still at TDC on No 1 cylinder as described in Section 3.

26 Make sure that the dowel sleeves are in position on the top VANOS adjustment unit securing studs in the cylinder head.

27 Apply a little Drei Bond 1209 sealant to the corners of the joint surfaces between the cylinder head and the VANOS adjustment unit, then fit a new gasket over the studs on the cylinder head **(see illustration).**

M52 engine

28 Ensure the exhaust camshaft sprocket and secondary timing chain are fully rotated clockwise to their stop position. On engines with two thrustwashers and a plate spring on the intake camshaft sprocket, it will be necessary to use the BMW tool (No 11 5 490) or home-made equivalent to rotate the sprocket – ensure neither camshaft rotates.

29 Using moderate hand pressure, push the splined shaft back into the VANOS adjustment unit as far as the stop **(see illustration).**

30 Offer the VANOS adjustment unit into position and, if necessary, rotate the splined shaft on the VANOS adjustment unit slightly

9.20 Use a pair of pliers to remove the sealing caps

9.21 The setscrews in the end of the camshafts have a *left-hand* thread

9.27 Apply a little sealant to the top of the gasket surface on each side of the cylinder head

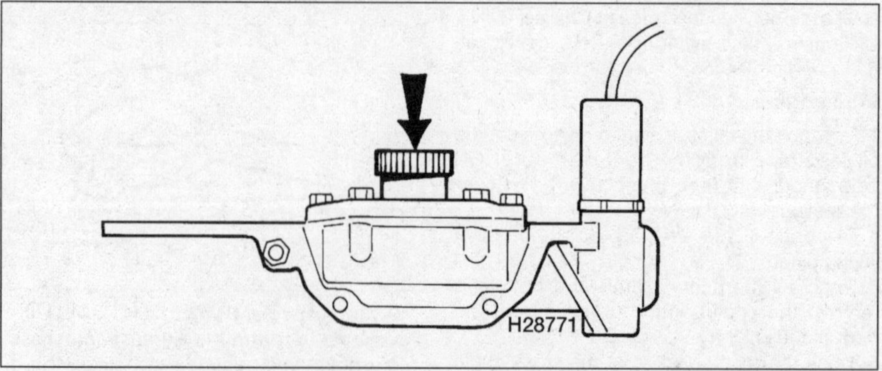

9.29 Push the splined shaft into the VANOS adjustment unit as far as the stop

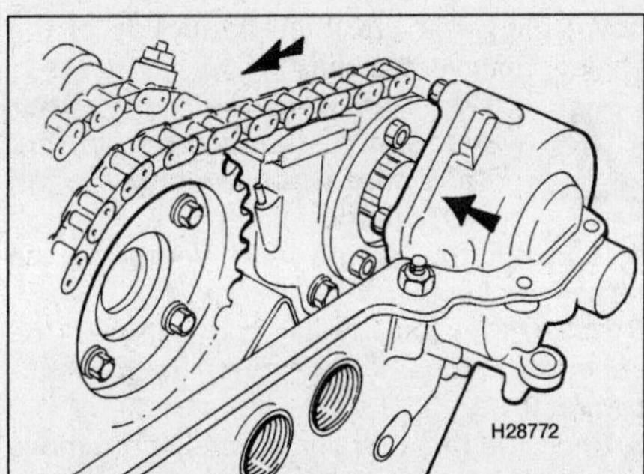

9.32 The sprockets and chain will turn anti-clockwise as the VANOS unit is fitted

until the internal splines on the VANOS unit shaft engage with the splines on the sprocket.

31 It is now necessary to engage the VANOS adjustment unit shaft splines with the internal splines in the camshaft. Turn the exhaust camshaft sprocket slowly anti-clockwise until the VANOS adjustment unit shaft splines mesh with the camshaft.

Warning: It is essential to ensure that the FIRST suitable spline meshes when the sprocket is turned back anti-clockwise from its clockwise stop.

32 Push the VANOS adjustment unit fully onto the mounting studs, noting that on engines with just one thrustwasher on the intake camshaft sprocket, the camshaft sprockets and chain will turn as the VANOS adjustment unit is pushed into position (this is due to the helical sprocket splines) **(see illustration)**. On engines with two thrustwashers and a plate spring on the intake camshaft sprocket, the exhaust camshaft sprocket and secondary chain must be slowly rotated anti-clockwise as the VANOS adjustment unit is pushed fully into place **(see illustration 9.13b)**. As the unit is pushed into position, guide the sprocket and chain anti-clockwise as necessary by hand.

33 Tighten the VANOS adjustment unit retaining nuts securely.

9.35 Unscrew the primary chain tensioner cover plug

34 Remove the tool locking the secondary timing chain tensioner in position.

35 Unscrew the primary timing chain tensioner plunger cover plug from the right-hand side of the engine **(see illustration)**. Recover the sealing ring.

Warning: The chain tensioner plunger has a strong spring. Take care when unscrewing the cover plug.

36 Fit special tool No 11 4 220 into the tensioner aperture and turn the adjuster screw on the tool until the end of the screw just touches the tensioner rail.

37 Using a torque wrench apply a torque of 1.3 Nm (1 lbf ft) to the adjusting screw on the special tool **(see illustration)**.

38 Tighten the exhaust camshaft sprocket bolts to the specified torque.

39 Remove the template from the camshafts, then withdraw the locking rod from the timing hole in the cylinder block.

40 Rotate the engine through two complete revolutions clockwise, then install the locking rod to the timing hole in the cylinder block, ensuring the tool engages with the flywheel.

41 Install the template to check the position of the camshafts. If the template cannot by fitted with the flywheel locked in position, the VANOS adjustment unit has been incorrectly installed.

42 Unscrew the special tool from the primary chain tensioner aperture.

43 Install the primary chain tensioner plunger, ensuring that the guide lugs engage with the tensioner rail.

44 Fit the tensioner spring, then fit the cover plug, using a new seal, and tighten it to the specified torque.

45 Install the camshaft sprocket securing bolts cover plugs to the front of the VANOS adjustment unit, using new sealing rings. Tighten the plugs to the specified torque.

46 At this point, BMW recommend that the operation of the VANOS adjustment unit is checked. As this procedure involves the use of special BMW tools, you may wish to entrust this task to a BMW dealer.

47 Fit special tool No 11 3 450 with a banjo bolt to the oil inlet port on the VANOS adjustment unit, and apply an air pressure (from a compressor) of 2.0 to 8.0 bar.

48 Using a pair of vernier calipers, measure the distance from the edge of the secondary chain tensioner and the edge of the intake camshaft sensor gear **(see illustration)**.

49 Connect the end of special tool No 12 6 411 to the connector from the VANOS solenoid valve, and the other end of the tool to the battery terminals.

Warning: If the polarity of the feed to the solenoid valve is reversed, the diode inside the valve will be destroyed.

50 Using a pair of vernier calipers, again measure the distance from the edge of the secondary chain tensioner and the edge of the intake camshaft sensor gear. The sensor gear must have a travel of at least 8.5 mm. If the distance travelled by the sensor gear is less that this, the VANOS adjustment unit must be removed and refitted.

51 The remainder of refitting is a reversal of removal.

M52TU and M54 engines

52 Refit the VANOS adjustment unit and tighten the nuts to the securely.

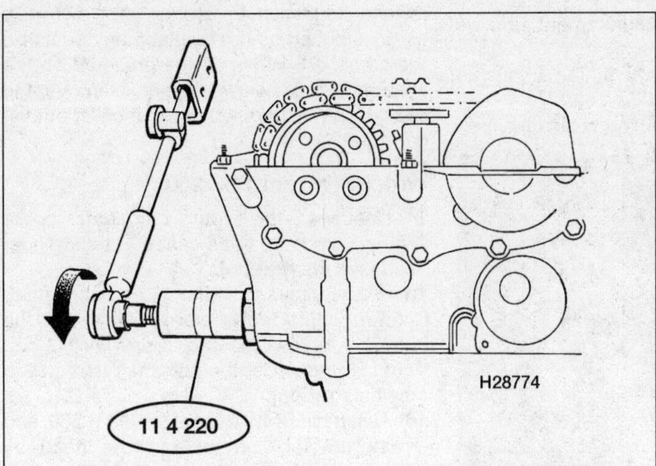

9.37 Apply the specified torque to the tool (see text)

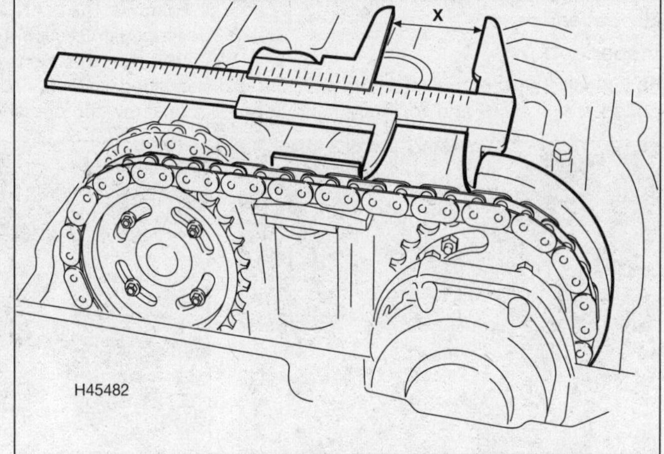

9.48 Measure the distance from the edge of the secondary chain tensioner to the edge of the intake camshaft sensor gear

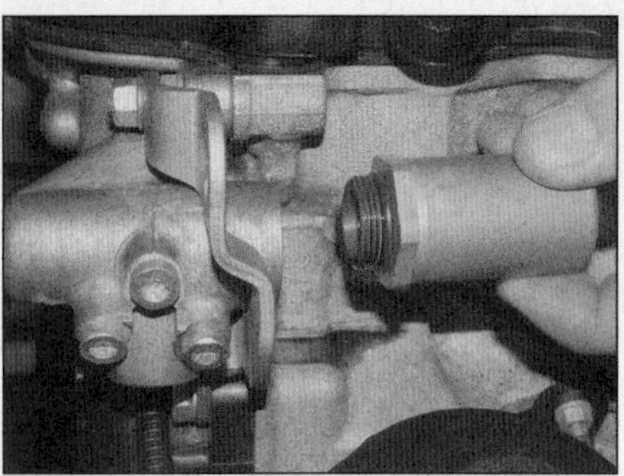
9.57 Unscrew the VANOS solenoid valve

53 Refit the setscrews into the ends of the camshafts and tighten them to the specified torque. Note that the setscrews are **left-hand thread**. Check the condition of the O-ring seals and refit the sealing caps into the ends of the camshafts.

54 The remainder of the refitting procedure is a reversal of removal, bearing in mind the following points.

a) Use new sealing rings when reconnecting the oil feed pipe to the VANOS adjustment unit.
b) Refit the cylinder head cover with reference to Section 4.
c) Refit the viscous cooling fan and cowl assembly as described in Chapter 3.
d) Ensure the crankshaft locking tool is removed prior to starting the engine.
e) If a new VANOS adjustment unit has been fitted, the camshaft timing must be checked as described in Section 3.

Solenoid valve

Note: *A new sealing ring will be required on refitting.*

Removal

55 Ensure that the ignition is switched off.

56 Disconnect the solenoid valve wiring connector, which is clipped to the engine wiring harness behind the oil filter assembly.

57 Using an open-ended spanner, unscrew the solenoid valve and recover the seal **(see illustration)**.

Inspection

58 Check that the solenoid plunger can be pulled freely back-and-forth by hand **(see illustration)**. If not, the solenoid must be renewed.

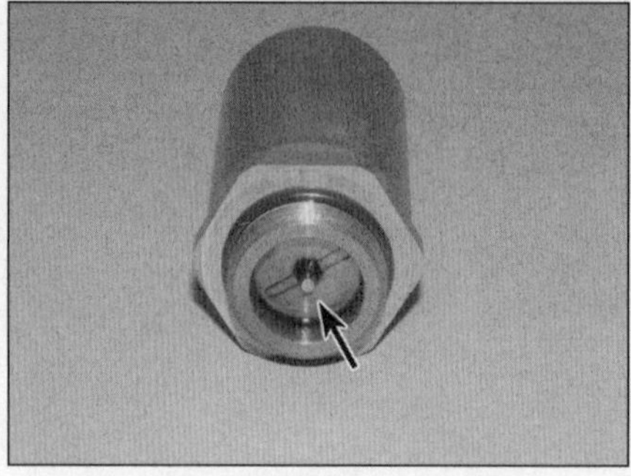
9.58 Check the solenoid plunger (arrowed) moves freely

59 On M52 engines, check that the hydraulic piston in the VANOS adjustment unit can be moved easily. If it's difficult to move the hydraulic piston, the complete VANOS adjustment unit must be renewed.

Refitting

60 Refitting is a reversal of removal, but use a new sealing ring, and tighten the solenoid to the specified torque.

10 Camshafts and followers – removal, inspection and refitting

Warning: BMW tool 11 3 260 may be required for this operation. This tool is extremely difficult to improvise due to its rugged construction and the need for accurate manufacture. It is possible to remove the camshafts without this tool, however, it is essential that the camshaft bearing caps are removed gradually and evenly. Failure to do so will result in damage to the camshaft(s).

Removal – M52 engine

1 Remove the VANOS adjustment unit as described in Section 9.

2 Remove the secondary timing chain as described in Section 7.

3 Unscrew the primary timing chain tensioner cover plug from the right-hand side of the engine. Recover the sealing ring.

Warning: The chain tensioner plunger has a strong spring. Take care when unscrewing the cover plug.

4 Recover the spring and withdraw the tensioner plunger.

5 Undo the four bolts and remove the secondary chain tensioner **(see illustration 8.13)**.

6 Undo the three retaining bolts and remove the secondary chain guide **(see illustration 7.36a)**.

7 Withdraw the primary chain sprocket from the exhaust camshaft, complete with chain. Remove the sprocket.

Caution: Keep tension on the chain, and tie up the end of the chain using wire or string to prevent it from dropping into the lower timing chain cover and/or disengaging from the crankshaft sprocket.

8 Remove the crankshaft locking pin then, holding the primary timing chain under tension with your hand, carefully rotate the crankshaft 30° anti-clockwise to prevent accidental piston-to-valve contact.

9 If required, undo the three 'screw-in' pins on the end of the intake camshaft and remove the thrustwasher and camshaft sensor gear **(see illustration 7.47)**.

10 Remove the template from the camshafts.

11 Unscrew the spark plugs from the cylinder head.

12 Check the camshaft bearing caps for identification marks. The caps are numbered from the timing chain end of the engine, and the marks can normally be read from the exhaust side of the engine. The exhaust camshaft bearing caps are marked A1 to A7, and the intake camshaft caps are marked E1 to E7.

Without BMW tool 11 3 260

13 Gradually, and evenly over the length of the camshaft, slacken the intake camshaft bearing caps a little at a time. The idea is to release the camshafts bearing caps as evenly as possible so as not to place any strain on the camshaft. When all the pressure on the camshaft has been released, remove the caps, lifting them out in order, then lift out the camshaft.

With BMW tool 11 3 260

14 Unscrew the four camshaft cover securing studs from the centre of the cylinder head **(see illustration)**.

10.14 Unscrew the four camshaft cover securing studs

15 As the intake camshaft No 1 bearing cap is fitted with adapter sleeves, unscrew the nuts and remove the cap to prevent the cap from binding whilst the camshaft is removed **(see illustration)**.

10.15 No 1 camshaft bearing cap is fitted with adapter sleeves

16 Assemble BMW special tool 11 3 260, and mount the tool on the cylinder head by screwing the mounting bolts into the spark plug holes. Position the tool so that the plungers are located over the relevant

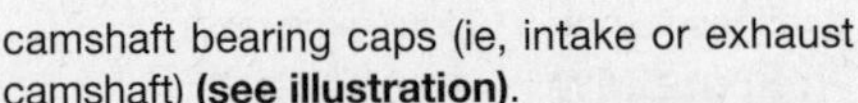

10.16 BMW special tool fitted to the cylinder head

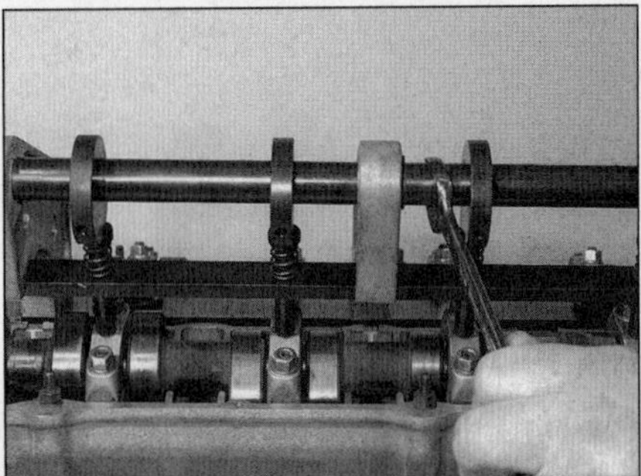

10.17 Use a spanner to turn the eccentric shaft, and apply pressure to the bearing caps

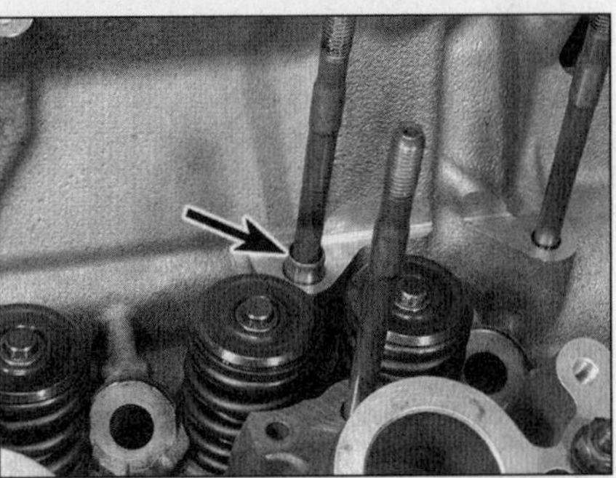

10.46 Bearing casting location dowel (arrowed) on the cylinder head stud at No 2 bearing location

camshaft bearing caps (ie, intake or exhaust camshaft) **(see illustration)**.

17 Apply pressure to the camshaft bearing caps by turning the eccentric shaft on the tools using a spanner **(see illustration)**.

18 Unscrew the remaining camshaft bearing cap nuts.

19 Release the pressure on the special tool shaft, then unbolt the tool from the cylinder head.

20 Lift off the bearing caps, keeping them in order, then lift out the camshaft.

All methods

21 The camshaft bearing casting can now be lifted from the cylinder head. This should be done very slowly, as the cam followers will be released as the casting is lifted off – if the casting is lifted off awkwardly, the cam followers may fall out. Do not allow the cam followers to fall out and get mixed up, as they must be fitted to their original locations.

22 With the bearing casting removed, lift the cam followers from the cylinder head. Identify the followers for location, and store them upright in a container of clean engine oil to prevent the oil from draining from inside the followers.

23 Repeat the procedure on the remaining camshaft. Do not forget to mark the cam followers Intake and Exhaust.

Removal – M52TU and M54 engines

24 Remove the VANOS adjustment unit as described in Section 9.

25 Remove the secondary timing chain as described in Section 7.

26 Remove the toothed shaft and sleeve from the centre of the exhaust camshaft sprocket.

27 Undo the four bolts and remove the secondary chain tensioner **(see illustration 8.13)**.

28 Undo the three 'screw-in' pins from the exhaust sprocket, lift the chain and remove the sprocket from the end of the camshaft. Note which way round the sprocket is fitted.

29 Remove the crankshaft locking pin then, holding the primary timing chain under tension with your hand, carefully rotate the crankshaft 30° anti-clockwise to prevent accidental piston-to-valve contact.

Caution: Use a length of wire or a cable tie through the primary timing chain and secure it to the cylinder head to prevent the chain falling down into the timing cover and/or disengaging from the crankshaft sprocket.

30 If required, undo the three 'screw-in' pins on the end of the intake camshaft and remove the thrustwasher and camshaft sensor gear **(see illustration 7.47)**.

31 Remove the template from the camshafts.

32 Unscrew the spark plugs from the cylinder head.

33 Check the camshaft bearing caps for identification marks. The caps are numbered from the timing chain end of the engine, and the marks can normally be read from the exhaust side of the engine. The exhaust camshaft bearing caps are marked A1 to A7, and the intake camshaft caps are marked E1 to E7.

Without BMW tool 11 3 260

34 Gradually, and evenly over the length of the camshaft, slacken the intake camshaft bearing caps a little at a time. The idea is to release the camshafts bearing caps as evenly as possible so as not to place any strain on the camshaft. When all the pressure on the camshaft has been released, remove the caps, lifting them out in order, then lift out the camshaft.

With BMW tool 11 3 260

35 Unscrew the four camshaft cover securing studs from the centre of the cylinder head **(see illustration 10.14)**.

36 As the intake camshaft No 1 bearing cap is fitted with adapter sleeves, unscrew the nuts and remove the cap to prevent the cap from binding whilst the camshaft is removed **(see illustration 10.15)**.

37 Assemble BMW special tool 11 3 260, and mount the tool on the cylinder head by screwing the mounting bolts into the spark plug holes. Position the tool so that the plungers are located over the relevant camshaft bearing caps (ie, intake or exhaust camshaft) **(see illustration 10.16)**.

38 Apply pressure to the camshaft bearing caps by turning the eccentric shaft on the tools using a spanner **(see illustration 10.17)**.

39 Unscrew the remaining camshaft bearing cap nuts.

40 Release the pressure on the special tool shaft, then unbolt the tool from the cylinder head.

41 Lift off the bearing caps, keeping them in order, then lift out the camshaft.

All methods

42 The camshaft bearing casting can now be lifted from the cylinder head. This should be done very slowly, as the cam followers will be released as the casting is lifted off – if the casting is lifted off awkwardly, the cam followers may fall out. Do not allow the cam followers to fall out and get mixed up, as they must be fitted to their original locations.

43 With the bearing casting removed, lift the cam followers from the cylinder head. Identify the followers for location, and store them upright in a container of clean engine oil to prevent the oil from draining from inside the followers.

44 Repeat the procedure on the remaining camshaft. Do not forget to mark the cam followers Intake and Exhaust.

Inspection

45 Clean all the components, including the bearing surfaces in the bearing castings and bearing caps. Examine the components carefully for wear and damage. In particular, check the bearing and cam lobe surfaces of the camshaft(s) for scoring and pitting. Examine the surfaces of the cam followers for signs wear or damage. Renew components as necessary.

Refitting

46 If the camshaft lower bearing castings have been removed, check that the mating faces of the bearing castings and the cylinder head are clean, and check that the bearing casting locating dowels are in position on the studs at Nos 2 and 7 bearing locations **(see illustration)**.

47 The bearing casting(s) and cam followers must now be refitted.

48 The simplest method of refitting these components is to retain the cam followers in

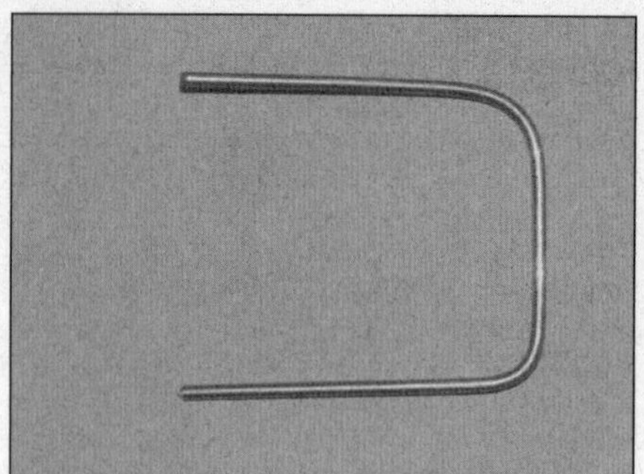

10.50a Using weld rod, make up 11 bucket retaining tools (approx 35 x 37 mm)

10.50b Retain the exhaust followers . . .

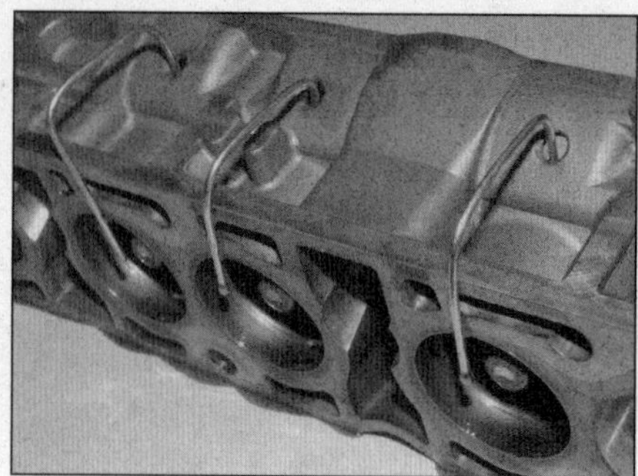

10.50c . . . and the intake followers

the bearing casting, and refit the components as an assembly.

49 Oil the bearing casting contact surfaces of the cam followers (avoid allowing oil onto the top faces of the followers at this stage), then fit each follower to its original location in the bearing casting.

50 Once all the followers have been fitted, they must be retained in the bearing casting so that they do not fall out as the assembly is refitted to the cylinder head. To retain the followers, cut 11 pieces of weld rod, and bend them to shape **(see illustration)**. With each follower fitted, retain them in place using a piece of the shaped weld rod **(see illustrations)**. **Note:** *No 1 intake cam follower can be held in place with your finger whilst the assembly is lowered into place. There is insufficient clearance to retain this follower with the welding rod.*

51 With the cam followers retained in the bearing casting, refit the casting to the cylinder head. Note that the exhaust side casting is marked A and the intake side casting is marked E. When the castings are refitted, the marks should face each other at the timing chain end of the cylinder head. Don't forget to remove the weld rod clips retaining the cam followers.

Warning: The cam followers expand when not subjected to load by the camshafts, and therefore require some time before they can be compressed. If the camshaft refitting operation is carried out rapidly, there is a possibility that the 'closed' valves will be forced open by the expanded cam followers, resulting in piston-to-valve contact.

52 To minimise the possibility of piston-to-valve contact after refitting the camshaft(s) observe the delays listed in the following table before turning the crankshaft back to the TDC position:

Temperature	Delay
Room temperature (20°C)	4 minutes
10°C to 20°C	11 minutes
0°C to 10°C	30 minutes

53 First identify the camshafts to ensure that they are fitted in the correct locations. The intake camshaft has a triangular front flange and the exhaust camshaft has a circular front flange. Ensure that the crankshaft is still positioned at 30° anti-clockwise from the TDC position. The flywheel end of the camshafts are also marked A (Exhaust) and E (Intake) **(see illustrations)**.

54 Position the camshaft on the cylinder head, so that the tips of the front cam lobes on the exhaust and intake camshafts face one another. Note also that the square flanges on the rear of the camshaft should be positioned with the sides of the flanges exactly at right-angles to the top surface of the cylinder head (this can be checked using a set-square), and the side of the flange with holes drilled into it uppermost. Feed the primary timing chain over the end of the exhaust camshaft as it is installed.

55 Place the bearing caps in position, noting that the caps carry identification marks. The exhaust camshaft caps are marked A1 to A7, and the intake camshaft caps are marked E1 to E7 (A1 and E1 at the timing chain end).

10.53a The intake camshaft has the triangular front flange (arrowed)

10.53b The intake camshaft is marked E and the exhaust camshaft is marked A

Place the bearing caps in their original locations as noted before removal.

Without BMW tool 11 3 260

56 Refit the nuts to the bearing cap studs. Note that it may be necessary to turn the camshafts slightly to allow them to sit low enough in the castings for the bearing cap retaining nuts to be initially fitted. As soon as the retaining nuts have been screwed on a few threads, turn the camshafts back to the position described in Paragraph 54. It is absolutely essential that the nuts are tightened down gradually and evenly, so the forces acting on the camshaft are spread out over its entire length. When the bearing casting is in full contact with the cylinder head, and all of the bearing caps are in full contact with the bearing casting, tighten the nuts to the specified torque.

With BMW tool 11 3 260

57 Re-assemble BMW special tool 11 3 260, and refit it to the cylinder head as during removal.

58 Apply pressure to the relevant bearing caps by turning the eccentric shaft on the tools using a 5spanner.

59 With pressure applied to the bearing caps, refit the bearing cap securing nuts, and tighten them as far as possible by hand.

60 Tighten the bearing cap nuts to the specified torque, working progressively in a diagonal sequence.

61 Once the bearing cap nuts have been tightened, unbolt the tool used to apply pressure to the bearing caps.

All methods

62 Repeat the procedure on the remaining camshaft.

63 Refit the spark plugs, and refit the camshaft cover studs to the cylinder head.

64 Refit the special tool/template used to check the position of the camshafts. If necessary, turn the camshaft(s) slightly using a spanner on the flats provided until the template can be fitted.

Warning: Note the warning in Paragraph 51 before proceeding.

65 Turn the crankshaft back 30° clockwise to the TDC position, then re-engage the locking tool with the flywheel to lock the crankshaft in position.

66 Refit the camshaft sprockets and timing chains as described in Section 7.

67 Refit the VANOS adjustment unit as described in Section 9.

68 To minimise the possibility of piston-to-valve contact, after refitting the camshaft(s), observe the following delays before cranking the engine:

Temperature	Delay
Room temperature (20°C)	10 minutes
10°C to 20°C	30 minutes
0°C to 10°C	75 minutes

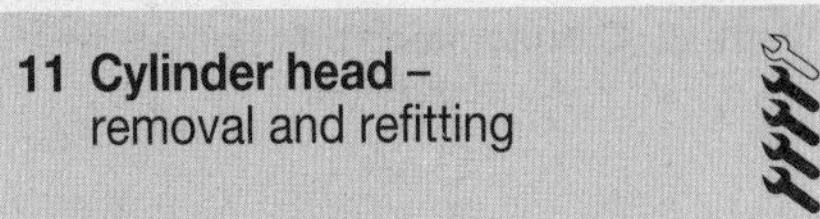

11 Cylinder head – removal and refitting

Note: *New cylinder head bolts and a new cylinder head gasket will be required on refitting.*

Removal

1 Drain the cooling system as described in Chapter 1.

2 Remove the intake and exhaust manifolds as described in Chapter 4A.

M52 engine

3 Remove the secondary timing chain as described in Section 7.

4 Undo the retaining bolts and remove the secondary timing chain tensioner **(see illustration 8.13)**.

5 Undo the two retaining bolts and remove the secondary timing chain guide **(see illustration 7.36a and 7.36b)**.

6 Unscrew the primary timing chain tensioner cover plug from the right-hand side of the engine. Recover the sealing ring.

Warning: The chain tensioner plunger has a strong spring. Take care when unscrewing the cover plug.

7 Recover the spring and withdraw the tensioner plunger.

8 Withdraw the primary chain sprocket from the exhaust camshaft, complete with chain. Remove the sprocket.

11.11 Disconnect the thermostat housing hoses (arrowed)

Caution: Keep tension on the chain, and tie up the end of the chain using wire or string to prevent it from dropping into the lower timing chain cover and/or disengaging from the crankshaft sprocket.

9 Trace the wiring back from the camshaft position sensor, then disconnect the sensor connector. Unscrew the securing bolt and remove the sensor from the cylinder head.

10 Unscrew the bolts securing the timing chain cover to the cylinder head (note that one of the bolts also secures the secondary timing chain tensioner).

11 Disconnect the two coolant hoses from the thermostat cover at the front of the cylinder head **(see illustration)**.

12 Disconnect the coolant hose from the rear left-hand corner of the cylinder head.

13 Disconnect the remaining small coolant hose from the left-hand side of the cylinder head, and remove the screw securing the wiring loom bracket to the cylinder head **(see illustration)**.

14 Disconnect the wiring plugs from the temperature sensors located in the left-hand side of the cylinder head.

M52TU and M54 engines

15 Remove the camshafts and followers as described in Section 10.

16 Trace the wiring back from the camshaft position sensors, then disconnect the sensor connectors. Unscrew the securing bolts, and remove the sensors from the cylinder head.

11.13 Undo the bolt securing the wiring loom bracket

17 Undo the two Torx screws and remove the secondary timing chain guide from the cylinder head **(see illustration)**.

18 Unscrew the bolts securing the lower timing chain cover to the cylinder head.

19 Remove the thermostat as described in Chapter 3.

20 Undo the two bolts and remove the coolant pipe from the intake side of the cylinder head. To improve access if necessary, undo the union bolt and disconnect the VANOS adjustment unit oil feed pipe from the rear of the oil filter housing **(see illustration)**. Recover the oil pipe sealing washers.

21 Disconnect wiring plugs from the temperature sensor located in the left-hand side of the cylinder head.

All engines

22 Remove the crankshaft locking pin then, holding the primary timing chain under tension with your hand, carefully rotate the crankshaft 30° anti-clockwise to prevent accidental piston-to-valve contact.

23 Progressively loosen the cylinder head bolts, working in the reverse of the tightening sequence **(see illustration 11.40)**.

24 Remove the cylinder head bolts, and recover the washers. Note that some of the

11.17 Undo the two Torx bolts securing the secondary timing chain guide (arrowed)

11.20 If necessary, undo the VANOS oil feed pipe from behind the oil filter housing (arrowed)

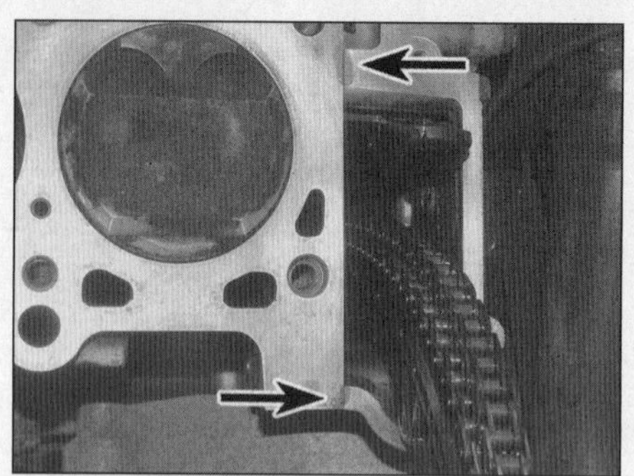
11.36 Apply sealant to the areas where the cylinder head meets the timing cover (arrowed)

11.37 Fit a new cylinder head gasket

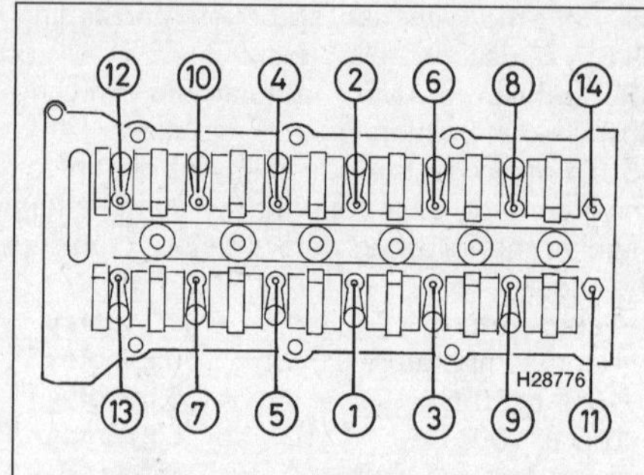

11.40 Cylinder head bolt tightening sequence

washers may be captive in the cylinder head, in which case they cannot be withdrawn.

25 Release the cylinder head from the cylinder block and locating dowels by rocking it. Do not prise between the mating faces of the cylinder head and block, as this may damage the gasket faces.

26 Ideally, two assistants will now be required to help remove the cylinder head. Have one assistant hold the timing chain up, clear of the cylinder head, making sure that tension is kept on the chain. With the aid of another assistant, lift the cylinder head from the block – take care, as the cylinder head is heavy. As the cylinder head is removed, feed the timing chain through the aperture in the front of the cylinder head, and support it from the cylinder block using the wire.

27 Recover the cylinder head gasket.

Inspection

28 Refer to Chapter 2B for details of cylinder head dismantling and reassembly.

29 The mating faces of the cylinder head and block must be perfectly clean before refitting the head. Use a scraper to remove all traces of gasket and carbon, and also clean the tops of the pistons. Take particular care with the aluminium cylinder head, as the soft metal is easily damaged. Make sure that debris is not allowed to enter the oil and water passages. Using adhesive tape and paper, seal the water, oil and bolt holes in the cylinder block. To prevent carbon entering the gap between the pistons and bores, smear a little grease in the gap. After cleaning each piston, rotate the crankshaft so that the piston moves **down** the bore, then wipe out the grease and carbon with a cloth rag.

30 Check the block and head for nicks, deep scratches and other damage. If slight, they may be removed from the cylinder block carefully with a file. More serious damage may be repaired by machining, but this is a specialist job.

31 If warpage of the cylinder head is suspected, use a straight-edge to check it for distortion, with reference to Chapter 2B.

32 Clean out the bolt holes in the block using a pipe cleaner or thin rag and a screwdriver. Make sure that all oil and water is removed, otherwise there is a possibility of the block being cracked by hydraulic pressure when the bolts are tightened.

33 Examine the bolt threads and the threads in the cylinder block for damage. If necessary, use the correct size tap to chase out the threads in the block.

Refitting

Warning: As the camshafts have been removed from the cylinder head, note the warnings given in Section 10, regarding expanded cam followers.

34 To minimise the possibility of piston-to-valve contact after refitting the camshaft(s), observe the following delays before refitting the cylinder head.

Temperature	Delay
Room temperature (20°C)	4 minutes
10°C to 20°C	11 minutes
0°C to 10°C	30 minutes

35 Ensure that the mating faces of the cylinder block and head are spotlessly clean, that the cylinder head bolt threads are clean and dry, and that they screw in and out of their locations. Check that the cylinder head locating dowels are correctly positioned in the cylinder block.

Warning: To avoid any possibility of piston-to-valve contact when refitting the cylinder head, it is necessary to ensure that none of the pistons are at TDC. Before proceeding further, if not already done, turn the crankshaft to position No 1 piston at TDC (check that the locking rod can be engaged with the flywheel, then remove the locking rod and turn the crankshaft approximately 30° anti-clockwise using a spanner or socket on the crankshaft pulley hub bolt.

36 Apply a thin bead of Drei Bond 1209 to the area where the cylinder block meets the timing cover **(see illustration)**.

37 Fit a new cylinder head gasket to the block, locating it over the dowels. Make sure that it is the correct way up **(see illustration)**. Note that 0.3 mm thicker-than-standard gaskets are available for use if the cylinder head has been machined (see Chapter 2B).

38 Lower the cylinder head onto the block, engaging it over the dowels.

39 Apply a light coat of clean engine oil to the threads and washer contact areas then fit the **new** cylinder head bolts, complete with new washers, where necessary, and tighten the bolts as far as possible by hand. Ensure that the washers are correctly seated in their locations in the cylinder head. **Note:** *Do not fit washers to any bolts which are fitted to locations where there are already captive washers in the cylinder head. If a new cylinder head is fitted (without captive washers), ensure that new washers are fitted to all the bolts.*

40 Tighten the bolts in the order shown, and in the stages given in the Specifications – ie, tighten all bolts in sequence to the Stage 1 torque, then tighten all bolts in sequence to the Stage 2 torque, and so on **(see illustration)**.

41 Refit and tighten the bolts securing the lower timing chain cover to the cylinder head.

42 On M52TU and M54 engines, refit the camshafts and followers as described in Section 10.

43 Turn the crankshaft 30° clockwise back to the TDC position, then re-engage the locking rod with the flywheel to lock the crankshaft in position.

44 The remainder of refitting is a reverse of removal. On completion, refill the cooling system as described in Chapter 1.

12 Sump – removal and refitting

Note: *A new sump gasket and/or a new dipstick tube sealing will be required on refitting, and suitable gasket sealant will be required.*

Removal

1 Apply the handbrake, then jack up the front of the vehicle and support securely on axle stands (see *Jacking and vehicle support*).

2 Undo the screws and remove the engine undershield and drain the engine oil, referring to Chapter 1.

3 Unscrew the securing bolts and/or nuts, and remove the alternator air ducting from the front of the vehicle.

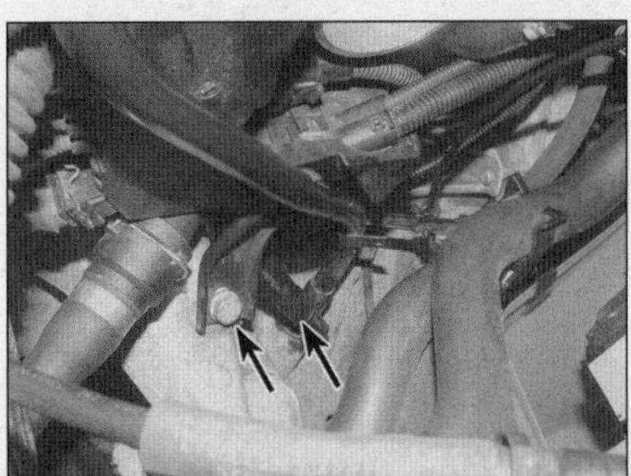

12.7 Dipstick guide tube oil return hose and mounting bracket bolt (arrowed)

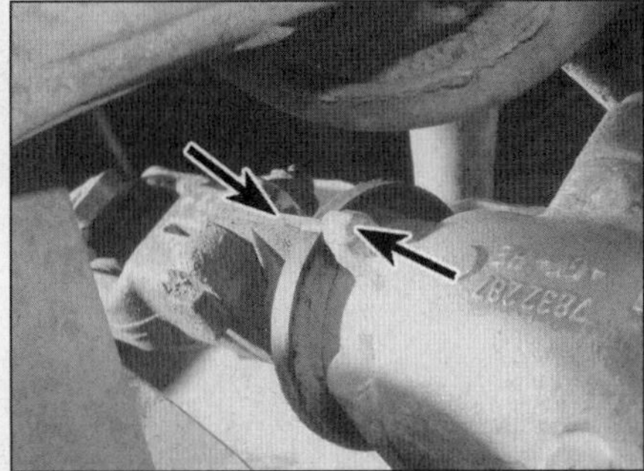

12.8 The steering is in the 'straight-ahead' position when the mark on the flange aligns with the pointer on the pinion casting (arrowed)

12.15 One of the rear subframe bolts is accessed through a hole in the subframe (arrowed)

4 Remove the air cleaner assembly as described in Chapter 4A.

5 In order to remove the sump, the front subframe must be lowered and, therefore, the engine suspended. Manoeuvre an engine lifting hoist or crane into position and attach a lifting chain or sling to the 'eye' at the front of the cylinder head. Take the weight of the engine.

6 On automatic transmission models, disconnect the oil pipes from the transmission oil pan. Be prepared for fluid spillage.

7 Undo the retaining bolt and detach the oil return hose from the oil separator. Unscrew the dipstick guide tube bolt, then pull the dipstick guide tube and return hose from the sump **(see illustration)**. Discard the O-ring seal, a new one must be fitted.

8 Ensure that the steering wheel is facing straight-ahead, and engage the steering lock. Make alignment marks between the steering column joint flange and the steering rack pinion, then undo the pinch-bolt, and pull the joint from the pinion. Whilst the column is separated from the rack it is essential that neither the steering wheel or roadwheels are moved from their positions **(see illustration)**.

9 Remove the auxiliary drivebelt as described in Chapter 1.

10 Unbolt the power steering support bracket from the rear of the pump, then unbolt the pump mounting bracket from the alternator mounting bracket, and move the pump to one side, clear of the engine, leaving

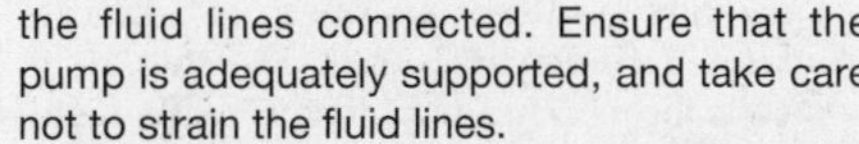

the fluid lines connected. Ensure that the pump is adequately supported, and take care not to strain the fluid lines.

11 Unscrew the nuts securing the left- and right-hand engine mountings to the subframe. Using the engine hoist or crane, raise the engine approximately 10 to 15 mm, ensuring that the rear of the cylinder head does not crush or trap the brake pipes along the engine compartment bulkhead.

12 Where applicable, unclip any pipes, hoses and/or wiring from the engine mounting brackets, and sump.

13 Disconnect the steering track rod end balljoints from the hub carriers as described in Chapter 10.

14 Disconnect the anti-roll bar from the drop links – see Chapter 10 if necessary.

15 Remove the subframe-to-chassis bolts and, using a trolley jack for support, lower the subframe, taking care not to strain the power steering hoses **(see illustration)**. Where fitted, remove the rubber damping block from between the subframe and the sump.

16 Working under the vehicle, progressively unscrew and remove all the sump securing bolts. Note that the rear sump securing bolts are accessible through the holes in the gearbox/transmission bellhousing **(see illustration)**. Also note that the three lower gearbox/transmission-to-engine bolts must be removed, as they screw into the sump.

17 Lower the sump to the ground.

18 Recover the sump gasket.

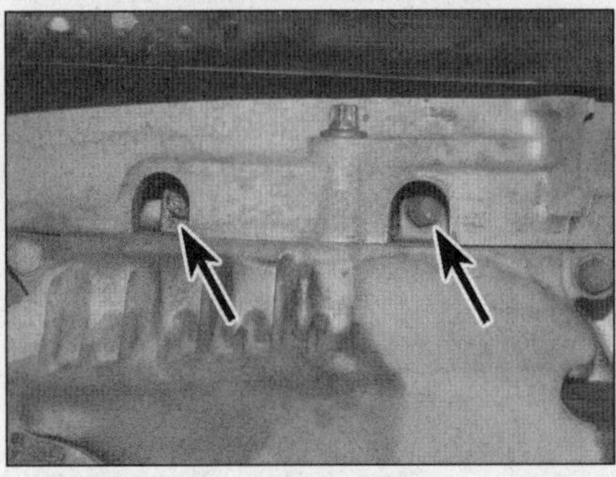

12.16 The rear sump bolts are accessible through the holes in the gearbox bellhousing (arrowed)

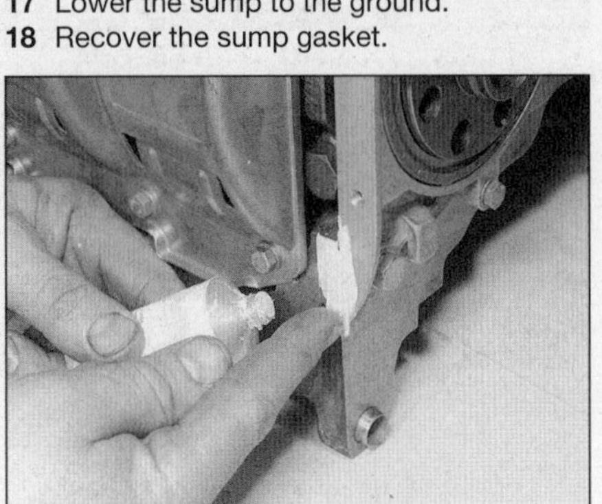

12.20 Apply sealant to the area where the rear oil seal housing and front timing chain cover join the cylinder block

Refitting

19 Commence refitting by thoroughly cleaning the mating faces of the sump and cylinder block.

20 Lightly coat the areas where the crankshaft rear oil seal housing and front timing chain cover join the cylinder block with Drei Bond 1209 sealant **(see illustration)**.

21 Place the gasket in position on the sump flange.

22 Offer the sump up to the cylinder block, ensuring that the gasket stays in place, and refit the sump securing bolts, tightening them finger-tight only at this stage.

23 Progressively tighten the sump-to-cylinder block bolts to the specified torque.

24 Tighten the sump-to-transmission-to-engine bolts to the specified torque.

25 Further refitting is a reversal of removal, noting the following points.

- a) *When raising the subframe into position, make sure that no pipes, hoses and/or wiring are trapped.*
- b) *Renew the subframe bolts.*
- c) *Tighten the engine mounting nuts securely.*
- d) *Refit and tension the auxiliary drivebelt as described in Chapter 1.*
- e) *When refitting the dipstick tube, renew the O-ring seal.*
- f) *On completion, refill the engine with oil as described in Chapter 1.*
- g) *On automatic transmission models, check the transmission fluid level as described in Chapter 7B.*

13 Oil pump and drive chain – removal, inspection and refitting

Oil pump

Note: *A new pick-up pipe O-ring, a new relief valve spring cap O-ring and a new relief valve circlip will be required on refitting.*

Removal and refitting

1 Remove the sump as described in Section 12.

13.2 Unscrew the oil pump sprocket securing nut – it has a *left-hand thread*

13.5 Unscrew the oil pick-up pipe bolts (arrowed)

13.6 Undo the four bolts (arrowed) and remove the oil pump

2 Unscrew the nut securing the sprocket to the oil pump shaft. Note that the nut is **left-hand thread** and unscrews clockwise **(see illustration)**.

3 Pull the sprocket and chain from the oil pump shaft.

4 On models where the pump is integral with the sump baffle plate, undo the bolts and remove the plate complete with the pump and pick-up tube.

13.7 Remove the cover from the oil pump

5 On models where the pump is separate from the baffle plate, undo the two bolts securing the pick-up pipe to the baffle plate, and the bolt securing the pipe to the pump **(see illustration)**. Remove the pipe.

6 Undo the four bolts and remove the oil pump **(see illustration)**.

Inspection

7 Unbolt the cover from the front of the pump **(see illustration)**.

8 Withdraw the driveshaft/rotor and the outer rotor from the pump body.

9 Check the pump body, rotors and cover for any signs of scoring, wear or cracks. If any wear or damage is evident, fit new rotors or renew the complete pump, depending on the extent of the damage. Note that it is wise to renew the complete pump as a unit.

10 Refit the rotors to the pump body, then using feeler blades, measure the clearance between the outer rotor and the pump body. Using the feeler blades and a straight-edge, measure the clearance (endfloat) between each of the rotors and the oil pump cover mating face **(see illustrations)**. Compare the measurements with the values given in the Specifications, and if necessary renew any worn components, or renew the complete pump as a unit.

11 To remove the pressure relief valve components, press the valve into its housing slightly, using a metal tool, then extract the circlip from the top of the housing using circlip pliers **(see illustration)**.

Warning: The relief valve has a strong spring. Take care when removing the circlip.

12 Withdraw the spring cap, spring and piston from the relief valve housing **(see illustrations)**.

13 Fit a new O-ring seal to the top of the

13.10a Measure the clearance between the outer oil pump rotor and the pump body . . .

13.10b . . . and the rotor endfloat

13.11 Extract the circlip . . .

13.12a . . . and withdraw the oil pressure relief valve spring cap . . .

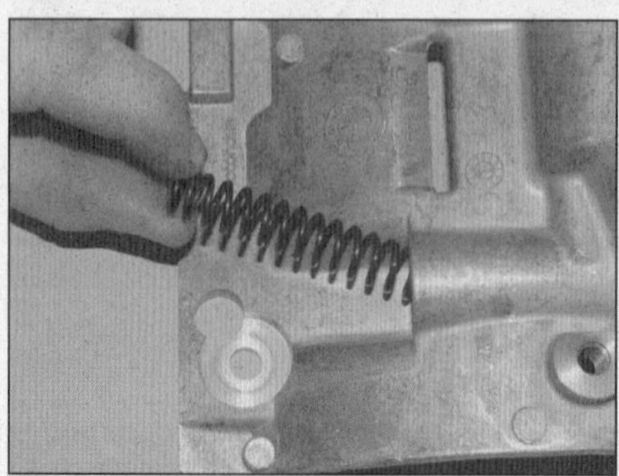
13.12b . . . spring . . .

13.12c . . . and piston

relief valve spring cap, then refit the components to the housing using a reversal of the removal procedure. Take care not to damage the surface of the spring cap during fitting, and secure the components using a new O-ring.

14 Refit the rotors to the pump body, then refit the cover to the pump. Ensure that the locating dowels are in position in the pump cover. Refit and tighten the cover bolts to the specified torque.

15 The remainder of refitting is a reversal of removal, noting the following points:

a) Where applicable renew the oil pick-up tube O-ring seal.

*b) Tighten the oil pump sprocket retaining nut **(left-hand thread)** to the specified torque.*

Oil pump drive chain

Removal

16 Remove the primary timing chain as described in Section 7.

17 Withdraw the chain from the crankshaft sprocket.

Inspection

18 Proceed as described for the secondary timing chain in Section 7.

Refitting

19 Refit the chain to the crankshaft sprocket, then refit the primary timing chain as described in Section 7.

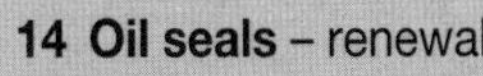

14 Oil seals – renewal

Crankshaft front oil seal

1 The procedure is described as part of the lower timing chain cover removal and refitting procedure in Section 6.

Crankshaft rear oil seal

Note: *A new oil seal housing gasket will be required on refitting.*

2 Remove the flywheel/driveplate, as described in Section 15.

3 Working at the bottom of the oil seal housing, unscrew the bolts securing the rear of the sump to the housing.

4 Unscrew the bolts securing the oil seal housing to the cylinder block.

5 If the housing is stuck to the sump gasket, run a sharp, thin blade between the housing and the sump gasket. Take care not to damage the sump gasket.

6 Withdraw the housing from the cylinder block. If the housing is stuck, tap it gently using a soft-faced mallet. Do not lever between the housing and the cylinder block, as this may damage the gasket surfaces.

7 Recover the gasket.

8 Thoroughly clean all traces of old gasket and sealant from the mating faces of the oil seal housing and the cylinder block. Again, take care not to damage the sump gasket. If the sump gasket has been damaged during removal, it is advisable to fit a new one with reference to Section 12.

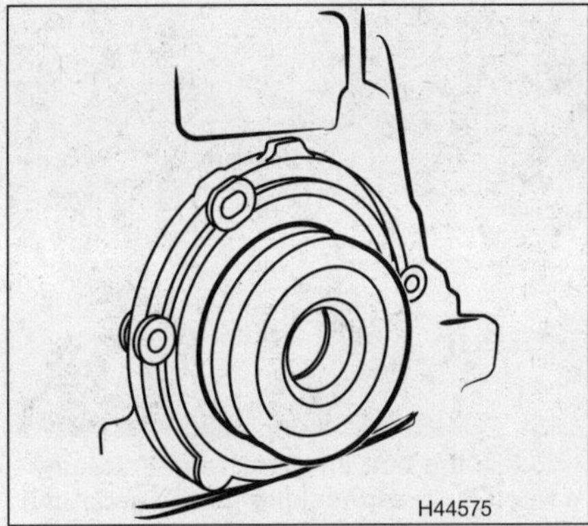

14.11 Leave the seal protector in the centre of the seal and drive it into place

9 Support the oil seal housing on blocks of wood, then drive out the seal from the rear of the housing using a hammer and drift.

10 Clean the seal mating surfaces in the housing.

11 From April 1998 a new type of oil seal is fitted. This seal can be identified by the lack of tension spring. This seal must only be fitted with the aid of the seal protector (supplied with the seal). Leave the seal protector fitted into the centre of the seal at this stage. Do not touch the sealing lip with your fingers, the lip is very sensitive and must not be kinked. Carefully drive it into position in the housing, using either a large tube of the correct diameter, or a block of wood, to avoid damage to the seal **(see illustration)**.

12 Ensure that the locating dowels are in position in the rear of the cylinder block, then locate a new oil seal housing gasket over the dowels.

13 Carefully offer the housing to the cylinder block, sliding the oil seal protector over the crankshaft flange, and push the seal and housing into place. Take care not to damage the oil seal lips.

14 Refit the housing-to-cylinder block and the sump-to-housing bolts, and tighten them lightly by hand.

15 Tighten the housing-to-cylinder block bolts to the specified torque, then tighten the sump-to-housing bolts to the specified torque.

16 Refit the flywheel/driveplate as described in Section 15.

Camshaft oil seals

17 No camshaft oil seals are fitted. Sealing is provided by the cylinder head cover gasket and the timing chain cover gaskets.

15 Flywheel/driveplate – removal and refitting

Note: *New flywheel/driveplate securing bolts will be required on refitting, and thread-locking compound may be required.*

Removal

1 Remove the manual gearbox as described in Chapter 7A, or the automatic transmission as described in Chapter 7B, as applicable.

2 On models with a manual gearbox, remove the clutch as described in Chapter 6.

3 In order to unscrew the bolts, the flywheel/driveplate must be locked in position. This can be done by bolting a toothed tool (engage the tooth with the starter ring gear) to the cylinder block using one of the engine-to-gearbox bolts **(see illustration)**.

4 Progressively unscrew the securing bolts, then withdraw the flywheel/driveplate from the crankshaft. Note that the flywheel/driveplate locates on dowels.

Warning: Take care as the flywheel/driveplate is heavy.

5 Recover the engine/transmission intermediate plate (where fitted), noting its orientation.

Refitting

6 Refit the engine/transmission intermediate plate (where fitted), ensuring that it is correctly located on the dowel(s) **(see illustration)**.

7 Refit the flywheel/driveplate to the end of the crankshaft, ensuring that the locating

15.3 Toothed tool used to lock the flywheel in position when unscrewing the flywheel bolts

15.6 Ensure the engine/transmission intermediate plate is correctly located

15.7 The notch (arrowed) indicates the position of the locating hole for the dowel

15.8 If the bolt threads are not already coated in thread-locking compound, then apply some

16.1 Crankshaft spigot bearing (arrowed)

dowel engages. Note that on dual-mass flywheels, the position of the dowel is indicated by one or two notches in the flywheel adjacent to the relevant locating hole **(see illustration)**.

8 Examine the threads of the **new** securing bolts. If the threads are not already coated with thread-locking compound, then apply suitable thread-locking compound to them, then refit the bolts **(see illustration)**.

9 Tighten the bolts progressively in a diagonal sequence to the specified torque. Counterhold the flywheel/driveplate by reversing the tool used during removal.

10 Where applicable, refit the clutch as described in Chapter 6.

11 Refit the manual gearbox or the automatic transmission, as applicable, as described in Chapter 7A or 7B respectively.

16 Crankshaft spigot bearing – renewal

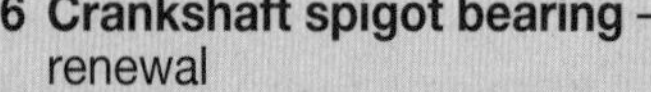

1 On manual gearbox models, a ball-bearing assembly is fitted to the end of the crankshaft to support the end of the gearbox input shaft **(see illustration)**.

2 To renew the bearing, proceed as follows.

3 Remove the flywheel as described in Section 15.

4 Pack the space behind, and the centre bore of the bearing with general purpose grease.

5 Position a metal rod or bolt in the entrance of the bearing internal bore. The rod/bolt diameter should be just less than the diameter of the bearing bore.

6 Strike the end of the rod/bolt with a hammer several times **(see illustration)**. As the rod/bolt is struck, the compressed grease forces the bearing from position. Continue until the bearing is removed.

7 Thoroughly clean the bearing housing in the end of the crankshaft.

8 Tap the new bearing into position, up to the stop, using a tube or socket on the bearing outer race.

9 Refit the flywheel as described in Section 15.

17 Engine/transmission mountings – inspection and renewal

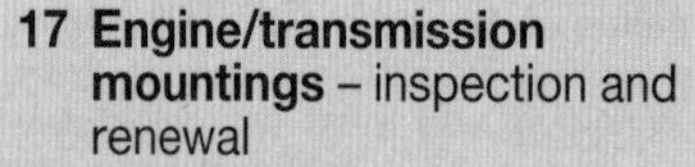

Inspection

1 Two engine mountings are used, one on either side of the engine.

2 If improved access is required, raise the front of the vehicle and support it securely on axle stands (see *Jacking and vehicle support*). Undo the screws and remove the engine undershield.

3 Check the mounting rubber to see if it is cracked, hardened or separated from the metal at any point. Renew the mounting if any such damage or deterioration is evident.

4 Check that all the mounting fasteners are securely tightened.

5 Using a large screwdriver or a crowbar, check for wear in the mounting by carefully levering against it to check for free play. Where this is not possible, enlist the aid of an assistant to move the engine/transmission back-and-forth, or from side-to-side, while you observe the mounting. While some freeplay is to be expected, even from new components, excessive wear should be obvious. If excessive freeplay is found, check first that the fasteners are correctly secured, then renew any worn components as required.

Renewal

6 Support the engine, either using a hoist and lifting tackle connected to the engine lifting brackets (refer to *Engine – removal and refitting* in Part B of this Chapter), or by positioning a jack and interposed block of wood under the sump. Ensure that the engine is adequately supported before proceeding.

7 Unscrew the nuts securing the left- and right-hand engine mounting brackets to the mounting rubbers, then unbolt the mounting brackets from the cylinder block, and remove the mountings. Disconnect and engine earth straps from the mountings **(see illustrations)**.

8 Unscrew the nuts securing the mountings to the body, then withdraw the mountings.

9 Refitting is a reversal of removal, but ensure that the metal protector plates are in position on the mountings, and securely tighten all fixings.

16.6 Use grease and a close-fitting rod to extract the spigot bearing

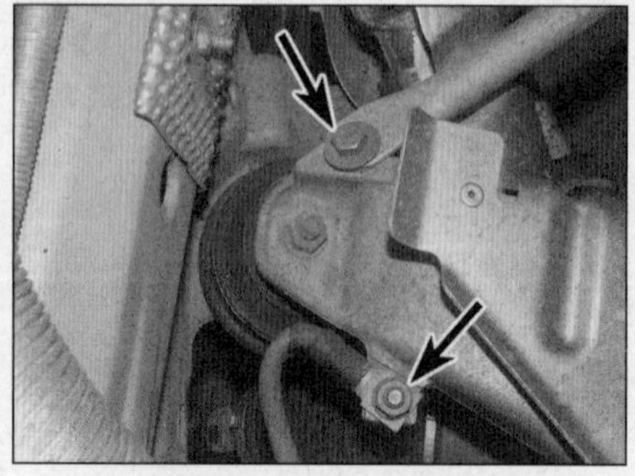

17.7a Disconnect the earth strap and support bracket (arrowed)

17.7b Unbolt the engine mounting bracket from the cylinder block

18.2 Disconnect the wiring plug from the oil pressure switch (arrowed)

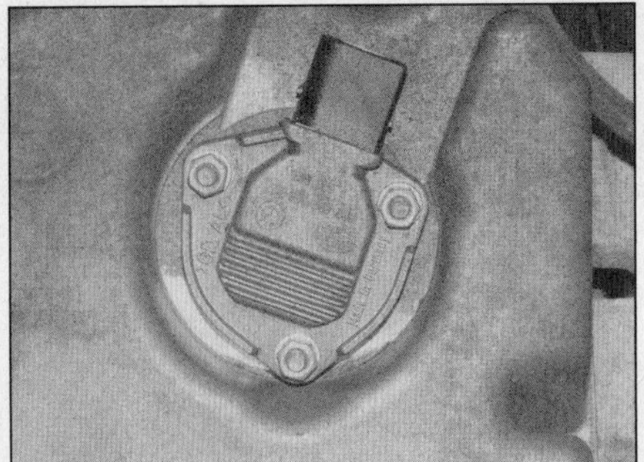
18.7 The oil level switch is retained by three nuts

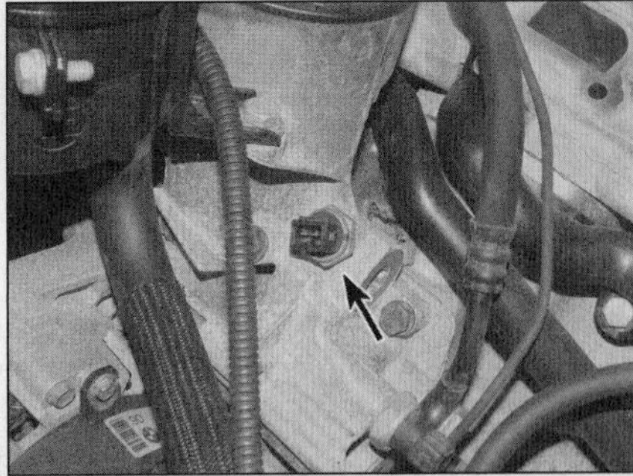
18.13 Disconnect the wiring plug from the oil temperature switch (arrowed)

18 Oil pressure, level and temperature switches – removal and refitting

Oil pressure switch

1 Unscrew the oil filter cap; this allows the oil within the filter to flow back into the sump, so reducing the amount lost during switch renewal.

2 Disconnect the wiring plug and unscrew the switch from the base of the oil filter housing **(see illustration)**.

3 Fit the new switch, and tighten it to the specified torque.

4 Refit the air filter housing and oil filter cap. Check the oil level as described in *Weekly Checks*.

Oil level switch

5 Drain the engine oil as described in Chapter 1.

6 Undo the screws and remove the engine undershield.

7 Disconnect the wiring plug, undo the three retaining nuts and remove the level switch **(see illustration)**.

8 Ensure that the sump mating surface is clean.

9 Complete with a new seal, install the oil level switch and tighten the retaining nuts securely.

10 Refit the engine undershield, and replenish the engine oil as described in Chapter 1.

Oil temperature switch

M52TU and M54 engines

11 Unscrew the oil filter cap; this allows the oil within the filter flows back into the sump, so reducing the amount lost during switch renewal.

12 Remove the air filter housing as described in Chapter 4A.

13 Disconnect the wiring plug and unscrew the switch from the base of the oil filter housing **(see illustration)**.

14 Fit the new switch, and tighten it to the specified torque.

15 Refit the air filter housing and oil filter cap. Check the oil level as described in *Weekly Checks*.

Chapter 2 Part B:
General engine overhaul procedures

Contents

Degrees of difficulty

Easy, suitable for novice with little experience 

Fairly easy, suitable for beginner with some experience 

Fairly difficult, suitable for competent DIY mechanic

Difficult, suitable for experienced DIY mechanic

Very difficult, suitable for expert DIY or professional 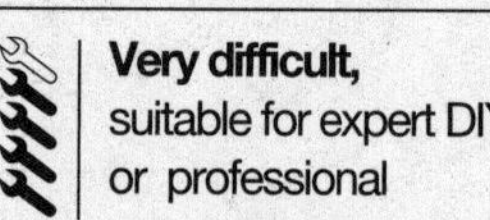

Specifications

Cylinder head

Maximum gasket face distortion	0.050 mm
New cylinder head height	140.00 mm
Minimum cylinder head height after machining	139.70 mm

Valves

Valve head diameter:	
M52, M52TU B20 and M54 B22:	
Intake	29.40 mm
Exhaust	26.40 mm
M52 B25 and B28:	
Intake	32.40 mm
Exhaust	29.40 mm
M52TU B25 and B28, M54 B25 and B30:	
Intake	32.40 mm
Exhaust	30.00 mm
Maximum side-to-side movement of valve in guide (measured at valve head with top of valve stem flush with guide)	0.50 mm

Cylinder block

Cylinder bore diameter:	
2.0 and 2.2 litre engines	80.00 mm (nominal)
All other engines	84.00 mm (nominal)
Maximum cylinder bore ovality	0.010 mm
Maximum cylinder bore taper	0.010 mm

Pistons

Piston diameter:	
M52 and M52TU B20 engines	79.985 mm (nominal); 0.25 mm oversize available
M54 B22 engine	79.980 mm (nominal); 0.25 mm oversize available
M52, M52TU B25 and B28 engines	83.980 mm (nominal); 0.25 mm oversize available
M54 B25, B30 engines	83.995 mm (nominal); 0.25 mm oversize available
Piston-to-cylinder bore running clearance	0.010 to 0.047 mm
Maximum play between piston and cylinder wall	0.150 mm

Connecting rods

Maximum weight difference between two connecting rods	4.000 g

Crankshaft

Endfloat	0.080 to 0.163 mm
Main bearing journal diameter	59.971 to 59.990 mm; 0.25 mm and 0.50 mm undersize bearing shells available
Big-end bearing journal diameter	44.50 to 45.00 mm; 0.25 mm and 0.50 mm undersize bearing shells available
Maximum run-out of centre main bearing	0.20 mm
Main bearing running clearance	0.020 to 0.058 mm
Big-end bearing running clearance	0.020 to 0.055 mm

Piston rings

End gaps:	
M52 and M52TU B20 engines:	
Top compression ring	0.10 to 0.30 mm
Second compression ring	0.20 to 0.40 mm
Oil control ring	0.20 to 0.40 mm
M52 B25 and B28 engines:	
Top compression ring	0.10 to 0.30 mm
Second compression ring	0.20 to 0.40 mm
Oil control ring	0.25 to 0.50 mm
M52TU B25 and B28 engines:	
Top compression ring	0.10 to 0.30 mm
Second compression ring	0.20 to 0.40 mm
Oil control ring	0.20 to 0.60 mm
M54 B22 engine:	
Top compression ring	0.10 to 0.30 mm
Second compression ring	0.20 to 0.40 mm
Oil control ring	0.25 to 0.50 mm
M54 B25 and B30 engines:	
Top compression ring	0.20 to 0.40 mm
Second compression ring	0.20 to 0.40 mm
Oil control ring	0.20 to 0.45 mm

Torque wrench settings

Refer to Chapter 2A Specifications

1 General information

Included in this Part of Chapter 2 are details of removing the engine/transmission from the car and general overhaul procedures for the cylinder head, cylinder block/crankcase and all other engine internal components.

The information given ranges from advice concerning preparation for an overhaul and the purchase of new parts, to detailed step-by-step procedures covering removal, inspection, renovation and refitting of engine internal components.

After Section 5, all instructions are based on the assumption that the engine has been removed from the car. For information concerning in-car engine repair, as well as the removal and refitting of those external components necessary for full overhaul, refer to Part A of this Chapter, and to Section 5. Ignore any preliminary dismantling operations described in Part A that are no longer relevant once the engine has been removed from the car.

Apart from torque wrench settings, which are given at the beginning of Part A, all specifications relating to engine overhaul are at the beginning of this Part of Chapter 2.

2 Engine overhaul – general information

1 It is not always easy to determine when, or if, an engine should be completely overhauled, as a number of factors must be considered.

2 High mileage is not necessarily an

indication that an overhaul is needed, while low mileage does not preclude the need for an overhaul. Frequency of servicing is probably the most important consideration. An engine which has had regular and frequent oil and filter changes, as well as other required maintenance, should give many thousands of miles of reliable service. Conversely, a neglected engine may require an overhaul very early in its life.

3 Excessive oil consumption is an indication that piston rings, valve seals and/or valve guides are in need of attention. Make sure that oil leaks are not responsible before deciding that the rings and/or guides are worn. Perform a compression test, as described in Part A of this Chapter, to determine the likely cause of the problem.

4 Check the oil pressure with a gauge fitted in place of the oil pressure switch, and compare it with that specified. If it is extremely low, the main and big-end bearings, and/or the oil pump, are probably worn out. It is a good idea to renew the oil pump whenever the engine is overhauled.

5 Loss of power, rough running, knocking or metallic engine noises, excessive valve gear noise, and high fuel consumption may also point to the need for an overhaul, especially if they are all present at the same time. If a complete service does not remedy the situation, major mechanical work is the only solution.

6 A full engine overhaul involves restoring all internal parts to the specification of a new engine. During a complete overhaul, the pistons and the piston rings are renewed, and the cylinder bores are reconditioned. New main and big-end bearings are generally fitted; if necessary, the crankshaft may be reground, to compensate for wear in the journals. The valves are also serviced as well, since they are usually in less-than-perfect condition at this point. Always pay careful attention to the condition of the oil pump when overhauling the engine, and renew it if there is any doubt as to its serviceability. The end result should be an as-new engine that will give many trouble-free miles.

7 Critical cooling system components such as the hoses, thermostat and water pump should be renewed when an engine is overhauled. The radiator should be checked carefully, to ensure that it is not clogged or leaking.

8 Before beginning the engine overhaul, read through the entire procedure, to familiarise yourself with the scope and requirements of the job. Overhauling an engine is not difficult if you follow carefully all of the instructions, have the necessary tools and equipment, and pay close attention to all specifications. It can, however, be time-consuming. Plan on the car being off the road for a minimum of two weeks, especially if parts must be taken to an engineering works for repair or reconditioning. Check on the availability of parts and make sure that any necessary special tools and equipment are obtained in advance. Most work can be done with typical hand tools, although a number of precision measuring tools are required for inspecting parts to determine if they must be renewed. Often the engineering works will handle the inspection of parts and offer advice concerning reconditioning and renewal.

9 Always wait until the engine has been completely dismantled, and until all components (especially the cylinder block/crankcase and the crankshaft) have been inspected, before deciding what service and repair operations must be performed by an engineering works. The condition of these components will be the major factor to consider when determining whether to overhaul the original engine, or to buy a reconditioned unit. Do not, therefore, purchase parts or have overhaul work done on other components until they have been thoroughly inspected. As a general rule, time is the primary cost of an overhaul, so it does not pay to fit worn or sub-standard parts.

10 As a final note, to ensure maximum life and minimum trouble from a reconditioned engine, everything must be assembled with care, in a spotlessly-clean environment.

3 Engine removal – methods and precautions

1 If you have decided that the engine must be removed for overhaul or major repair work, several preliminary steps should be taken.

2 Locating a suitable place to work is extremely important. Adequate work space, along with storage space for the car, will be needed. If a workshop or garage is not available, at the very least, a flat, level, clean work surface is required.

3 Cleaning the engine compartment and engine/transmission before beginning the removal procedure will help keep tools clean and organised.

4 An engine hoist or A-frame will also be necessary. Make sure the equipment is rated in excess of the weight of the engine. Safety is of primary importance, considering the potential hazards involved in lifting the engine/transmission out of the car.

5 If this is the first time you have removed an engine, an assistant should ideally be available. Advice and aid from someone more experienced would also be helpful. There are many instances when one person cannot simultaneously perform all of the operations required when lifting the engine out of the vehicle.

6 Plan the operation ahead of time. Before starting work, arrange for the hire of or obtain all of the tools and equipment you will need. Some of the equipment necessary to perform engine/transmission removal and installation safely and with relative ease (in addition to an engine hoist) is as follows: a heavy duty trolley jack, complete sets of spanners and sockets (see *Tools and working facilities*), wooden blocks, and plenty of rags and cleaning solvent for mopping-up spilled oil, coolant and fuel. If the hoist must be hired, make sure that you arrange for it in advance, and perform all of the operations possible without it beforehand. This will save you money and time.

7 Plan for the car to be out of use for quite a while. An engineering works will be required to perform some of the work which the do-it-yourselfer cannot accomplish without special equipment. These places often have a busy schedule, so it would be a good idea to consult them before removing the engine, in order to accurately estimate the amount of time required to rebuild or repair components that may need work.

8 Always be extremely careful when removing and refitting the engine/transmission. Serious injury can result from careless actions. Plan ahead and take your time, and a job of this nature, although major, can be accomplished successfully.

9 On all models, then engine is removed by first removing the transmission, then lifting the engine out from above the vehicle.

4 Engine – removal and refitting

Note: *This is an involved operation. Read through the procedure thoroughly before starting work, and ensure that adequate lifting tackle and jacking/support equipment is available. Make notes during dismantling to ensure that all wiring/hoses and brackets are correctly repositioned and routed on refitting.*

Removal

1 Remove the bonnet as described in Chapter 11.

2 Depressurise the fuel system as described in Chapter 4A, then disconnect the battery negative lead (see Chapter 5A).

3 Drain the cooling system as described in Chapter 1.

4 Drain the engine oil, referring to Chapter 1.

5 Remove the manual gearbox (Chapter 7A) or the automatic transmission (Chapter 7B), as applicable.

6 Unless a hoist is available which is capable of lifting the engine out over the front of the vehicle with the vehicle raised, it will now be necessary to remove the axle stands and lower the vehicle to the ground. Ensure that the engine is adequately supported during the lowering procedure.

7 To improve access and working room, temporarily support the engine from underneath the sump, using a trolley jack and interposed block of wood, then disconnect and withdraw the hoist and lifting tackle used to support the engine during transmission removal.

Warning: Ensure that the engine is securely and safely supported by the jack before disconnecting the lifting tackle.

8 Remove the radiator cooling fan and viscous coupling as described in Chapter 3.
9 Remove the radiator (see Chapter 3).
10 Remove the air cleaner/airflow meter assembly as described in Chapter 4A.
11 Unbolt the power steering reservoir, and move the reservoir to one side, leaving the fluid lines connected.
12 Unbolt the air conditioning compressor from the engine where applicable, release the pipes from the retaining clips, and support the compressor clear of the working area, as described in Chapter 3.

Warning: Do not disconnect the refrigerant lines – refer to Chapter 3 for precautions to be taken.

13 Unbolt the power steering pump as described in Chapter 10, and move it to one side, leaving the fluid lines connected. If necessary, release the power steering flexible hose from the steering rack mounting to allow the pump and reservoir to be moved from the work area.
14 Unbolt the earth lead(s) from the engine mounting bracket(s).
15 If not already done so, remove the inlet manifold as described in Chapter 4A.
16 Note their fitted positions, then disconnect all engine coolant/vacuum hoses. Note the hose routing to aid refitting.
17 To reduce the risk of damage during engine removal, remove the oil dipstick guide tube. Discard the O-ring seal, a new one must be fitted.
18 Note their fitted positions, then unplug all electrical connectors from the engine. Note also the harness routing and bracket fitment to aid refitting.
19 Unscrew the securing bolts, and release any clips (noting their locations) and release the wiring harness/wiring ducting assembly from the engine. Move the assembly to one side, clear of the engine.
20 Check that all relevant wiring has been disconnected from the engine to enable engine removal.
21 Make a final check to ensure that all relevant hoses, pipes and wiring have been disconnected from the engine and moved clear to allow the engine to be lifted out.
22 Reposition the lifting tackle and hoist to support the engine both from the lifting eye at the rear left-hand corner of the cylinder block, and from the lifting bracket at the front of the cylinder head **(see illustration)**. Raise the hoist to just take the weight of the engine.
23 Unscrew the nuts securing the left- and right-hand engine mounting brackets to the mounting rubbers, then unbolt the mounting brackets from the cylinder block, and remove the mountings.
24 With the aid of an assistant, raise the hoist, and lift the engine from the engine compartment.

Refitting

25 Refitting is a reversal of removal, bearing in mind the following points.

a) Tighten all fixings to the specified torque where given.
b) Ensure that all wiring, hoses and brackets are positioned and routed as noted before removal.
c) Refit the auxiliary drivebelt with reference to Chapter 1.
d) Refit the inlet manifold as described in Chapter 4A.
e) Refit the radiator, referring to Chapter 3.
f) Refit the manual gearbox or automatic transmission as described in Chapter 7A or 7B respectively.
g) On completion, refill the engine with oil, and refill the cooling system as described in Chapter 1.

5 Engine overhaul – dismantling sequence

1 It is much easier to dismantle and work on the engine if it is mounted on a portable engine stand. These stands can often be hired from a tool hire shop. Before the engine is mounted on a stand, the flywheel/driveplate should be removed, so that the stand bolts can be tightened into the end of the cylinder block/crankcase.
2 If a stand is not available, it is possible to dismantle the engine with it blocked up on a sturdy workbench, or on the floor. Be extra-careful not to tip or drop the engine when working without a stand.
3 If you are going to obtain a reconditioned engine, all the external components must be removed first, to be transferred to the new engine (just as they will if you are doing a complete engine overhaul yourself). These components include the following:

a) Ancillary unit mounting brackets (oil filter, starter, alternator, etc).
b) Thermostat and housing (Chapter 3).
c) Dipstick tube.

4.22 Attach lifting tackle to the front and rear lifting eyes

d) All electrical switches and sensors.
e) Inlet and exhaust manifolds – where applicable (Chapter 4A).
f) Ignition coils and spark plugs – as applicable (Chapters 5B and 1).
g) Flywheel/driveplate (Part A of this Chapter).

Note: *When removing the external components from the engine, pay close attention to details that may be helpful or important during refitting. Note the fitted position of gaskets, seals, spacers, pins, washers, bolts, and other small items.*

4 If you are obtaining a 'short' engine (which consists of the engine cylinder block/crankcase, crankshaft, pistons and connecting rods all assembled), then the cylinder head, sump, oil pump, and timing chain will have to be removed also.
5 If you are planning a complete overhaul, the engine can be dismantled, and the internal components removed, in the order given below, referring to Part A of this Chapter unless otherwise stated.

a) Inlet and exhaust manifolds – where applicable (Chapter 4A).
b) Timing chains, sprockets and tensioner(s).
c) Cylinder head.
d) Flywheel/driveplate.
e) Sump.
f) Oil pump.
g) Piston/connecting rod assemblies (Section 9).
h) Crankshaft (Section 10).

6 Before beginning the dismantling and overhaul procedures, make sure that you have all of the correct tools necessary. Refer to *Tools and working facilities* for further information.

6 Cylinder head – dismantling

Note: *New and reconditioned cylinder heads are available from the manufacturer, and from engine overhaul specialists. Be aware that some specialist tools are required for the dismantling and inspection procedures, and new components may not be readily available. It may therefore be more practical and economical for the home mechanic to purchase a reconditioned head, rather than dismantle, inspect and recondition the original head. A valve spring compressor tool will be required for this operation.*

1 Remove the cylinder head as described in Part A of this Chapter.
2 Remove the camshafts (M52 engine), cam followers and camshaft bearing castings as described in Part A of this Chapter.
3 Using a valve spring compressor, compress the spring on each valve in turn until the split collets can be removed. Release the compressor, and lift off the spring retainer, spring and spring seat. Using a pair of pliers,

6.3a Compressing a valve spring using a spring compressor tool

6.3b Remove the valve stem oil seals

6.6 Place each valve and its associated components in a labelled plastic bag

carefully extract the valve stem oil seal from the top of the guide **(see illustrations)**.

4 If, when the valve spring compressor is screwed down, the spring retainer refuses to free and expose the split collets, gently tap the top of the tool, directly over the retainer, with a light hammer. This will free the retainer.

5 Withdraw the valve through the combustion chamber.

6 It is essential that each valve is stored together with its collets, retainer, spring, and spring seat. The valves should also be kept in their correct sequence, unless they are so badly worn that they are to be renewed. If they are going to be kept and used again, place each valve assembly in a labelled polythene bag or similar small container **(see illustration)**. Note that No 1 valve is nearest to the timing chain end of the engine.

7 Cylinder head and valves – cleaning and inspection

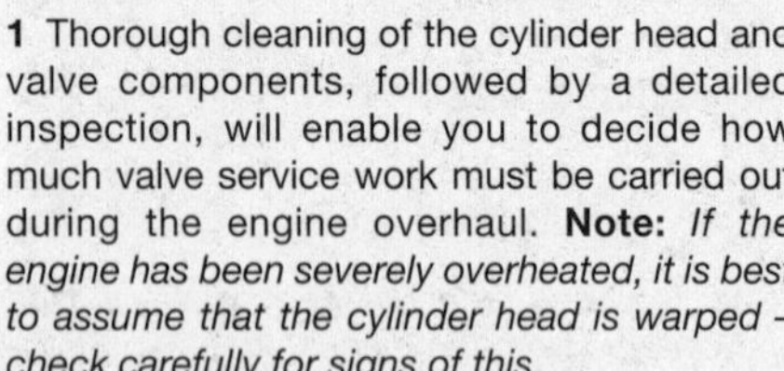

1 Thorough cleaning of the cylinder head and valve components, followed by a detailed inspection, will enable you to decide how much valve service work must be carried out during the engine overhaul. **Note:** *If the engine has been severely overheated, it is best to assume that the cylinder head is warped – check carefully for signs of this.*

Cleaning

2 Scrape away all traces of old gasket material from the cylinder head.

3 Scrape away the carbon from the combustion chambers and ports, then wash the cylinder head thoroughly with paraffin or a suitable solvent.

4 Scrape off any heavy carbon deposits that may have formed on the valves, then use a power-operated wire brush to remove deposits from the valve heads and stems.

Inspection

Note: *Be sure to perform all the following inspection procedures before concluding that the services of a machine shop or engine overhaul specialist are required. Make a list of all items that require attention.*

Cylinder head

5 Inspect the head very carefully for cracks, evidence of coolant leakage, and other damage. If cracks are found, a new cylinder head should be obtained.

6 Use a straight-edge and feeler blade to check that the cylinder head gasket surface is not distorted **(see illustration)**. If it is, it may be possible to have it machined, provided that the cylinder head is not reduced to less than the specified height. **Note:** *If 0.3 mm is machined off the cylinder head, a 0.3 mm thicker cylinder head gasket must be fitted when the engine is reassembled. This is necessary in order to maintain the correct dimensions between the valve heads, valve guides and cylinder head gasket face.*

7 Examine the valve seats in each of the combustion chambers. If they are severely pitted, cracked, or burned, they will need to be renewed or recut by an engine overhaul specialist. If they are only slightly pitted, this can be removed by grinding-in the valve heads and seats with fine valve-grinding compound, as described later in this Section.

8 Check the valve guides for wear by inserting the relevant valve, and checking for side-to-side motion of the valve. A very small amount of movement is acceptable. If the movement seems excessive, renew the valve. Separate valve guides are not available, although different grades (sizes) of valves (stems) are.

9 Unscrew the oil pressure check valve from the bottom of the cylinder head. Check that the valve can be blown through from bottom-to-top, but not from top-to-bottom. Thoroughly clean the valve and fit a new O-ring, then refit the valve to the cylinder head and tighten securely **(see illustration)**.

10 Examine the bearing surfaces in the cylinder head or bearing castings (as applicable) and the bearing caps for signs of wear or damage.

11 Check the camshaft bearing casting mating faces on the cylinder head for distortion. Use a straight-edge and feeler blade to check that the cylinder head faces are not distorted. If the distortion is outside the specified limit, the cylinder head and bearing castings must be renewed.

Valves

Warning: The exhaust valves fitted to some engines are filled with sodium to improve their heat transfer. Sodium is a highly reactive metal, which will ignite or explode spontaneously on contact with water (including water vapour in the air). These valves must NOT be disposed of as ordinary scrap. Seek advice from a BMW dealer or your local authority when disposing of the valves.

12 Examine the head of each valve for pitting, burning, cracks, and general wear. Check the valve stem for scoring and wear ridges. Rotate the valve, and check for any obvious indication that it is bent. Look for pits or excessive wear on the tip of each valve stem. Renew any valve that shows any such signs of wear or damage.

13 If the valve appears satisfactory at this stage, measure the valve stem diameter at

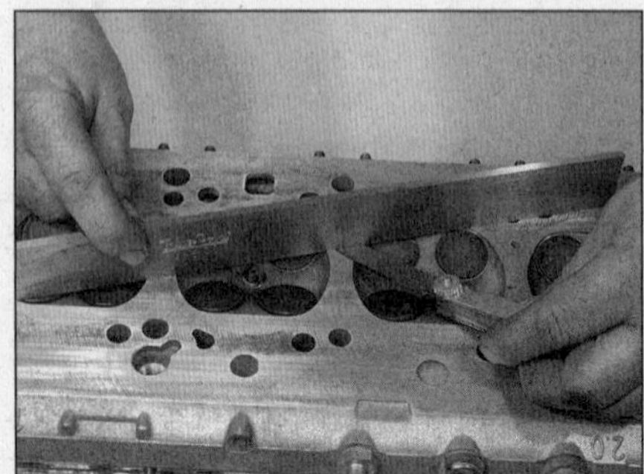

7.6 Check the cylinder head gasket face for distortion

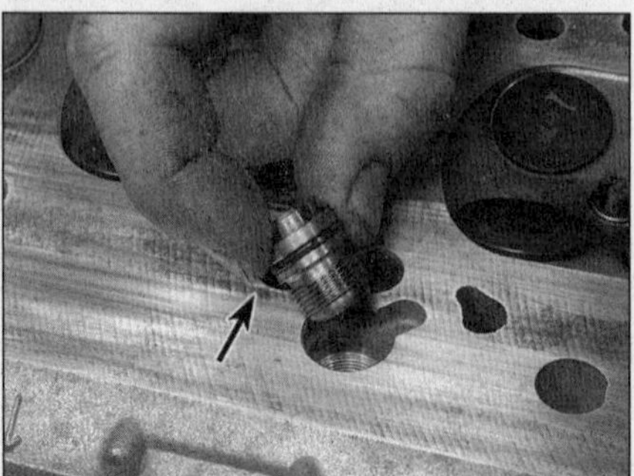

7.9 Fit a new O-ring (arrowed) to the cylinder head oil pressure check valve

7.13 Measure the valve stem diameter

several points using a micrometer **(see illustration)**. Any significant difference in the readings obtained indicates wear of the valve stem. Should any of these conditions be apparent, the valve(s) must be renewed.

14 If the valves are in satisfactory condition, they should be ground (lapped) into their respective seats, to ensure a smooth, gas-tight seal. If the seat is only lightly pitted, or if it has been recut, fine grinding compound *only* should be used to produce the required finish. Coarse valve-grinding compound should *not* be used, unless a seat is badly burned or deeply pitted. If this is the case, the cylinder head and valves should be inspected by an expert, to decide whether seat recutting, or even the renewal of the valve or seat insert (where possible) is required.

15 Valve grinding is carried out as follows. Place the cylinder head upside-down on a bench.

16 Smear a trace of (the appropriate grade of) valve-grinding compound on the seat face, and press a suction grinding tool onto the valve

7.16 Grinding-in a valve

head **(see illustration)**. With a semi-rotary action, grind the valve head to its seat, lifting the valve occasionally to redistribute the grinding compound. A light spring placed under the valve head will greatly ease this operation.

17 If coarse grinding compound is being used, work only until a dull, matt even surface is produced on both the valve seat and the valve, then wipe off the used compound, and repeat the process with fine compound. When a smooth unbroken ring of light grey matt finish is produced on both the valve and seat, the grinding operation is complete. *Do not* grind-in the valves any further than absolutely necessary, or the seat will be prematurely sunk into the cylinder head.

18 When all the valves have been ground-in, carefully wash off *all* traces of grinding compound using paraffin or a suitable solvent, before reassembling the cylinder head.

Valve components

19 Examine the valve springs for signs of damage and discoloration. No minimum free length is specified by BMW, so the only way of judging valve spring wear is by comparison with a new component.

20 Stand each spring on a flat surface, and check it for squareness. If any of the springs are damaged, distorted or have lost their tension, obtain a complete new set of springs. It is normal to renew the valve springs as a matter of course if a major overhaul is being carried out.

21 Renew the valve stem oil seals regardless of their apparent condition.

Cam followers/valve lifters

22 Examine the contact surfaces for wear or scoring. If excessive wear is evident, the component(s) should be renewed.

8 Cylinder head – reassembly

Note: *New valve stem oil seals should be fitted, and a valve spring compressor tool will be required for this operation.*

1 Lubricate the stems of the valves, and insert the valves into their original locations **(see illustration)**. If new valves are being fitted, insert them into the locations to which they have been ground.

2 Working on the first valve, dip the new valve stem seal in fresh engine oil. New seals are normally supplied with protective sleeves which should be fitted to the tops of the valve stems to prevent the collet grooves from damaging the oil seals. If no sleeves are supplied, wind a little thin tape round the top of the valve stems to protect the seals. Carefully locate the seal over the valve and onto the guide. Take care not to damage the seal as it is passed over the valve stem. Use a suitable socket or metal tube to press the seal firmly onto the guide **(see illustrations)**.

3 Refit the spring seat **(see illustration)**.

4 Locate the valve spring on top of the seat, then refit the spring retainer **(see illustrations)**. Where the spring diameter is different at each end, the larger diameter end of the valve spring fits against the seat on the cylinder head.

5 Compress the valve spring, and locate the split collets in the recess in the valve stem. Release the compressor, then repeat the procedure on the remaining valves.

8.1 Lubricate the valve stem

8.2a Fit the protective sleeve to the valve stem . . .

8.2b . . . then fit the oil seal using a socket

8.3 Refit the spring seat

8.4a Fit the valve spring . . .

8.4b . . . followed by the spring retainer

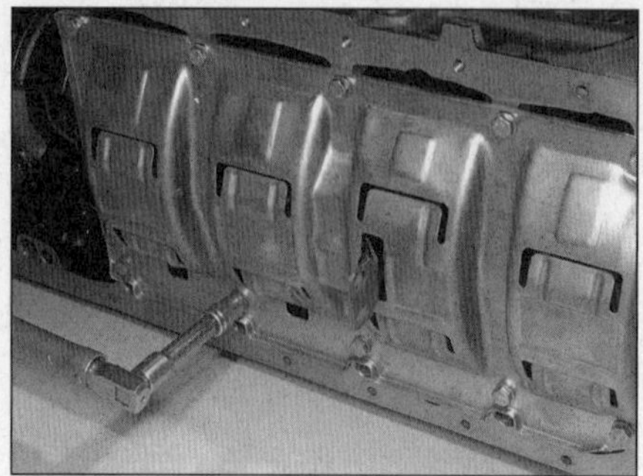
9.2 Unbolt the oil baffle plate from the cylinder block

9.4 Big-end bearing cap marks

6 With all the valves installed, support the cylinder head on blocks of wood and, using a hammer and interposed block of wood, tap the end of each valve stem to settle the components.

7 Refit the camshaft bearing castings, cam followers and camshafts (as applicable) as described in Part A of this Chapter.

8 Refit the cylinder head as described in Part A of this Chapter.

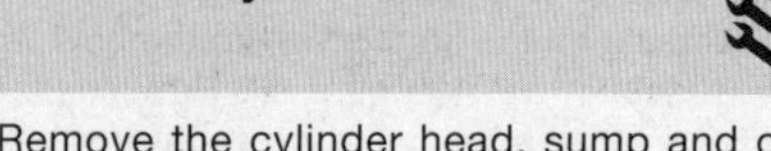

9 Piston/connecting rod assembly – removal

1 Remove the cylinder head, sump and oil pump as described in Part A of this Chapter.

2 Where applicable, unbolt the oil baffle from the bottom of the cylinder block **(see illustration)**.

3 If there is a pronounced wear ridge at the top of any bore, it may be necessary to remove it with a scraper or ridge reamer, to avoid piston damage during removal. Such a ridge indicates excessive wear of the cylinder bore.

4 Check the connecting rods and big-end caps for identification marks. Both rods and caps should be marked with the cylinder number. Note that No 1 cylinder is at the timing chain end of the engine. If no marks are present, using a hammer and centre-punch, paint or similar, mark each connecting rod and big-end bearing cap with its respective cylinder number on the flat machined surface provided **(see illustration)**.

5 Turn the crankshaft to bring pistons 1 and 6 to BDC (bottom dead centre).

6 Unscrew the bolts from No 1 piston big-end bearing cap. Take off the cap, and recover the bottom half bearing shell **(see illustration)**. If the bearing shells are to be re-used, tape the cap and the shell together.

7 Using a hammer handle, push the piston up through the bore, and remove it from the top of the cylinder block. Recover the bearing shell, and tape it to the connecting rod for safe-keeping. Take care not to damage the oil spray jets.

8 Loosely refit the big-end cap to the connecting rod, and secure with the bolts – this will help to keep the components in their correct order.

9 Remove No 6 piston assembly in the same way.

10 Turn the crankshaft as necessary to bring the remaining pistons to BDC, and remove them in the same way.

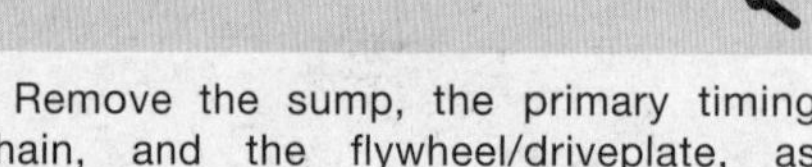

10 Crankshaft – removal

1 Remove the sump, the primary timing chain, and the flywheel/driveplate, as described in Part A of this Chapter.

2 Remove the pistons and connecting rods, as described in Section 9. If no work is to be done on the pistons and connecting rods, there is no need to remove the cylinder head, or to push the pistons out of the cylinder bores. The pistons should just be pushed far enough up the bores so that they are positioned clear of the crankshaft journals.

9.6 Remove the big-end bearing cap

Warning: If the pistons are pushed up the bores, and the cylinder head is still fitted, take care not to force the pistons into the open valves.

3 Check the crankshaft endfloat as described in Section 13, then proceed as follows.

4 Slacken and remove the retaining bolts, and remove the oil seal carrier from the rear (flywheel/driveplate) end of the cylinder block, along with its gasket **(see illustration)**.

5 If not already done, remove the oil pump drive chain and, if necessary, remove the crankshaft sprocket with reference to Part A of this Chapter.

6 The main bearing caps should be numbered 1 to 7 on the exhaust side of the engine, starting from the timing chain end of the engine **(see illustration)**. If not, mark them accordingly using a centre-punch.

7 Slacken and remove the main bearing cap retaining bolts, and lift off each bearing cap **(see illustration)**. Recover the lower bearing

10.4 Remove the oil seal carrier from the rear of the cylinder block

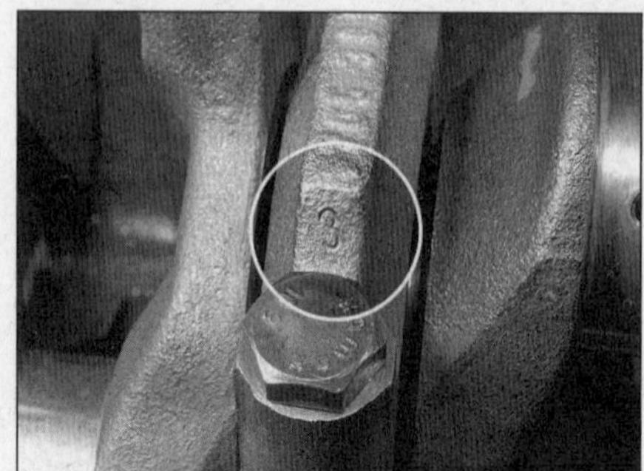
10.6 Main bearing cap identification number

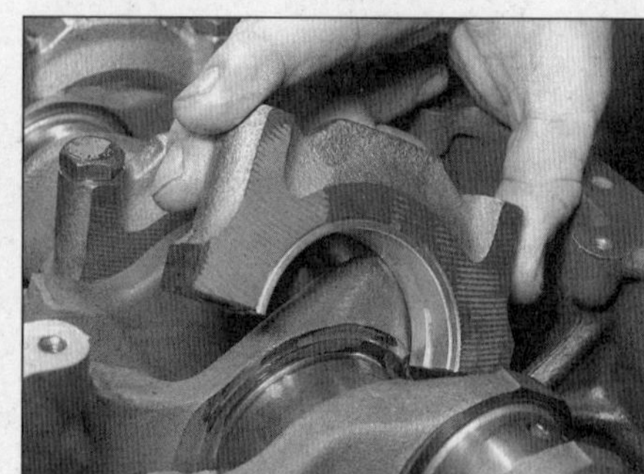
10.7 Lift off the main bearing caps

10.10 Lift the upper main bearing shells from the cylinder block

shells, and tape them to their respective caps for safe-keeping. Note that on engines with an aluminium cylinder block and a one-piece oil pump and baffle plate, reinforcement plates are fitted from the cylinder block to the main bearing caps. Unscrew and remove these as the main bearing caps are removed.

8 Note that the lower thrust bearing shell, which controls crankshaft endfloat, is fitted to No 6 main bearing cap. Also note that on engines with a cast-iron cylinder block, the oil pick-up tube support bracket, which is secured by the No 5 main bearing cap bolts.

9 Lift out the crankshaft. Take care as the crankshaft is heavy.

10 Recover the upper bearing shells from the cylinder block **(see illustration)**, and tape them to their respective caps for safe-keeping. Again, note the location of the upper thrust bearing shell.

11.2a Remove the piston oil spray jets tubes from the main bearing locations – 2.0 and 2.2 litre engines

11.8 Clean the cylinder block threaded holes using a suitable tap

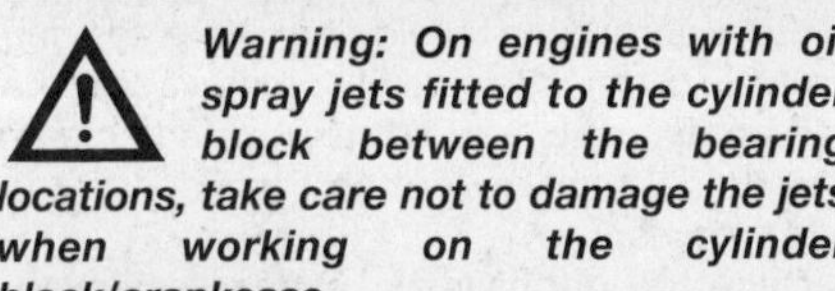

11 Cylinder block/crankcase – cleaning and inspection

Warning: On engines with oil spray jets fitted to the cylinder block between the bearing locations, take care not to damage the jets when working on the cylinder block/crankcase.

Cleaning

1 Remove all external components and electrical switches/sensors from the block. For complete cleaning, the core plugs should ideally be removed. Drill a small hole in the plugs, then insert a self-tapping screw into the hole. Pull out the plugs by pulling on the screw with a pair of grips, or by using a slide hammer.

2 Pull/unscrew the piston oil jet spray tubes from their locations in the cylinder block. The tubes are fitted to Nos 2 to 7 bearing locations on 2.0 litre and 2.2 litre engines, and to the underside of the cylinder block between the main bearing seats on 2.5 litre, 2.8 litre and 3.0 litre engines **(see illustrations)**. Discard the retaining bolts, new ones must be fitted.

3 Scrape all traces of gasket from the cylinder block/crankcase, taking care not to damage the gasket/sealing surfaces.

4 Remove all oil gallery plugs (where fitted). The plugs are usually very tight – they may have to be drilled out, and the holes retapped.

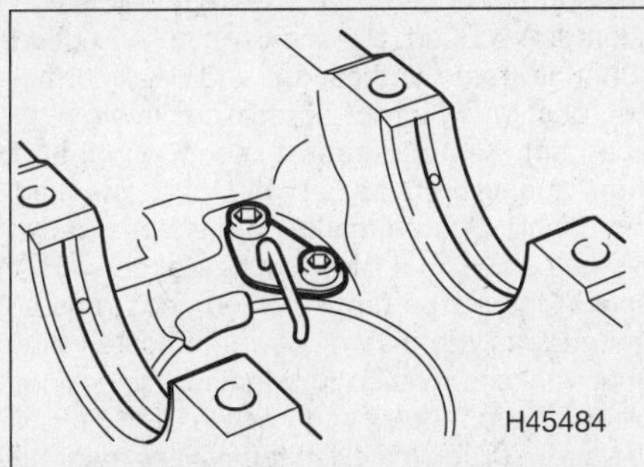

11.2b On 2.5, 2.8 and 3.0 litre engines, the piston oil spray jets are bolted to the underside of the cylinder block between the main bearing locations

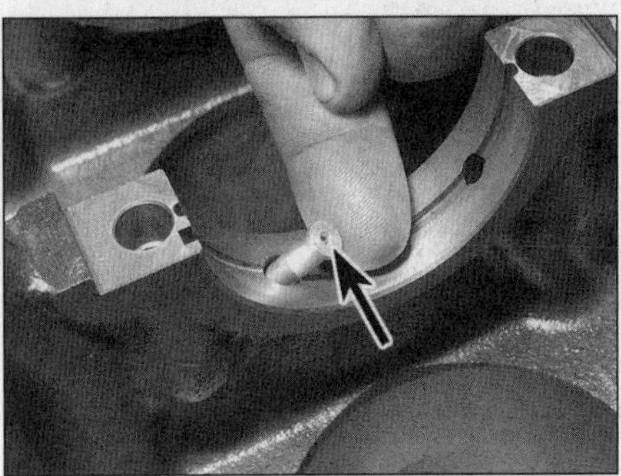

11.12 Clean the holes (arrowed) in the oil spray tubes

Use new plugs when the engine is reassembled.

5 If any of the castings are extremely dirty, all should be steam-cleaned.

6 After the castings are returned, clean all oil holes and oil galleries one more time. Flush all internal passages with warm water until the water runs clear. Dry thoroughly, and apply a light film of oil to all mating surfaces, to prevent rusting. Also oil the cylinder bores. If you have access to compressed air, use it to speed up the drying process, and to blow out all the oil holes and galleries.

Warning: Wear eye protection when using compressed air.

7 If the castings are not very dirty, you can do an adequate cleaning job with hot (as hot as you can stand), soapy water and a stiff brush. Take plenty of time, and do a thorough job. Regardless of the cleaning method used, be sure to clean all oil holes and galleries very thoroughly, and to dry all components well. Protect the cylinder bores as described above, to prevent rusting.

8 All threaded holes must be clean, to ensure accurate torque readings during reassembly. To clean the threads, run the correct-size tap into each of the holes to remove rust, corrosion, thread sealant or sludge, and to restore damaged threads **(see illustration)**. If possible, use compressed air to clear the holes of debris produced by this operation.

HAYNES HiNT ***A good alternative is to inject aerosol-applied water-dispersant lubricant into each hole, using the long spout usually supplied.***

Warning: Wear eye protection when cleaning out these holes in this way.

9 Ensure that all threaded holes in the cylinder block are dry.

10 After coating the mating surfaces of the new core plugs with suitable sealant, fit them to the cylinder block. Make sure that they are driven in straight and seated correctly, or leakage could result.

HAYNES HiNT ***A large socket with an outside diameter which will just fit into the core plug can be used to drive core plugs into position.***

11 Apply suitable sealant to the new oil gallery plugs, and insert them into the holes in the block. Tighten them securely.

12 Thoroughly clean the piston oil spray tubes, then refit them to their locations. When refitting the type which are bolted in place, use new bolts and apply a little locking compound to the threads before tightening securely **(see illustration)**.

13 If the engine is not going to be reassembled right away, cover it with a large plastic bag to keep it clean; protect all mating surfaces and the cylinder bores as described above, to prevent rusting.

Inspection

14 Visually check the castings for cracks and corrosion. Look for stripped threads in the threaded holes. If there has been any history of internal water leakage, it may be worthwhile having an engine overhaul specialist check the cylinder block/crankcase with special equipment. If defects are found, have them repaired if possible, or renew the assembly.

15 Check each cylinder bore for scuffing and scoring. Check for signs of a wear ridge at the top of the cylinder, indicating that the bore is excessively worn.

16 Have the bores of the engine block measured by a BMW dealer or automotive engineering workshop. Then if the bore wear exceeds the permitted tolerances, or if the bore walls are badly scuffed or scored, then the cylinders must be rebored. Have the work carried out by a BMW dealer or automotive engineering workshop, who will also be able to supply suitable oversize pistons and rings.

12 Piston/connecting rod assembly – inspection

1 Before the inspection process can begin, the piston/connecting rod assemblies must be cleaned, and the original piston rings removed from the pistons.

2 Carefully expand the old rings over the top of the pistons. The use of two or three old feeler blades will be helpful in preventing the rings dropping into empty grooves **(see illustration)**. Be careful not to scratch the piston with the ends of the ring. The rings are brittle, and will snap if they are spread too far. They are also very sharp – protect your hands and fingers. Note that the third ring incorporates an expander. Always remove the rings from the top of the piston. Keep each set of rings with its piston if the old rings are to be re-used. Note which way up each ring is fitted.

3 Scrape away all traces of carbon from the top of the piston. A hand-held wire brush (or a piece of fine emery cloth) can be used, once the majority of the deposits have been scraped away.

4 Remove the carbon from the ring grooves in the piston, using an old ring. Break the ring in half to do this. Be careful to remove only the carbon deposits – do not remove any metal, and do not nick or scratch the sides of the ring grooves.

5 Once the deposits have been removed, clean the piston/connecting rod assembly with paraffin or a suitable solvent, and dry thoroughly. Make sure that the oil return holes in the ring grooves are clear.

6 If the pistons and cylinder bores are not damaged or worn excessively, and if the cylinder block does not need to be rebored, the original pistons can be refitted. Measure the piston diameters, and check that they are within limits for the corresponding bore diameters. If the piston-to-bore clearance is excessive, the block will have to be rebored, and new pistons and rings fitted. Normal piston wear shows up as even vertical wear on the piston thrust surfaces, and slight looseness of the top ring in its groove. New piston rings should always be used when the engine is reassembled.

7 Carefully inspect each piston for cracks around the skirt, around the gudgeon pin holes, and at the piston ring 'lands' (between the ring grooves).

8 Look for scoring and scuffing on the piston skirt, holes in the piston crown, and burned areas at the edge of the crown. If the skirt is scored or scuffed, the engine may have been suffering from overheating, and/or abnormal combustion which caused excessively high operating temperatures. The cooling and lubrication systems should be checked thoroughly. Scorch marks on the sides of the pistons show that blow-by has occurred. A hole in the piston crown, or burned areas at the edge of the piston crown, indicates that abnormal combustion (pre-ignition, knocking, or detonation) has been occurring. If any of the above problems exist, the causes must be investigated and corrected, or the damage will occur again. The causes may include incorrect ignition timing, inlet air leaks, or incorrect air/fuel mixture.

9 Corrosion of the piston, in the form of pitting, indicates that coolant has been leaking into the combustion chamber and/or the crankcase. Again, the cause must be corrected, or the problem may persist in the rebuilt engine.

10 New pistons can be purchased from a BMW dealer or engine reconditioning specialist.

11 Examine each connecting rod carefully for signs of damage, such as cracks around the big-end and small-end bearings. Check that the rod is not bent or distorted. Damage is highly unlikely, unless the engine has been seized or badly overheated. Detailed checking of the connecting rod assembly can only be carried out by a BMW dealer or engine repair specialist with the necessary equipment.

12 The gudgeon pins are of the floating type, secured in position by two circlips. The pistons and connecting rods can be separated as follows.

13 Using a small flat-bladed screwdriver, prise out the circlips, and push out the gudgeon pin **(see illustrations)**. Hand pressure should be sufficient to remove the pin. Identify the piston and rod to ensure correct reassembly. Discard the circlips – new ones must be used on refitting. Note that BMW recommend that gudgeon pins must not be renewed separately – they are matched to their respective pistons.

14 Examine the gudgeon pin and connecting rod small-end bearing for signs of wear or damage. It should be possible to push the gudgeon pin through the connecting rod by hand, without noticeable play. Wear can only be cured by renewing both the pin and piston.

15 The connecting rods themselves should not be in need of renewal, unless seizure or some other major mechanical failure has occurred. Check the alignment of the connecting rods visually, and if the rods are not straight, take them to an engine overhaul specialist for a more detailed check.

16 Examine all components, and obtain any new parts from your BMW dealer. If new pistons are purchased, they will be supplied complete with gudgeon pins and circlips. Circlips can also be purchased individually.

17 Position the piston in relation to the connecting rod, so that when the assembly is

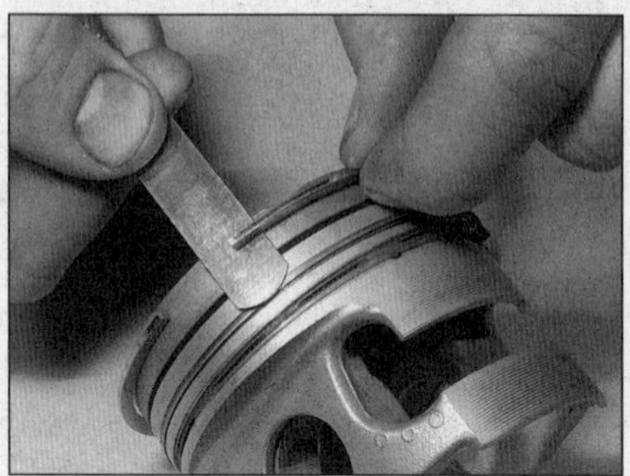

12.2 Remove the piston rings with the aid of a feeler gauge

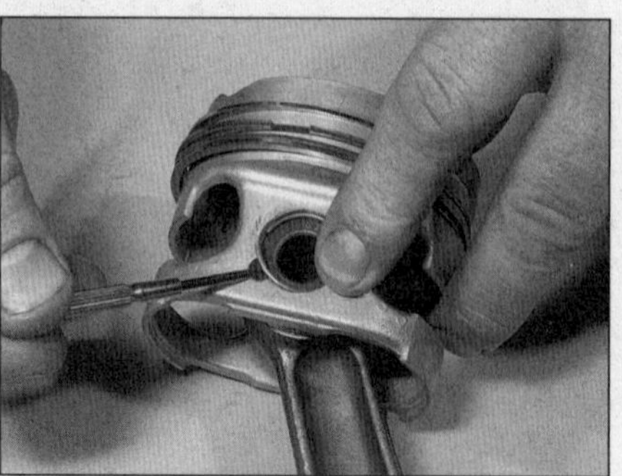

12.13a Prise out the circlips . . .

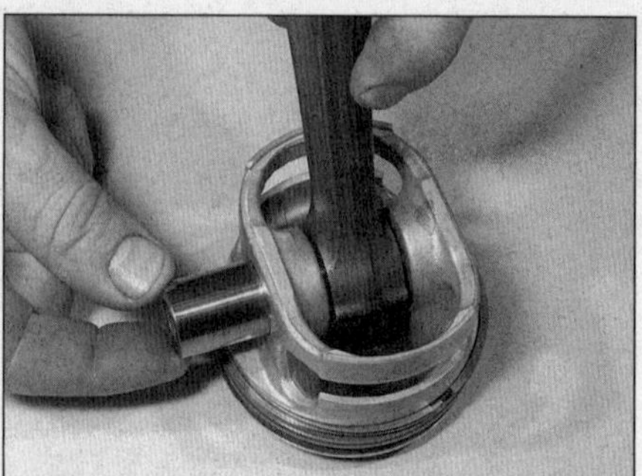

12.13b . . . and remove the gudgeon pins from the pistons

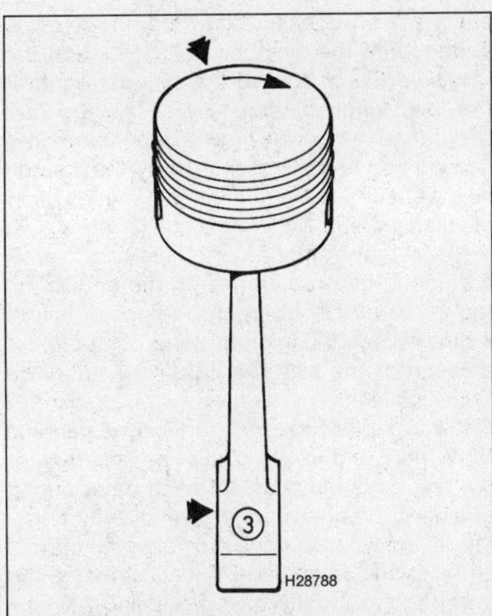

12.17a The cylinder number markings should be on the exhaust manifold side of the engine, and the arrow on the piston crown should point towards the timing chain end of the engine

refitted to the engine, the identifying cylinder numbers on the connecting rod and big-end cap are positioned on the exhaust manifold side of the engine, and the installation direction arrow on the piston crown points towards the timing chain end of the engine **(see illustrations)**.

18 Apply a smear of clean engine oil to the gudgeon pin. Slide it into the piston and through the connecting rod small-end. Check that the piston pivots freely on the rod, then secure the gudgeon pin in position with two new circlips. Ensure that each circlip is correctly located in its groove in the piston.

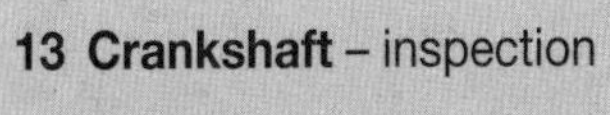

13 Crankshaft – inspection

Checking endfloat

1 If the crankshaft endfloat is to be checked, this must be done when the crankshaft is still installed in the cylinder block/crankcase, but is free to move.

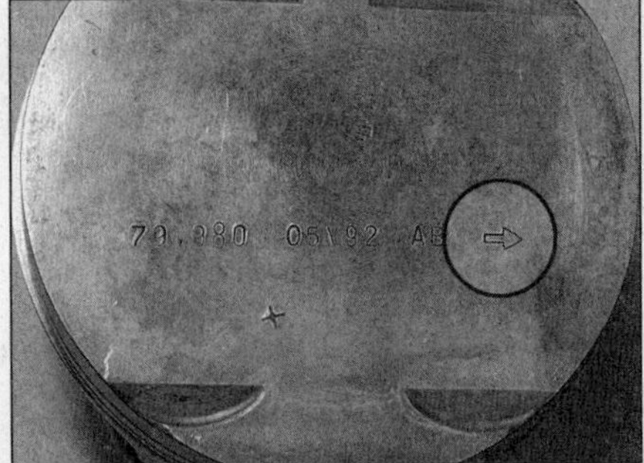

12.17b Installation direction arrow (highlighted)

2 Check the endfloat using a dial gauge in contact with the end of the crankshaft. Push the crankshaft fully one way, and then zero the gauge. Push the crankshaft fully the other way, and check the endfloat. The result can be compared with the specified amount, and will give an indication as to whether new thrust bearing shells are required **(see illustration)**.

3 If a dial gauge is not available, feeler blades can be used. First push the crankshaft fully towards the flywheel/driveplate end of the engine, then use feeler blades to measure the gap between the web of No 6 crankpin and the thrust bearing shell **(see illustration)**.

Inspection

4 Clean the crankshaft using paraffin or a suitable solvent, and dry it, preferably with compressed air if available. Be sure to clean the oil holes with a pipe cleaner or similar probe, to ensure that they are not obstructed.

Warning: Wear eye protection when using compressed air.

5 Check the main and big-end bearing journals for uneven wear, scoring, pitting and cracking.

6 Big-end bearing wear is accompanied by distinct metallic knocking when the engine is running (particularly noticeable when the engine is pulling from low speed) and some loss of oil pressure.

7 Main bearing wear is accompanied by severe engine vibration and rumble – getting progressively worse as engine speed increases – and again by loss of oil pressure.

8 Check the bearing journal for roughness by running a finger lightly over the bearing surface. Any roughness (which will be accompanied by obvious bearing wear) indicates that the crankshaft requires regrinding (where possible) or renewal.

9 If the crankshaft has been reground, check for burrs around the crankshaft oil holes (the holes are usually chamfered, so burrs should not be a problem unless regrinding has been carried out carelessly). Remove any burrs with a fine file or scraper, and thoroughly clean the oil holes as described previously.

10 Have the crankshaft journals measured by a BMW dealer or automotive engineering workshop. If the crankshaft is worn or damaged, they may be able to regrind the journals and supply suitable undersize bearing shells. If no oversize shells are available and the crankshaft has worn beyond the specified limits, it will have to be renewed. Consult your BMW dealer or engine specialist for further information on parts availability.

14 Main and big-end bearings – inspection

1 Even though the main and big-end bearings should be renewed during the engine overhaul, the old bearings should be retained for close examination, as they may reveal valuable information about the condition of the engine. The bearing shells are graded by thickness, the grade of each shell being indicated by the colour code marked on it.

2 Bearing failure can occur due to lack of lubrication, the presence of dirt or other foreign particles, overloading the engine, or corrosion **(see illustration)**. Regardless of the

13.2 Measure the crankshaft endfloat using a dial gauge . . .

13.3 . . . or feeler gauges

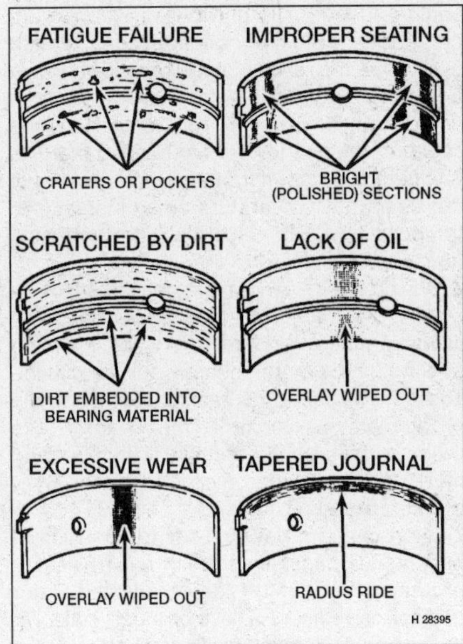

14.2 Typical bearing failures

cause of bearing failure, the cause must be corrected (where applicable) before the engine is reassembled, to prevent it from happening again.

3 When examining the bearing shells, remove them from the cylinder block/crankcase, the connecting rods and the connecting rod big-end bearing caps. Lay them out on a clean surface in the same general position as their location in the engine. This will enable you to match any bearing problems with the corresponding crankshaft journal. *Do not* touch any shell's bearing surface with your fingers while checking it, or the delicate surface may be scratched.

4 Dirt and other foreign matter gets into the engine in a variety of ways. It may be left in the engine during assembly, or it may pass through filters or the crankcase ventilation system. It may get into the oil, and from there into the bearings. Metal chips from machining operations and normal engine wear are often present. Abrasives are sometimes left in engine components after reconditioning, especially when parts are not thoroughly cleaned using the proper cleaning methods. Whatever the source, these foreign objects often end up embedded in the soft bearing material, and are easily recognised. Large particles will not embed in the bearing, and will score or gouge the bearing and journal. The best prevention for this cause of bearing failure is to clean all parts thoroughly, and keep everything spotlessly-clean during engine assembly. Frequent and regular engine oil and filter changes are also recommended.

5 Lack of lubrication (or lubrication breakdown) has a number of interrelated causes. Excessive heat (which thins the oil), overloading (which squeezes the oil from the bearing face) and oil leakage (from excessive bearing clearances, worn oil pump or high engine speeds) all contribute to lubrication breakdown. Blocked oil passages, which usually are the result of misaligned oil holes in a bearing shell, will also oil-starve a bearing, and destroy it. When lack of lubrication is the cause of bearing failure, the bearing material is wiped or extruded from the steel backing of the bearing. Temperatures may increase to the point where the steel backing turns blue from overheating.

6 Driving habits can have a definite effect on bearing life. Full-throttle, low-speed operation (labouring the engine) puts very high loads on bearings, tending to squeeze out the oil film. These loads cause the bearings to flex, which produces fine cracks in the bearing face (fatigue failure). Eventually, the bearing material will loosen in pieces, and tear away from the steel backing.

7 Short-distance driving leads to corrosion of bearings, because insufficient engine heat is produced to drive off the condensed water and corrosive gases. These products collect in the engine oil, forming acid and sludge. As the oil is carried to the engine bearings, the acid attacks and corrodes the bearing material.

8 Incorrect bearing installation during engine assembly will lead to bearing failure as well. Tight-fitting bearings leave insufficient bearing running clearance, and will result in oil starvation. Dirt or foreign particles trapped behind a bearing shell result in high spots on the bearing, which lead to failure.

9 *Do not* touch any shell's bearing surface with your fingers during reassembly; there is a risk of scratching the delicate surface, or of depositing particles of dirt on it.

10 As mentioned at the beginning of this Section, the bearing shells should be renewed as a matter of course during engine overhaul; to do otherwise is false economy.

15 Engine overhaul – reassembly sequence

1 Before reassembly begins, ensure that all new parts have been obtained, and that all necessary tools are available. Read through the entire procedure to familiarise yourself with the work involved, and to ensure that all items necessary for reassembly of the engine are at hand. In addition to all normal tools and materials, thread-locking compound will be needed. A suitable tube of Drei Bond 1209 sealant (available from BMW dealers) will also be required.

2 In order to save time and avoid problems, engine reassembly can be carried out in the following order, referring to Part A of this Chapter unless otherwise stated:

a) Crankshaft (Section 17).
b) Piston/connecting rod assemblies (Section 18).
c) Oil pump.
d) Sump.
e) Flywheel/driveplate.
f) Cylinder head.
g) Timing chain, tensioner and sprockets.
h) Engine external components.

3 At this stage, all engine components should be absolutely clean and dry, with all faults repaired. The components should be laid out (or in individual containers) on a completely clean work surface.

16 Piston rings – refitting

1 Before fitting new piston rings, the ring end gaps must be checked as follows.

2 Lay out the piston/connecting rod assemblies and the new piston ring sets, so that the ring sets will be matched with the same piston and cylinder during the end gap measurement and subsequent engine reassembly.

3 Insert the top ring into the first cylinder, and push it down the bore using the top of the piston. This will ensure that the ring remains square with the cylinder walls. Position the ring near the bottom of the cylinder bore, at the lower limit of ring travel. The top and second compression rings are different. The second ring is easily identified by the step on its lower surface, and by the fact that its outer face is tapered.

4 Measure the end gap using feeler blades.

5 Repeat the procedure with the ring at the top of the cylinder bore, at the upper limit of its travel **(see illustration)**, and compare the measurements with the figures given in the Specifications.

6 If the gap is too small (unlikely if genuine BMW parts are used), it must be enlarged, or the ring ends may contact each other during engine operation, causing serious damage. Ideally, new piston rings providing the correct end gap should be fitted. As a last resort, the end gap can be increased by filing the ring ends very carefully with a fine file. Mount the file in a vice equipped with soft jaws, slip the ring over the file with the ends contacting the file face, and slowly move the ring to remove material from the ends. Take care, as piston rings are sharp, and are easily broken.

7 With new piston rings, it is unlikely that the end gap will be too large. If the gaps are too large, check that you have the correct rings for your engine and for the particular cylinder bore size.

8 Repeat the checking procedure for each ring in the first cylinder, and then for the rings in the remaining cylinders. Remember to keep rings, pistons and cylinders matched up.

9 Once the ring end gaps have been checked and if necessary corrected, the rings can be fitted to the pistons.

10 Fit the piston rings using the same technique as for removal. Fit the bottom (oil control) ring first, and work up. When fitting a three-piece oil control ring, first insert the expander, then fit the lower rail with its gap positioned 120° from the expander gap, then fit the upper rail with its gap positioned 120° from the lower rail. When fitting a two-piece oil control ring, first insert the expander, then fit the control ring with its gap positioned 180° from the expander gap. Ensure that the second compression ring is fitted the correct way up, with its identification mark (either a dot of paint or the word TOP stamped on the

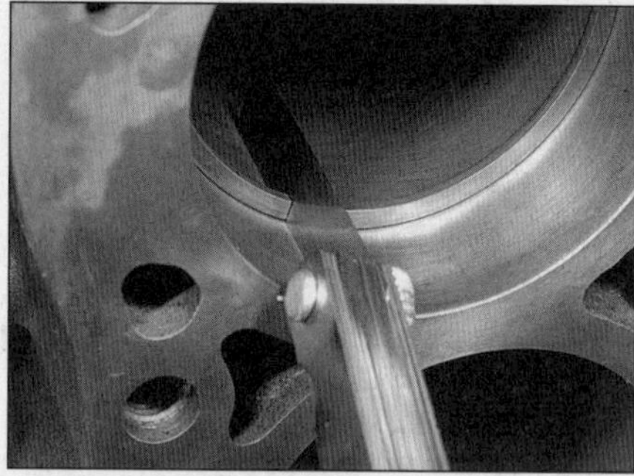

16.5 Measure the piston ring end gaps

ring surface) at the top, and the stepped surface at the bottom **(see illustration)**. Arrange the gaps of the top and second compression rings 120° either side of the oil control ring gap, but make sure that none of the rings' gaps are positioned over the gudgeon pin hole. **Note:** *Always follow any instructions supplied with the new piston ring sets – different manufacturers may specify different procedures. Do not mix up the top and second compression rings, as they have different cross-sections.*

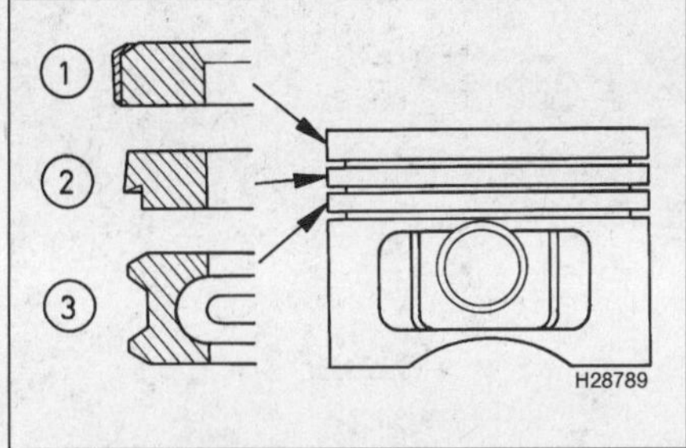

16.10 Typical piston ring fitting

1 Top compression ring
2 2nd compression ring
3 Control ring

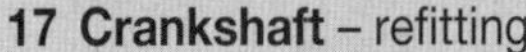

17 Crankshaft – refitting

Selection of bearing shells

1 Have the crankshaft inspected and measured by a BMW dealer or automotive engineering workshop. They will be able to carry out any regrinding/repairs, and supply suitable main and big-end bearing shells.

Crankshaft refitting

Note: *New main bearing cap bolts must be used when refitting the crankshaft.*

2 Ensure that the oil spray jets are fitted to the bearing locations in the cylinder block – see Section 11.

3 Clean the backs of the bearing shells, and the bearing locations in both the cylinder block/crankcase and the main bearing caps/lower crankcase.

4 Press the bearing shells into their locations, ensuring that the tab on each shell engages in the notch in the cylinder block/crankcase or bearing cap/lower crankcase. Take care not to touch any shell's bearing surface with your fingers. Note that the upper bearing shells have an oil groove running along the full length of the bearing surface, whereas the lower shells have a short, tapered oil groove at each end. The thrust bearing shells fit in No 6 bearing location **(see illustrations)**. Ensure that all traces of protective grease are cleaned off using paraffin. Wipe dry the shells with a lint-free cloth. Liberally lubricate each bearing shell in the cylinder block/crankcase and cap/lower crankcase with clean engine oil **(see illustration)**.

5 Lower the crankshaft into position so that Nos 1 and 6 cylinder crankpins will be at BDC, ready for fitting No 1 piston. Check the crankshaft endfloat as described in Section 13.

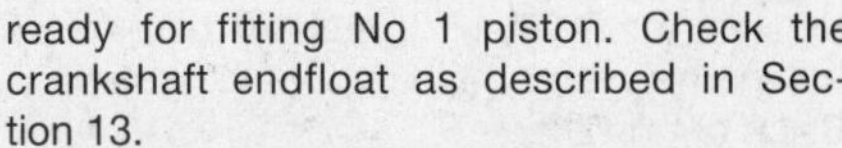

6 Lubricate the lower bearing shells in the main bearing caps with clean engine oil. Make sure that the locating lugs on the shells engage with the corresponding recesses in the caps.

7 Fit the main bearing caps to their correct locations, ensuring that they are fitted the correct way round (the bearing shell tab recesses in the block and caps must be on the same side). Where applicable, refit the bearing cap reinforcement plates. Thoroughly clean the new main bearing bolts, apply a little threadlocking compound to the threads, then insert the bolts, tightening them only loosely at this stage. Ensure that the oil pick-up tube support bracket (where applicable) is correctly in position on the No 5 main bearing cap bolts **(see illustrations)**.

8 Tighten the main bearing cap bolts to the specified torque, in the two stages given in the Specifications **(see illustration)**. Where applicable, tighten the reinforcement plates outer bolts securely.

9 Check that the crankshaft rotates freely.

10 Fit a new crankshaft rear oil seal to the oil seal carrier, then refit the oil seal carrier using a new gasket, as described in Part A of this Chapter.

11 Refit the crankshaft sprocket and the oil pump drive chain, as described in Part A of this Chapter.

12 Refit the piston/connecting rod assemblies as described in Section 18.

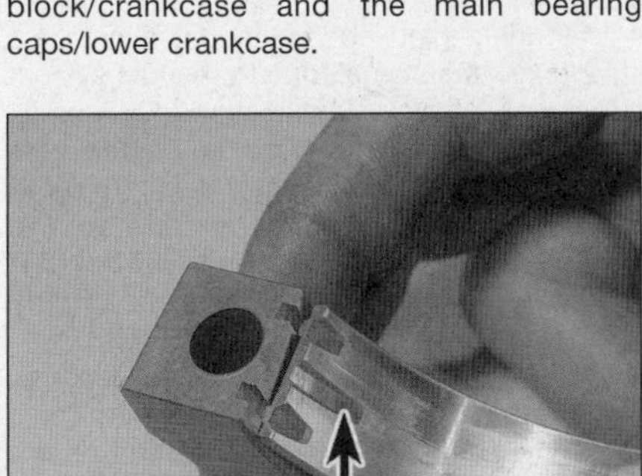

17.4a The lower bearing shells have short tapered oil grooves (arrowed)

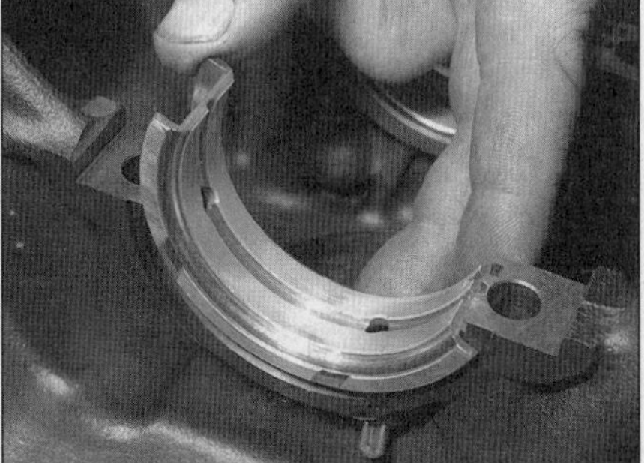

17.4b The thrust bearing shell is fitted to No 6 bearing location

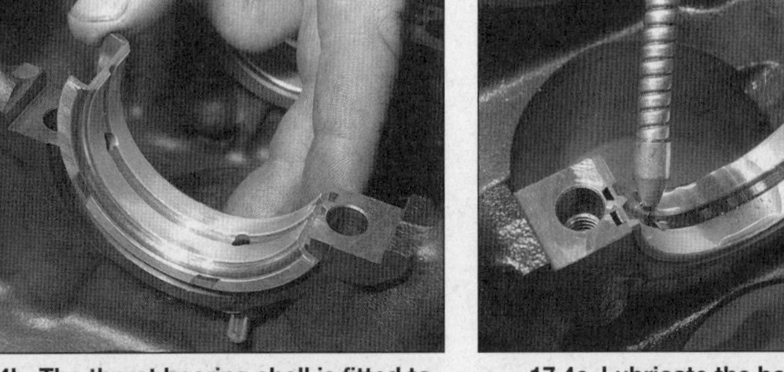

17.4c Lubricate the bearing shells

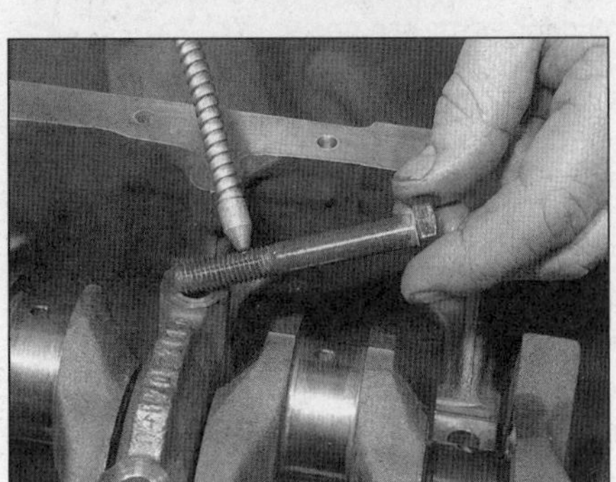

17.7a Lightly oil the threads of the main bearing cap bolts

17.7b Ensure the oil pick-up tube support bracket is in position on the No 5 main bearing cap bolts

17.8 Tighten the main bearing cap bolts to the specified torque

13 Refit the flywheel/driveplate, the primary timing chain, and the sump, as described in Part A of this Chapter.

18 Piston/connecting rod assembly – refitting

Warning: On engines with oil spray jets fitted to the cylinder block, take care not to damage the jets as the piston/connecting rod assemblies are refitted.

Selection of bearing shells

1 There are a number of sizes of big-end bearing shell produced by BMW; a standard size for use with the standard crankshaft, and oversizes for use once the crankshaft journals have been reground.

2 Have the crankshaft inspected and measured by a BMW dealer or automotive engineering workshop. They will be able to carry out any regrinding/repairs, and supply suitable main and big-end bearing shells.

Piston/connecting rod refitting

Note: *New big-end cap bolts must be used when finally refitting the piston/connecting rod assemblies. A piston ring compressor tool will be required for this operation.*

3 Note that the following procedure assumes that the main bearing caps are in place (see Section 17).

4 Press the bearing shells into their locations, ensuring that the tab on each shell engages in the notch in the connecting rod and cap. Take care not to touch any shell's bearing surface with your fingers. Ensure that all traces of the protective grease are cleaned off using paraffin. Wipe dry the shells and connecting rods with a lint-free cloth.

5 Lubricate the cylinder bores, the pistons, and piston rings, then lay out each piston/connecting rod assembly in its respective position.

6 Start with assembly No 1. Make sure that the piston rings are still spaced as described in Section 16, then clamp them in position with a piston ring compressor.

7 Insert the piston/connecting rod assembly into the top of cylinder No 1. Ensure that the arrow on the piston crown points towards the timing chain end of the engine, and that the identifying marks on the connecting rods and big-end caps are positioned as noted before removal. Using a block of wood or hammer handle against the piston crown, tap the assembly into the cylinder until the piston crown is flush with the top of the cylinder **(see illustrations)**.

18.7a Insert the piston/connecting rod assembly into the cylinder bore . . .

18.7b . . . then lightly tap the assembly into the cylinder

8 Ensure that the bearing shell is still correctly installed. Liberally lubricate the crankpin and both bearing shells. Taking care not to mark the cylinder bores, pull the piston/connecting rod assembly down the bore and onto the crankpin. Refit the big-end bearing cap. Note that the bearing shell locating tabs must abut each other.

9 Fit new bearing cap securing bolts, then tighten the bolts evenly and progressively to the Stage 1 torque setting. Once both bolts have been tightened to the Stage 1 setting, angle-tighten them through the specified Stage 2 angle, using a socket and extension bar. It is recommended that an angle-measuring gauge is used during this stage of the tightening, to ensure accuracy. If a gauge is not available, use a dab of white paint to make alignment marks between the bolt and bearing cap prior to tightening; the marks can then be used to check that the bolt has been rotated sufficiently during tightening.

10 Once the bearing cap bolts have been correctly tightened, rotate the crankshaft. Check that it turns freely; some stiffness is to be expected if new components have been fitted, but there should be no signs of binding or tight spots.

11 Refit the remaining piston/connecting rod assemblies in the same way.

12 Where applicable, refit the oil baffle to the bottom of the cylinder block.

13 Refit the cylinder head, oil pump and sump as described in Part A of this Chapter.

19 Engine – initial start-up after overhaul

Warning: If the camshafts have been removed, observe the recommended delays between refitting the camshafts and starting the engine – refer to the relevant camshaft removal and refitting procedure in Chapter 2A for details.

1 With the engine refitted in the vehicle, double-check the engine oil and coolant levels. Make a final check that everything has been reconnected, and that there are no tools or rags left in the engine compartment.

2 Disable the ignition and fuel injection systems by removing the engine management relay (located in the engine electrical box), and the fuel pump fuse (located in the main fusebox – see Chapter 12), then turn the engine on the starter motor until the oil pressure warning light goes out.

3 Refit the relays (and ensure that the fuel pump fuse is fitted), and switch on the ignition to prime the fuel system.

4 Start the engine, noting that this may take a little longer than usual, due to the fuel system components having been disturbed.

Caution: When first starting the engine after overhaul, if there is a rattling noise from the valve-gear, this is probably due to the hydraulic valve lifters partially draining. If the rattling persists, do not run the engine above 2000 rpm until the rattling stops.

5 While the engine is idling, check for fuel, water and oil leaks. Don't be alarmed if there are some odd smells and smoke from parts getting hot and burning off oil deposits.

6 Assuming all is well, keep the engine idling until hot water is felt circulating through the top hose, then switch off the engine.

7 After a few minutes, recheck the oil and coolant levels as described in *Weekly checks*, and top-up as necessary.

8 If new pistons, rings or crankshaft bearings have been fitted, the engine must be treated as new, and run-in for the first 500 miles (800 km). *Do not* operate the engine at full-throttle, or allow it to labour at low engine speeds in any gear. It is recommended that the oil and filter are changed at the end of this period.

Chapter 3
Cooling, heating and ventilation systems

Contents

Degrees of difficulty

Easy, suitable for novice with little experience 	**Fairly easy,** suitable for beginner with some experience 	**Fairly difficult,** suitable for competent DIY mechanic	**Difficult,** suitable for experienced DIY mechanic 	**Very difficult,** suitable for expert DIY or professional

Specifications

General

Expansion tank cap opening pressure	2.0 ± 0.2 bar

Thermostat

Opening temperatures:	
M52 engine	92°C
M52TU and M54 engines	97°C

Torque wrench settings	**Nm**	**lbf ft**
Coolant pump nuts/bolts:		
M6 nuts/bolts	10	7
M8 nuts/bolts	22	16
Cooling fan viscous coupling to coolant pump **(left-hand thread)**	40	30
Thermal switch to radiator	15	11
Thermostat cover bolts	10	7

1 General information and precautions

General information

The cooling system is of pressurised type, comprising of a pump, an aluminium crossflow radiator, cooling fan, and a thermostat. The system functions as follows. Cold coolant from the radiator passes through the hose to the coolant pump where it is pumped around the cylinder block and head passages. After cooling the cylinder bores, combustion surfaces and valve seats, the coolant reaches the underside of the thermostat, which is initially closed. The coolant passes through the heater and is returned through the cylinder block to the coolant pump. On M54 engines, an auxiliary electrically-operated cool pump is fitted to the base of the radiator.

When the engine is cold the coolant circulates only through the cylinder block, cylinder head, expansion tank and heater. When the coolant reaches a predetermined temperature, the thermostat opens and the coolant passes through to the radiator. As the coolant circulates through the radiator it is cooled by the inrush of air when the car is in forward motion. Airflow is supplemented by the action of the cooling fan. Upon reaching the radiator, the coolant is now cooled and the cycle is repeated.

All models are fitted with a belt driven cooling fan. The belt is driven by the crankshaft pulley via a viscous fluid coupling. The viscous coupling varies the fan speed according to the engine temperature. At low temperatures, the coupling provides very little resistance between the fan and pump pulley so only a slight amount of drive is transmitted to the cooling fan. As the temperature of the coupling increases, so does its internal resistance therefore increasing the drive to the cooling fan. On all engines an additional electrically-operated cooling fan may fitted on the bumper side of the radiator.

Refer to Section 11 for information on the air conditioning system.

Precautions

Warning: Do not attempt to remove the expansion tank filler cap or disturb any part of the cooling system while the engine is hot, as there is a high risk of scalding. If the expansion tank filler cap must be removed before the engine and radiator have fully cooled (even though this is not recommended) the pressure in the cooling system must first be relieved. Cover the cap with a thick layer of cloth, to avoid scalding, and slowly unscrew the filler cap until a hissing sound can be heard. When the hissing has stopped, indicating that the pressure has reduced, slowly unscrew the filler cap until it can be removed; if more hissing sounds are heard, wait until they have stopped before unscrewing the cap completely. At all times keep well away from the filler cap opening.

• Do not allow antifreeze to come into contact with skin or painted surfaces of the vehicle. Rinse off spills immediately with plenty of water. Never leave antifreeze lying around in an open container or in a puddle in the driveway or on the garage floor. Children and pets are attracted by its sweet smell. Antifreeze can be fatal if ingested.

• Refer to Section 11 for precautions to be observed when working on models equipped with air conditioning.

2 Cooling system hoses – disconnection and renewal

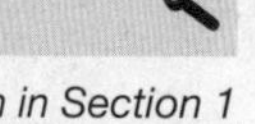

Note: *Refer to the warnings given in Section 1 of this Chapter before proceeding.*

1 If the checks described in Chapter 1 reveal a faulty hose, it must be renewed as follows.

2 First drain the cooling system (see Chapter 1). If the coolant is not due for renewal, it may be re-used if it is collected in a clean container.

3 To disconnect a hose, prise up the wire retaining clip and pull the hose from its fitting **(see illustrations)**. Some hoses may be secured using traditional hose clips. To disconnect these hoses, release its retaining clips, then move them along the hose, clear of the relevant inlet/outlet union. Carefully work the hose free. While the hoses can be removed with relative ease when new, or when hot, do not attempt to disconnect any part of the system while it is still hot.

4 Note that the radiator inlet and outlet unions are fragile; do not use excessive force when attempting to remove the hoses. If a hose proves to be difficult to remove, try to release it by rotating the hose ends before attempting to free it.

5 To refit a hose, simply push the end over the fitting until the retaining clip engages and lock the hose in place. Pull the hose to make sure its locked in place. When fitting a hose with traditional hose clips, first slide the clips onto the hose, then work the hose into position. If clamp type clips were originally fitted, it is a good idea to use screw type clips when refitting the hose. If the hose is stiff, use a little soapy water as a lubricant, or soften the hose by soaking it in hot water. Work the hose into position, checking that it is correctly routed, then slide each clip along the hose until it passes over the flared end of the relevant inlet/outlet union, before securing it in position with the retaining clip.

6 Refill the cooling system with reference to Chapter 1.

7 Check thoroughly for leaks as soon as possible after disturbing any part of the cooling system.

3 Radiator – removal, inspection and refitting

Removal

1 Disconnect the battery negative lead (see Chapter 5A).

2.3a Prise up the wire locking clip . . .

2.3b . . . and pull the hose from the fitting

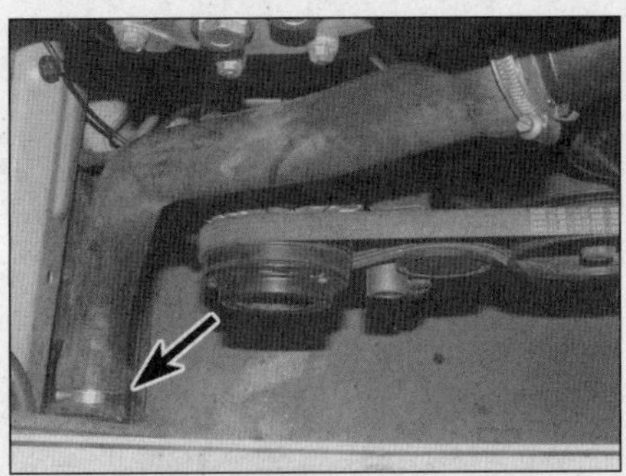

3.4a Slacken the lower hose clip (arrowed) . . .

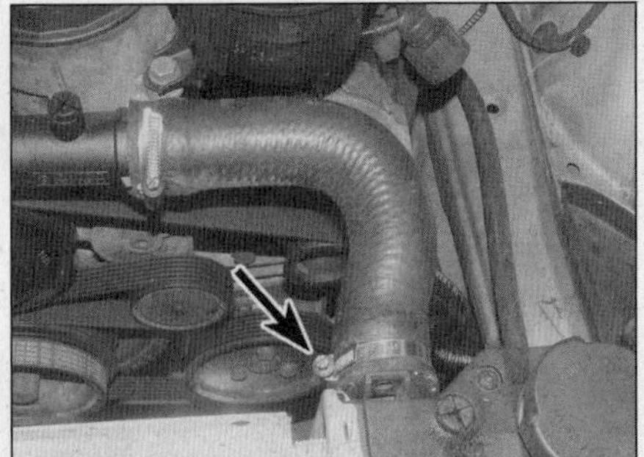

3.4b . . . and the upper hose clip (arrowed)

3.6 Undo the bolt (arrowed) and remove the radiator bracket from each side

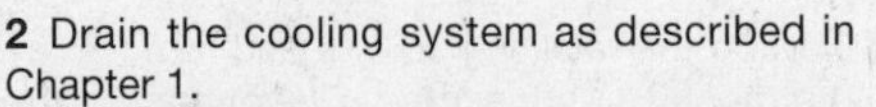

2 Drain the cooling system as described in Chapter 1.

3 Remove the cooling fan and viscous coupling (Section 5).

M52 engine

4 Slacken the hose clamp or prise out the locking wire clips (as applicable) and disconnect the upper and lower coolant hoses from the radiator **(see illustrations)**.

5 Slacken the hose clamp or prise out the locking wire clip (as applicable) and disconnect the hose from the expansion tank.

6 Undo the two screws, and remove the two retaining brackets from the upper edge of the radiator **(see illustration)**.

7 Lift the radiator upwards and remove it from the engine compartment. Note the rubber mountings at the lower corners of the radiator **(see illustration)**.

8 Reach underneath the coolant expansion tank and disconnect the wiring from the coolant level sensor (where fitted). On models with air conditioning, disconnect the wiring plug from the temperature switch mounted on the side of the radiator **(see illustration)**.

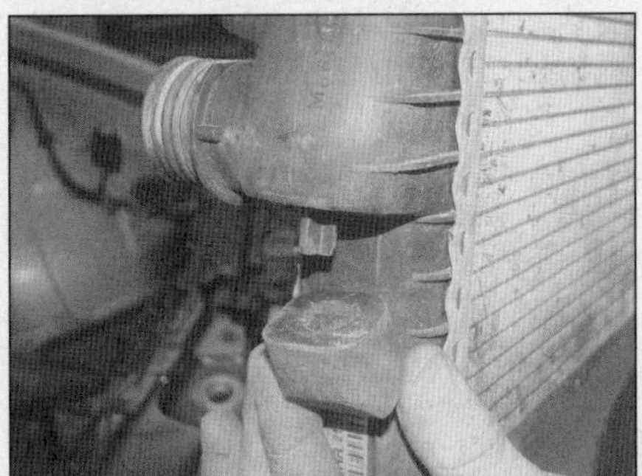

3.7 Radiator rubber mounting

M54 and M52TU engines

9 Prise out the locking wire and disconnect the upper coolant hose from the radiator **(see illustration)**.

10 Undo the two screws and remove the two retaining brackets from the upper edge of the radiator **(see illustration 3.6)**.

11 Disconnect the wiring plug from the sensor mounted in the lower coolant hose, then prise out the locking wire clip and disconnect the hose from the radiator.

12 Lift the radiator upwards and remove it from the engine compartment. Note the rubber mountings at the sides of the radiator **(see illustration 3.7)**. **Note:** *On automatic transmission models, undo the bolt and disconnect the transmission cooling pipes from the cooling cassette to allow sufficient clearance for the radiator to be lifted. Be prepared for fluid spillage, and plug the openings.*

Inspection

13 If the radiator has been removed due to suspected blockage, reverse flush it as described in Chapter 1.

14 Clean dirt and debris from the radiator fins, using an air line (in which case, wear eye protection) or a soft brush. Be careful, as the fins are easily damaged, and are sharp.

15 If necessary, a radiator specialist can perform a 'flow test' on the radiator, to establish whether an internal blockage exists.

16 A leaking radiator must be referred to a specialist for permanent repair. Do not attempt to weld or solder a leaking radiator, as damage may result.

17 Inspect the radiator lower mounting rubbers for signs of damage or deterioration and renew if necessary.

Refitting

18 Refitting is the reverse of removal, noting the following points.

a) *Ensure that the lower mounting rubbers are correctly located then lower the radiator into position, engage it with the mountings and secure it in position with the retaining clip* ***(see illustration)****.*

b) *Ensure that the fan cowl is correctly located with the lugs on the radiator and secure it in position with the clips.*

d) *Reconnect the hoses and ensure the retaining clips engage securely.*

e) *Check the condition of the O-ring seals (where applicable) in the end of the radiator fittings. Renew any that are defective.*

f) *On completion, reconnect the battery and refill the cooling system (see Chapter 1).*

g) *Where applicable, check and top-up the automatic transmission fluid.*

3.8 Disconnect the temperature switch (air conditioned models only)

3.9 Prise out the clip and disconnect the upper hose

3.18 Ensure the radiator mounting is firmly pressed over the retaining lug (arrowed)

4.3 Slacken the thermostat hose clamps (arrowed)

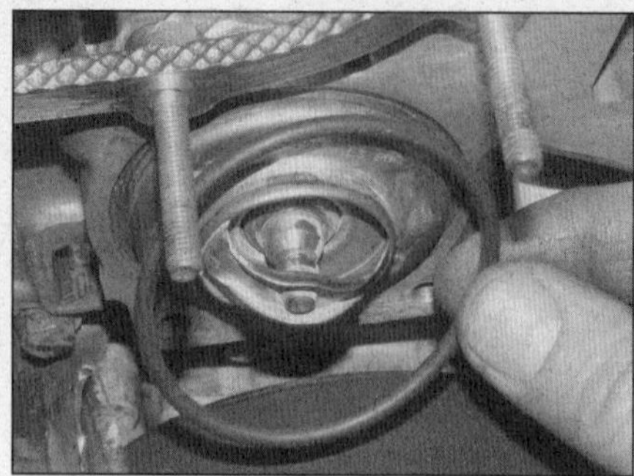
4.6 Recover the thermostat seal

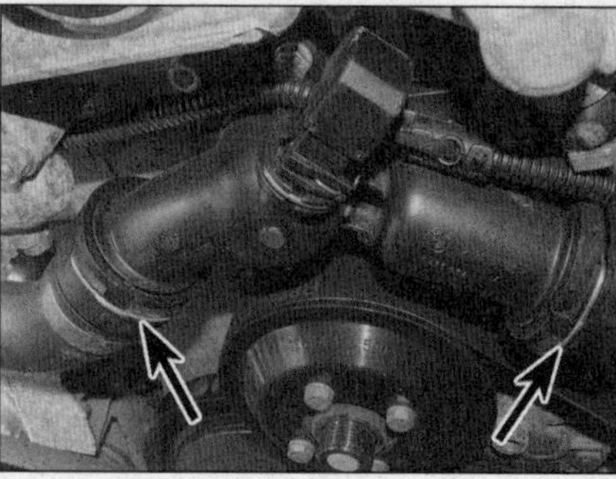
4.7 Prise out the locking clips (arrowed)

4.9 Renew the thermostat housing O-ring seal

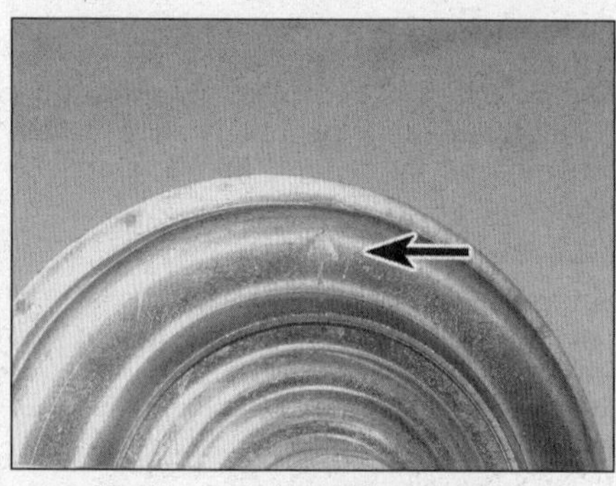
4.10 The arrow must be uppermost (arrowed)

4 Thermostat – removal and refitting

Note: *A new thermostat sealing ring and (where fitted) housing gasket/seal will be required on refitting.*

Removal

1 Drain the cooling system as described in Chapter 1.

2 To improve access to the thermostat housing, remove the cooling fan and coupling as described in Section 5.

M52 engine

3 Slacken the securing clamps, and disconnect the coolant hoses from the thermostat housing on the front of the timing chain cover **(see illustration)**.

4 Undo the bolt/nut, and remove the engine lifting bracket above the thermostat housing.

5 Unclip the wiring harness guide from above the thermostat housing, by sliding it to the right.

6 Slacken and remove the retaining screws and remove the thermostat housing. Recover the housing gasket/seal **(see illustration)**. Remove the thermostat.

M52TU and M54 engines

7 Prise out the locking wire clips and disconnect the two coolant hoses from the thermostat housing **(see illustration)**.

8 Undo the bolt/nut and remove the engine lifting bracket from above the thermostat housing.

9 Undo the retaining screws and remove the thermostat housing. Disconnect the thermostat heater wiring plug (where fitted). Note that the thermostat is integral with the housing, and cannot be renewed separately. Recover the seal **(see illustration)**.

Refitting

10 Refitting is a reversal of removal, bearing in mind the following points.

a) When refitting the thermostat on M52 engines, note that the arrow on the edge of the thermostat flange must be uppermost ***(see illustration)****.*

a) Renew the thermostat cover O-ring seal.

b) Tighten the thermostat cover bolts to the specified torque.

c) Refit the cooling fan as described in Section 5.

d) On completion refill the cooling system as described in Chapter 1.

5 Cooling fan and viscous coupling – removal and refitting

Note: *A special 32 mm narrow open-ended spanner (BMW tool No 11 5 040) may be required to remove the fan and viscous coupling assembly.*

Removal

1 Using an open-ended spanner unscrew the viscous coupling from the coolant pump **(see illustrations). Note:** *The viscous coupling has a* ***left-hand thread*** and unscrews clockwise. Use a second spanner or socket on the crankshaft pulley bolt to prevent the pulley from turning. If necessary use a strip of metal with two slots to fit over the pulley bolt heads to counterhold the nut.

M52 engine

2 Release the fan shroud upper retaining clips by pulling out their centre pins. Gently pull the shroud upwards to release the guide tabs each side of the radiator, then lift the

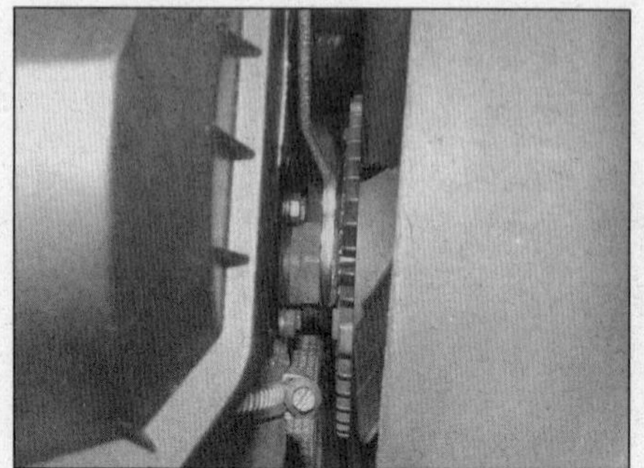
5.1a Using a special slim 32 mm spanner

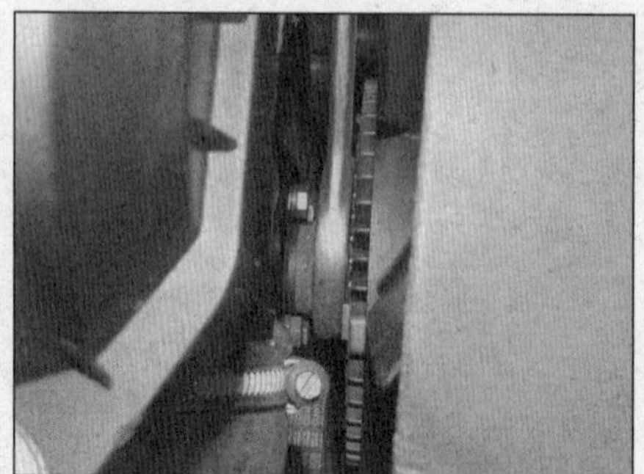
5.1b Most 'normal' 32 mm spanners will also fit

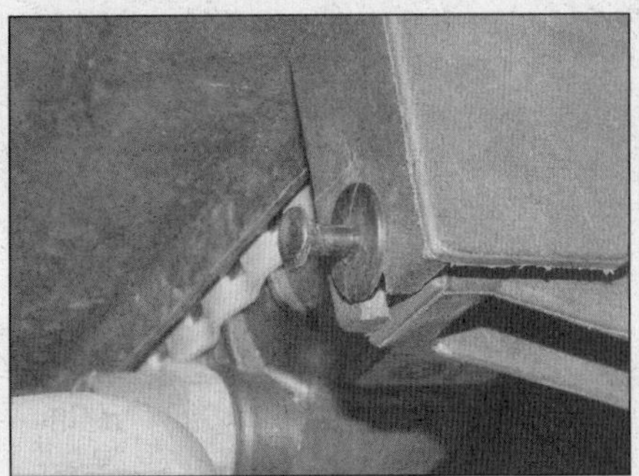

5.2a Prise up the centre pins then remove the complete plastic rivet

5.2b Lift the shroud and fan from place

5.4 Unscrew the vent plug, and unclip the bracket

5.5 Disconnect the hose from the expansion tank

5.8 Disconnect the auxiliary pump wiring plug

5.10 Unclip the AUC sensor (arrowed) from the fan shroud

shroud and fan assembly upwards and out of position **(see illustrations)**.

M54 and M52TU engines

3 Drain the cooling system as described in Chapter 1. Disconnect the level sensor wiring plug from the base of the expansion tank (where fitted), then prise out the locking wires and disconnect the coolant hose(s) from the base of the expansion tank .

4 Remove the cap from the expansion tank, unscrew and remove the vent plug, then remove the tank retaining bracket **(see illustration)**.

Caution: Ensure the cooling system is cold before removing the cap.

5 Pull the top of the tank slightly to the rear and disconnect the vent hose **(see illustration)**. It may be necessary to cut the metal pipe clip from the hose. In this case substitute the clip with a worm-drive clamp.

6 Lift the expansion tank upwards to disengage it from the lower retaining lugs.

7 Jack up the front of the vehicle and support it securely on axle stands (see *Jacking and vehicle support*). Release the screws and remove the engine undershield.

8 Working underneath the vehicle, disconnect the auxiliary coolant pump wiring plug **(see illustration)**.

9 Release the auxiliary pump from its mounting, and the coolant hoses from the clips on the shroud.

10 Unclip the AUC sensor from the left-hand side of the shroud **(see illustration)**.

11 Release the fan shroud upper retaining clips by pulling out their centre pins, then detach the sealing strip from the front upper edge of the shroud.

12 Lift the shroud upwards, and remove it along with the cooling fan and coupling. Note the shroud retaining lugs at the bottom and sides of the radiator.

All engines

13 If necessary, slacken and remove the retaining bolts and separate the cooling fan from the coupling noting which way around the fan is fitted.

Refitting

14 Where necessary, refit the fan to the viscous coupling and securely tighten its retaining bolts. Make sure the fan is fitted the correct way around. **Note:** *If the fan is fitted the wrong way around the efficiency of the cooling system will be significantly reduced.*

15 Refit the fan, shroud and cooling fan assembly. Screw the fan onto the coolant pump and tighten it securely. Engage the fan shroud with the tabs on the radiator and secure it in position with the retaining clips.

16 The remainder of refitting is a reversal of removal.

17 Reconnect the air ducts (where removed).

6 Electric cooling fan and shroud – removal and refitting

Removal

1 Remove the front bumper as described in Chapter 11.

2 Remove both front headlamps as described in Chapter 12, Section 7.

3 Undo the three screws securing the air duct(s) to the cooling fan shroud **(see illustration)**.

4 Unclip and disconnect the fan motor wiring plug **(see illustration)**.

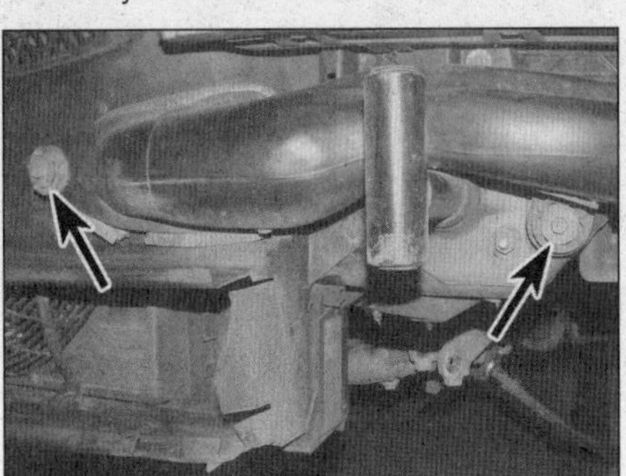

6.3 The air duct is secured by 3 screws (inner 2 arrowed)

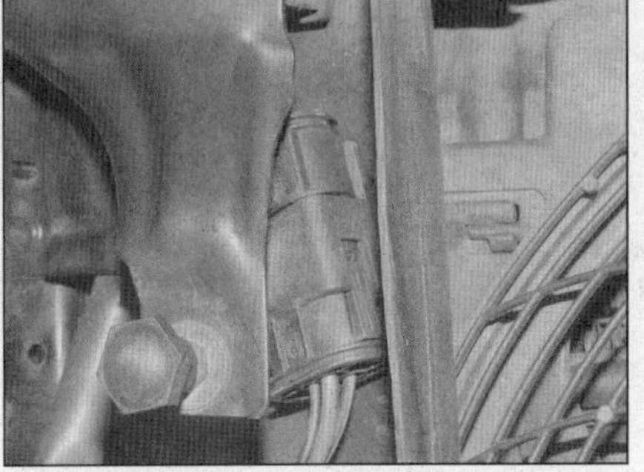

6.4 Unclip and disconnect the fan wiring plug

6.6 Push in the centre pins and prise out the plastic rivets (arrowed)

6.7 Undo the four bolts and remove the fan assembly

5 Unclip the wiring harness from the front air ducting/cowling.
6 Undo the three retaining screws, remove the three plastic expansion rivets from the top/side of the ducting/cowling, and lower the air ducting/cowling and remove it from the vehicle **(see illustration)**. Where plastic expansion rivets are fitted, push the centre pins down through the rivet, then prise the entire rivet from place.
7 Undo the four retaining nuts, and lower the cooling fan and shroud assembly from position **(see illustration)**.

Refitting

8 Refitting is a reversal of removal.

7 Cooling system electrical switches – testing, removal and refitting

Coolant level sensor

Note: *Not all models are equipped with a coolant level sensor.*

Testing

1 Testing of the switch should be entrusted to a BMW dealer.

Removal

2 The sensor is located in the base of the coolant expansion tank. Drain the coolant to below the level of the expansion tank (see Chapter 1).
3 Jack up the front of the vehicle and support it securely on axle stands (see *Jacking and vehicle support*). Release the screws and remove the engine undershield.
4 Disconnect the sensor wiring plug, then unscrew the sensor from the tank. Recover the sealing ring where fitted.

Refitting

5 Refitting is a reversal of removal using a new sealing ring (where fitted). On completion, refill the cooling system as described in Chapter 1 or top-up as described in *Weekly checks*.

Radiator temperature sensor

Removal

6 The switch is located in the radiator lower hose on some models, and on the right-hand side of the radiator on others. The engine and radiator should be cold before removing the switch.
7 Either drain the cooling system to below the level of the switch (as described in Chapter 1), or have ready a suitable plug which can be used to plug the switch aperture in the radiator whilst the switch is removed. If a plug is used, take great care not to damage the radiator, and do not use anything which will allow foreign matter to enter the radiator.
8 Disconnect the wiring plug from the switch **(see illustration)**.
9 Release the retaining clip, and remove the switch. Recover the sealing ring.

Refitting

10 Refitting is a reversal of removal using a new sealing washer. On completion, refill the cooling system as described in Chapter 1 or top-up as described in *Weekly checks*.
11 Start the engine and run it until it reaches normal operating temperature, then continue to run the engine and check that the cooling fan cuts in and functions correctly.

Coolant temperature sensor

Testing

12 Testing of the sensor should be entrusted to a BMW dealer.

Removal

13 Either partially drain the cooling system to just below the level of the sensor (as described in Chapter 1), or have ready a suitable plug which can be used to plug the sensor aperture whilst it is removed. If a plug is used, take great care not to damage the sensor unit aperture, and do not use anything which will allow foreign matter to enter the cooling system.
14 The sensor is screwed into the left-hand side of the cylinder head, under the intake manifold. Remove the inlet manifold as described in Chapter 4A.
15 Disconnect the wiring from the sensor. Unscrew the sensor unit from the cylinder head and recover its sealing washer **(see illustration)**.

Refitting

16 Fit a new sealing washer to the sensor unit and refit the sensor, tightening it securely.
17 Refit the intake manifold with reference to Chapter 4A.
18 Reconnect the wiring connector then refill the cooling system as described in Chapter 1 or top-up as described in *Weekly checks*.

8 Coolant pump – removal and refitting

Note: *A new sealing ring will be required on refitting.*

Removal

1 Drain the cooling system as described in Chapter 1.
2 Remove the cooling fan and coupling as described in Section 5.
3 Slacken the coolant pump pulley bolts then remove the auxiliary drivebelt as described in Chapter 1.
4 Unscrew the retaining bolts and remove the pulley from the pump, noting which way around it is fitted **(see illustration)**.

7.8 Coolant temperature sensor located in the lower hose

7.15 Unscrew the temperature sensor from the cylinder head (shown with the intake manifold removed)

8.4 Undo the pulley retaining bolts

8.5 If the coolant pump is a tight fit, draw the pump out of position using two jacking bolts (arrowed)

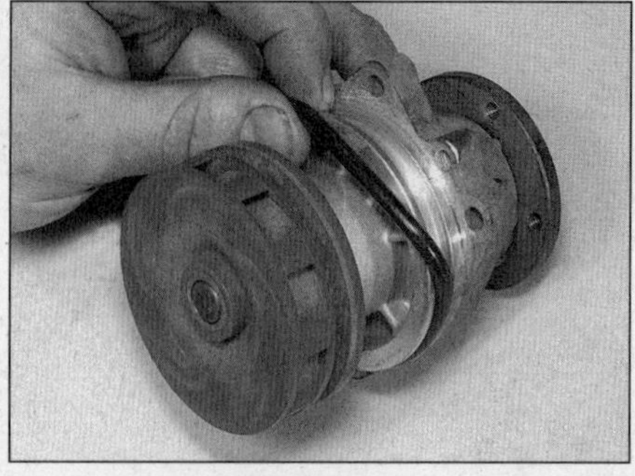

8.6 Recover the coolant pump sealing ring

8.17 Undo the Torx screw (arrowed), and remove the auxiliary pump

5 Slacken and remove the pump retaining bolts/nuts (as applicable) and withdraw the pump. If the pump is a tight fit, screw two M6 bolts into the jacking holes on either side of the pump and use the bolts to draw the pump out of position **(see illustration)**.

6 Recover the sealing ring from the rear of the pump **(see illustration)**.

Refitting

7 Fit the new sealing ring to the rear of the pump and lubricate it with a smear of grease to ease installation.

8 Locate the pump in position and refit the retaining bolts/nuts. Tighten the bolts/nuts evenly and progressively to the specified torque, making sure the pump is drawn squarely into position.

9 Refit the pulley to the pump, making sure it is the correct way around, and screw in its retaining bolts.

10 Refit the auxiliary drivebelt as described in Chapter 1 then securely tighten the pulley bolts.

11 Refit the cooling fan assembly as described in Section 5.

12 Refill the cooling system as described in Chapter 1.

Auxiliary water pump – M54 engine

Removal

13 Drain the cooling system as described in Chapter 1.

14 Jack up the front of the vehicle, and support it securely on axle stands (see *Jacking and vehicle support*). Release the screws and remove the engine undertray.

15 Disconnect the wiring plug from the pump **(see illustration 5.8)**.

16 Prise out the wire locking clips and disconnect the coolant hoses from the pump.

17 Undo the Torx screw, lift the pump from its mounting and remove it from the vehicle **(see illustration)**.

Refitting

18 Refitting is a reversal of removal, remembering to top-up the cooling system as described in Chapter 1.

9 Heating and ventilation system – general information

1 The heating/ventilation system consists of a variable speed blower motor, face-level vents in the centre and at each end of the facia, and air ducts to the front and rear footwells. On some models, a second blower motor is located in the centre console between the front seats to provide airflow to the rear seat occupants.

2 The control unit is located in the facia, and the controls operate flap valves to deflect and mix the air flowing through the various parts of the heating/ventilation system. The flap valves are contained in the air distribution housing, which acts as a central distribution unit, passing air to the various ducts and vents.

3 Cold air enters the system through the grille at the rear of the engine compartment. Two pollen filters are fitted to the inlet to remove dust, spores and soot from the incoming air.

4 The airflow, which can be boosted by the blower, then flows through the various ducts, according to the settings of the controls. Stale air is expelled through ducts at the rear of the vehicle. If warm air is required, the cold air is passed through the heater matrix, which is heated by the engine coolant.

5 If necessary, the outside air supply can be closed off, allowing the air inside the vehicle to be recirculated. This can be useful to prevent unpleasant odours entering from outside the vehicle, but should only be used briefly, as the recirculated air quality inside the vehicle will soon deteriorate. On some models, automatic air recirculation is fitted. This system identifies unpleasant odours and pollutants, and shuts off the supply of air to the interior of the car temporarily. As soon as the odour/pollutant dissipates, the air supply is restored.

6 Certain models are fitted with heated front seats. The heat is produced by electrically-heated mats in the seat and backrest cushions (see Chapter 12). The temperature is regulated automatically by a thermostat, and can be set at one of three levels, controlled by switches on the facia.

7 On certain models steering wheel heating is available. The heat is provided by an electrical element embedded in the steering wheel, and controlled by a button also on the wheel.

8 Some models are equipped with a 'latent heat accumulator'. This is a system whereby heat from the coolant system is stored in a facia-mounted insulated reservoir. The reservoir contains a salt mixture, which is converted from a solid state to a liquid state by the hot engine coolant. This system is capable of retaining heat for several days, even at very low outside temperatures. When the engine is restarted, the liquid salt mixture converts back to a solid state – the latent heat released is available for immediate use to defrost the windows, heat the passenger cabin, and reduce the engine warm-up time.

10 Heater/ventilation components – removal and refitting

Without air conditioning

Heater/ventilation control panel

1 Disconnect the battery negative lead (see Chapter 5A).

2 Using a wooden or plastic tool, carefully prise the switch panel below the heater control panel downwards and to the rear. Disconnect the switches wiring plugs as the panel is withdrawn.

3 Press the two retaining clips upwards, and remove the heater control panel to the rear.

4 Note their fitted positions, then disconnect the control panel wiring plugs and control cables.

5 Refitting is reversal of removal. Ensure that the control cables are correctly routed and reconnected to the control panel, as noted before removal. Clip the outer cables in position and check the operation of each knob/lever before refitting the switch panel.

Heater/ventilation control cables

6 Remove the heater/ventilation control unit from the facia as described above in paragraphs 1 to 4, detaching the relevant

10.10 Release the clip(s) and disconnect the passenger's side air duct

10.12 Clamp the three hoses at the bulkhead

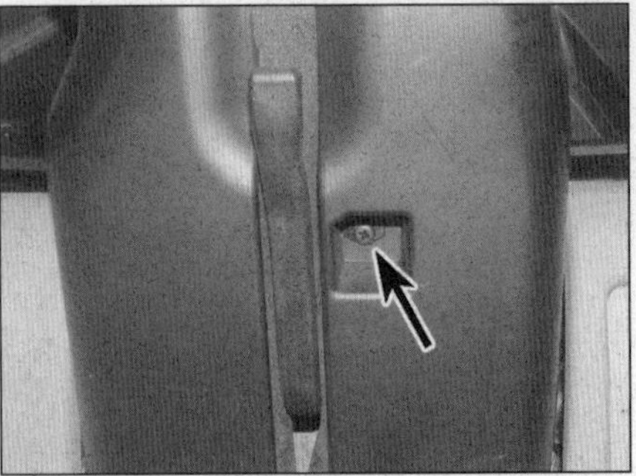
10.15 The lower steering column shroud is secured by 3 screws (upper screw arrowed)

cable from the control unit. Note their correct fitted positions to aid refitment.

7 On right-hand drive models, undo the retaining screws then unclip the driver's side lower facia panel and remove it from the vehicle. On left-hand drive models, remove the glovebox as described in Chapter 11, Section 26.

8 Follow the run of the cable behind the facia, taking note of its routing, and disconnect the cable from the air distribution housing.

9 Fit the new cable by reversing the removal procedure, ensuring that it is correctly routed and free from kinks and obstructions. Check the operation of the control knob then refit the control unit as described previously in this Section.

Heater matrix – models up to 03/99

10 Working in the engine compartment, release the retaining clip, and pull the left-hand air duct from the pollen filter housing, then rotate it upwards and disconnect it from the engine compartment bulkhead **(see illustration)**.

11 Unscrew the expansion tank cap (referring to the **Warning** note in Section 1) to release any pressure present in the cooling system then securely refit the cap.

12 Clamp all three heater hoses as close to the bulkhead as possible to minimise coolant loss **(see illustration)**. Alternatively, drain the cooling system as described in Chapter 1.

13 Disconnect the heater hoses at the bulkhead.

14 Remove the centre console and facia lower panel as described in Chapter 11.

15 Undo the screws and remove the lower steering column shroud **(see illustration)**.

16 Remove the two retaining screws and pull away the passenger side air duct from the heater housing.

17 Undo the screws/nuts and disconnect the heater pipes from the matrix. Be prepared for coolant spillage.

18 Undo the screw and remove the heater pipe bracket from the heater box.

19 Unhook the servo motor for the footwell ventilation flap from the heater box and move it to one side.

20 Undo the two screws and remove the right-hand footwell air outlet duct from the heater box.

21 Undo the three screws, release the retaining clip and remove the matrix cover from the heater housing.

22 Release the clips/screws and remove the rear passenger compartment outlet air duct. Slide the matrix from the heater box. **Note:** *Keep the matrix unions uppermost as the matrix is removed to prevent coolant spillage. Mop-up any spilt coolant immediately and wipe the affected area with a damp cloth to prevent staining.*

23 Refitting is the reverse of removal, using new sealing rings. On completion, refill the cooling system as described in Chapter 1.

Heater matrix – models from 03/99

24 Proceed as described in Paragraphs 10 to 19.

25 Release the three retaining clips and remove the right-hand footwell outlet air vent.

26 Undo the four retaining screws, release the clip and slide the heater matrix cover downwards out of its guides, to remove it. If necessary, close the footwell air flap to enable the matrix to be slid out from the heater housing. **Note:** *Keep the matrix unions uppermost as the matrix is removed to prevent coolant spillage. Mop-up any spilt coolant immediately and wipe the affected area with a damp cloth to prevent staining.*

27 Refitting is the reverse of removal, using new sealing rings. On completion, refill the cooling system as described in Chapter 1.

Heater blower motor

28 Remove the complete facia panel, as described in Chapter 11.

29 Remove the foam rubber mat from around the facia central air vent.

30 Depress the clip and slide the vent distribution motor spindle to the left, then release the two retaining clips and prise out the facia windscreen air vent **(see illustrations)**.

31 Slide the connecting rail to one side, then pull both linkages out of the distribution flaps **(see illustration)**.

32 Release the retaining clips and pull the

10.30a Depress the clip and slide the motor spindle to the left

10.30b Note how the front edge of the centre vent engages with the clips (arrowed)

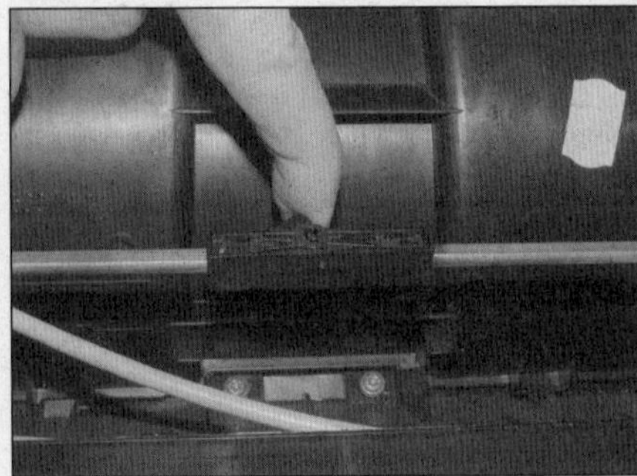
10.31 Slide the connecting rail to one side

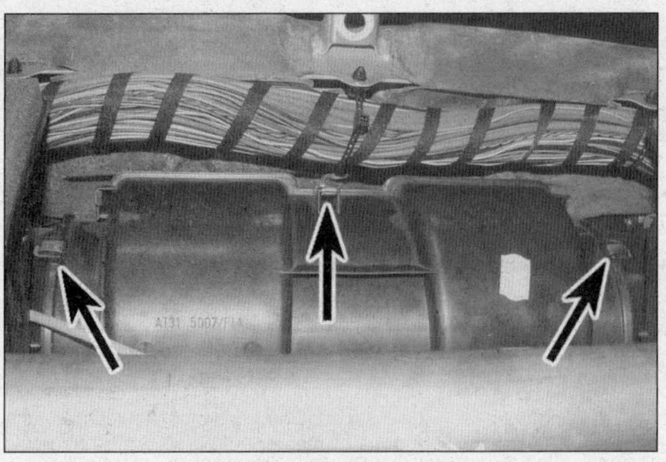

10.32 Release the three clips

10.33 Undo the three motor retaining screws

top of the motor cover to the rear, disengaging the lower lugs **(see illustration)**.

33 Undo the three retaining screws and lift out the blower motor **(see illustration)**. Disconnect the wiring plug as the motor is withdrawn.

34 Refitting is a reversal of the removal procedure making sure the motor is correctly clipped into the housing and the housing covers are securely refitted.

Heater blower motor resistor/ limit switch

35 Remove the driver's side lower facia panel, and footwell centre console panel as described in Chapter 11.

36 Release the retaining clip and disconnect the resistor/switch wiring plug **(see illustration)**.

37 Press the retaining clip downwards and pull the resistor/switch from the heater housing.

38 Refitting is the reverse of removal.

Heater matrix coolant valve(s)

39 The coolant valve(s) is mounted onto the left-hand inner wing. Note that some models are fitted with an auxiliary pump adjacent to the valve(s) **(see illustration)**. Unscrew the expansion tank cap (referring to the **Warning** note in Section 1) to release any pressure present in the cooling system then securely refit the cap.

40 On M52 and M54 engines, remove the air cleaner housing as described in Chapter 4A.

41 Clamp both heater hoses as close to the coolant valve(s) as possible to minimise coolant loss.

42 Disconnect the valve(s) wiring connector(s).

43 Slacken the retaining clips and disconnect the hoses from the valve(s) then unclip the valve(s) and remove it from the engine compartment.

44 Refitting is the reverse of removal.

Heater housing

45 Working in the engine compartment, release the retaining clip, and pull the left- and right-hand air duct from the pollen housing, then rotate it upwards and disconnect it from the engine compartment bulkhead **(see illustration 10.10)**.

46 Unscrew the expansion tank cap (referring to the **Warning** note in Section 1) to release any pressure present in the cooling system then securely refit the cap.

47 Clamp all three heater hoses as close to the bulkhead as possible to minimise coolant loss **(see illustration 10.12)**. Alternatively, drain the cooling system as described in Chapter 1.

48 Disconnect the heater hoses at the bulkhead.

49 Working in the engine compartment, slacken and remove the three screws securing the heater housing to the bulkhead **(see illustrations)**.

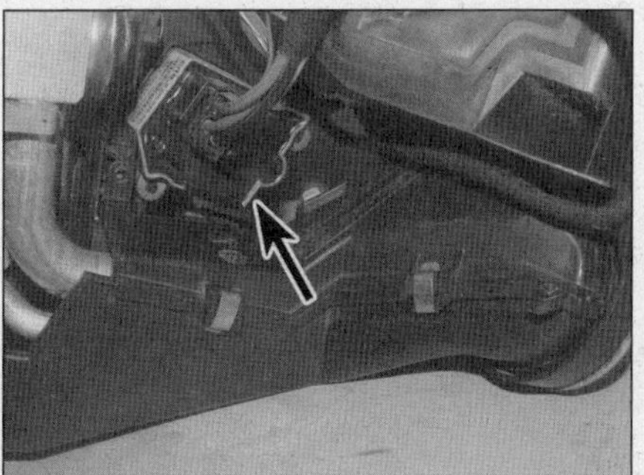

10.36 Disconnect the limit switch wiring plug (arrowed)

10.39 Coolant valves and auxiliary pump

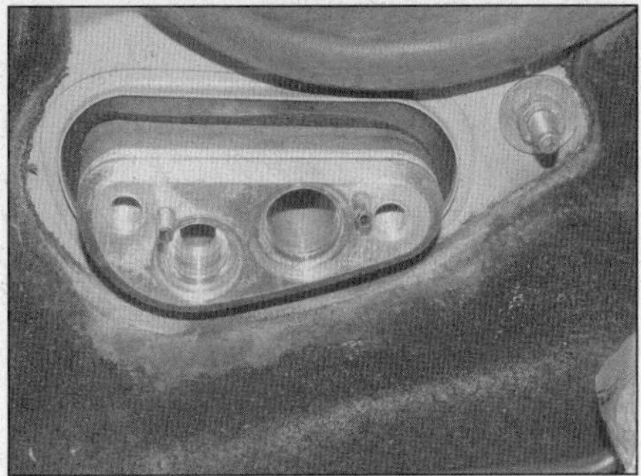

10.49a Undo the right-hand . . .

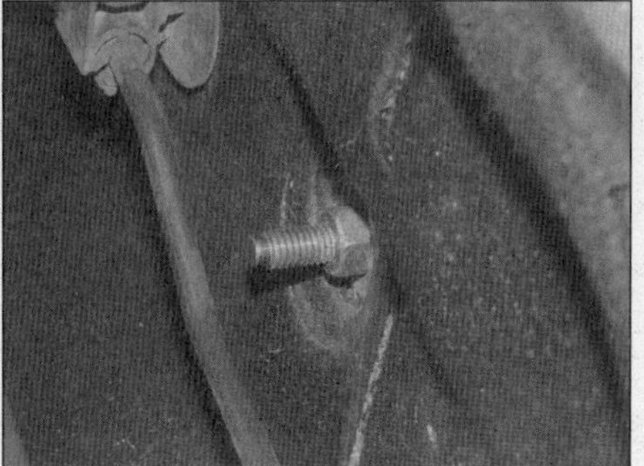

10.49b . . . centre . . .

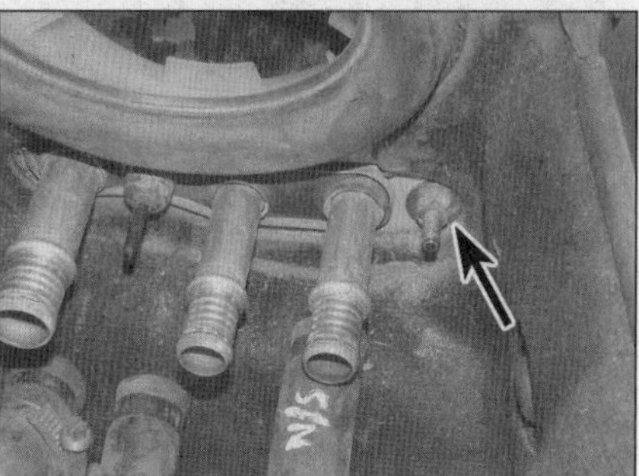

10.49c . . . and left-hand heater housing retaining nuts (arrowed)

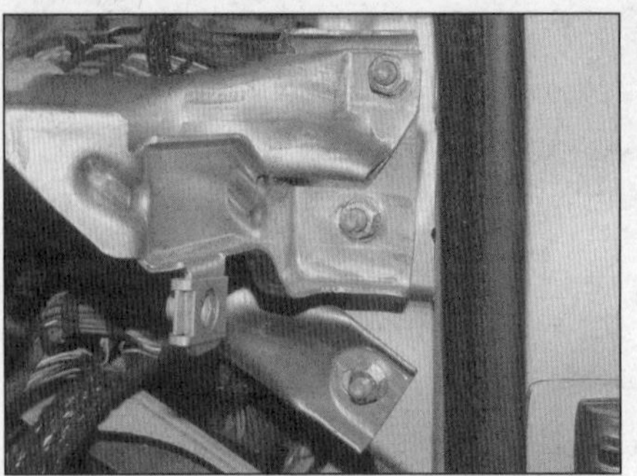

10.53a Undo the crossmember nuts/bolts at the right-hand end . . .

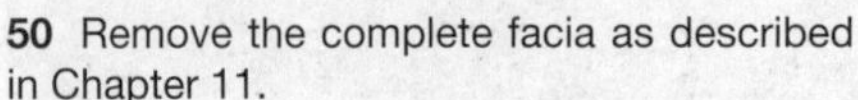

10.53b . . . left-hand end . . .

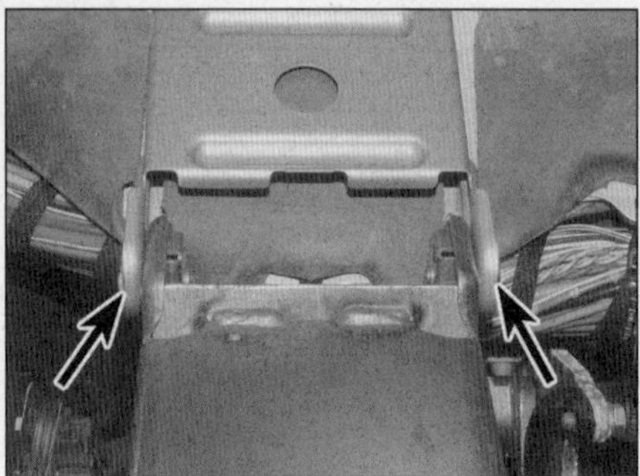

10.53c . . . above the steering column (arrowed) . . .

50 Remove the complete facia as described in Chapter 11.

51 Remove the bolts securing the steering column to the facia crossmember. Use a block of wood or similar to support the column and steering wheel.

52 Note their fitted positions, then release the cable ties securing the wiring harnesses to the facia crossmember,

53 Undo the nuts securing the facia crossmember at the left- and right-hand ends, above the steering column, and either side of the centre console **(see illustrations)**. Depress the two clips and detach the fuse holder assembly from the fusebox lid and lift out the facia crossmember.

54 Remove the plastic expanding rivet and detach the rear cabin air duct from the heater housing.

55 Check around the heater housing to ensure all wiring plugs have been disconnected, undo the two nuts at the rear of the housing, then lift the housing to the rear and remove it from the vehicle **(see illustration)**.

With air conditioning

Heater control unit – models with manual air conditioning

56 The procedure is as described in Paragraphs 1 to 5 of this Section.

Heater control unit – models with automatic air conditioning

57 Remove the facia-mounted MID/IRIS unit as described in Chapter 12.

58 Using two flat-bladed tools inserted at each side of the control panel, then push the panel from place **(see illustration)**.

59 Note their fitted locations, unlock the lever and disconnect the wiring plugs. To remove the control panel front plate, use a feeler gauge or similar to release the clips around the plate edge and detach it. If necessary, the buttons of the control panel can be removed by carefully prising them out at their lower edge **(see illustration)**.

60 Refitting is a reversal of removal. **Note:** *If the control panel is renewed, the new unit must be reprogrammed using dedicated test equipment via the vehicle's diagnostic socket. Entrust this task to a BMW dealer or suitably-equipped specialist.*

Heater matrix

61 Remove the lower facia panel as described in Chapter 11.

62 Undo the six screws and three retaining clips, then remove the heater outlet ducts each side **(see illustration)**.

63 Release the clips and detach the rear heater ducts from the housing **(see illustration)**.

64 Undo the nut securing the pipes to the matrix **(see illustration)**.

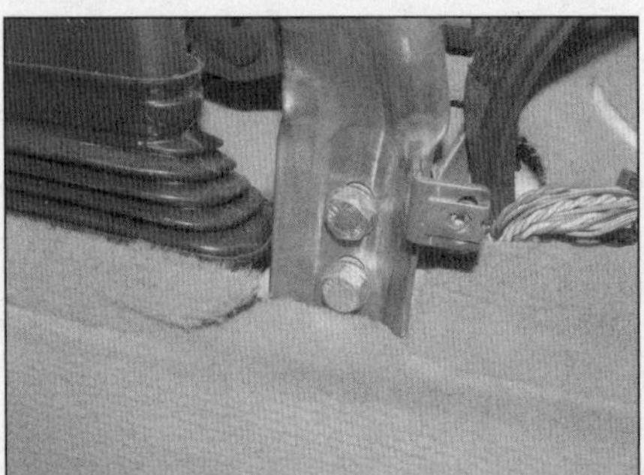

10.53d . . . and either side of the centre console

10.55 Undo the two nuts (arrowed) at the rear of the heater housing

10.58 Use a flat-bladed tool either side of the heater control panel

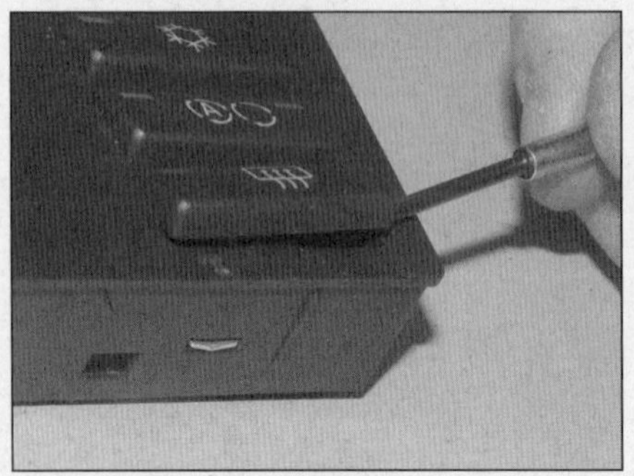

10.59 Carefully prise out the lower edge of the buttons

10.62 Release the clips, undo the screws and remove the air vent (arrowed) each side

10.63 Release the clips and detach the rear heater vents

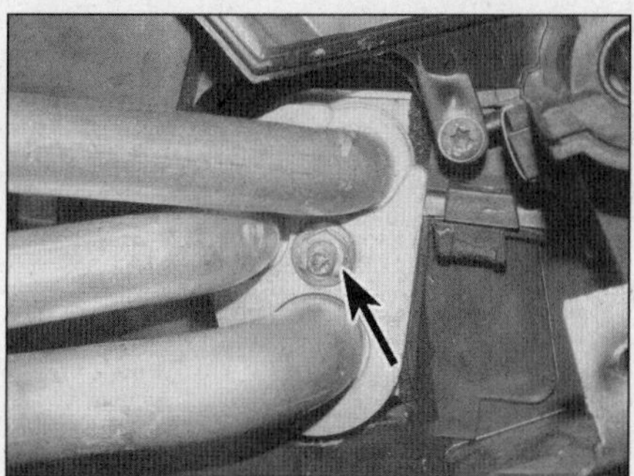

10.64 Undo the nut securing the pipes to the matrix (arrowed)

10.65a Undo the three screws (arrowed), release the clip and remove the matrix cover

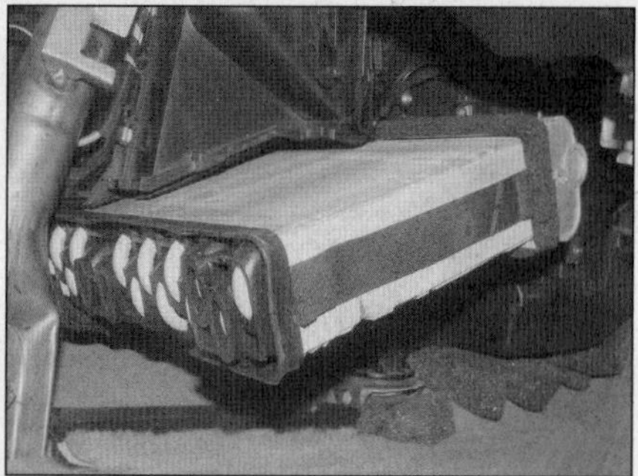

10.65b Pull the matrix from the housing

65 Release the screws/clip and remove the matrix cover **(see illustrations)**. Pull the matrix from the housing.

66 Refitting is a reversal of removal. Renew the matrix pipe seals.

Heater housing

67 Have the air conditioning refrigerant discharged by a BMW dealer or suitably-equipped specialist.

68 Working in the engine compartment, release the retaining clips, and pull the left- and right-hand air ducts from the pollen filter housings, then rotate them upwards and disconnect them from the engine compartment bulkhead **(see illustration 10.10)**.

69 Unscrew the expansion tank cap (referring to the **Warning** note in Section 1) to release any pressure present in the cooling system then securely refit the cap.

70 Clamp all three heater hoses as close to the bulkhead as possible to minimise coolant loss **(see illustration 10.12)**. Alternatively, drain the cooling system as described in Chapter 1.

71 Disconnect the heater hoses at the bulkhead. Pull away the rubber grommet and undo the heater housing retaining nut.

72 Undo the two screws and disconnect the air conditioning pressure and suction pipes from the engine compartment bulkhead. Discard the pipe seals, new ones must be fitted. Pull back the rubber grommet around the pipes and undo the heater housing retaining nut **(see illustrations)**. Plug or cover the ends of the pipes to minimise moisture ingress.

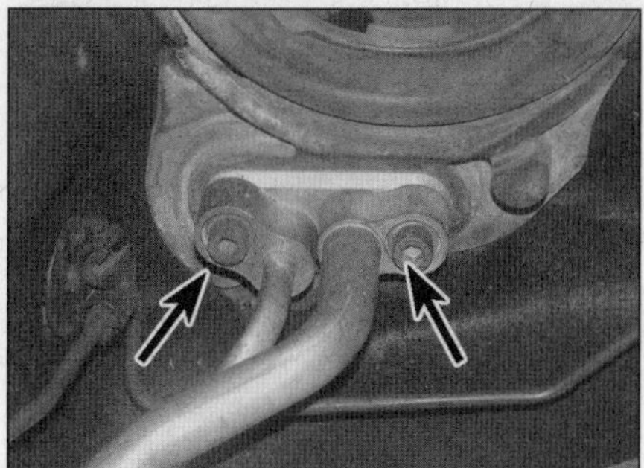

10.72a Undo the two bolts (arrowed) and disconnect the air conditioning pipes (arrowed)

73 The remainder of the heater housing removal procedure is as described from Paragraph 49 to 55 of this Section.

Heater blower motor

74 The heater blower motor is as described in Paragraphs 28 to 34 of this Section.

Heater blower motor resistor/ limit switch

75 Refer to the information given in Paragraphs 35 to 38 of this Section.

Heater matrix coolant valve

76 Refer to the information given in Paragraphs 39 to 44 of this Section.

All models

Rear blower motor

77 Remove the centre console as described in Chapter 11.

78 Unscrew the two retaining bolt, disconnect the wiring plug, and pull the blower motor out towards the rear.

79 Refitting is a reversal of removal.

Rear blower motor controller

80 Remove the rear blower motor as previously described.

81 Disconnect the wiring plug, undo the two screws, and remove the controller.

82 Refitting is a reversal of removal.

Latent heat accumulator

83 Remove the passenger side glovebox as described in Chapter 11, Section 26.

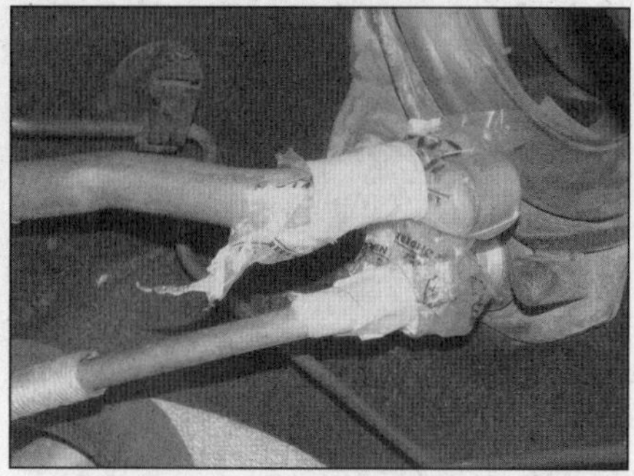

10.72b Plug or cover the pipes to prevent moisture ingress

84 Drain the cooling system as described in Chapter 1.

85 Carefully unclip the passenger side door sill trim.

86 Pull back the carpet from under the passenger's side facia. BMW suggest that the carpet underheater is cut to allow the carpet to be pulled back. Take care to only cut the carpet where the cut will not show.

87 Undo the two screws, and disconnect the coolant pipes from the accumulator – discard the seals, new ones must be fitted. Be prepared for coolant spillage.

88 Unscrew the retaining nut, unhook the retaining strap, and lift out the accumulator. Try to keep the accumulator is a vertical position to prevent coolant escaping.

89 Refitting is a reversal of removal. Prior to refitting, fill the accumulator with coolant and try to keep it as vertical as possible to minimise coolant loss. Upon completion, refill the cooling system as described in Chapter 1.

11 Air conditioning system – general information and precautions

General information

1 An air conditioning system is available on all models. It enables the temperature of incoming air to be lowered, and dehumidifies the air, which makes for rapid demisting and increased comfort.

2 The cooling side of the system works in the same way as a domestic refrigerator. Refrigerant gas is drawn into a belt-driven compressor and passes into a condenser mounted in front of the radiator, where it loses heat and becomes liquid. The liquid passes through an expansion valve to an evaporator, where it changes from liquid under high pressure to gas under low pressure. This change is accompanied by a drop in temperature, which cools the evaporator. The refrigerant returns to the compressor and the cycle begins again.

3 Air blown through the evaporator passes to the air distribution unit, where it is mixed with hot air blown through the heater matrix to achieve the desired temperature in the passenger compartment.

4 The heating side of the system works in the same way as on models without air conditioning (see Section 9).

5 The operation of the system is controlled by an electronic control unit, with a self-diagnosis system. Any problems with the system should be referred to a BMW dealer or suitably-equipped specialist.

Precautions

6 When an air conditioning system is fitted, it is necessary to observe special precautions whenever dealing with any part of the system, its associated components and any items which require disconnection of the system. If for any reason the system must be disconnected, entrust this task to your BMW dealer or a suitably-equipped specialist.

Warning: The refrigerant is potentially dangerous and should only be handled by qualified persons. If it is splashed onto the skin it can cause frostbite. It is not itself poisonous, but in the presence of a naked flame (including a cigarette) it forms a poisonous gas. Uncontrolled discharging of the refrigerant is dangerous and potentially damaging to the environment.

Warning: Do not operate the air conditioning system if it is known to be short of refrigerant, as this may damage the compressor.

12 Air conditioning system components – removal and refitting

Warning: Do not attempt to open the refrigerant circuit. Refer to the precautions given in Section 11.

Evaporator

1 Remove the heater housing as described in Section 10.

2 Undo the screws, and remove the left- and right-hand footwell air ducts **(see illustration 10.63)**.

3 Undo the screws and remove the expansion valve cover **(see illustration)**.

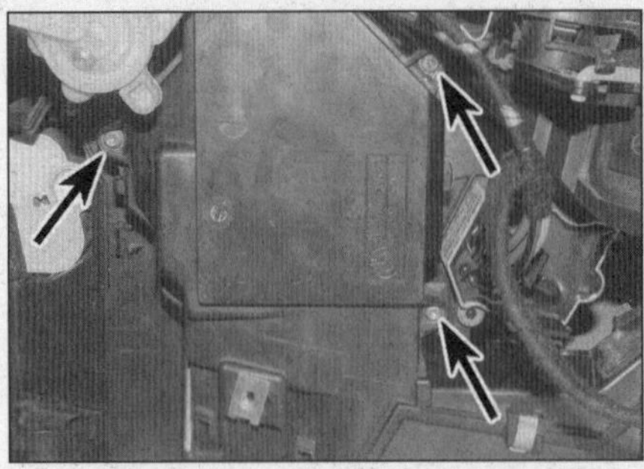

12.3 Undo the screws (arrowed) and remove the expansion valve cover

4 Release the clips and remove the evaporator pipes cover.

5 Undo the screws/clips and remove the heater matrix cover **(see illustration 10.65a)**.

6 Undo the two screws, release the two clips securing the central air vent outlet **(see illustration)**.

7 Turn the assembly upside down, then undo the four screws, release the clips and remove the lower section of the heater housing **(see illustration)**.

8 Undo the screws, pull the pipes slightly apart and remove the expansion valve **(see illustration)**.

9 Pull the evaporator from the housing. **Note:** *Take care not to damage any of the evaporator cooling fins. If necessary straighten any that are bent.*

10 Refitting is a reversal of removal. Have the system recharged by a BMW dealer or suitably-equipped specialist.

Expansion valve

11 Have the air conditioning system discharged by a BMW dealer or suitably-equipped specialist.

12 Working in the engine compartment, release the retaining clip, and remove the right-hand air duct using a combination of prising and twisting **(see illustration 10.12)**.

13 Undo the two screws and remove the air conditioning pressure and return pipes from the engine compartment bulkhead. Discard the O-ring seals, new ones must be fitted.

14 Remove the centre console and trim panel above the pedals as described in Chapter 11.

15 Undo the screws and remove the right-hand footwell air duct **(see illustration 10.63)**.

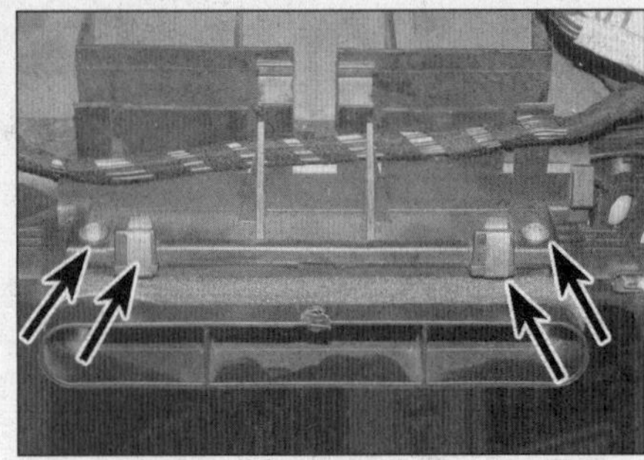

12.6 Undo the two screws, release the two clips and remove the central air vent (arrowed)

16 Undo the four screws, and remove the cover from the expansion valve **(see illustration 12.3)**.

17 Undo the two screws securing the pipes to the valve, pull the pipes apart slightly, and remove the expansion valve **(see illustration 12.8)**. Discard the O-ring seals, new ones must be fitted.

18 Refitting is a reversal of removal. Have the refrigerant recharged by a BMW dealer or specialist, and top-up the coolant level as described in *Weekly checks*.

Receiver/drier

19 The receiver/drier should be renewed when:

a) There is dirt in the air conditioning system.
b) The compressor has been renewed.
c) The condenser or evaporator has been renewed.
d) A leak has emptied the air conditioning system.
e) The air conditioning system has been opened for more than 24 hours.

20 Have the air conditioning refrigerant discharged by a BMW dealer or suitably-equipped specialist.

21 The receiver/drier is located in the right-hand corner of the engine compartment.

22 Remove the right-hand headlight as described in Chapter 12, Section 7.

23 Undo the two screws, and remove the headlamp mounting bracket from the aperture.

24 Undo the two retaining screws, and lift the pipes and coupling from the top of the unit **(see illustration)**. Discard the O-ring seals,

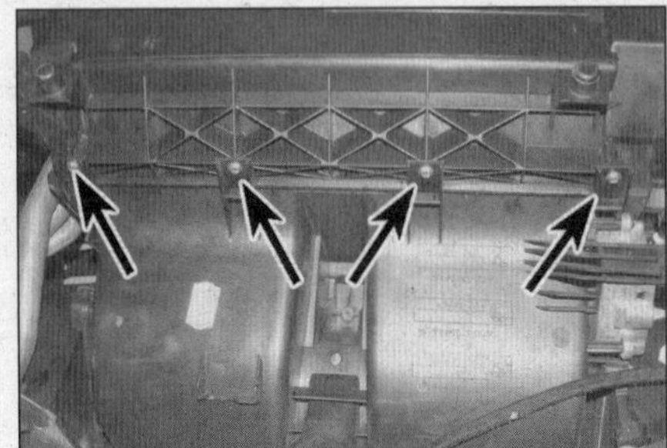

12.7 Undo the screws (arrowed), release the clips and remove the lower section of the heater housing

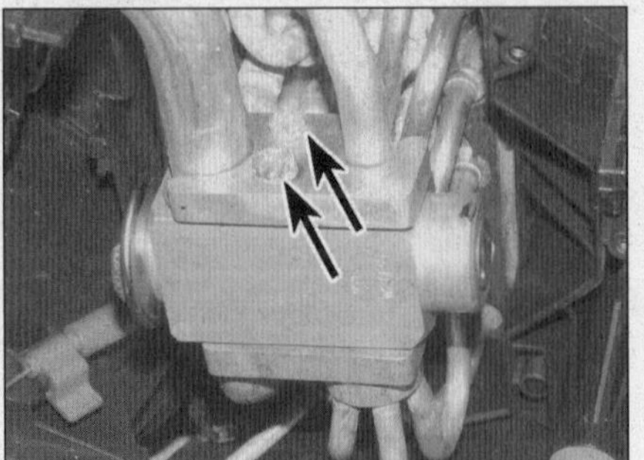

12.8 Undo the screws (arrowed) and remove the expansion valve

12.24 Undo the two screws and disconnect the pipes from the receiver/drier

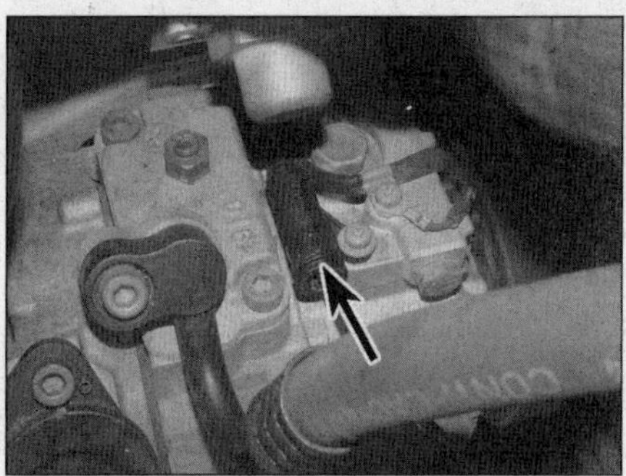
12.29 Disconnect the compressor wiring plug (arrowed)

12.30 Undo the two bolts and disconnect the compressor pipes

12.34 Undo the two screws and remove the trim panel

new ones must be fitted. **Note:** *If the drier is to be left unconnected for more than one hour, plug the openings.*

25 Undo the three screws, and lift the receiver/drier from position.

Compressor

26 Have the air conditioning refrigerant discharged by a BMW dealer or suitably-equipped specialist.

27 Firmly apply the handbrake, then jack up the front of the car and support it on axle stands. Undo the screws and remove the engine undershield.

28 Remove the auxiliary drivebelt as described in Chapter 1.

29 Disconnect the compressor wiring plug **(see illustration)**.

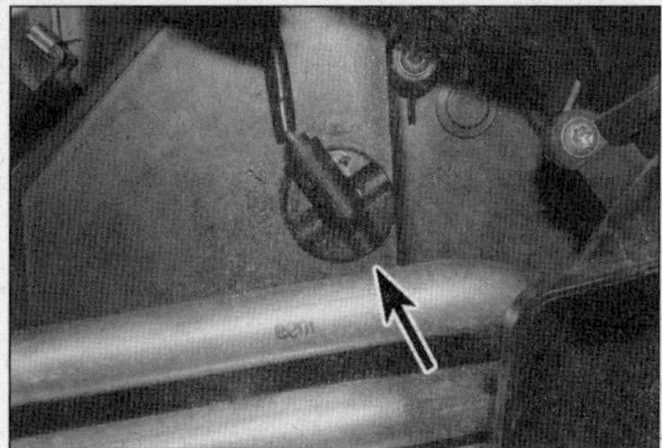
12.37 Pull the evaporator temperature sensor from place (arrowed)

30 Undo the two screws and disconnect the air conditioning pipes from the compressor **(see illustration)**. Discard the O-ring seals, new ones must be fitted.

31 Working underneath the vehicle, undo the mounting bolts, and remove the compressor. Note that on some models the compressor is retained by 3 bolts, whilst other models have 4 securing bolts.

32 Refitting is a reversal of removal, noting the following points:

a) *Prior to refitting the compressor, it is essential that the correct amount of refrigerant oil is added – refer to your dealer or specialist for the correct amount and specification.*

b) *Always use new seals when reconnecting the refrigerant pipes.*

c) *Upon completion, have the refrigerant recharged by a BMW dealer or specialist.*

Evaporator temperature sensor

Models with manual control

33 Remove the passenger's glovebox as described in Chapter 11, Section 26.

34 Undo the two screws and remove the glovebox inner trim **(see illustration)**.

35 Undo and remove the left-hand footwell air duct.

36 Disconnect the sensor wiring plug, and release it from its retaining clip.

37 Using a thin-nosed pair of pliers, pull the sensor from its position **(see illustration)**.

38 Refitting is a reversal of removal.

Models with automatic control

39 Working in the passenger's side footwell, undo the bolt, and pull back the carpet adjacent to the centre console.

40 Unclip the footwell air duct.

41 Undo the two screws and remove the retaining bracket at the front edge of the console.

42 Disconnect the sensor wiring plug, and pull the sensor from position.

43 Refitting is a reversal of removal, ensure the sensor grommet fully engages with the housing.

Condenser

44 Have the air conditioning refrigerant discharged by a BMW dealer or suitably-equipped specialist.

45 The condenser is located in front of the radiator. Remove the radiator as described in Section 3.

46 Undo the bolts, and disconnect the power steering, engine oil cooler and automatic transmission oil cooler pipes from the condenser 'cassette' **(see illustration)**. Discard the sealing rings, new ones must be fitted.

47 Undo the two bolts and disconnect the air conditioning pipes at the condenser. Discard the seals, new ones must be fitted **(see illustration)**.

12.46 Power steering cooler pipes connection

12.47 Undo the two bolts and disconnect the pipes from the condenser

48 Reach underneath the left-hand condenser mounting, release the clip and remove the mounting. Tilt the condenser 'cassette' slightly to the rear at the top, and lift it from position.

49 Unclip all the coolers from the 'cassette', then unclip the condenser **(see illustrations)**.

50 Refitting is a reversal of removal, noting the following points:

a) *Prior to refitting the condenser it is essential that the correct amount of refrigerant oil is added – refer to your dealer for the correct amount and specification.*

b) *Always use new seals when reconnecting the refrigerant pipes.*

c) *Upon completion, have the refrigerant recharged by a BMW dealer or specialist.*

12.49a Unclip the coolers from the cassette . . .

12.49b . . . then unclip the condenser

Chapter 4 Part A:
Fuel and exhaust systems

Contents

Degrees of difficulty

Easy, suitable for novice with little experience 

Fairly easy, suitable for beginner with some experience 

Fairly difficult, suitable for competent DIY mechanic

Difficult, suitable for experienced DIY mechanic

Very difficult, suitable for expert DIY or professional 

Specifications

System type

M52 engine	DME (Digital Motor Electronics) MS41 engine management
M52TU engine	DME (Digital Motor Electronics) MS42 engine management
M54 engine	DME (Digital Motor Electronics) MS43 engine management

Fuel system data

Fuel pump type	Electric, immersed in tank
Fuel pressure regulator rating	3.5 ± 0.2 bar
Specified idle speed:	
M52 engine	750 ± 50 rpm (not adjustable – controlled by ECM)
M52TU engine	750 ± 50 rpm (not adjustable – controlled by ECM)
M54 engine	No information available
Specified idle mixture CO content	Not adjustable – controlled by ECM
Tank capacity	78 litres
Fuel tank level sensor resistance:	
Empty	50 to 70 ohms
Full	401 to 415 ohms

Torque wrench settings

Torque wrench settings	Nm	lbf ft
Camshaft position sensor bolt*	7	5
Coolant temperature sensor	13	10
Crankshaft position sensor screw*	10	7
Exhaust manifold nuts*:		
M6 nuts	10	7
M7 nuts	15	11
M8 nuts	22	16
Fuel rail-to-inlet manifold bolts	10	7
Fuel tank mounting bolts	23	17
Fuel tank retaining strap bolts	8	6
Inlet manifold nuts:		
M6 nuts	10	7
M7 nuts	15	11
M8 nuts	22	16

** Do not re-use*

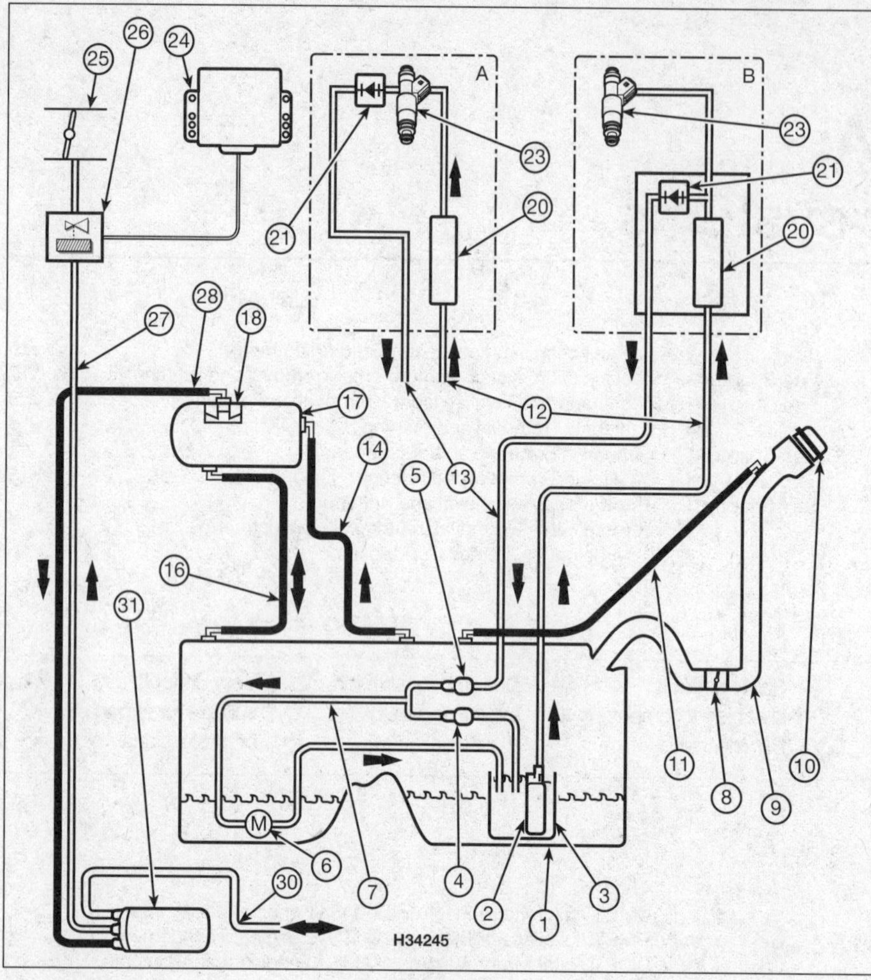

1.1 Fuel system

A M52 and M52 TU engines
B M54 engines
1 Fuel tank
2 Electric pump
3 Surge chamber
4 Pressure limiting valve
5 Outlet protection valve
6 Suction jet pump
7 Tank expansion pipe
8 Non-return valve
9 Filler neck
10 Filler cap
11 Breather hose
12 Fuel supply pipe
13 Fuel return pipe
14 Breather hose
16 Breather hose
17 Expansion tank
18 Roll-over valve
20 Fuel filter
21 Pressure regulator
23 Fuel rail
24 ECM
25 Intake manifold
26 Tank vent valve
27 Purge pipe
28 Vent pipe
30 Evaporation pipe
31 Carbon canister

2.2a The resonator chamber is secured to the air filter housing by two screws (arrowed – shown with the air filter housing removed)

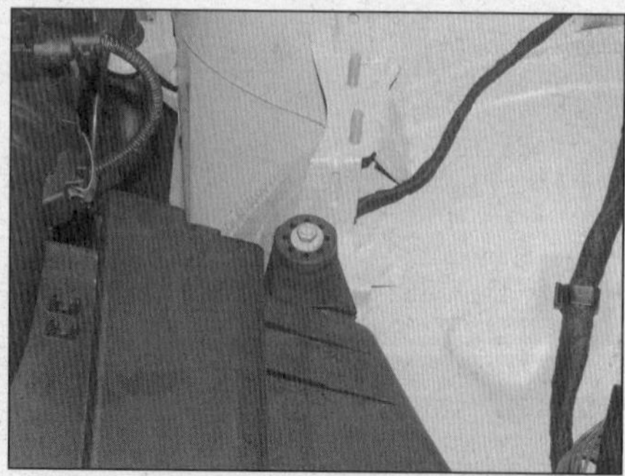

2.2b Air filter housing retaining bolt

1 General information and precautions

General information

The fuel supply system consists of a fuel tank (which is mounted under the rear of the vehicle, with an electric fuel pump immersed in it), a fuel filter, fuel feed and return lines. The fuel pump supplies fuel to the fuel rail, which acts as a reservoir for the six fuel injectors which inject fuel into the inlet tracts. The fuel filter incorporated in the feed line from the pump to the fuel rail ensures that the fuel supplied to the injectors is clean. On M52 and M52TU engines, the fuel pressure regulator is fitted to the fuel injection rail. On M54 engines, the pressure regulator is incorporated into the fuel filter assembly **(see illustration)**.

Refer to Section 7 for further information on the operation of the fuel injection system, and to Section 14 for information on the exhaust system.

Precautions

Warning: Many of the procedures in this Chapter required the disconnection of fuel lines and connections, which may result in some fuel spillage. Before carrying out any operation on the fuel system, refer to the precautions given in 'Safety first!', and follow then implicitly. Petrol is a highly dangerous and volatile liquid, and the precautions necessary when handling it cannot be overstressed.

Warning: Residual pressure will remain in the fuel lines long after the vehicle was last used. When disconnecting any fuel line, first depressurise the fuel system as described in Section 8.

2 Air cleaner assembly – removal and refitting

Removal

1 Remove the airflow meter as described in Section 12.

2 If not already done so, undo the two screws securing the intake resonator chamber to the air filter housing, and the air filter housing retaining bolt **(see illustrations)**.

M52 engine

3 Pull the intake snorkel from the inner wing as the housing is removed.

M52TU and M54 engines

4 Slacken the clamp and disconnect the intake snorkel from the air cleaner housing

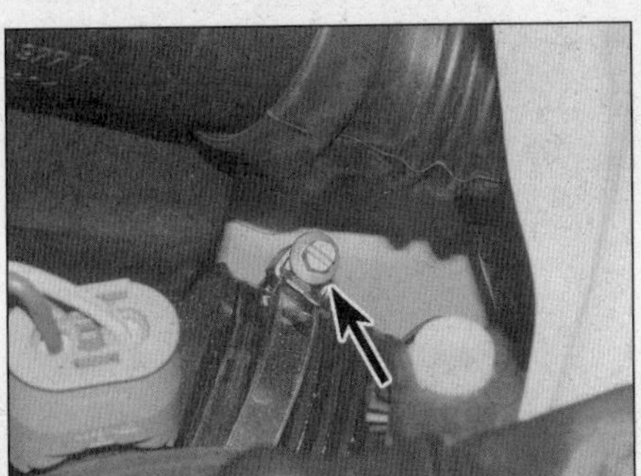

2.4 Undo the intake snorkel clamp (arrowed)

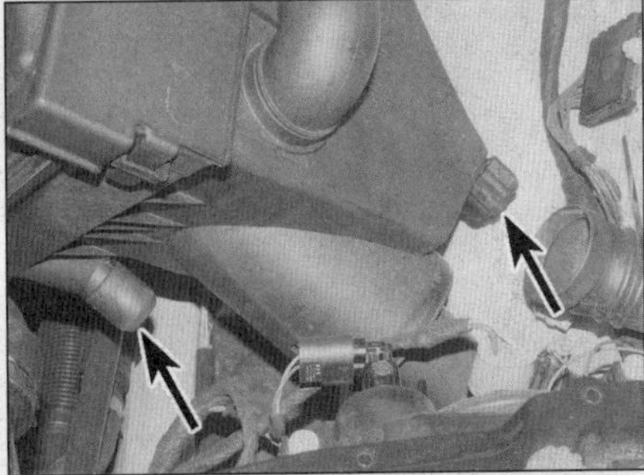

2.5 Air filter housing mounting rubbers (arrowed)

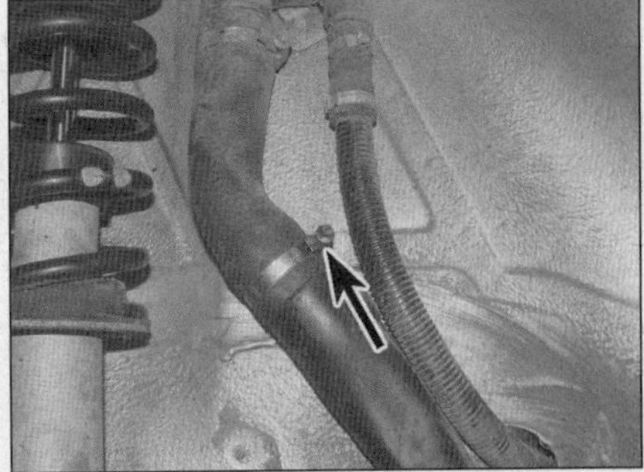

3.7 Slacken the clamp and disconnect the fuel filler hose (arrowed)

(see illustration). Pull the housing from its locating lug.

Refitting

5 Refitting is a reversal of removal, but ensure that the lower mountings engage with the lugs on the body **(see illustration)**, and where a rubber seal is fitted between the intake hose and the housing, apply a little petroleum jelly to the seal to ease refitting.

3 Fuel tank – removal and refitting

Removal

1 Disconnect the battery negative lead as described in Chapter 5A.

2 Before removing the fuel tank, all fuel should be drained from the tank. Since a fuel tank drain plug is not provided, it is preferable to carry out the removal operation when the tank is nearly empty.

3 Jack up the rear of the vehicle, and support it securely on axle stands (see *Jacking and vehicle support*). Remove the right-hand rear wheel.

4 Detach the handbrake cables from the handbrake lever as described in Chapter 9.

5 Remove the propeller shaft as described in Chapter 8.

6 Release the retaining clips/screws, and remove the right-hand rear wheel arch liner (see Chapter 11, Section 22).

7 Slacken the clamp and disconnect the fuel filler neck **(see illustration)**.

8 Undo the nuts and remove the heat shield from the tank/vehicle body underside.

9 Pull the handbrake cables from the guide tubes **(see illustration)**.

10 Undo the retaining screw each side and remove the covers (where fitted) from the rear axle mounting.

11 Mark them to aid refitment, then release the clips and disconnect the fuel supply and return hoses **(see illustration)**. Be prepared for fuel spillage, and clamp or plug the open ends of the hoses and pipes to prevent dirt entry and further fuel spillage.

12 Support the fuel tank using a trolley jack and an interposed block of wood.

13 Undo the Allen retaining bolts at the left- and right-hand rear of the tank, and the Allen bolts securing the tank front retaining straps.

14 Lower the tank slightly, note their fitted positions then disconnect the wiring plug(s).

15 Release the clamps and disconnect the breather hoses from the tank **(see illustration)**. Lower the tank, and manoeuvre it from under the vehicle.

Refitting

16 Refitting is a reversal of removal. Note that once the tank is refitted, at least 5 litres of fuel must be added to allow the fuel system to function correctly.

4 Fuel expansion tank – removal and refitting

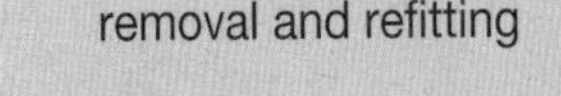

Removal

1 Jack up the left-hand rear side of the vehicle and support it on axle stands (see *Jacking and vehicle support*). Remove the left-hand rear roadwheel.

2 Undo the plastic nuts/screws/expansion rivets and remove the left-hand rear wheel arch liner as described in Chapter 11, Section 22.

3 Release the clip and disconnect the return pipe from the tank.

4 Undo the retaining nut, and lower the expansion tank.

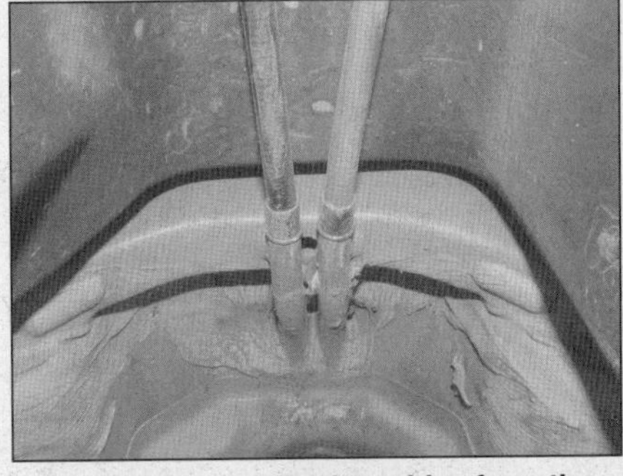

3.9 Pull the handbrake cables from the guide tubes

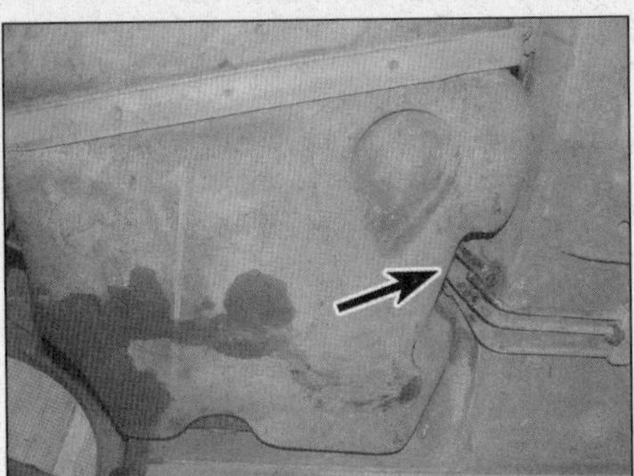

3.11 Disconnect the fuel supply and return hoses (arrowed)

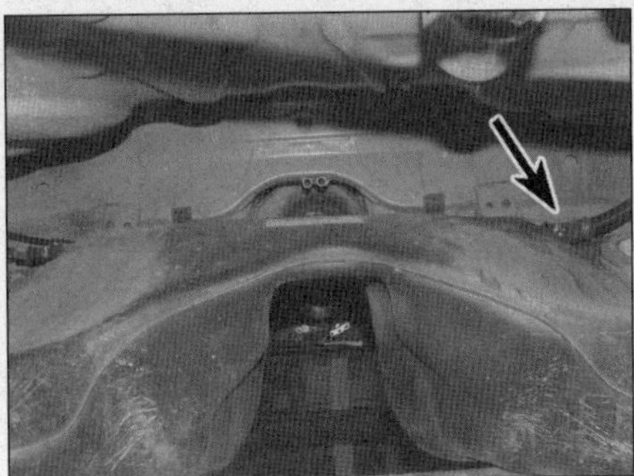

3.15a Disconnect the breather hose (arrowed) . . .

3.15b . . . and expansion tank hose as the tank is lowered

5.1 Disengage the inner cable end fitting from the throttle lever

5 Note their fitted positions, then release the clips and disconnect the remaining two breather hoses from the tank. Remove the tank.

Refitting

6 Refitting is a reversal of removal.

5 Throttle cable – removal, refitting and adjustment

Note: *The M54 engine is equipped with a fully electronic throttle, and therefore is not fitted with a throttle cable.*

Removal

M52 engine

1 Operate the throttle lever by hand and pull the throttle inner cable end fitting from the throttle lever **(see illustration)**.

2 Pull the outer cable end fitting from the grommet in the support bracket.

3 Working inside the vehicle, release the retaining clips/screws, and withdraw the driver's side lower facia panel (see Chapter 11).

4 Pull the inner throttle cable fitting from the grommet at the top of the operating lever on the accelerator pedal **(see illustration)**.

5 Working under the facia, squeeze together the top and bottom of the end fitting to release the retaining clips, and push the cable outer end fitting from the mounting in the bulkhead **(see illustration)**.

6 Note the correct routing, then free the cable from any retaining clips/grommets and manoeuvre it from the engine compartment.

5.4 Pull the inner cable fitting from the grommet in the accelerator pedal operating lever

M52TU engine

7 Pull the outer cable and fitting upwards from the support bracket adjacent to the throttle body, then disconnect the inner cable end fitting from the throttle lever.

8 Proceed as described in Paragraphs 3 to 6.

Refitting

9 Refitting is a reversal of removal, ensuring that the cable is routed as before. Fit the grommet to the top of the throttle operating lever, then insert the cable end fitting. Carry out the adjustment procedure as follows.

Adjustment

M52 engine

10 Check that the accelerator pedal and throttle quadrant are in the idle position.

11 Rotate the knurled cable adjustment sleeve on the outer cable to eliminate free play in the cable.

12 Screw the sleeve a quarter of a turn to allow a little free play in the cable.

13 Have an assistant fully depress the accelerator pedal, and then release it. Check that with there is 0.5 to 1.0 mm of free play in the cable. Adjust as necessary.

M52TU engine

14 In order to accurately adjust the throttle cable, access to specialised BMW diagnostic equipment is required, to establish the throttle potentiometer position expressed as a percentage. However, the basic position for manual transmission models can be established as follows, providing the setting is checked by a BMW dealer or suitably-equipped specialist afterwards. **Note:** *On automatic transmission models, have the cable adjusted by a BMW dealer or suitably-equipped specialist.*

5.5 Squeeze together the clips (arrowed) and pull the fitting from the bulkhead (shown with the cable removed for clarity)

15 Check that the accelerator pedal and throttle quadrant are in the idle position.

16 Rotate the knurled cable adjustment sleeve on the outer cable to eliminate any free play in the cable.

17 Screw in the sleeve a quarter of a turn to allow a little free play in the cable.

18 Have an assistant fully depress the accelerator pedal, and check that with the pedal fully depressed, there is still 0.5 mm of free play at the throttle valve in the throttle body.

19 If necessary, turn the pedal full-throttle stop (screwed into the floor) to give the correct amount of free-play. on some models, it will be necessary to slacken a locknut before the stop can be adjusted.

6 Throttle pedal – removal and refitting

Warning: Once the throttle pedal has been removed, it MUST be renewed. Removal will damage the pedal retaining clips, and if the original pedal is refitted, it could work loose, causing an accident.

Models with throttle cable

1 Reach behind the throttle pedal and pull the retaining clip tab forwards, then release the pedal from the floor **(see illustration)**. Manoeuvre the pedal and free it from the throttle cable operating lever.

2 Engage the new pedal with the throttle cable operating lever.

3 Push the pedal down to engage the lower retaining clip with the floor plate. Ensure that the clip snaps securely into place.

4 Check the throttle cable adjustment as described in Section 5.

Models with electronic throttle

5 Using a flat-bladed screwdriver, depress the retaining clip and slide the pedal assembly towards the centre of the cabin **(see illustration)**. Disconnect the wiring plug as the assembly is withdrawn.

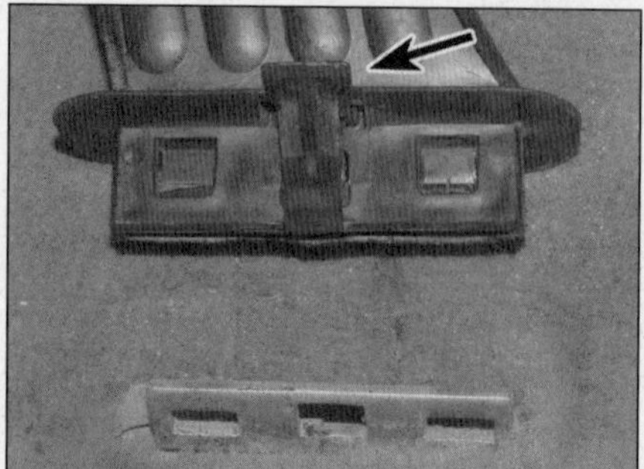

6.1 Pull the clip (arrowed) forward, and remove the pedal

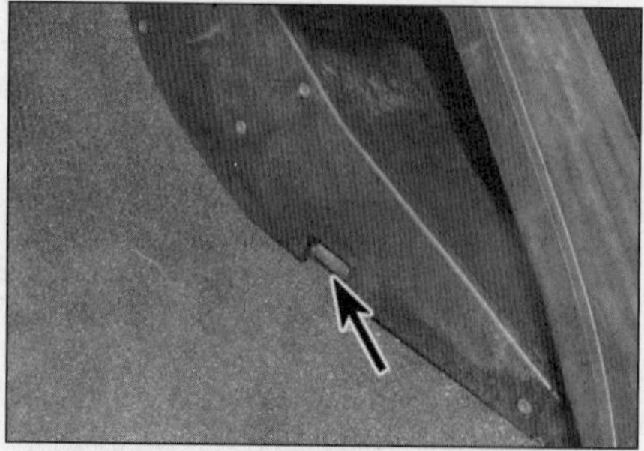

6.5 Depress the clip (arrowed), and slide the pedal assembly towards the centre of the cabin

6 To fit, reconnect the wiring plug and slide the assembly into the mounting, ensuring that it is correctly located. When correctly located, two 'clicks' should be heard as the clips engage, and the right-hand side of the assembly is flush with the side of the mounting.

7 Fuel injection system – general information

1 An integrated engine management system known as DME (Digital Motor Electronics) is fitted to all models, and the system controls all fuel injection and ignition system functions using a central ECM (Electronic Control Module).

2 On all models, the system incorporates a closed-loop catalytic converter and an evaporative emission control system, and complies with the very latest emission control standards. Refer to Chapter 5B for information on the ignition side of the system; the fuel side of the system operates as follows.

3 The fuel pump (which is immersed in the fuel tank) supplies fuel from the tank to the fuel rail, via a filter. Fuel supply pressure is controlled by the pressure regulator in the fuel rail/under the vehicle body on M52 and M52TU engines, and integral with the fuel filter on M54 engines. When the optimum operating pressure of the fuel system is exceeded, the regulator allows excess fuel to return to the tank.

4 The electrical control system consists of the ECM, along with the following sensors:

a) *Hot film air mass meter – informs the ECM of the quantity and temperature of air entering the engine.*
b) *Throttle position sensor – informs the ECM of the throttle position, and the rate of throttle opening/closing.*
c) *Coolant temperature sensor(s) – informs the ECM of engine temperature.*
d) *Crankshaft position sensor – informs the ECM of the crankshaft position and speed of rotation.*
e) *Camshaft position sensor(s) – informs the ECM of the camshaft(s) position.*
f) *Oxygen sensor(s) – informs the ECM of the oxygen content of the exhaust gases (explained in greater detail in Part B of this Chapter).*
g) *Vehicle speed sensor – informs the ECM of the vehicle's roadspeed.*
h) *Intake air temperature sensor – informs the ECM of the temperature of the air entering the engine (M52TU and M54 engines).*
i) *Oil temperature – informs the ECM of the engine oil temperature.*

5 All the above signals are analysed by the ECM which selects the fuelling response appropriate to those values. The ECM controls the fuel injectors (varying the pulse width – the length of time the injectors are held open – to provide a richer or weaker mixture, as appropriate). The mixture is constantly varied by the ECM, to provide the best setting for cranking, starting (with a hot or cold engine), warm-up, idle, cruising and acceleration.

6 The ECM also has full control over the engine idle speed, via an auxiliary air valve which bypasses the throttle valve. When the throttle valve is closed, the ECM controls the opening of the valve, which in turn regulates the amount of air entering the manifold, and so controls the idle speed.

7 The ECM controls the exhaust and evaporative emission control systems, which are described in Part B of this Chapter.

8 On M52TU and M54 engines, a Differential Air Inlet System (DISA) is fitted. Variable length inlet tracts incorporated in the inlet manifold are operated by a butterfly valve according to engine speed and load. This improves engines torque at low and medium engine speeds. The butterfly valve is operated by a vacuum actuator fitted under the manifold.

9 If there is an abnormality in any of the readings obtained from the sensors, the ECM enters its back-up mode. In this event, it ignores the abnormal sensor signal and assumes a preprogrammed value which will allow the engine to continue running (albeit at reduced efficiency). If the ECM enters this back-up mode, the relevant fault code will be stored in the ECM memory.

10 If a fault is suspected, the vehicle should be taken to a BMW dealer or suitably-equipped specialist at the earliest opportunity. A complete test of the engine management system can then be carried out, using a special electronic diagnostic test unit which is simply plugged into the system's diagnostic connector. The 16-pin OBD socket is located in the storage compartment under the facia on the driver's side on models from 2001, whilst on models up to 2001, the BMW diagnostic socket is located in the right-hand corner of the engine compartment or under the facia on the driver's side **(see illustrations 10.2a and 10.2b)**.

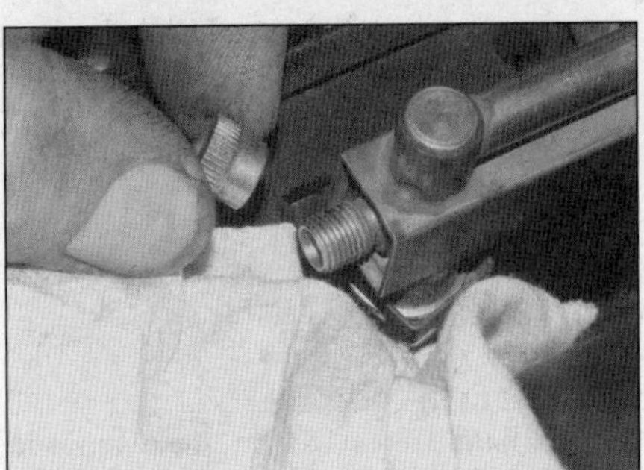
8.2 Undo the cap from the valve

9.4 Unclip the rubber grommet

8 Fuel injection system – depressurisation and priming

Depressurisation

1 Prise out the cover caps, undo the two retaining screws, and remove the plastic cover from above the fuel rail and injectors.

2 Undo the cap over the valve at the front of the fuel rail **(see illustration)**.

3 Place absorbent rags around the valve, then depress the valve core with a small screwdriver to relive the residual pressure. Be prepared for fuel spillage.

4 The fuel system is now depressurised. **Note:** *Place a wad of rag around fuel lines before disconnecting, to prevent any residual fuel from spilling onto the engine.*

5 Disconnect the battery negative lead before working on any part of the fuel system (see Chapter 5A).

Priming

6 Refit the fuel pump fuse, then switch on the ignition and wait for a few seconds for the fuel pump to run, building-up fuel pressure. Switch off the ignition unless the engine is to be started.

9 Fuel pump/fuel level sensors – removal and refitting

Removal

1 There are two level sensors fitted to the fuel tank – one in the left-hand side of the tank, and one in the right-hand side. The pump is integral with the right-hand side sensor, and at the time of writing, can only be renewed as a complete unit.

Right-hand sensor/fuel pump

2 Before removing the fuel level sensor/pump, all fuel should be drained from the tank. Since a fuel tank drain plug is not provided, it is preferable to carry out the removal operation when the tank is nearly empty.

3 Remove the rear bench seat as described in Chapter 11.

4 Unclip the rubber wiring grommet, and cut along the perforations, and fold back the rubber matting to expose the access cover **(see illustration)**.

9.6a Slide out the locking element and disconnect the wiring plug . . .

9.6b . . . then cut off the clamp from the fuel hose

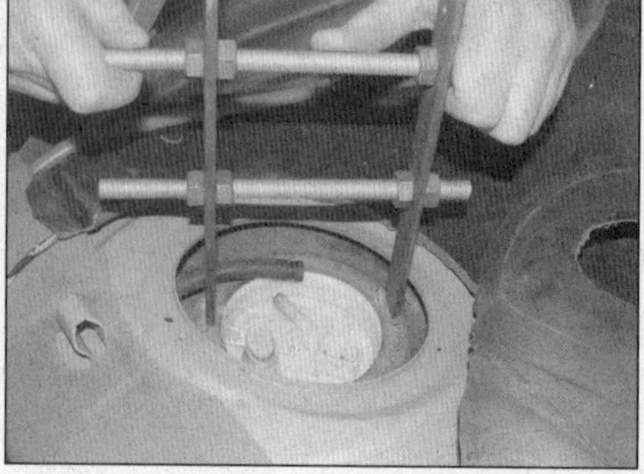
9.7 Unscrew the fuel pump/level sensor locking ring

9.8a Lift the level sensor from place . . .

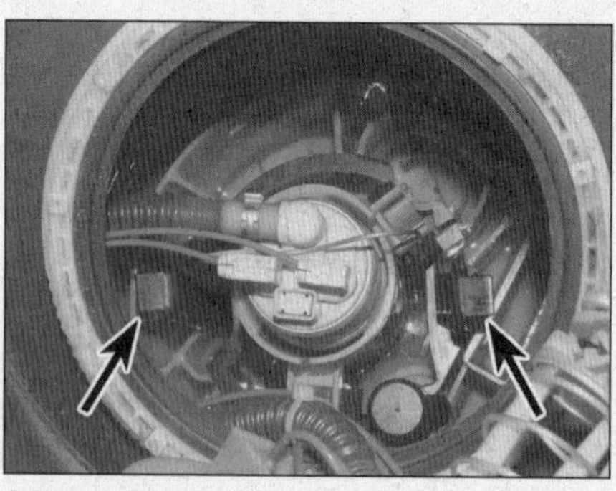
9.8b . . . then squeeze together the retaining clips (arrowed) and remove the pump

5 Undo the three screws, and remove the access cover from the floor. Recover the gasket.

6 Slide out the locking element to disconnect the wiring plug, then cut the original metal hose clamp from place using side-cutters (or similar) and disconnect the fuel hose **(see illustrations)**. Be prepared for fuel spillage.

7 Unscrew the fuel pump/level sensor unit locking ring and remove it from the tank. Although a BMW tool 16 1 020 is available for this task, it can be accomplished using a large pair of grips to push on two opposite raised ribs on the locking ring. Alternatively, a home-made tool can be fabricated to engage with the raised ribs of the locking ring. Turn the ring anti-clockwise until it can be unscrewed by hand **(see illustration)**.

8 Carefully lift the level sensor unit from the tank, taking care not to bend the sensor float arm (gently push the float arm towards the unit if necessary). To remove the pump, squeeze together the retaining clips and pull it up from the mounting. Recover the sealing ring. If necessary the strainer on the base of the pump can cleaned **(see illustrations)**, but no further dismantling is recommended.

Left-hand sensor

9 Removal of the left-hand sensor is almost identical to the right-hand sensor described previously, except that the wiring plug is clipped into place. When lifting out the sensor unit, depress the detent and disconnect the expansion tank pipe from the unit.

Refitting

10 Refitting is a reversal of removal, noting the following points:

a) Use a new sealing ring.
b) To allow the unit to pass through the aperture in the fuel tank, press the float arm against the fuel pick-up strainer.
c) When the unit is fitted, the locating lug on the unit must engage with the corresponding slot in the fuel tank collar ***(see illustration).***
d) Tighten the locking collar securely.
e) Use a new hose clamp to secure the fuel hose.

10 Fuel injection system – testing and adjustment

Testing

1 If a fault appears in the fuel injection system, first ensure that all the system wiring connectors are securely connected and free of corrosion. Ensure that the fault is not due to poor maintenance; ie, check that the air cleaner filter element is clean, the spark plugs are in good condition and correctly gapped, the cylinder compression pressures are correct, and that the engine breather hoses are clear and undamaged, referring to the relevant Parts of Chapters 1, 2 and 5 for further information.

2 If these checks fail to reveal the cause of the problem, the vehicle should be taken to a BMW dealer or suitably-equipped specialist for testing. A wiring block connector is incorporated in the engine management circuit, into which a special electronic diagnostic tester can be plugged. The BMW diagnostic connector is clipped to the right-hand suspension turret on some models up to 2001 **(see illustration)**, whilst on others it is

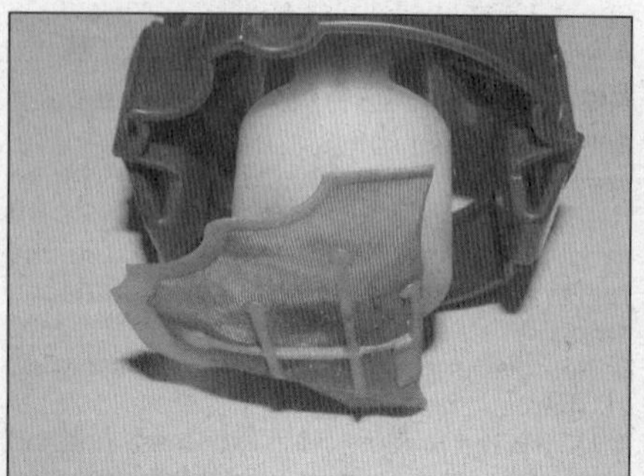
9.8c If necessary, clean the strainer

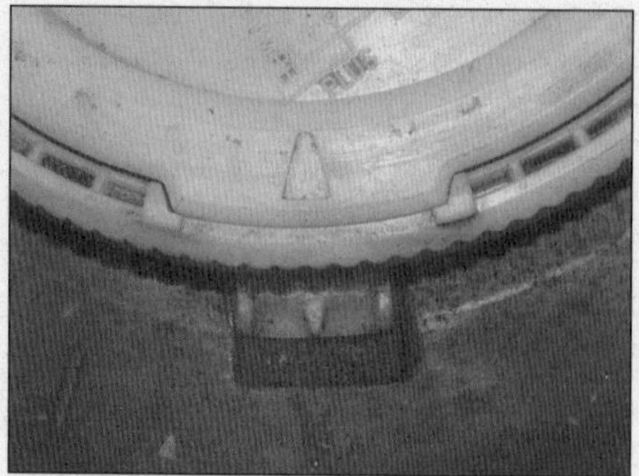
9.10 The cover must engage with the locating slot in the collar

10.2a On models up to 2001, the diagnostic plug is in the engine compartment, just in front of the right-hand suspension turret

10.2b On models from 2001, the diagnostic plug is behind a cover in the driver's side facia storage compartment

located above the pedals in the driver's footwell along with the OBD (On-Board Diagnostic) 16-pin socket **(see illustration)**. The tester will locate the fault quickly and simply, alleviating the need to test all the system components individually, which is a time-consuming operation that also carries a risk of damaging the ECM.

Adjustment

3 Experienced home mechanics with a considerable amount of skill and equipment (including a tachometer and an accurately calibrated exhaust gas analyser) may be able to check the exhaust CO level and the idle speed. However, if these are found to be in need of adjustment, the car *must* be taken to a BMW dealer or specialist for further testing.

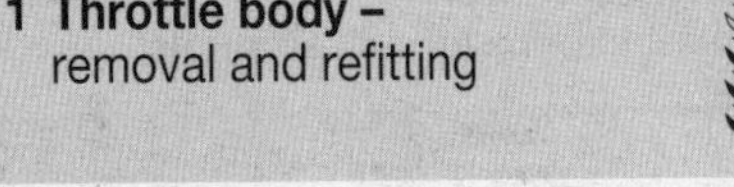

11 Throttle body – removal and refitting

M52 engine

Removal

1 Remove the mass airflow meter as described in Section 12.

2 Slacken the hose clamps and remove the intake hose from the throttle body and idle speed control valve.

3 Disconnect the throttle cable from the throttle lever, and move the cable to one side, with reference to Section 5. Where fitted, disconnect the ASC+T control cable from the outer throttle body.

4 Slacken the hose clamps, and disconnect the coolant hoses from the base of the throttle body, Be prepared for coolant spillage, and plug or clamp the open ends of the hoses **(see illustration)**.

5 Disconnect the wiring plug(s) from the throttle position sensor(s) **(see illustration)**. Note that the wiring plug with the corrugated outer cable sleeve connects to the inner throttle position sensor.

6 On models with ASC+T, undo the two Allen bolts and remove the outer throttle body **(see illustration)**.

7 Undo the four securing bolts, and remove the throttle body from the intake manifold **(see illustration)**.

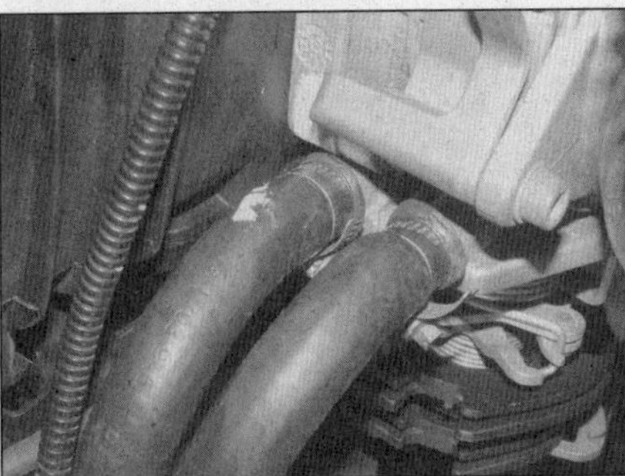

11.4 Disconnect the hoses from the base of the throttle body

8 Discard the sealing ring(s), a new one(s) must be fitted.

Refitting

9 Refitting is a reversal of removal, but fit a new sealing ring. Check the coolant level as described in Chapter 1.

M52TU engines

Removal

10 Disconnect the battery negative lead as described in Chapter 5A.

11 Remove the air cleaner housing as described in Section 2.

12 Remove the mass airflow sensor and ducting as described in Section 12.

13 Disconnect the throttle cable(s) from the throttle quadrant and support bracket.

14 Release the retaining clips, and disconnect the air intake ducting from the throttle body and the idle speed control valve.

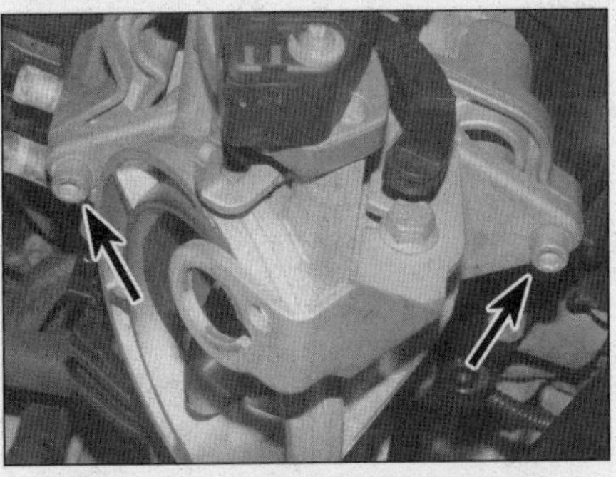

11.6 Undo the two bolts (arrowed) and remove the ASC+T throttle body

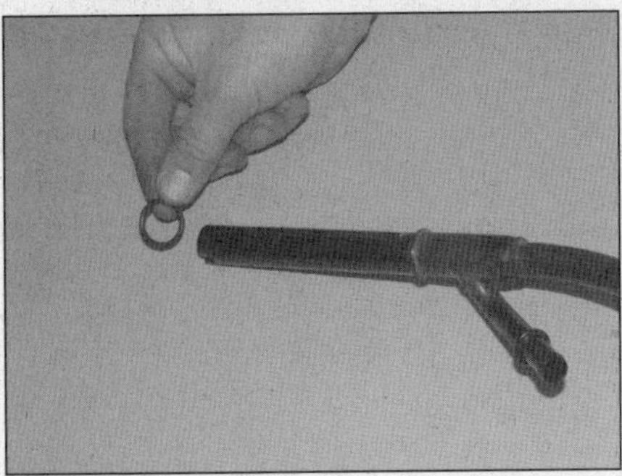

11.18 Discard the oil dipstick tube O-ring

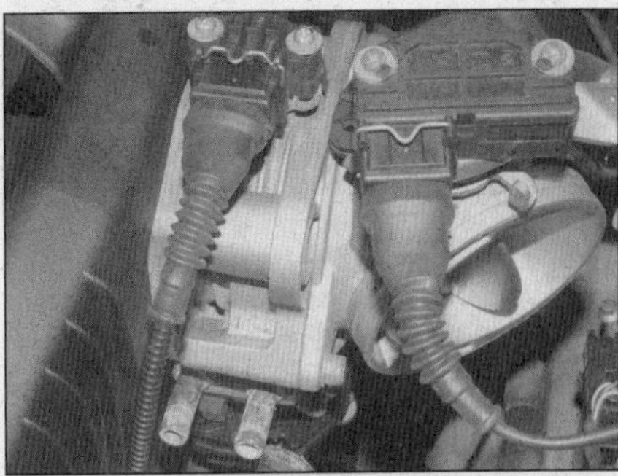

11.5 Disconnect the wiring plugs from the throttle position sensors

15 Note their fitted locations, and disconnect any wiring plugs attached to the throttle body.

16 Disconnect the oil pressure and oil temperature switches wiring plugs adjacent to the oil filter housing.

17 Unclip the fuel pipes and fuel regulator vacuum hose (where fitted) from the retaining bracket on the oil dipstick guide tube.

18 Disconnect the oil return pipe from the dipstick guide tube, undo the retaining bolt and remove the guide tube. Discard the O-ring seal, a new one must be fitted **(see illustration)**.

19 Undo the three screws/nuts securing the cable duct mounting.

20 Rotate the plug collar anti-clockwise, and disconnect the wiring plug from the throttle body (M52TU engines) or release the retaining clip and disconnect the wiring plug (M54 engines), undo the four screws and remove the body from the intake manifold **(see illustration)**.

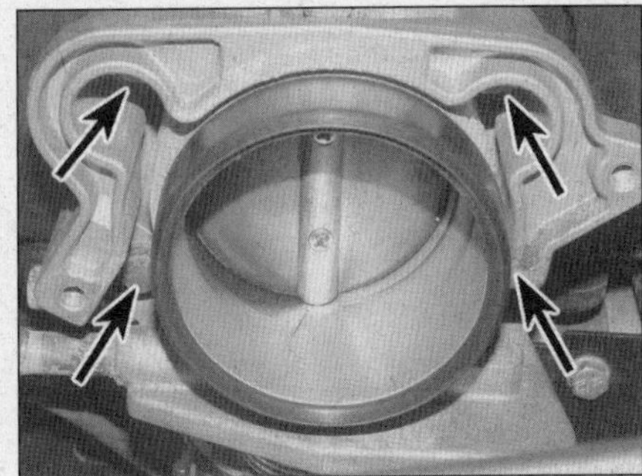

11.7 Undo the four bolts (arrowed) and remove the throttle body

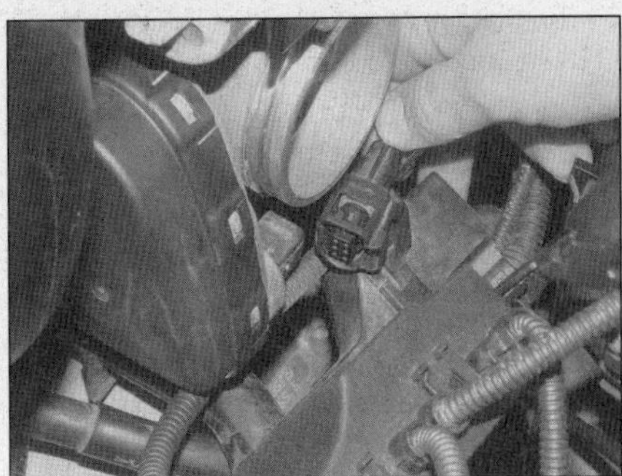

11.20 Disconnect the throttle body wiring plug – M54 engine

Refitting

21 Examine the throttle body-to-intake manifold O-ring seal. If it is good condition, it can be re-used. Refit the throttle body to the manifold, and tighten the four bolts securely.

22 Prior to reconnecting the throttle body wiring plug on M52TU engines, rotate the plug collar until the red locking pin is visible though the opening in the collar. Align the arrow on the collar with the arrow on the throttle body terminal. Push the wiring plug on, rotating the collar clockwise until the second arrow on the collar aligns **(see illustration)**. On M54 engines, simply refit the wiring plug.

23 The remainder of refitting is a reversal of removal. Note that if a new throttle body has been fitted, the 'learnt adaption' values stored in the engine management ECM, must be reset using dedicated test equipment. Have this carried out be a BMW dealer or suitably-equipped specialist.

M54 engines

Removal

24 Disconnect the battery negative lead as described in Chapter 5A.

25 Remove the air cleaner housing as described in Section 2.

26 Release the retaining clips, disconnect the vacuum hose, and remove air cleaner housing-to-connecting piece intake ducting.

27 Disconnect the wiring plug, undo the two mounting Torx screws, and remove the Differential Air Inlet System (DISA) adjustment unit from the intake manifold **(see illustration)**.

28 Unscrew the bolt securing the suction jet tube to the intake manifold **(see illustration)**.

29 Release the clamps, and disconnect the intake ducting from the throttle body and idle speed control valve.

30 Disconnect the idle speed control valve wiring plug.

31 Disconnect the wiring plugs for the oil temperature and oil pressure switches adjacent to the oil filter housing.

32 Press in the retaining clip to unlock the wiring plug, and detach it from the tank venting valve **(see illustration)**.

33 Proceed as described from Paragraph 18 to 20.

Refitting

34 Refitting is as described in Paragraphs 21 to 23.

12 Fuel injection system components – removal and refitting

Electronic control module

1 Disconnect the battery negative lead, as described in Chapter 5A. **Note:** *Disconnecting the battery will erase any fault codes stored in the ECM. It is recommended that the fault code memory of the module is interrogated using special test equipment prior to battery disconnection. Entrust this task to a BMW dealer or suitably-equipped specialist.*

2 Working in the left-hand corner of the engine compartment, release the clip(s) and remove the left-hand air ducting from the pollen filter housing, remove the filter cover, then release the clip and remove the filter housing. Remove the rain deflector then undo the four screws, and remove the cover from the electrical box **(see illustrations)**.

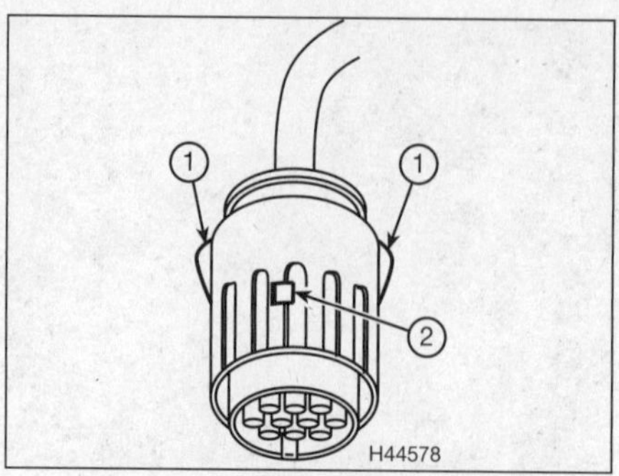

11.22 Wiring connector arrows (1) and opening (2)

11.27 Undo the screws (arrowed) and remove the DISA adjustment unit

11.28 Undo the bolt securing the suction jet tube (arrowed)

11.32 Disconnect the tank vent valve wiring plug

12.2a Release the single clip . . .

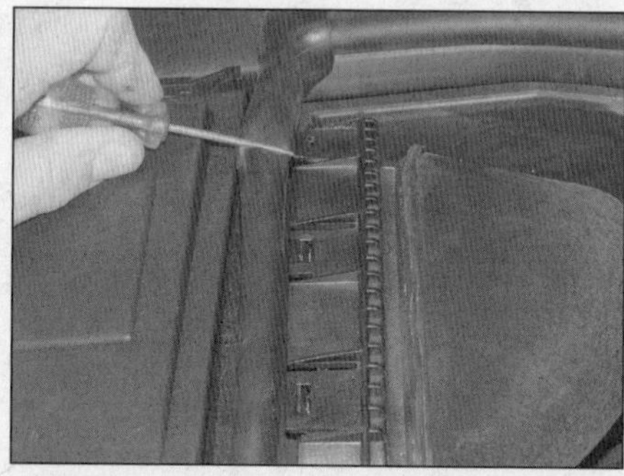

12.2b . . . or 3 clips (depending on model) and disconnect the left-hand air duct

12.2c Release the clip and remove the pollen filter cover . . .

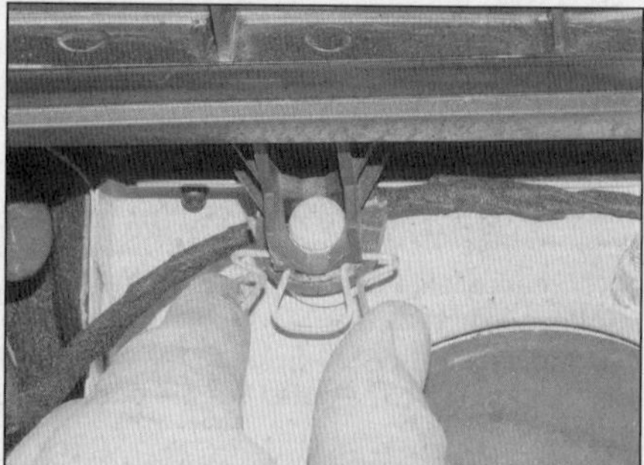

12.2d . . . then unclip and remove the pollen filter housing

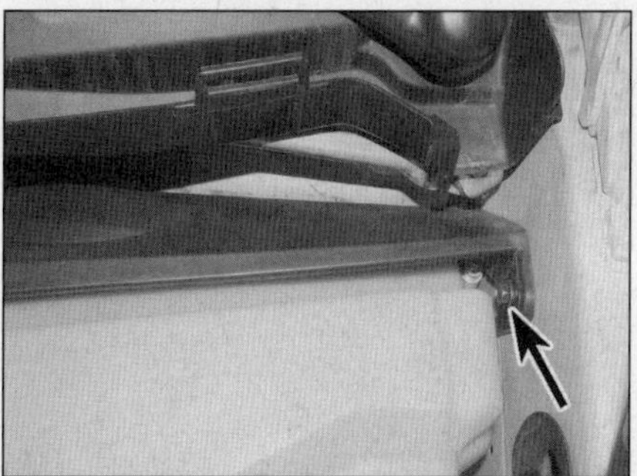

12.2e Undo the bolt (arrowed) and remove the rain deflector . . .

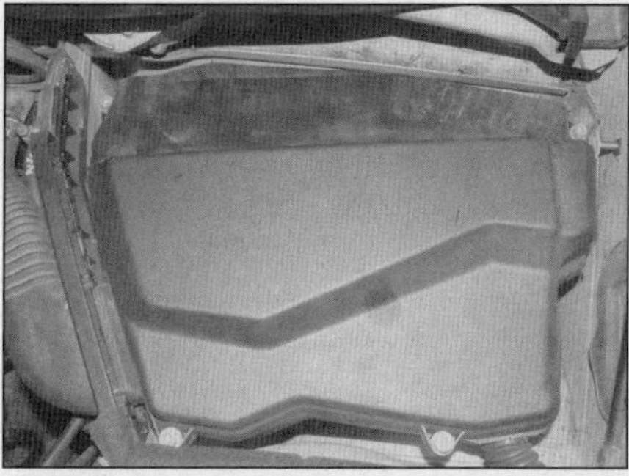

12.2f . . . then undo the four screws and remove the E-box cover

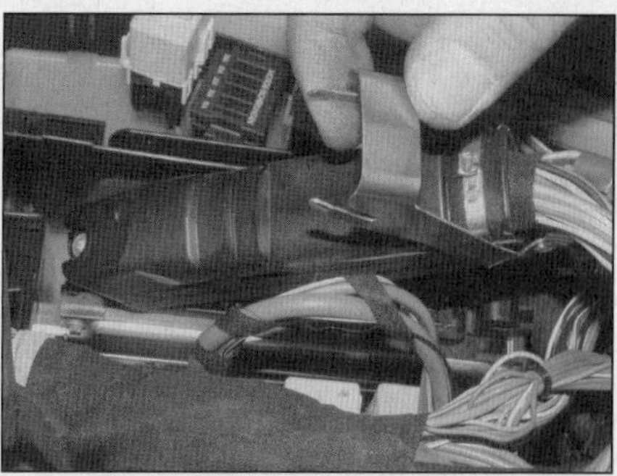

12.3 Unlock the ECM wiring plug

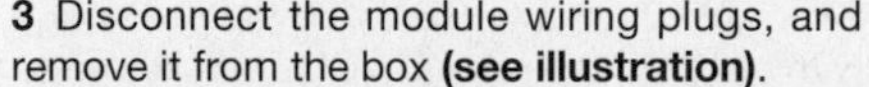

3 Disconnect the module wiring plugs, and remove it from the box **(see illustration)**.

4 Refitting is a reversal of removal. **Note:** *If a new module has been fitted, it will need to be coded using special test equipment. Entrust this task to a BMW dealer or suitably-equipped specialist. After reconnecting the battery, the vehicle must be driven for several miles so that the ECM can learn its basic settings. If the engine still runs erratically, the basic settings may be reinstated by a BMW dealer or specialist using special diagnostic equipment.*

Fuel rail and injectors

Warning: Refer to the warning notes in Section 1 before proceeding.

5 Depressurise the fuel system as described in Section 8, then disconnect the battery negative lead (see Chapter 5A).

M52 engine

6 Prise out the plastic caps, undo the two screws, and remove the plastic cover from the over the injectors **(see illustration)**.

7 Squeeze together the sides of the cylinder head cover breather hose collar and disconnect it. Release the retaining clips and pull the wiring rail from the fuel injectors, then disconnect the VANOS solenoid wiring plug **(see illustrations)**.

8 Mark the two oxygen sensor wiring connectors to aid refitting, unplug them and release them from the retaining clips.

9 Press in the locking collar, and detach the fuel supply and return pipes from the fuel rail. Be prepared for fuel spillage, and take adequate fire precautions. Plug the open ends of the pipe and hose to prevent dirt entry and further fuel spillage **(see illustration)**.

10 Disconnect the fuel regulator vacuum hose.

11 Undo the four screws and remove the fuel rail complete with the injectors **(see illustration)**.

12 Prise out the retaining clips and remove the injectors from the fuel rail **(see illustration)**.

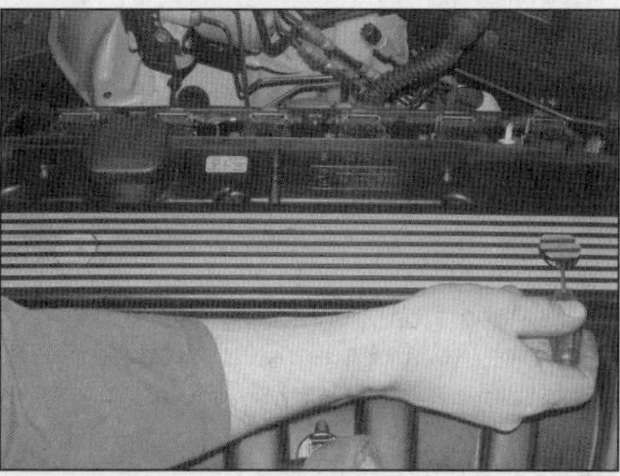

12.6 Prise up the caps, undo the screws and remove the cover over the injectors

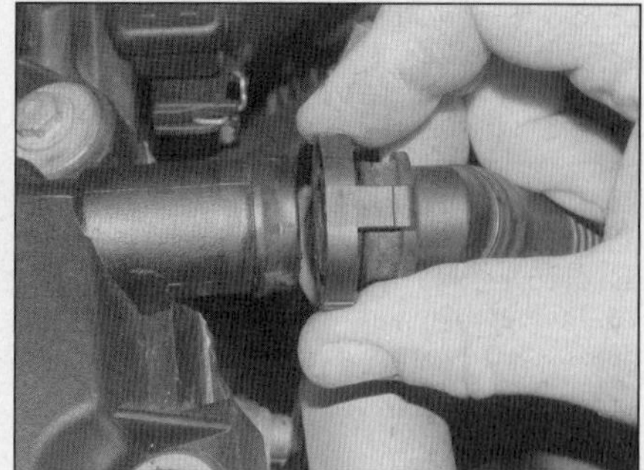

12.7a Disconnect the breather hose . . .

12.7b . . . release the clips and pull the wiring rail from the injectors . . .

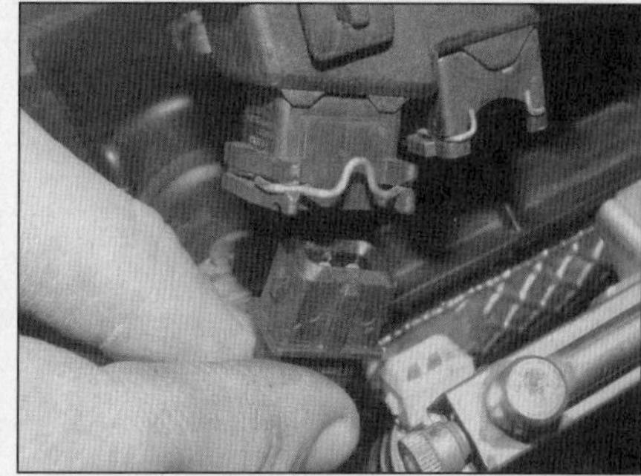

12.7c . . . then disconnect the VANOS wiring plug from the rail

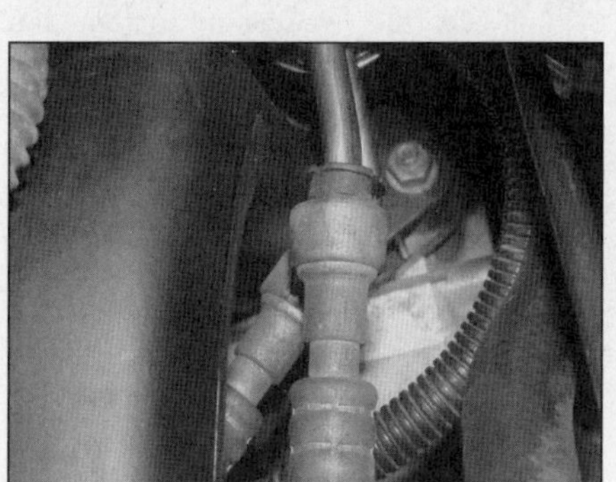

12.9 Press-in the black collar and disconnect the fuel supply and return pipes

12.11 Undo the four fuel rail bolts (arrowed)

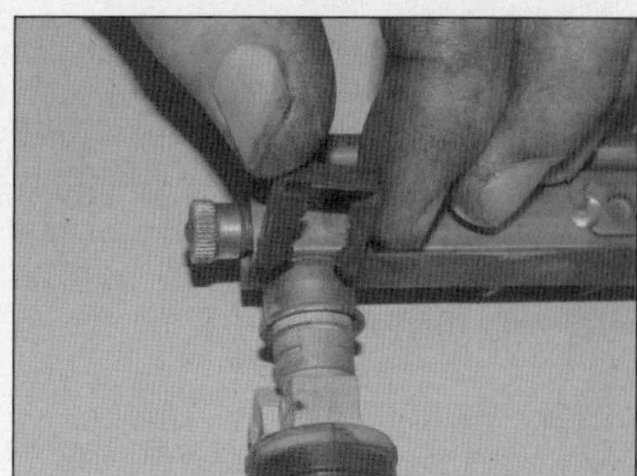

12.12 Prise out the clip and detach the injector from the rail

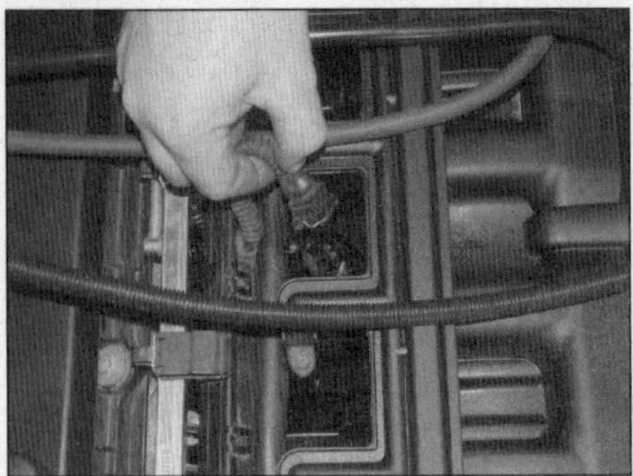
12.19a Disconnect the air intake temperature sensor . . .

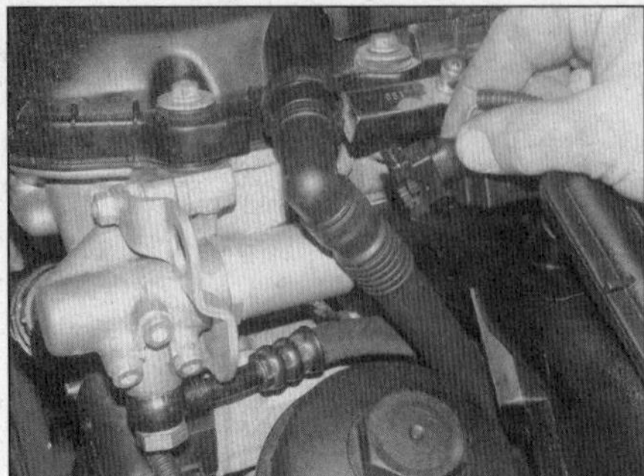
12.19b . . . and the VANOS solenoid . . .

12.19c . . . then release the wiring rail plug clips

Check the condition of the O-ring seals, and renew if necessary.

13 Lightly lubricate the fuel injector O-rings with a little petroleum jelly, or SAE 90 transmission oil.

14 Refit the injectors to the fuel rail, and retain them in place with the clips pushed into the grooves.

15 Further refitting is a reversal of removal.

M52TU and M54 engines

16 Pull up the rubber weatherstrip from the bulkhead at the rear of the engine compartment. Undo the four rotary fasteners, and three clips, and remove the housing at the centre of the bulkhead. Release the cables from the housing as it is withdrawn.

17 Prise out the plastic caps, undo the two screws, and remove the plastic cover from the over the injectors **(see illustration 12.6)**.

18 Disconnect the fuel regulator vacuum hose on the M52TU engine.

19 Disconnect the intake air temperature sensor wiring plug, and VANOS solenoid wiring plug, then pull the wiring rail from the fuel injectors **(see illustrations)**.

20 Mark the two oxygen sensor wiring connectors to aid refitting, unplug them and release them from the retaining clips.

21 Label the fuel supply and return pipes, then disconnect the pipes at the quick-release connectors. **Note:** *The M54 engine is equipped only with a supply hose to the fuel rail.*

22 Undo the four screws and remove the fuel rail complete with the injectors **(see illustration)**.

23 To remove a fuel injector from the fuel rail, proceed as follows.

a) Prise off the metal securing clip, using a screwdriver.

b) Pull the fuel injector from the fuel rail.

12.22 Undo the screws (arrowed) and remove the fuel rail

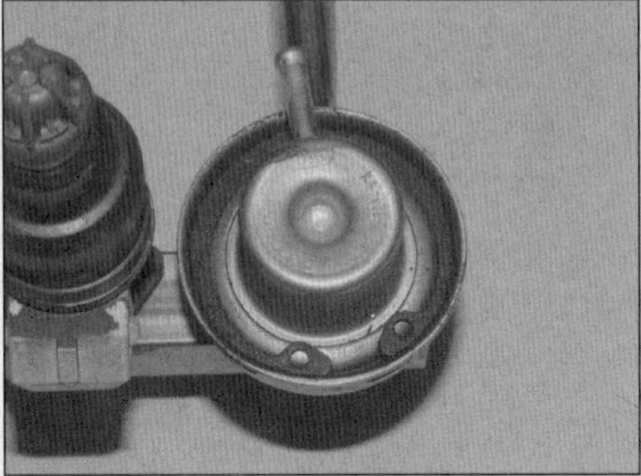
12.28a Note the position of the vacuum connection, then remove the circlip

12.28b Renew the regulator O-ring (arrowed)

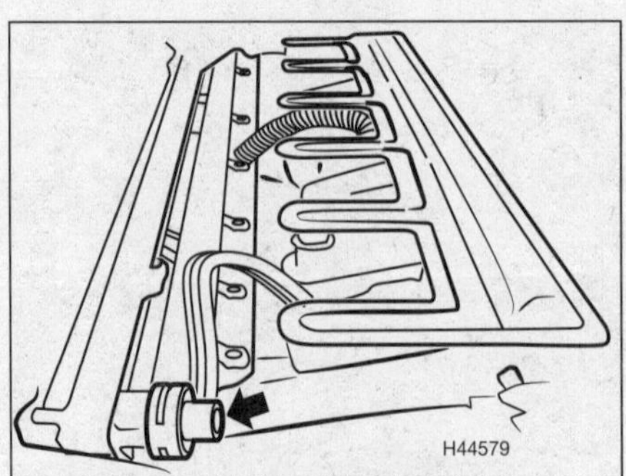

12.37 Fuel regulator (arrowed) – M52TU engine

24 Lightly lubricate the fuel injector O-rings with a little petroleum jelly, or acid-free grease.

25 Refit the injectors to the fuel rail, and retain them in place with the clips pushed into the grooves.

26 Further refitting is a reversal of removal.

Fuel pressure regulator

Warning: Refer to the warning notes in Section 1 before proceeding.

M52 engine – fuel rail-mounted

27 Remove the fuel rail and injectors as described previously in this Section.

28 Remove the retaining circlip, note the position of the vacuum connection, then remove the regulator from the fuel rail **(see illustrations)**. Discard the O-ring seals, new ones must be fitted.

29 Refitting is a reversal of removal.

M52 engine – underbody-mounted

30 Jack up the front of the vehicle and support it securely using axle stands (see *Jacking and vehicle support*).

31 Undo the four screws and remove the cover from the regulator.

32 Disconnect the vacuum pipe from the regulator.

33 Prise out the retaining clip and remove the regulator from the housing. Be prepared for fuel spillage. Discard the regulator O-ring seals, new ones must be fitted.

M52TU engine

34 Pull up the weatherstrip from the bulkhead at the rear of the engine compartment, then undo the four rotary fasteners and remove the housing from the centre of the bulkhead. Release the cables from the housing as it is withdrawn.

35 Prise out the plastic caps, undo the two screws, and remove the plastic cover from the over the injectors **(see illustration 12.6)**.

36 Disconnect the fuel regulator vacuum hose.

37 Note the position of the regulator vacuum connection, then remove the circlip and withdraw the regulator from the fuel rail **(see illustration)**. Discard the O-ring seals, new ones must be fitted.

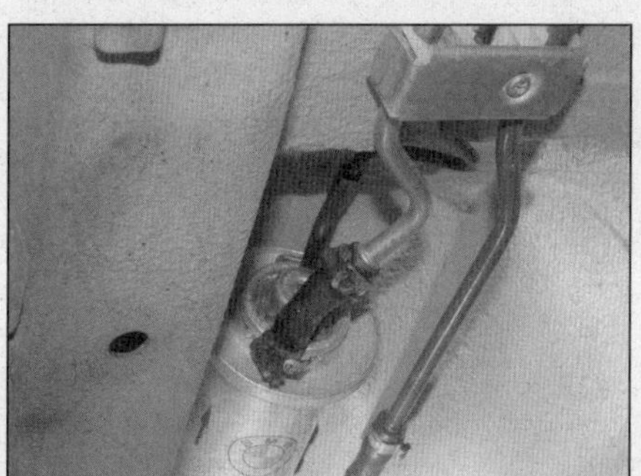
12.41 On M54 engines, the regulator is fitted to the end of the fuel filter

12.43a Disconnect the airflow sensor wiring plug – M52 engines . . .

12.43b . . . and M54 engines

38 Refitting is a reversal of removal, bearing in mind the following points.
- a) *Ensure that the regulator is pushed firmly into position in the end of the fuel rail.*
- b) *Make sure that the circlip correctly engages with the recess in the fuel rail..*
- c) *On completion, pressurise the fuel system (refit the fuel pump fuse and switch on the ignition) and check for leaks before starting the engine.*

M54 engine

39 On these engines, the regulator is fitted to the fuel filter assembly, adjacent to the left-hand chassis rail next to the transmission. Jack up the front of the vehicle and support it securely on axle stands (see *Jacking and vehicle support*).

40 Undo the six screws, and remove the filter cover.

41 Disconnect the regulator vacuum hose, prise out the circlip and withdraw the regulator from the filter body **(see illustration)**. Check the condition of the O-ring seals, and renew them if there is any sign of damage or wear.

42 Refitting is a reversal of removal, bearing in mind the following points.
- a) *Ensure that the regulator is pushed firmly into position in the end of the fuel filter.*
- b) *On completion, pressurise the fuel system (refit the fuel pump fuse and switch on the ignition) and check for leaks before starting the engine.*

Mass airflow sensor

Note: *A new airflow sensor seal may be required on refitting.*

M52 and M54 engines

43 Ensure the ignition is turned off, and disconnect the wiring plug from the sensor **(see illustrations)**.

44 Slacken the hose clamp, release the retaining clips and remove the sensor from the intake ducting and the air cleaner housing. Recover the seal. To improve access if required, remove the air filter housing retaining bolt, and the two screws securing the intake resonator chamber to the air filter housing as described earlier in this Chapter.

45 Refitting is a reversal of removal, but check the condition of the seal and renew if necessary.

M52TU engine

46 Ensure the ignition is turned off, and disconnect the wiring plug from the sensor.

47 Pull the vacuum hose from the intake ducting, release the retaining clips, and remove the sensor complete with the intake ducting. Recover the seal.

48 Refitting is a reversal of removal, but check the condition of the seal and renew if necessary.

Throttle position sensor

M52 engine

Note: *A new O-ring may be required on refitting.*

49 Ensure the ignition is turned off.

50 Disconnect the wiring plug from the sensor **(see illustration 11.5)**.

51 Unscrew the two securing screws, and withdraw the sensor from the throttle body. Where applicable, recover the O-ring

52 Refitting is a reversal of removal, but where applicable, check the condition of the O-ring and renew if necessary, and ensure that the O-ring is correctly positioned.

53 Note that adjustment of the unit is not necessary.

M52TU and M54 engines

54 The throttle position sensor is integral with the throttle body. Remove the throttle body as described in Section 11.

55 Refitting is a reversal of removal.

12.57 Coolant temperature sensor

56 Note that if a new throttle body/position sensor has been fitted, it will be necessary to clear the adaption values stored in the engine management ECM using specialist test equipment. Entrust this task to a BMW dealer or suitably-equipped specialist. Once cleared, new adaption values will be 'learnt' as the engine is started and used.

Coolant temperature sensor

57 See Chapter 3, Section 7 **(see illustration)**.

Crankshaft position sensor

58 On some engines, the sensor is located above the crankshaft pulley at the front of the engine, whilst on other engines, the sensor is located under the starter motor, and is accessible from under the vehicle.

Sensor above crankshaft pulley

59 Slacken the banjo bolt and disconnect the oil feed pipe to the VANOS adjustment unit. Recover the sealing washers.

60 Undo the bolt/nut and remove the engine lifting bracket from above the thermostat housing at the front of the engine.

61 Remove the wiring guide channelling from above the thermostat housing. The guide channel is unclipped by sliding it to the right.

62 Undo the retaining bolt, and remove the sensor **(see illustration)**. Disconnect the sensor wiring plug.

Sensor at the under the starter motor

63 Jack up the front of the vehicle and support it securely on axle stands (see

12.62 On some engines the crankshaft position sensor is located above the crankshaft pulley . . .

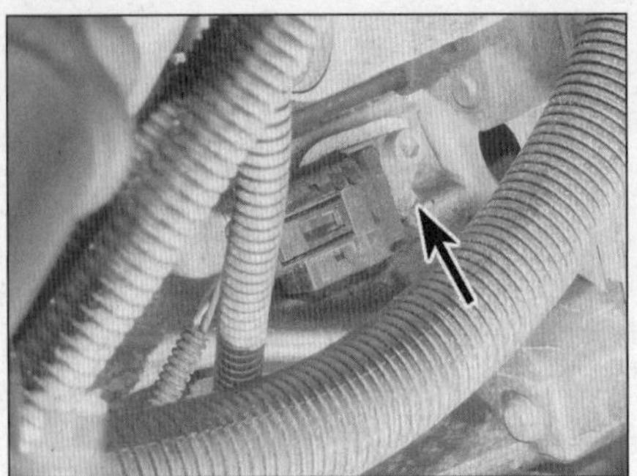

12.64 . . . whilst on others, it's below the starter motor (arrowed)

12.69 Renew the camshaft position sensor O-ring if necessary

12.71 Unscrew the VANOS solenoid

Jacking and vehicle support). Undo the screws and remove the engine undershield.

64 The sensor is located below the starter motor. Disconnect the sensor wiring plug, undo the retaining screw and remove the sensor **(see illustration)**. Recover the seal.

65 Refitting is a reversal of removal. Check the condition of the seal and renew if necessary.

Camshaft position sensor(s)

M52 engine

66 The sensor is located on the front left-hand side of the cylinder head. The sensor is fitted only to the intake camshaft. To access the sensor, first remove the VANOS solenoid valve as described in Chapter 2A.

67 With the solenoid removed, slacken the VANOS oil feed pipe banjo bolt.

68 Undo the retaining screw, and remove the sensor. Disconnect the wiring plug. Discard the screw, a new one must be fitted.

69 Refitting is a reversal of removal. Check the condition of the sealing ring, and renew if necessary **(see illustration)**. Tighten the new retaining screw to the specified torque.

M52TU and M54 engines – intake camshaft

70 Ensure the ignition is turned off, and remove the air cleaner housing as described in Section 2.

71 Disconnect the wiring plug, then unscrew the VANOS solenoid valve to access the sensor **(see illustration)**.

72 Trace the wiring back from the sensor, and disconnect the wiring plug where it clips to the cable ducting behind the alternator.

73 Undo the retaining screw and remove the sensor from the cylinder head **(see illustration)**. Recover the seal.

M52TU and M54 engines – exhaust camshaft

74 Ensure the ignition is switched off.

75 Disconnect the sensor wiring plug, undo the retaining screw and remove the sensor **(see illustration)**. Recover the seal.

76 Refitting is a reversal of removal. Check the condition of the seal and renew it if necessary.

Oxygen sensor

77 Refer to Chapter 4B.

Idle speed control valve

M52 engine

78 The valve is mounted on the underside of the intake manifold.

79 Ensure the ignition is switched off.

80 Remove the throttle body as described in Section 11.

81 Undo the bolt securing the oil dipstick guide tube to the manifold. **Note:** *Not all engines are fitted with a bolt securing the guide tube to the manifold.*

82 Undo the two screws and remove the idle speed control valve from the rubber sleeve in the manifold **(see illustration)**. Slacken the clip and detach the valve from the hose.

83 Refitting is a reversal of removal, but clean the sealing face of the valve, and check the condition of the seal. Renew the seal if necessary.

M52TU and M54 engines

84 Disconnect the battery negative lead as described in Chapter 5A.

85 The idle speed control valve is located below the intake manifold, and above the throttle body.

86 Remove the air cleaner housing as described in Section 2.

87 Pull the throttle cable outer (where fitted) from the support bracket on the throttle body.

88 Undo the two clamps and disconnect the intake ducting from the throttle body and idle speed control valve.

89 Disconnect the wiring plugs from the idle speed control valve and the manifold resonance flap actuator solenoid valve.

90 Undo the nut securing the cable support bracket, and the two screws securing the idle speed control valve bracket. Manoeuvre the valve from the manifold **(see illustration)**.

12.73 Undo the screw and remove the intake camshaft position sensor

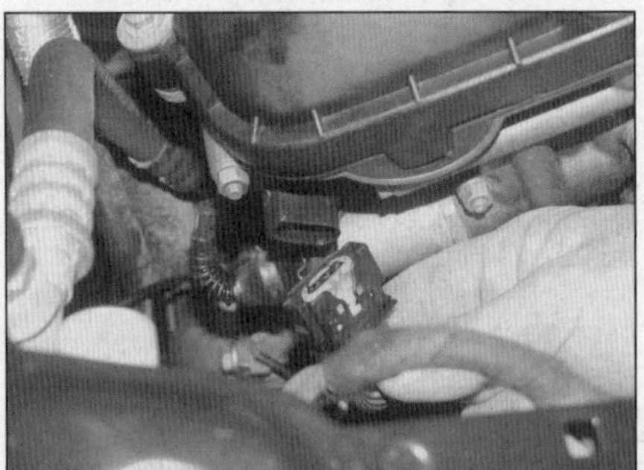

12.75 Disconnect the exhaust camshaft position sensor wiring plug

12.82 Undo the two screws (arrowed) and remove the idle speed control valve – M52 engine

12.90 Undo the two screws (arrowed) and remove the idle speed control valve – M52TU and M54 engines

12.99 Disconnect the intake air temperature sensor wiring plug (arrowed) – M52 engine

12.102 Intake air temperature sensor (arrowed) – M52TU and M54 engines

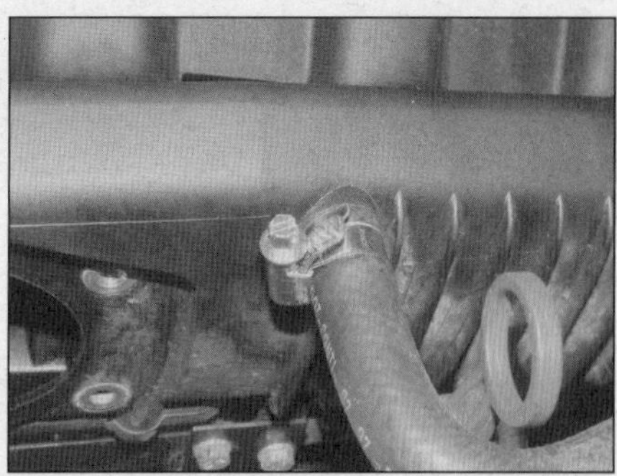

13.7 When refitting the servo vacuum hose, use a traditional hose clamp

Discard the seal between the valve and the manifold, a new one must be fitted.

91 Smear the new seal with grease and fit it to the intake manifold. Push the idle speed control valve into place and securely tighten the bracket retaining screws/nuts.

92 The remainder of refitting is a reversal of removal.

Main engine management relay

93 Ensure the ignition is switched off. Release the clip(s) and pull the left-hand air duct from the pollen filter housing. Rotate the air duct upwards and disconnect it from the engine compartment bulkhead. Disconnect the bonnet light switch, release the clip and remove the pollen filter cover, then release the clip and remove the pollen filter housing.

94 Working in the left-hand corner of the engine compartment, undo the four screws, and remove the cover from the electrical box **(see illustration 12.2f)**.

95 Pull the relay from the relay socket.

96 Refitting is a reversal of removal.

Throttle pedal position sensor

97 The throttle pedal position sensor is integral with the pedal assembly. Refer to Section 6 for the removal procedure.

Intake air temperature sensor

M52 engine

98 Remove the throttle body as described in Section 11.

99 Disconnect the sensor wiring plug, then depress the catch and remove the sensor from the manifold **(see illustration)**. Check the condition of the sealing ring, and renew if necessary.

100 Refitting is a reversal of removal.

M52 and M54 engines

101 Prise out the plastic caps, undo the two screws, and remove the plastic cover from the over the injectors **(see illustration 12.6)**.

102 Disconnect the sensor wiring plug, then depress the catch and pull the sensor from the manifold **(see illustration)**. Check the condition of the sealing ring, and renew if necessary.

103 Refitting is a reversal of removal.

13 Manifolds – removal and refitting

Intake manifold

M52 engine

Note: *New manifold seals will be required on refitting.*

1 Ensure the ignition is switched off.

2 To allow sufficient clearance, remove the left- and right-hand air ducting from the engine compartment **(see illustration 12.2a)**.

3 Remove both pollen filters (see Chapter 1), then disconnect the bonnet light switch, release the clip at the front of each pollen filter housing, then lift the housings away disengaging the rubber strips as the housings are removed.

4 Remove the 3 clips at the top, then rotate the 4 fasteners underneath a quarter turn, and remove the rear bulkhead cover. Unclip the various pipes from the cover as it is withdrawn, noting their fitted positions.

5 Remove the air cleaner housing and mass airflow sensor as previously described in this Chapter.

6 Remove the fuel injection rail (Section 12) and throttle body (Section 11).

7 Carefully cut the metal clip and disconnect the vacuum servo hose from the manifold **(see illustration)**. When refitting, secure the hose with a normal worm-drive clamp.

8 Squeeze together the two opposite sides of the collar, and disconnect the crankcase breather pipe from the cylinder head cover **(see illustration 12.7a)**.

9 Undo the bolt securing the oil dipstick guide tube to the manifold. **Note:** *Not all engines have a bolt securing the guide tube to the manifold.*

10 Release the clip and disconnect the return hose from the cyclone oil separator at the dipstick guide tube **(see illustration)**.

11 Undo the nuts securing the support bracket to the cylinder block at the front of the manifold, and the nut securing the support bracket to the cylinder block at the rear of the manifold **(see illustration)**. At the front support bracket, release the wiring harness from the retaining clips.

12 Remove the plastic cover, unscrew the battery positive connection bolt, squeeze together the side of the retaining clip and push the connection downwards **(see illustration)**.

13.10 Disconnect the oil return hose (arrowed)

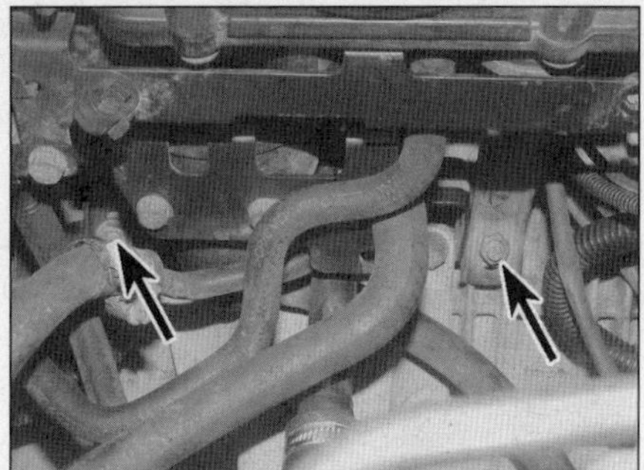

13.11 Undo the nuts (arrowed) securing the manifold front and rear support brackets

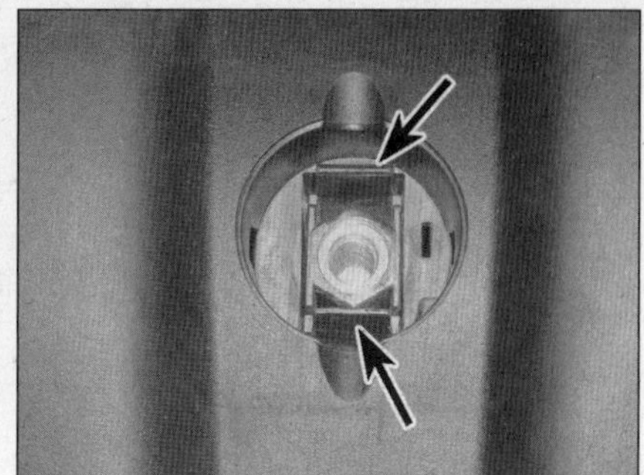

13.12 Squeeze together the retaining clips (arrowed) and push it downwards

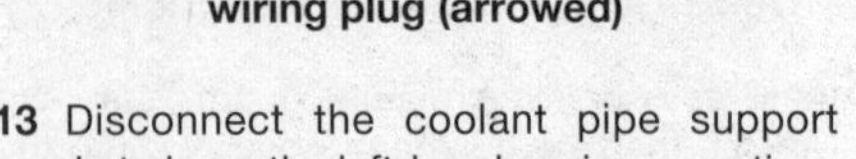

13.15 Disconnect the tank vent valve wiring plug (arrowed)

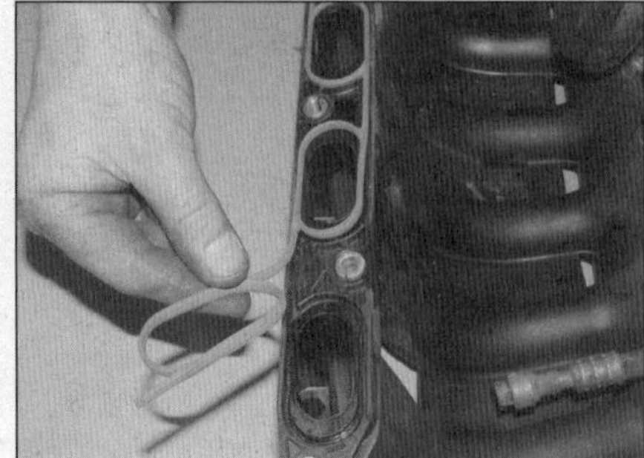

13.17 If necessary, renew the intake manifold seals

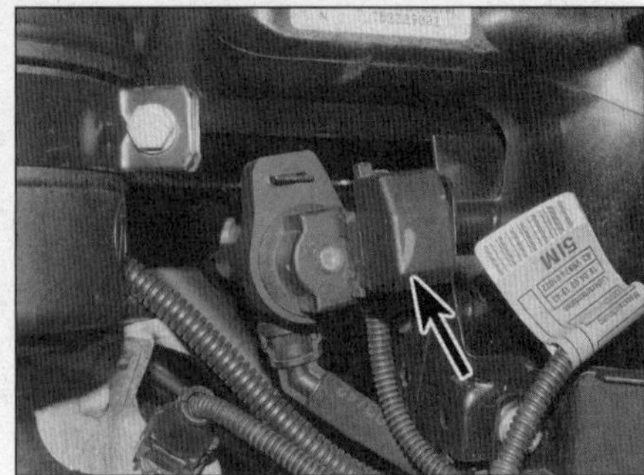

13.28 Disconnect the tank vent valve wiring plug (arrowed)

13 Disconnect the coolant pipe support bracket above the left-hand engine mounting.

14 Disconnect the wiring plugs from the intake air temperature sensor, and idle speed control valve.

15 Disconnect the tank vent valve wiring plug, then push the valve downwards through its rubber mounting **(see illustration)**. Disconnect the valve lower hose as it is withdrawn.

16 Release the hoses at the rear of the manifold from their retaining clips, then depress the collars, and disconnect the fuel supply and return hoses from the pipes on the inner wing, having marked them for refitting, or note their fitted positions.

17 Undo the bolts/nuts and lift off the manifold **(see illustration)**. Recover the seals.

18 Refitting is a reversal of removal, bearing in mind the following points.

a) Check the condition of the seals, and renew if necessary.

b) Ensure that all wires and hoses are correctly routed and reconnected as noted before removal.

c) Reconnect and if necessary adjust the throttle cable with reference to Section 5.

M52TU and M54 engines

19 Ensure the ignition is switched off.

20 To allow sufficient clearance, remove the left- and right-hand air ducting from the engine compartment **(see illustration 12.2a)**.

21 Remove both pollen filters (see Chapter 1), then disconnect the bonnet light switch, release the clip at the front of each pollen filter housing, then lift the housings away disengaging the rubber strips as the housings are removed.

22 Remove the 3 clips at the top, then rotate the 4 fasteners underneath a quarter turn, and remove the rear bulkhead cover.

23 Remove the air cleaner housing and mass airflow sensor as previously described in this Chapter.

24 Remove the fuel injection rail (Section 12) and throttle body (Section 11).

25 Disconnect the vacuum servo hose from the check valve.

26 Squeeze together the two opposite sides of the collar, and disconnect the crankcase breather pipe from the cylinder head cover **(see illustration 12.7a)**.

27 Undo the bolt securing the oil dipstick guide tube to the mounting.

28 Disconnect the tank venting valve wiring plug, and detach the valve from the bracket on the manifold **(see illustration)**.

29 On M52TU engines, unclip the fuel supply and return hoses from the support bracket on the manifold.

30 Unclip the knock sensor(s) wiring plug from the mounting bracket on the underside of the manifold.

31 Disconnect the VANOS solenoid wiring plug at the left-hand front side of the cylinder head (if not already done so).

32 Note their fitted positions, then release any wiring harness(s) from the retaining clips on the manifold and support bracket (under the manifold).

33 Undo the nine nuts securing the manifold to the cylinder head, and the nut securing the manifold support bracket to the cylinder block (under the manifold), and remove the manifold from the cylinder head. As the manifold is withdrawn, feed the starter motor cable through the manifold **(see illustration)**. Recover the seals.

34 Check the condition of the seals and renew if necessary.

35 Refitting is a reversal of removal.

Exhaust manifold

36 Jack up the front of the vehicle, and support it securely on axle stands (see *Jacking and vehicle support*). Undo the screws and remove the engine undershield.

37 Undo the nuts/bolts, and separate the exhaust pipe from the manifold **(see illustration)**.

38 Prise out the plastic caps, undo the two screws, and remove the plastic cover from the over the injectors.

39 Prise out the plastic caps, undo the two nuts, remove the oil filler cap, and remove the plastic cover from the cylinder head.

40 Trace back the wiring from the oxygen sensor(s), and disconnect the wiring plugs. Label the plugs to ensure correct refitting. Unclip the cable harness from any retainers on the manifolds.

41 Starting with the front exhaust manifold, undo the nuts and manoeuvre the manifold from the engine compartment **(see illustration)**. Take great care not to damage the oxygen sensor fitted to the manifold. Discard the gasket.

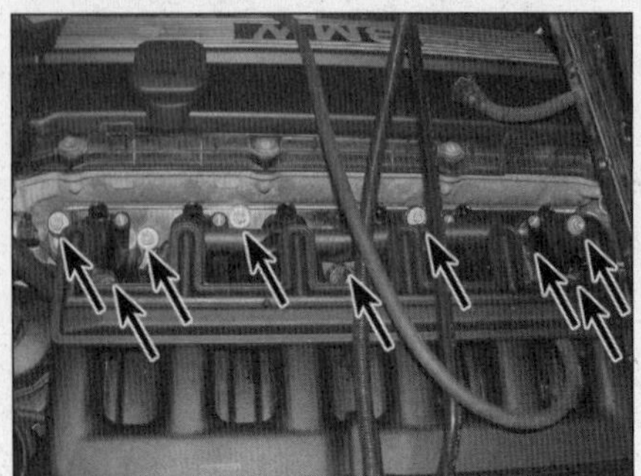

13.33 Intake manifold nuts (arrowed)

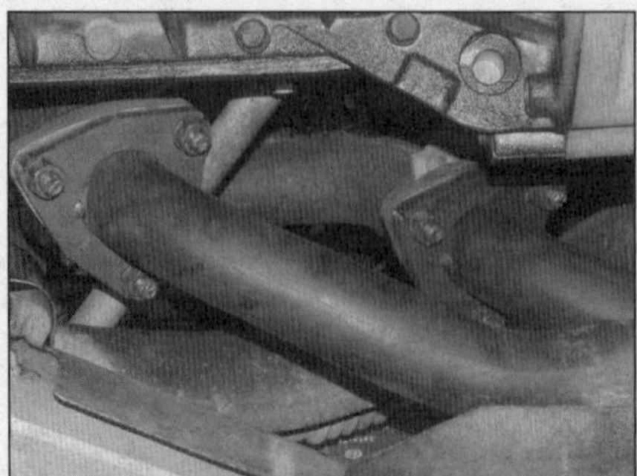

13.37 Undo the nuts and separate the exhaust pipe from the manifold

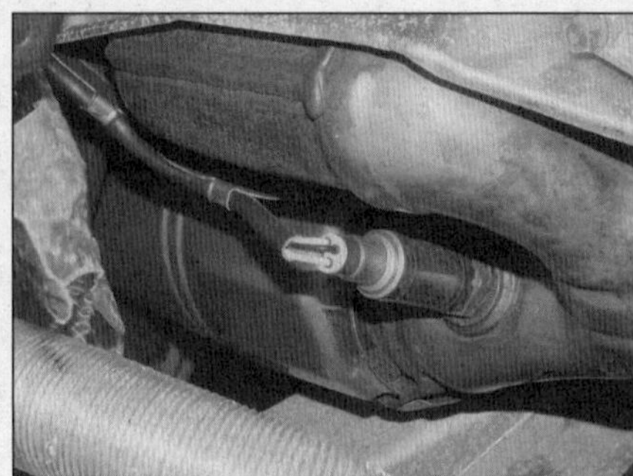

13.41 Take care not to damage the oxygen sensors

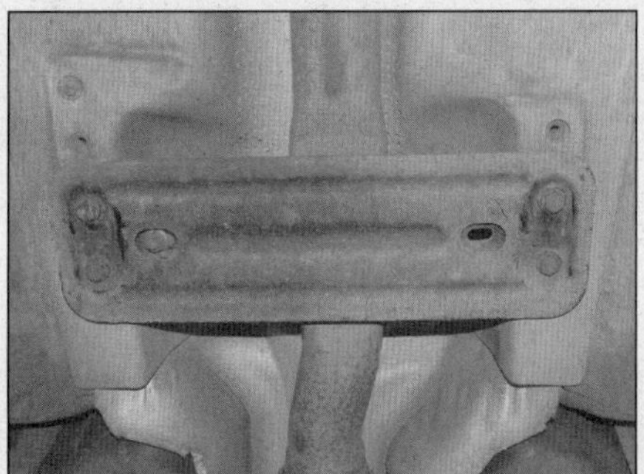

14.3 The rear plate is attached to the exhaust by rubber mountings

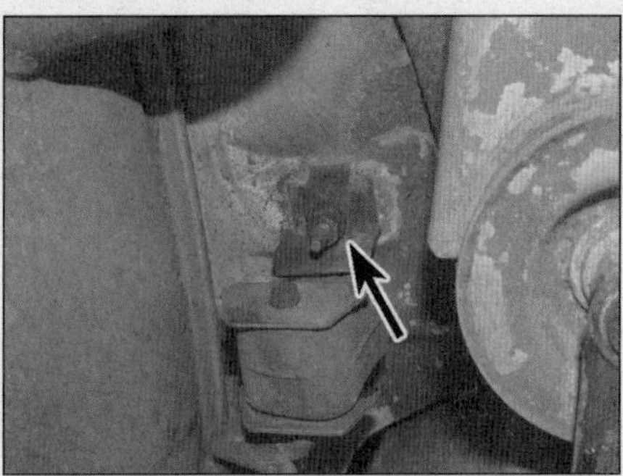

14.5 Undo the nut (arrowed) and detach the mounting from the vehicle body

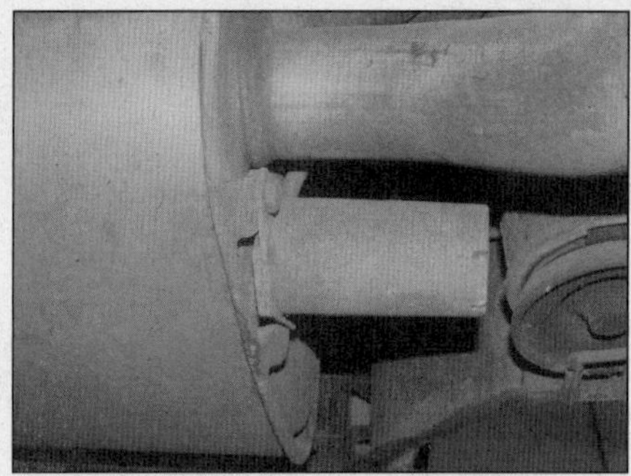

14.7 On M54 engines, the vibration damper can be unbolted for re-use

42 Undo the nuts and remove the rear exhaust manifold. Again take great care not to damage the oxygen sensor. Discard the gasket.

43 Refitting is a reversal of removal, noting the following points:

a) Apply some anti-seize high-temperature grease to the manifold studs.

b) Always renew the manifold gaskets.

c) Tighten the manifold nuts to the specified torque.

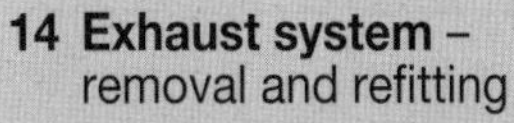

14 Exhaust system – removal and refitting

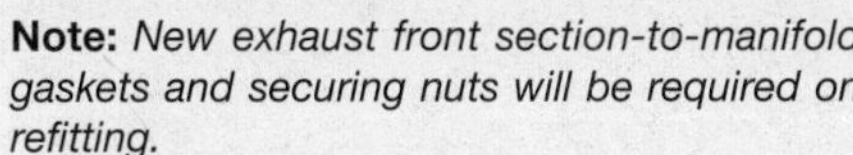

Note: *New exhaust front section-to-manifold gaskets and securing nuts will be required on refitting.*

Removal

1 Jack up the vehicle and support securely on axle stands (see *Jacking and vehicle support*). Undo the screws and remove the engine undershield.

2 Trace back the oxygen sensor(s) wiring and disconnect the plug(s). Free the wiring from the guide.

3 Undo the bolts, and remove the reinforcement plates from across the transmission tunnel. Note that the rear reinforcement plate is attached to the exhaust system by rubber mountings **(see illustration)**.

4 Unscrew the securing nuts, and disconnect the exhaust front section from the manifolds. Recover the gaskets **(see illustration 13.37)**.

5 Slacken the retaining nut securing the exhaust system rear mounting bracket **(see illustration)**. **Note:** *On M54 engines, undo the bolt securing the central silencer mounting bracket to the body.*

6 Withdraw the complete exhaust system from under the vehicle.

Caution: Enlist the help of an assistant, then complete exhaust system weighs in excess of 40 kgs.

7 To remove the heat shield, undo the nuts and bolts, then lower it to the ground. On M54 engine, the vibration damper fitted to the existing rear silencer of the exhaust system can be unbolted and fitted to the new silencer **(see illustration)**.

Refitting

8 Refitting is a reversal of removal, bearing in mind the following points:

a) Use new gaskets when reconnecting the exhaust front section to the manifold. Also use new nuts, and coat the threads of the new nuts with copper grease.

b) Check the position of the tailpipes in relation to the cut-out in the rear valence, and if necessary adjust the exhaust mountings to give sufficient clearance between the system and the valence.

Chapter 4 Part B:
Emission control systems

Contents

Degrees of difficulty

Easy, suitable for novice with little experience 	**Fairly easy,** suitable for beginner with some experience 	**Fairly difficult,** suitable for competent DIY mechanic	**Difficult,** suitable for experienced DIY mechanic	**Very difficult,** suitable for expert DIY or professional

Specifications

Torque wrench setting	Nm	lbf ft
Oxygen sensor to exhaust system	50	37

1 General information

1 All models have various built-in fuel system features which help to minimise emissions, including a crankcase emission control system, catalytic converter, and an evaporative emission control system.

2 Note that leaded fuel or LRP must not be used.

Crankcase emission control

3 To reduce the emission of unburned hydrocarbons from the crankcase into the atmosphere, the engine is sealed, and the blow-by gases and oil vapour are drawn from the crankcase and the cylinder head cover, through an oil separator, into the inlet tract to be burned by the engine during normal combustion.

4 Under conditions of high manifold depression (idling, deceleration) the gases will be sucked positively out of the crankcase. Under conditions of low manifold depression (acceleration, full-throttle running) the gases are forced out of the crankcase by the (relatively) higher crankcase pressure; if the engine is worn, the raised crankcase pressure (due to increased blow-by) will cause some of the flow to return under all manifold conditions.

Exhaust emission control

5 To minimise the amount of pollutants which escape into the atmosphere, all models are fitted with a catalytic converter in the exhaust system. The system is of the 'closed-loop' type; two or three oxygen (lambda) sensors in the exhaust system provides the fuel injection/ignition system ECM with constant feedback, enabling the ECM to adjust the mixture to provide the best possible conditions for the converter to operate.

6 The oxygen sensor(s) has a built-in heating element, controlled by the ECM, to quickly bring the sensor's tip to an efficient operating temperature. The sensor's tip is sensitive to oxygen, and sends the ECM a varying voltage depending on the amount of oxygen in the exhaust gases. If the inlet air/fuel mixture is too rich, the exhaust gases are low in oxygen, so the sensor sends a low-voltage signal. The voltage rises as the mixture weakens and the amount of oxygen in the exhaust gases rises. Peak conversion efficiency of all major pollutants occurs if the inlet air/fuel mixture is maintained at the chemically-correct ratio for the complete combustion of petrol – 14.7 parts (by weight) of air to 1 part of fuel (the 'stoichiometric' ratio). The sensor output voltage alters in a large step at this point, the ECM using the signal change as a reference point, and correcting the inlet air/fuel mixture accordingly by altering the fuel injector pulse width (the length of time that the injector is open).

Evaporative emission control

7 To minimise the escape into the atmosphere of unburned hydrocarbons, an evaporative emissions control system is fitted to all models. The fuel tank filler cap is sealed, and a charcoal canister, mounted under the rear of the vehicle, collects the petrol vapours generated in the tank when the car is parked. The canister stores them until they can be cleared from the canister (under the control of the fuel injection/ignition system ECM) via the purge solenoid valve. When the valve is opened, the fuel vapours pass into the inlet tract, to be burned by the engine during normal combustion.

8 To ensure that the engine runs correctly when it is cold and/or idling, the ECM does not open the purge control valve until the engine has warmed-up and is under load; the valve solenoid is then modulated on and off, to allow the stored vapour to pass into the inlet tract.

Secondary air injection

9 M52TU engine models may be equipped with a system which is designed to shorten the amount of time the catalytic converter takes to warm-up. In order to function correctly, the catalytic converter needs to be at a temperature of at least 300°C. This temperature level is achieved by the action of the exhaust gases passing through. In order to reduce the catalyst warm-up phase, a secondary air injection pump injects fresh air just behind the exhaust valves in the exhaust manifold. This oxygen rich mixture causes an 'afterburning' effect in the exhaust, greatly increasing the gas temperature, and therefore the catalyst temperature. The system is only active during cold starts (up to 33°C coolant temperature), and only operates for approximately 2 minutes.

2 Emission control systems – component renewal

Crankcase emission control

1 The components of this system require no routine attention, other than to check that the hoses are clear and undamaged at regular intervals.

Charcoal canister renewal

2 The canister is located behind the left-hand rear wheel arch liner. Jack up the rear and support it securely on axle stands (see *Jacking and vehicle support*). Remove the left-hand rear roadwheel.

3 Remove the left-hand rear wheel arch liner as described in Chapter 11, Section 22.

4 Disconnect the hoses from the canister. If the hoses are secured by plastic locking clips, squeeze the sides of the clips to release them from the connection on the canister. Note the hose locations to ensure correct refitting.

5 The canister is removed by lifting it up from position. Note the three mountings, with corresponding locating holes.

6 Refitting is a reversal of removal, but ensure that the hoses are correctly reconnected as noted before removal, and make sure that the hose securing clips are correctly engaged.

Purge solenoid valve renewal

M52 engine

7 The valve is located on a bracket, adjacent to the left-hand suspension turret in the engine compartment.

8 Ensure the ignition is switched off.

9 Squeeze together the sides of the locking collar, and disconnect the hose from the side of the valve.

10 Disconnect the wiring plug from the valve **(see illustration)**.

11 Pull the valve up, so that the remaining hose can be disconnected.

12 Pull the valve from its mounting.

13 Refitting is a reversal of removal, but make sure that all hoses are correctly reconnected as noted before removal.

M52TU and M54 engines

14 The valve is located under the intake manifold. Remove the air cleaner housing as described in Chapter 4A.

15 Reach under the manifold, and disconnect the valve wiring plug **(see illustration)**.

16 Depress the locking catch and disconnect the hose from the underside of the valve.

17 Disconnect the remaining hose and pull the valve from the rubber holder.

18 Refitting is a reversal of removal.

Catalytic converter renewal

M52 engine

19 The catalytic converters are integral with the front section of the exhaust system. In order to renew a catalytic converter, it is necessary to renew the front section of the exhaust system.

M52TU and M54 engines

20 The catalytic converters are integral with the exhaust manifolds. In order to renew them, it is necessary to renew the manifolds.

Oxygen sensor renewal

Note: *Ensure that the exhaust system is cold before attempting to remove the oxygen sensor.*

21 The oxygen sensor(s) is screwed into the front exhaust down pipes before and after the catalytic converters.

2.10 Disconnect the solenoid valve wiring plug (arrowed) – M52 engine

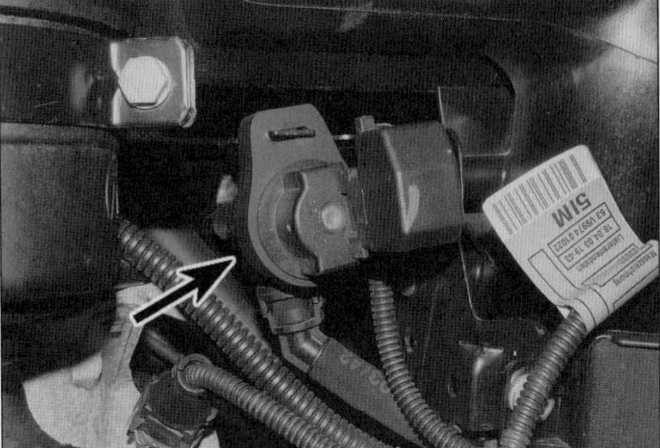

2.15 Purge solenoid valve (arrowed) – M52TU and M54 engines

2.25a Oxygen sensor connectors – M52 engine

2.25b Oxygen sensor connectors – M52TU and M54 engines

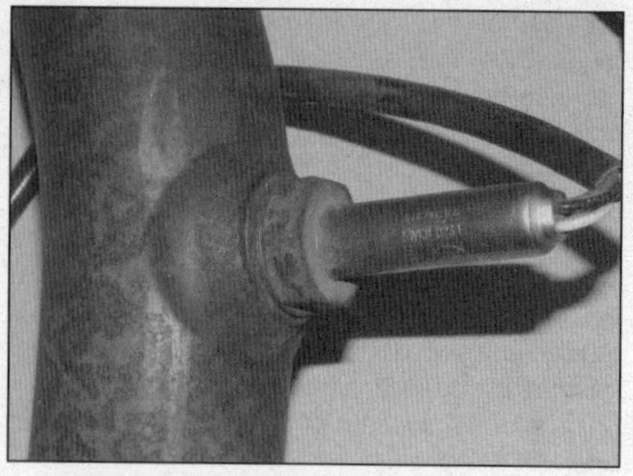

2.27 Unscrew the oxygen sensor – M52 engine

22 Ensure the ignition is switched off.

23 Apply the handbrake, then jack up the front of the vehicle and support securely on axle stands (see *Jacking and vehicle support*). Undo the screws and remove the engine undershield.

Note: *Due to the limited access, if the sensor for cylinders 4 to 6 is to be removed, the complete exhaust system must be removed.*

24 Prise out the plastic caps, undo the two screws, and remove the plastic cover from over the injectors.

25 Unclip the oxygen sensor cables from the retainer, and disconnect the wiring plugs. Label the connectors to ensure they are refitted to their original locations **(see illustrations)**.

26 Remove the exhaust manifolds as described in Chapter 4A.

27 Using a oxygen sensor removal socket, unscrew the sensor and remove it from the exhaust pipe **(see illustration)**.

28 Refitting is a reverse of the removal procedure, noting the following points:

a) Tighten the sensor to the specified torque.

b) Check that the wiring is correctly routed, and in no danger of contacting the exhaust system.

c) Ensure that no lubricant or dirt comes into contact with the sensor probe.

d) Apply a smear of copper based, high-temperature anti-seize grease to the sensor threads prior to refitting.

3 Catalytic converter – general information and precautions

The catalytic converter is a reliable and simple device, which needs no maintenance in itself, but there are some facts of which an owner should be aware, if the converter is to function properly for its full service life.

a) DO NOT use leaded petrol or LRP in a car equipped with a catalytic converter – the lead will coat the precious metals, reducing their converting efficiency, and will eventually destroy the converter.

b) Always keep the ignition and fuel systems well-maintained in accordance with the manufacturer's schedule.

c) If the engine develops a misfire, do not drive the car at all (or at least as little as possible) until the fault is cured.

d) DO NOT push- or tow-start the car – this will soak the catalytic converter in unburned fuel, causing it to overheat when the engine does start.

e) DO NOT switch off the ignition at high engine speeds.

f) DO NOT use fuel or engine oil additives – these may contain substances harmful to the catalytic converter.

g) DO NOT continue to use the car if the engine burns oil to the extent of leaving a visible trail of blue smoke.

h) Remember that the catalytic converter operates at very high temperatures. DO NOT, therefore, park the car in dry undergrowth, or over long grass or piles of dead leaves after a long run.

i) Remember that the catalytic converter is FRAGILE – do not strike it with tools during servicing work.

j) In some cases, a sulphurous smell (like that of rotten eggs) may be noticed from the exhaust. This is common to many catalytic converter-equipped cars, and once the car has covered a few thousand miles the problem should disappear.

k) The catalytic converter, used on a well-maintained and well-driven car, should last for between 50 000 and 100 000 miles – if the converter is no longer effective, it must be renewed.

Chapter 5 Part A:
Starting and charging systems

Contents

Degrees of difficulty

Easy, suitable for novice with little experience 	**Fairly easy,** suitable for beginner with some experience 	**Fairly difficult,** suitable for competent DIY mechanic	**Difficult,** suitable for experienced DIY mechanic	**Very difficult,** suitable for expert DIY or professional

Specifications

System type	12 volt negative earth	
Alternator		
Regulated voltage (at 1500 rpm engine speed with no electrical equipment switched on)	13.5 to 14.2 volts	
Starter motor		
Rated output	1.4 kW	
Torque wrench settings	**Nm**	**lbf ft**
Starter motor support bracket-to-engine bolts	47	35
Starter motor support bracket-to-starter motor nuts	5	4
Starter motor-to-gearbox/transmission nuts and bolts	47	35

* *Do not re-use*

1 General information and precautions

General information

The engine electrical system consists mainly of the charging and starting systems. Because of their engine-related functions, these components are covered separately from the body electrical devices such as the lights, instruments, etc (which are covered in Chapter 12). For information on the ignition system refer to Part B of this Chapter.

The electrical system is of the 12 volt negative earth type.

The battery is of the low maintenance or 'maintenance-free' (sealed for life) type and is charged by the alternator, which is belt-driven from the crankshaft pulley.

The starter motor is of the pre-engaged type incorporating an integral solenoid. On starting, the solenoid moves the drive pinion into engagement with the flywheel ring gear before the starter motor is energised. Once the engine has started, a one-way clutch prevents the motor armature being driven by the engine until the pinion disengages from the flywheel.

An earth strap is fitted between the right-hand engine mounting and the vehicle chassis **(see illustration)**.

Precautions

Further details of the various systems are given in the relevant Sections of this Chapter. While some repair procedures are given, the usual course of action is to renew the component concerned. The owner whose interest extends beyond mere component renewal should obtain a copy of the *Automotive Electrical & Electronic Systems Manual*, available from the publishers of this manual.

Warning: It is necessary to take extra care when working on the electrical system to avoid damage to semi-conductor devices (diodes and transistors), and to avoid the risk of personal injury. In addition to the precautions given in 'Safety first!' at the beginning of this manual, observe the following when working on the system:

- ***Always remove rings, watches, etc, before working on the electrical system. Even with the battery disconnected, capacitive discharge could occur if a component's live terminal is earthed through a metal object. This could cause a shock or nasty burn.***
- ***Do not reverse the battery connections. Components such as the alternator, electronic control units, or any other components having semi-conductor circuitry could be irreparably damaged.***
- ***If the engine is being started using jump leads and a slave battery, make use of the built-in jump lead connections points (see 'Jump starting', at the beginning of this manual). This also applies when connecting a battery charger.***
- ***Never disconnect the battery terminals, the alternator, any electrical wiring or any test instruments when the engine is running.***
- ***Do not allow the engine to turn the alternator when the alternator is not connected.***
- ***Never 'test' for alternator output by 'flashing' the output lead to earth.***
- ***Never use an ohmmeter of the type incorporating a hand-cranked generator for circuit or continuity testing.***
- ***Always ensure that the battery negative lead is disconnected when working on the electrical system.***
- ***Before using electric-arc welding equipment on the car, disconnect the battery, alternator and components such as the fuel injection/ignition electronic control unit to protect them from the risk of damage.***
- ***If a radio/cassette/CD unit with a built-in security code is fitted, note the following precautions. If the power source to the unit is cut, the anti-theft system will activate. Even if the power source is immediately reconnected, the radio/cassette unit will not function until the correct security code has been entered. Therefore, if you do not know the correct security code for the radio/cassette unit do not disconnect the battery negative terminal of the battery or remove the radio/cassette/CD unit from the vehicle. Refer to 'Audio unit anti-theft system' Section for further information.***

2 Electrical fault finding – general information

Refer to Chapter 12.

3 Battery – testing and charging

Note: *The following is intended as a guide only. Always refer to the manufacturer's recommendations (often printed on a label attached to the battery) before charging a battery.*

1 All models are fitted with a maintenance-free battery in production, which should require no maintenance under normal operating conditions.

2 If the condition of the battery is suspect, remove the battery as described in Section 4, and check that the electrolyte level in each cell is up to the MAX mark on the outside of the battery case (about 5.0 mm above the tops of the plates in the cells). If necessary, the electrolyte level can be topped-up by removing the cell plugs from the top of the battery and adding distilled water (not acid).

1.1 An earth strap is bolted from the right-hand engine mounting (arrowed) to the vehicle body

3 An approximate check on battery condition can be made by checking the specific gravity of the electrolyte, using the following as a guide.

4 Use a hydrometer to make the check and compare the results with the following table. The temperatures quoted are ambient (air) temperatures. Note that the specific gravity readings assume an electrolyte temperature of 15°C (60°F); for every 10°C (18°F) below 15°C (60°F) subtract 0.007. For every 10°C (18°F) above 15°C (60°F) add 0.007.

	Above 25°C(77°F)	Below 25°C (77°F)
Fully-charged	*1.210 to 1.230*	*1.270 to 1.290*
70% charged	*1.170 to 1.190*	*1.230 to 1.250*
Discharged	*1.050 to 1.070*	*1.110 to 1.130*

5 If the battery condition is suspect, first check the specific gravity of electrolyte in each cell. A variation of 0.040 or more between any cells indicates loss of electrolyte or deterioration of the internal plates.

6 If the specific gravity variation is 0.040 or more, the battery should be renewed. If the cell variation is satisfactory but the battery is discharged, it should be charged in accordance with the manufacturer's instructions.

7 If testing the battery using a voltmeter, connect the voltmeter across the battery. A fully-charged battery should give a reading of 12.5 volts or higher. The test is only accurate if the battery has not been subjected to any kind of charge for the previous six hours. If this is not the case, switch on the headlights for 30 seconds, then wait four to five minutes before testing the battery after switching off the headlights. All other electrical circuits must be switched off, so check that the doors and tailgate are fully shut when making the test.

8 Generally speaking, if the voltage reading is less than 12.2 volts, then the battery is discharged, whilst a reading of 12.2 to 12.4 volts indicates a partially-discharged condition.

9 If the battery is to be charged with a trickle charger, locate the earth point connection on

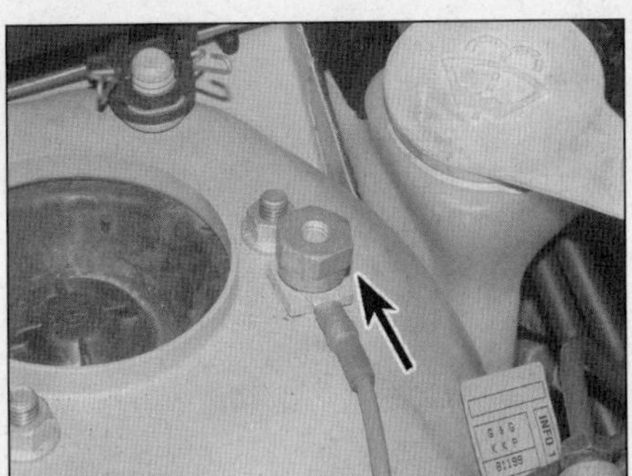

3.9 Connect the charger negative lead to the earth point connection (arrowed) on the right-hand suspension turret in the engine compartment

the right-hand front suspension turret, and the positive connection point unto the plastic cover on the intake manifold, and connect the charger leads to the connections **(see illustration)**. If a rapid, or boost charger is used (or if in doubt as to which type of charger you have), remove the battery from the vehicle (Section 4) and charge it in accordance with its maker's instructions.

4 Battery – removal and refitting

Note: *When the battery is disconnected, any fault codes stored in the engine management ECM memory will be erased. If any faults are suspected, do not disconnect the battery until the fault codes have been read by a BMW dealer or specialist. If the vehicle is fitted with a code-protected radio, refer to 'Audio unit anti-theft system'.*

Note: *After reconnecting the battery, it may be necessary to carry out the sunroof initialisation procedure as described in Section 21 of Chapter 11.*

Removal

1 The battery is located beneath a cover on the right-hand side of the luggage compartment.

2 Open the boot lid/tailgate, and open the right-hand side storage panel.

3 Slacken the clamp nut, and disconnect the clamp from the battery negative (earth) terminal **(see illustrations)**.

4 Remove the insulation cover (where fitted) and disconnect the positive terminal lead in the same way **(see illustrations)**.

5 Slacken the clamping plate bolt, then unscrew the bolts, and remove the battery retaining clamp **(see illustrations)**.

6 Lift the battery from its housing, disconnect the vent hose as the battery is removed. Take care as the battery is heavy!

Refitting

7 Refitting is a reversal of removal, but smear petroleum jelly on the terminals after reconnecting the leads to combat corrosion, and always reconnect the positive lead first and the negative lead last.

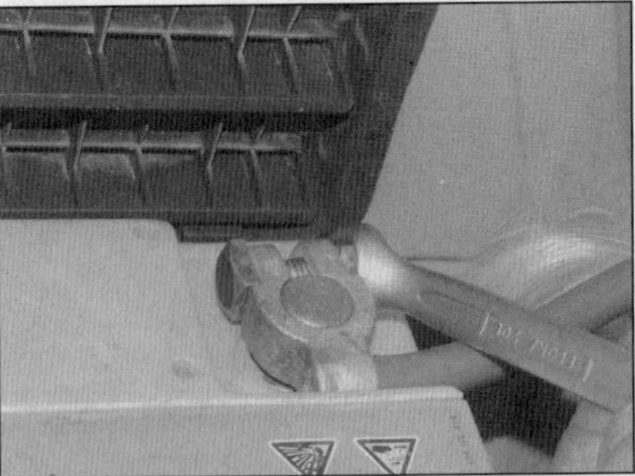

4.3a Slacken the negative terminal clamp bolt . . .

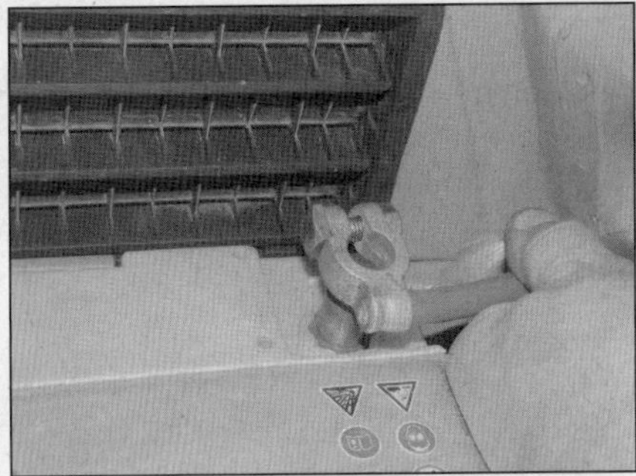

4.3b . . . and disconnect the clamp from the terminal

5 Charging system – testing

Note: *Refer to the warnings given in 'Safety first!' and in Section 1 of this Chapter before starting work.*

1 If the ignition warning light fails to illuminate when the ignition is switched on, first check the alternator wiring connections for security. If satisfactory, check that the warning light bulb has not blown, and that the bulbholder is secure in its location in the instrument panel. If the light still fails to illuminate, check the continuity of the warning light feed wire from the alternator to the bulbholder. If all is satisfactory, the alternator is at fault and should be renewed or taken to an auto-electrician for testing and repair.

2 If the ignition warning light illuminates when the engine is running, stop the engine and check that the drivebelt is correctly tensioned (see Chapter 1) and that the alternator connections are secure. If all is so far satisfactory, have the alternator checked by an auto-electrician for testing and repair.

3 If the alternator output is suspect even though the warning light functions correctly, the regulated voltage may be checked as follows.

4 Connect a voltmeter across the battery terminals and start the engine.

5 Increase the engine speed until the voltmeter reading remains steady; the reading should be approximately 12 to 13 volts, and no more than 14.2 volts.

6 Switch on as many electrical accessories

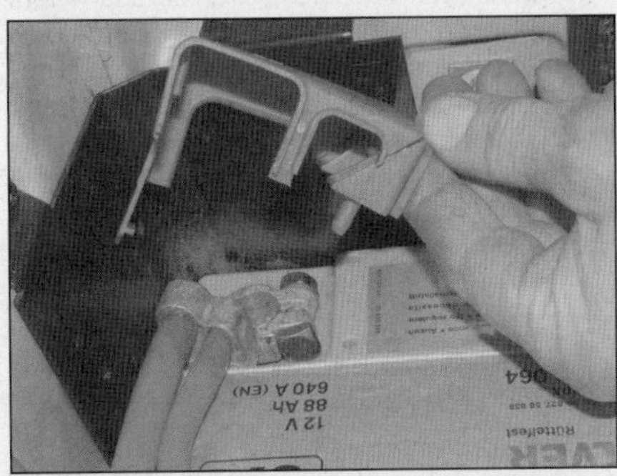

4.4a Lift off the positive terminal cover . . .

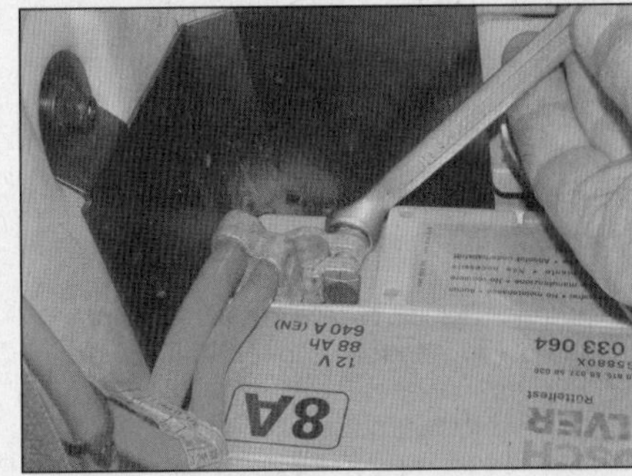

4.4b . . . and slacken the positive clamp bolt

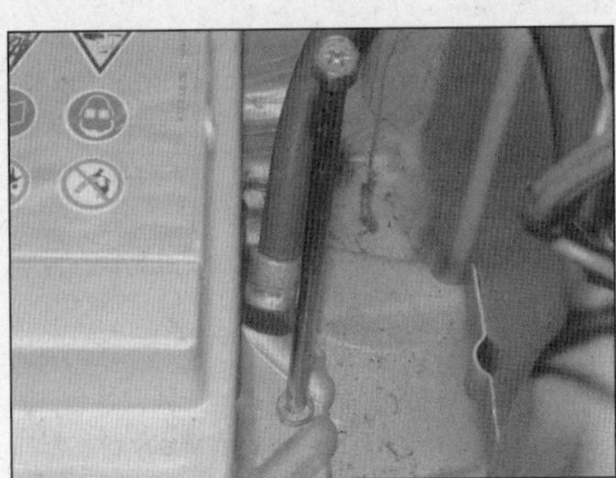

4.5a Slacken the clamping plate bolt . . .

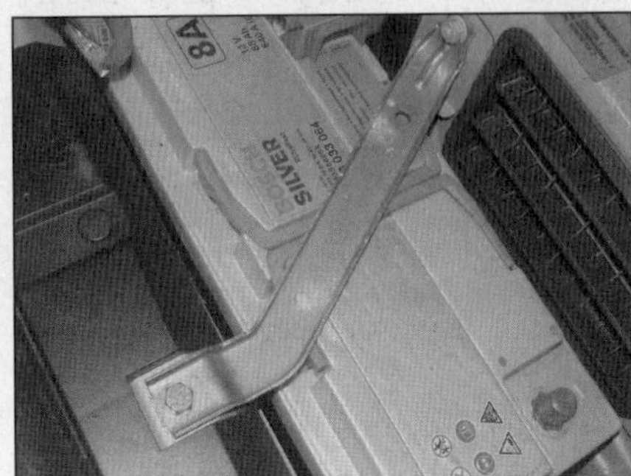

4.5b . . . then undo the bolts and remove the battery retaining strap

7.7 Pull back the rubber cover, and disconnect the alternator wiring

7.8 Alternator upper and lower mountings (arrowed)

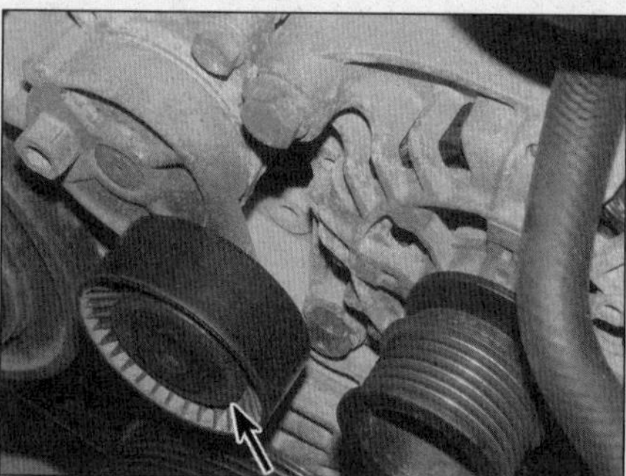

7.9 Prise off the plastic cover (arrowed) and undo the pulley retaining bolt

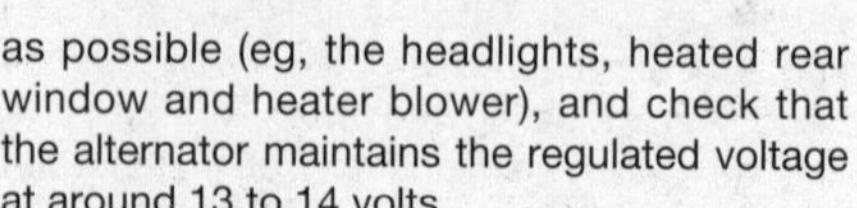

as possible (eg, the headlights, heated rear window and heater blower), and check that the alternator maintains the regulated voltage at around 13 to 14 volts.

7 If the regulated voltage is not as stated, the fault may be due to worn alternator brushes, weak brush springs, a faulty voltage regulator, a faulty diode, a severed phase winding or worn or damaged slip-rings. The alternator should be renewed or taken to an auto-electrician for testing and repair.

6 Alternator drivebelt – removal, refitting and tensioning

Refer to the procedure given for the auxiliary drivebelt(s) in Chapter 1.

7 Alternator – removal and refitting

Removal

1 Disconnect the battery negative lead (see Section 4).

2 Remove the air cleaner assembly and the mass airflow sensor as described in Chapter 4A, Section 12.

3 Remove the viscous cooling fan coupling as described in Chapter 3.

4 Remove the auxiliary drivebelt as described in Chapter 1.

5 Remove the power steering pump reservoir mounting bolts, and position the reservoir to one side. There is no need to disconnect the fluid hoses.

6 Reach beneath the alternator and pull the air cooling hose (where fitted) down and off of the alternator rear cover.

7 Pull off the cover (where fitted), then unscrew the nut and disconnect the wiring from the rear of the alternator **(see illustration)**.

8 On models without an auxiliary belt idler pulley, undo the upper and lower alternator securing bolts **(see illustration)**.

9 On models with an auxiliary belt idler pulley, undo the retaining bolt and remove the pulley for access to the alternator upper securing bolt **(see illustration)**. Undo the two bolts securing the alternator.

10 Withdraw the alternator from the engine.

Refitting

11 Refitting is a reversal of removal, bearing in mind the following points.

a) When refitting the tensioner idler pulley, ensure that the lug on the rear of the pulley assembly engages with the corresponding cut-out in the mounting bracket.

b) Refit the auxiliary drivebelt (see Chapter 1).

8 Alternator – testing and overhaul

If the alternator is thought to be suspect, it should be removed from the vehicle and taken to an auto-electrician for testing. Most auto-electricians will be able to supply and fit brushes at a reasonable cost. However, check on the cost of repairs before proceeding as it may prove more economical to obtain a new or exchange alternator.

9 Starting system – testing

Note: *Refer to the precautions given in 'Safety first!' and in Section 1 of this Chapter before starting work.*

1 If the starter motor fails to operate when the ignition key is turned to the appropriate position, the following possible causes may be to blame.

a) The battery is faulty.

b) The electrical connections between the switch, solenoid, battery and starter motor are somewhere failing to pass the necessary current from the battery through the starter to earth.

c) The solenoid is faulty.

d) The starter motor is mechanically or electrically defective.

2 To check the battery, switch on the headlights. If they dim after a few seconds, this indicates that the battery is discharged – recharge (see Section 3) or renew the battery. If the headlights glow brightly, operate the ignition switch and observe the lights. If they dim, then this indicates that current is reaching the starter motor, therefore the fault must lie in the starter motor. If the lights continue to glow brightly (and no clicking sound can be heard from the starter motor solenoid), this indicates that there is a fault in the circuit or solenoid – see following paragraphs. If the starter motor turns slowly when operated, but the battery is in good condition, then this indicates that either the starter motor is faulty, or there is considerable resistance somewhere in the circuit.

3 If a fault in the circuit is suspected, disconnect the battery leads (including the earth connection to the body), the starter/solenoid wiring and the engine/transmission earth strap. Thoroughly clean the connections, and reconnect the leads and wiring, then use a voltmeter or test lamp to check that full battery voltage is available at the battery positive lead connection to the solenoid, and that the earth is sound. Smear petroleum jelly around the battery terminals to prevent corrosion – corroded connections are amongst the most frequent causes of electrical system faults.

4 If the battery and all connections are in good condition, check the circuit by disconnecting the wire from the solenoid blade terminal. Connect a voltmeter or test lamp between the wire end and a good earth (such as the battery negative terminal), and check that the wire is live when the ignition switch is turned to the 'start' position. If it is, then the circuit is sound – if not the circuit wiring can be checked as described in Chapter 12.

5 The solenoid contacts can be checked by connecting a voltmeter or test lamp between the battery positive feed connection on the starter side of the solenoid, and earth. When the ignition switch is turned to the 'start' position, there should be a reading or lighted bulb, as applicable. If there is no reading or lighted bulb, the solenoid is faulty and should be renewed.

6 If the circuit and solenoid are proved sound, the fault must lie in the starter motor.

In this event, it may be possible to have the starter motor overhauled by a specialist, but check on the cost of spares before proceeding, as it may prove more economical to obtain a new or exchange motor.

10 Starter motor – removal and refitting

Removal – M52 engine

1 Disconnect the battery negative lead (see Section 4).

Manual transmission models

2 Apply the handbrake, then jack up the front of the vehicle and support it on axle stands (see *Jacking and vehicle support*).

3 Release the screws/clips and remove the engine undertray.

4 Undo the two bolts and remove the chassis cross-brace fitted behind the engine oil sump, then unclip the cover and release the fuel pipes and reversing light cable from their support bracket.

Automatic transmission models

5 Remove the intake manifold as described in Chapter 4A.

All models

6 Unscrew the nuts and disconnect the wiring from the rear of the starter motor. Note the fitted positions and routing of the cables **(see illustration)**.

7 Using a socket, ratchet and long extension, undo the starter motor mounting bolts from the transmission bellhousing.

8 Manoeuvre the starter from the engine, taking care not to damage the fuel hoses.

Refitting – M52 engine

9 Refitting is a reversal of removal. Tighten the starter motor mounting bolts to the specified torque.

Removal – M52TU engine

10 Disconnect the battery negative lead (see Section 4).

11 Disconnect the mass airflow sensor wiring and the vacuum hose, release the retaining clips, and remove the air filter housing (see Chapter 4A).

12 Pull the throttle outer cable up and manoeuvre it from the retaining bracket on the throttle body. Disconnect the inner cable end from the throttle valve quadrant – refer to Chapter 4A if necessary.

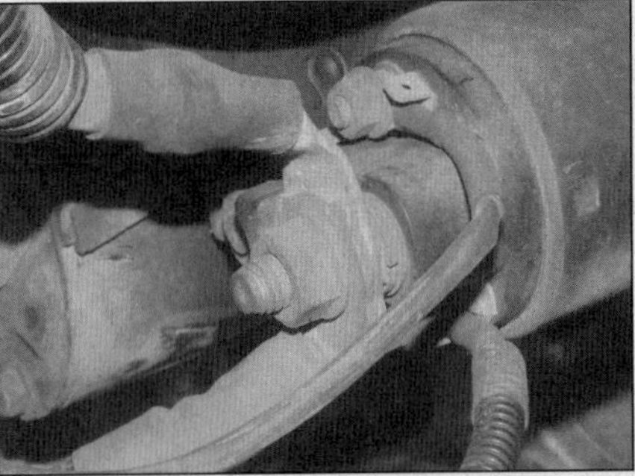

10.6 Undo the starter motor wiring connections – M52 engine

13 Undo the hose clamps and detach the intake hoses from the throttle body and idle speed control valve.

14 Apply the handbrake, then jack up the front of the vehicle and support securely on axle stands (see *Jacking and vehicle support*). Remove the engine undershield.

15 To improve access, unclip the fuel hoses from the retaining clips under the starter motor, depress the tabs and disconnect the quick-release couplings. Be prepared for fuel spillage.

16 Unscrew the nuts and disconnect the wiring from the rear of the starter motor.

17 Using a socket, ratchet and long extension, undo the starter motor mounting bolts from the transmission bellhousing.

18 Pull the motor forward and manoeuvre it downwards, taking care not to damage the fuel hoses.

Refitting – M52TU engine

19 Refitting is a reversal of removal. Tighten the starter motor mounting bolts to the specified torque.

Removal – M54 engine

20 Disconnect the battery negative lead (see Section 4).

21 Apply the handbrake, then jack up the front of the vehicle and support securely on axle stands (see *Jacking and vehicle support*). Undo the screws and remove the engine/transmission undershields.

22 Working underneath the vehicle, disconnect the crankshaft position sensor (beneath the starter motor) wiring plug.

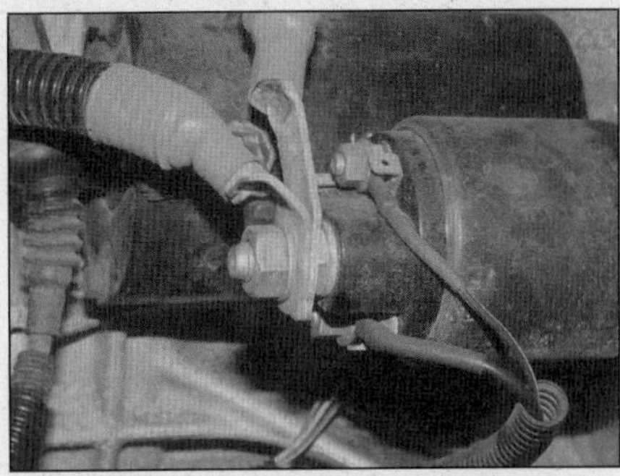

10.23 Starter motor connections – M54 engine

23 Note their fitted positions, then undo the nuts and disconnect the wiring from the starter motor **(see illustration)**.

24 Using a socket, ratchet, universal joint and long extension, undo the starter motor mounting bolts from the transmission bellhousing.

25 Pull the motor forward and manoeuvre it downwards.

Refitting – M54 engine

26 Refitting is a reversal of removal. Tighten the starter motor mounting bolts to the specified torque.

11 Starter motor – testing and overhaul

If the starter motor is thought to be suspect, it should be removed from the vehicle and taken to an auto-electrician for testing. Most auto-electricians will be able to supply and fit brushes at a reasonable cost. However, check on the cost of repairs before proceeding as it may prove more economical to obtain a new or exchange motor.

12 Ignition switch – removal and refitting

The ignition switch is integral with the steering column lock, and can be removed as described in Chapter 10.

Notes

Chapter 5 Part B: Ignition systems

Contents

Degrees of difficulty

Easy, suitable for novice with little experience 	**Fairly easy,** suitable for beginner with some experience 	**Fairly difficult,** suitable for competent DIY mechanic	**Difficult,** suitable for experienced DIY mechanic 	**Very difficult,** suitable for expert DIY or professional

Specifications

Firing order		
6-cylinder engines	1-5-3-6-2-4	
Ignition timing	Electronically-controlled by DME – no adjustment possible	
Torque wrench settings	**Nm**	**lbf ft**
Knock sensor securing bolt	20	15
Spark plugs:		
M12 thread	23	17
M14 thread	30	22

1 General information and precautions

General information

The ignition system is controlled by the engine management system (see Chapter 4A), known as DME (Digital Motor Electronics). The DME system controls all ignition and fuel injection functions using a central ECM (Electronic Control Module).

The ignition timing is based on inputs provided to the ECM by various sensors supplying information on engine load, engine speed, coolant temperature and inlet air temperature (see Chapter 4A).

All engines are fitted with two knock sensors to detect 'knocking' (also known as 'pinking' or pre-ignition). One sensor is for cylinders 1 to 3, and the second for cylinder 4 to 6. The knock sensors are sensitive to vibration and detect the knocking which occurs when a cylinder starts to pre-ignite. The knock sensors provides a signal to the ECM which in turn retards the ignition advance setting until the knocking ceases.

A distributorless ignition system is used, with a separate HT coil for each cylinder. No distributor is used, and the coils provide the high voltage signal direct to each spark plug.

The ECM uses the inputs from the various sensors to calculate the required ignition advance and the coil charging time.

Precautions

Refer to the precautions in Chapter 5A.

Testing of ignition system components should be entrusted to a BMW dealer or suitably-equipped specialist. Improvised testing techniques are time-consuming and run the risk of damaging the engine management ECM.

2 Ignition system – testing

1 If a fault appears in the engine management (fuel/injection) system, first ensure that the fault is not due to a poor electrical connection, or to poor maintenance, ie, check that the air cleaner filter element is clean, that the spark plugs are in good condition and correctly gapped, and that the engine breather hoses are clear and undamaged.

2 Due to the design of the coils, it is not possible to test the resistance of the HT leads in the traditional manner.

3 Check that the throttle cable is correctly adjusted as described in Chapter 4A.

4 If the engine is running very roughly, check the compression pressures as described in Chapter 2A.

5 If these checks fail to reveal the cause of the problem, then the vehicle should be taken to a BMW dealer or specialist for testing using the appropriate specialist diagnostic equipment. The ECM incorporates a self-diagnostic function which stores fault codes in the system memory (note that stored fault codes are erased if the battery is disconnected). These fault codes can be read using the appropriate BMW diagnosis equipment. Improvised testing techniques are time-consuming and run the risk of damaging the engine management ECM.

3 Ignition HT coil – removal and refitting

Removal

1 Each spark plug is fed by its own coil, and the coils are mounted directly on top of the spark plugs, in the cylinder head cover.

2 Ensure the ignition is switched off.

3 Remove the engine oil filler cap.

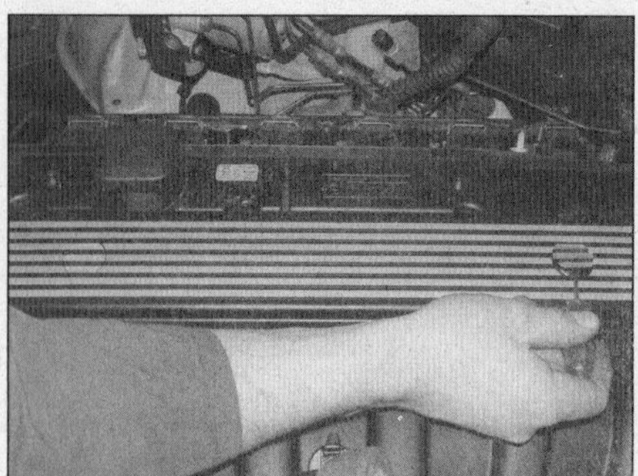

3.4 **Prise up the plastic caps to access the injectors cover retaining screws**

3.5 **Prise up the plastic caps and undo the coil's cover retaining nuts**

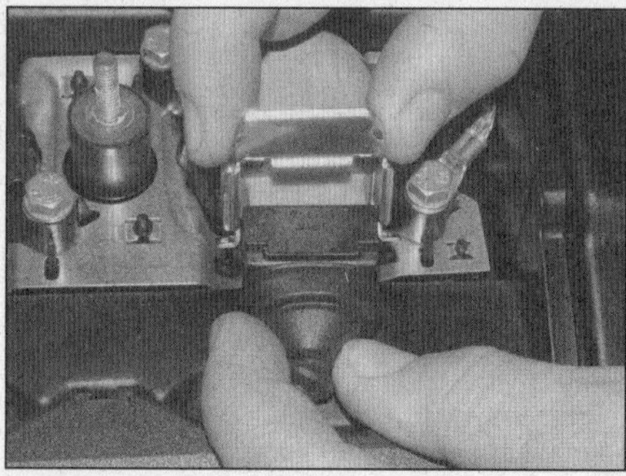

3.6 **Lift the clip and disconnect the wiring plug**

4 Prise up the plastic caps, undo the retaining screws, and remove the plastic cover from above the injectors **(see illustration)**.

5 Remove the plastic cover from the top of the cylinder head cover. To remove the cover, prise out the cover plates and unscrew the two securing nuts, then lift and pull the cover forwards. Manipulate the cover over the oil filler neck **(see illustration)**.

Single-spark type coils

6 Lift the securing clip, and disconnect the wiring plug from the relevant coil **(see illustration)**.

7 Unscrew the two coil securing nuts/bolts, noting the locations of any earth leads and/or brackets secured by the nuts **(see illustration)**. Note that the coil connectors are spring-loaded, so the coil will lift as the nuts are unscrewed.

3.7 **Unscrew the coil retaining bolts, noting any earth leads attached**

Rod-type coils

8 Lift the locking catch, and disconnect the coil wiring plug **(see illustration)**.

All types

9 Pull the coil from the camshaft cover and spark plug, and withdraw it from the engine **(see illustration)**.

Refitting

10 Refitting is a reversal of removal, but where applicable, ensure that any earth leads and brackets are in position as noted before removal.

4 Knock sensor – removal and refitting

Removal

1 Two knock sensors are fitted, screwed into the left-hand side of the cylinder block. One sensor detects knocking in Nos 1 to 3 cylinders, and the other sensor detects knocking in Nos 4 to 6 cylinders.

2 Disconnect the battery negative lead (see Chapter 5A).

3 Remove the intake manifold as described in Chapter 4A.

4 Locate the sensor connector bracket which is located beneath the idle speed control valve.

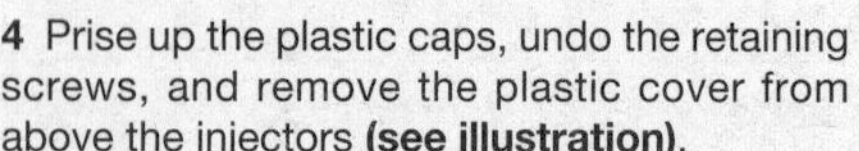

Warning: If both knock sensors are to be removed, mark the wiring connectors to ensure correct refitting. Incorrect reconnection may result in engine damage.

5 Unclip the connector from the retaining clip, and disconnect the sensor wiring connector(s).

6 Unscrew the securing bolt and remove the knock sensor, noting the routing of the wiring. The sensor for cylinders 1 to 3 is located beneath the temperature sensors in the cylinder head **(see illustration)**. The sensor for cylinders 4 to 6 is located to the rear of the sensor wiring connector bracket.

Refitting

7 Commence refitting by thoroughly cleaning the mating faces of the sensor and the cylinder block.

8 Refit the sensor to the cylinder block, tightening the securing bolt to the specified torque.

9 Route the wiring as noted before removal, then reconnect the connector(s), and clip the connector to the bracket, ensuring that the connectors are positioned as noted before removal.

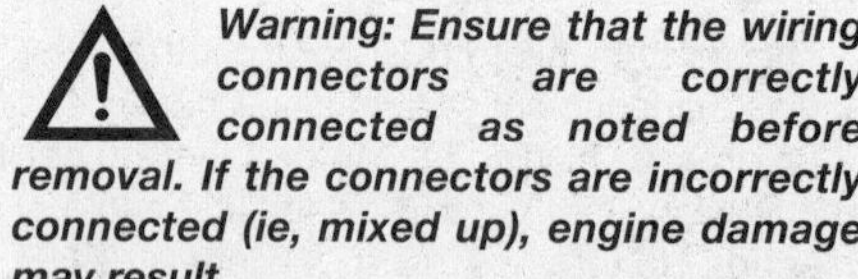

Warning: Ensure that the wiring connectors are correctly connected as noted before removal. If the connectors are incorrectly connected (ie, mixed up), engine damage may result.

10 Refit the inlet manifold as described in Chapter 4A.

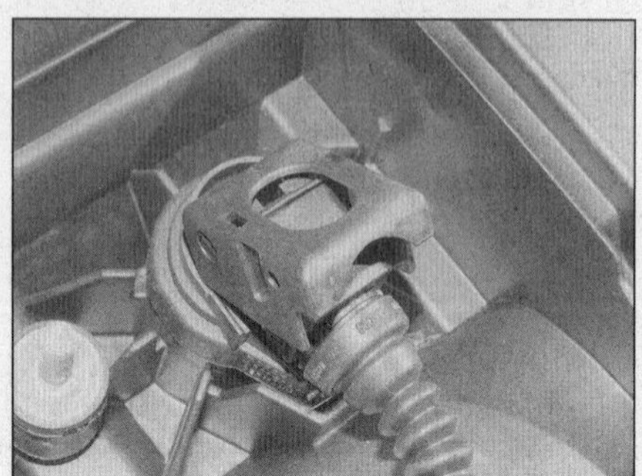

3.8 **Lift the locking catch and disconnect the wiring plug**

3.9 **Pull the coil from the cover and spark plug**

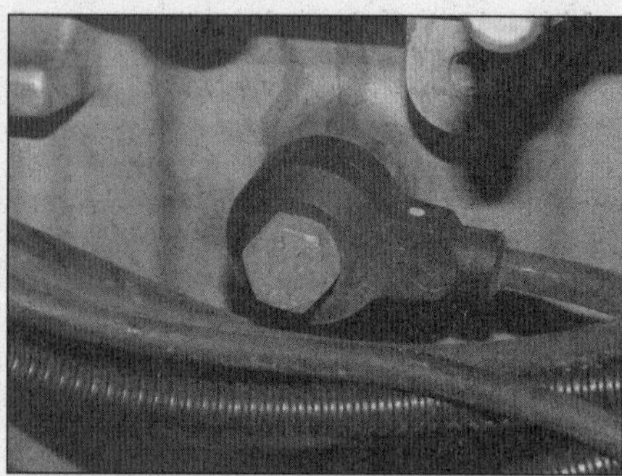

4.6 **Undo the bolt and remove the knock sensor**

Chapter 6
Clutch

Contents

Degrees of difficulty

Easy, suitable for novice with little experience 	**Fairly easy,** suitable for beginner with some experience 	**Fairly difficult,** suitable for competent DIY mechanic	**Difficult,** suitable for experienced DIY mechanic	**Very difficult,** suitable for expert DIY or professional

Specifications

Type	Single dry plate with diaphragm spring, hydraulically-operated	
Driveplate		
Minimum lining thickness above rivet head	1.0 mm	
Torque wrench settings	**Nm**	**lbf ft**
Clutch cover-to-flywheel bolts	24	18
Clutch master cylinder bolts	22	16
Clutch slave cylinder nuts	22	16
Hydraulic pipe union bolts	20	15

1 General information

All models are fitted with a single dry plate clutch, which consists of five main components; friction disc, pressure plate, diaphragm spring, cover and release bearing.

The friction disc is free to slide along the splines of the gearbox input shaft, and is held in position between the flywheel and the pressure plate by the pressure exerted on the pressure plate by the diaphragm spring. Friction lining material is riveted to both sides of the friction disc. Models up to 09/1997 are fitted with a traditional clutch, whereas, all models after this date are fitted with a Self-Adjusting Clutch (SAC), which compensates for friction disc wear by altering the attitude of the diaphragm spring fingers by means of a sprung mechanism within the pressure plate cover. This ensures a consistent clutch pedal 'feel' over the life of the clutch.

The diaphragm spring is mounted on pins, and is held in place in the cover by annular fulcrum rings.

The release bearing is located on a guide sleeve at the front of the gearbox, and the bearing is free to slide on the sleeve, under the action of the release arm which pivots inside the clutch bellhousing.

The release mechanism is operated by the clutch pedal, using hydraulic pressure. The pedal acts on the hydraulic master cylinder pushrod, and a slave cylinder, mounted on the gearbox bellhousing, operates the clutch release lever via a pushrod.

When the clutch pedal is depressed, the release arm pushes the release bearing forwards, to bear against the centre of the diaphragm spring, thus pushing the centre of the diaphragm spring inwards. The diaphragm spring acts against the fulcrum rings in the cover and so, as the centre of the spring is pushed in, the outside of the spring is pushed out, so allowing the pressure plate to move backwards away from the friction disc.

When the clutch pedal is released, the diaphragm spring forces the pressure plate into contact with the friction linings on the friction disc, and simultaneously pushes the friction disc forwards on its splines, forcing it against the flywheel. The friction disc is now firmly sandwiched between the pressure plate and the flywheel, and drive is taken up.

2 Clutch assembly – removal, inspection and refitting

Warning: Dust created by clutch wear and deposited on the clutch components may contain asbestos, which is a health hazard. DO NOT blow it out with compressed air, or inhale any of it. DO NOT use petrol (or petroleum-based solvents) to clean off the dust. Brake system cleaner or methylated spirit should be used to flush the dust into a suitable receptacle. After the clutch components are wiped clean with rags, dispose of the contaminated rags and cleaner in a sealed, marked container.

Note: *On models with a self-adjusting clutch (SAC), if the clutch pressure plate is to be re-used, BMW tools 21 2 180 and 21 2 170 will be required to compress the diaphragm spring prior to removal of the clutch cover/pressure plate assembly. Tool 21 2 142 may be required to centre the friction plate.*

Removal

1 Remove the gearbox, as described in Chapter 7A.

2 If the original clutch is to be refitted, make alignment marks between the clutch cover and the flywheel, so that the clutch can be refitted in its original position.

3 Progressively unscrew the bolts securing the clutch cover/pressure plate assembly to the flywheel, and where applicable recover the washers.

4 Withdraw the clutch cover from the flywheel. Be prepared to catch the clutch friction disc, which may drop out of the cover as it is withdrawn, and note which way round the friction disc is fitted – the two sides of the disc are normally marked 'Engine side' and 'Transmission side'. The greater projecting side of the hub faces away from the flywheel.

Inspection

5 With the clutch assembly removed, clean off all traces of dust using a dry cloth. Although most friction discs now have asbestos-free linings, some do not, and it is wise to take suitable precautions; *asbestos dust is harmful, and must not be inhaled.*

6 Examine the linings of the friction disc for wear and loose rivets, and the disc for distortion, cracks, and worn splines. The surface of the friction linings may be highly glazed, but, as long as the friction material pattern can be clearly seen, this is satisfactory. If there is any sign of oil contamination, indicated by a continuous, or patchy, shiny black discolouration, the disc must be renewed. The source of the contamination must be traced and rectified before fitting new clutch components; typically, a leaking crankshaft rear oil seal or gearbox input shaft oil seal – or both – will be to blame (renewal procedures are given in Chapter 2A, and Chapter 7A respectively). The disc must also be renewed if the lining thickness has worn down to, or just above, the level of the rivet heads. Note that BMW specify a minimum friction material thickness above the heads of the rivets (see Specifications).

7 Check the machined faces of the flywheel and pressure plate. If either is grooved, or heavily scored, renewal is necessary. The pressure plate must also be renewed if any cracks are apparent, or if the diaphragm spring is damaged or its pressure suspect.

8 With the clutch removed, it is advisable to check the condition of the release bearing, as described in Section 3.

9 Check the spigot bearing in the end of the crankshaft. Make sure that it turns smoothly and quietly. If the gearbox input shaft contact face on the bearing is worn or damaged, fit a new bearing, as described in Chapter 2A.

Refitting

10 If new clutch components are to be fitted, where applicable, ensure that all anti-corrosion preservative is cleaned from the friction material on the disc, and the contact surfaces of the pressure plate.

11 It is important to ensure that no oil or grease gets onto the friction disc linings, or the pressure plate and flywheel faces. It is advisable to refit the clutch assembly with clean hands, and to wipe down the pressure plate and flywheel faces with a clean rag before assembly begins.

12 Apply a smear of molybdenum disulphide grease to the splines of the friction disc hub, then offer the disc to the flywheel, with the greater projecting side of the hub facing away from the flywheel (most friction discs will have an 'Engine side' or 'Transmission side' marking which should face the flywheel or gearbox as applicable) **(see illustration)**. Using tool BMW tool 21 2 142, centre the friction disc in the flywheel **(see illustration)**. If the tool is not available, an alternative may be fabricated.

Models without self-adjusting clutch

13 Refit the pressure plate/cover assembly, aligning the marks made on disassembly (if the original pressure plate is re-used), and aligning the locating dowels with the corresponding holes in the pressure plate. Fit the cover bolts, and tighten them in a diagonal pattern, evenly and gradually to the specified torque setting **(see illustration)**.

Models with self-adjusting clutch

14 If the original pressure plate and cover is to be refitted, engage the legs of BMW tool 21 2 170 with the cover in the area of the adjusting springs. Screw down the knurled collar to lock the legs in place, then tighten down the spindle to compress the diaphragm spring. Using a screwdriver, reset the self-adjusting mechanism by pushing the adjustment ring thrust pieces fully anti-clockwise, whilst undoing the special tool spindle only enough to allow the adjustment ring to move. With the adjustment ring reset, tighten down the special tool spindle to compress the spring fingers, whilst preventing the adjustment ring thrust pieces from moving by inserting metal spacers in the gap between the thrust pieces and the cover. Note that a

2.12a The clutch friction disc marking

2.12b Use BMW tool 21 2 142 (or similar) to centre the friction disc

2.13 Tighten the cover gradually and evenly

2.14a Use BMW tool 21 2 170 to compress the diaphragm spring

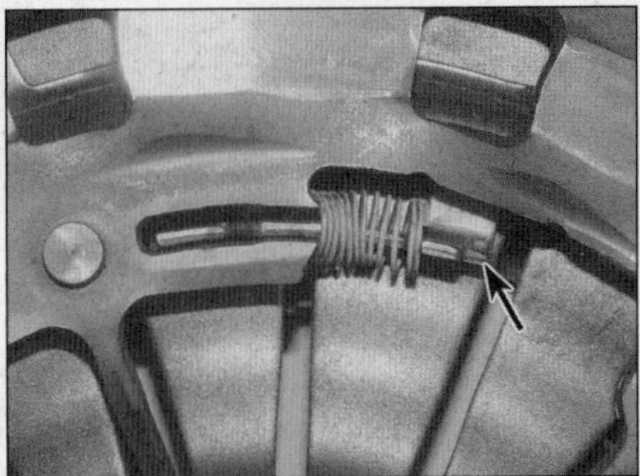

2.14b Push the adjustment ring thrust pieces (arrowed) fully anti-clockwise . . .

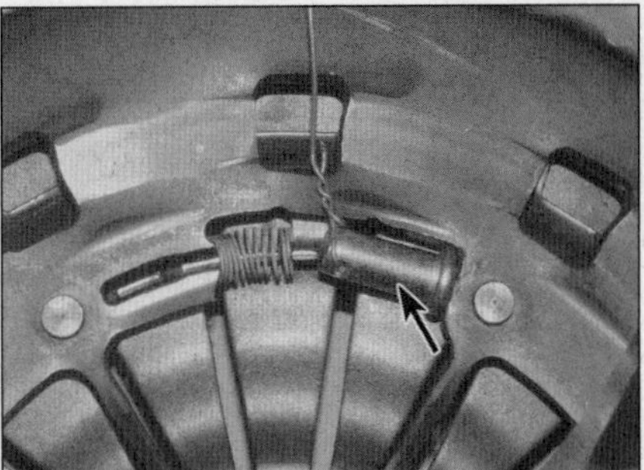

2.14c . . . and insert metal spacers (arrowed) between the thrust pieces and the cover

2.14d A special BMW tool is available to reset the adjustment ring thrust pieces

2.15 Ensure the cover locates over the flywheel dowels

special tool is available from BMW to reset the adjustment ring **(see illustrations)**

15 Fit the clutch cover assembly, where applicable aligning the marks on the flywheel and clutch cover. Ensure that the clutch cover locates over the dowels on the flywheel **(see illustration)**. Insert the securing bolts and washers, and tighten them to the specified torque.

16 If a new pressure plate cover was fitted, insert a 14 mm Allen key into the centre of the diaphragm spring locking piece, and turn it clockwise and remove it to release the spring.

17 Where the original pressure plate cover was refitted, undo the spindle and knurled collar, then remove the compression tool from the cover. Prise out the metal spacers holding the adjustment ring thrust pieces in place **(see illustration)**.

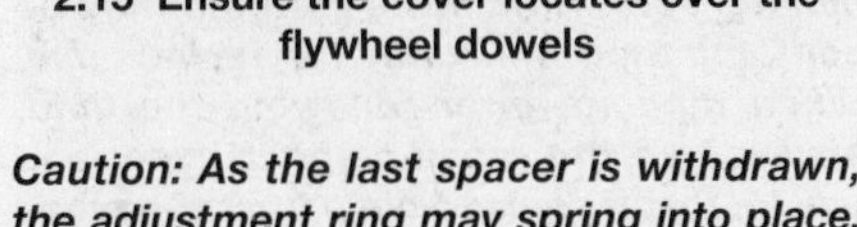

Caution: As the last spacer is withdrawn, the adjustment ring may spring into place. Ensure all fingers are clear of the area.

All models

18 If the BMW centring tool was used, remove the tool by screwing a 10 mm bolt into its end and pulling using a pair of pliers or similar **(see illustration)**.

19 Refit the gearbox as described in Chapter 7A.

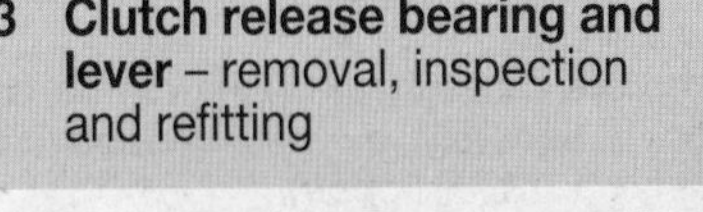

3 Clutch release bearing and lever – removal, inspection and refitting

Warning: Dust created by clutch wear and deposited on the clutch components may contain asbestos, which is a health hazard. DO NOT blow it out with compressed air, or inhale any of it. DO NOT use petrol (or petroleum-based solvents) to clean off the dust. Brake system cleaner or methylated spirit should be used to flush the dust into a suitable receptacle. After the clutch components are wiped clean with rags, dispose of the contaminated rags and cleaner in a sealed, marked container.

Release bearing

Removal

1 Remove the gearbox as described in Chapter 7A.

2 Pull the bearing forwards, and slide it from the guide sleeve in the gearbox bellhousing **(see illustration)**.

Inspection

3 Spin the release bearing, and check it for excessive roughness. Hold the outer race, and attempt to move it laterally against the inner race. If any excessive movement or roughness is evident, renew the bearing. If a new clutch has been fitted, it is wise to renew the release bearing as a matter of course.

Refitting

4 Clean and then lightly apply clutch assembly grease to the release bearing contact surfaces on the release lever and guide sleeve.

5 Slide the bearing into position on the guide sleeve, ensuring that the bearing engages correctly with the release lever.

6 Refit the gearbox, referring to Chapter 7A.

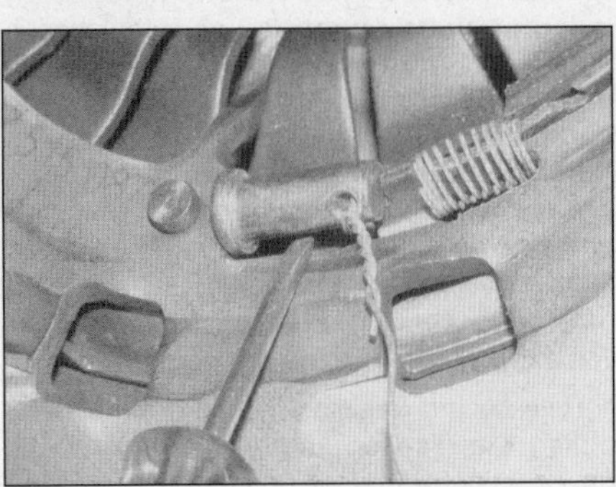

2.17 Keep all fingers away when removing the metal spacers

2.18 Thread the bolt into the end of the BMW centring tool and pull it out

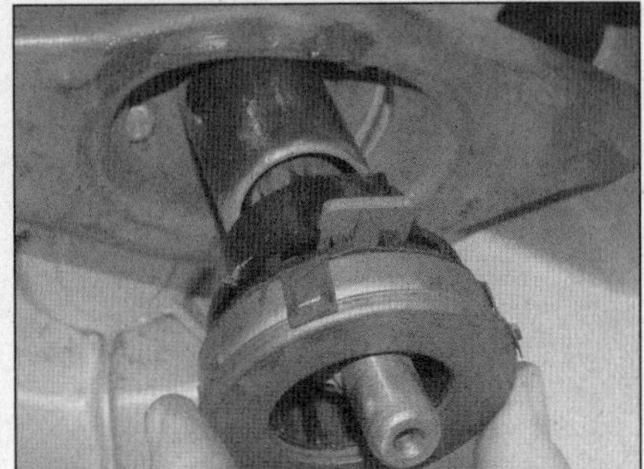

3.2 Pull the release bearing from the guide sleeve

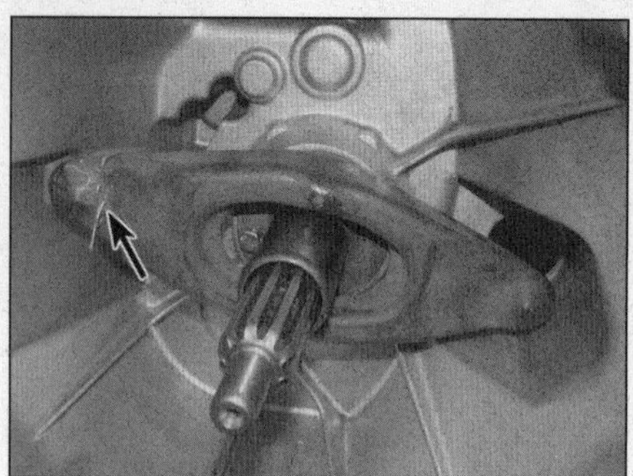
3.8 Slide the release lever sideways to disengage the retaining clip (arrowed)

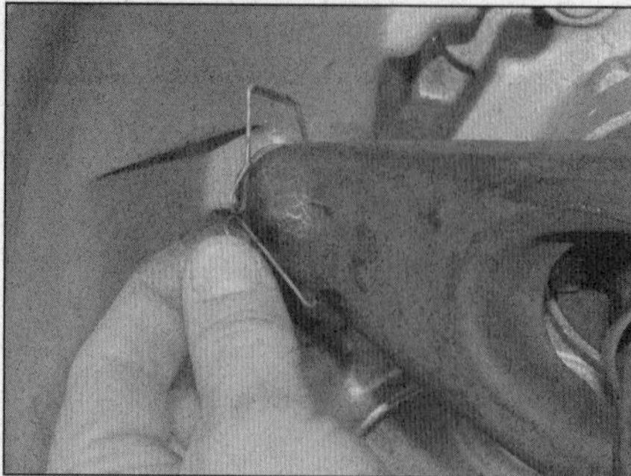
3.11 Ensure the lever engages correctly with the retaining clip

Release lever

Removal

7 Remove the release bearing, as described previously in this Section.

8 Slide the release lever sideways to release it from the retaining spring clip and pivot, then pull the lever forwards from the guide sleeve **(see illustration)**.

Inspection

9 Inspect the release bearing, pivot and slave cylinder pushrod contact faces on the release lever for wear. Renew the lever if excessive wear is evident.

10 Check the release lever retaining spring clip, and renew if necessary. It is advisable to renew the clip as a matter of course.

Refitting

11 Slide the release lever into position over the guide sleeve, then push the end of the lever over the pivot, ensuring that the retaining spring clip engages correctly over the end of the release lever **(see illustration)**.

12 Refit the release bearing as described previously in this Section.

4 Hydraulic slave cylinder – removal, inspection and refitting

Warning: Hydraulic fluid is poisonous; wash off immediately and thoroughly in the case of skin contact, and seek immediate medical advice if any fluid is swallowed or gets into the eyes. Certain types of hydraulic fluid are inflammable, and may ignite when allowed into contact with hot components; when servicing any hydraulic system, it is safest to assume that the fluid is inflammable, and to take precautions against the risk of fire as though it is petrol that is being handled. Hydraulic fluid is also an effective paint stripper, and will attack plastics; if any is spilt, it should be washed off immediately, using copious quantities of fresh water. Finally, it is hygroscopic (it absorbs moisture from the air) – old fluid may be contaminated and unfit for further use. When topping-up or renewing the fluid, always use the recommended type, and ensure that it comes from a freshly-opened sealed container.

Removal

1 Remove the brake fluid reservoir cap, and use a poultry baster or similar to syphon out sufficient hydraulic fluid so that the fluid level is below the level of the reservoir fluid hose connection to the clutch master cylinder (the brake fluid reservoir feeds both the brake and clutch hydraulic systems). **Do not** empty the reservoir, as this will draw air into the brake hydraulic circuits.

2 To improve access, jack up the vehicle, and support it securely on axle stands (see *Jacking and vehicle support*).

3 Release the screws and remove the underbody shield (where fitted) for access to the gearbox bellhousing.

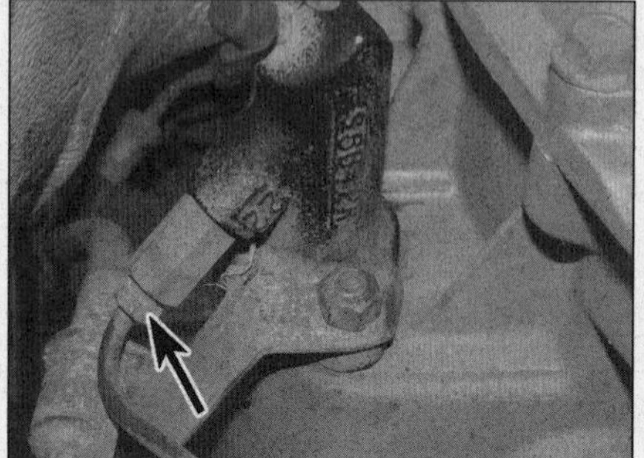
4.4 Unscrew the clutch slave cylinder union nut (arrowed)

5.1 Release the clip and remove the driver's side pollen filter cover

4 Place a container beneath the hydraulic pipe connection on the clutch slave cylinder to catch escaping hydraulic fluid. Unscrew the union nut and disconnect the fluid pipe **(see illustration)**

5 Unscrew the securing nuts, and withdraw the slave cylinder from the mounting studs on the bellhousing.

Inspection

6 Inspect the slave cylinder for fluid leaks and damage, and renew if necessary. At the time of writing, no spare parts are available for the slave cylinder, and if faulty, the complete unit must be renewed. Check with your dealer or specialist.

Refitting

7 Refitting is a reversal of removal, bearing in mind the following points.

a) Before refitting, clean and then lightly grease the end of the slave cylinder pushrod.

b) Tighten the mounting nuts to the specified torque.

c) On completion, top-up the hydraulic fluid level and bleed the clutch hydraulic circuit as described in Section 6.

5 Hydraulic master cylinder – removal, inspection and refitting

Warning: Hydraulic fluid is poisonous; wash off immediately and thoroughly in the case of skin contact, and seek immediate medical advice if any fluid is swallowed or gets into the eyes. Certain types of hydraulic fluid are inflammable, and may ignite when allowed into contact with hot components; when servicing any hydraulic system, it is safest to assume that the fluid is inflammable, and to take precautions against the risk of fire as though it is petrol that is being handled. Hydraulic fluid is also an effective paint stripper, and will attack plastics; if any is spilt, it should be washed off immediately, using copious quantities of fresh water. Finally, it is hygroscopic (it absorbs moisture from the air) – old fluid may be contaminated and unfit for further use. When topping-up or renewing the fluid, always use the recommended type, and ensure that it comes from a freshly-opened sealed container.

Removal

1 Release the retaining clip, and remove the pollen filter cover and element from the driver's side of the engine compartment **(see illustration)**.

2 Release the retaining clips and carefully rotate

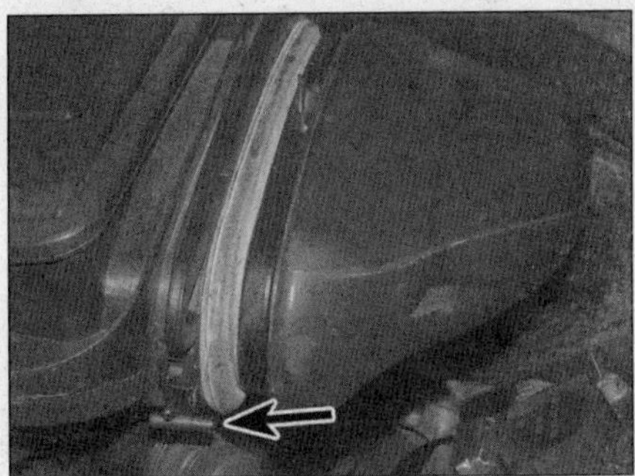
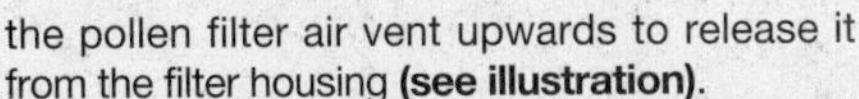

5.2 Release the clip (arrowed) and remove the air duct

5.3 Squeeze together the sides of the clip (arrowed) and remove the pollen filter housing

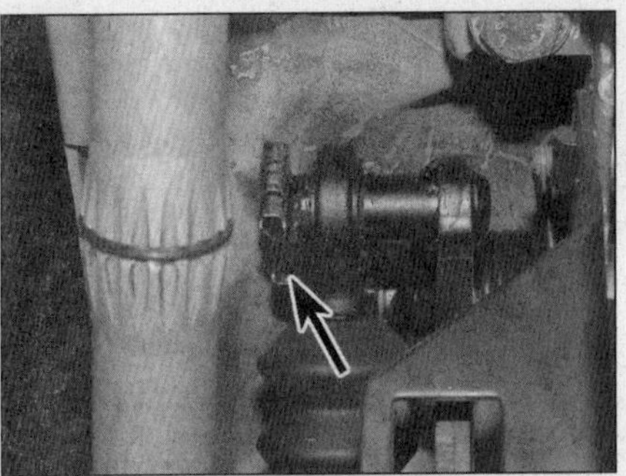

5.7 Prise open and slide off the clip (arrowed) securing the master cylinder pushrod to the pedal

the pollen filter air vent upwards to release it from the filter housing **(see illustration)**.

3 Release the clip and remove the pollen filter housing **(see illustration)**.

4 Remove the brake fluid reservoir cap, and use a poultry baster or similar to syphon out sufficient hydraulic fluid so that the fluid level is below the level of the reservoir fluid hose connection to the clutch master cylinder (the brake fluid reservoir feeds both the brake and clutch hydraulic systems). **Do not** empty the reservoir, as this will draw air into the brake hydraulic circuits.

5 Disconnect the clutch master cylinder hose from the brake fluid reservoir. Be prepared for fluid spillage, and plug the open end of the hose to prevent dirt entry.

6 Working inside the vehicle, remove the securing screws, and remove the driver's side lower facia trim panel (see Chapter 11).

7 Carefully prise and slide off the retaining clip, then press out the master cylinder pushrod pivot pin from the clutch pedal **(see illustration)**.

8 Unscrew the two bolts and nut securing the master cylinder to the pedal bracket in the footwell.

9 Using a small screwdriver, prise out the retaining clip and then pull the master cylinder from the hydraulic pressure pipe **(see illustration)**. Withdraw the master cylinder, and ease the fluid supply hose through the bulkhead grommet, taking care not to strain the pipe. Be prepared for fluid leaks.

10 Depress the locking tab, and disconnect the master cylinder switch wiring plug (where fitted). If required, carefully release the clips and detach the switch from the cylinder.

Inspection

11 Inspect the master cylinder for fluid leaks and damage, and renew if necessary. At the time of writing, no spare parts were available for the master cylinder, and if faulty the complete unit must be renewed. Check with your local dealer or parts supplier.

Refitting

12 Refitting is a reversal of removal, bearing in mind the following points.

a) Take care not to strain the master cylinder fluid pipe during refitting.

b) On completion, top-up the level in the brake fluid reservoir, then bleed the clutch hydraulic system (see Section 6).

6 Hydraulic system – bleeding

Warning: Hydraulic fluid is poisonous; wash off immediately and thoroughly in the case of skin contact, and seek immediate medical advice if any fluid is swallowed or gets into the eyes. Certain types of hydraulic fluid are inflammable, and may ignite when allowed into contact with hot components; when servicing any hydraulic system, it is safest to assume that the fluid is inflammable, and to take precautions against the risk of fire as though it is petrol that is being handled. Hydraulic fluid is also an effective paint stripper, and will attack plastics; if any is spilt, it should be washed off immediately, using copious quantities of fresh water. Finally, it is hygroscopic (it absorbs moisture from the air) – old fluid may be contaminated and unfit for further use. When topping-up or renewing the fluid, always use the recommended type, and ensure that it comes from a freshly-opened sealed container.

Note: *BMW recommend that pressure-bleeding equipment is used to bleed the clutch hydraulic system.*

General

1 The correct operation of any hydraulic system is only possible after removing all air from the components and circuit; this is achieved by bleeding the system.

2 During the bleeding procedure, add only clean, unused hydraulic fluid of the recommended type; never re-use fluid that has already been bled from the system. Ensure that sufficient fluid is available before starting work.

3 If there is any possibility of incorrect fluid being already in the system, the brake and clutch components and circuit must be flushed completely with uncontaminated, correct fluid, and new seals should be fitted to the various components.

4 If hydraulic fluid has been lost from the system, or air has entered because of a leak, ensure that the fault is cured before proceeding further.

5 To improve access, apply the handbrake, then jack up the front of the vehicle, and support it securely on axle stands (see *Jacking and vehicle support*).

6 Undo the screws and remove the underbody shield (where fitted) for access to the gearbox bellhousing.

7 Check that the clutch hydraulic pipe(s) and hose(s) are secure, that the unions are tight, and that the bleed screw on the rear of the clutch slave cylinder (mounted under the vehicle on the lower left-hand side of the gearbox bellhousing) is closed. Clean any dirt from around the bleed screw **(see illustration)**.

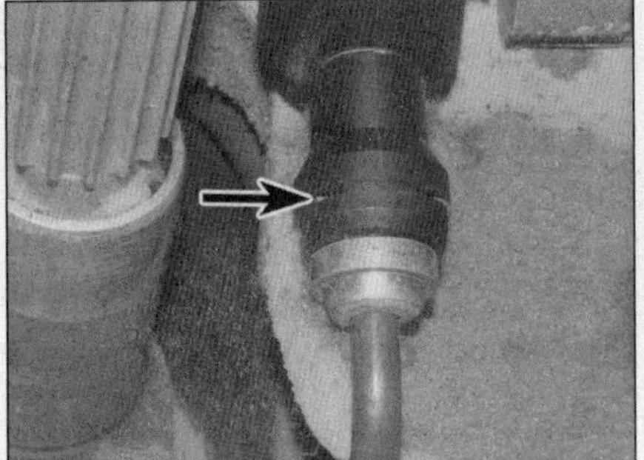

5.9 Prise out the clip (arrowed) and pull the master cylinder from the pipe

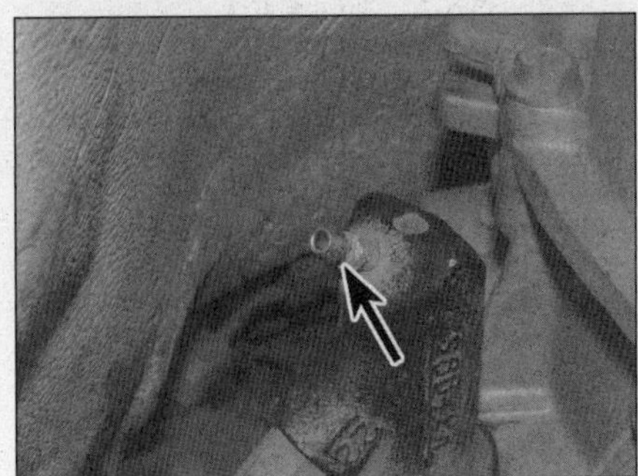

6.7 Ensure the area around the bleed screw (arrowed) is clean

8 Release the retaining clip and remove the driver's side air duct between the pollen filter housing and the bulkhead, then release the clip and remove the pollen filter cover **(see illustrations 5.1 and 5.2)**.

9 Release the retaining clip and remove the pollen filter housing **(see illustration 5.3)**.

10 Unscrew the brake fluid reservoir cap, and top the fluid up to the MAX level line; refit the cap loosely, and remember to maintain the fluid level at least above the MIN level line throughout the procedure, or there is a risk of further air entering the system. Note that the brake fluid reservoir feeds both the brake and clutch hydraulic systems.

11 It is recommended that pressure-bleeding equipment is used to bleed the system. Alternatively, there are a number of one-man, do-it-yourself brake bleeding kits currently available from motor accessory shops. These kits greatly simplify the bleeding operation, and also reduce the risk of expelled air and fluid being drawn back into the system. If such a kit is not available, the basic (two-man) method must be used, which is described in detail below.

12 If pressure-bleeding equipment or a one-man kit is to be used, prepare the vehicle as described previously, and follow the equipment/kit manufacturer's instructions, as the procedure may vary slightly according to the type being used; generally, they are as outlined below in the relevant sub-section.

13 Whichever method is used, the same basic process must be followed to ensure that the removal of all air from the system.

Bleeding

Basic (two-man) method

14 Collect a clean glass jar, a suitable length of plastic or rubber tubing which is a tight fit over the bleed screw, and a ring spanner to fit the screw. The help of an assistant will also be required.

15 Where applicable, remove the dust cap from the bleed screw. Fit the spanner and tube to the screw, place the other end of the tube in the jar, and pour in sufficient fluid to cover the end of the tube.

16 Ensure that the reservoir fluid level is maintained at least above the MIN level line throughout the procedure.

17 Have the assistant fully depress the clutch pedal several times to build-up pressure, then maintain it on the final downstroke.

18 While pedal pressure is maintained, unscrew the bleed screw (approximately one turn) and allow the compressed fluid and air to flow into the jar. The assistant should maintain pedal pressure, following it down to the floor if necessary, and should not release it until instructed to do so. When the flow stops, tighten the bleed screw again, have the assistant release the pedal slowly, and recheck the reservoir fluid level.

19 Repeat the steps given in paragraphs 17 and 18 until the fluid emerging from the bleed screw is free from air bubbles.

20 When no more air bubbles appear, tighten the bleed screw securely. Do not overtighten the bleed screw.

21 Temporarily disconnect the bleed tube from the bleed screw, and move the container of fluid to one side.

22 Unscrew the two securing nuts, and withdraw the slave cylinder from the bellhousing, taking care not to strain the fluid hose.

23 Reconnect the bleed tube to the bleed screw, and submerge the end of the tube in the container of fluid.

24 With the bleed screw pointing vertically upwards, unscrew the bleed screw (approximately one turn), and slowly push the slave cylinder pushrod into the cylinder until no more air bubbles appear in the fluid.

25 Hold the pushrod in position, then tighten the bleed screw.

26 Slowly allow the pushrod to return to its rest position. Do not allow the pushrod to return quickly, as this will cause air to enter the slave cylinder.

27 Remove the tube and spanner, and refit the dust cap to the bleed screw.

28 Refit the slave cylinder to the bellhousing, and tighten the securing nuts to the specified torque.

Using a one-way valve kit

29 As their name implies, these kits consist of a length of tubing with a one-way valve fitted, to prevent expelled air and fluid being drawn back into the system; some kits include a translucent container, which can be positioned so that the air bubbles can be more easily seen flowing from the end of the tube.

30 The kit is connected to the bleed screw, which is then opened. The user returns to the driver's seat, depresses the clutch pedal with a smooth, steady stroke, and slowly releases it; this is repeated until the expelled fluid is clear of air bubbles.

31 Note that these kits simplify work so much that it is easy to forget the reservoir fluid level; ensure that this is maintained at least above the MIN level line at all times.

Using a pressure-bleeding kit

32 These kits are usually operated by the reservoir of pressurised air contained in the spare tyre. However, note that it will probably be necessary to reduce the pressure to a lower level than normal; refer to the instructions supplied with the kit.

33 By connecting a pressurised, fluid-filled container to the fluid reservoir, bleeding can be carried out simply by opening the bleed screw, and allowing the fluid to flow out until no more air bubbles can be seen in the expelled fluid.

34 This method has the advantage that the large reservoir of fluid provides an additional safeguard against air being drawn into the system during bleeding.

All methods

35 If after following the instructions given, it is suspected that air is still present in hydraulic system, remove the slave cylinder (Section 4) without disconnecting the hydraulic pipes, push the cylinder piston all the way in, and holding the cylinder with the bleed screw uppermost, bleed the system again. **Note:** *Steps must be taken to ensure that the slave cylinder piston is prevented from extending during the bleeding procedure. If necessary, use a metal strip and two threaded bars to fabricate a tool to hold the piston in.*

36 When bleeding is complete, and firm pedal feel is restored, wash off any spilt fluid, check that the bleed screw is tightened securely, and refit the dust cap.

37 Check the hydraulic fluid level in the reservoir, and top-up if necessary (*Weekly checks*).

38 Discard any hydraulic fluid that has been bled from the system; it will not be fit for re-use.

39 Check the feel of the clutch pedal. If it feels at all spongy, air must still be present in the system, and further bleeding is required. Failure to bleed satisfactorily after a reasonable repetition of the bleeding procedure may be due to worn master or slave cylinder seals.

40 On completion, where applicable refit the underbody shield (where fitted) and lower the vehicle to the ground.

7 Clutch pedal – removal and refitting

Removal

1 Working inside the vehicle, release the retaining clips/screws, and withdraw the driver's side lower facia panel (see Chapter 11).

2 Undo the bolt and nut, then remove the clutch pedal switch – where fitted.

3 Prise up and slide off the retaining clip, then press out the master cylinder rod pivot pin from the pedal arm **(see illustration 5.7)**.

4 Using a small flat-bladed screwdriver, prise the circlip off and detach the over-centre spring (where fitted) from the pedal arm.

5 Undo the screws and move the clutch master cylinder to one side. There no need to disconnect the fluid pipe.

6 Prise off the clip securing the pedal to the pivot shaft, then slide the pedal from the shaft. Recover the pivot bushes if they are loose. Where, fitted release the return coil spring.

Refitting

7 Before refitting the pedal to the pivot shaft, check the condition of the pivot bushes, and renew if necessary. Apply a little grease to the bushes.

8 Refitting is a reversal of removal. Ensure that the clutch switch plunger is fully extended prior to refitment (where fitted).

Chapter 7 Part A:
Manual gearbox

Contents

Degrees of difficulty

Easy, suitable for novice with little experience 

Fairly easy, suitable for beginner with some experience 

Fairly difficult, suitable for competent DIY mechanic

Difficult, suitable for experienced DIY mechanic 

Very difficult, suitable for expert DIY or professional

Specifications

Type . . . . Getrag or ZF S5D 5 speed

Torque wrench settings	**Nm**	**lbf ft**
Gearbox crossmember-to-body bolts:		
M8 bolts	21	15
M10 bolts	42	31
Gearbox mounting-to-gearbox nuts:		
M8 nuts	21	15
M10 nuts	42	31
Gearbox-to-engine bolts:		
Hexagon head bolts:		
M8 bolts	25	18
M10 bolts	49	36
M12 bolts	74	55
Torx head bolts:		
M8 bolts	22	16
M10 bolts	43	32
M12 bolts	72	53
Oil drain plug	50	37
Oil filler/level plug	50	37
Output flange-to-output shaft nut:		
Stage 1	190	140
Stage 2	Remove nut and apply locking compound (see text)	
Stage 3	120	89
Reversing light switch	21	15

1 General information

The gearbox is a 5- speed unit, and is contained in a cast-alloy casing bolted to the rear of the engine. The gearbox code is constructed as follows, eg, S5D 200G:

S = manual transmission.
5 = number of forward gears.
D/S = direct drive/overdrive.
200 = maximum input torque (Nm).
G/Z = Getrag/ZF.

Drive is transmitted from the crankshaft via the clutch to the input shaft, which has a splined extension to accept the clutch friction disc. The output shaft transmits the drive via the propeller shaft to the rear differential.

The input shaft runs in line with the output shaft. The input shaft and output shaft gears are in constant mesh with the layshaft gear cluster. Selection of gears is by sliding synchromesh hubs, which lock the appropriate output shaft gears to the output shaft.

Gear selection is via a floor-mounted lever and selector mechanism. The selector mechanism causes the appropriate selector fork to move its respective synchro-sleeve along the shaft, to lock the gear pinion to the synchro-hub. Since the synchro-hubs are splined to the output shaft, this locks the pinion to the shaft, so that drive can be transmitted. To ensure that gearchanging can be made quickly and quietly, a synchromesh system is fitted to all forward gears, consisting of baulk rings and spring-loaded fingers, as well as the gear pinions and synchro-hubs. The synchromesh cones are formed on the mating faces of the baulk rings and gear pinions.

The transmission is filled with oil during production, and is then considered 'filled for life', with BMW making no recommendations concerning the changing of the fluid.

2 Manual gearbox oil level check

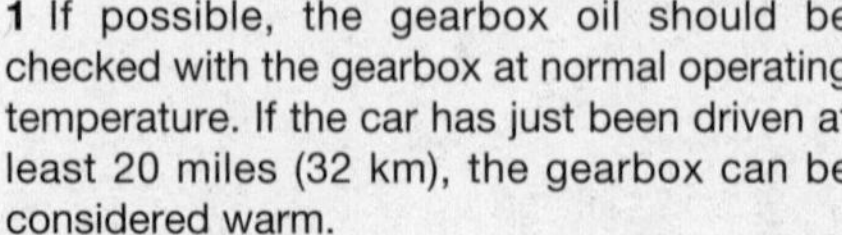

1 If possible, the gearbox oil should be checked with the gearbox at normal operating temperature. If the car has just been driven at least 20 miles (32 km), the gearbox can be considered warm.
2 To improve access, jack up the vehicle and support on axle stands (see *Jacking and vehicle support*). Ensure that the car is level. Where fitted, undo the screws and remove the undershield from beneath the transmission.
3 Unscrew the gearbox oil level/filler plug from the right-hand side of the gearbox casing **(see illustration)**.
4 The oil level should be up to the bottom of the level/filler plug hole.
5 If necessary, top-up the level, using the correct type of fluid (see *Lubricants and fluids*) until the oil overflows from the filler/level plug hole.

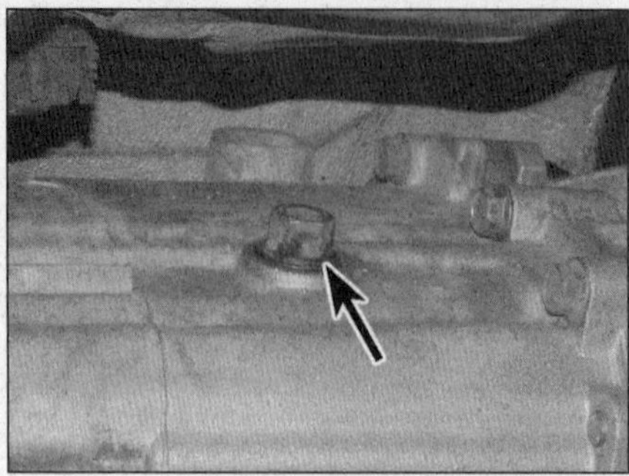

2.3 Unscrew the oil filler plug (arrowed)

6 Wipe away any spilt oil, then refit the filler/level plug, and tighten to the specified torque. Where applicable, refit the undershield.
7 Lower the vehicle to the ground.

3 Manual gearbox oil renewal

Note: *New gearbox oil drain plug and oil filler/level plug sealing rings may be required on refitting.*
1 The gearbox oil should be drained with the gearbox at normal operating temperature. If the car has just been driven at least 20 miles (32 km), the gearbox can be considered warm.
2 Immediately after driving the car, park it on a level surface, apply the handbrake. If desired, jack up the car and support on axle stands (see *Jacking and vehicle support*) to improve access, but make sure that the car is level. Remove the transmission undershield (where fitted).
3 Working under the car, slacken the gearbox oil drain plug about half a turn **(see illustration)**. Position a draining container under the drain plug, then remove the plug completely. If possible, try to keep the plug pressed into the gearbox while unscrewing it by hand the last couple of turns.

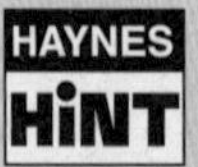

As the plug releases from the threads, move it away sharply so the stream of fluid from the gearbox runs into the container, not up your sleeve.

4 Where applicable, recover the sealing ring from the drain plug.
5 Refit the drain plug, using a new sealing ring where applicable, and tighten to the specified torque.
6 Unscrew the oil filler/level plug from the side of the gearbox, and recover the sealing ring, where applicable.
7 Fill the gearbox through the filler/level plug hole with the specified quantity and type of oil (see Chapter 1 and *Lubricants and fluids*), until the oil overflows from the filler/level plug hole.

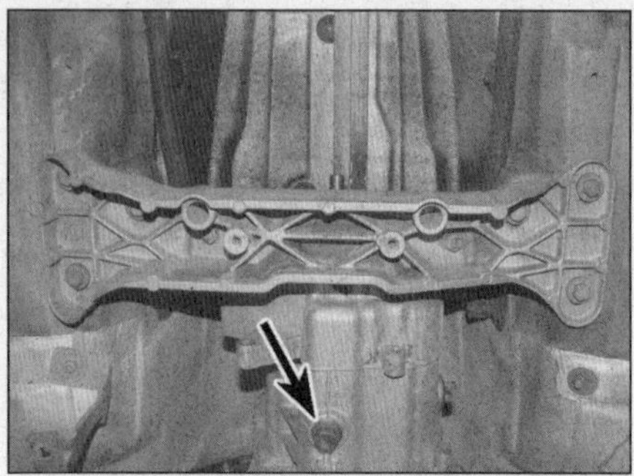

3.3 Undo the gearbox drain plug (arrowed)

8 Refit the filler/level plug, using a new sealing ring where applicable, and tighten to the specified torque.
9 If applicable, lower the car to the ground.

4 Gearchange components – removal and refitting

Gear lever

Note: *A new gear lever bearing maybe required on refitting.*
1 Jack up the car and support securely on axle stands (see *Jacking and vehicle support*).
2 Remove the knob from the gear lever by pulling it sharply upwards. **Note:** *Do not twist the knob or damage will result to the turning lock.*
3 Squeeze together the sides of the gaiter slightly, detach it from the centre console, and withdraw the gaiter over the gear lever. Where applicable, also remove the foam insulation.
4 Working under the vehicle, prise the securing clip from the end of the gear selector rod pin. Withdraw the selector rod pin from the eye on the end of the gear lever, and recover the washers **(see illustration)**.
5 It is now necessary to release the gear lever lower bearing retaining ring from the gear selector arm. A special tool is available for this purpose, but two screwdrivers, with the tips engaged in opposite slots in the bearing ring can be used instead. To unlock the bearing

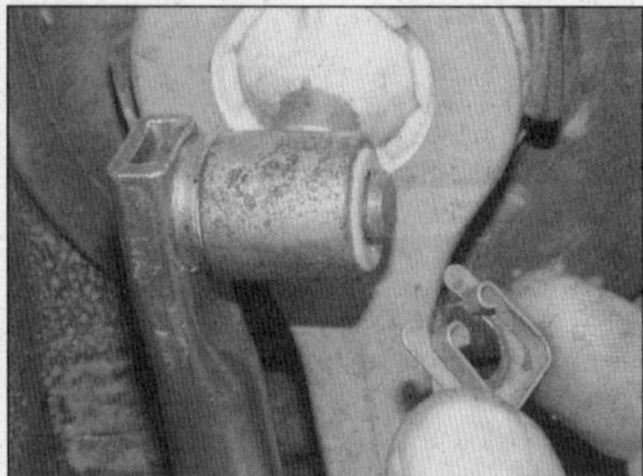

4.4 Slide the clip from the gearchange rod pin

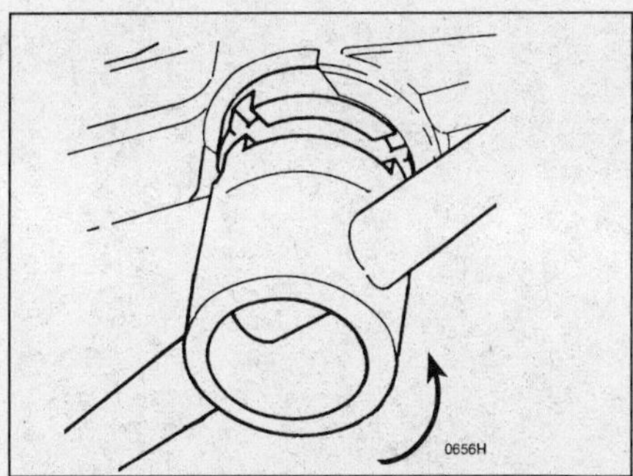

4.5 Turn the bearing ring anti-clockwise – special tool shown

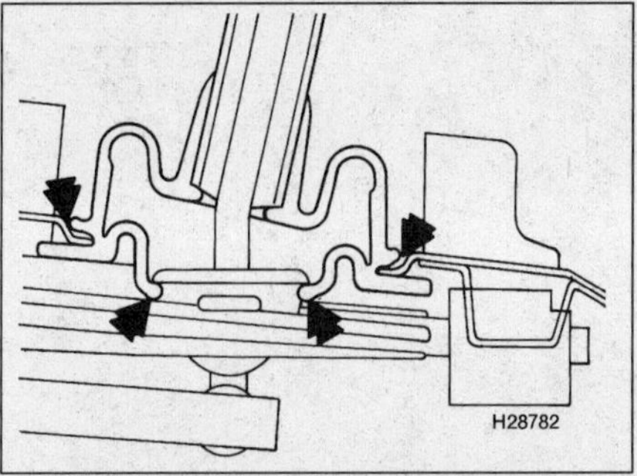

4.9 Gear lever grommet correctly engaged with the selector arm and vehicle floor

4.13 Slide back the circlip (arrowed) and drive out the locking pin

ring, turn it a quarter-turn anti-clockwise **(see illustration).**

6 The bearing can now be pushed up through the housing, and the gear lever can be withdrawn from inside the vehicle.

7 If desired, the bearing can be removed from the gear lever ball by pressing it downwards. To withdraw the bearing over the lever eye, rotate the bearing until the eye passes through the slots provided in the bearing. Note that if the bearing is removed from the lever, it must be renewed.

8 Fit a new bearing using a reversal of the removal process. Ensure that the bearing is pressed securely into position on the gear lever ball.

9 Refit the lever using a reversal of the removal process, bearing in mind the following points.

a) Grease the contact faces of the bearing before refitting.

b) Lower the gear lever into position, ensuring that the arrow on the gear lever gaiter points towards the front of the vehicle.

c) Make sure that the gear lever grommet is correctly engaged with the gear selector arm and with the opening in the vehicle floor ***(see illustration).***

d) When engaging the bearing with the selector arm, make sure that the retaining lugs of the bearing are aligned transversely (across the vehicle).

e) To lock the bearing in position in the selector arm, press down on the top of the bearing retaining tab locations until the tabs are heard to click into position.

f) Grease the selector rod pin before engaging it with the gear lever eye.

Selector shaft eye

Note: *A new selector shaft eye securing roll-pin will be required on refitting.*

10 Jack up the car and support securely on axle stands (see *Jacking and vehicle support*). Where fitted, undo the screws and remove the undershield from beneath the transmission.

11 Disconnect the propeller shaft from the gearbox flange, and support it clear of the gearbox using wire or string. Refer to Chapter 8 for details.

12 Prise the retaining clip from the end of the gear selector rod pin. Withdraw the selector rod pin from the selector shaft eye, and recover the washers.

13 Slide back the locking sleeve, then drive out the roll-pin securing the gear selector shaft eye to the end of the gear selector shaft **(see illustration)**.

14 Pull the gear selector shaft eye off the end of the selector shaft.

15 Refitting is a reversal of removal, bearing in mind the following points.

a) Before refitting, check the condition of the rubber washer in the end of the selector shaft eye and renew if necessary.

b) Use a new roll-pin to secure the eye to the selector shaft.

c) Grease the selector rod pin.

d) Reconnect the propeller shaft to the gearbox flange as described in Chapter 8.

Selector arm rear mounting

16 Jack up the car and support securely on axle stands (see *Jacking and vehicle support*).

17 Disconnect the propeller shaft from the gearbox flange, and support it clear of the gearbox using wire or string. See Chapter 8 for details.

18 Remove the gear lever as described previously in this Section.

19 Using a screwdriver or a small pin-punch, lever the mounting sleeve from the bracket on the body **(see illustration)**.

20 Pull the mounting from the selector arm.

21 Grease the mounting, then push the mounting onto the selector arm, with the cut-out facing the rear of the vehicle, and the arrow pointing vertically upwards.

22 Clip the mounting into position in the bracket, making sure that the mounting is securely located.

23 Reconnect the propeller shaft to the gearbox flange as described in Chapter 8, then lower the vehicle to the ground.

Selector shaft front mounting

24 Remove the rear mounting from the vehicle body as described in Paragraphs 16 to 20.

25 Undo the screws/nuts and remove the underbody heat shield to allow access to the transmission crossmember mounting bolts.

26 In order to remove the selector shaft front mounting pin, the transmission must be lowered slightly. Support the rear of the transmission casing with a trolley jack, then undo the bolts securing the transmission crossmember to the body, and the nuts securing the rubber mounts to the transmission casing **(see illustration)**.

27 Lower the transmission slightly, then prise up the retaining clip and slide out the selector shaft pivot pin **(see illustration)**. Manoeuvre the shaft from under the vehicle.

28 Refitting is a reversal of removal.

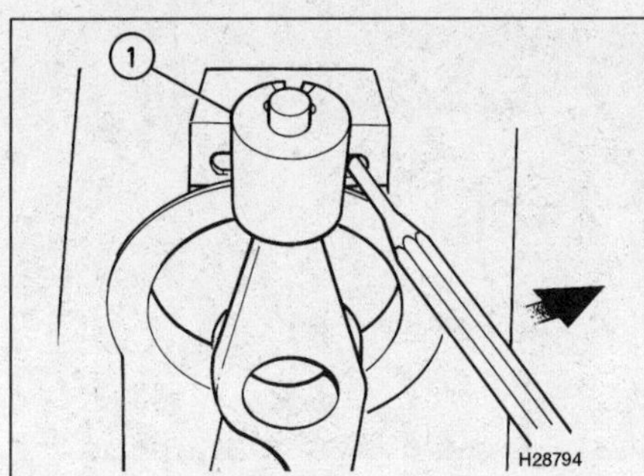

4.19 Lever the gear selector arm rear mounting sleeve (1) from the body bracket

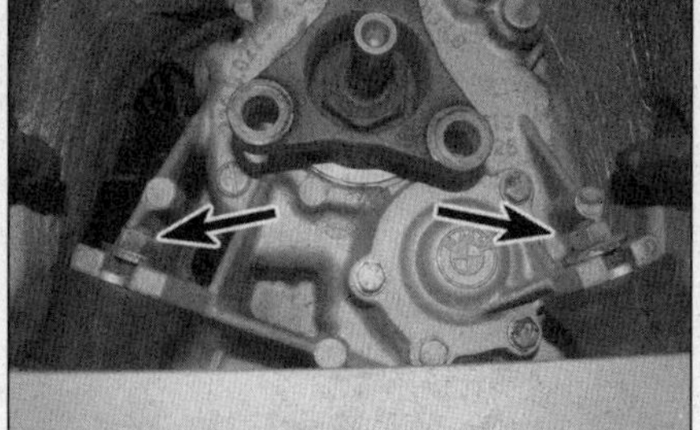
4.26 Undo the crossmember-to-body bolts, and the crossmember rubber mounting nuts (arrowed)

4.27 Prise up the clip with a screwdriver, then slide out the selector shaft pivot pin

Selector shaft bush

29 Remove the selector shaft from the vehicle by remove the front and rear mountings as previously described in this Section. Examine the bush for wear or damage. If required, the old bush can be pressed out, and a new bush pressed in. BMW recommend that the new bush is coated with Circolight (available from BMW dealers) prior to fitting. When correctly positioned, the new bush side edges should protruded equally on both sides of the shaft.

5 Oil seals – renewal

Input shaft oil seal

1 With the gearbox removed as described in Section 7, proceed as follows.

2 Remove the clutch release bearing and lever as described in Chapter 6.

3 Unscrew the securing bolts and withdraw the clutch release bearing guide sleeve from the gearbox bellhousing **(see illustration)**.

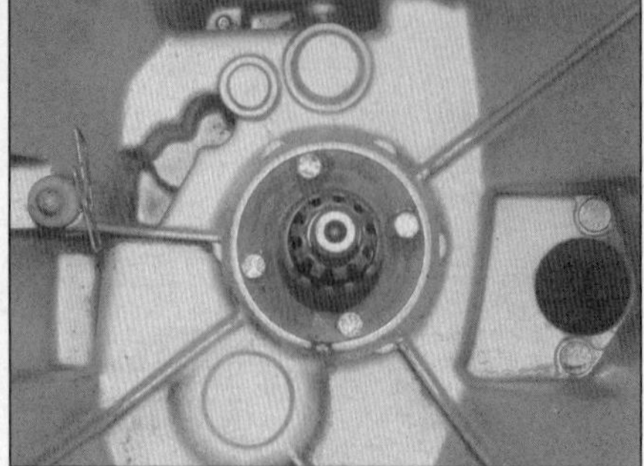

5.3 Undo the four bolts and remove the release bearing guide sleeve

4 Note the fitted depth of the now-exposed input shaft oil seal.

5 Drill one small hole in the oil seal (two small pilot holes should be provided at opposite points on the seal). Coat the end of the drill bit with grease to prevent any swarf from the holes entering the gearbox **(see illustration)**.

5.5 Drill a small hole in the oil seal

6 Using a small drift, tap one side of the seal (opposite to the hole) into the bellhousing as far as the stop.

7 Screw a small self-tapping screw into the drilled hole, and use pliers to pull out the seal **(see illustration)**.

5.7 Screw a self-tapping screw into the hole, and pull the seal from place using a pair of pliers

8 Clean the oil seal seating surface, then wind a length of tape over the splines on the shaft to prevent damage to the new seal as it is slid over the shaft.

9 Lubricate the lips of the new oil seal with a little clean gearbox oil, then carefully slide the seal over the input shaft into position in the bellhousing.

10 Tap the oil seal into the bellhousing to the previously noted depth.

11 Refit the guide sleeve to the gearbox housing, tighten the retaining bolts securely,

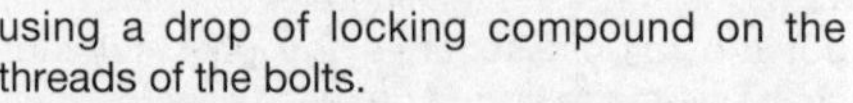

using a drop of locking compound on the threads of the bolts.

12 Refit the clutch release lever and bearing as described in Chapter 6.

13 Refit the gearbox as described in Section 7, then check the gearbox oil level as described in Section 2.

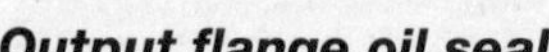

Output flange oil seal

Note: *Thread-locking compound will be required for the gearbox flange nut on refitting.*

14 Jack up the vehicle and support securely on axle stands (see *Jacking and vehicle support*).

15 Disconnect the propeller shaft from the gearbox flange, and support it clear of the gearbox using wire or string. See Chapter 8 for details.

16 Where applicable, prise the gearbox flange nut cover plate from the flange using a screwdriver. Discard the cover plate – it is not required on refitting. If necessary, support the transmission, and remove the transmission crossmember to improve access.

17 Counterhold the gearbox flange by bolting a forked or two-legged tool to two of the flange bolt holes, then unscrew the flange securing nut using a deep socket and extension bar **(see illustration)**.

5.17 Counterhold the output flange and undo the nut using a deep socket

18 Using a puller, draw the flange from the end of the gearbox output shaft **(see illustration)**. Be prepared for oil spillage.

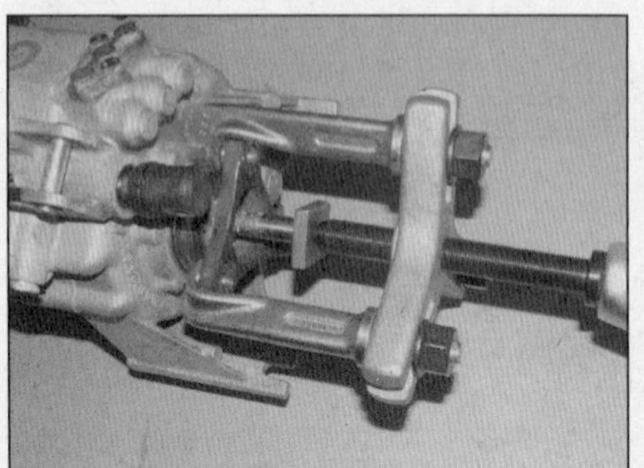

5.18 Use a three-legged puller to remove the output flange

19 Note the fitted depth of the oil seal then, using a puller (take care to avoid damage to the gearbox output shaft), pull the oil seal from the gearbox casing **(see illustration)**.

5.19 Carefully pull the seal from place

20 Clean the oil seal seating surface.

21 Lubricate the lips of the new oil seal with a little clean gearbox oil, then carefully tap the seal into the gearbox casing to the to the previously noted depth **(see illustration)**.

5.21 Tap the new seal into place using a tubular spacer or socket which bears only on the hard outer edge of the seal

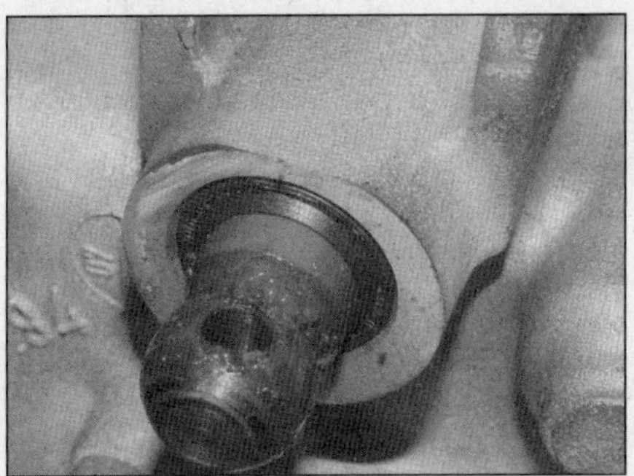
5.31 Tap the new selector shaft seal into position

22 Refit the flange to the output shaft. **Note:** *To ease refitment of the flange, immerse it in hot water for a few minutes, then install it on the shaft.*
23 Tighten the flange nut to the Stage one torque setting, then slacken and remove the nut (Stage two). Coat the threads of the flange nut with thread-locking compound, then tighten the nut to the Stage three torque as specified. Counterhold the flange as during removal.
24 If a flange nut cover plate was originally fitted, discard it. There is no need to fit a cover plate on refitting.
25 Reconnect the propeller shaft to the gearbox flange as described in Chapter 8, then check the gearbox oil level as described in Section 2, and lower the vehicle to the ground.

Selector shaft oil seal

Note: *A new selector shaft eye securing roll-pin will be required on refitting.*
26 Jack up the vehicle and support securely on axle stands (see *Jacking and vehicle support*).
27 Disconnect the propeller shaft from the gearbox flange, and support it clear of the gearbox using wire or string. See Chapter 8 for details. For improved access, support the transmission, and remove the transmission crossmember.
28 Slide back the locking collar, then slide out the pin securing the gear selector shaft eye to the end of the gear selector shaft.
29 Pull the gear selector shaft eye (complete with gear linkage) off the end of the selector shaft, and move the linkage clear of the selector shaft.
30 Using a small flat-bladed screwdriver, prise the selector shaft oil seal from the gearbox casing.
31 Clean the oil seal seating surface, smear the inner lip of the new oil seal with clean transmission oil, then tap the new seal into position using a small socket or tube of the correct diameter **(see illustration)**.
32 Check the condition of the rubber washer in the end of the selector shaft eye and renew if necessary.
33 Push the selector shaft eye back onto the end of the selector shaft, then align the holes in the eye and shaft and secure the eye to the shaft using the pin.

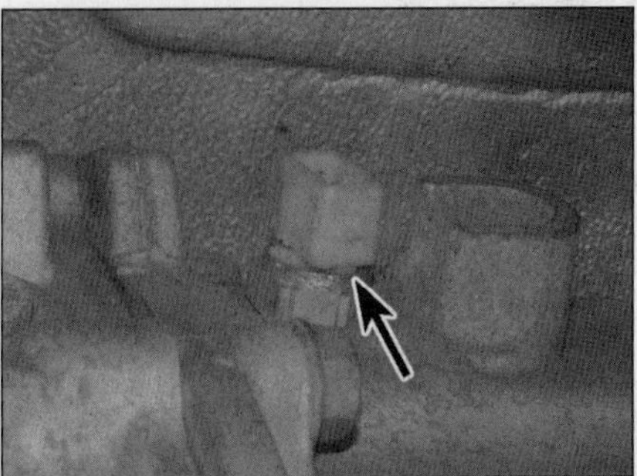
6.4 Unscrew the switch (arrowed) from the gearbox casing

34 Slide the locking collar into position over the roll-pin.
35 Reconnect the propeller shaft to the gearbox flange as described in Chapter 8.
36 Check the gearbox oil level as described in Section 2, then lower the vehicle to the ground.

6 Reversing light switch – testing, removal and refitting

Testing

1 The reversing light circuit is controlled by a plunger-type switch screwed into the left-hand side of the Getrag gearbox casing, and the right-hand side of the ZF gearbox casing. If a fault develops in the circuit, first ensure that the circuit fuse has not blown.
2 To test the switch, disconnect the wiring connector, and use a multimeter (set to the resistance function) or a battery-and-bulb test circuit to check that there is continuity between the switch terminals only when reverse gear is selected. If this is not the case, and there are no obvious breaks or other damage to the wires, the switch is faulty, and must be renewed.

Removal

3 Jack up the vehicle and support securely on axle stands (see *Jacking and vehicle support*).
4 Disconnect the wiring connector, then unscrew the switch from the gearbox casing **(see illustration)**.

Refitting

5 Screw the switch back into position in the gearbox housing and tighten it securely. Reconnect the wiring connector, and test the operation of the circuit.
6 Lower the vehicle to the ground.

7 Manual gearbox –

Note: *This is an involved operation. Read through the procedure thoroughly before starting work, and ensure that adequate lifting tackle and/or jacking/support equipment is available.*

Removal

1 Disconnect the battery negative lead (see Chapter 5A).
2 Jack up the car and support securely on axle stands (see *Jacking and vehicle support*). Note that the car must be raised sufficiently to allow clearance for the gearbox to be removed from under the car. Undo the screws and remove the engine/transmission undershields.
3 Using a socket, ratchet and long extension, undo the starter motor mounting bolts from the transmission bellhousing.
4 Remove the propeller shaft as described in Chapter 8.
5 Working under the car, prise the retaining clip from the end of the gear selector rod pin. Withdraw the selector rod pin from the eye on the end of the gearbox selector shaft, and recover the washers. Similarly, disconnect the selector rod pin from the end of the gear lever, and withdraw the selector rod.
6 Working at the gearbox bellhousing, unscrew the nuts, and withdraw the clutch slave cylinder from the studs on the bellhousing. Support the slave cylinder clear of the working area, but do not strain the hose.
7 Note their fitted locations, then disconnect all wiring plugs, and release any wiring harnesses from the gearbox casing.
8 Undo the nuts and remove the heat shield bracket from the transmission tunnel.
9 Undo the nuts, and disconnect the front anti-roll bar from the drop-links at each end (refer to Chapter 10 if necessary). Swivel the ends of the anti-roll bar upwards to position the bar out of the way of the gearbox.
10 Connect the lifting tackle to the engine lifting eye at the rear left-hand corner of the cylinder block (incorporated in the rear flange of the cylinder block casting).
11 Place a trolley jack under the gearbox casing, just behind the bellhousing. Use a block of wood to spread the load, then raise the jack to just take the weight of the gearbox.
12 Remove the crossmember and mountings from the rear of the transmission.
13 Using the jack(s) and engine hoist (where applicable), lower the engine and gearbox until the rear of the engine cylinder head/manifold assembly is almost touching the engine compartment bulkhead. Check that the assembly is not resting against any hoses/pipes on the bulkhead.
14 Working at the top of the gearbox, prise up the clip securing the gear selector arm pivot pin to the gearbox casing, then pull out the pivot pin to release the selector arm from the gearbox **(see illustration 4.27)**.
15 Where applicable, unscrew the bolt securing the engine/gearbox adapter plate to the right-hand side of the gearbox bellhousing

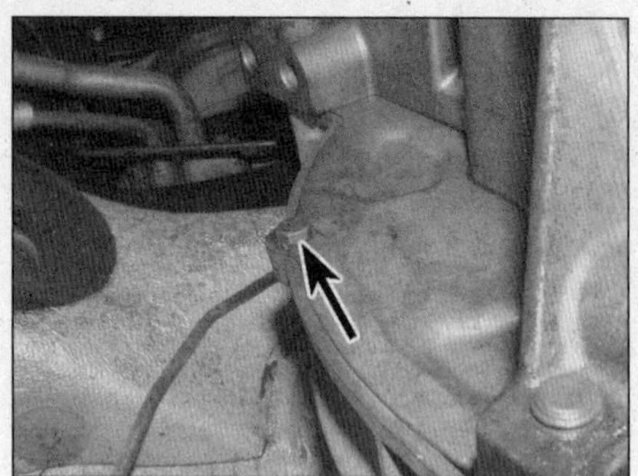

7.15 Undo the bolt (arrowed) securing the adapter plate to the gearbox casing

7.20 Ensure the adapter plate is position correctly over the locating dowels

and/or remove the flywheel lower cover plate **(see illustration)**.

16 Unscrew the engine-to-gearbox bolts, and recover the washers, then slide the gearbox rearwards to disengage the input shaft from the clutch. Take care during this operation to ensure that the weight of the gearbox is not allowed to hang on the input shaft. As the gearbox is released from the engine, check to make sure that the engine is not forced against the heater hose connections or the bulkhead.

17 Lower the gearbox and carefully withdraw it from under the car. If the gearbox is to be removed for some time, ensure that the engine is adequately supported in the engine compartment.

Refitting

18 Commence refitting by checking that the clutch friction disc is centralised as described in Chapter 6.

19 Before refitting the gearbox, it is advisable to inspect and grease the clutch release bearing and lever as described in Chapter 6.

20 The remainder of the refitting procedure is a reversal of removal, bearing in mind the following points.

a) Check that the gearbox positioning dowels are securely in place at the rear of the engine.

*b) Make sure that the engine/gearbox adapter plate is fitted correctly over the positioning dowels **(see illustration)**.*

c) Tighten all fixings to the specified torque.

d) Lightly grease the gear selector arm pivot pin and the gear selector rod pin before refitting.

e) Reconnect the propeller shaft to the gearbox flange as described in Chapter 8.

8 Manual gearbox overhaul – general information

Overhauling a manual gearbox is a difficult and involved job for the DIY home mechanic. In addition to dismantling and reassembling many small parts, clearances must be precisely measured and, if necessary, changed by selecting shims and spacers. Internal gearbox components are also often difficult to obtain, and in many instances, extremely expensive. Because of this, if the gearbox develops a fault or becomes noisy, the best course of action is to have the unit overhauled by a specialist repairer, or to obtain an exchange reconditioned unit. Be aware that some gearbox repairs can be carried out with the gearbox in the car.

Nevertheless, it is not impossible for the more experienced mechanic to overhaul the gearbox, provided the special tools are available, and the job is done in a deliberate step-by-step manner, so that nothing is overlooked.

The tools necessary for an overhaul include internal and external circlip pliers, bearing pullers, a slide hammer, a set of pin punches, a dial test indicator, and possibly a hydraulic press. In addition, a large, sturdy workbench and a vice will be required.

During dismantling of the gearbox, make careful notes of how each component is fitted, to make reassembly easier and more accurate.

Before dismantling the gearbox, it will help if you have some idea what area is malfunctioning. Certain problems can be closely related to specific areas in the gearbox, which can make component examination and renewal easier. Refer to the *Fault finding* Section at the end of this manual for more information.

Chapter 7 Part B: Automatic transmission

Contents

Degrees of difficulty

Easy, suitable for novice with little experience 

Fairly easy, suitable for beginner with some experience 

Fairly difficult, suitable for competent DIY mechanic

Difficult, suitable for experienced DIY mechanic

Very difficult, suitable for expert DIY or professional 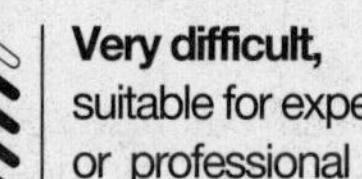

Specifications

Transmission fluid level

Fluid temperature °C	Fluid level height (mm)
20	3 to 15
25	5 to 17
30	8 to 20
35	11 to 22
40	13 to 25
45	14 to 26
50	16 to 27
55	17 to 28
60	19 to 29
65	21 to 32
70	22 to 35
75	24 to 36
80	26 to 38
85	29 to 41
90	31 to 43

Torque wrench settings

Torque wrench settings	Nm	lbf ft
Engine-to-transmission bolts:		
Hexagon bolts:		
M8 bolts	24	18
M10 bolts	45	33
M12 bolts	82	61
Torx bolts:		
M8 bolts	21	15
M10 bolts	42	31
M12 bolts	72	53
Engine/transmission adapter plate bolt	23	17
Torque-converter-to-driveplate bolts:		
M8 bolts	26	19
M10 bolts	49	36
Transmission crossmember-to-body bolts	21	15
Transmission mounting-to-transmission nuts	21	15
Transmission oil drain plug:		
M10 thread	16	12
M14 thread	18	13
M16 thread	35	26
Transmission oil filler/level plug	40	30

** Use thread-locking compound*

2.2 Undo the selector cable clamping nut (arrowed)

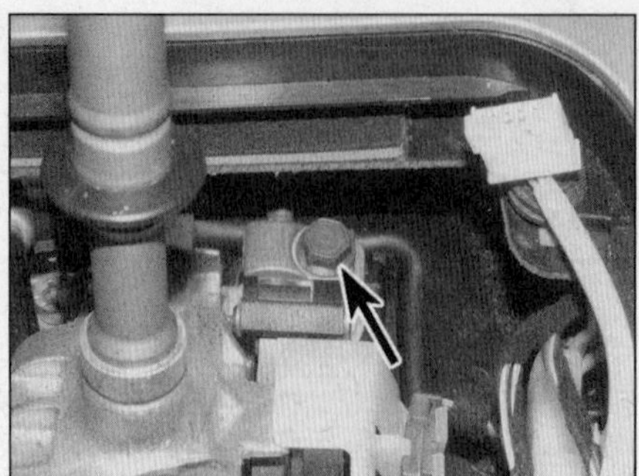
2.7 Slacken the interlock cable clamp bolt (arrowed)

2.8 Undo the three bolts (arrowed) securing the selector lever assembly

1 General information

A five-speed automatic transmission is fitted, consisting of a torque converter, an epicyclic geartrain and hydraulically-operated clutches and brakes.

The torque converter provides a fluid coupling between engine and transmission, acting as a clutch, and also provides a degree of torque multiplication when accelerating.

The epicyclic geartrain provides either of the forward or reverse gear ratio, according to which of its component parts are held stationary or allowed to turn. The components of the geartrain are held or released by brakes and clutches which are activated by a hydraulic control unit. A fluid pump within the transmission provides the necessary hydraulic pressure to operate the brakes and clutches.

Driver control of the transmission is by a floor-mounted selector lever. The transmission is equipped with Adaptive Transmission Control (ATC), which ensures an accurate response to the driver's needs by automatically selecting various driving programs. The system evaluates a number of factors before selecting the optimum shift points. These factors include accelerator pedal position/rate of change, braking rate, lateral acceleration, engine load, etc. Four driving programs are available to the ECU, from comfort-orientated to performance-orientated shift points.

Certain models are available with Steptronic gearchange where the driver is able to make gearchanges with a simple movement of the lever – forward to change up, and back to change down. Refer to the Owners Handbook supplied with the vehicle.

Due to the complexity of the automatic transmission, any repair or overhaul work must be left to a BMW dealer or specialist with the necessary special equipment for fault diagnosis and repair. The contents of the following Sections are therefore confined to supplying general information, and any service information and instructions that can be used by the owner.

2 Gear selector lever – removal and refitting

Removal

1 Jack up the car and support securely on axle stands (see *Jacking and vehicle support*). Ensure the selector lever is in position P. Where applicable, undo the screws and remove the transmission undershield.

2 Working underneath the vehicle, slacken the selector cable clamping nut on the transmission lever **(see illustration)**.

3 Undo the locknut securing the selector outer cable and remove the cable from the support bracket on the transmission.

4 Working in the passenger cabin, pull the knob straight upwards from the selector lever. **Note:** *Do not twist the knob or damage will result to the turning lock in the lever.*

5 Carefully prise up the lever trim (complete with lever gaiter) from the centre console. Note the fitted location(s), and disconnect the wiring plug(s) from the underside of the trim.

6 On non-Steptronic models, undo the two screws, and remove the position switch from the right-hand side of the selector lever housing.

7 On Steptronic models, slacken the screw securing the interlock cable **(see illustration)**.

8 Slacken and remove the three bolts securing the selector lever housing to the floor **(see illustration)**.

9 In order to remove the housing, the centre console must be moved to the rear approximately 20 mm. With reference to Chapter 11, remove the fasteners securing the centre console in position, and slide it back.

10 Lift the selector lever housing and manoeuvre it from the centre console along with the selector cable. Note their fitted positions, then disconnect any wiring plugs attached to the selector lever assembly. No further dismantling of the selector lever and housing is recommended.

Refitting

11 Refitting is a reversal of removal, noting the following points:

a) When refitting the position switch, the pin on the switch must locate in the recess on the selector lever.

b) Prior to refitting the gear knob, push the gaiter down the lever until the locking groove in the lever is exposed.

c) On completion, adjust the selector cable as described in Section 3.

3 Gear selector cable – removal, refitting and adjustment

Removal

1 Remove the selector lever and housing (complete with cable) as described in Section 2.

2 On non-Steptronic models, remove the circlip, then slide the cable inner end and plastic fitting from the lever **(see illustrations)**.

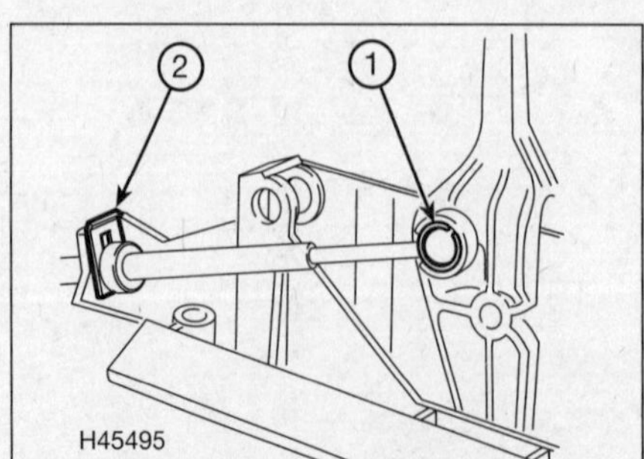

3.2a On non-Steptronic models, the cable is secured to the lever by circlip (1), and to the housing by clip (2)

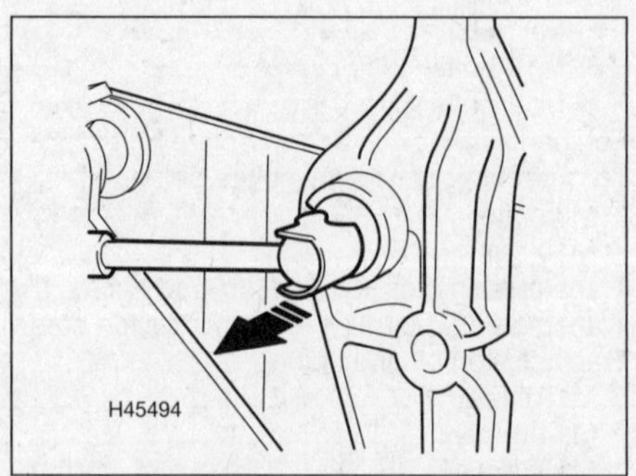

3.2b With the circlip removed, slide the cable end and plastic fitting from the lever

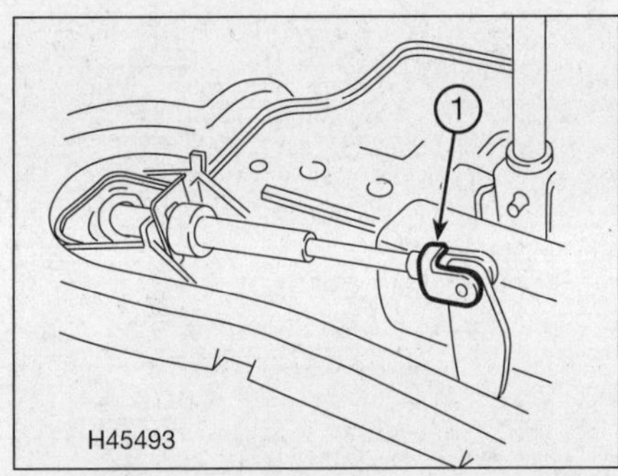

3.3 On Steptronic models, lift up the retaining catch (1) and slide out the pin

3 On Steptronic models, lift up the retaining catch and slide out the pin securing the inner cable to the selector lever **(see illustration)**. Note the location of the damping rubber between the cable end and the selector lever.

4 On all models, slide up the outer cable retaining clip, and remove the cable from the housing.

Refitting

5 Refitting is a reversal of removal, bearing in mind the following points.

a) *BMW insist that on non-Steptronic models, the inner cable plastic end fitting should not be re-used – a new one must be fitted.*

b) *Refit the selector lever housing along with the cable as described in Section 2.*

c) *Reconnect the cable to the selector lever assembly with reference to Section 2.*

d) *On completion, adjust the cable as described in the following paragraphs.*

Adjustment

6 Move the selector lever to position P.

7 If not already done, counterhold clamp bolt and loosen the clamp nut securing the cable to the end fitting (the car should be raised for access).

8 Push the operating lever on the transmission away from the cable bracket on the transmission (towards the Park position).

9 Press the end of the cable in the opposite direction (ie, towards the cable bracket), then release the cable and tighten the clamp nut (again, counterhold the bolt).

10 Check that the cable is correctly adjusted by starting the engine, applying the brakes firmly, and moving the selector lever through all the selector positions.

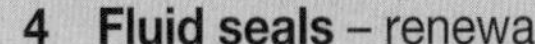

4 Fluid seals – renewal

Torque converter seal

1 Remove the transmission and the torque converter as described in Section 5.

2 On some models, the oil seal is retained by a circular plate, secured by Torx screws. Undo the screws and remove the plate.

3 Using a hooked tool, prise the old oil seal from the transmission bellhousing. Alternatively, drill a small hole, then screw a self-tapping screw into the seal and use pliers to pull out the seal.

4 Lubricate the lip of the new seal with clean fluid, then carefully drive it into place using a large socket or tube.

5 Remove the old O-ring seal from the input shaft, and slide a new one into place. Apply a smear of petroleum jelly to the new O-ring.

6 Refit the torque converter and transmission as described in Section 5.

Output flange oil seal

7 Renewal of the oil seal involves partial dismantling of the transmission, which is a complex operation – see Section 6. Oil seal renewal should be entrusted to a BMW dealer or specialist.

5 Automatic transmission – removal and refitting

Note: *This is an involved operation. Read through the procedure thoroughly before starting work, and ensure that adequate lifting tackle and/or jacking/support equipment is available. A suitable tool will be required to align the torque converter when refitting the transmission, and new fluid pipe O-rings may be required.*

Removal

1 Disconnect the battery negative lead – see Chapter 5A.

2 Jack up the car and support securely on axle stands (see *Jacking and vehicle support*). Note that the car must be raised sufficiently to allow clearance for the transmission to be removed from under the car. Undo the screws and remove the engine/transmission undertray from the vehicle.

3 Unscrew the nuts, and disconnect the front anti-roll bar from the drop-links. Refer to Chapter 10 if necessary.

4 Remove the starter motor as described in Chapter 5A.

5 Remove the exhaust system and heat shield, then unbolt the exhaust mounting crossmember from under the car.

6 Remove the propeller shaft as described in Chapter 8.

7 Drain the automatic transmission fluid as described in Section 9.

8 Where applicable, unscrew the union nut, and remove the fluid filler pipe from the transmission fluid pan.

9 Disconnect the selector cable from the transmission with reference to Section 3.

10 Note their fitted locations, then disconnect the transmission wiring harness plugs **(see illustration)**. Release the wiring harness from the brackets and clips on the transmission.

11 Where applicable, release the oxygen sensor from the bracket on the transmission.

12 Unbolt the fluid cooler pipe brackets and clamps. Undo the unions and disconnect the fluid pipes – be prepared for fluid spillage. Where O-ring seals are fitted, discard them – new ones must be fitted.

13 Prise the plug from the aperture in the engine/transmission adapter plate/crankcase, depending on model, for access to the torque converter securing bolts **(see illustrations)**.

14 Unscrew the three torque converter bolts, turning the crankshaft using a spanner or socket on the pulley hub bolt for access to each bolt in turn.

15 Support the transmission using a trolley jack and interposed block of wood.

Caution: The transmission is heavy, so ensure that it is adequately supported.

16 Support the engine using a trolley jack under the sump, with a block of wood between the jack and sump to spread the load. Raise the jack to just touch the sump.

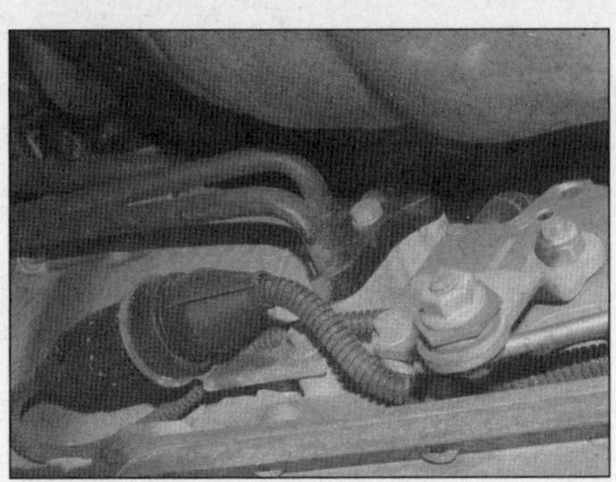

5.10 Disconnect the transmission wiring plugs

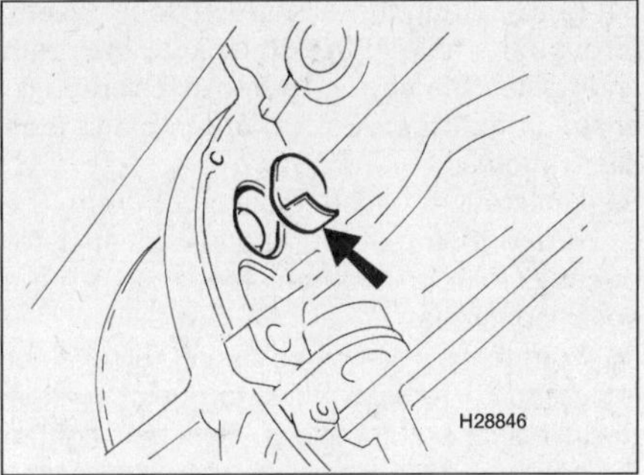

5.13a Prise the plug (arrowed) from the engine/transmission adapter plate . . .

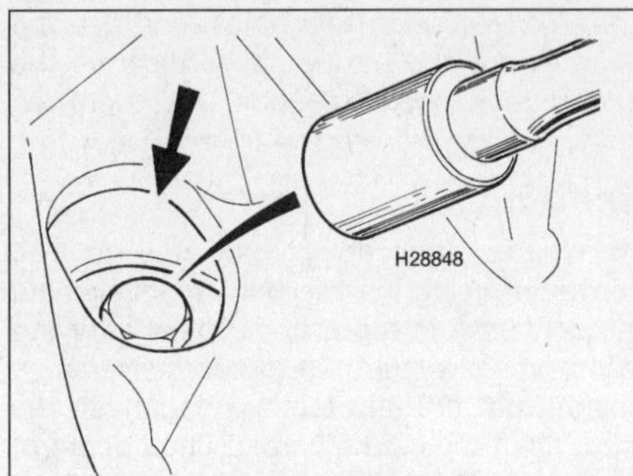

5.13b . . . or from the aperture in the crankcase

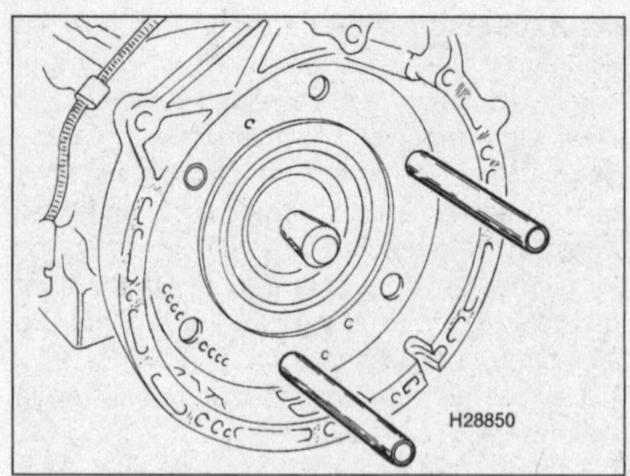

5.24 Fit two long bolts to lift out the torque converter

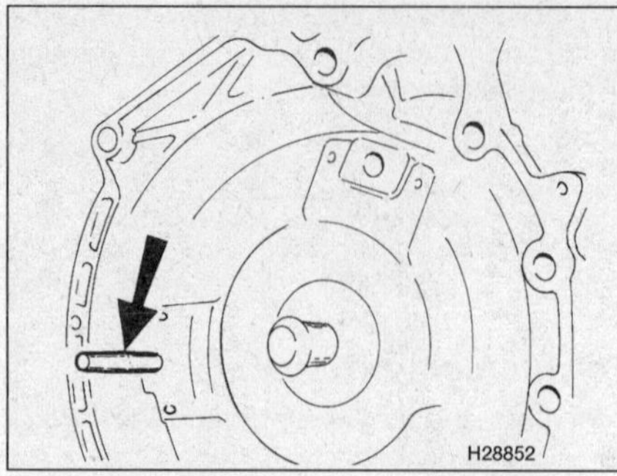

5.30 Alignment tool screws into the driveplate aligned with the aperture in the engine/transmission adapter plate

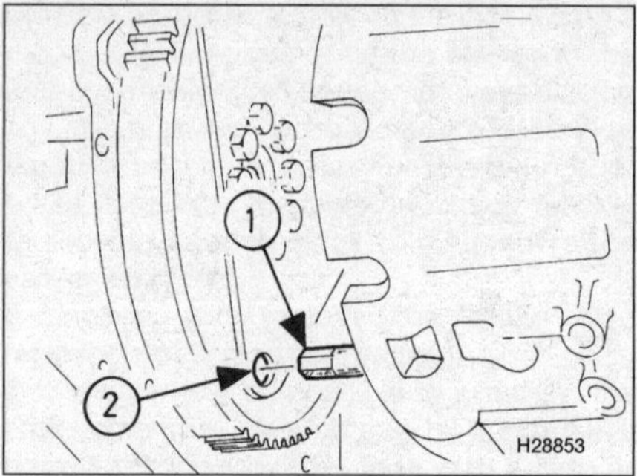

5.34 Ensure that the alignment tool (1) passes through the hole (2) in the torque converter

17 Check to ensure that the engine and transmission are adequately supported then, working under the car, unscrew the nuts securing the transmission rubber mountings to the lugs on the transmission casing.

18 Remove the bolts securing the transmission crossmember to the body, then withdraw the crossmember from under the car. If necessary, bend back or unbolt the exhaust heat shield for access to the crossmember bolts.

19 Using the jack(s) and engine hoist (where applicable), lower the engine and transmission until the rear of the engine cylinder head/manifold assembly is almost touching the engine compartment bulkhead. Check that the assembly is not resting against the heater hose connections on the bulkhead.

20 Unscrew the engine-to-transmission bolts, and recover the washers, then slide the transmission rearwards.

21 Insert a suitable metal or wooden lever through the slot in the bottom of the bellhousing to retain the torque converter. As the transmission is released from the engine, check to make sure that the engine is not forced against the heater hose connections or the bulkhead.

22 Lower the transmission and carefully withdraw it from under the car, making sure that the torque converter is held in position. If the transmission is to be removed for some time, ensure that the engine is adequately supported in the engine compartment.

23 To remove the torque converter, first remove the retaining lever.

24 Fit two long bolts to two of the torque converter securing bolt holes, and use the bolts to pull the torque converter from the transmission **(see illustration)**. Pull evenly on both bolts. Be prepared for fluid spillage.

Refitting

25 Where applicable, refit the torque converter, using the two bolts to manipulate the converter into position. Whilst applying slight pressure, turn the torque converter to ensure that the hub teeth engage with the input shaft teeth. The correct fitted depth of the torque converter is 31 mm (approx) from the bellhousing face to the forward edge of the torque converter securing bolt holes.

26 Ensure that the transmission locating dowels are in position on the engine.

27 Before mating the transmission with the engine, it is essential that the torque converter is perfectly aligned with the driveplate. Once the engine and transmission have been mated, it is no longer possible to turn the torque converter to allow re-alignment.

28 To align the driveplate with the torque converter, BMW use a special tapered tool (No 24 4 000) which screws into the converter. It may be possible to improvise a suitable tool using an old torque converter-to-driveplate bolt with the head cut off, or a length of threaded bar – note that the end of the bolt or bar must either have a slot cut in the end, or flats machined on it to allow it to be unscrewed once the engine and transmission have been mated.

29 Turn the flywheel to align one of the torque converter-to-driveplate bolt holes with the aperture in the crankcase/transmission adapter plate (as applicable). This is essential to enable the alignment stud to be removed after the engine and transmission have been mated.

30 Screw the alignment tool into the relevant hole in the converter **(see illustration)**.

31 Where applicable, remove the retaining lever from the torque converter.

32 Ensure that the transmission is adequately supported, and manoeuvre it into position under the car.

33 Turn the torque converter to align one of the torque converter-to-driveplate bolt holes with the alignment tool fitted to the converter, then offer the transmission into position.

34 Ensure that the alignment tool passes through the hole in the driveplate, then refit and tighten the engine-to-transmission bolts, ensuring that the washers are in place **(see illustration)**.

35 Unscrew the alignment tool from the converter, then refit the torque converter-to-driveplate bolt. Tighten the bolt to the specified torque.

36 Turn the crankshaft as during removal for access to the remaining two torque converter-to-driveplate bolt locations. Refit and tighten the bolts.

37 Further refitting is a reversal of removal, bearing in mind the following points.

a) Tighten all fixings to the specified torques, where applicable.
b) Check the condition of the transmission fluid pipe O-rings and renew if necessary.
c) Refit the propeller shaft (see Chapter 8).
d) Refit the starter motor (see Chapter 5A).
e) Reconnect and adjust the selector cable as described in Section 3.
f) On completion, refill the transmission with fluid as described in Section 9.

6 Automatic transmission overhaul – general information

In the event of a fault occurring with the transmission, it is first necessary to determine whether it is of an electrical, mechanical or hydraulic nature, and to do this special test equipment is required. It is therefore essential to have the work carried out by a BMW dealer or suitably-equipped specialist if a transmission fault is suspected.

Do not remove the transmission from the car for possible repair before professional fault diagnosis has been carried out, since most tests require the transmission to be in the car.

7 Electronic components/sensors – removal and refitting

1 The turbine speed sensor, output speed sensor and transmission range switch are all contained within the transmission casing. Renewal of the components involves removal and the sump and partial dismantling of the transmission, therefore this should be entrusted to a BMW dealer or suitably-equipped specialist.

2 The transmission electronic control module (ECM) is located in the 'E-box' in the left-hand corner of the engine compartment.

3 To remove the ECM, release the clip(s) and disconnect the air duct from the passenger's side pollen filter housing. Release the retaining clip and remove the filter housing cover.

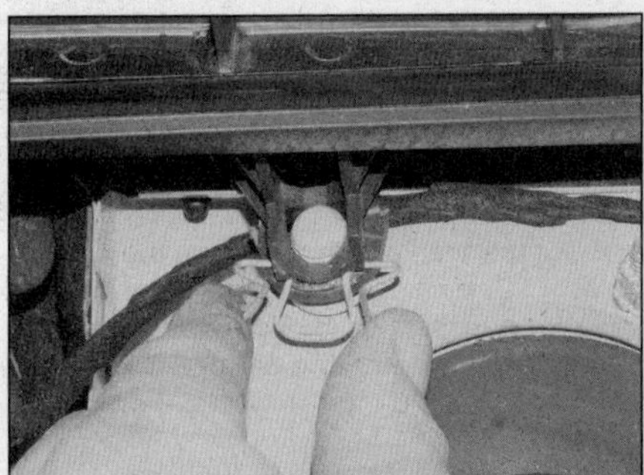

7.4 Release the clip and remove the pollen filter housing

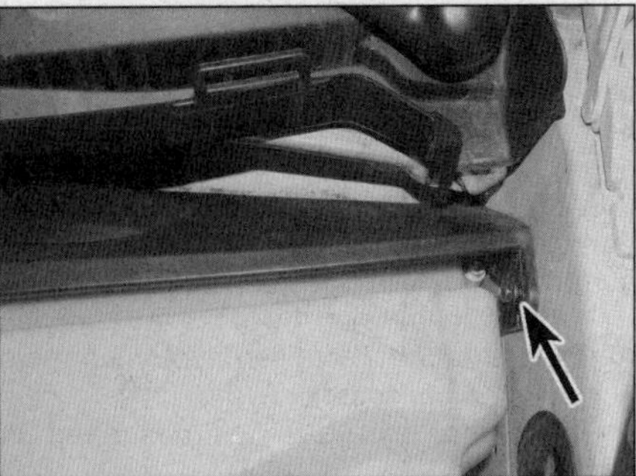

7.5 Undo the bolt (arrowed\ and remove the panel

7.6 Automatic transmission ECM (arrowed)

4 Release the clip and remove the filter housing **(see illustration)**.

5 Undo the bolt and remove the panel over the rear of the E-box **(see illustration)**.

6 Undo the screws, remove the E-box lid, disconnect the wiring plug and remove the ECM **(see illustration)**.

8 Automatic transmission fluid level check

Models with dipstick

1 Park the vehicle on a level surface, apply the handbrake and start the engine. While the engine is idling, depress the brake pedal and move the selector lever through all the gear positions, beginning and ending in P.

2 The automatic transmission fluid dipstick is located in the rear left-hand corner of the engine compartment.

3 The level of the fluid within the transmission depends on its temperature. To establish this temperature BMW technicians use special diagnostic equipment plugged into the vehicle diagnostic socket in the right-hand corner of the engine compartment. However, with care the temperature of the fluid can be taken by inserting a thermometer or thermocouple from a digital multimeter down into the dipstick hole.

4 Whilst the engine is still idling, pull the dipstick out of the tube, wipe it off with a clean, lint-free cloth, push it all the way back into the tube, and withdraw it again, then note the fluid level.

5 Measure the distance from the bottom of the dipstick to the fluid level, and compare with the table given in the Specifications at the start of this Chapter. If the level is low, add the specified automatic transmission fluid through the dipstick tube – use a clean funnel, preferably equipped with a fine mesh filter, to prevent spills.

Caution: Be careful not to introduce dirt into the transmission when topping-up.

6 Add just enough of the recommended fluid to fill the transmission to the proper level. Add the fluid a little at a time, and keep checking the level until it is correct.

7 On completion, stop the engine.

8 The condition of the fluid should also be checked along with the level. If the fluid is black or a dark reddish-brown colour, or if it smells burned, it should be renewed (see Section 9).

Models without dipstick

Note: *A new filler/level plug sealing ring will be required on refitting.*

9 The fluid level is checked by removing the filler/level plug from the transmission fluid pan. If desired, jack up the car and support on axle stands (see *Jacking and vehicle support*) to improve access, but make sure that the car is level.

10 While the engine is idling, depress the brake pedal and move the selector lever through all the gear positions, beginning and ending in P.

11 Working under the car, place a container under the transmission fluid pan, then unscrew the filler/level plug **(see illustration)**. Recover the sealing ring.

12 The fluid level should be up to the edge of the filler/level plug hole.

13 If necessary, top-up the fluid until it overflows from the plug hole. Use a metal filler tube to overcome the spring-loaded plate covering the filler hole. Refit the filler plug.

14 Depress the brake pedal and move the selector lever through all the gear positions, beginning and ending in P.

15 Ascertain that the fluid temperature is between 30°C and 55°C. BMW technicians use diagnostic equipment plugged into the vehicle's diagnostic socket, but is should also be possible to measure the temperature with a thermometer or thermocouple (from a digital multimeter) through the filler aperture. If the temperature of the fluid has only been approximately established, have the level rechecked by a BMW dealer or suitably-equipped specialist.

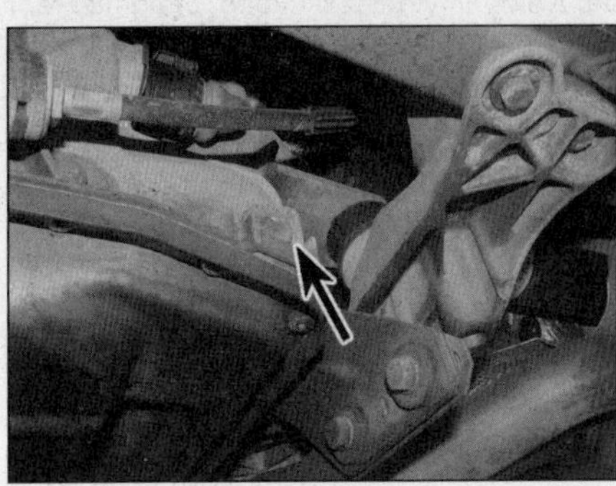

8.11 Automatic transmission oil filler/level plug (arrowed)

16 Again, the fluid level should be up to the edge of the filler/level plug hole. If necessary, top-up the fluid until it overflows from the plug hole.

17 The condition of the fluid should also be checked along with the level. If the fluid is black or a dark reddish-brown colour, or if it smells burned, it should be renewed (see Section 9).

18 Refit the filler/level plug, using a new sealing ring; tighten to the specified torque.

19 Stop the engine and, where applicable, lower the car to the ground.

9 Automatic transmission fluid renewal

Note: *A new drain plug sealing ring will be required on refitting.*

1 The transmission fluid should be drained with the transmission at operating temperature. If the car has just been driven at least 20 miles (32 km), the transmission can be considered warm.

2 Immediately after driving the car, park it on a level surface, apply the handbrake. If desired, jack up the car and support on axle stands (see Jacking and vehicle support) to improve access, but make sure that the car is level.

3 Working under the car, slacken the transmission fluid pan drain plug about half a turn **(see illustration)**. Position a draining

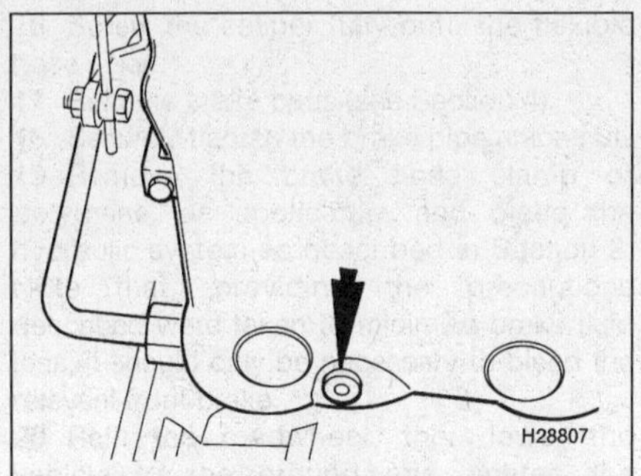

9.3 Automatic transmission drain plug (arrowed)

container under the drain plug, then remove the plug completely. If possible, try to keep the plug pressed into the fluid pan while unscrewing it by hand the last couple of turns.

As the plug releases from the threads, move it away sharply so the stream of fluid issuing from the fluid pan runs into the container, not up your sleeve.

4 Recover the sealing ring from the drain plug.

5 Refit the drain plug, using a new sealing ring, and tighten to the specified torque.

6 With reference to Section 8, fill the transmission with the specified quantity of the correct type of fluid (see *Lubricants and fluids*) – fill the transmission through the dipstick tube or through the filler/level plug hole according to transmission type.

7 Check the fluid level as described in Section 8, bearing in mind that the new fluid will not yet be at operating temperature.

8 With the handbrake applied, and the transmission selector lever in position P, start the engine and run it at idle for a few minutes to warm up the new fluid, then recheck the fluid level as described in Section 8. Note that it may be necessary to drain off a little fluid once the new fluid has reached operating temperature.

Chapter 8
Final drive, driveshafts and propeller shaft

Contents

Degrees of difficulty

Easy, suitable for novice with little experience 	**Fairly easy,** suitable for beginner with some experience 	**Fairly difficult,** suitable for competent DIY mechanic	**Difficult,** suitable for experienced DIY mechanic	**Very difficult,** suitable for expert DIY or professional

Specifications

Final drive

Type	Unsprung, attached to rear suspension crossmember

Driveshaft

Type	Steel shafts with ball-and-cage type constant velocity joints at each end
Constant velocity joint grease capacity	80g in each joint

Propeller shaft

Type	Two-piece tubular shaft with centre bearing, centre and rear universal joint. Front joint is either rubber coupling or universal joint (depending on model)

Torque wrench settings

Note: *On some fixings different grades of bolt can be used; the grade of each bolt is stamped on the bolt head. Ensure that each bolt is tightened to the correct torque for its specific grade.*

	Nm	lbf ft
Final drive unit		
Mounting bolts:		
Front bolt	150	111
Rear bolts	105	77
Oil filler and drain plug	60	44
Propeller shaft flange retaining nut (approximate – see text):		
M20 nut	175	129
M22 nut	185	137
Vibration damper on bracket (where fitted)	77	57
Driveshaft		
Driveshaft retaining nut*:		
M22 nut	200	148
M24 nut	250	185
M27 nut	300	221
Shaft-to-final drive flange bolts*:		
Allen bolts:		
M10 bolts:		
Bolts with serrations under bolt head	96	71
Bolts without serrations	83	61
M12 bolts	110	81
Torx bolts:		
M10 bolts:		
Plain bolts	83	61
Black bolts with serrations under bolt head	100	74
Silver bolts with serrations under bolt head	80	59
M8 bolts:		
Black bolts	64	47
Silver bolts	52	38
M12 bolts	135	100
Propeller shaft		
Centre UJ-to-propshaft bolt	97	72
Front (rubber) coupling:		
M10 bolts:		
Strength grade 8.8 (see head of bolt)	48	35
Strength grade 10.9 (see head of bolt)	64	47
Torx bolt	70	52
M12 bolts:		
Strength grade 8.8 (see head of bolt)	81	60
Strength grade 10.9 (see head of bolt)	100	74
M14 bolts	140	103
Rear CV joint nuts:		
M8 compression nut	32	24
M8 finned nut	43	32
M10 compression nut	64	47
M10 finned nut	70	52
Support bearing bracket nuts	21	15
Roadwheels		
Wheel bolts	110	81

* *Do not re-use*

1 General information

Power is transmitted from the transmission to the rear axle by a two-piece propeller shaft, joined behind the centre bearing. The slip-joint allows slight fore-and-aft movement of the propeller shaft. The forward end of the propeller shaft is attached to the output flange of the transmission by a flexible rubber coupling. The middle of the propeller shaft is supported by the centre bearing which is bolted to the vehicle body. A universal joint is located at the centre bearing, and a constant velocity (CV) joint is located at the rear of the shaft to compensate for movement of the transmission and differential on their mountings and for any flexing of the chassis.

The final drive assembly includes the drive pinion, the ring gear, the differential and the output flanges. The drive pinion, which drives the ring gear, is also known as the differential input shaft and is connected to the propeller shaft via an input flange. The differential is bolted to the ring gear and drives the rear wheels through a pair of output flanges bolted to driveshafts with constant velocity (CV) joints at either end. The differential allows the wheels to turn at different speeds when cornering.

The driveshafts deliver power from the final drive unit output flanges to the rear wheels. The driveshafts are equipped with constant velocity (CV) joints at each end. The inner CV

2.3 Make alignment marks (arrowed) then remove the Torx bolts and plates

2.7a Slacken and remove the front . . .

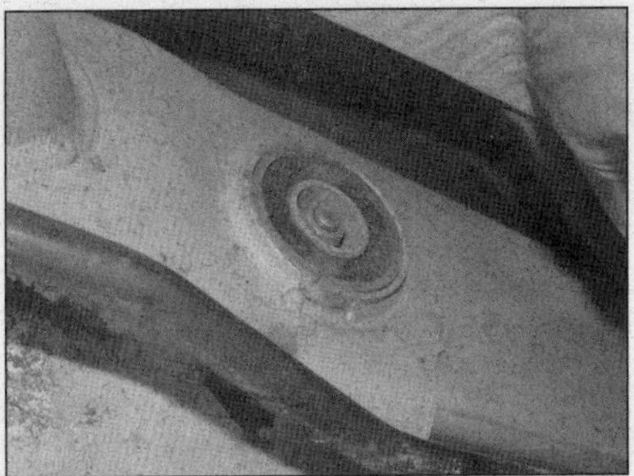

2.7b . . . and rear final drive mounting bolts

joints are bolted to the differential flanges. and the outer CV joints engage the splines of the wheel hubs, and are secured by a large nut.

Major repair work on the differential assembly components (drive pinion, ring-and-pinion and differential) requires many special tools and a high degree of expertise, and therefore should not be attempted by the home mechanic. If major repairs become necessary, we recommend that they be performed by a BMW service department or other suitably-equipped automotive engineer.

2 Final drive unit – removal and refitting

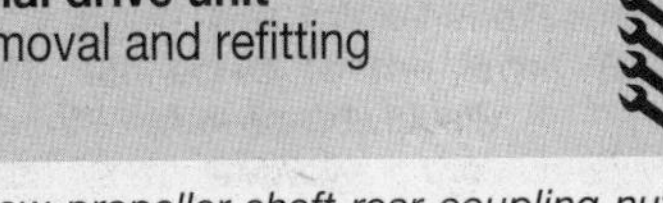

Note: *New propeller shaft rear coupling nuts and driveshaft retaining bolts will be required on refitting.*

Removal

1 Chock the front wheels. Jack up the rear of the vehicle and support it on axle stands (see *Jacking and vehicle support*). Remove both rear wheels. If necessary, drain the final drive unit as described in Section 10.

2 Using paint or a suitable marker pen, make alignment marks between the propeller shaft and final drive unit flange. Unscrew the nuts securing the propeller shaft to the final drive unit and discard them; new ones must be used on refitting.

3 Slacken and remove the retaining bolts and plates securing the right-hand driveshaft to the final drive unit flange and support the driveshaft by tying it to the vehicle underbody using a piece of wire **(see illustration)**. **Note:** *Do not allow the driveshaft to hang under its own weight as the CV joint may be damaged.* Discard the bolts, new ones should be used on refitting.

4 Disconnect the left-hand driveshaft from the final drive as described in Paragraph 3.

5 Remove the rear section of the exhaust system (see Chapter 4A).

6 Move a jack and interposed block of wood into position and raise it so that it is supporting the weight of the final drive unit.

7 Making sure the final drive unit is safely supported, slacken and remove the two bolts securing the rear of the unit in position and the single bolt securing the front of the unit in position **(see illustrations)**.

8 Carefully lower the final drive unit out of position and remove it from underneath the vehicle. Examine the final drive unit mounting rubbers for signs of wear or damage and renew if necessary.

Refitting

9 Refitting is a reversal of removal noting the following.

a) Raise the final drive unit into position and engage it with the propeller shaft rear joint, making sure the marks made prior to removal are correctly aligned.

b) Finger tighten the final drive mounting bolts, remove the jack, and then tighten the rear mounting bolts to the specified torque, followed by the front bolt.

c) Fit the new propeller shaft joint nuts and tighten them to the specified torque.

e) Fit the new driveshaft joint retaining bolts and plates and tighten them to the specified torque.

f) On completion, refill/top-up the final drive unit with oil as described in Section 10.

3 Final drive unit oil seals – renewal

Propeller shaft flange seal

Note: *A new flange nut retaining plate will be required.*

1 Drain the final drive unit as described in Section 10.

2 Remove the final drive unit as described in Section 2 and secure the unit in a vice.

3 Remove the retaining plate and make alignment marks between the propeller flange nut, the drive flange and pinion **(see illustration)**. Discard the retaining plate; a new one must be used on refitting.

4 Hold the drive flange stationary by bolting a length of metal bar to it, then unscrew the nut noting the exact number of turns necessary to remove it.

5 Using a suitable puller, draw the drive flange from the pinion and remove the dust cover. If the dust cover shows signs of wear, renew it.

6 Lever the oil seal from the final drive casing with a screwdriver. Wipe clean the oil seal seating.

7 Smear a little oil on the sealing lip of the new oil seal, then press it squarely into the casing until flush with the outer face. If necessary the seal can be tapped into position using a metal tube which bears only on its hard outer edge.

8 Fit the dust cover and locate the drive flange on the pinion aligning the marks made on removal. Refit the flange nut, screwing it on by the exact number of turns counted on removal, so that the alignment marks align.

Warning: Do not overtighten the flange nut. If the nut is overtightened, the collapsible spacer behind the flange will be deformed necessitating its renewal. This is a complex operation requiring the final drive unit to be dismantled (see Section 1).

9 Secure the nut in position with the new retaining plate, tapping it squarely into position.

10 Refit the final drive unit as described in Section 2 and refill it with oil as described in Section 10.

Driveshaft flange seal

Note: *New driveshaft joint retaining bolts and a driveshaft flange circlip will be required.*

11 Drain the final drive unit oil as described in Section 10.

12 Slacken and remove the bolts securing the driveshaft constant velocity joint to the final drive unit and recover the retaining plates. Position the driveshaft clear of the flange and tie it to the vehicle underbody using a piece of wire. **Note:** *Do not allow the*

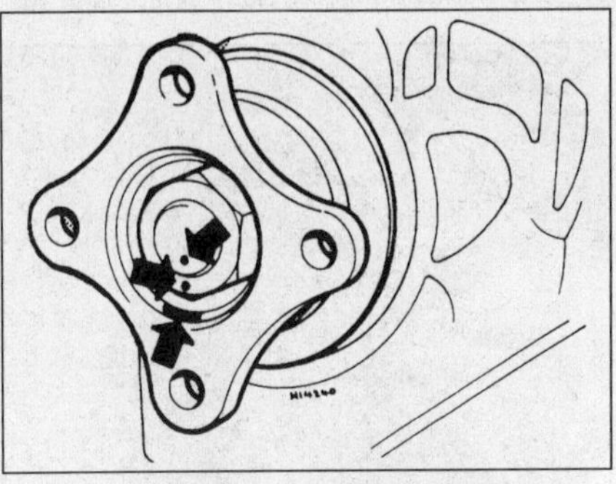

3.3 Make alignment marks (arrowed) on the flange, the pinion shaft and nut to ensure proper reassembly

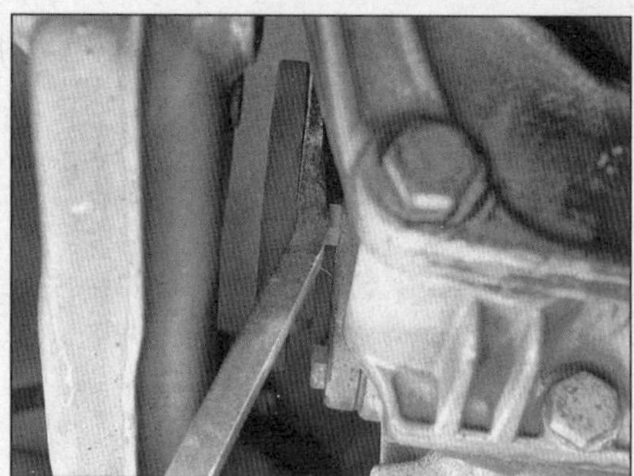
3.13 Use a suitable lever to remove the driveshaft flange from the final drive unit

driveshaft to hang under its own weight as the CV joint may be damaged.

13 Using a suitable lever, carefully prise the driveshaft flange out from the final drive unit taking care not to damage the dust seal or casing **(see illustration)**. Remove the flange and recover dust seal. If the dust seal shows signs of damage, renew it.

14 Carefully lever the oil seal out from the final drive unit. Wipe clean the oil seal seating.

15 With the flange removed, prise out the circlip from the end of the splined shaft **(see illustration)**.

16 Fit a new circlip, making sure it is correctly located in the splined shaft groove.

17 Smear a little final drive oil on the sealing lip of the new oil seal, then press it squarely into the casing until it reaches its stop. If necessary the seal can be tapped into position using a metal tube which bears only on its hard outer edge **(see illustration)**.

4.6 When the driveshaft nut has been fully tightened, stake the nut using a punch

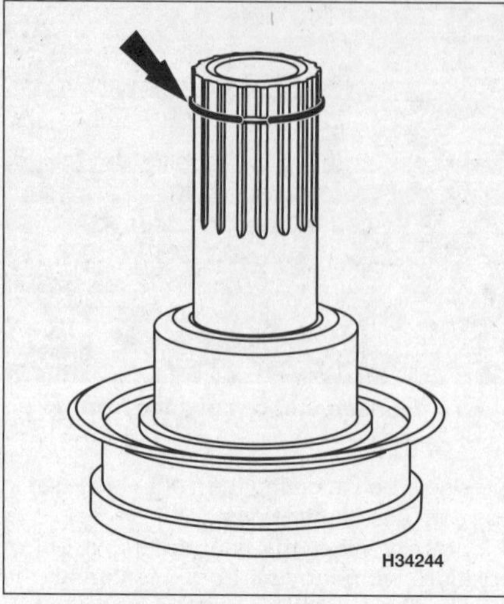

3.15 Renew the output flange circlip (arrowed)

18 Fit the dust cover and insert the drive flange. Push the drive flange fully into position and check that it is securely retained by the circlip.

19 Align the driveshaft with the flange and refit the new retaining bolts and plates, tightening them to the specified torque.

20 Refill the final drive unit with oil as described in Section 10.

4 Driveshaft – removal and refitting

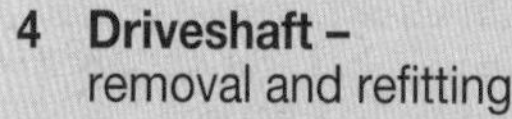

Note: *A new driveshaft retaining nut and bolts will be required on refitting.*

Removal

1 Remove the final drive unit as described in Section 2.

2 Remove the relevant rear roadwheel.

3 Unscrew and remove the driveshaft nut.

4 Withdraw the driveshaft outer constant velocity joint from the hub assembly. The outer joint will be very tight, tap the joint out of the hub using a soft-faced mallet. If this fails to free it from the hub, the joint will have to be pressed out using a suitable tool which is bolted to the hub.

5 Remove the driveshaft from underneath the vehicle.

3.17 Tap the new seal into position using a socket which bears only on the hard outer edge of the seal

Refitting

6 Refitting is the reverse of removal noting the following points.

a) *Ensure the splines of the driveshaft outer joint and hub are clean. Apply a little anti-seize grease to the splines prior to refitting.*

b) *Lubricate the threads of the new driveshaft nut with clean engine oil prior to fitting and tighten it to the specified torque. If necessary, wait until the vehicle is lower to the ground and then tighten the nut to the specified torque. Once tightened, use a hammer and punch to stake the nut **(see illustration)**.*

c) *Fit new inner joint retaining bolts and plates (where fitted) and tighten to the specified torque.*

5 Driveshaft gaiters – renewal

1 Remove the driveshaft (see Section 4).

2 Clean the driveshaft and mount it in a vice.

3 Lever off the sealing cover from the end of the inner constant velocity (CV) joint **(see illustration)**.

4 Release the two inner joint gaiter retaining clips and free the gaiter and dust cover from the joint **(see illustration)**.

5 Scoop out excess grease and remove the inner joint circlip from the end of the driveshaft **(see illustration)**.

5.3 Carefully remove the sealing cover from the inner end of the joint

5.4 Release the gaiter retaining clips and slide the gaiter down the shaft

5.5 Remove the inner joint circlip from the driveshaft

5.6 Support the inner joint member, then tap the driveshaft out of position . . .

5.7 . . . and slide off the gaiter

5.20a Fill the inner joint with the grease supplied . . .

6 Securely support the joint inner member and tap the driveshaft out of position using a hammer and suitable drift **(see illustration)**. If the joint is a tight fit, a suitable puller will be required to draw off the joint. Do not dismantle the inner joint.
7 With the joint removed, slide the inner gaiter and dust cover off from the end of the driveshaft **(see illustration)**.
8 Release the outer joint gaiter retaining clips then slide the gaiter along the shaft and remove it.
9 Thoroughly clean the constant velocity joints using paraffin, or a suitable solvent, and dry thoroughly. Carry out a visual inspection as follows.
10 Move the inner splined driving member from side-to-side to expose each ball in turn at the top of its track. Examine the balls for cracks, flat spots or signs of surface pitting.
11 Inspect the ball tracks on the inner and outer members. If the tracks have widened, the balls will no longer be a tight fit. At the same time check the ball cage windows for wear or cracking between the windows.
12 If any of the constant velocity joint components are found to be worn or damaged, it must be renewed. The inner joint is available separately but if the outer joint is worn it will be necessary to renew the complete joint and driveshaft assembly. If the joints are in satisfactory condition, obtain new gaiter repair kits which contain gaiters, retaining clips, an inner constant velocity joint circlip and the correct type and quantity of grease required.
13 Tape over the splines on the end of the driveshaft.
14 Slide the new outer gaiter onto the end of the driveshaft.
15 Pack the outer joint with the grease supplied in the gaiter kit. Work the grease well into the bearing tracks whilst twisting the joint, and fill the rubber gaiter with any excess.
16 Ease the gaiter over the joint and ensure that the gaiter lips are correctly located on both the driveshaft and constant velocity joint. Lift the outer sealing lip of the gaiter to equalise air pressure within the gaiter.
17 Fit the large retaining clip to the gaiter. Pull the retaining clip tight then bend it back to secure it in position and cut off any excess clip. Secure the small retaining clip using the same procedure.
18 Engage the new inner gaiter with its dust cover and slide the assembly onto the driveshaft.
19 Remove the tape from the driveshaft splines and fit the inner constant velocity joint. Press the joint fully onto the shaft and secure it in position with a new circlip.
20 Work the grease supplied fully into the inner joint and fill the gaiter with any excess **(see illustrations)**.
21 Slide the inner gaiter into position and press the dust cover onto the joint, making sure the retaining bolt holes are correctly aligned. Lift the outer sealing lip of the gaiter, to equalise air pressure within the gaiter, and secure it in position with the retaining clips (see paragraph 17).
22 Apply a smear of suitable sealant (BMW recommend BMW sealing gel) and press the new sealing cover fully onto the end of the inner joint.
23 Check that both constant velocity joints are free to move easily then refit the driveshaft as described in Section 4.

6 Propeller shaft – removal and refitting

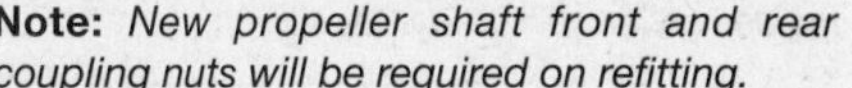

Note: *New propeller shaft front and rear coupling nuts will be required on refitting.*

Removal

1 Chock the front wheels. Jack up the rear of the vehicle and support it on axle stands (see *Jacking and vehicle support*).
2 Remove the exhaust system and heat shield as described in Chapter 4A. Where necessary, unbolt the exhaust system mounting bracket(s) in order to gain the necessary clearance required to remove the propeller shaft.
3 Remove the crossmember under the front section of the propeller shaft **(see illustration)**.
4 Make alignment marks between the shaft, transmission flange and rubber coupling at the front of the shaft. Slacken and remove the nuts and bolts securing the coupling to the transmission **(see illustration)**. The nuts can be accessed by inserting a spanner between the end of the transmission and the crossmember. Discard the nuts, new ones should be used on refitting.

5.20b . . . and work it into the bearing tracks

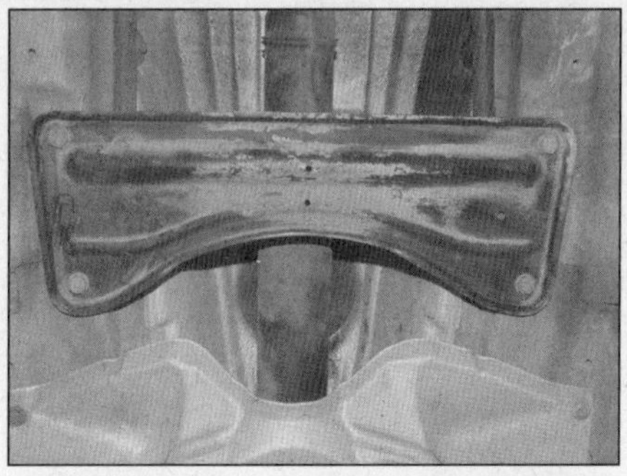

6.3 Remove the crossmember under the front section of the propeller shaft

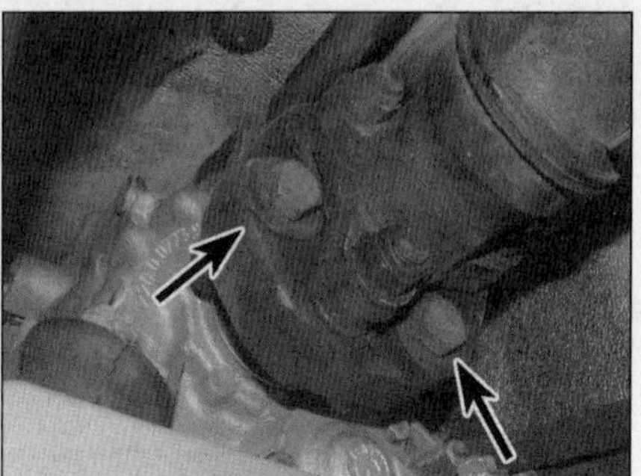

6.4 Remove the nuts and bolts securing the coupling to the transmission (two arrowed)

6.5 Make alignment marks between the CV joint flange and the final drive flange (arrowed)

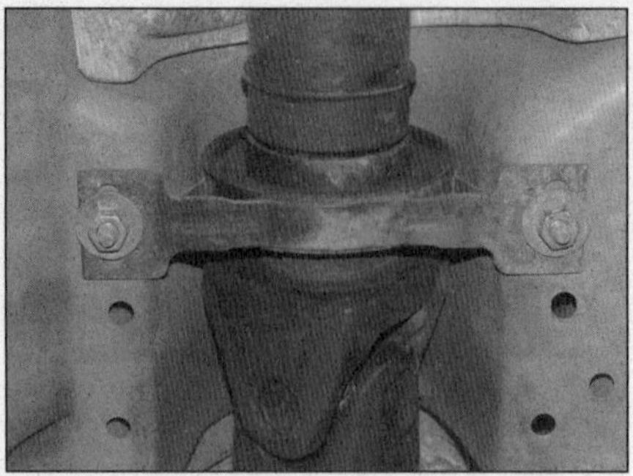

6.7 Unscrew the centre support bearing bracket retaining nuts

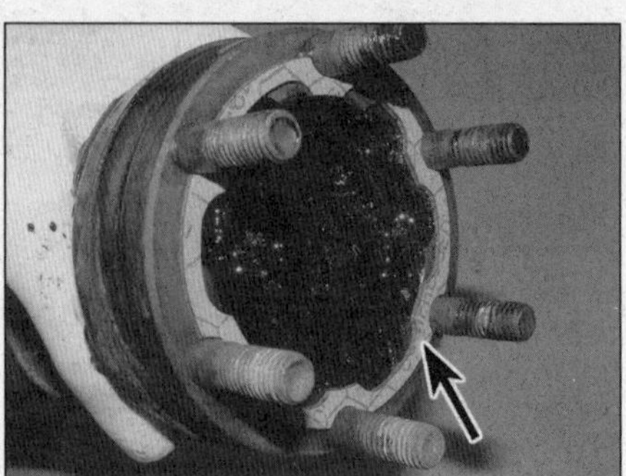

6.11 Fit a new seal (arrowed) to the CV joint

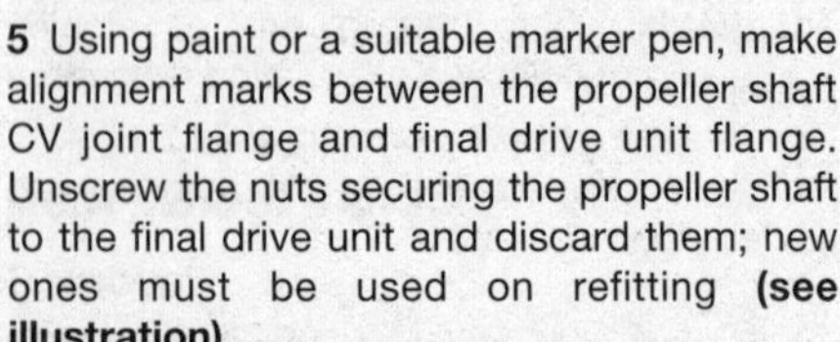

5 Using paint or a suitable marker pen, make alignment marks between the propeller shaft CV joint flange and final drive unit flange. Unscrew the nuts securing the propeller shaft to the final drive unit and discard them; new ones must be used on refitting **(see illustration)**.

6 Use a flat-bladed screwdriver to prise the CV joint flange from the final drive flange. **Note:** *If the CV joint flange is forced to an extreme angle in relation to the shaft, the joint rubber gaiter can be damaged.*

7 With the aid of an assistant, support the propeller shaft then unscrew the centre support bearing bracket retaining nuts **(see illustration)**. Lower the centre of the shaft and disengage it from the transmission and final drive unit. Remove the shaft from underneath the vehicle.

8 Inspect the rubber coupling (where fitted), the support bearing and shaft joints as described in Sections 7, 8 and 9. Inspect the transmission flange locating pin and propeller shaft bush for signs of wear or damage and renew as necessary.

Refitting

9 Apply a smear of molybdenum disulphide grease (BMW recommend Molykote Long-term 2) to the transmission pin and shaft bush and manoeuvre the shaft into position.

10 Pull the CV joint outer flange outwards to its full extension, then pack the CV joint with the correct grease (available from BMW dealers).

7.4 Remove the bolts/nuts securing the coupling to the shaft

11 Discard the seal between the CV joint and the final drive flange, and fit a new one **(see illustration)**. Apply a little grease to the sealing faces of the CV joint and the final drive flange.

12 Align the marks made prior to removal and engage the shaft with the transmission and final drive unit flanges. Try not to compress the CV joint outer flange, as this would cause the packed grease to be expelled. With the marks correctly aligned, refit the support bracket retaining nuts, tightening them lightly only at this stage.

13 Fit new retaining nuts to the rear CV joint of the propeller shaft, and tighten them evenly, working in a diagonal pattern, to the specified torque.

14 Insert the bolts through the rubber coupling, and into the transmission output flange, then fit the new retaining nuts. Tighten them to the specified torque, noting that only the nuts should be rotated to avoid stressing the rubber coupling.

15 Tighten the centre support bearing bracket to the specified torque,

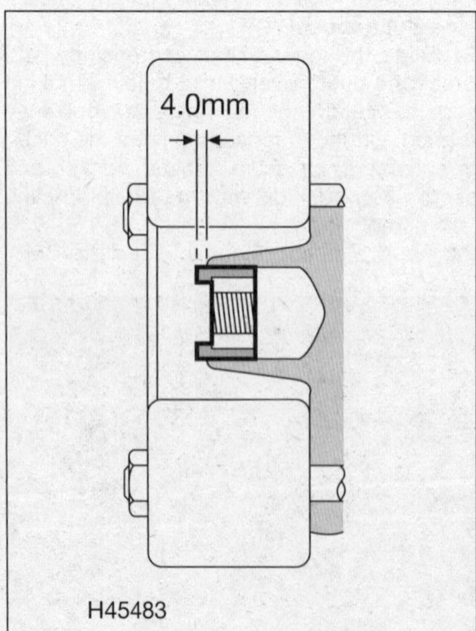

7.9 The centring guide is correctly located when it protrudes 4.0 mm from the end of the propshaft tube

16 Refit the exhaust system and associated components as described in Chapter 4A.

7 Propeller shaft rubber coupling and centring guide – check and renewal

Check

1 Firmly apply the handbrake, then jack up the front of the vehicle and support it on axle stands (see *Jacking and vehicle support*).

2 Closely examine the rubber coupling linking the propeller shaft to the transmission, looking for signs of damage such as cracking or splitting or for signs of general deterioration. If necessary, renew the coupling as follows.

Renewal

3 Remove the propeller shaft as described in the previous Section.

4 Slacken and remove the nuts securing the coupling to the shaft and remove it **(see illustration)**.

5 Check the centring guide for damage or wear.

6 If the centring guide is to be renewed, pack the cavity behind the guide with grease, until the grease is flush with the lower edge of the guide.

7 Insert a 14 mm diameter rod into the guide, and then strike end of the rod with a hammer to force the guide out from the shaft. It may be necessary to refill the cavity with grease during the procedure.

8 With the old guide removed, remove the grease from the cavity.

9 Lubricate the new centring guide with molybdenum disulphide grease (BMW recommend Molykote Long-term 2), and using a suitable tubular spacer (socket) which acts only on the outer edge of the guide, drive it into position. The guide is correctly fitted when it protrudes 4.0 mm from the end of the propshaft tube **(see illustration)**.

10 Fit the new rubber coupling noting that the arrows on the side of the coupling must point towards the propeller shaft/transmission

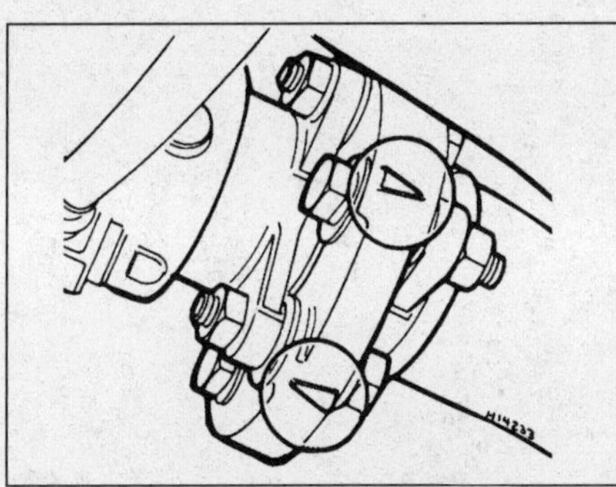

7.10 The arrows on the side of the coupling must point towards the propeller shaft/transmission flanges

flanges **(see illustration)**. Fit the new retaining nuts and tighten them to the specified torque. When tightening the nuts, ensure that the bolts do not rotate, as this may stress the rubber coupling.

11 Apply a smear of molybdenum disulphide grease (BMW recommend Molykote Long-term 2) to the transmission pin and shaft bush and manoeuvre the shaft into position.

12 Refit the propeller shaft as described in Section 6.

8 Propeller shaft support bearing – check and renewal

Check

1 Wear in the support bearing will lead to noise and vibration when the vehicle is driven. The bearing is best checked with the propeller shaft removed (see Section 6). To gain access to the bearing with the shaft in position, remove the exhaust system and heat shields as described in Chapter 4A.

2 Rotate the bearing and check that it turns smoothly with no sign of free play; if it's difficult to turn, or if it has a gritty feeling, renew it. Also inspect the rubber portion. If it's cracked or deteriorated, renew it.

Renewal

3 Remove the propeller shaft as described in Section 6.

4 Paint alignment marks between the central universal joint yoke and the propeller shaft, then undo the bolt securing the yoke to the shaft.

5 Slide off the shim and support bearing rear dust cover.

6 Press/drive the new bearing and bracket assembly fully onto the shaft until it reaches the stop, using a suitable tubular spacer which bears only on the inner race of the bearing.

7 Check that the bearing is free to rotate smoothly, then fit the new rear dust seal.

8 Refit the shim to the end of the shaft.

9 Refit the universal joint yoke to the shaft, aligning the previously made marks, then apply a little thread-locking compound to the threads, and tighten the retaining bolt to the specified torque.

10 Refit the propeller shaft as described in Section 6.

9 Propeller shaft universal joint – check and renewal

Check

1 Wear in the universal joint is characterised by vibration in the transmission, noise during acceleration, and metallic squeaking and grating sounds as the bearings disintegrate. The joints can be checked with the propeller shaft still fitted noting that it will be necessary to remove the exhaust system and heat shields (see Chapter 4A) to gain access.

2 If the propeller shaft is in position on the vehicle, try to turn the propeller shaft while holding the transmission/final drive flange. Free play between the propeller shaft and the front or rear flanges indicates excessive wear.

3 If the propeller shaft is already removed, you can check the universal joints by holding the shaft in one hand and turning the yoke or flange with the other. If the axial movement is excessive, renew the propeller shaft.

Renewal

4 At the time of writing, no spare parts were available to enable renewal of the universal joints to be carried out. Therefore, if any joint shows signs of damage or wear the complete propeller shaft assembly must be renewed. Consult your BMW dealer for latest information on parts availability.

10.2 Final drive filler plug (arrowed)

5 If renewal of the propeller shaft is necessary, it may be worthwhile seeking the advice of an automotive engineering specialist. They may be able to repair the original shaft assembly or supply a reconditioned shaft on an exchange basis.

10 Final drive oil renewal

1 Park the car on level ground.

2 Locate the filler/level plug in the centre of the final drive unit rear cover **(see illustration)**. Unscrew the plug and recover the sealing washer.

3 Place a suitable container beneath the final drive unit, then unscrew the drain plug from the base of the rear cover and allow the oil to drain. Recover the sealing washer. **Note:** *On some vehicles manufactured from 03/2003, no drain plug is fitted to the final drive, as there is no requirement in the maintenance schedule for the oil's renewal.*

4 Inspect the sealing washers for signs of damage and renew if necessary.

5 When the oil has finished draining, refit the drain plug and sealing washer and tighten it to the specified torque.

6 Refill the final drive unit through the filler/level plug hole with the exact amount of the specified type of oil (see Chapter 1); this should bring the oil level up to the base of the filler/level plug hole. If the correct amount was poured into the transmission and a large amount flows out on checking the level, refit the filler/level plug and take the car on a short journey so that the new oil is distributed fully around the final drive components.

7 On return, park on level ground and allow the car to stand for a few minutes. Unscrew the filler/level plug again. The oil level should reach the lower edge of the filler/level hole. To ensure a true level is established, wait until the initial trickle stops, then add oil as necessary until a trickle of new oil can be seen emerging. The level will be correct when the flow ceases; use only good-quality oil of the specified type (see *Lubricants and fluids*).

8 When the level is correct, refit the filler/level plug and sealing washer and tighten it to the specified torque.

Chapter 9
Braking system

Contents

Degrees of difficulty

Easy, suitable for novice with little experience 

Fairly easy, suitable for beginner with some experience 

Fairly difficult, suitable for competent DIY mechanic 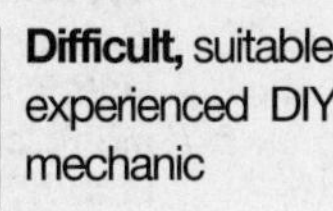

Difficult, suitable for experienced DIY mechanic

Very difficult, suitable for expert DIY or professional

Specifications

Front brakes

Disc diameter:	
530i	324 mm
All other models	296 mm
Disc minimum thickness (stamped on disc):	
530i	28.4 mm
All other models	20.4 mm
Maximum disc run-out	0.2 mm
Brake pad friction material minimum thickness	3.0 mm

Rear disc brakes

Disc diameter	298 mm
Disc minimum thickness (stamped on disc):	
Solid disc	8.4 mm
Ventilated disc	18.4 mm
Maximum disc run-out	0.2 mm
Brake pad friction material minimum thickness	3.0 mm
Handbrake drum diameter	185 mm
Handbrake shoe friction material minimum thickness	1.5 mm

Torque wrench settings

Torque wrench settings	Nm	lbf ft
ABS pressure sensors to master cylinder	19	14
ABS wheel sensor retaining bolts	8	6
Brake disc retaining screw	16	12
Brake hose unions:		
M10 thread	17	13
M12 thread	19	14
Front brake caliper:		
Guide pin bolts	35	26
Mounting bracket bolts	110	81

Torque wrench settings (continued)

	Nm	lbf ft
Master cylinder mounting nuts*	26	19
Rear brake caliper:		
Guide pin bolts	35	26
Mounting bracket bolts	67	49
Roadwheel bolts	110	81
Servo unit mounting nuts	31	23

** Do not re-use*

1 General information

The braking system is of the servo-assisted, dual-circuit hydraulic type. Under normal circumstances, both circuits operate in unison. However, if there is hydraulic failure in one circuit, full braking force will still be available at two wheels.

All models are fitted with front and rear disc brakes. ABS is fitted as standard to all models (refer to Section 19 for further information on ABS operation). **Note:** *On models also equipped with Automatic Stability Control plus Traction (ASC+T), the ABS system also operates the traction control side of the system.*

The front disc brakes are actuated by single-piston sliding type calipers, which ensure that equal pressure is applied to each disc pad.

All models are fitted with rear disc brakes, actuated by single-piston sliding calipers, whilst a separate drum brake arrangement is fitted in the centre of the brake disc to provide a separate means of handbrake application.

Note: *When servicing any part of the system, work carefully and methodically; also observe scrupulous cleanliness when overhauling any part of the hydraulic system. Always renew components (in axle sets, where applicable) if in doubt about their condition, and use only genuine BMW parts, or at least those of known good quality. Note the warnings given in 'Safety first!' and at relevant points in this Chapter concerning the dangers of asbestos dust and hydraulic fluid.*

2 Hydraulic system – bleeding

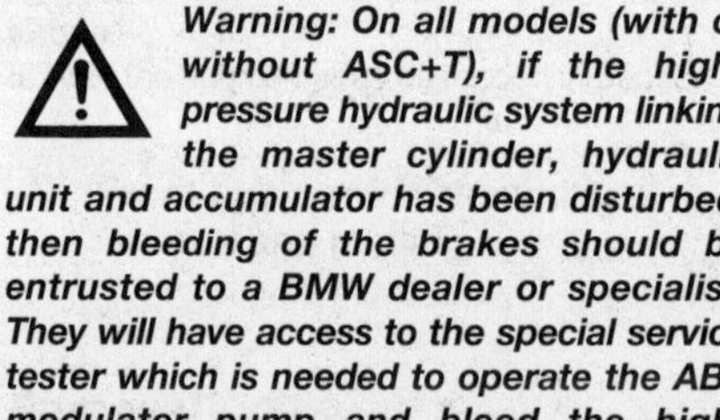

Warning: Hydraulic fluid is poisonous; wash off immediately and thoroughly in the case of skin contact, and seek immediate medical advice if any fluid is swallowed or gets into the eyes. Certain types of hydraulic fluid are flammable, and may ignite when allowed into contact with hot components; when servicing any hydraulic system, it is safest to assume that the fluid is flammable, and to take precautions against the risk of fire as though it is petrol that is being handled. Hydraulic fluid is also an effective paint stripper, and will attack plastics; if any is spilt, it should be washed off immediately, using copious quantities of fresh water. Finally, it is hygroscopic (it absorbs moisture from the air) – old fluid may be contaminated and unfit for further use. When topping-up or renewing the fluid, always use the recommended type, and ensure that it comes from a freshly-opened sealed container.

Warning: On all models (with or without ASC+T), if the high-pressure hydraulic system linking the master cylinder, hydraulic unit and accumulator has been disturbed, then bleeding of the brakes should be entrusted to a BMW dealer or specialist. They will have access to the special service tester which is needed to operate the ABS modulator pump and bleed the high-pressure hydraulic system safely.

General

1 The correct operation of any hydraulic system is only possible after removing all air from the components and circuit; this is achieved by bleeding the system.

2 During the bleeding procedure, add only clean, unused hydraulic fluid of the recommended type; never re-use fluid that has already been bled from the system. Ensure that sufficient fluid is available before starting work.

3 If there is any possibility of incorrect fluid being already in the system, the brake components and circuit must be flushed completely with uncontaminated, correct fluid, and new seals should be fitted to the various components.

4 If hydraulic fluid has been lost from the system, or air has entered because of a leak, ensure that the fault is cured before continuing further.

5 Park the vehicle on level ground, switch off the engine and select first or reverse gear, then chock the wheels and release the handbrake.

6 Check that all pipes and hoses are secure, unions tight and bleed screws closed. Clean any dirt from around the bleed screws.

7 Release the clip and remove the pollen filter cover from the driver's side. Release the clip and disconnect the air duct from the filter housing. Unclip and remove the driver's side pollen filter housing **(see illustrations)**. Unscrew the master cylinder reservoir cap, and top the master cylinder reservoir up to the MAX level line; refit the cap loosely, and remember to maintain the fluid level at least above the MIN level line throughout the procedure, or there is a risk of further air entering the system.

2.7a Release the clip (arrowed) and disconnect the air duct from the pollen filter housing . . .

2.7b . . . then release the clip (arrowed), open the cover . . .

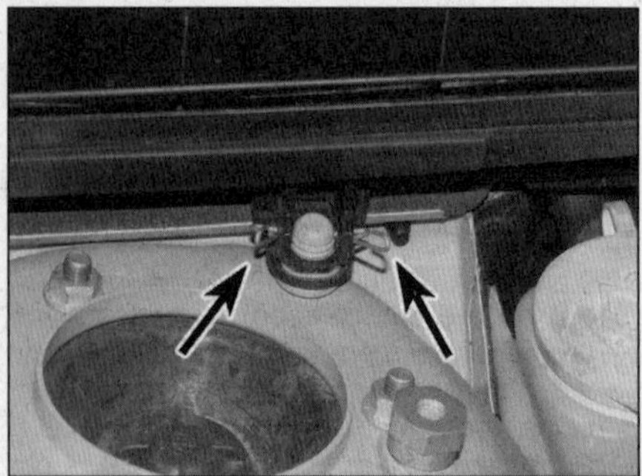

2.7c . . . squeeze together the sides of the clip (arrowed) and remove the pollen filter housing

2.21 Bleeding a rear brake caliper using one-way valve kit

8 There is a number of one-man, do-it-yourself brake bleeding kits currently available from motor accessory shops. It is recommended that one of these kits is used whenever possible, as they greatly simplify the bleeding operation, and reduce the risk of expelled air and fluid being drawn back into the system. If such a kit is not available, the basic (two-man) method must be used, which is described in detail below.

9 If a kit is to be used, prepare the vehicle as described previously, and follow the kit manufacturer's instructions, as the procedure may vary slightly according to the type being used; generally, they are as outlined below in the relevant sub-section.

10 Whichever method is used, the same sequence must be followed (paragraphs 11 and 12) to ensure the removal of all air from the system.

Bleeding

Sequence

11 If the system has been only partially disconnected, and suitable precautions were taken to minimise fluid loss, it should be necessary only to bleed that part of the system.

12 If the complete system is to be bled, then it should be done working in the following sequence:

a) Right-hand rear brake.
b) Left-hand rear brake.
c) Right-hand front brake.
d) Left-hand front brake.

Warning: After bleeding, the operation of the braking system should be checked at the earliest possible opportunity by a BMW dealer or suitably-equipped specialist.

Basic (two-man) method

13 Collect a clean glass jar, a suitable length of plastic or rubber tubing which is a tight fit over the bleed screw, and a ring spanner to fit the screw. The help of an assistant will also be required.

14 Remove the dust cap from the first screw in the sequence. Fit the spanner and tube to the screw, place the other end of the tube in the jar, and pour in sufficient fluid to cover the end of the tube.

15 Ensure that the master cylinder reservoir fluid level is maintained at least above the MIN level line throughout the procedure.

16 Have the assistant fully depress the brake pedal several times to build-up pressure, then maintain it on the final downstroke.

17 While pedal pressure is maintained, unscrew the bleed screw (approximately one turn) and allow the compressed fluid and air to flow into the jar. The assistant should maintain pedal pressure, following it down to the floor if necessary, and should not release it until instructed to do so. When the flow stops, tighten the bleed screw again, have the assistant release the pedal slowly, and recheck the reservoir fluid level.

18 Repeat the steps in paragraphs 16 and 17 until the fluid emerging from the bleed screw is free from air bubbles. If the master cylinder has been drained and refilled, and air is being bled from the first screw in the sequence, allow about 5 seconds between cycles for the master cylinder passages to refill.

19 When no more air bubbles appear, tighten the bleed screw securely, remove the tube and spanner, and refit the dust cap. Do not overtighten the bleed screw.

20 Repeat the procedure on the remaining screws in the sequence, until all air is removed from the system and the brake pedal feels firm again.

Using a one-way valve kit

21 As their name implies, these kits consist of a length of tubing with a one-way valve fitted, to prevent expelled air and fluid being drawn back into the system; some kits include a translucent container, which can be positioned so that the air bubbles can be more easily seen flowing from the end of the tube **(see illustration)**.

22 The kit is connected to the bleed screw, which is then opened. The user returns to the driver's seat, depresses the brake pedal with a smooth, steady stroke, and slowly releases it; this is repeated until the expelled fluid is clear of air bubbles.

23 Note that these kits simplify work so much that it is easy to forget the master cylinder reservoir fluid level; ensure that this is maintained at least above the MIN level line at all times.

Using a pressure-bleeding kit

24 These kits are usually operated by the reservoir of pressurised air contained in the spare tyre. However, note that it will probably be necessary to reduce the pressure to a lower level than normal; refer to the instructions supplied with the kit. **Note:** *BMW specify that a pressure of 2 bar (29 psi) should not be exceeded.*

25 By connecting a pressurised, fluid-filled container to the master cylinder reservoir, bleeding can be carried out simply by opening each screw in turn (in the specified sequence), and allowing the fluid to flow out until no more air bubbles can be seen in the expelled fluid.

26 This method has the advantage that the large reservoir of fluid provides an additional safeguard against air being drawn into the system during bleeding.

27 Pressure-bleeding is particularly effective when bleeding 'difficult' systems, or when bleeding the complete system at the time of routine fluid renewal.

All methods

28 When bleeding is complete, and firm pedal feel is restored, wash off any spilt fluid, tighten the bleed screws securely, and refit their dust caps.

29 Check the hydraulic fluid level in the master cylinder reservoir, and top-up if necessary (*Weekly checks*).

30 Discard any hydraulic fluid that has been bled from the system; it will not be fit for re-use.

31 Check the feel of the brake pedal. If it feels at all spongy, air must still be present in the system, and further bleeding is required. Failure to bleed satisfactorily after a reasonable repetition of the bleeding procedure may be due to worn master cylinder seals.

3 Hydraulic pipes and hoses – renewal

Warning: Under no circumstances should the hydraulic pipes/hoses linking the master cylinder, hydraulic unit and the accumulator be disturbed. If these unions are disturbed and air enters the high-pressure hydraulic system, bleeding of the system can only be safely carried out by a BMW dealer or suitably-equipped specialist using the special service tester.

Note: *Before starting work, refer to the warnings at the beginning of Section 2.*

1 If any pipe or hose is to be renewed, minimise fluid loss by first removing the master cylinder reservoir cap, then tightening it down onto a piece of polythene to obtain an airtight seal. Alternatively, flexible hoses can be sealed, if required, using a proprietary brake hose clamp; metal brake pipe unions can be plugged (if care is taken not to allow dirt into the system) or capped immediately they are disconnected. Place a wad of rag under any union that is to be disconnected, to catch any spilt fluid.

2 If a flexible hose is to be disconnected, unscrew the brake pipe union nut before removing the spring clip which secures the hose to its mounting bracket.

3 To unscrew the union nuts, it is preferable to obtain a brake pipe spanner of the correct size; these are available from most large motor accessory shops. Failing this, a close-fitting open-ended spanner will be required, though if the nuts are tight or corroded, their flats may be rounded-off if the spanner slips. In such a case, using self-locking pliers is often the only way to unscrew a stubborn

union, but it follows that the pipe and the damaged nuts must be renewed on reassembly. Always clean a union and surrounding area before disconnecting it. If disconnecting a component with more than one union, make a careful note of the connections before disturbing any of them.

4 If a brake pipe is to be renewed, it can be obtained, cut to length and with the union nuts and end flares in place, from BMW dealers. All that is then necessary is to bend it to shape, following the line of the original, before fitting it to the car. Alternatively, most motor accessory shops can make up brake pipes from kits, but this requires very careful measurement of the original, to ensure that the new one is of the correct length. The safest answer is usually to take the original to the shop as a pattern.

5 On refitting, do not overtighten the union nuts. It is not necessary to exercise brute force to obtain a sound joint.

6 Ensure that the pipes and hoses are correctly routed, with no kinks, and that they are secured in the clips or brackets provided. After fitting, remove the polythene from the reservoir, and bleed the hydraulic system as described in Section 2. Wash off any spilt fluid, and check carefully for fluid leaks.

4 Front brake pads – renewal

Warning: Renew both sets of front brake pads at the same time – never renew the pads on only one wheel, as uneven braking may result. Note that the dust created by wear of the pads may contain asbestos, which is a health hazard. Never blow it out with compressed air, and do not inhale any of it. An approved filtering mask should be worn when working on the brakes. DO NOT use petrol or petroleum-based solvents to clean brake parts; use brake cleaner or methylated spirit only.

1 Apply the handbrake, then jack up the front of the vehicle and support it on axle stands (see *Jacking and vehicle support*). Remove the front roadwheels.

2 Using a screwdriver, carefully unclip the retaining spring from the side of the brake caliper, noting its correct fitted position **(see illustration)**.

3 Slide the brake pad wear sensor from the brake pad (where fitted) and remove it from the caliper aperture **(see illustrations)**.

4 Remove the plastic plugs from the caliper guide bushes to gain access to the guide pin bolts **(see illustration)**.

5 Slacken and remove the guide pin bolts, noting that a suitable Allen key will be needed **(see illustrations)**. Lift the caliper away from the caliper mounting bracket, and tie it to the suspension strut using a suitable piece of wire. Do not allow the caliper to hang unsupported on the flexible brake hose.

6 Unclip the inner brake pad from the caliper piston, and withdraw the outer pad from the caliper mounting bracket **(see illustration)**.

7 First measure the thickness of each brake pad's friction material **(see illustration)**. If either pad is worn at any point to the specified

4.2 Lever the spring away from the hub, then pull it sideways from the caliper

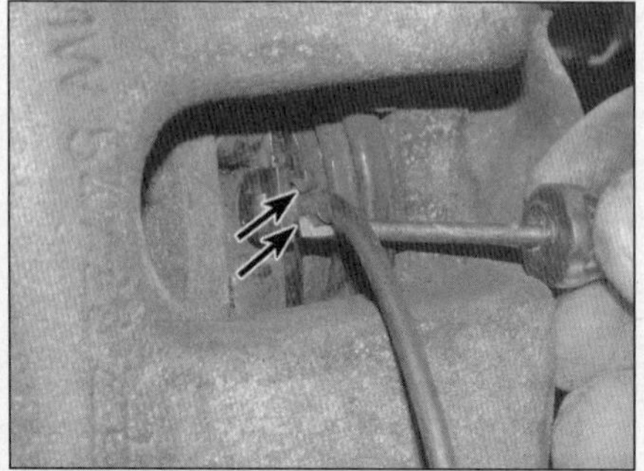

4.3a Release the clips (arrowed) . . .

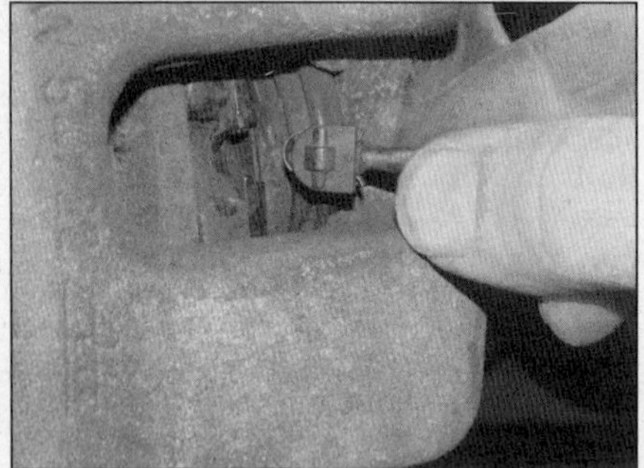

4.3b . . . and slide the wear sensor from the brake pad

4.4 Prise off the plastic caps

4.5a Use an Allen key to slacken the guide pin bolts . . .

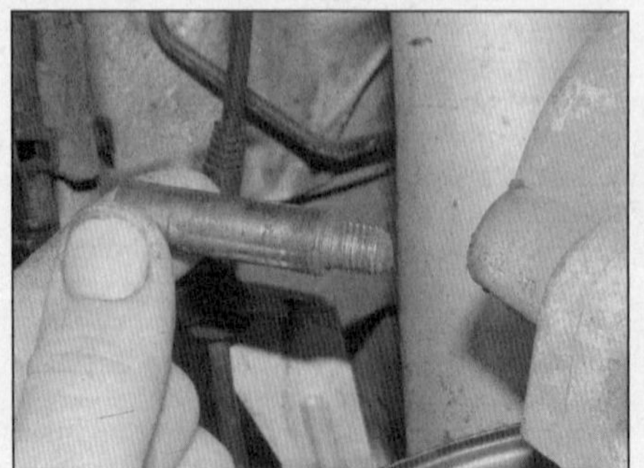

4.5b . . . then remove them

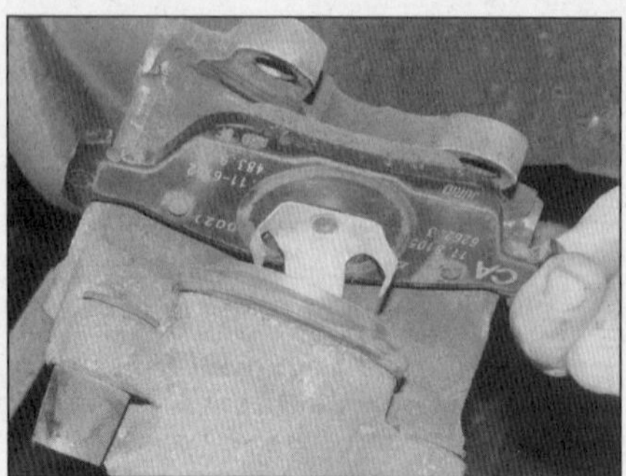

4.6 The inner pad clips into the piston

4.7 Measure the thickness of the friction material

4.10 Using a piston retraction tool

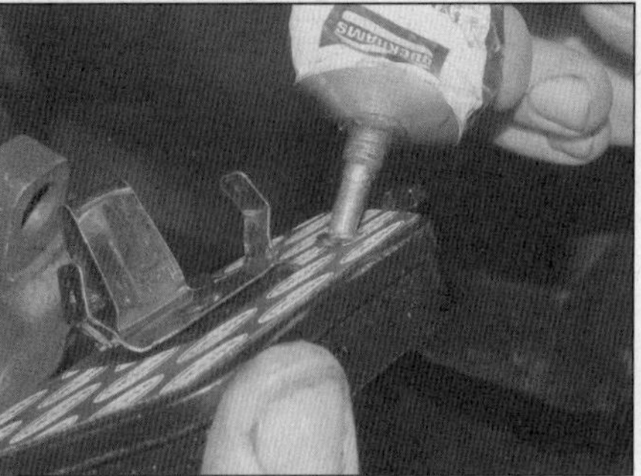
4.11 Apply a little anti-squeak compound to the rear of the brake pads

4.12 Fit the outer pad to the caliper bracket

minimum thickness or less, all four pads must be renewed. Also, the pads should be renewed if any are fouled with oil or grease; there is no satisfactory way of degreasing friction material, once contaminated. If any of the brake pads are worn unevenly, or are fouled with oil or grease, trace and rectify the cause before reassembly.

8 If the brake pads are still serviceable, carefully clean them using a clean, fine wire brush or similar, paying particular attention to the sides and back of the metal backing. Clean out the grooves in the friction material (where applicable), and pick out any large embedded particles of dirt or debris. Carefully clean the pad locations in the caliper body/mounting bracket.

9 Prior to fitting the pads, check that the guide pins are a light, sliding fit in the caliper body bushes, with little sign of free play. If any of the guide pins appear to worn or damaged, renew them all **(see illustration 4.5b)**. Brush the dust and dirt from the caliper and piston, but *do not* inhale it, as it is a health hazard. Inspect the dust seal around the piston for damage, and the piston for evidence of fluid leaks, corrosion or damage. If attention to any of these components is necessary, refer to Section 8.

10 If new brake pads are to be fitted, the caliper piston must be pushed back into the cylinder to make room for them. Either use a piston retraction tool, a G-clamp or use suitable pieces of wood as levers **(see illustration)**. Provided that the master cylinder reservoir has not been overfilled with brake fluid, there should be no spillage, but keep a careful watch on the fluid level while retracting the piston. If the fluid level rises above the MAX level line at any time, the surplus should be syphoned off or ejected through a plastic tube connected to the bleed nipple (see Section 2). **Note:** *Do not syphon the fluid by mouth, as it is poisonous; use a syringe or a hand-held vacuum pump.*

11 Apply a smear of brake anti-squeak compound to the backing plate of each pad, and the pad backing plate contact points on the caliper bracket; do not apply excess grease, nor allow the grease to contact the friction material **(see illustration)**.

12 Fit the outer pad to the caliper mounting bracket, ensuring that its friction material is against the brake disc **(see illustration)**.

13 Clip the inner pad into the caliper piston, and manoeuvre the caliper assembly into position **(see illustrations)**.

14 Install the caliper guide pin bolts, and tighten them to the specified torque setting. Refit the plugs to the ends of the caliper guide pins.

15 Clip the pad wear sensor back into position in the outer pad, making sure its wiring is correctly routed **(see illustrations 4.3a and 4.3b)**.

16 Clip the retaining spring into position in the caliper **(see illustration 4.2)**. Depress the brake pedal repeatedly, until the pads are pressed into firm contact with the brake disc, and normal (non-assisted) pedal pressure is restored.

17 Repeat the above procedure on the remaining front brake caliper.

18 Refit the roadwheels, then lower the vehicle to the ground and tighten the roadwheel bolts to the specified torque setting.

19 Turn the ignition key to position I and hold it there for at least 30 seconds without starting the engine. This clears the brake pad warning fault stored in the ECM, and turns out the brake pad thickness warning light in the instrument cluster.

New pads will not give full braking efficiency until they have bedded-in. Be prepared for this, and avoid hard braking as far as possible for the first hundred miles or so after pad renewal.

4.13a Clip the inner pad to the piston . . .

4.13b . . . then refit the caliper

5 Rear brake pads – renewal

The rear brake calipers are virtually identical to those fitted at the front. Refer to Section 4 for pad inspection and renewal details.

6 Front brake disc – inspection, removal and refitting

Note: *Before starting work, refer to the note at the beginning of Section 4 concerning the dangers of asbestos dust.*

Note: *If either disc requires renewal, BOTH should be renewed at the same time, to ensure even and consistent braking. New brake pads should also be fitted.*

Inspection

1 Apply the handbrake, then jack up the front of the car and support it on axle stands. Remove the appropriate front roadwheel.

2 Slowly rotate the brake disc so that the full area of both sides can be checked; remove the brake pads if better access is required to the inboard surface (see Section 4). Light scoring is normal in the area swept by the brake pads, but if heavy scoring or cracks are found, the disc must be renewed.

6.3 Use a micrometer to measure the disc thickness

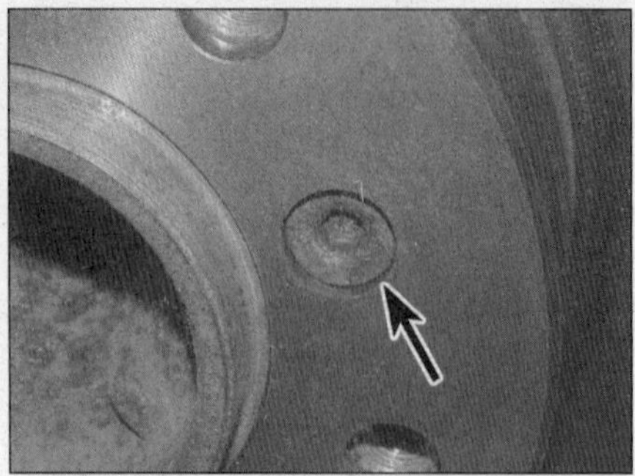

6.7 Remove the screw (arrowed) securing the disc to the hub

3 It is normal to find a lip of rust and brake dust around the disc's perimeter; this can be scraped off if required. If, however, a lip has formed due to excessive wear of the brake pad swept area, then the disc's thickness must be measured using a micrometer **(see illustration)**. Take measurements at several places around the disc, at the inside and outside of the pad swept area; if the disc has worn at any point to the specified minimum thickness or less, the disc must be renewed.

4 If the disc is thought to be warped, it can be checked for run-out. Either use a dial gauge mounted on any convenient fixed point, while the disc is slowly rotated, or use feeler blades to measure (at several points all around the disc) the clearance between the disc and a fixed point, such as the caliper mounting bracket. If the measurements obtained are at the specified maximum or beyond, the disc is excessively warped, and must be renewed; however, it is worth checking first that the hub bearing is in good condition (Chapter 10). If the run-out is excessive, the disc must be renewed.

5 Check the disc for cracks, especially around the wheel bolt holes, and any other wear or damage, and renew if necessary.

Removal

6 Unscrew the two bolts securing the brake caliper mounting bracket to the hub carrier, then slide the caliper assembly off the disc. Using a piece of wire or string, tie the caliper to the front suspension coil spring, to avoid placing any strain on the hydraulic brake hose.

7 Use chalk or paint to mark the relationship of the disc to the hub, then remove the screw securing the brake disc to the hub, and remove the disc **(see illustration)**. If the disc is tight, lightly tap its rear face with a hide or plastic mallet. **Note:** *Where ventilated discs are fitted, do not remove the balance weight from the inside diameter of the disc.*

Refitting

8 Refitting is the reverse of the removal procedure, noting the following points:

a) Ensure that the mating surfaces of the disc and hub are clean and flat.

b) Align (if applicable) the marks made on removal, and tighten the disc retaining screw to the specified torque.

c) If a new disc has been fitted, use a suitable solvent to wipe any preservative coating from the disc, before refitting the caliper.

d) Slide the caliper into position over the disc, making sure the pads pass either side of the disc. Tighten the caliper mounting bolts to the specified torque setting.

e) Refit the roadwheel, then lower the vehicle to the ground and tighten the roadwheel bolts to the specified torque. On completion, repeatedly depress the brake pedal until normal (non-assisted) pedal pressure returns.

7 Rear brake disc – inspection, removal and refitting

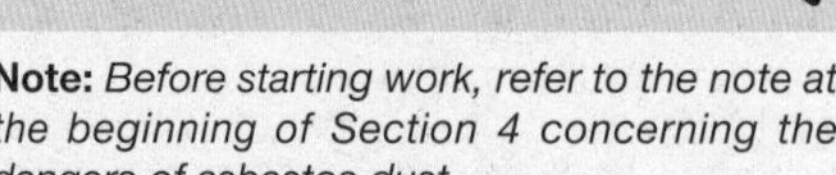

Note: *Before starting work, refer to the note at the beginning of Section 4 concerning the dangers of asbestos dust.*

Note: *If either disc requires renewal, BOTH should be renewed at the same time, to ensure even and consistent braking. New brake pads should also be fitted.*

Inspection

1 Firmly chock the front wheels, then jack up the rear of the car and support it on axle stands. Remove the appropriate rear roadwheel. Release the handbrake.

2 Inspect the disc as described in Section 6.

Removal

3 Unscrew the two bolts securing the brake caliper mounting bracket in position, then slide the caliper assembly off the disc. Using a piece of wire or string, tie the caliper to the rear suspension coil spring, to avoid placing any strain on the hydraulic brake hose **(see illustration)**. If necessary unclip the rubber brake hose from the lower mounting bracket to provide enough slack to manoeuvre the caliper and bracket.

4 Slacken and remove the brake disc retaining screw **(see illustration)**.

5 It should now be possible to withdraw the brake disc from the stub axle by hand. If it is tight, lightly tap its rear face with a hide or plastic mallet. If the handbrake shoes are binding, first check that the handbrake is fully released, then continue as follows.

6 Referring to Section 14 for further details, fully slacken the handbrake adjustment to obtain maximum free play in the cable.

7 Insert a screwdriver through one of the wheel bolt holes in the brake disc, and rotate the adjuster knurled wheel on the upper pivot to retract the shoes **(see illustration 14.5)**. The brake disc can then be withdrawn.

Refitting

8 If a new disc is been fitted, use a suitable solvent to wipe any preservative coating from the disc.

9 Align (if applicable) the marks made on removal, then fit the disc and tighten the retaining screw to the specified torque.

10 Slide the caliper into position over the disc, making sure the pads pass either side of the disc. Tighten the caliper bracket mounting bolts to the specified torque setting.

11 Adjust the handbrake shoes and cable as described in Section 14.

12 Refit the roadwheel, then lower the car to the ground, and tighten the roadwheel bolts to the specified torque. On completion, repeatedly depress the brake pedal until normal (non-assisted) pedal pressure returns. Recheck the handbrake adjustment.

8 Front brake caliper – removal, overhaul and refitting

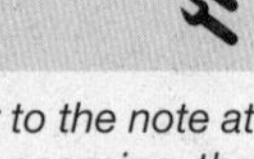

Note: *Before starting work, refer to the note at the beginning of Section 2 concerning the dangers of hydraulic fluid, and to the warning*

7.3 Using a cable tie (arrowed) to suspend the caliper from the brake pipe bracket

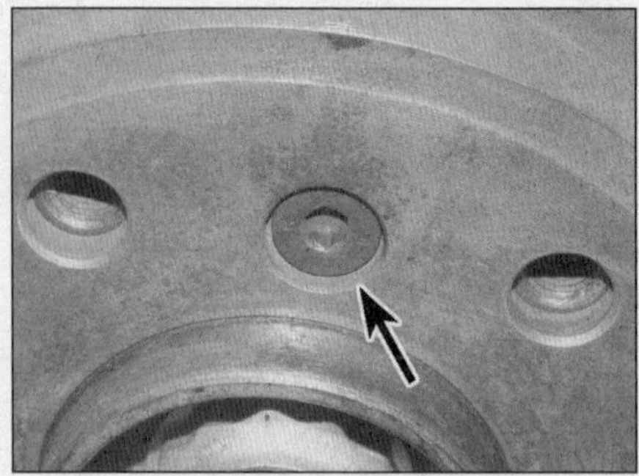

7.4 Remove the disc retaining screw (arrowed)

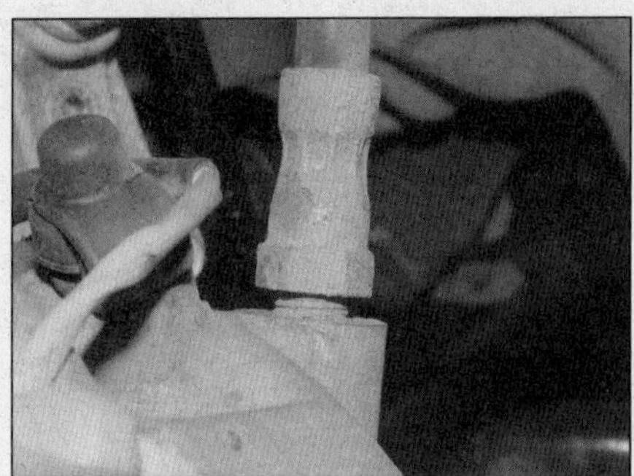

8.3 Slacken the hose union nut

at the beginning of Section 4 concerning the dangers of asbestos dust.

Removal

1 Apply the handbrake, then jack up the front of the vehicle and support it on axle stands (see *Jacking and vehicle support*). Remove the appropriate roadwheel.

2 Minimise fluid loss by using a brake hose clamp, a G-clamp or a similar tool to clamp the flexible hose.

3 Clean the area around the union, then loosen the brake hose union nut **(see illustration)**.

4 Remove the brake pads (see Section 4).

5 Unscrew the caliper from the end of the brake hose and remove it from the vehicle.

Overhaul

6 With the caliper on the bench, wipe away all traces of dust and dirt, but *avoid inhaling the dust, as it is a health hazard.*

7 Withdraw the partially-ejected piston from the caliper body, and remove the dust seal **(see illustration)**. **Note:** *If the piston cannot be withdrawn by hand, it can be pushed out by applying compressed air to the brake hose union hole. Only low pressure should be required, such as is generated by a foot pump. As the piston is expelled, take great care not to trap your fingers between the piston and caliper.*

8 Using a small screwdriver, extract the piston hydraulic seal, taking great care not to damage the caliper bore **(see illustration)**.

9 Thoroughly clean all components, using only methylated spirit, isopropyl alcohol or clean hydraulic fluid as a cleaning medium. Never use mineral-based solvents such as petrol or paraffin, as they will attack the hydraulic system's rubber components. Dry the components immediately, using compressed air or a clean, lint-free cloth. Use compressed air to blow clear the fluid passages.

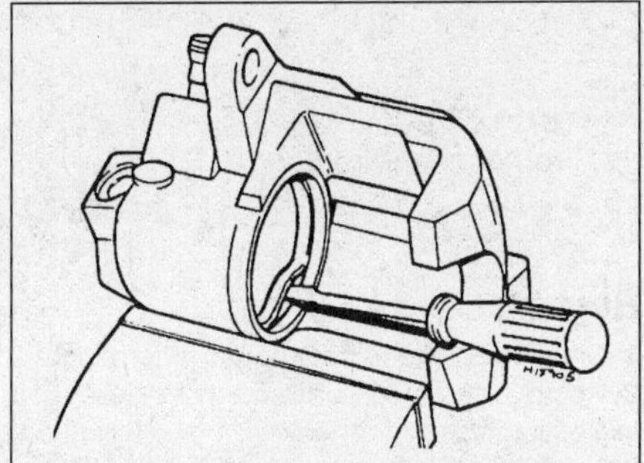

8.8 Extract the piston seal – take care not to scratch the surface of the bore

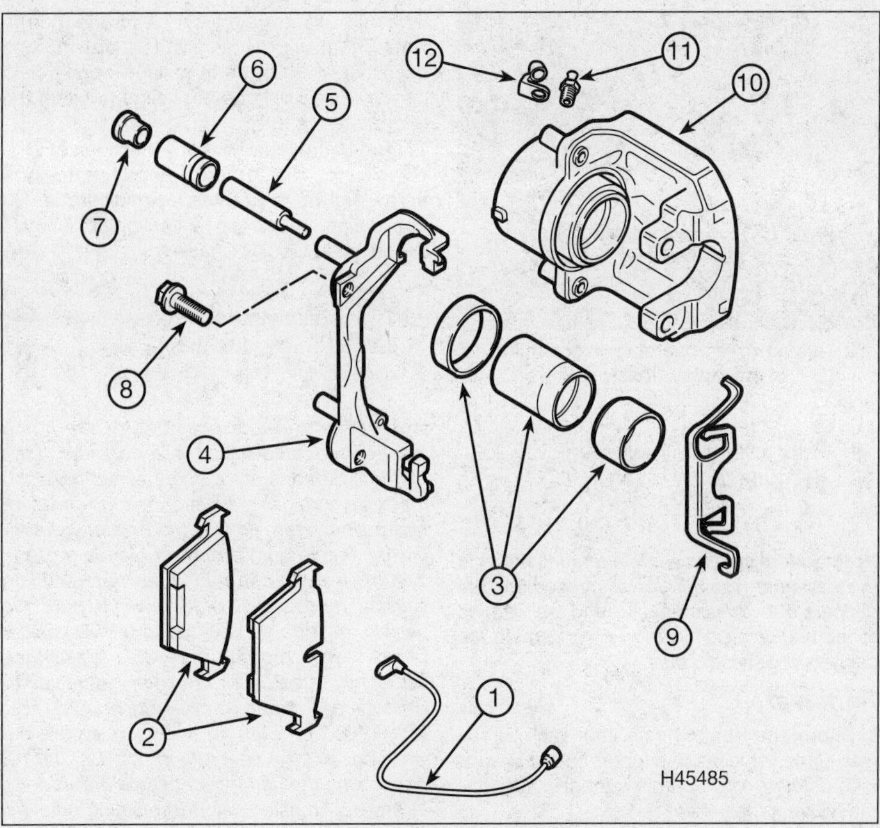

8.7 Front brake caliper

1 Brake pad wear sensor
2 Brake pads
3 Piston and seal assembly
4 Caliper mounting bracket
5 Guide bolt
6 Sleeve
7 Cap
8 Bolt
9 Spring retainer
10 Caliper
11 Bleed nipple
12 Dust cap

10 Check all components, and renew any that are worn or damaged. Check particularly the cylinder bore and piston; these should be renewed (note that this means the renewal of the complete body assembly) if they are scratched, worn or corroded in any way. Similarly check the condition of the guide pins and their bushes; both pins should be undamaged and (when cleaned) a reasonably tight sliding fit in the bushes. If there is any doubt about the condition of any component, renew it.

11 If the assembly is fit for further use, obtain the appropriate repair kit; the components are available from BMW dealers in various combinations. All rubber seals should be renewed as a matter of course; these should never be re-used.

12 On reassembly, ensure that all components are clean and dry.

13 Soak the piston and the new piston (fluid) seal in clean hydraulic fluid. Smear clean fluid on the cylinder bore surface.

14 Fit the new piston (fluid) seal, using only your fingers (no tools) to manipulate it into the cylinder bore groove.

15 Fit the new dust seal to the piston. Locate the rear of the seal in the recess in the caliper body, and refit the piston to the cylinder bore using a twisting motion. Ensure that the piston enters squarely into the bore, and press it fully into the bore.

Refitting

16 Screw the caliper fully onto the flexible hose union.

17 Refit the brake pads (see Section 4).

18 Securely tighten the brake pipe union nut.

19 Remove the brake hose clamp or polythene, as applicable, and bleed the hydraulic system as described in Section 2. Note that, providing the precautions described were taken to minimise brake fluid loss, it should only be necessary to bleed the relevant front brake.

20 Refit the roadwheel, then lower the vehicle to the ground and tighten the roadwheel bolts to the specified torque. On completion, check the hydraulic fluid level as described in *Weekly Checks*.

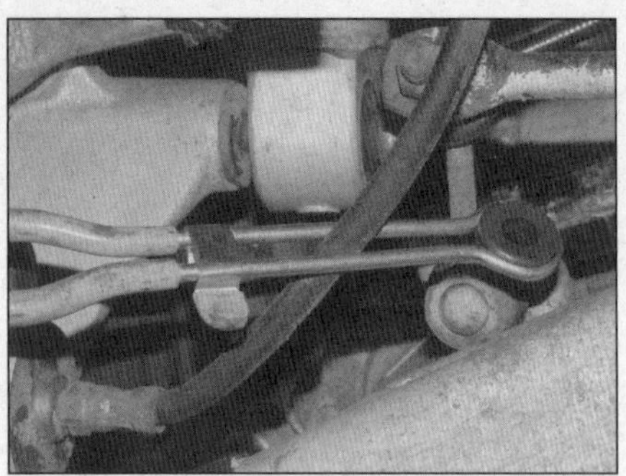

9.2 Use a brake hose clamp (or similar) to minimise fluid loss

9 Rear brake caliper – removal, overhaul and refitting

Note: *Before starting work, refer to the note at the beginning of Section 2 concerning the dangers of hydraulic fluid, and to the warning at the beginning of Section 4 concerning the dangers of asbestos dust.*

Removal

1 Chock the front wheels, then jack up the rear of the vehicle and support on axle stands (see *Jacking and vehicle support*). Remove the relevant rear wheel.

2 Minimise fluid loss by using a brake hose clamp, a G-clamp or a similar tool to clamp the flexible hose **(see illustration)**.

3 Clean the area around the union, then loosen the brake hose union nut.

4 Remove the brake pads as described in Section 4.

5 Unscrew the caliper from the end of the flexible hose, and remove it from the vehicle.

Overhaul

6 Refer to Section 8.

Refitting

7 Screw the caliper fully onto the flexible hose union.

8 Refit the brake pads (refer to Section 4).

9 Securely tighten the brake pipe union nut.

10 Remove the brake hose clamp or polythene, as applicable, and bleed the hydraulic system as described in Section 2. Note that, providing the precautions described were taken to minimise brake fluid loss, it should only be necessary to bleed the relevant rear brake.

11 Refit the roadwheel, then lower the vehicle to the ground and tighten the roadwheel bolts to the specified torque. On completion, check the hydraulic fluid level as described in *Weekly Checks*.

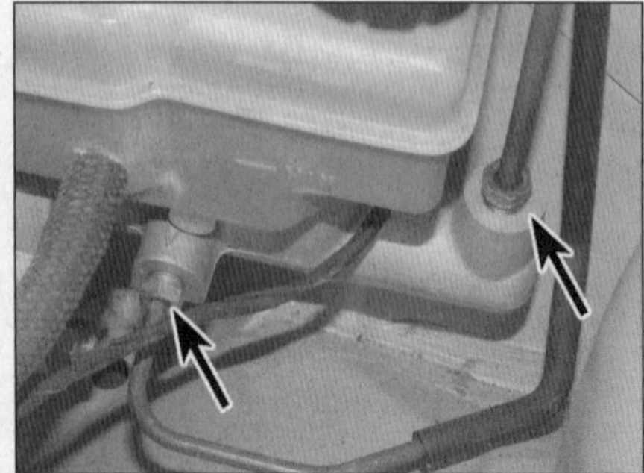

10.6 Unscrew the pipe unions (arrowed)

10 Master cylinder – removal, overhaul and refitting

Note: *Although it is possible for the home mechanic to remove the master cylinder, if the hydraulic unions are disconnected from the master cylinder air will enter the high-pressure hydraulic system linking the master cylinder and hydraulic unit. If manual bleeding of the system (see Section 2) does not result in satisfactory operation of the brake system, the vehicle must be transported to a BMW dealer or specialist who has access to the service tester which actuates the solenoid valves to dislodge any trapped air (see Section 2).*

Note: *Before starting work, refer to the warning at the beginning of Section 2 concerning the dangers of hydraulic fluid.*

Note: *New master cylinder retaining nuts will be required on refitting.*

Removal

1 To allow access to the master cylinder, unclip the driver's side air duct, unclip the pollen filter cover and remove the filter.

2 Release the clip and remove the filter housing.

3 Remove the master cylinder reservoir cap, and syphon the hydraulic fluid from the reservoir. **Note:** *Do not syphon the fluid by mouth, as it is poisonous; use a syringe or a hand-held vacuum pump.* Alternatively, open any convenient bleed screw in the system, and gently pump the brake pedal to expel the fluid through a plastic tube connected to the screw until the level of fluid drops below that of the reservoir (see Section 2).

4 Disconnect the fluid hose(s) from the side of the reservoir, plug the hose end(s) to minimise fluid loss, and disconnect the level sensor wiring plug. **Note:** *On models equipped with DSC (Dynamic Stability Control), disconnect the precharge pump supply hose from the reservoir, and secure it in a vertical position to prevent fluid loss.*

5 Carefully ease the fluid reservoir out from the top of the master cylinder. Recover the reservoir seals, and plug the cylinder ports to prevent dirt entry.

6 Wipe clean the area around the brake pipe unions on the side of the master cylinder, and place absorbent rags beneath the pipe unions to catch any surplus fluid. Make a note of the correct fitted positions of the unions, then undo the union nuts **(see illustration)**. Plug or tape over the pipe ends and master cylinder orifices, to minimise the loss of brake fluid, and to prevent the entry of dirt into the system. Wash off any spilt fluid immediately with cold water.

7 Slacken and remove the two nuts and washers securing the master cylinder to the vacuum servo unit, then separate the two. Remove the O-ring from the rear of the master cylinder. Discard the retaining nuts, new ones should be used on refitting.

Overhaul

8 If the master cylinder is faulty, it must be renewed. At the time of writing, repair kits are not available from BMW dealers so the cylinder must be treated as a sealed unit. Check with your local dealer or motor factors for overhaul kit availability before purchasing a new master cylinder. Renew the master cylinder O-ring seal and reservoir seals regardless of their apparent condition.

Refitting

9 Remove all traces of dirt from the master cylinder and servo unit mating surfaces, and fit a new O-ring to the groove on the master cylinder body.

10 Fit the master cylinder to the servo unit, ensuring that the servo unit pushrod enters the master cylinder bore centrally. Fit the new master cylinder retaining nuts and washers, and tighten them to the specified torque.

11 The remainder of the procedure is a reversal of removal noting the following points:

a) Wipe clean the brake pipe unions, then refit them to the master cylinder ports and tighten them securely.

b) Press the new reservoir seals firmly into the master cylinder ports, then ease the reservoir into position. Tighten the reservoir retaining bolt securely. Reconnect the fluid hose(s) to the reservoir, and reconnect the wiring connector(s).

c) Refit and adjust the stop-light switch as described in Section 18.

d) Refill the master cylinder reservoir with new fluid, and bleed the complete hydraulic system as described in Section 2.

11 Brake pedal – removal and refitting

Removal

1 Disconnect the battery negative terminal.

2 Remove the stop-light switch as described in Section 18.

3 Using a pair of pliers, carefully unhook the return spring from the brake pedal.

4 Slide off the retaining clip and remove the

clevis pin securing the brake pedal to the servo unit pushrod **(see illustration)**.

5 Slide off the pedal pivot pin retaining clip and remove the pedal from the pivot.

6 Carefully clean and inspect all components, renewing any that are worn or damaged.

Refitting

7 Refitting is the reverse of removal. Apply a smear of multi-purpose grease to the pedal pivot and clevis pin.

12 Vacuum servo unit – testing, removal and refitting

Testing

1 To test the operation of the servo unit, depress the footbrake several times to exhaust the vacuum, then start the engine whilst keeping the pedal firmly depressed. As the engine starts, there should be a noticeable 'give' in the brake pedal as the vacuum builds-up. Allow the engine to run for at least two minutes, then switch it off. If the brake pedal is now depressed it should feel normal, but further applications should result in the pedal feeling firmer, with the pedal stroke decreasing with each application.

2 If the servo does not operate as described, first inspect the servo unit check valve as described in Section 13.

3 If the servo unit still fails to operate satisfactorily, the fault lies within the unit itself. Repairs to the unit are not possible – if faulty, the servo unit must be renewed.

Removal

Note: *New retaining nuts will be required on refitting.*

4 Although it is possible for the home mechanic to remove the servo unit, if the hydraulic unions are disconnected from the master cylinder, air will enter the high-pressure hydraulic system linking the master cylinder and hydraulic unit. If manual bleeding of the system (see Section 2) does not result in satisfactory operation of the brake system, the vehicle must be transported to a BMW dealer or specialist who has access to the service tester which actuates the solenoid valves to dislodge any trapped air (see Section 2).

5 Remove the master cylinder as described in Section 10.

6 Disconnect the vacuum hose from the servo unit check valve.

7 Remove the stop-light switch as described in Section 18.

8 Remove the retaining clip, and withdraw the servo pivot pin from the brake pedal **(see illustration)**.

9 Unhook the brake pedal return spring.

10 Undo the 5 retaining nuts and pull the pedal assembly away from the bulkhead slightly **(see illustration)**.

11 Working in the engine compartment, carefully remove the servo unit assembly from the bulkhead. Take great care not to damage the servo pushrod rubber gaiter as the unit is removed.

Refitting

12 Refitting is the reverse of removal, noting the following points.

a) *Check the servo unit check valve sealing grommet for signs of damage or deterioration, and renew if necessary.*
b) *If a new servo unit is being installed, remove the sound insulation material from the original, and transfer it to the new one.*
c) *Ensure that the servo unit pushrod is correctly engaged with the brake pedal, then fit the new retaining nuts and tighten them to the specified torque.*

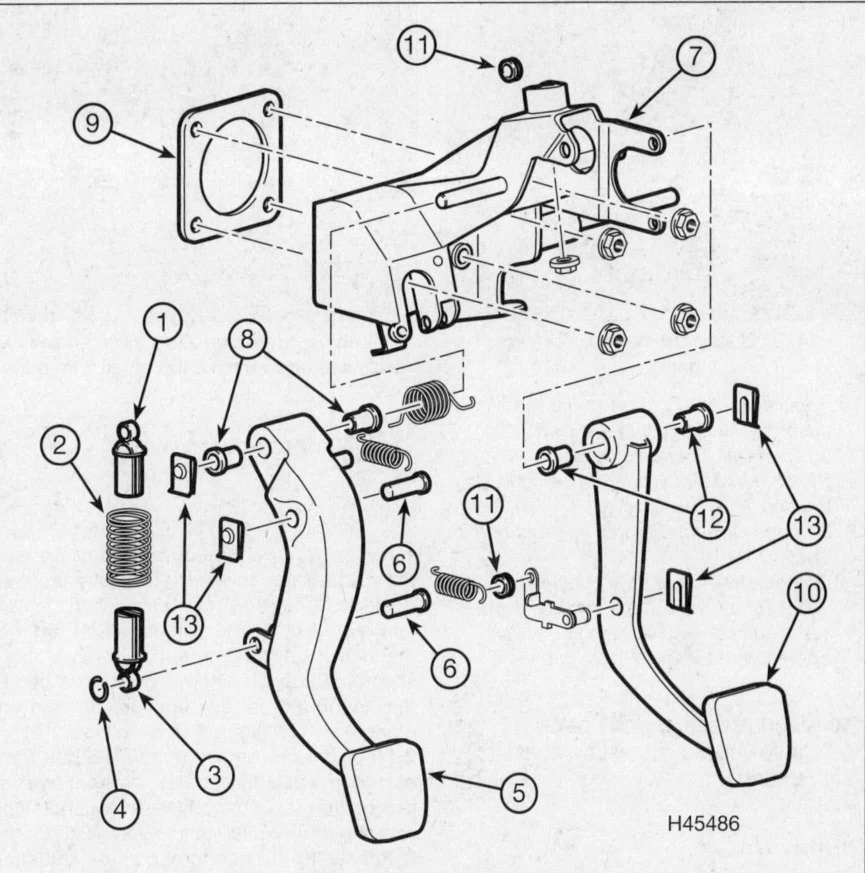

11.4 Brake and clutch pedal assemblies

1 Bracket
2 Spring
3 Bracket
4 Retainer
5 Clutch pedal
6 Pin
7 Mounting bracket
8 Bushes
9 Seal
10 Brake pedal
11 Grommet
12 Bushes
13 Retaining clips

12.8 Remove the servo pivot pin clip (arrowed)

12.10 The pedal assembly is secured by 5 nuts (4 arrowed – the remaining nut is above the bracket)

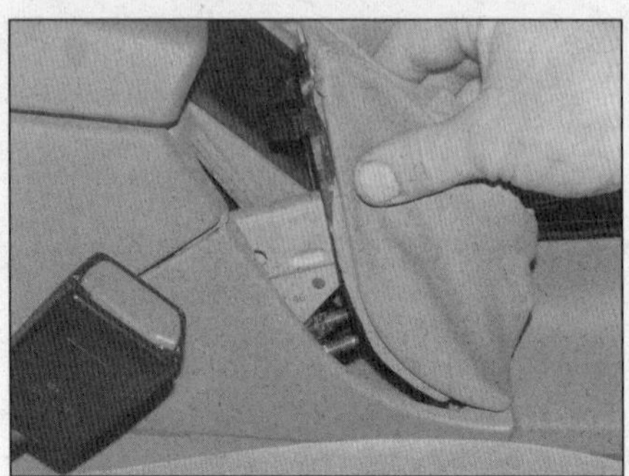

14.3a Unclip the handbrake lever gaiter . . .

d) *Apply a smear of grease to the servo pushrod clevis pin, and secure it in position with the retaining clip.*
e) *Refit the master cylinder as described in Section 10 of this Chapter.*
f) *Refit the stop-light switch as described in Section 18.*
g) *On completion, start the engine and check for air leaks at the vacuum hose-to-servo unit connection; check the operation of the braking system.*

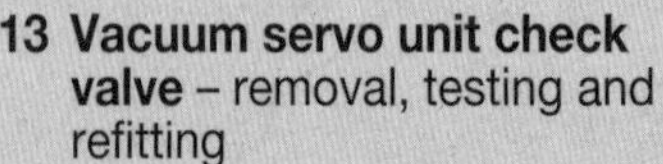

13 Vacuum servo unit check valve – removal, testing and refitting

Removal

1 Before starting, depress the brake pedal several times, to collapse any vacuum in the servo.

2 Working in the engine compartment, unclip the hoses to and from the check valve and remove it.

Testing

3 Examine the check valve for signs of damage, and renew if necessary.

4 The valve may be tested by blowing through it in both directions; air should flow through the valve in one direction only – when blown through from the servo unit end of the valve. Renew the valve if this is not the case.

Refitting

5 Reconnect the vacuum hoses securely to the valve, using new clips.

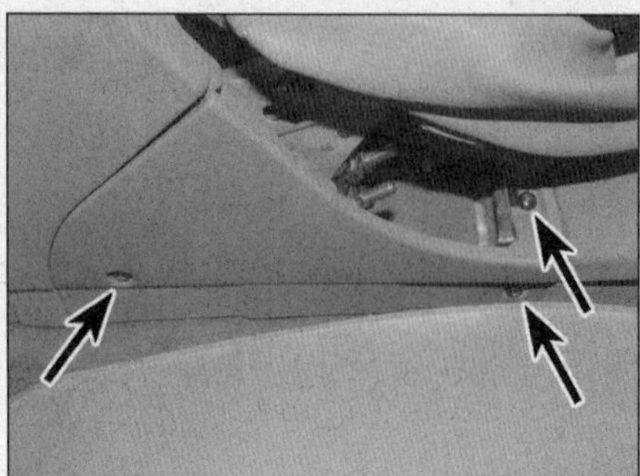

14.3b . . . then undo the three screws (arrowed) and remove the small trim panel

14 Handbrake – adjustment

1 Applying normal moderate pressure, pull the handbrake lever to the fully applied position, counting the number of clicks emitted from the handbrake ratchet mechanism. If adjustment is correct, there should be approximately 7 or 8 clicks before the handbrake is fully applied. If there are more than 10 clicks, adjust as follows.

2 Slacken and remove one wheel bolt from each rear wheel then chock the front wheels, jack up the rear of the vehicle and support it on axle stands (see *Jacking and vehicle support*).

3 Access to the handbrake cable adjusting nuts can be gained by removing the handbrake lever gaiter from the centre console, then undoing three screws and removing the trim panel adjacent to the handbrake lever **(see illustrations)**. If greater access is required, the centre console will have to be removed (Chapter 11).

4 With the handbrake fully released, undo the cable locknuts and release the adjusting nuts until all tension in the cables is released **(see illustration)**.

5 Starting on the left-hand rear wheel, position the wheel/disc so the exposed bolt hole is positioned at the bottom (6 o'clock position). Make sure the handbrake lever is fully released, then insert a screwdriver in through the bolt hole and fully expand the handbrake shoes by rotating the adjuster knurled ring. When the wheel/disc can no longer be turned, back the knurled ring off by 12 teeth (catches) so that the wheel is free to rotate easily **(see illustration)**.

6 Repeat paragraph 5 on the right-hand wheel.

7 Depress the handbrake lever release button, and apply the handbrake 5 times.

8 With the handbrake set on the second notch of the ratchet mechanism, rotate the cables adjusting nuts equally until it is difficult to turn both rear wheels. Once this is so, fully release the handbrake lever, and check that the wheels rotate freely and, with the ignition switched on, the handbrake warning light is not illuminated. Slowly apply the handbrake, and check that the brake shoes start to contact the drums when the handbrake is set to the second notch of the ratchet mechanism. Check the adjustment by applying the handbrake fully, counting the clicks emitted from the handbrake ratchet and, if necessary, re-adjust.

9 Once adjustment is correct, hold the adjusting nuts and securely tighten the locknuts. Check the operation of the handbrake warning light switch, then refit the centre console section/handbrake lever gaiter (as applicable). Refit the roadwheels, then lower the vehicle to the ground and tighten the wheel bolts to the specified torque.

15 Handbrake lever – removal and refitting

Removal

1 Remove the centre console as described in Chapter 11 to gain access to the handbrake lever.

2 Slacken and remove both the handbrake cable locknuts/adjusting nuts, and detach the cables from the lever.

3 Undo the retaining bolts, disconnect the handbrake warning switch wiring plug, and remove the lever from the vehicle **(see illustration)**.

Refitting

4 Refitting is a reversal of the removal. Prior to refitting the centre console, adjust the handbrake as described in Section 14.

14.4 Undo the cable locknuts

14.5 With a wheel bolt hole at the 6 o'clock position, rotate the adjuster knurled wheel with a flat-bladed screwdriver

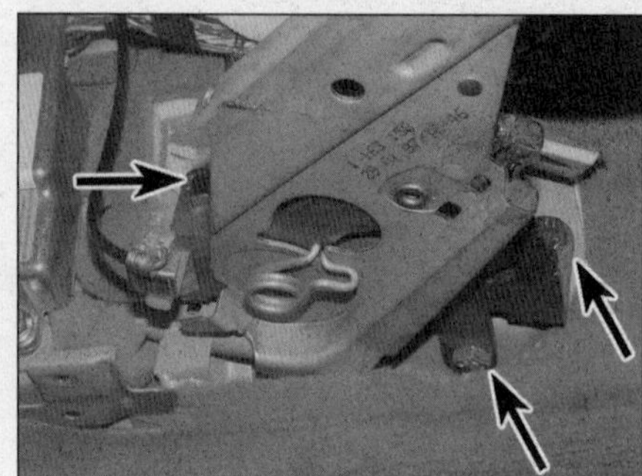

15.3 Undo the three bolts (arrowed) and remove the handbrake lever assembly

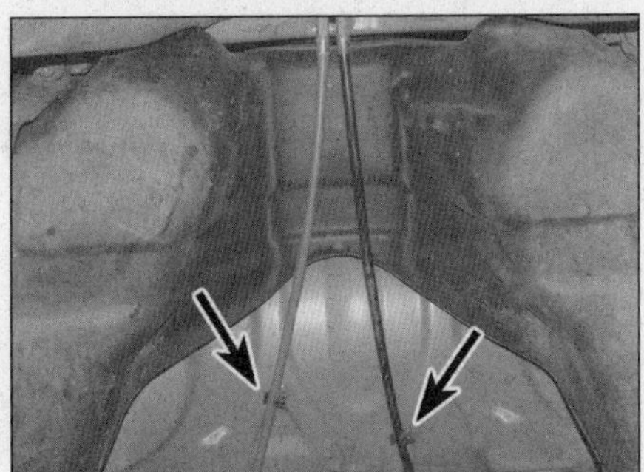

16.8 Pull the handbrake cables from the guides tubes and free them from the retaining clips (arrowed)

16.11a Slide the inner cable towards the hub flange, and free it from the expander assembly

16.11b If the outer cable is seized in place, apply penetrating fluid, and carefully twist it from place using self-grip pliers

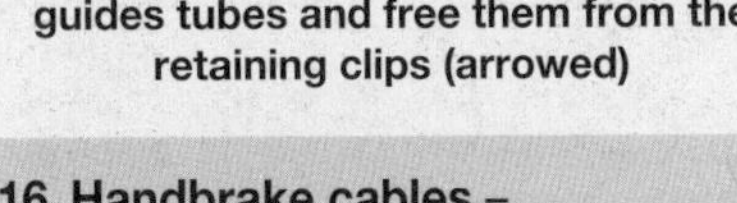

16 Handbrake cables – removal and refitting

Removal

1 Unclip the handbrake lever gaiter from the centre console **(see illustration 14.3a)**.

2 Undo the three screws and remove the handbrake lever surround trim **(see illustration 14.3b)**.

The handbrake cable consists of two sections, a right- and a left-hand section, which are connected to the lever. Each section can be removed individually.

3 Slacken and remove the relevant handbrake cable locknut and adjusting nut, and disengage the inner cable from the handbrake lever.

4 Firmly chock the front wheels, then jack up the rear of the car and support it on axle stands (see *Jacking and vehicle support*).

5 Remove the exhaust system as described in Chapter 4A.

6 Remove the propeller shaft as described in Chapter 8.

7 Release the nuts and remove the exhaust heat shield.

8 Free the front end of the outer cable from the body, and withdraw the cable from its support guide **(see illustration)**.

9 Working back along the length of the cable, noting its correct routing, and free it from all the relevant retaining clips.

10 Remove the relevant rear disc as described in Section 7.

11 Slide the inner cable in the direction of the hub flange up to the stop, and manoeuvre the cable end fitting from the expander assembly. If the outer cable is seized in the hub carrier casing, apply some penetrating fluid and twist the fitting using a pair of self-grip pliers **(see illustrations)**.

Refitting

12 Insert the cable into the brake carrier/guard plate, and push it in up to the stop on the cable outer sleeve.

13 Grip the sleeve of the cable end, and push it in to the expander until it snaps into place.

14 Refitting is a reversal of the removal procedure. Prior to refitting the centre console, adjust the handbrake as described in Section 14.

17 Handbrake shoes – removal and refitting

Removal

1 Remove the rear brake disc as described in Section 7, and make a note of the correct fitted position of all components.

2 Using a pair of pliers, carefully unhook and remove the handbrake shoe return springs **(see illustrations)**.

3 Release the shoe retaining pins using an Allen key by depressing them and rotating them through 90°, then remove the pins and springs **(see illustration)**.

4 Remove both handbrake shoes, and recover the shoe adjuster mechanism, noting which way around it is fitted **(see illustrations)**.

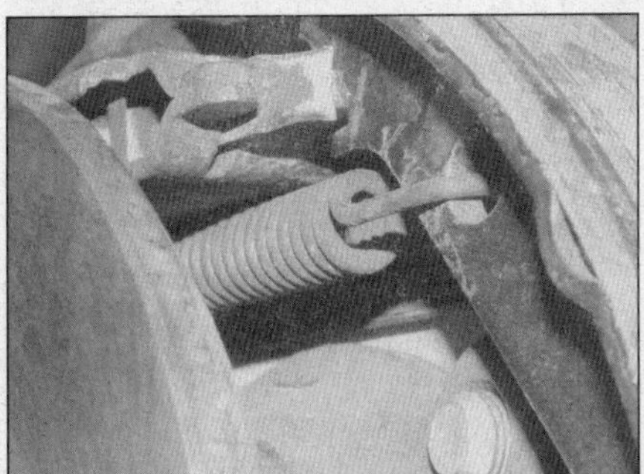

17.2a Use pliers to disconnect the upper . . .

17.2b . . . and lower handbrake shoe return springs

17.3 Using an Allen key, push the retaining clips/springs in, then rotate them 90° anti-clockwise to release them

17.4a Remove the brake shoes . . .

17.4b . . . followed by the expander assembly (left-hand brake shown)

17.9 Ensure the lower ends of the shoes engage correctly with the adjuster

5 Inspect the handbrake shoes for wear or contamination, and renew if necessary. It is recommended that the return springs are renewed as a matter of course.

6 While the shoes are removed, clean and inspect the condition of the shoe adjuster and expander mechanisms, renew them if they show signs of wear or damage. If all is well, apply a fresh coat of brake grease (BMW recommend Molykote Paste G) to the threads of the adjuster and sliding surfaces of the expander mechanism. Do not allow the grease to contact the shoe friction material.

Refitting

7 Prior to installation, clean the backplate, and apply a thin smear of high-temperature brake grease or anti-seize compound to all those surfaces of the backplate which bear on the shoes. Do not allow the lubricant to foul the friction material.

8 Offer up the handbrake shoes, and secure them in position with the retaining pins and springs.

9 Make sure the lower ends of the shoes are correctly engaged with the adjuster, then slide the adjuster mechanism into position between the upper ends of the shoes **(see illustration)**.

10 Check all components are correctly fitted, and fit the upper and lower return springs using a pair of pliers.

11 Centralise the handbrake shoes, and refit the brake disc as described in Section 7.

12 Prior to refitting the roadwheel, adjust the handbrake as described in Section 14.

18 Stop-light switch – removal and refitting

Removal

1 The stop-light switch is located on the pedal bracket behind the facia.

2 Slacken and remove the retaining screws/fasteners securing the driver's side lower facia panel. Unclip the panel and remove it from the vehicle (see Chapter 11).

3 Reach up behind the facia and disconnect the wiring connector from the switch.

Models up to 09/98

4 Depress the brake pedal, pull the switch plunger fully out, pull the red collar forwards, then squeeze together the retaining tabs and pull the switch from the mounting **(see illustrations)**. Note that on this type of switch there are no moving parts. The brake lights are triggered by the proximity of the pedal to the switch.

Models from 09/98

5 Pull the switch from the mounting. If required, squeeze together the sides of the clips and withdraw the switch mounting from the pedal bracket **(see illustration)**.

Refitting

6 Fully depress the brake pedal and hold it down, then manoeuvre the switch into position. Slide the switch as far as it will go into the bracket, then **slowly** release the brake pedal and allow it to return to its starting position. **Note:** *If the pedal is released too quickly, the switch will be incorrectly adjusted. On models with DSC, a gap of 0.7 mm must exist between the brake pedal and the switch* ***(see illustration)****.*

7 Reconnect the wiring connector, and check the operation of the stop-lights. **Note:** *If the operation of the stop-lights is unsatisfactory on models with DSC, try reducing the gap between the switch and the pedal to 0.6 mm.*

8 On completion, refit the driver's side lower facia panel.

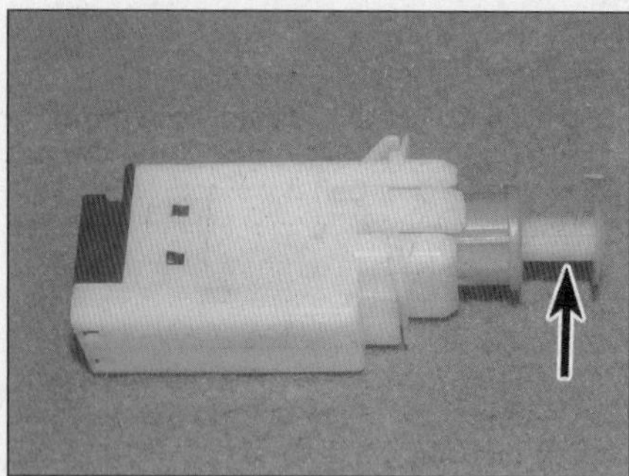

18.4a Shown with the switch removed – pull out the plunger (arrowed) . . .

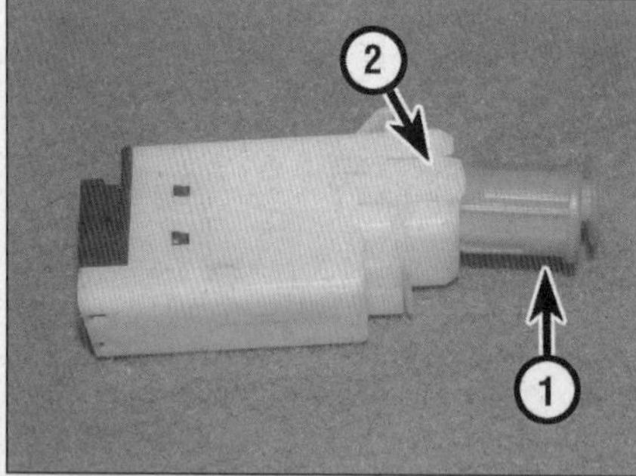

18.4b . . . then pull out the red collar (1) and depress the clips (2)

18.5 Note the locating guide (arrowed) which locates into the corresponding slot in the mounting

18.6 Use a feeler gauge to set the correct clearance – see text

19 Anti-lock braking system (ABS) – general information

Note: *On models equipped with traction control, the ABS unit is a dual function unit, and works both the anti-lock braking system (ABS) and traction control function of the Automatic Stability Control plus Traction (ASC+T) system. On models so equipped, the unit also controls the function of the Dynamic Stability Control (DSC) system.*

1 ABS is fitted to all models as standard. The system comprises a hydraulic block which contains the hydraulic solenoid valves and the electrically-driven pump, the four roadwheel sensors (one fitted to each wheel), and the electronic control unit (ECU). The purpose of the system is to prevent the wheel(s) locking during heavy braking. This is achieved by automatic release of the brake on the relevant wheel, followed by re-application of the brake.

2 The solenoids are controlled by the ECU, which itself receives signals from the four wheel sensors, which monitor the speed of rotation of each wheel. By comparing these signals, the ECU can determine the speed at which the vehicle is travelling. It can then use this speed to determine when a wheel is decelerating at an abnormal rate, compared to the speed of the vehicle, and therefore predicts when a wheel is about to lock. During normal operation, the system functions in the same way as a non-ABS braking system.

3 If the ECU senses that a wheel is about to lock, it operates the relevant solenoid valve in the hydraulic unit, which then isolates the brake caliper on the wheel which is about to lock from the master cylinder, effectively sealing-in the hydraulic pressure.

4 If the speed of rotation of the wheel continues to decrease at an abnormal rate, the ECU switches on the electrically-driven pump, and pumps the hydraulic fluid back into the master cylinder, releasing pressure on the brake caliper so that the brake is released. Once the speed of rotation of the wheel returns to an acceptable rate, the pump stops and the solenoid valve opens, allowing the hydraulic master cylinder pressure to return to the caliper, which then re-applies the brake. This cycle can be carried out at up to 10 times a second.

5 The action of the solenoid valves and return pump creates pulses in the hydraulic circuit. When the ABS system is functioning, these pulses can be felt through the brake pedal.

6 The operation of the ABS system is entirely dependent on electrical signals. To prevent the system responding to any inaccurate signals, a built-in safety circuit monitors all signals received by the ECU. If an inaccurate signal or low battery voltage is detected, the ABS system is automatically shut down, and the warning light on the instrument panel is illuminated, to inform the driver that the ABS system is not operational. Normal braking should still be available, however.

7 If a fault does develop in the ABS system, the vehicle must be taken to a BMW dealer or suitably-equipped specialist for fault diagnosis and repair.

8 On models equipped with ASC+T, an accumulator is also incorporated into the hydraulic system. As well as performing the ABS function as described above, the hydraulic unit also works the traction control side of the ASC+T system. If the ECU senses that the wheels are about to lose traction under acceleration, the hydraulic unit momentarily applies the rear brakes to prevent the wheel(s) spinning. In the same way as the ABS, the vehicle must be taken to a BMW dealer or suitably-equipped specialist for testing if a fault develops in the ASC+T system.

9 All models may be equipped with a DSC system, which monitors the dynamic situation of the vehicle via lateral acceleration, steering angle, and yaw rate sensors. If the system detects oversteer or understeer, it can reduce the engine output, and apply the brakes at one or more wheel, to avoid skidding and stabilise the vehicle. The various components of the DSC system are covered in Chapter 10, with the exception of the hydraulic unit, ECU, and wheel speed sensors, which are shared by the ABS system.

20.4 Undo the two screws and remove the trim panel

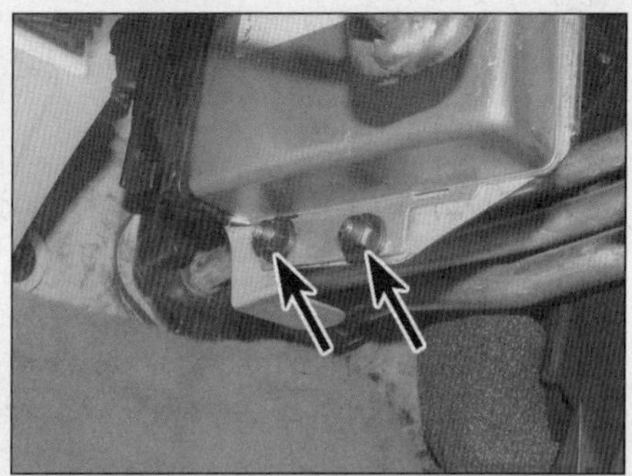

20.5 Undo the two nuts (arrowed) at the base of the ABS ECU

20 Anti-lock braking system (ABS) components – removal and refitting

Hydraulic unit

1 Although it is possible for the home mechanic to remove the hydraulic unit, the unit's self-diagnosis system must be interrogated by dedicated test equipment before and after removal, and the unit must be bled by BMW service test equipment. Consequently, we recommend that removal and refitting the hydraulic unit should be entrusted to a BMW dealer or suitably-equipped specialist.

Accumulator

2 For the same reasons given in Paragraph 1, we recommend that removal and refitting of the accumulator should be entrusted to a BMW dealer or suitable-equipped specialist.

Electronic control unit (ECU)

Models up to 09/98

Note: *Before removing the ECU, BMW recommend that the systems self-diagnosis system is interrogated to retrieve any stored fault codes.*

3 Remove the passenger side glovebox as described in Chapter 11, Section 26.

4 Undo the two bolts, and remove the inner trim panel adjacent to the glovebox lid strut **(see illustration)**.

5 Undo the two plastic retaining nuts at the base, and manoeuvre it from the mounting bracket **(see illustration)**.

6 Lever open the locking catch and disconnect the ECU's wiring plug **(see illustration)**.

7 Refitting is a reversal of removal.

Models from 09/98

8 In order to remove the ABS/ASC+T/DSC ECU, the hydraulic unit must first be disturbed, as the ECU is screwed to the side of the hydraulic unit. Consequently, we recommend that removal and refitting of the ECU is entrusted to a BMW dealer or suitably-equipped specialist.

Front wheel sensor

Removal

9 Chock the rear wheels, then firmly apply the handbrake, jack up the front of the vehicle and support on axle stands (see *Jacking and vehicle support*). Remove the appropriate front roadwheel.

10 Trace the wiring back from the sensor to the connector which is situated in a protective plastic box. Unclip the lid, then free the wiring connector and disconnect it from the main harness **(see illustration)**. Release the lead and grommet from any retaining bracket on the suspension strut.

11 Slacken and remove the bolts securing the sensor to the hub carrier, and remove the sensor and lead assembly from the vehicle **(see illustration)**. **Note:** *On vehicles*

20.6 Lift the locking catch and disconnect the wiring plug

20.10 Open the plastic box and disconnect the ABS sensor wiring plug

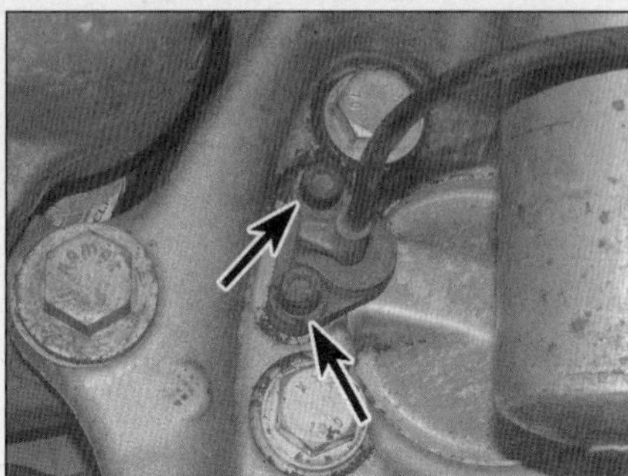

20.11 Remove the ABS wheel speed sensor bolts (arrowed)

manufactured after 03/2000 the sensor is secured by a single bolt.

Refitting

12 Prior to refitting, apply a thin coat of multi-purpose grease to the sensor tip (BMW recommend the use of Staborax NBU 12/k).

13 Ensure that the sensor and hub carrier sealing faces are clean, then fit the sensor to the hub. Refit the retaining bolt(s) and tighten it to the specified torque.

14 Ensure that the sensor wiring is correctly routed and retained by all the necessary clips, and reconnect it to its wiring connector. Refit the sensor connector into the box and securely clip the lid in position.

15 Refit the roadwheel, then lower the vehicle to the ground and tighten the roadwheel bolts to the specified torque.

Rear wheel sensor

Removal

16 Chock the front wheels, then jack up the rear of the vehicle and support it on axle stands (see *Jacking and vehicle support*). Remove the appropriate roadwheel.

20.17 Rear ABS sensor connector

20.18 Rear wheel speed sensor bolt

17 Trace the wiring back from the sensor to the connector which is situated in a protective plastic box. Unclip the lid, then free the wiring connector and disconnect it from the main harness **(see illustration)**. Release the sensor lead from the plastic guide on the suspension arm.

18 Slacken and remove the bolt securing the sensor to the hub carrier, and remove the sensor and lead assembly from the vehicle **(see illustration)**.

Refitting

19 Refit the sensor as described above in paragraphs 12 to 15.

Reluctor rings

20 The front reluctor rings are integral with the wheel bearing oil seals (see Chapter 10).

Chapter 10
Suspension and steering

Contents

Degrees of difficulty

Easy, suitable for novice with little experience 

Fairly easy, suitable for beginner with some experience

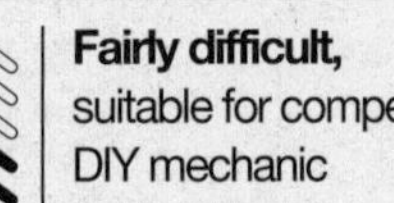

Fairly difficult, suitable for competent DIY mechanic

Difficult, suitable for experienced DIY mechanic 

Very difficult, suitable for expert DIY or professional

Specifications

Front suspension

Type . . . Independent, with MacPherson struts incorporating coil springs and telescopic shock absorbers, located by aluminium lower control arm and tension arm. Anti-roll bar fitted to all models

Rear suspension

Type . . . Independent, aluminium swinging arm with aluminium upper control arms, coil springs and shock absorbers (Touring models) or MacPherson struts incorporating coil springs and telescopic shock absorbers (Saloon models). Self-levelling electro-pneumatic shock absorbers available as an option. Anti-roll bar fitted to all models

Steering

Type . . . Rack-and-pinion. Power assistance standard on all models

Wheel alignment and steering angles

Vehicle must be laden to simulate front and rear passengers, and have a full fuel tank.

Front wheel:	
Camber angle:	
Standard	-36' ± 30'
Models with Sports suspension	-36' ± 30'
Models with air suspension	-13' ± 30'
Maximum difference between sides	40'
Castor angle (with 10° wheel lock):	
Standard	6° 28' ± 30'
Models with Sports suspension	6° 41' ± 30'
Models with air suspension	6° 28' ± 30'
Maximum difference between sides	30'
Toe setting (total)	0° 05' ± 10'
Rear wheel:	
Camber angle:	
Saloon models:	
Standard	-2° 10' ± 20'
Sports suspension	-2° 10' ± 25'
Air suspension	-2° 10' ± 25'
Touring models	-1° 50' ± 20'
Maximum difference between sides	15'
Toe setting (total)	0° 16' ± 10'

Roadwheels

Type	Aluminium alloy
Size	6.5J x 15, 7J x 15, 7J x 16, 8J x 17, 9J x 17, 8J x 18 or 9J x 18

Tyres

Size	From 205/65 R 15 to 265/35 ZR 18 depending on model and wheel type*
Pressures	See the label affixed to the driver's door aperture

**Consult your handbook, a BMW dealer or a suitable tyre dealer for the correct size for your vehicle.*

Torque wrench settings

	Nm	lbf ft
Front suspension		
Anti-roll bar connecting link nuts*	65	48
Anti-roll bar mounting clamp nuts*	22	16
Hub-to-carrier bolts*	110	81
Lower control arm balljoint nut*	80	59
Lower control arm to subframe	110	81
Strut mounting-to-body nuts*:		
Nuts with 18 mm diameter flange	24	18
Nuts with 21 mm diameter flange	34	25
Strut upper mounting plate/piston rod nut:		
M12 thread:		
Piston with an external hexagon end (retain with socket)	64	47
Piston with an internal hexagon end (retain with Allen key)	44	32
M14 thread	64	47
Strut-to-hub carrier nut*	81	60
Subframe*:		
M10:		
8.8 strength grade (see head of bolt)	42	31
9.8 strength grade (see head of bolt)	47	35
M12:		
8.8 strength grade (see head of bolt)	77	57
10.9 strength grade (see head of bolt)	110	81
12.9 strength grade (see head of bolt)	105	77
Lower tension arm balljoint nut*	80	59
Lower tension arm to subframe	110	81
Rear suspension		
Air suspension unit on hub carrier	20	15
Anti-roll bar/link nuts*	65	47
Control arm to hub carrier*	142	105
Control arm-to-subframe nut*	110	81
Driveshaft flange nut*:		
M27	300	221
M24	250	185
M22	200	148

Torque wrench settings (continued)	Nm	lbf ft
Integral link to hub carrier	105	77
Shock absorber upper mounting nuts (Touring)*	25	18
Shock absorber lower mounting bolt (Touring)	127	94
Shock absorber piston rod nut*:		
M10	23	17
M14	27	20
Strut mounting-to-body nuts (Saloon)*	25	18
Strut to hub carrier (Saloon)*	127	94
Subframe bolts	163	120
Swinging arm-to-integral link/hub carrier nut*	256	189
Swinging arm to rear subframe:		
Front bolt	58	43
Rear nut (camber adjustment)*:		
Saloon models	115	85
Touring models	174	128
Traction arm-to-hub carrier nut*	55	41
Traction arm-to-subframe nut*	60	44
Wheel bearing hub-to-hub carrier bolts*:		
Stage 1	30	22
Stage 2	Angle-tighten a further 90°	
Steering		
Lateral acceleration sensor	8	6
Power steering pump bolts	22	16
Power steering pipe union bolts:		
M10 union bolt	12	9
M14 union bolt	35	26
M16 union bolt	40	30
M18 union bolt	45	33
Steering column universal joint clamp bolt*	19	14
Steering rack mounting nuts*:		
Stage 1	50	37
Stage 2	Angle-tighten a further 90°	
Steering wheel:		
Bolt	63	46
Nut	80	59
Track rod to rack	71	52
Track rod balljoint:		
Retaining nut*	65	48
Locknut	51	37
Roadwheels		
Roadwheel bolts	110	81

** Do not re-use*

1 General information

The independent front suspension is of the MacPherson strut type, incorporating coil springs and integral telescopic shock absorbers. The MacPherson struts are located by transverse lower suspension arms, which use rubber inner mounting bushes, and incorporate a balljoint at the outer ends. The forward-most suspension lower arm is the Tension arm, whilst the rear-most is the Control arm. The front hub carriers, which carry the brake calipers and the hub/disc assemblies, are bolted to the MacPherson struts, and connected to the lower arms through balljoints. A front anti-roll bar is fitted to all models. The anti-roll bar is rubber-mounted and is connected to both suspension struts/lower arms (as applicable) by connecting links.

The rear suspension is of the fully independent type consisting of swinging arms, and upper suspension arms which locate the hub carriers. The forward-most arm is the Traction arm, whilst the rear-most is the Control arm. On Saloon models, MacPherson struts incorporating coil springs and integral telescopic shock absorbers are fitted between the hub carriers and the vehicle body. On Touring models, coil springs are fitted between the hub carrier and vehicle body, and shock absorbers are connected to the vehicle body and swinging arms. A rear anti-roll bar is fitted on all models. The anti-roll bar is rubber-mounted, and is connected to the swinging arms by connecting links **(see illustration overleaf)**. Electropneumatic self-levelling rear suspension shock absorbers are available as an option.

The steering column is connected to the steering rack by an intermediate shaft, which incorporates a universal joint.

The steering rack is mounted onto the front subframe, and is connected by two track rods, with balljoints at their outer ends, to the steering arms projecting forwards from the hub carriers. The track rod ends are threaded, to facilitate adjustment.

Power-assisted steering is fitted as standard to all models. The hydraulic steering system is powered by a belt-driven pump, which is driven off the crankshaft pulley.

Note: *The information contained in this Chapter is applicable to the standard suspension set-up. On models with M-Technic Sports suspension, slight differences will be found. Refer to your BMW dealer for details.*

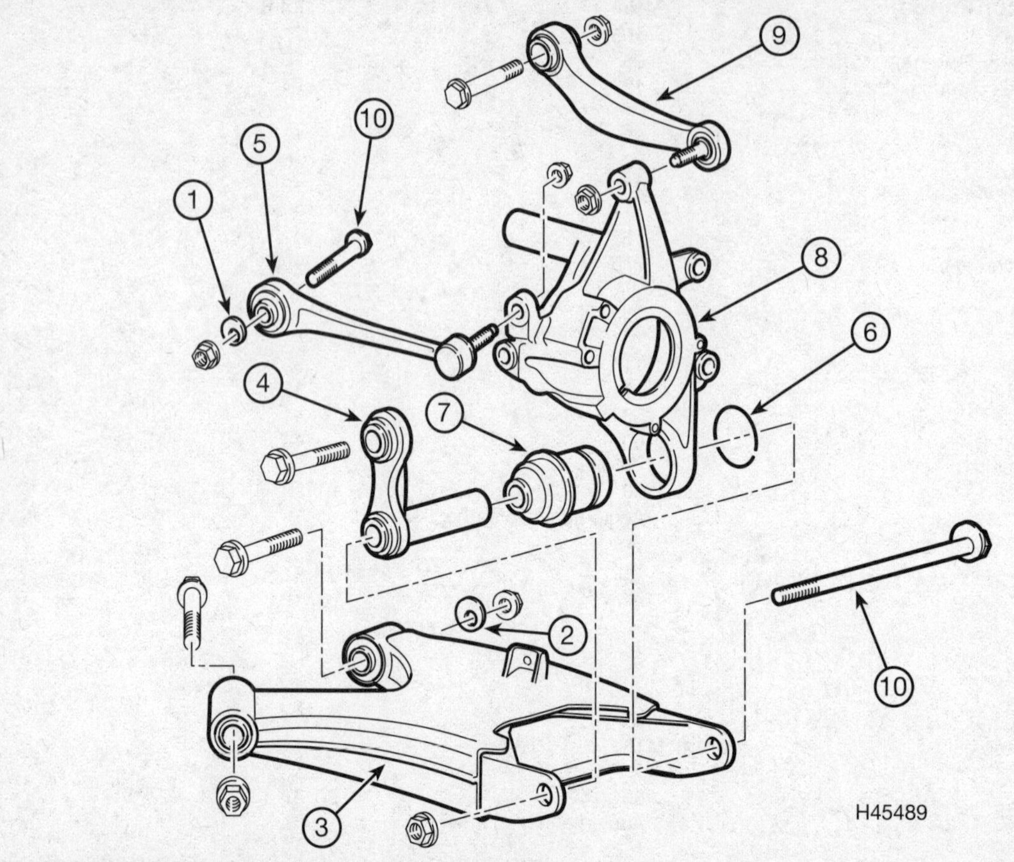

1.1 Rear suspension components – all models

1 Eccentric washer
2 Eccentric washer
3 Swinging arm
4 Integral link
5 Traction arm
6 Circlip
7 Balljoint
8 Hub carrier
9 Control arm
10 Bolt with integral eccentric washer

2 Front hub and bearing assembly – removal and refitting

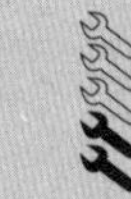

Removal

1 Remove the hub carrier as described in Section 3.

2 Undo the four retaining bolts, and remove the hub assembly from the carrier **(see illustration)**. Discard the bolts, new ones must be fitted.

3 The wheel bearing is integral with the hub assembly, and is not available separately. No further dismantling of the hub assembly is recommended.

2.2 The front hub assembly is secured by four bolts to the hub carrier

Refitting

4 Ensure the contact faces of the hub carrier and hub assembly are clean and free of grease. Refit the hub to the carrier, and tighten the new retaining bolts to the specified torque.

5 Refit the hub carrier as described in Section 3.

3 Front hub carrier assembly – removal and refitting

Removal

1 Firmly apply the handbrake, then jack up the front of the car and support it on axle stands (see *Jacking and vehicle support*). Remove the relevant front roadwheel.

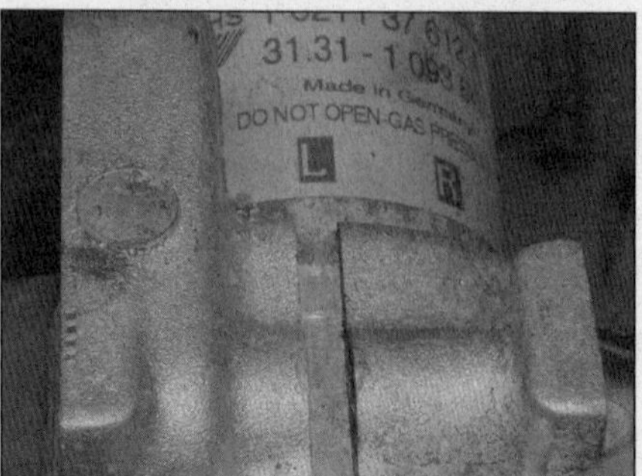

3.7 L is for the installation position of the left-hand strut, and R for the right-hand

2 Remove the brake disc as described in Chapter 9.

3 Undo the bolt(s) and remove the wheel speed sensor from the hub carrier (see Chapter 9).

4 Slacken and remove the nut securing the steering rack track rod balljoint to the hub carrier, and release the balljoint tapered shank using a universal balljoint separator.

5 Unscrew the control arm balljoint nut, and release the balljoint tapered shank from the hub carrier using a universal balljoint separator (see Section 5).

6 Unscrew the tension arm balljoint nut, and release the balljoint tapered shank from the hub carrier using a universal balljoint separator (see Section 5).

7 When the suspension struts are fitted in the factory, painted L or R alignment marks are made to indicate the correct fitted position of the struts in relation to the hub carrier – L is the installation position of the left-hand strut, and R is for right-hand fitment **(see illustration)**. If these marks are no longer visible, paint new alignment marks to ensure the strut is fitted to its original position.

8 Slacken and remove the nut/bolt securing the suspension strut to the hub carrier. Slide the hub carrier down and off from the end of the strut. Don't twist the strut as it's removed as this may cause damage to it. To ease

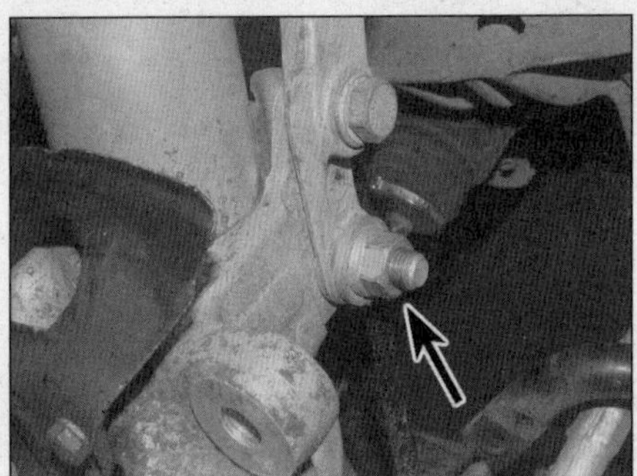
3.8a Slacken and remove the strut securing bolt/nut (arrowed)

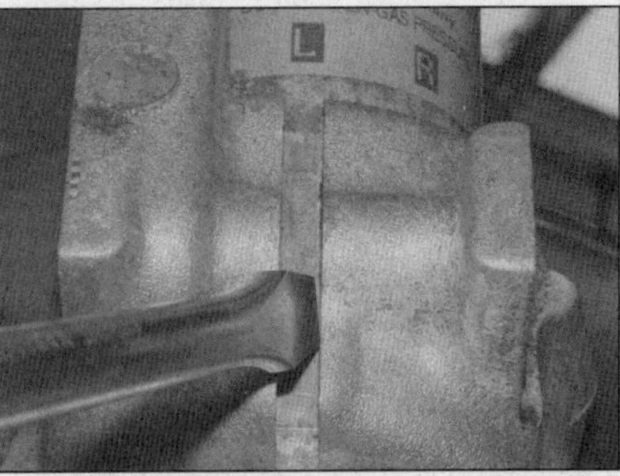
3.8b Use a large flat-bladed screwdriver to slightly spread the hub carrier clamp

removal, insert a large screwdriver into the slot on the back of the hub carrier and slightly spread the hub carrier clamp **(see illustrations)**. Take care to spread the carrier clamp only as much as absolutely necessary, as excessive force will cause damage.

9 If necessary, the hub and bearing assembly can now be removed as described in Section 2.

10 Examine the hub carrier for signs of wear or damage, and renew if necessary.

Refitting

11 If removed, refit the hub and bearing assembly as described in Section 2.

12 Locate the hub carrier correctly with the suspension strut, ensuring that the marks made prior to removal are correctly aligned **(see illustration 3.7)**. Slide the hub carrier up until it contacts the 'stop' on the strut. Fit the strut-to-hub carrier bolt and new nut, then tighten it to the specified torque.

13 Engage the hub carrier with the tension arm balljoint stud, and fit the new retaining nut with the washer. Tighten the nut to the specified torque.

14 Engage the hub carrier with the control arm balljoint stud, and fit the new retaining nut with the washer. Tighten the nut to the specified torque.

15 Engage the track rod balljoint in the hub carrier, then fit a new retaining nut with the washer and tighten it to the specified torque.

16 The remainder of refitting is a reversal of removal. Have the front wheel alignment checked at the earliest opportunity.

4 Front suspension strut – removal, overhaul and refitting

Note: *New suspension strut upper mounting nuts and strut-to-hub carrier bolt will be required on refitting.*

Removal

1 Chock the rear wheels, apply the handbrake, then jack up the front of the car and support on axle stands (see *Jacking and vehicle support*). Remove the appropriate roadwheel.

2 Remove the brake caliper (see Chapter 9). There is no need to disconnect the flexible brake hose. Tie the caliper to the inner wheel arch/body to prevent any strain on the hose.

3 Unclip the brake hose and wiring harness from its clips on the base of the strut **(see illustration)**.

4 Trace the wiring back from the wheel speed sensor to the connector which is situated in a protective plastic box. Unclip the lid, then free the wiring connector and disconnect it from the main harness

5 Slacken and remove the retaining nut and washer, then disconnect the anti-roll bar link from the strut. Use an open-ended spanner to counterhold the anti-roll bar link balljoint whilst undoing the nut. Discard the nut, a new one must be fitted.

6 On models fitted with a ride height sensor for headlamp range adjustment, undo the nut and remove the link bracket from the lower control arm.

7 Slacken and remove the nut securing the steering rack track rod balljoint to the hub carrier, and release the balljoint tapered shank using a universal balljoint separator.

8 When the suspension struts are fitted in the factory, painted L or R alignment marks are made to indicate the correct fitted position of the struts in relation to the hub carrier – L is the installation position of the left-hand strut, and R is for right-hand fitment **(see illustration 3.7)**. If these marks are no longer visible, paint new alignment marks to ensure the strut is fitted to its original position.

9 Slacken and remove the nut/bolt securing the suspension strut to the hub carrier. Discard the nut, a new one must be fitted.

10 Place a trolley jack under the hub carrier to take the weight of the strut and carrier assembly, and turn the steering wheel to full lock to the opposite side, ie, if the right-hand side strut is to be removed, turn the steering to full left-hand lock. This prevents the track rod from being damaged.

11 Working in the engine compartment, prise up the protective cap (where fitted), then slacken and remove the nuts securing the strut to the wheel arch **(see illustration)**. Discard the nuts, new ones must be fitted. On models with EDC (Electronic Damper Control), disconnect the wiring plug and release the cable from the cap.

12 Lower the hub carrier/strut assembly until the top of the strut is clear of the underside of the wheel arch aperture, then pull the strut outwards to the side **(see illustration)**.

13 Now the strut must be pulled upwards and out from the hub carrier. To ease removal, insert a large screwdriver into the slot on the back of the hub carrier and slightly spread the hub carrier clamp **(see illustration 3.8b)**. Take care to spread the carrier clamp only as much as absolutely necessary, as excessive force will cause damage. It's essential that the strut is pulled upwards with no turning motion, as this can cause irreparable damage.

Overhaul

Warning: Before attempting to dismantle the front suspension strut, a suitable tool to hold the coil spring in compression must be obtained. Adjustable coil spring compressors are readily available, and are

4.3 Unclip the wiring harness from the bracket

4.11 Undo the nuts securing the strut to the wheel arch

4.12 Push the suspension arms down, and pull the strut outwards

4.15 Compress the spring until all tension on the upper seat is relieved

4.16a Remove the plastic cap . . .

4.16b . . . then slacken the piston nut

recommended for this operation. Any attempt to dismantle the strut without such a tool is likely to result in damage or personal injury.

Note: *A new mounting plate nut will be required.*

14 With the strut removed from the car, clean away all external dirt, then mount it in a vice.

15 Fit the spring compressor, and compress the coil spring until all tension is relieved from the upper spring seat **(see illustration)**.

16 Remove the plastic cap, then slacken the piston nut whilst retaining the strut piston with an Allen key **(see illustrations)**.

17 Remove the mounting nut and washer, followed by the mounting plate complete with thrust bearing, washer, upper spring plate and upper spring seat.

18 Lift off the coil spring, followed by the bump stop, gaiter and lower spring seat.

19 With the strut assembly now completely dismantled, examine all the components for wear, damage or deformation, and check the upper mounting bearing for smoothness of operation. Remove the conical washer from the base of the thrust bearing and examine the condition of the bearing – if necessary, repack the bearing race with multi-purpose grease **(see illustration)**. Renew any of the components as necessary.

20 Examine the strut for signs of fluid leakage. Check the strut piston for signs of pitting along its entire length, and check the strut body for signs of damage. While holding it in an upright position, test the operation of the strut by moving the piston up-and-down. Due to the design of the shock absorber, it will not be possible to move the piston through a full stroke by hand. However, the resistance felt should be smooth. If the resistance is jerky, or uneven, or if there is any visible sign of wear or damage to the strut, renewal is necessary.

21 If any doubt exists about the condition of the coil spring, carefully remove the spring compressors, and check the spring for distortion and signs of cracking. Renew the spring if it is damaged or distorted, or if there is any doubt as to its condition.

22 Inspect all other components for damage or deterioration, and renew any that are suspect.

23 Refit the lower spring seat, and slide the bump stop and gaiter onto the strut piston **(see illustrations)**.

24 Fit the coil spring onto the strut, making sure the rubber seat and spring are correctly located.

25 Fit the upper spring seat, seat plate, washer and mounting plate. Ensure that the spring end is against the seat stop **(see illustrations)**.

26 Fit the washer and new mounting plate nut then tighten it to the specified torque

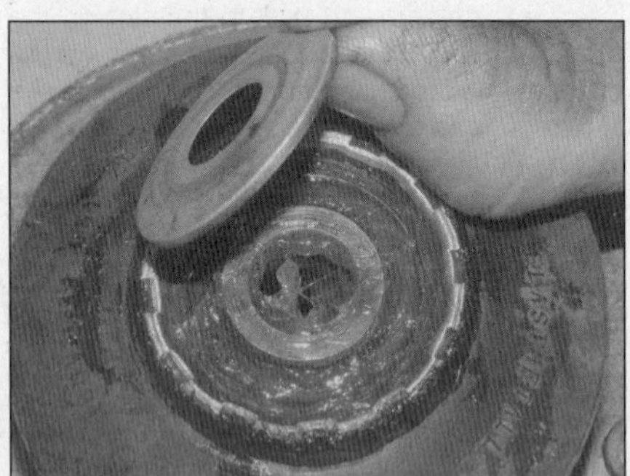
4.19 Lift the conical washer, and repack the bearing with grease

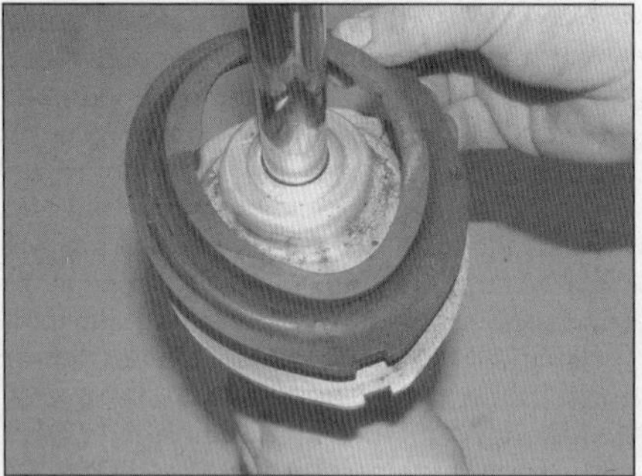
4.23a Refit the lower spring seat . . .

4.23b . . . followed by the bump stop and gaiter

4.25a Ensure the end of the spring locates correctly against the step in the rubber seat and plate

4.25b Refit the washer . . .

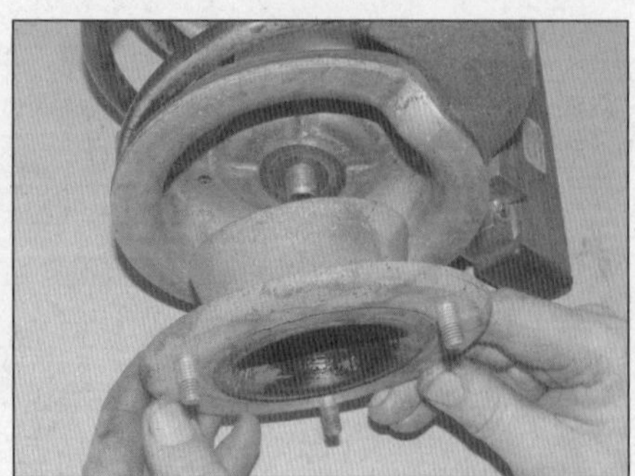
4.25c . . . and mounting plate

(see illustrations). If the damper rod rotates whilst attempting to tighten the nut, a special 'cut-away' socket is available from BMW dealers and good tool retailers that allows an Allen key to be inserted into the top of the damper rod whilst the torque wrench is fitted.

27 Ensure the spring ends and seats are correctly located, then carefully release the compressor and remove it from the strut.

Refitting

28 Locate the hub carrier correctly with the suspension strut (see Section 3, paragraph 12), and insert the retaining bolt and new nut. Tighten the bolt/nut to the specified torque.

29 Manoeuvre the strut assembly into position, and fit the new upper mounting nuts **(see illustration 4.11)**.

30 Tighten the strut upper mounting nuts to the specified torque.

31 Where applicable, refit the suspension height sensor link bracket to the lower control arm, and tighten the retaining nut securely.

32 The remainder of refitting is a reversal of removal.

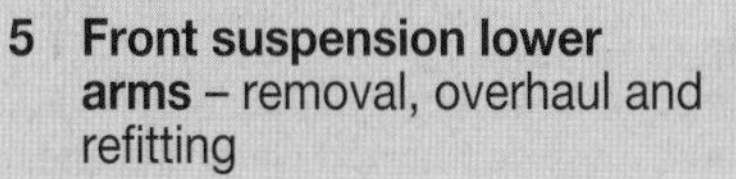

5 Front suspension lower arms – removal, overhaul and refitting

Control arm

Removal

1 Chock the rear wheels, firmly apply the handbrake, then jack up the front of the car and support on axle stands (see *Jacking and vehicle support*). Remove the appropriate front roadwheel.

2 Undo the screws and remove the engine undershield.

3 On models fitted with suspension ride height sensors, undo the retaining nut and remove the sensor link bracket from the lower arm.

4 Unscrew the lower arm balljoint nut, and release the arm from the hub carrier using a universal balljoint separator **(see illustration)**. Recover the washer.

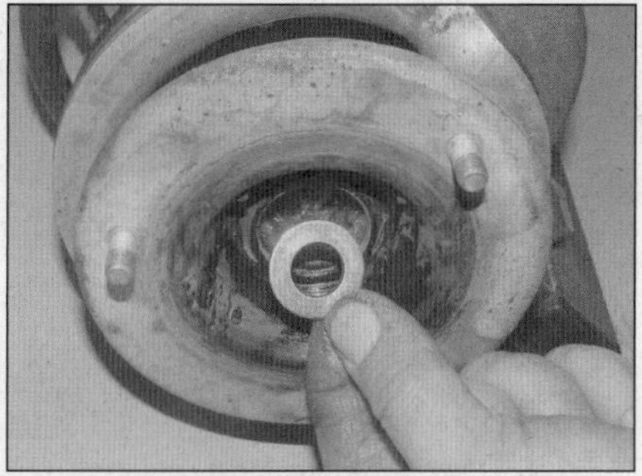

4.26a Fit the washer . . .

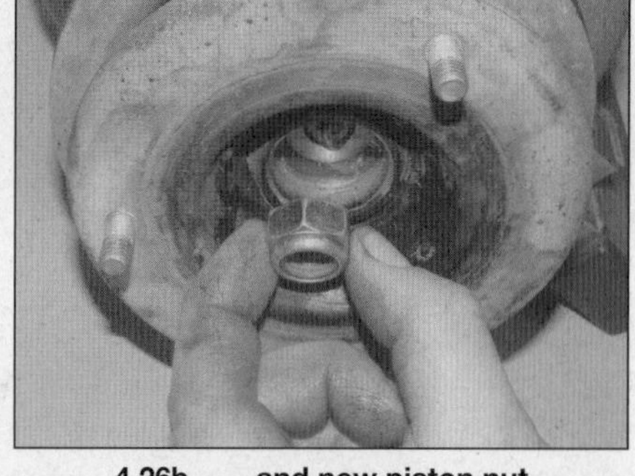

4.26b . . . and new piston nut

5 Slacken and remove the nut/bolt securing the control arm to the subframe and remove the arm from the vehicle **(see illustration)**.

Overhaul

6 Thoroughly clean the lower arm and the area around the arm mountings, removing all traces of dirt and underseal if necessary, then check carefully for cracks, distortion or any other signs of wear or damage, paying particular attention to the mounting bushes and balljoint. At the time of writing, the bush and the balljoint were not available as separate parts. If either bush or the balljoint requires renewal, the lower arm should be renewed. Check with your local BMW dealer or specialist.

Refitting

7 Ensure the balljoint studs and mounting holes are clean and dry, then offer up the lower arm.

8 Locate the inner end of the arm in the subframe mounting, and insert the bolt. Only tighten the new nut finger-tight at this stage.

9 Engage the balljoint stud with the hub carrier, fit a new nut with the washer and tighten it to the specified torque.

10 On models equipped with suspension ride height sensors, refit the sensor link bracket to the lower arm and tighten the retaining nut securely.

11 Refit the roadwheel, then lower the car to the ground and tighten the wheel bolts to the specified torque.

12 The nut/bolt securing the inner end of the control arm must be tightened when the vehicle is in the 'normal' position. This is with a full tank of fuel, a 68 kg load on each front seat, a 68 kg load in the centre of the rear seat and a 21 kg load in the luggage compartment. The loads on the seats are intended to simulate the weight of an adult. Tighten the nut/bolt to the specified torque.

13 Jack up the front of the car and support on axle stands (if necessary), then refit the engine undershield.

Tension arm

Removal

14 Chock the rear wheels, firmly apply the handbrake, then jack up the front of the car and support on axle stands (see *Jacking and vehicle support*). Remove the appropriate front roadwheel.

15 Undo the screws and remove the engine undershield.

16 Undo the screws and remove the wheel arch lower front liner, then undo the 3 screws and remove the air duct from the appropriate side.

17 Undo the two screws, and unclip the cover from the front of the tension arm **(see illustration)**.

18 Slacken and remove the nut/bolt securing

5.4 Use a large universal balljoint separator to detach the control arm from the hub carrier

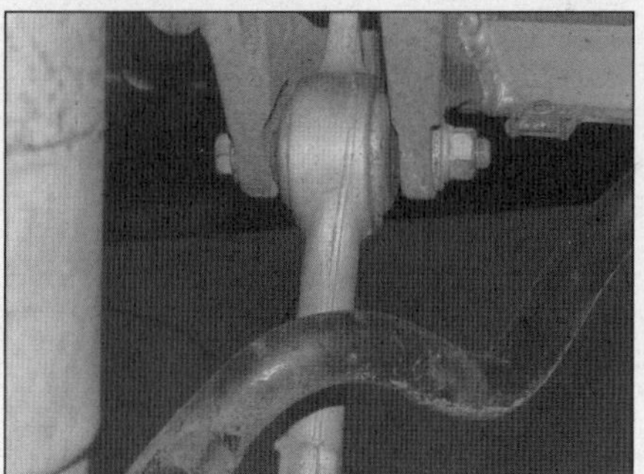

5.5 Remove the nut/bolt securing the control arm to the subframe

5.17 Undo the two screws securing the cover over the inner end of the tension arm

5.18 Undo the nut/bolt securing the inner end of the tension arm to the subframe

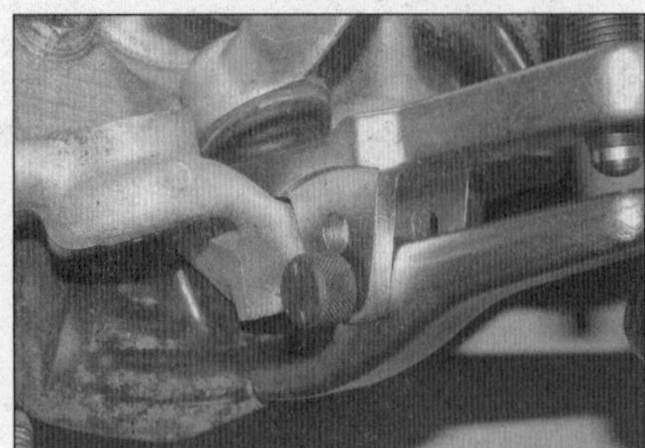

5.19 Use a large universal balljoint separator to detach the tension arm from the hub carrier

the tension arm to the subframe **(see illustration)**.

19 Unscrew the tension arm balljoint nut, and release the balljoint tapered shank from the hub carrier using a universal balljoint separator **(see illustration)**.

20 In order to remove the arm from the hub carrier, the suspension strut must be moved upwards in the carrier clamp. When the suspension struts are fitted in the factory, painted L or R alignment marks are made to indicate the correct fitted position of the struts in relation to the hub carrier – L is the installation position of the left-hand strut, and R is for right-hand fitment **(see illustration 3.7)**. If these marks are no longer visible, paint new alignment marks to ensure the strut is fitted to its original position.

21 Slacken and remove the nut/bolt securing the suspension strut to the hub carrier. Slide the hub carrier down until there is sufficient clearance for the tension arm to be removed. To ease movement of the strut, insert a large screwdriver into the slot on the back of the hub carrier and slightly spread the hub carrier clamp **(see illustration 3.8b)**. Take care to spread the carrier clamp only as much as absolutely necessary, as excessive force will cause damage.

Overhaul

22 Thoroughly clean the lower arm and the area around the arm mountings, removing all traces of dirt and underseal if necessary, then check carefully for cracks, distortion or any other signs of wear or damage, paying particular attention to the mounting bushes and balljoint. If the balljoint requires renewal, a new tension arm must be fitted – the balljoint is not available separately. However, the bush can be renewed independently of the arm. The process requires the use of an hydraulic press and suitable spacers. For this reason we recommend the task is entrusted to a BMW dealer of suitably-equipped specialist.

Refitting

23 Ensure the balljoint stud and mounting hole is clean and dry, then offer up the lower arm.

24 Locate the inner end of the arm in the subframe mounting, and insert the bolt. Only tighten the new nut finger-tight at this stage.

25 Slide the hub carrier upwards on the strut, ensuring that the marks made prior to removal are correctly aligned **(see illustration 3.7)**. Slide the hub carrier up until it contacts the 'stop' on the strut. Fit the strut-to-hub carrier bolt and new nut, then tighten it to the specified torque.

26 Fit a new nut with the washer to the balljoint stud, and tighten it to the specified torque.

27 Refit the roadwheel, then lower the car to the ground and tighten the wheel bolts to the specified torque.

28 The nut/bolt securing the inner end of the tension arm must be tightened when the vehicle is in the 'normal' position. This is with a full tank of fuel, a 68 kg load on each front seat, a 68 kg load in the centre of the rear seat and a 21 kg load in the luggage compartment. The loads on the seats are intended to simulate the weight of an adult. Tighten the nut/bolt to the specified torque.

29 Refit the air ducting, securely tighten the retaining screws, then refit the wheel arch liner.

30 Jack up the front of the car and support on axle stands (if necessary), refit the cover over the arm front mounting, then refit the engine undershield.

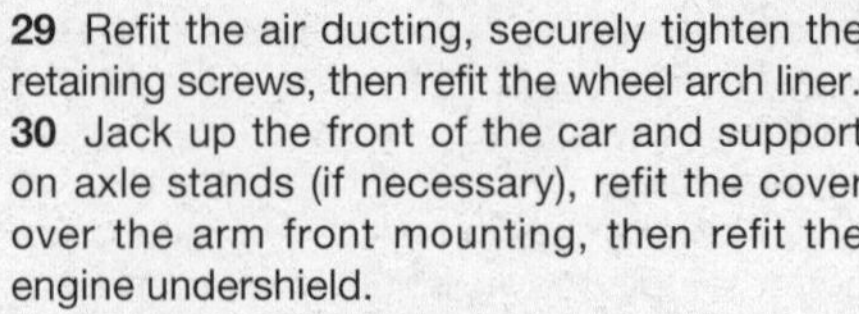

6 Front suspension lower arms balljoints – renewal

The front suspension lower arm balljoints are integral with the arms and are not available separately. If the balljoints shows signs of wear or damage, the arms must be renewed as described in Section 5.

7 Front suspension anti-roll bar – removal and refitting

Removal

1 Chock the rear wheels, firmly apply the handbrake, then jack up the front of the car and support on axle stands (see *Jacking and vehicle support*). Undo the screws and remove the engine undershield, then remove both front roadwheels.

2 In order to remove the anti-roll bar, the front subframe must be lowered whilst the engine remains in place. Partially remove the trim beside the rear subframe bolts.

3 Support the engine using a hoist or cross beam, with chains attached to the lifting brackets (see Chapter 2B).

4 Support the subframe using a trolley jack and the length of wood.

5 Unscrew the three bolts either side securing the subframe to the body **(see illustration)**.

6 Detach the left- and right-hand engine mountings (see Chapter 2A).

7 Unscrew the retaining nuts, and free the connecting link from each end of the anti-roll bar using a second spanner to counterhold the balljoint stud **(see illustration)**.

8 Make alignment marks between the mounting bushes and anti-roll bar, then slacken and remove the anti-roll bar mounting clamp retaining nuts **(see illustration)**.

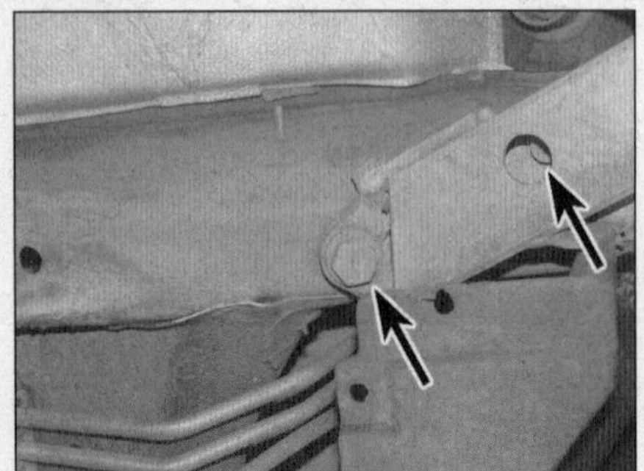

7.5 Front subframe rear mounting bolts (arrowed)

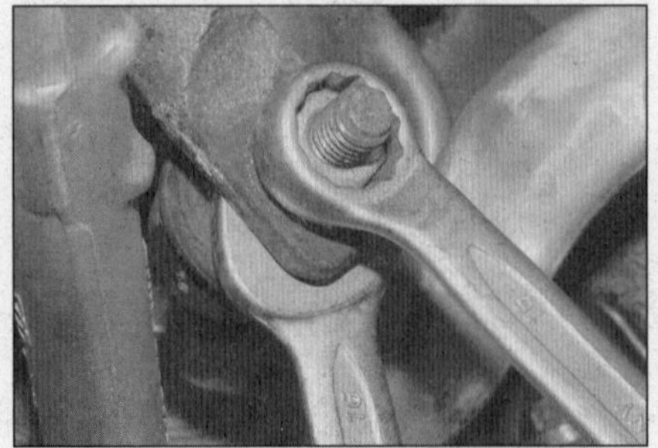

7.7 Use a second spanner to counterhold the balljoint shank whilst slackening the anti-roll bar link nut

7.8 Anti-roll bar clamp nut/bolt (arrowed)

9 Remove both clamps from the subframe, then lower the subframe and manoeuvre the anti-roll bar out from underneath the car. Remove the mounting bushes from the bar.
10 Carefully examine the anti-roll bar components for signs of wear, damage or deterioration, paying particular attention to the mounting bushes. Renew worn components as necessary.

Refitting

11 Fit the rubber mounting bushes to the anti-roll bar, aligning them with the marks made prior to removal. Rotate each bush so that its flat surface is uppermost, and the split side on the underside.
12 Offer up the anti-roll bar, and manoeuvre it into position. Refit the mounting clamps, ensuring that their ends are correctly located in the hooks on the subframe, and fit the new retaining nuts. Ensure that the bush markings are still aligned with the marks on the bars, only finger-tighten the nuts at this stage.
13 Manoeuvre the subframe back into position and fit new bolts. Tighten the bolts to the specified torque.
14 Align the engine mountings and tighten the bolts/nuts to the specified torque (see Chapter 2A).
15 Engage the anti-roll bar connecting links with the bar, then fit the new retaining nuts and tighten to the specified torque.
16 Refit the roadwheels then lower the car to the ground and tighten the wheel bolts to the specified torque.
17 The nut/bolts securing the clamps to the anti-roll bar must be tightened when the vehicle is in the 'normal' position. This is with a full tank of fuel, a 68 kg load on each front seat, a 68 kg load in the centre of the rear seat and a 21 kg load in the luggage compartment. The loads on the seats are intended to simulate the weight of an adult. Tighten the nut/bolts to the specified torque.
18 Jack up the front of the car and support on axle stands (if necessary), then refit the engine undershield.

8 Front suspension anti-roll bar connecting link – removal and refitting

Note: *New connecting link nuts will be required on refitting.*

Removal

1 Firmly apply the handbrake, then jack up the front of the car and support it on axle stands.
2 Unscrew the retaining nut, and free the connecting link from the anti-roll bar using a second spanner to counterhold the link balljoint stud.
3 Slacken and remove the nut securing the link to the suspension strut, using a second spanner to counterhold the link balljoint stud **(see illustration 7.7)**.

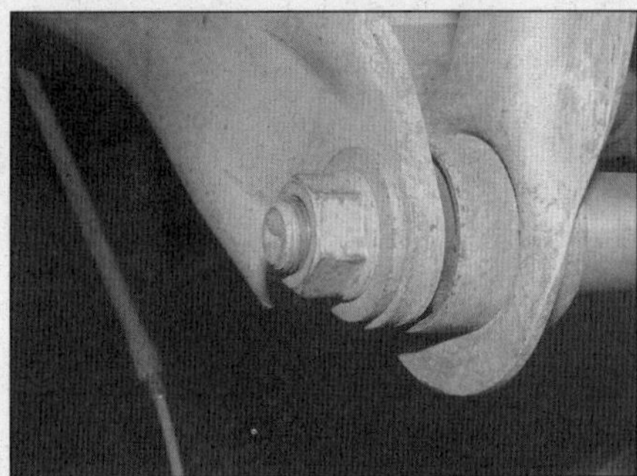

9.7 Undo the nut and withdrawn the bolt securing the swinging arm to the hub carrier/integral link

4 Check the connecting link balljoints for signs of wear. Check that each balljoint is free to move easily, and that the rubber gaiters are undamaged. If necessary renew the connecting link.

Refitting

5 Refitting is a reverse of the removal sequence, using new nuts and tightening them to the specified torque setting.

9 Rear hub carrier assembly – removal and refitting

Removal

Saloon models

1 On vehicles equipped with air suspension, remove the spare wheel, and disconnect the air supply unit wiring plug **(see illustration 9.14)**.
2 Check the front wheels, then jack up the rear of the vehicle and support it securely on axle stands (see *Jacking and vehicle support*). Remove the relevant rear roadwheel.
3 On models with air suspension, working in the spare wheel recess, slacken the air pipe unions at the distribution block to relieve any system pressure **(see illustration 9.16)**.
4 On all models, slacken and remove the driveshaft flange nut. This nut is very tight – have an assistant apply the brake, and take great care not to push or pull the vehicle from the axle stands.
5 Remove the handbrake shoes and expander mechanism as described in Chapter 9.
6 Undo the bolt(s) and remove the wheel speed sensor from the hub carrier (see Chapter 9).
7 Undo the nut and remove the bolt securing the lower swinging arm to the integral link/hub carrier **(see illustration)**. Discard the nut, a new one must be fitted.
8 Slacken and remove the securing bolt, and disconnect the shock absorber from the hub carrier **(see illustration)**.
9 The driveshaft must now be pressed in from the drive flange. Special BMW tools (Nos 33 2 111, 116 and 117) are available which bolt to the drive flange, and push the shaft in through the flange. In the absence of the tools, it may be possible to pull the lower edge of the hub carrier outwards and tap the driveshaft through the flange using a soft-faced hammer – take great care not to damage the driveshaft.
10 Position a trolley jack under the hub carrier and take the weight.
11 Undo the retaining nut and disconnect the control arm from the hub carrier **(see illustration)**. Discard the nut, a new one must be fitted.
12 Undo the nut and disconnect the traction arm from the hub carrier **(see illustration)**. Discard the nut, a new one must be fitted.
13 Remove the hub carrier from the vehicle.

9.8 Undo the shock absorber lower mounting bolt

9.11 Undo the nut and disconnect the control arm from the hub carrier

9.12 Undo the nut (arrowed) and disconnect the traction arm from the hub carrier

9.13 Undo the bolt (arrowed) and pull the integral link from the hub carrier

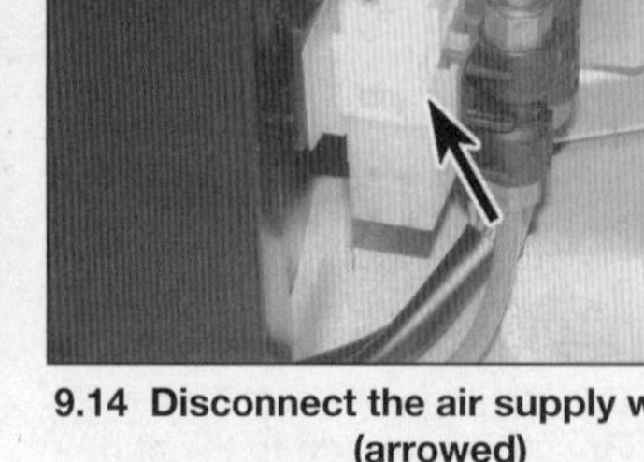

9.14 Disconnect the air supply wiring plug (arrowed)

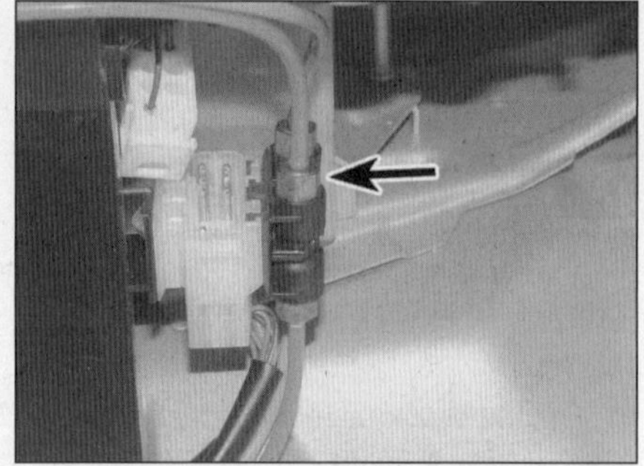

9.16 Slacken the air pipe unions (arrowed) to relieve any system pressure

If required, the integral link can be removed from the carrier by unscrewing the retaining bolt and pulling the link from the balljoint **(see illustration)**.

Touring models

Note: *On models with traditional (non-air suspension) in order to remove the hub carrier, the suspension coil springs must be either removed, or left on the vehicle in a tensioned (compressed) state. Tensioning the spring requires the use of special BMW tools Nos 33 2 302, 303, 304, 305 and 306. If these tools are not available, both coil springs must be removed as described in Section 12.*

14 On vehicles equipped with air suspension, remove spare wheel, and disconnect the air supply unit wiring plug **(see illustration)**.

15 Chock the front wheels, jack up the rear of the vehicle, and support it securely on axle stands (see *Jacking and vehicle support*).

16 On models with air suspension, slacken the air pipe unions on the distributor block to release any system pressure **(see illustration)**. Once the pressure has been relieved, tighten the unions securely.

17 Slacken and remove the driveshaft flange nut. This nut is very tight – have an assistant apply the brake, and take great care not to push or pull the vehicle from the axle stands.

18 On non-air suspension models, remove or pretension the coils springs as described in Section 12.

19 Place a trolley jack under the hub carrier and take its weight.

20 On models with air suspension, undo the bolt securing the air spring unit to the hub carrier **(see illustration)**.

21 Remove the handbrake shoes as described in Chapter 9.

22 Remove the wheel speed sensor as described in Chapter 9.

23 Undo the nut and remove the bolt securing the lower swinging arm to the integral link/hub carrier **(see illustration)**. Discard the nut, a new one must be fitted.

24 The driveshaft must now be pressed in from the drive flange. Special BMW tools (Nos 33 2 111, 116 and 117) are available which bolt to the drive flange, and push the shaft in through the flange. In the absence of the tools, it may be possible to pull the lower edge of the hub carrier outwards and tap the driveshaft through the flange using a soft-faced hammer – take great care not to damage the driveshaft.

25 Undo the retaining nuts, and disconnect the control arm and traction arm from the hub carrier **(see illustrations 9.11 and 9.12)**. Remove the hub carrier from the vehicle.

26 If required, the integral link can be removed from the carrier by unscrewing the retaining bolt and pulling the link from the balljoint **(see illustration 9.13)**.

Overhaul

27 Check the hub carrier for damage and wear, particularly around the control/traction arm mounting points. Check the balljoint in the lower part of the assembly for cracks, roughness and distortion. If renewal is required, entrust the task to a BMW dealer or suitably-equipped specialist – this requires special tools.

Refitting

28 Refitting is a reversal of removal, noting the following points:

a) *Tighten all fasteners to their specified torque.*
b) *Fit new self locking nuts to the control and traction arms.*
c) *Lubricate the threads of the new driveshaft nut with clean engine oil prior to fitting and tighten it to the specified torque. If necessary, wait until the vehicle is lower to the ground and then tighten the nut to the specified torque. Once tightened, use a hammer and punch to stake the nut **(see illustration)**.*
d) *Tighten the air pipes unions securely (where applicable).*

10 Rear hub and bearings – renewal

Note: *The hub assembly should not be removed unless it, or the hub bearing, is to be renewed. The hub is a press fit in the bearing inner race, and removal of the hub will almost certainly damage the bearings. If the hub is to be removed, be prepared to renew the hub bearing at the same time.*

1 Chock the front wheels, jack up the rear of the vehicle and support it securely on axle stands (see *Jacking and vehicle support*).

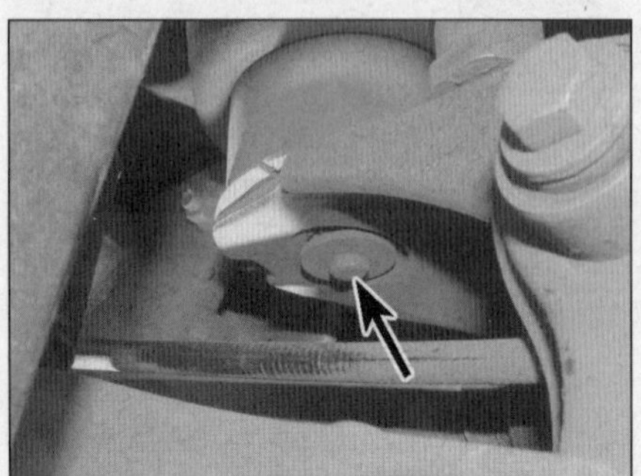

9.20 Undo the bolt (arrowed) securing the air spring to the hub carrier

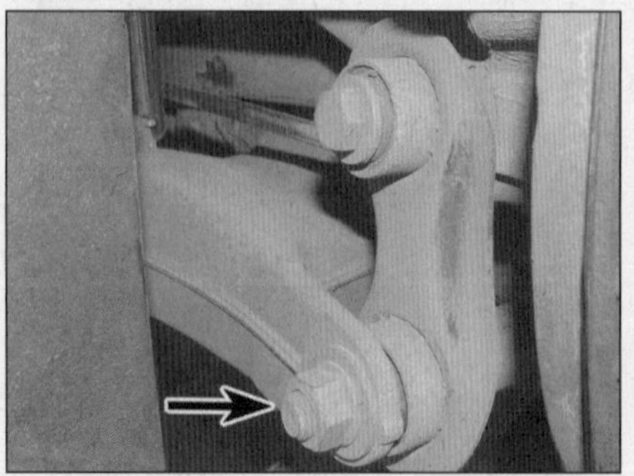

9.23 Undo the swinging arm-to-hub carrier/integral link bolt (arrowed)

9.28 When the driveshaft nut has been fully tightened, use a punch to stake the nut

2 Slacken and remove the driveshaft flange nut. This nut is very tight – have an assistant apply the brake, and take great care not to push or pull the vehicle from the axle stands.
3 Remove the brake disc as described in Chapter 9.
4 Bolt a slide hammer to the driveshaft flange, and pull the flange from the hub/shaft. If necessary, use a puller to draw the bearing inner race from the flange.
5 Undo the four retaining bolts, and remove the hub and bearing assembly from the hub carrier. Discard the bolts, new ones must be fitted.
6 Ensure the mating face between the hub and hub carrier are clean and free of grease. Position the new hub/bearing assembly, fit the new bolts and tighten them to the Stage 1 torque setting, followed by the Stage 2 tightening angle.
7 The driveshaft flange must now be drawn onto the driveshaft. On the project vehicle, the shaft was simply pushed into the hub and the driveshaft nut was used to pull the shaft into place. Alternatively, BMW recommend special tools Nos 33 2 115, 116 and 118. These tools bolt to the flange and the end of the driveshaft. Apply a little clean engine oil to the splines of the driveshaft, then turn the central threaded rod and draw the flange onto the shaft.
8 The remainder of refitting is a reversal of removal, noting the following points:

a) *Tighten all fasteners to their specified torque.*
b) *Lubricate the threads of the new driveshaft nut with clean engine oil prior to fitting and tighten it to the specified torque. If necessary, wait until the vehicle is lower to the ground and then tighten the nut to the specified torque. Once tightened, use a hammer and punch to stake the nut* **(see illustration 9.28)**.

11 Rear suspension shock absorber/strut – removal, overhaul and refitting

Saloon models

Note: *This procedure is only applicable to vehicles with traditional suspension (non-air suspension). For models with air suspension, refer to Section 17.*

Removal

1 Check the front wheels, then jack up the rear of the car and support it on axle stands (see *Jacking and vehicle support*). Remove the rear roadwheels.
2 Remove the rear parcel shelf and plastic wheel arch liner as described in Chapter 11.
3 Undo the two retaining screws, lift the front edge of the rear speaker up and disengage it from the lug at the rear **(see illustration)**. Disconnect the speaker wiring plug as it is withdrawn.

11.3 Undo the two screws (arrowed) and remove the speaker assembly

4 Undo the retaining nut and remove the seat belt inertia reel from each side.
5 Prise off the protective cap from the top of the strut, and (where applicable) disconnect the electronic damper control wiring plug.
6 Position a jack underneath the hub carrier, and raise the jack so that it is supporting the weight of the assembly. This will prevent the assembly dropping when the shock absorber is unbolted.
7 Slacken and remove the bolt securing the shock absorber to the hub carrier **(see illustration)**.
8 Unscrew the upper mounting nuts **(see illustration)**. Lower the shock absorber out from underneath the car, and recover the gasket which is fitted between the upper mounting and body. Discard the mounting nuts, new ones must be fitted.

Overhaul

Warning: Before attempting to dismantle the front suspension strut, a suitable tool to hold the coil spring in compression must be obtained. Adjustable coil spring compressors are readily available, and are recommended for this operation. Any attempt to dismantle the strut without such a tool is likely to result in damage or personal injury.

Note: *A new piston nut will be required.*
9 With the strut removed from the car, clean away all external dirt, then mount it upright in a vice.
10 Fit the spring compressor, and compress the coil spring until all tension is relieved from the upper spring seat.

11.8 Undo the three shock absorber upper mounting nuts

11.7 Undo the shock absorber lower mounting bolt

11 Slacken the piston nut whilst retaining the strut piston with a suitable tool **(see illustration)**.
12 Remove the mounting nut and washer, then lift off the mounting plate complete with thrust bearing and upper spring seat.
13 Lift off the coil spring, followed by the bump stop/gaiter and lower spring seat. **Note:** *Small diameter springs are fitted. With the spring compressors fitted, the bump stop/gaiter were trapped by the compressor legs and were therefore removed from the shock absorber still 'inside' the spring. If only the damper assembly is to be renewed, the bump stop/gaiter can be left in the spring, and refitted at the same time.*
14 With the strut assembly now completely dismantled, examine all the components for wear, damage or deformation, and check the upper mounting bearing for smoothness of operation. Renew any of the components as necessary.
15 Examine the strut for signs of fluid leakage. Check the strut piston for signs of pitting along its entire length, and check the strut body for signs of damage. While holding it in an upright position, test the operation of the strut by attempting to move the piston. Smooth stiff resistance should be felt, although it should not be possible to move the piston much as the damper is of the 'self-centring' type. If the resistance is jerky, or uneven, or if there is any visible sign of wear or damage to the strut, renewal is necessary.
16 If any doubt exists about the condition of the coil spring, carefully remove the spring compressors, and check the spring for

11.11 Counterhold the strut piston whilst slackening the nut

11.18 Fit the lower spring seat

11.19a Insert the bump stop/gaiter into the spring . . .

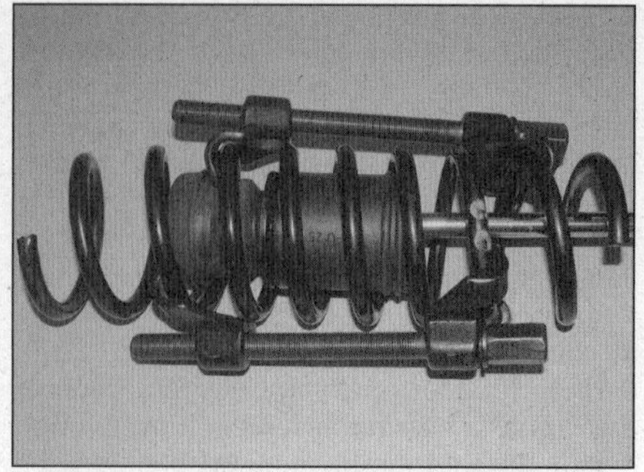

11.19b . . . then compress the spring . . .

11.19c . . . the fit it to the strut, making sure the spring locates correctly with the lower seat

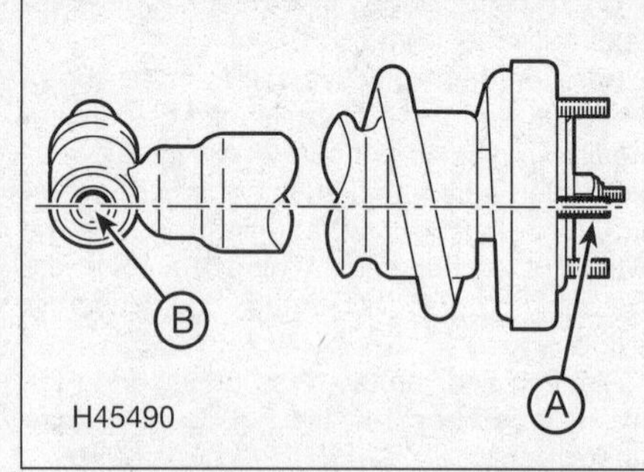

11.20 When refitting the upper spring seat assembly, ensure one of the upper mounting studs (A) is in-line with the bore (B) of the lower mounting

distortion and signs of cracking. Renew the spring if it is damaged or distorted, or if there is any doubt as to its condition.

17 Inspect all other components for damage or deterioration, and renew any that are suspect.

18 Refit the lower spring seat **(see illustration)**.

19 Insert the bump stop/gaiter into the spring, compress the spring, then fit it onto the strut, making sure the rubber seat and spring are correctly located **(see illustrations)**.

20 Fit the upper spring seat and mounting plate. Ensure that the spring end is against the seat stop **(see illustration)**.

21 Fit the new mounting plate nut and tighten it to the specified torque. If the damper rod rotates whilst attempting to tighten the nut, a special 'cut-away' socket is available from BMW dealers and good tool retailers that allows an Allen key to be inserted into the top of the damper rod whilst the torque wrench is fitted.

22 Ensure the spring ends and seats are correctly located, then carefully release the compressor and remove it from the strut.

Refitting

23 Manoeuvre the shock absorber into position, and fit the new upper mounting nuts.

24 Ensure the lower end of the shock absorber is positioned correctly. Screw in the lower mounting bolt, tightening it by hand only at this stage.

25 Tighten the upper mounting nuts to the specified torque setting then reconnect the electronic damper control wiring plug (where applicable). Refit the protective cap, speaker, wheel arch liner, and parcel shelf.

26 Refit the roadwheel and lower the car to the ground.

27 The bolt securing the lower end of the strut to the hub carrier must be tightened when the vehicle is in the 'normal' position. This is with a full tank of fuel, a 68 kg load on each front seat, a 68 kg load in the centre of the rear seat and a 21 kg load in the luggage compartment. The loads on the seats are intended to simulate the weight of an adult. Tighten the bolt to the specified torque.

Touring models

Note: *On Touring models, the shock absorber is separate from the coil spring. Therefore the following procedure is applicable only to the shock absorber.*

Note: *On vehicles equipped with air suspension, remove the spare wheel from the luggage compartment, and disconnect the air supply unit wiring plug **(see illustration 9.14)**.*

Removal

28 Remove the luggage compartment floor covering.

29 Undo the three screws and remove the access cover from the luggage compartment floor **(see illustration)**.

30 Squeeze together the sides of the protective cap, and pull it from the shock absorber mounting **(see illustration)**.

31 Undo the three shock absorber upper mounting nuts **(see illustration)**. Discard the nuts, new ones must be fitted.

32 Undo the lower mounting bolt/nut, and

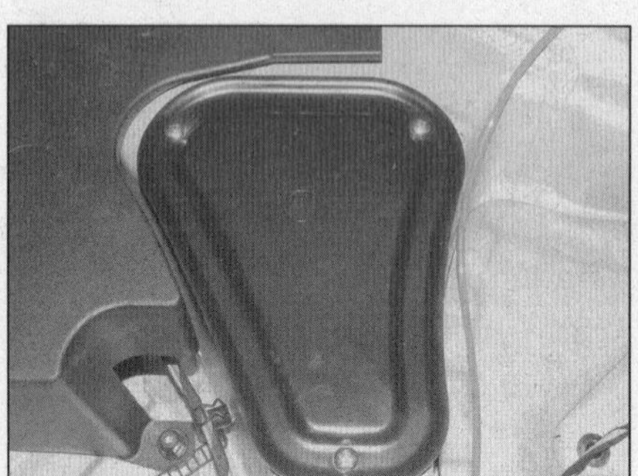

11.29 Undo the three screws and remove the access cover

11.30 Remove the protective cap

11.31 Undo the three upper mounting nuts

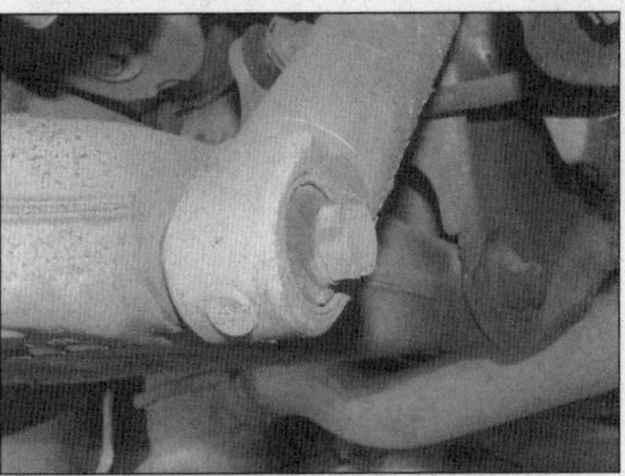

11.32 Undo the lower mounting bolt

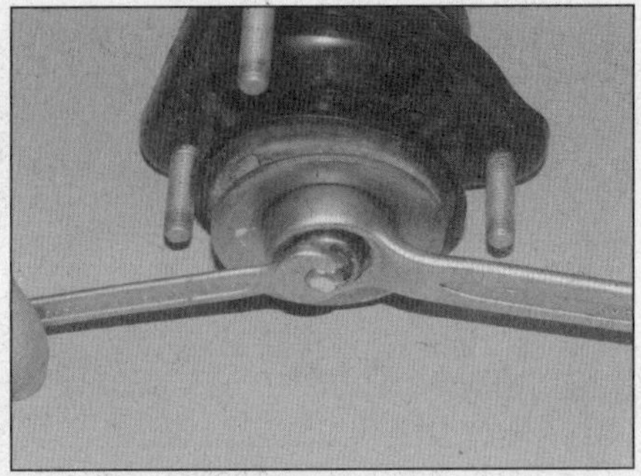

11.33 Counterhold the damper piston whilst undoing the nut

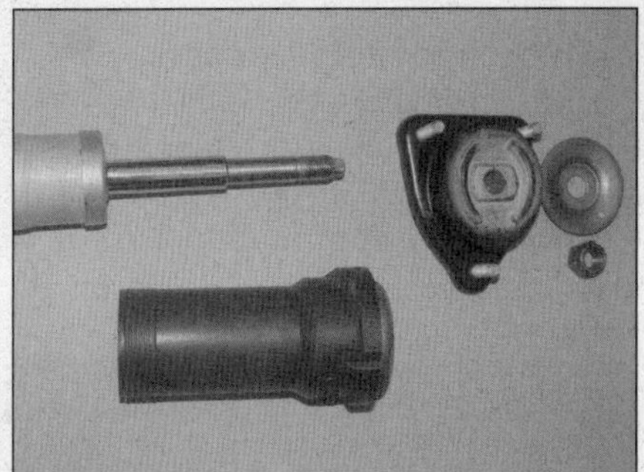

11.34 Shock absorber bump stop/dust cover, upper mounting, washer and nut

remove the shock absorber from the vehicle **(see illustration)**.

Overhaul

33 Slacken and remove the piston rod nut, using a second spanner to counterhold the piston whilst slackening the nut **(see illustration)**.

34 Remove the upper mounting assembly, and the dust cover/bump stop assembly **(see illustration)**.

35 Examine the shock absorber for signs of fluid leakage. Check the piston rod for signs of pitting along its entire length, and check the body for signs of damage. While holding it in an upright position, test the operation of the shock absorber by attempting to move the piston rod. The shock absorber is 'self-centring', and it should not be possible to move the piston rod more than a few millimetres by hand. If the piston rod is easy to move, or if there is any visible sign of wear or damage, renewal is necessary.

36 Slide the bump stop/dust cover, and upper mounting assembly onto the piston rod. Fit a new retaining nut and tighten it to the specified torque.

Refitting

37 Position the shock absorber on the vehicle, ensuring the lower mounting bush engages correctly with the swinging arm **(see illustration)**. Hand tighten the bolt only at this stage.

38 Ensure the upper mounting plate studs are correctly located corresponding holes in the vehicle body. Fit the new nuts and tighten it to the specified torque.

39 Check the luggage compartment access cover seal and renew it if damaged. Refit the cover and tighten the screws securely.

40 Refit the luggage compartment floor covering.

41 The bolt securing the lower end of the shock absorber to the swinging arm must be tightened when the vehicle is in the 'normal' position. This is with a full tank of fuel, a 68 kg load on each front seat, a 68 kg load in the centre of the rear seat and a 21 kg load in the luggage compartment. The loads on the seats are intended to simulate the weight of an adult. Tighten the bolt to the specified torque.

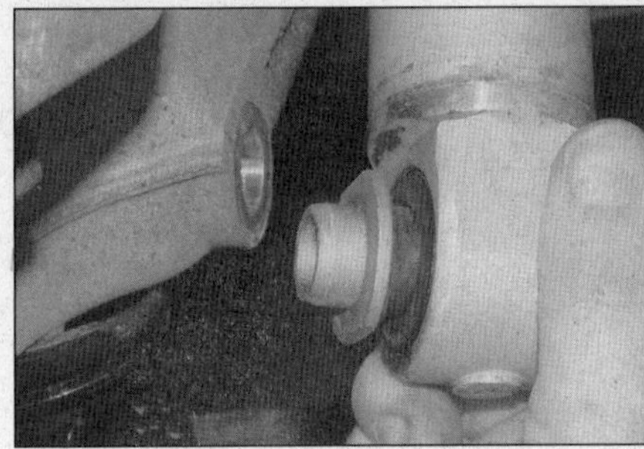

11.37 Ensure the lower shock absorber bush engages correctly with the swinging arm

12 Rear suspension coil spring – removal and refitting

Note: *On Saloon models, as MacPherson struts are fitted, the coil spring removal procedure is included in the procedure described in Section 11. The following procedure applies only to the Touring models with conventional suspension (non-air suspension).*

Removal

1 Chock the front wheels, then jack up the rear of the car and support it on axle stands. Note that the final drive and rear subframe must be lowered to remove the springs – ensure there is sufficient clearance below the rear of the vehicle. Remove both roadwheels.

2 Remove the exhaust system as described in Chapter 4A.

3 Remove the rear brake calipers from both sides, and tie them to the vehicle body (see Chapter 9). There is no need to disconnect the fluid hoses.

12.7 Left-hand subframe mounting bolt (arrowed)

4 Remove the propeller shaft as described in Chapter 8.

5 Disconnect both handbrake cables from the actuating mechanisms as described in Chapter 9.

6 Position a trolley jack under the final drive/rear subframe, and take the weight. Use a length of wood between the jack head and final drive/subframe to prevent any damage.

7 Slacken and remove the four bolts securing the rear subframe to the vehicle body. Recover the rubber-coated washers fitted under the bolt heads **(see illustration)**.

8 Ensure there are no hoses or wires attached which may be damaged as the assembly is lowered.

9 Slowly lower the trailing final drive/rear subframe assembly, until it is possible to withdraw the coil spring. We recommend the help of an assistant to steady the assembly as it is lowered.

10 Recover the spring seats from the car body and hub carrier.

11 Inspect the spring closely for signs of damage, such as cracking, and check the spring seats for signs of wear. Renew worn components as necessary.

Refitting

12 Fit the upper and lower spring seats.

13 Apply a little grease to the spring ends and engage the spring with its upper seat. Note that the spring is fitted with the smaller diameter opening at the top.

14 With the help of an assistant, hold the springs in position and carefully raise the final drive/subframe assembly whilst aligning the coil springs with their seats.

15 Raise the assembly fully and refit the subframe mounting bolts. Tighten the bolts to the specified torque.

16 Reconnect the handbrake cables (see Chapter 9).

17 Refit the propeller shaft (Chapter 8).

18 Refit the rear brake calipers (Chapter 9).

19 Refit the exhaust system (Chapter 4A).

20 Refit the roadwheels then lower the car to the ground. Tighten the wheel bolts to the specified torque.

13 Rear suspension swinging arm – removal and refitting

Removal – Saloon models

Note: *On models equipped with air suspension, remove the spare wheel and disconnect the air supply unit wiring plug* ***(see illustration 9.14)****.*

1 Chock the front wheels, then jack up the rear of the car and support it on axle stands (see *Jacking and vehicle support*). Remove the relevant roadwheel.

2 Trace the wiring back from the ABS wheel speed sensor to the connector which is situated in a protective plastic box. Unclip the lid, then free the wiring connector and disconnect it from the main harness.

3 On models equipped with self-levelling air suspension, disconnect the ride height sensor control arm – see Section 17.

4 Disconnect the anti-roll bar link from the swinging arm (see Section 16). Discard the nut, a new one must be fitted.

5 Paint alignment marks between the swinging arm rear inboard eccentric bolt and the rear subframe, so the rear axle alignment can be preserved **(see illustration)**.

6 Slacken and remove the swinging arm rear inboard mounting nut and remove the eccentric screw. Recover the eccentric washer under the nut. Discard the nut, and new one must be fitted.

7 Slacken and remove the swinging arm front inboard mounting bolt **(see illustration)**.

8 Support the hub carrier with a trolley jack, then slacken and remove the swinging arm-to-hub carrier/integral link nut and withdraw the bolt **(see illustration 9.13)**. Discard the nut, a new one must be fitted. Withdraw the swinging arm from the vehicle.

Removal – Touring models

Note: *On models with conventional suspension (non-air suspension), in order to remove the swinging arm the suspension coil springs must be either removed, or left on the vehicle in a tensioned (compressed) state. Tensioning the spring requires the use of special BMW tools Nos 33 2 302, 303, 304, 305 and 306. If these tools are not available, both coil springs must be removed as described in Section 12. The following procedure assumes the coil springs have been removed.*

Models with air suspension

9 Remove spare wheel, and disconnect the air supply unit wiring plug **(see illustration 9.14)**.

10 Chock the front wheels, jack up the rear of the vehicle, and support it securely on axle stands (see *Jacking and vehicle support*).

11 Slacken the air pipe unions on the distributor block to release any system pressure **(see illustration 9.16)**. Once the pressure has been relieved, tighten the unions securely.

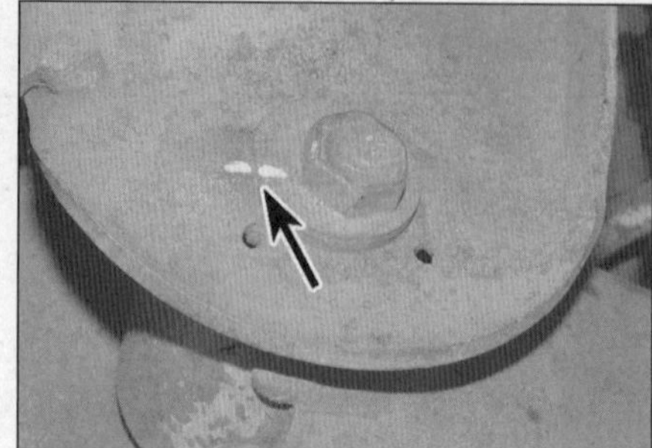

13.5 Paint alignment marks between the swinging arm eccentric washer and the subframe (arrowed)

All models

12 Slacken and remove the bolt securing the shock absorber to the swinging arm **(see illustration 9.8)**.

13 Disconnect the anti-roll bar link from the swinging arm as described in Section 16. Discard the nut, a new one must be fitted.

14 Paint alignment marks between the swinging arm rear inboard eccentric bolt and the rear subframe, so the rear axle alignment can be preserved **(see illustration 13.5)**.

15 Slacken and remove the swinging arm rear inboard mounting nut and remove the eccentric screw. Recover the eccentric washer under the nut. Discard the nut, and new one must be fitted.

16 Slacken and remove the swinging arm front inboard mounting bolt **(see illustration 13.7)**.

17 Support the hub carrier with a trolley jack, then slacken and remove the swinging arm-to-hub carrier/integral link nut and withdraw the bolt **(see illustration 9.13)**. Discard the nut, a new one must be fitted. Withdraw the swinging arm from the vehicle.

Overhaul

18 Thoroughly clean the swinging arm and the area around the arm mountings, removing all traces of dirt and underseal if necessary, then check carefully for cracks, distortion or any other signs of wear or damage, paying particular attention to the mounting bushes. If the bushes requires renewal, a new swinging arm must be fitted – at the time of writing, the bushes are not available separately. Check with your local BMW dealer or specialist.

Refitting – Saloon models

19 Offer up the swinging arm assembly, and refit the outer mounting bolt and new nut. Only finger-tighten the nut at this stage.

20 Align the swinging arm with the subframe, then insert the front mounting bolt. Ensure the locking arm of the captive nut is correctly located **(see illustration 13.7)**. Only finger-tighten the bolt at this stage.

21 Refit the rear mounting bolt, aligning the previously made marks. Fit the eccentric washer and new nut, but only finger-tighten them at this stage.

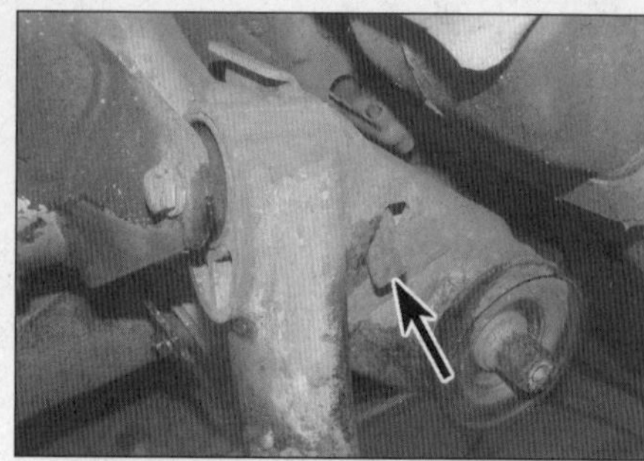

13.7 Slacken and remove the front swinging arm bolt. Note how the captive nut is locked with the strip of metal through the slot in the subframe (arrowed)

22 Reconnect the anti-roll bar link, and tighten the new nut to the specified torque.

23 Where applicable, reconnect the ride height sensor control arm.

24 Reconnect the ABS wheel speed sensor.

25 Refit the roadwheel, then lower the car to the ground and tighten the wheel bolts to the specified torque.

26 The nuts/bolts securing the swinging arm to the hub carrier and rear subframe must be tightened when the vehicle is in the 'normal' position. This is with a full tank of fuel, a 68 kg load on each front seat, a 68 kg load in the centre of the rear seat and a 21 kg load in the luggage compartment. The loads on the seats are intended to simulate the weight of an adult. Tighten the nuts/bolts to the specified torque. **Note:** *On completion, it is advisable to have the camber angle checked and, if necessary, adjusted.*

Refitting – Touring models

27 Offer up the swinging arm assembly, and refit the outer mounting bolt and new nut. Only finger-tighten the nut at this stage.

28 Align the swinging arm with the subframe, then insert the front mounting bolt. Ensure the locking arm off the captive nut is correctly located **(see illustration 13.7)**. Only finger-tighten the bolt at this stage.

29 Refit the rear mounting bolt, aligning the previously made marks. Fit the eccentric washer and new nut, ensuring the washer spigots correctly locate in the holes in the subframe **(see illustration)**. Only finger-tighten them at this stage.

13.29 Ensure the eccentric washer locates correctly in the subframe slots (arrowed)

Models without air suspension

30 Refit the coil springs as described in Section 12.

Models with air suspension

31 Reconnect the air supply unit wiring plug, and refit the spare wheel.

All models

32 Refit the roadwheel, then lower the car to the ground and tighten the wheel bolts to the specified torque.

33 The nuts/bolts securing the swinging arm to the hub carrier and rear subframe must be tightened when the vehicle is in the 'normal' position. This is with a full tank of fuel, a 68 kg load on each front seat, a 68 kg load in the centre of the rear seat and a 21 kg load in the luggage compartment. The loads on the seats are intended to simulate the weight of an adult. Tighten the nuts/bolts to the specified torque. **Note:** *On completion, it is advisable to have the camber angle checked and, if necessary, adjusted.*

14 Rear suspension control arm – removal, overhaul and refitting

Removal – Saloon models

1 Chock the front wheels, then jack up the rear of the car and support it on axle stands (see *Jacking and vehicle support*). Remove the relevant roadwheel.

2 Slacken and remove the control arm-to-subframe pivot bolt **(see illustration)**. Note its direction of fitting, and discard the nut, a new one must be fitted.

3 Release the brake hose from the retaining clips on the control arm.

4 Slacken and remove the nut from the control arm-to-hub carrier pivot bolt, and remove the control arm from underneath the car. Discard the nut, a new one must be fitted. Note that it may be necessary to counterhold the tapered pin whilst unscrewing the nut **(see illustration 9.11)**.

Removal – Touring models

Note: *On models without air suspension, in order to remove the swinging arm the suspension coil springs must be either removed, or left on the vehicle in a tensioned (compressed) state. Tensioning the spring requires the use of special BMW tools Nos 33 2 302, 303, 304, 305 and 306. If these tools are not available, both coil springs must be removed as described in Section 12. The following procedure assumes the coil springs have been removed.*

Models with air suspension

5 Remove spare wheel, and disconnect the air supply unit wiring plug **(see illustration 9.14)**.

6 Chock the front wheels, jack up the rear of the vehicle, and support it securely on axle stands (see *Jacking and vehicle support*).

7 Slacken the air pipe unions on the distributor block to release any system pressure **(see illustration 9.15)**. Once the pressure has been relieved, tighten the unions securely.

All models

8 Remove the relevant rear shock absorber as described in Section 11.

9 Unscrew the nut, and pull out the inner control arm pivot bolt **(see illustration)**. Discard the nut, a new one must be fitted.

10 Release the brake hose from the retaining clips on the control arm.

11 Undo the nut securing the control arm to the hub carrier. If necessary, use a second spanner to counterhold the nut **(see illustration 9.11)**. Discard the nut, a new one must be fitted.

Overhaul

12 Thoroughly clean the control arm and the area around the arm mountings, removing all traces of dirt and underseal if necessary, then check carefully for cracks, distortion or any other signs of wear or damage, paying particular attention to the mounting bushes and balljoint. If the balljoint or bush requires renewal, a new arm must be fitted – at the time of writing the balljoint/bush is not available separately. Check with your local BMW dealer or specialist.

13 Inspect the pivot bolts for signs of wear or damage, and renew as necessary.

Refitting

14 Manoeuvre the control arm into position, ensure the balljoint pin is clean and free from grease, then fit the new nut. Tighten the nut to the specified torque.

Touring models

15 Insert the inner pivot bolt with the head of the bolt pointing to the rear of the vehicle **(see illustration 14.9)**. Fit the new nut, but only finger-tighten it at this stage.

16 Align the lower end of the shock absorber with the swinging arm, fit the new nut, but only finger-tighten it at this stage.

17 Refit the brake hose into its retaining clips on the control arm.

18 Refit the coil springs as described in Section 12.

Saloon models

19 Insert the inner pivot bolt with the head of the bolt pointing to the front of the vehicle **(see illustration 14.2)**. Fit the new nut, but only finger-tighten it at this stage.

20 Refit the brake hose into the retaining clips.

All models

21 Refit the roadwheel, then lower the car to the ground and tighten the wheel bolts to the specified torque. On Touring models with air suspension, reconnect the air supply unit wiring plug and refit the spare wheel.

22 The inner pivot bolt/nut securing the control arm to the subframe and lower shock absorber bolt (Touring models) must be

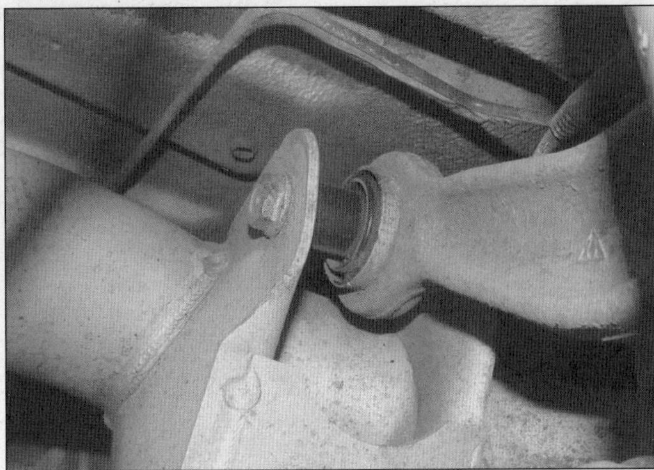

14.2 The control arm inner mounting bolt is inserted from the front

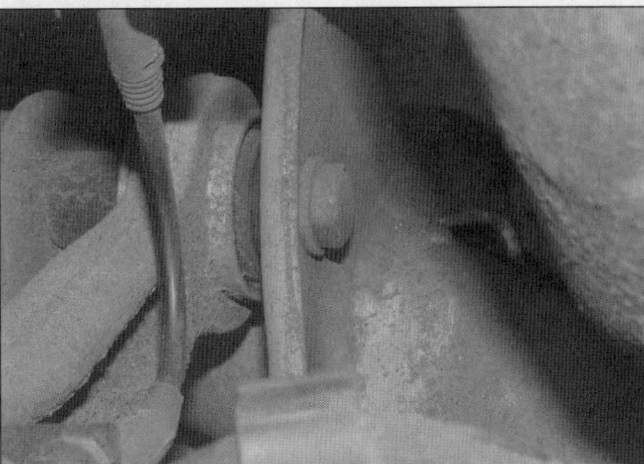

14.9 Slacken and remove the control arm inner pivot bolt

tightened when the vehicle is in the 'normal' position. This is with a full tank of fuel, a 68 kg load on each front seat, a 68 kg load in the centre of the rear seat and a 21 kg load in the luggage compartment. The loads on the seats are intended to simulate the weight of an adult. Tighten the nut/bolt to the specified torque. **Note:** *On completion, it is advisable to have the camber angle checked and, if necessary, adjusted.*

15 Rear suspension traction arm – removal, overhaul and refitting

Removal

1 Chock the front wheels, then jack up the rear of the car and support it on axle stands (see *Jacking and vehicle support*). Remove the relevant rear roadwheel.

2 Using paint or a suitable marker pen, make alignment marks between the traction arm bolt eccentric washer and the subframe. This is necessary to ensure that the rear wheel alignment and camber are correct on refitting **(see illustration)**.

3 Undo the nut securing the traction arm to the hub carrier. If necessary, use a second spanner to counterhold the nut **(see illustration 9.12)**. Discard the nut, a new one must be fitted.

Overhaul

4 Thoroughly clean the traction arm and the area around the arm mountings, removing all traces of dirt and underseal if necessary, then check carefully for cracks, distortion or any other signs of wear or damage, paying particular attention to the mounting bushes and balljoint. If the balljoint or bush requires renewal, a new arm must be fitted – at the time of writing the balljoint/bush is not available separately. Check with your local BMW dealer or specialist.

5 Inspect the pivot bolt for signs of wear or damage, and renew as necessary.

Refitting

6 Manoeuvre the traction arm into position, ensure the balljoint pin is clean and free from grease, then fit the new nut. Tighten the nut to the specified torque.

7 Align the inner end of the arm with the subframe and refit the bolt, eccentric washer, and new nut. Align the previously made marks. The bolt head must point to the front of the vehicle **(see illustration 15.2)**. Only finger-tighten the nut at this stage.

8 Refit the roadwheel and lower the car to the ground.

9 The inner pivot bolt/nut securing the traction arm to the subframe and lower shock absorber bolt (Touring models) must be tightened when the vehicle is in the 'normal' position. This is with a full tank of fuel, a 68 kg load on each front seat, a 68 kg load in the centre of the rear seat and a 21 kg load in the luggage compartment. The loads on the seats are intended to simulate the weight of an adult. Tighten the nut/bolt to the specified torque

16 Rear suspension anti-roll bar – removal and refitting

Note: *New mounting clamp nuts and connecting link nuts will be required on refitting.*

Removal

1 Chock the front wheels, then jack up the rear of the car and support it on axle stands (see *Jacking and vehicle support*). To improve access, remove the rear roadwheels.

2 Mark the left-hand end of the anti-roll bar with paint to aid refitment. Slacken and remove the nut and bolt securing each connecting link to the swinging arms **(see illustration)**.

3 Make alignment marks between the mounting bushes and anti-roll bar, then slacken the anti-roll bar mounting clamp retaining nuts and bolts **(see illustration)**.

4 Remove both clamps from the subframe, and manoeuvre the anti-roll bar and connecting link assembly out from underneath the car. Remove the mounting bushes and connecting links from the bar.

5 Carefully examine the anti-roll bar components for signs of wear, damage or deterioration, paying particular attention to the mounting bushes. Renew any worn components as necessary.

Refitting

6 Fit the rubber mounting bushes to the anti-roll bar, aligning them with the marks made prior to removal. Rotate each bush so that its flat surface is facing forwards.

7 Offer up the anti-roll bar, and manoeuvre it into position. Locate the connecting links in the upper control arms, and fit the new retaining nuts and tighten securely.

8 Refit the mounting clamps, ensuring that their ends are correctly located in the hooks on the subframe, and fit the bolts and new retaining nuts. Ensure that the bush markings are still aligned with the marks on the bars, then securely tighten the mounting clamp retaining nuts.

9 Refit the roadwheels then lower the car to the ground and tighten the wheel bolts to the specified torque.

17 Air suspension system – general information and component renewal

General information

Available as an option, electro-pneumatic self-levelling rear suspension may be fitted to Saloon and Touring models. Sensors attached to control arms at the front, and the rear swinging arms, monitor the ride height of the vehicle. This information is passed to the air supply unit, which is located in the centre of the spare wheel recess in the luggage compartment. The air supply unit incorporates a control unit and pump, and supplies or withdraws air pressure to and from air suspension units. The air suspension units are fitted in place of the conventional springs and shock absorbers on Saloon models, but only the springs on Touring models.

If any fault with the system is suspected, take the vehicle to a BMW dealer or specialist, who will be able to interrogate the vehicle's self diagnosis system using dedicated test equipment.

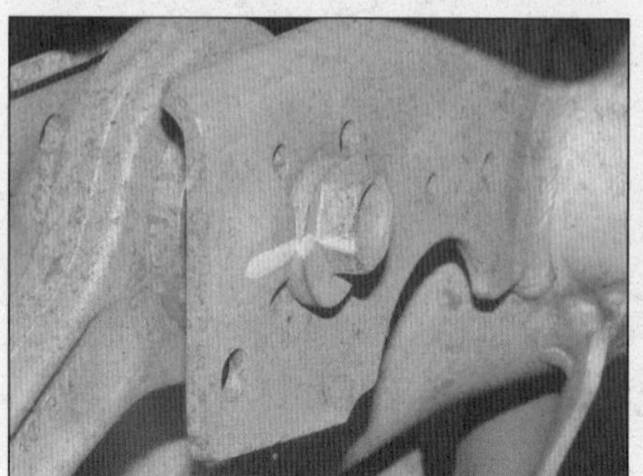

15.2 Make alignment marks between the eccentric washer and the subframe

16.2 Undo the nut securing the anti-roll bar to the link rod (arrowed)

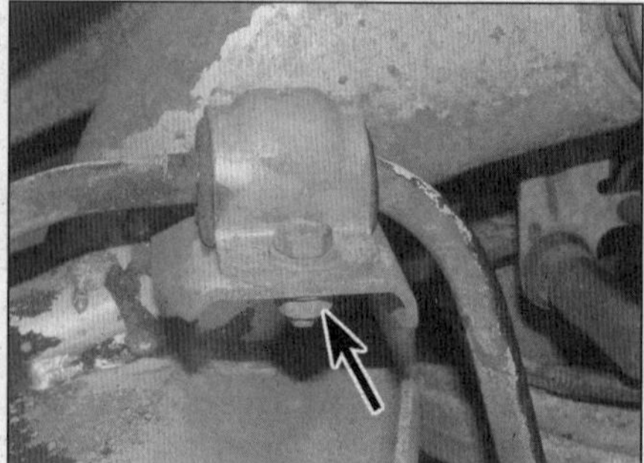

16.3 Undo the anti-roll bar clamp nut/bolt (arrowed)

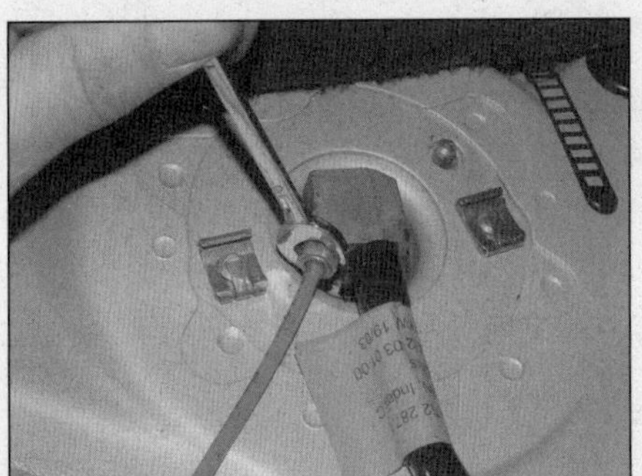

17.12 Slacken the air pipe union to relieve any system pressure

17.13a Push the coupling down, squeeze together the clips (arrowed) . . .

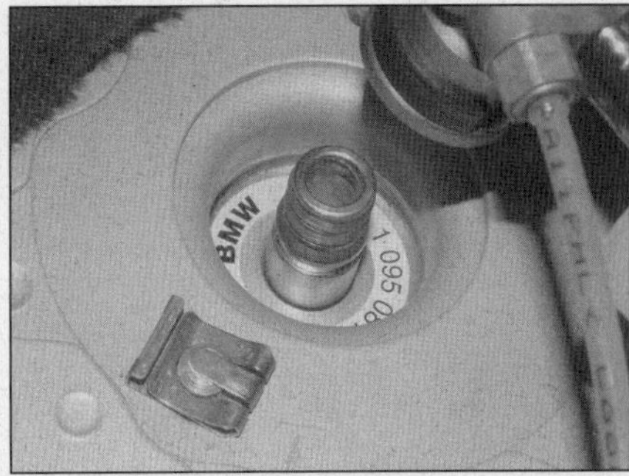

17.13b . . . and pull it from the top of the air spring

Caution: When working on any part of the air suspension system, absolute cleanliness must be observed. Even the smallest particle of dirt entering the system may cause irreparable damage to the system's components.

Caution: Do not drive the vehicle with the system depressurised, or irreparable damage will be caused to the suspension struts

Spring/strut renewal

Saloon models

1 Remove the spare wheel, disconnect the air supply unit wiring plug **(see illustration 9.14)**.

2 Chock the front wheels, jack up the rear of the vehicle and support it securely on axle stands (see *Jacking and vehicle support*). Remove the appropriate roadwheel.

3 Working in the spare wheel recess, slacken the air pipe unions at the distribution assembly to relieve any pressure in the system **(see illustration 9.15)**. With the system pressure relieved, tighten the unions securely.

4 Unscrew the union, and disconnect the air pipe from the strut/spring. Do not remove the union from the pipe, or the pipe will have to be renewed. Tape over the open end of the pipe to prevent dirt ingress.

5 Position a trolley jack under the hub carrier and take the weight.

6 Remove the parcel shelf and wheel arch trim from the luggage compartment as described in Chapter 11.

7 Prise up the protective cap and unscrew the three nuts securing the top of the strut. Discard the nuts, new ones must be fitted.

8 Undo the bolt securing the strut/spring to the hub carrier, and remove it from the vehicle.

9 Refitting is a reversal of removal, noting the following points:

a) New struts/springs are supplied with the pipe connections plugged. Unscrew the connector and remove the plug prior to reconnecting the pipe.

b) The strut/spring lower mounting bolt must be tightened when the vehicle is in the 'normal' position. This is with a full tank of fuel, a 68 kg load on each front seat, a 68 kg load in the centre of the rear seat and a 21 kg load in the luggage compartment. The loads on the seats are intended to simulate the weight of an adult. Tighten the bolt to the specified torque.

c) Fit new nuts to the upper mounting and tighten them to the specified torque.

Touring models

10 Remove the spare wheel, disconnect the air supply unit wiring plug **(see illustration 9.14)**.

11 Chock the front wheels, jack up the rear of the vehicle and support it securely on axle stands (see *Jacking and vehicle support*). Remove the appropriate roadwheel. Place a trolley jack under the hub carrier.

12 Working in the luggage compartment, slacken the air pipe union at the top of each air spring unit to relieve any pressure in the system **(see illustration)**. With the system pressure relieved, tighten the union securely.

13 Press the quick-release coupling down, and squeeze together the tabs of the retaining clip, then pull the coupling upwards to disconnect it **(see illustrations)**. Plug or tape over the connector opening to prevent dirt ingress.

14 Remove the retaining clips securing the air spring unit to the vehicle body **(see illustration)**.

15 Raise the hub carrier a little, then undo the bolt securing the air spring unit to the hub carrier **(see illustration 9.20)**. Manoeuvre the unit from the vehicle. Note that the units are colour coded: Red for the left-hand spring, and blue for the right-hand spring.

16 To refit the spring unit, manoeuvre the unit into position and secure it to the vehicle body using the two retaining clips.

17 Check the condition of the air connection sealing rings, and renew if necessary. Remove the plug/tape and push the quick-release coupling into the connector until the clip and be heard to engage.

18 Check that the lug on the underside of the air spring unit engages correctly with the recess in the hub carrier, then tighten the bolt to the specified torque **(see illustrations)**.

19 Reconnect the air supply unit wiring plug and lower the vehicle to the ground.

Air supply unit renewal

20 Remove the spare wheel from the luggage compartment.

21 Working on the right-hand side of the luggage compartment, paint alignment marks on the air pipes and distribution block to aid

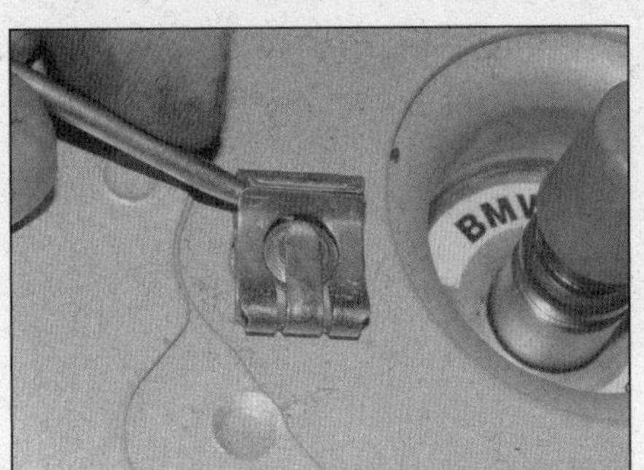

17.14 Remove the air spring retaining clips

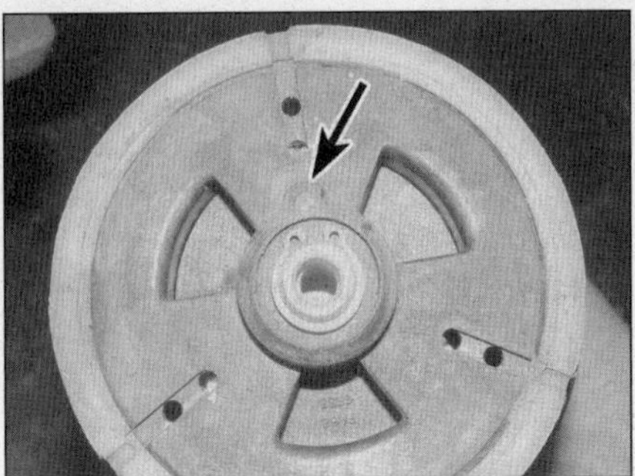

17.18a The lug (arrowed) on the base of the spring must align . . .

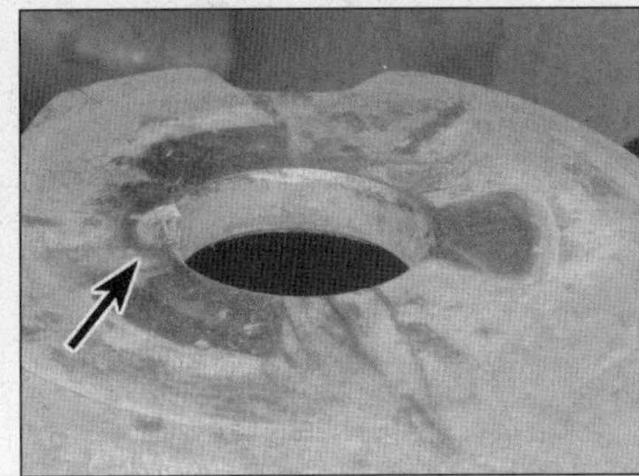

17.18b . . . with the cut-out (arrowed) in the hub carrier

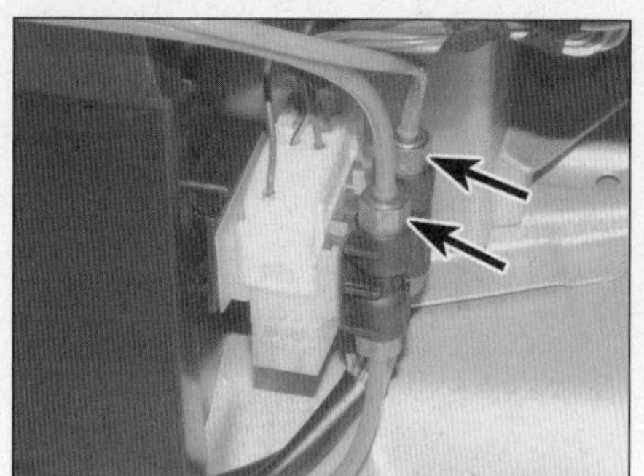

17.21 Undo the unions and disconnect the air pipes (arrowed)

refitment, then undo the unions and disconnect the pipes. Release the cable ties securing the pipes **(see illustration)**.

22 Rotate the distribution block 45° anti-clockwise and remove it.

23 Disconnect the wiring plug, then rotate the wiring connector housing 45° anti-clockwise and remove it **(see illustration)**.

24 Undo the four screws/nuts and remove the air supply unit **(see illustration)**. Take care not to twist or kink any of the air pipes as the unit is withdrawn. No further dismantling of the unit is recommended. Consult your local BMW dealer or specialist.

25 Refitting is a reversal of removal. **Note:** *After renewing the air supply unit, it is recommended that the system height calibration is carried out. This requires dedicated test equipment, and should be entrusted to a BMW dealer or specialist.*

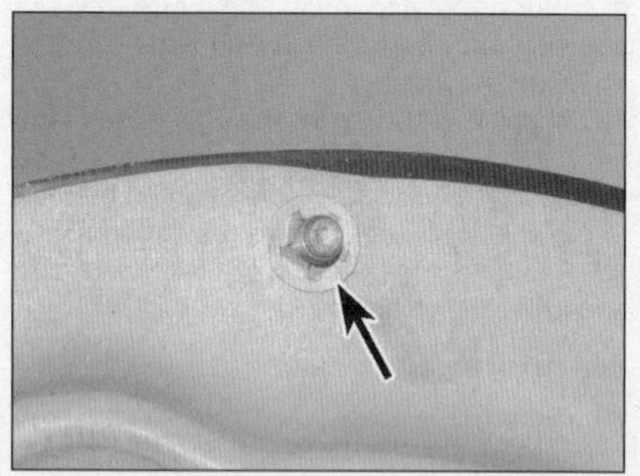

17.27 Release the bolt clips (arrowed) and remove the lower cover

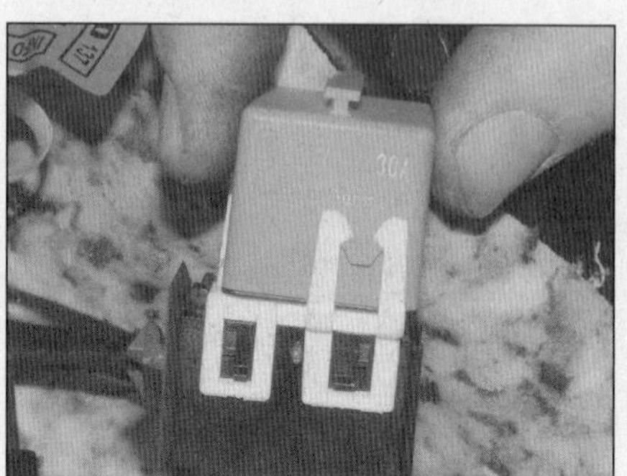

17.28b . . . then pull the relay from the holder

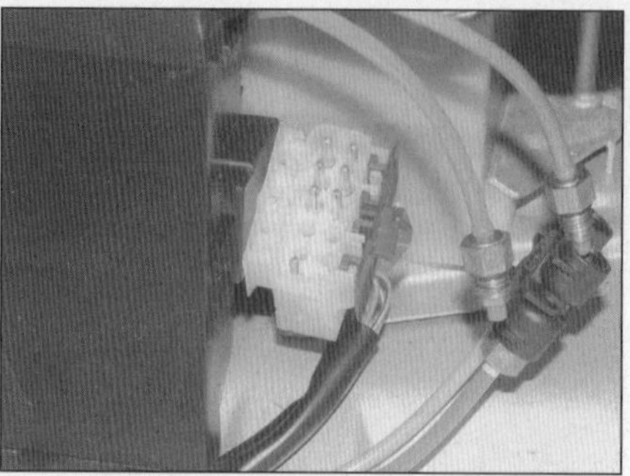

17.23 Disconnect the wiring plug, then rotate the wiring connector 45° to release it from its mounting

Air supply unit relay renewal

26 Remove the spare wheel from the luggage compartment.

27 Undo the four screws securing the air supply unit to the vehicle body, and carefully invert it **(see illustration 17.24)**. Release the bolt retaining clips and remove the lower cover **(see illustration)**.

28 Rotate the relay holder 45° clockwise and remove it **(see illustrations)**.

29 Refitting is a reversal of removal.

Front ride height sensor renewal

30 Jack up the front of the vehicle and support it securely on axle stands (see *Jacking and vehicle support*). Remove the relevant front roadwheel.

31 Disconnect the sensor wiring plug.

17.28a Rotate the relay holder (arrowed) 45° to release it . . .

17.37 Disconnect the ride height sensor wiring plug (arrowed)

17.24 Undo the four screws/nuts (arrowed) and remove the air supply unit

32 Undo the nut and disconnect the sensor arm from the lower arm link.

33 Undo the nut securing the sensor bracket to the control arm and remove the sensor.

34 Refitting is a reversal of removal, tightening all fasteners securely. **Note:** *After renewing one or more of the ride height sensors, it is recommended that the system height calibration is carried out. This requires dedicated test equipment, and should be entrusted to a BMW dealer or specialist.*

Rear ride height sensor renewal

35 Chock the front wheels, jack up the rear of the vehicle and support it securely on axle stands (see *Jacking and vehicle support*).

36 On Saloon models, working underneath the vehicle, undo the two screws and remove the trim adjacent to the swinging arm.

37 Disconnect the sensor wiring plug **(see illustration)**.

38 Undo the nut and disconnect the sensor arm from the swinging arm link.

39 Undo the two screws and remove the sensor.

40 Refitting is a reversal of removal, tightening all fasteners securely. **Note:** *After renewing one or more of the ride height sensors, it is recommended that the system height calibration is carried out. This requires dedicated test equipment, and should be entrusted to a BMW dealer or specialist.*

Control unit renewal

41 Remove the spare wheel from the luggage compartment.

42 Release the clips and remove the cover from the control unit **(see illustration)**.

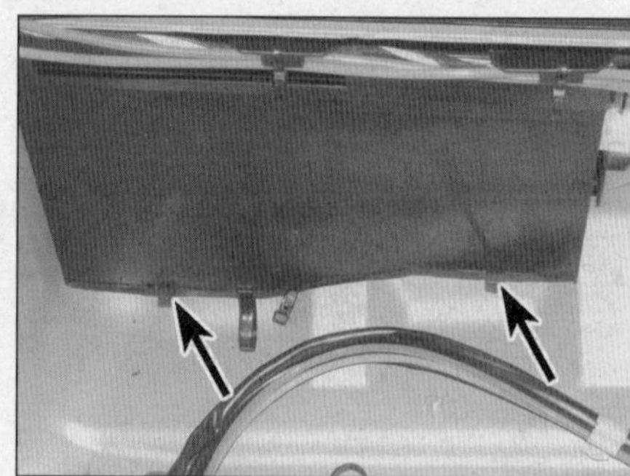

17.42 Release the cover clips (arrowed)

43 Unlock the wiring plug and disconnect it **(see illustration)**.

44 Pull the control unit from its mounting place.

45 Refitting is a reversal of removal. **Note:** *After renewing the control unit, it is recommended that the system height calibration is carried out. This requires dedicated test equipment, and should be entrusted to a BMW dealer or specialist.*

Air reservoirs renewal

46 Chock the front wheels, jack up the rear of the vehicle and support it securely on axle stands (see *Jacking and vehicle support*).

47 Remove the spare wheel from the luggage compartment.

48 Slacken the union securing the air pipes to the distribution block to relieve the system pressure. When the pressure has been relieved, tighten the unions securely.

49 Undo the two screws securing each reservoir in place **(see illustration)**. If required to improve access, remove the exhaust mounting from the subframe.

50 To disconnect the air pipe from a reservoir, pull back the protective cap, squeeze together the tabs of the retaining clip, and pull the coupling from the reservoir. **Note:** *On vehicles manufactured after 09/99, the air pipe cannot be disconnected from the reservoirs, and must be removed complete with supply pipe.*

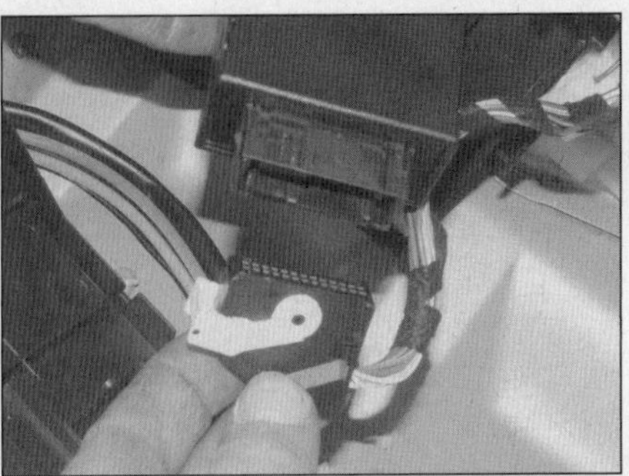

17.43 Unlock the catch and disconnect the control unit wiring plug

51 Manoeuvre the reservoir from position. **Note:** *An identification number is stamped onto each reservoir: odd number for the left-hand reservoir, and an even number for the right-hand reservoir.*

52 Refitting is a reversal of removal, noting the following points:

a) *Check the condition of the reservoir connection sealing rings, and renew if necessary.*

b) *New reservoirs are supplied with a protective cap fitted over the air pipe connection, which must be removed before connecting the pipe.*

c) *Take great care not to twist or kink the air pipes.*

17.49 Undo the two reservoir retaining bolts (arrowed)

18 Steering wheel – removal and refitting

Removal

1 Remove the airbag unit from the centre of the steering wheel, referring to Chapter 12, Section 25.

2 Set the front wheels in the straight-ahead position. This can be verified by observing the position of the alignment marks between the steering rack and pinion **(see illustration)**.

3 Fully extend the steering column and set it in its lowest position.

Models up to 03/99

4 Remove the driver's side facia lower trim panel as described in Chapter 11.

5 Undo the screw, and prise out the rivet securing the upper column shroud, then squeeze together the sides of the shroud and lift it upwards, disengaging the hooks at the front **(see illustrations)**.

6 Undo the screw, prise out the plastic rivet and remove the lower steering column shroud **(see illustration)**.

7 Disconnect the wiring plugs for the airbag and steering wheel switch(es)from the underside of the column **(see illustration)**.

18.2 The steering is in the 'straight-ahead' position when the pinion mark aligns with the casting mark (arrowed)

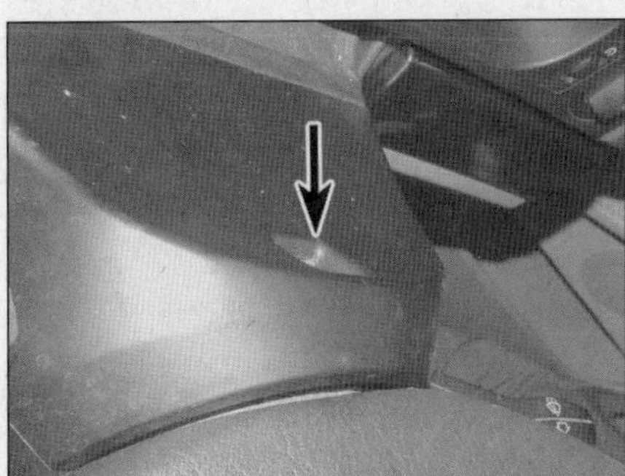

18.5a Undo the screw and prise out the rivet (arrowed)

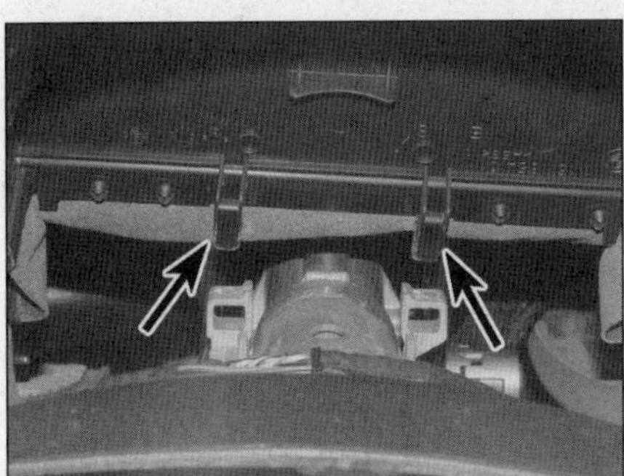

18.5b Disengage the shroud hooks at the front (arrowed)

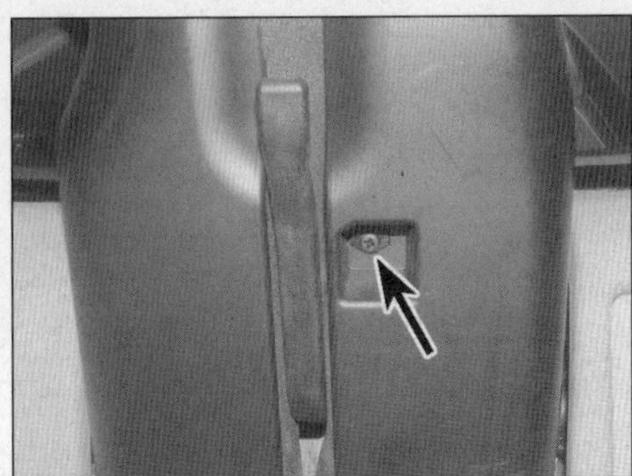

18.6 Undo the screw (arrowed) and prise out the plastic rivet

18.7 Disconnect the airbag and steering wheel switches

18.8 Undo the steering wheel bolt

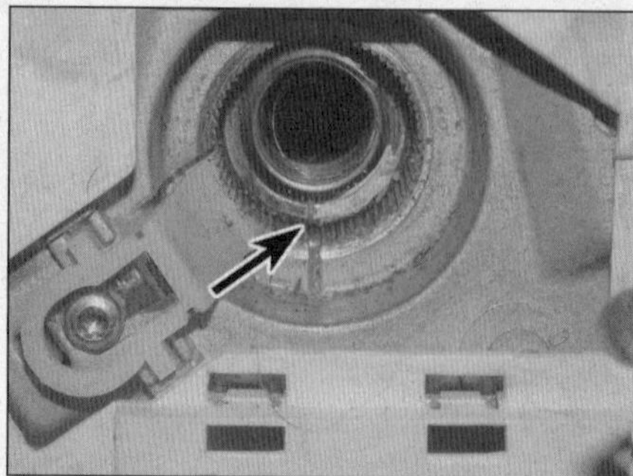
18.9 Make alignment marks between the steering wheel and column (arrowed)

18.10a On pre-03/99 vehicles, ensure the single pin (arrowed) engages with the contact unit

18.10b On vehicles after 03/99, two pins (arrowed) on the contact unit must engage with the holes in the back of the steering wheel

All models

8 Slacken and remove the steering wheel retaining bolt/nut **(see illustration)**. **Note:** *On vehicles manufactured prior to 03/99, when the steering wheel bolt is slackened a torsion spring automatically secures the contact ring in the central position. Once the bolt is slackened, the steering wheel must not be rotated at all, or the contact ring will be damaged. On vehicles manufactured after this date, when the steering wheel is removed, the contact unit remains in place on the steering column.*

9 Mark the steering wheel and steering column shaft in relation to each other, then lift the steering wheel off the column splines. If it is tight, tap it up near the centre, using the palm of your hand, whilst pulling upwards to release it from the shaft splines, **do not** twist it from side-to-side **(see illustration)**. Disconnect any wiring plugs as the steering wheel is removed.

Refitting

10 Refitting is the reverse of removal, noting the following points.

a) If the contact unit has been rotated with the wheel removed, centralise it by pressing down on the locking spring, and rotating the contact unit centre fully anti-clockwise. From this position, rotate the centre fully clockwise, counting the number of turns. Turn the centre back anti-clockwise half the number of turns.

b) Prior to refitting, ensure the indicator switch stalk is in the central (OFF) position. Failure to do so could lead to the steering wheel lug breaking the switch tab.

*c) On vehicles manufactured prior to 03/99, ensure the pin on the steering column engages with the recess in the contact unit as the steering wheel is refitted. On vehicles manufactured after this date, there are two pins on the contact unit which must engage with the recesses in the back of the steering wheel **(see illustrations)**.*

d) Engage the wheel with the column splines, aligning the marks made on removal, and tighten the steering wheel retaining bolt/nut to the specified torque.

e) Refit the airbag unit (see Chapter 12).

19 Steering column – removal, inspection and refitting

Note: *New steering column shear-bolt(s), and an intermediate shaft clamp bolt/nut, will be required on refitting.*

Removal

1 Disconnect the battery negative terminal (see Chapter 5A).

2 Remove the steering wheel as described in Section 18.

3 Remove the collar from the top of the steering column **(see illustration)**.

4 Unscrew the collar, and disconnect the interlock cable (where fitted) from the steering lock **(see illustration)**.

5 Make alignment marks between the column and the intermediate shaft, then slacken and remove the nut and clamp bolt, push down the intermediate shaft, and disengage the column from the shaft **(see illustration)**. Discard the clamp nut, a new one must be fitted.

6 Note their fitted positions, then disconnect the all the wiring connectors from the

19.3 Remove the collar (arrowed) from the top of the steering column

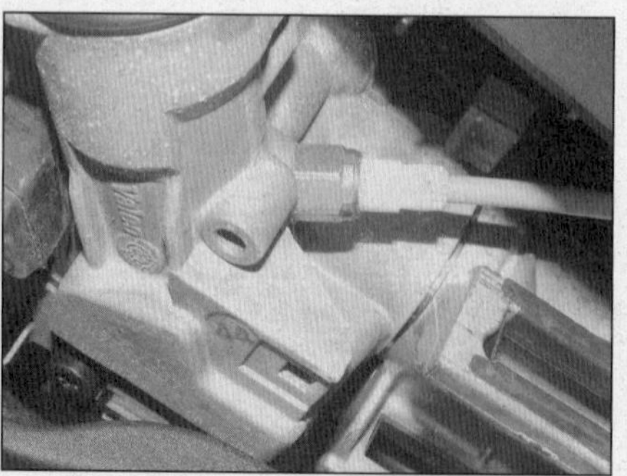
19.4 Disconnect the interlock cable

19.5 Make alignment marks (arrowed) between the shaft and clamp

steering column. Release the connectors from their retaining brackets **(see illustrations)**.

7 The steering column is secured in position with one or two shear-bolts at its base, and two bolts at the top. The shear-bolt(s) can be extracted using a hammer and suitable chisel to tap the bolt heads around until they can be unscrewed by hand. Alternatively, drill a hole in the centre of the bolt heads and extract them using a bolt/stud extractor (sometimes called an 'Easy-out'). Unscrew the remaining mounting bolt **(see illustrations)**.

8 Pull the column upwards and away from the bulkhead.

19.6a Disconnect all the wiring plugs from the steering column . . .

19.6b . . . and release them from their retaining brackets

Inspection

9 The steering column incorporates a telescopic safety feature. In the event of a front-end crash, the shaft collapses and prevents the steering wheel injuring the driver. Before refitting the steering column, examine the column and mountings for damage and deformation, and renew as necessary.

10 Check the steering shaft for signs of free play in the column bushes. If any damage or wear is found on the steering column bushes, the column should be overhauled. Overhaul of the column is a complex task requiring several special tools, and should be entrusted to a BMW dealer.

19.7a Using a chisel to extract the shear bolt

19.7b Undo the two bolts (arrowed) at the top of the colum

Refitting

11 Manoeuvre the column into position and engage it with the intermediate shaft splines, aligning the marks made prior to removal.

12 Locate the lower end of the column in its seat and screw in the mounting bolts and new shear-bolt(s); tighten them lightly only at this stage.

13 Tighten the column shear-bolt(s) until their heads breaks off. Tighten the remaining column mounting bolts securely

14 Reconnect all the wiring connectors, and secure the wiring to the column, ensuring it is correctly routed.

15 Ensure the intermediate shaft and column marks are correctly aligned, and insert the column into the shaft. Fit the new clamp bolt nut and tighten it to the specified torque.

16 Where necessary, reconnect the interlock cable to the switch and secure it in position.

17 Refit the steering wheel as described in Section 18.

20 Ignition switch/steering column lock – removal and refitting

Lock assembly

1 Renewal of the lock assembly requires the steering column to be dismantled. This task requires the use of several special tools, and for this reason should be entrusted to a BMW dealer or suitably-equipped specialist.

Lock cylinder

Removal

2 Undo the three screws, and prise out the plastic rivet securing the lower steering column shroud **(see illustration 18.6)**. Squeeze together the sides of the upper shroud to release the retaining clips, and pull the lower shroud downwards.

3 Remove the retaining screw, prise out the plastic rivet and remove the upper steering column shroud **(see illustration 18.5a)**.

4 Using two screwdrivers, carefully prise the transponder ring over the end of the ignition switch **(see illustration)**.

5 Detach the interlock cable (where fitted) from the ignition switch **(see illustration 19.4)**.

6 Turn the ignition key to the accessory position, then insert a suitable rod (eg, straightened paper clip) into the hole in the cylinder and depress the lock cylinder detent. Slide the lock cylinder out of position **(see illustrations)**.

20.4 Prise the transponder ring from the ignition switch, and recover the rubber ring

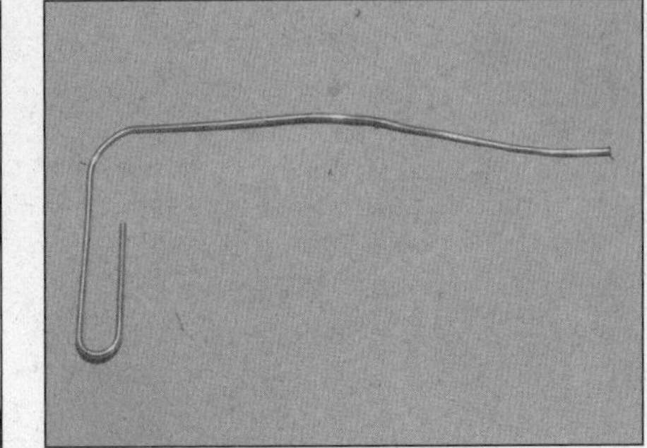

20.6a Straighten out a paper clip . . .

20.6b . . . turn the key to the accessory position and insert the clip into the hole

20.7 Position the lock cylinder as shown

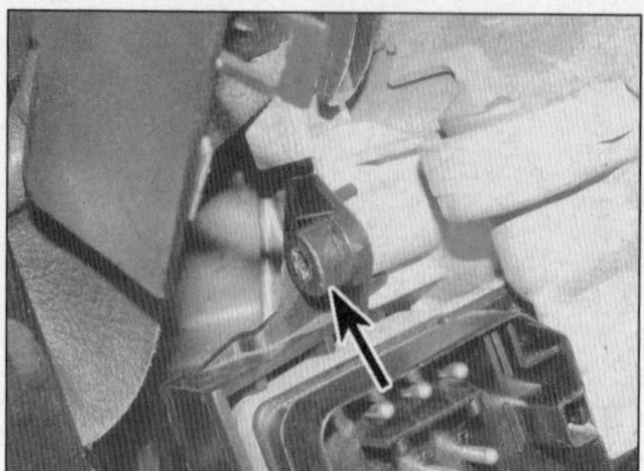

20.9 Undo the wiring loom support bracket screw (arrowed)

20.10 Undo the two grub screws (arrowed) and remove the ignition switch

Refitting

7 Position the lock cylinder as shown **(see illustration)**, and insert the cylinder into the housing until it clicks in to position.

Ignition switch block

Removal

8 Remove the upper and lower steering column shrouds as previously described in this Section.

9 Disconnect the ignition switch connector block, then undo the screw and remove the plastic wiring loom support **(see illustration)**.

10 Undo the two grub screws and remove the switch block from the lock assembly **(see illustration)**.

Refitting

11 Refitting is the reverse of removal, noting the following points:

a) *Apply varnish to the switch grub screws prior to refitting, to lock them in position.*
b) *Check the operation of the switch prior to refitting the steering column shrouds.*

21 Steering column intermediate shaft – removal and refitting

Note: *New intermediate shaft clamp bolts will be required on refitting.*

Removal

1 Chock the rear wheels, firmly apply the handbrake, then jack up the front of the car and support on axle stands. Set the front wheels in the straight-ahead position. Undo the screws and remove the engine undershield.

2 Remove the driver's side lower facia panel as described in Chapter 11.

3 Using paint or a suitable marker pen, make alignment marks between the intermediate shaft universal joint and the steering column, the shaft and flexible coupling, and the flexible coupling and the steering rack pinion. **Note:** *On some models an alignment mark is already provided on the pinion flange, which aligns with a mark cast into the pinion housing **(see illustrations 19.5 and 18.2)**.*

4 Slacken and remove the clamp bolts/nuts, then slide the two halves of the shaft together, unseat the rubber grommet, and remove the shaft assembly from the car **(see illustration)**.

5 Inspect the intermediate shaft universal joint for signs of roughness in its bearings and ease of movement. Also examine the shaft rubber coupling for signs of damage or deterioration, and check that the rubber is securely bonded to the flanges. If the universal joint or rubber coupling are suspect, the complete intermediate shaft should be renewed.

Refitting

6 Check that the front wheels are still in the straight-ahead position, and that the steering wheel is correctly positioned.

7 Align the marks made on removal, and engage the intermediate shaft joint with the steering column and the coupling with the steering rack.

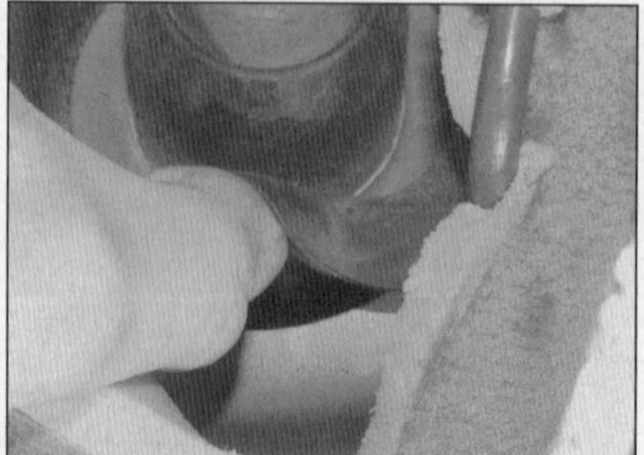

21.4 Unseat the rubber grommet at the base of the column

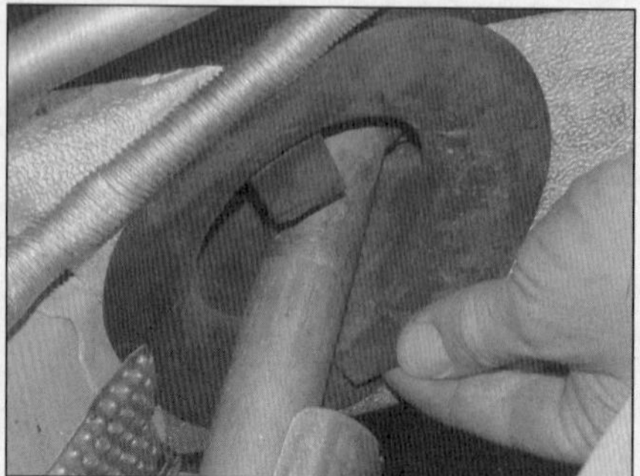

21.8 Ensure the rubber grommet is correctly fitted to the bulkhead

8 Ensure the rubber grommet is correctly refitted **(see illustration)**.

9 Insert the clamp bolts, fit the new upper clamp nut, and tighten them to the specified torque setting. Lower the car to the ground.

22 Steering rack assembly – removal, overhaul and refitting

Note: *New track rod balljoint nuts, steering rack mounting nuts, intermediate shaft clamp bolt, and fluid pipe union bolt sealing washers will be required on refitting.*

Removal

1 Chock the rear wheels, firmly apply the handbrake, then jack up the front of the car and support on axle stands (see *Jacking and vehicle support*). Remove both front roadwheels, then undo the screws and remove the engine undershield.

2 In order to remove the steering rack, then engine must be lifted approximately 40 mm. Release the engine mounting brackets from the front subframe and, using a trolley jack with a block of wood between the jack head and sump, carefully raise the engine 40 mm.

3 Slacken and remove the nuts securing the steering rack track rod balljoints to the hub carriers, and release the balljoint tapered shanks using a universal balljoint separator – see Section 26.

4 Using paint or a suitable marker pen, make alignment marks between the intermediate shaft coupling and the steering rack pinion. **Note:** *On some models an alignment mark is already provided on the pinion flange, which aligns with a mark cast into the pinion housing **(see illustration 18.2)**.*

5 Slacken and remove the universal joint pinch-bolt. Discard the bolt, a new one must be fitted.

6 Using brake hose clamps, clamp both the supply and return hoses near the power steering fluid reservoir. This will minimise fluid loss. Mark the unions to ensure they are correctly positioned on reassembly, then slacken and remove the feed and return pipe union bolts and recover the sealing washers. Be prepared for fluid spillage, and position a suitable container beneath the pipes whilst unscrewing the bolts. Plug the pipe ends and steering rack orifices to prevent fluid leakage and to keep dirt out of the hydraulic system.

7 Slacken and remove the steering rack mounting bolts and nuts, and remove the steering rack through the driver's side of the engine compartment **(see illustration)**. Discard the nuts, new ones must be fitted.

Overhaul

8 Examine the steering rack assembly for signs of wear or damage, and check that the rack moves freely throughout the full length of its travel, with no signs of roughness or excessive free play between the steering rack pinion and rack. It is not possible to overhaul the steering rack assembly housing components; if it is faulty, the assembly must be renewed. The only components which can be renewed individually are the steering rack gaiters, the track rod balljoints and the track rods. These procedures are covered later in this Chapter.

Refitting

9 Offer up the steering rack, and insert the mounting bolts. Fit new nuts to the bolts, and tighten them to the specified Stage 1 torque setting, followed by the Stage 2 angle.

10 Position a new sealing washer on each side of the pipe hose unions and refit the union bolts. Tighten the union bolts to the specified torque.

11 Lower the engine, and secure the engine mounting brackets to the subframe.

12 Align the marks made on removal, and connect the intermediate shaft coupling to the steering rack. Insert the new clamp bolt then tighten it to the specified torque.

13 Locate the track rod balljoints in the hub carriers, then fit the new nuts and tighten them to the specified torque.

14 Refit the roadwheels, and the engine undershield, then lower the car to the ground and tighten the wheel bolts to the specified torque.

15 Bleed the hydraulic system as described in Section 24.

16 If a new rack has been fitted, BMW recommend that the front wheel alignment is checked, and if necessary, adjusted.

23 Power steering pump – removal and refitting

Note: *New feed pipe union bolt sealing washers will be required on refitting*

Removal

1 Chock the rear wheels, then jack up the front of the car and support it on axle stands (see *Jacking and vehicle support*). Undo the screws and remove the engine undershield.

2 Working as described in Chapter 1, release the drivebelt tension and unhook the drivebelt from the pump pulley.

3 Using brake hose clamps, clamp both the supply and return hoses near the power steering fluid reservoir. This will minimise fluid loss during subsequent operations.

4 Mark the unions to ensure they are correctly positioned on reassembly, then slacken and remove the feed and return pipe union bolts and recover the sealing washers. Be prepared for fluid spillage, and position a suitable container beneath the pipes whilst unscrewing the bolts. Plug the pipe ends and steering pump orifices, to prevent fluid leakage and to keep dirt out of the hydraulic system.

5 Slacken and remove the mounting bolts and remove the pump.

6 If the power steering pump is faulty, seek the advice of your BMW dealer as to the availability of spare parts. If spares are available, it may be possible to have the pump overhauled by a suitable specialist, or alternatively obtain an exchange unit. If not, the pump must be renewed.

Refitting

7 Prior to refitting, ensure that the pump is primed by injecting the specified type of fluid in through the supply hose union and rotating the pump shaft.

8 Manoeuvre the pump into position and refit the mounting bolts, tightening them securely.

9 Position a new sealing washer on each side of the pipe hose unions and refit the union bolts. Tighten the union bolts to the specified torque.

10 Remove the hose clamps.

11 Refit the auxiliary drivebelt and tension it as described in Chapter 1.

12 Refit the engine undershield.

13 On completion, lower the car to the ground and bleed the hydraulic system as described in Section 24.

24 Power steering system – bleeding

1 With the engine stopped, fill the fluid reservoir right up to the top with the specified type of fluid.

2 With the engine running, slowly move the steering from lock-to-lock twice to purge out the trapped air, then stop the engine and top-up the level in the fluid reservoir. Repeat this procedure until the fluid level in the reservoir does not drop any further.

3 If, when turning the steering, an abnormal noise is heard from the fluid lines, it indicates that there is still air in the system. Check this by turning the wheels to the straight-ahead position and switching off the engine. If the fluid level in the reservoir rises, then air is present in the system and further bleeding is necessary.

25 Steering rack rubber gaiters – renewal

1 Disconnect the track rod balljoint from the hub carrier as described in Section 26. Undo the screws and remove the engine undershield.

2 Note the correct fitted position of the gaiter on the track rod, then release the retaining clip(s) and slide the gaiter off the steering rack housing and track rod end **(see illustration)**.

3 Thoroughly clean the track rod and the

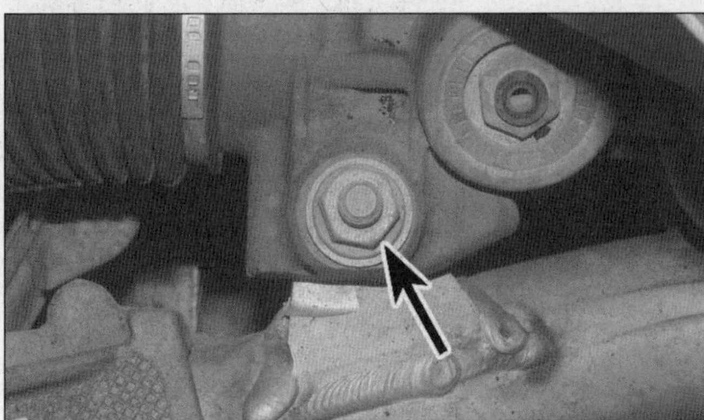

22.7 Right-hand steering rack mounting bolt/nut (arrowed) – viewed from underneath

25.2 Slide the gaiter over the track rod end

25.5a Lift the outer lip to equalise pressure . . .

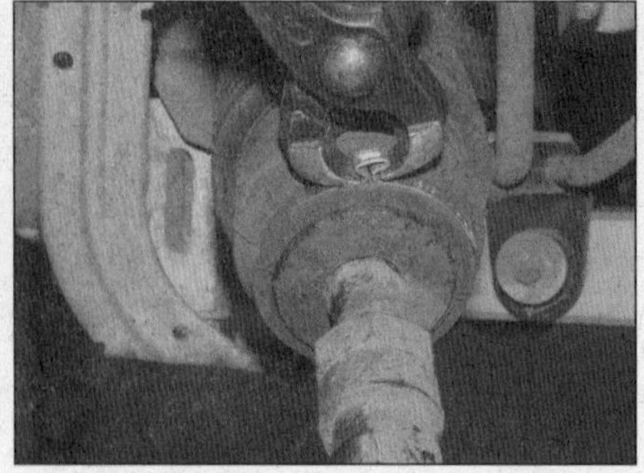

25.5b . . . then crimp the new outer . . .

25.5c . . . and inner gaiter clips in place

steering rack housing, using fine abrasive paper to polish off any corrosion, burrs or sharp edges, which might damage the new gaiter's sealing lips on installation. Scrape off all the grease from the old gaiter, and apply it to the track rod inner balljoint. (This assumes that grease has not been lost or contaminated as a result of damage to the old gaiter. Use fresh grease if in doubt.)

4 Carefully slide the new gaiter onto the track rod end, and locate it on the steering rack housing. Position the outer edge of the gaiter on the track rod, as was noted prior to removal.

5 Make sure the gaiter is not twisted, then lift the outer sealing lip of the gaiter to equalise air pressure within the gaiter. Secure the gaiter in position with the new retaining clip(s) **(see illustrations)**.

6 Refit the track rod balljoint as described in Section 26.

26 Track rod balljoint – removal and refitting

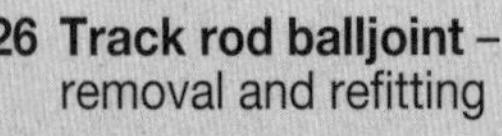

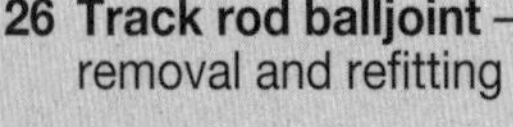

Note: *A new balljoint retaining nut will be required on refitting.*

Removal

1 Apply the handbrake, then jack up the front of the car and support it on axle stands (see *Jacking and vehicle support*). Remove the appropriate front roadwheel.

2 Make a mark on the track rod and measure the distance from the mark to the centre of the balljoint **(see illustration)**. Note this measurement down, as it will be needed to ensure the wheel alignment remains correctly set when the balljoint is installed.

3 Hold the track rod, and unscrew the balljoint locknut.

4 Slacken and remove the nut securing the track rod balljoint to the hub carrier, and release the balljoint tapered shank using a universal balljoint separator **(see illustration)**.

5 Counting the exact number of turns necessary to do so, unscrew the balljoint from the track rod end.

6 Carefully clean the balljoint and the threads. Renew the balljoint if its movement is sloppy or too stiff, if excessively worn, or if damaged in any way; carefully check the stud taper and threads. If the balljoint gaiter is damaged, the complete balljoint assembly must be renewed; it is not possible to obtain the gaiter separately.

Refitting

7 If necessary, transfer the locknut and collar to the new track rod balljoint.

8 Screw the balljoint onto the track rod by the number of turns noted on removal. This should position the balljoint at the relevant distance from the track rod mark that was noted prior to removal.

9 Refit the balljoint shank to the hub carrier, then fit a new retaining nut and tighten it to the specified torque.

10 Refit the roadwheel, then lower the car to the ground and tighten the roadwheel bolts to the specified torque.

11 Check and, if necessary, adjust the front wheel toe setting as described in Section 29, then tighten the balljoint locknut to the specified torque setting.

27 Track rod – renewal

1 Remove the steering rack gaiter as described in Section 25.

2 Unscrew the track rod from the end of the steering rack **(see illustration)**.

3 Screw in the track rod and tighten it to the specified torque.

4 Refit the steering gaiter as described in Section 25.

28 Dynamic Stability Control – general information and component renewal

General information

1 Dynamic Stability Control (DSC) is standard on most models, and available as an option on all other models. Strictly speaking, DSC includes ABS and Traction control, but this Section is concerned with Cornering Brake Control (CBC). By monitoring steering wheel

26.2 Make a mark on the track rod (arrowed) and measure from here to the centre of the balljoint

26.4 Use a large balljoint separator to release the track rod end

27.2 Unscrew the collar (arrowed) from the end of the rack

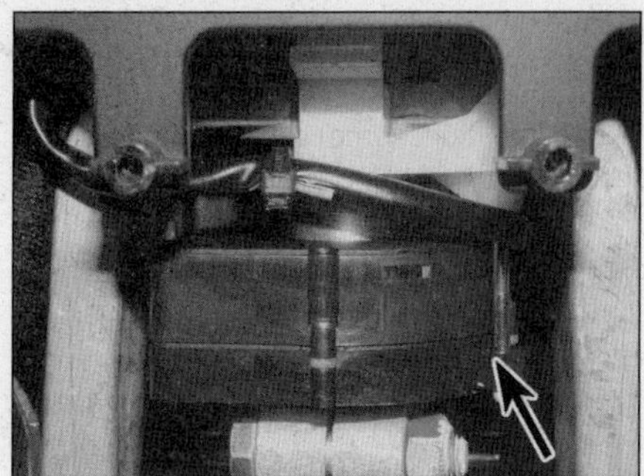

28.4 Steering angle sensor (arrowed)

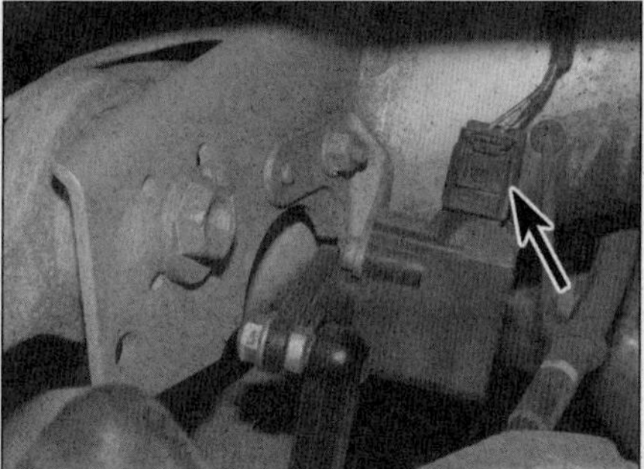

28.13 Disconnect the ride height sensor wiring plug (arrowed)

28.18 The preboost pump (arrowed) is adjacent to the brake master cylinder

movements, suspension ride heights, roadspeed, lateral acceleration and yaw rate, the system controls the pressure in the brake lines to each of the four brake calipers, reducing the possibility of understeer or oversteer.

Component renewal

Steering angle sensor

2 Remove the driver's side lower facia panel, as described in Chapter 11.

3 Make alignment marks between the column and the intermediate shaft, then slacken and remove the nut and clamp bolt, push down the intermediate shaft, and disengage the column from the shaft **(see illustration 19.5)**. Discard the clamp nut, a new one must be fitted.

4 Carefully pull the sensor from the lower end of the column **(see illustration)**.

5 When refitting the sensor, the pivot mounting pin must engage with the corresponding hole in the sensor. **Note:** *After renewing the steering angle sensor, the 'steering angle offset' procedure must be carrier out using dedicated diagnostic equipment. Have this procedure carried out by a BMW dealer or suitably-equipped specialist.*

Front ride height sensor

6 Jack up the front of the vehicle, and support it securely on axle stands (see *Jacking and vehicle support*). Remove the relevant front roadwheel.

7 Disconnect the sensor wiring plug.

8 Undo the nut securing the link rod to the sensor arm.

9 Remove the two retaining screws, and withdraw the ride sensor

10 Refitting is a reversal of removal. Have the headlight alignment checked on completion. **Note:** *After renewing one or more of the ride height sensors, it is recommended that the system height calibration is carried out. This requires dedicated test equipment, and should be entrusted to a BMW dealer or specialist.*

Rear ride height sensor

11 Chock the front wheel, jack up the rear of the vehicle and support it securely on axle stands (see *Jacking and vehicle support)*.

12 Working underneath the vehicle, undo the two screws and remove the trim (where fitted) adjacent to the swinging arm.

13 Disconnect the sensor wiring plug **(see illustration)**.

14 Undo the nut and disconnect the sensor arm from the swinging arm link.

15 Undo the two screws and remove the sensor.

16 Refitting is a reversal of removal, tightening all fasteners securely. **Note:** *After renewing one or more of the ride height sensors, it is recommended that the system height calibration is carried out. This requires dedicated test equipment, and should be entrusted to a BMW dealer or specialist.*

DSC control unit

17 The DSC control unit is integral with the ABS control unit, renewal of which should be entrusted to a BMW dealer or suitably-equipped specialist – see Chapter 9.

DSC preboost pump

Note: *After renewing the preboost pump, the brake high pressure hydraulic system needs to be bled. This necessitates the use of dedicated service equipment. Have the procedure carried out by a BMW dealer or suitably-equipped specialist.*

18 The DSC preboost pump is located alongside the brake master cylinder **(see illustration)**. Clamp the supply hose from the master cylinder reservoir to the pump, and disconnect the hose from the pump. Be prepared for fluid spillage.

19 Undo the union and disconnect the outlet pipe from the pump. **Note:** *The two pipe connections to the pump are marked HZ – connection to master cylinder, and BA – connection to the brake fluid reservoir* ***(see illustration)****.*

28.19 The connection to the master cylinder is marked HZ and the connection to the reservoir is marked BA

20 Disconnect the wiring plug from the pump.

21 Undo the three bolts, and remove the pump complete with mounting.

22 Refitting is a reversal of removal. Bleed the brake hydraulic system as described in Chapter 9.

Yaw rate/lateral acceleration sensor

23 Remove the driver's seat as described in Chapter 11.

24 Pull the driver's side sill panel trim upwards from its retaining clips and fold back the carpet to expose the sensor.

25 Disconnect the wiring plug, undo the two screws and remove the sensor.

26 Refitting is a reversal of removal. **Note:** *If the sensor has been renewed, the sensor values must set using dedicated test equipment. Entrust this task to a BMW dealer or suitably equipped specialist.*

29 Wheel alignment and steering angles – general information

Definitions

1 A car's steering and suspension geometry is defined in four basic settings – all angles are expressed in degrees; the steering axis is defined as an imaginary line drawn through the axis of the suspension strut, extended where necessary to contact the ground.

2 Camber is the angle between each roadwheel and a vertical line drawn through its centre and tyre contact patch, when viewed from the front or rear of the car. Positive camber is when the roadwheels are tilted outwards from the vertical at the top; negative camber is when they are tilted inwards.

3 The front camber angle is not adjustable, and is given for reference only (see paragraph 5). The rear camber angle is adjustable and can be adjusted using a camber angle gauge.

4 Castor is the angle between the steering

axis and a vertical line drawn through each roadwheel's centre and tyre contact patch, when viewed from the side of the car. Positive castor is when the steering axis is tilted so that it contacts the ground ahead of the vertical; negative castor is when it contacts the ground behind the vertical.

5 Castor is not adjustable, and is given for reference only; while it can be checked using a castor checking gauge, if the figure obtained is significantly different from that specified, the car must be taken for careful checking by a professional, as the fault can only be caused by wear or damage to the body or suspension components.

6 Toe is the difference, viewed from above, between lines drawn through the roadwheel centres and the car's centre-line. 'Toe-in' is when the roadwheels point inwards, towards each other at the front, while 'toe-out' is when they splay outwards from each other at the front.

7 The front wheel toe setting is adjusted by screwing the track rods in or out of their balljoint, to alter the effective length of the track rod assembly.

8 Rear wheel toe setting and camber setting is also adjustable. The camber setting is adjusted by slackening the locknut, and rotating the swinging arm-to-rear subframe bolt, which has an integral eccentric washer. The toe setting are adjusted by slackening the locknut, and rotating the traction arm-to-rear subframe pivot bolt, which also has in integral eccentric washer.

Checking and adjustment

Front wheel toe setting

9 Due to the special measuring equipment necessary to check the wheel alignment, and the skill required to use it properly, the checking and adjustment of these settings is best left to a BMW dealer or similar expert. Note that most tyre-fitting shops now possess sophisticated checking equipment.

10 To check the toe setting, a tracking gauge must first be obtained. Two types of gauge are available, and can be obtained from motor accessory shops. The first type measures the distance between the front and rear inside edges of the roadwheels, as previously described, with the car stationary. The second type, known as a 'scuff plate', measures the actual position of the contact surface of the tyre, in relation to the road surface, with the car in motion. This is achieved by pushing or driving the front tyre over a plate, which then moves slightly according to the scuff of the tyre, and shows this movement on a scale. Both types have their advantages and disadvantages, but either can give satisfactory results if used correctly and carefully.

11 Make sure that the steering is in the straight-ahead position when making measurements.

12 If adjustment is necessary, apply the handbrake then jack up the front of the car and support it securely on axle stands.

13 First clean the track rod threads; if they are corroded, apply penetrating fluid before starting adjustment. Release the rubber gaiter outer clips, peel back the gaiters and apply a smear of grease so that both are free and will not be twisted or strained as their respective track rods are rotated.

14 Retain the track rod with a suitable spanner and slacken the balljoint locknut. Alter the length of the track rod, by screwing them into or out of the balljoints by rotating the track rod using an open-ended spanner fitted to the track rod flats provided; shortening the track rods (screwing them onto their balljoints) will reduce toe-in/increase toe-out.

15 When the setting is correct, hold the track rod and tighten the balljoint locknut to the specified torque setting. If after adjustment, the steering wheel spokes are no longer horizontal when the wheels are in the straight-ahead position, remove the steering wheel and reposition it (see Section 18).

16 Check that the toe setting has been correctly adjusted by lowering the car to the ground and rechecking the toe setting; re-adjust if necessary. Ensure that the rubber gaiters are seated correctly and are not twisted or strained, and secure them in position with the retaining clips; where necessary fit a new retaining clip (see Section 25).

Rear wheel toe setting

Note: *Prior adjusting the toe setting, the camber angle should first be checked.*

17 The procedure for checking the rear toe setting is same as described for the front in paragraph 10.

18 To adjust the setting, slacken the locknut, and rotate the traction arm-to-rear subframe pivot bolt, which has an integral eccentric washer. Once the toe setting is correct, tighten the locknut to the specified torque. **Note:** *BMW insist that when the pivot bolt locknut has been slackened and tightened 10 times it must be renewed.*

Rear wheel camber angle

19 Checking and adjusting of the camber angle should be entrusted to a BMW dealer or other suitably-equipped specialist. Note that most tyre-fitting shops now possess sophisticated checking equipment. For reference, adjustments are made by slackening the locknut and rotating the swinging arm-to-rear subframe pivot bolt, which has an integral eccentric washer. Once adjustment is correct, tighten the locknut to the specified torque. **Note:** *BMW insist that when the pivot bolt locknut has been slackened and tightened 10 times it must be renewed.*

Chapter 11
Bodywork and fittings

Contents

Degrees of difficulty

Easy, suitable for novice with little experience 	**Fairly easy,** suitable for beginner with some experience 	**Fairly difficult,** suitable for competent DIY mechanic 	**Difficult,** suitable for experienced DIY mechanic 	**Very difficult,** suitable for expert DIY or professional

Specifications

Torque wrench settings	**Nm**	**lbf ft**
Door window regulator fixings	9	7
Exterior mirror bolts	6	4
Seat belt mounting bolts	48	35
Seat belt mounting on B-pillar	31	23
Seat belt tensioner stalk on seat	48	35
Seat mounting bolts	42	31

1 General information

The bodyshell is made of pressed-steel sections. Most components are welded together, but some use is made of structural adhesives.

The bonnet, door and some other vulnerable panels are made of zinc-coated metal, and are further protected by being coated with an anti-chip primer before being sprayed.

Extensive use is made of plastic materials, mainly in the interior, but also in exterior components. The front and rear bumpers and front grille are injection-moulded from a synthetic material that is very strong and yet light. Plastic components such as wheel arch liners are fitted to the underside of the vehicle, to improve the body's resistance to corrosion.

2 Maintenance – bodywork and underframe

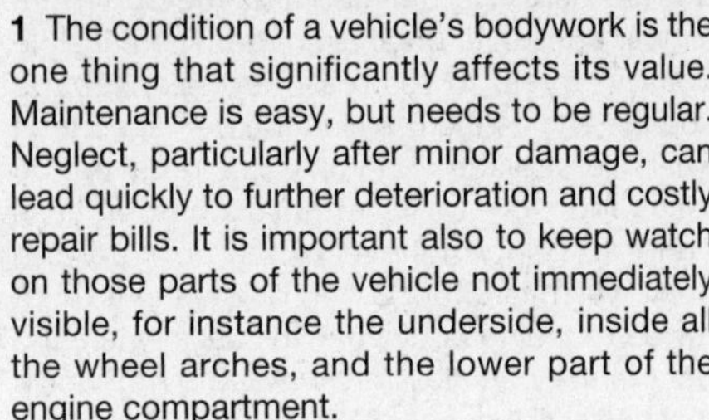

1 The condition of a vehicle's bodywork is the one thing that significantly affects its value. Maintenance is easy, but needs to be regular. Neglect, particularly after minor damage, can lead quickly to further deterioration and costly repair bills. It is important also to keep watch on those parts of the vehicle not immediately visible, for instance the underside, inside all the wheel arches, and the lower part of the engine compartment.

2 The basic maintenance routine for the bodywork is washing – preferably with a lot of water, from a hose. This will remove all the loose solids which may have stuck to the vehicle. It is important to flush these off in such a way as to prevent grit from scratching the finish. The wheel arches and underframe need washing in the same way, to remove any accumulated mud which will retain moisture and tend to encourage rust. Oddly enough, the best time to clean the underframe and wheel arches is in wet weather, when the mud is thoroughly wet and soft. In very wet weather, the underframe is usually cleaned of large accumulations automatically, and this is a good time for inspection.

3 Periodically, except on vehicles with a wax-based underbody protective coating, it is a good idea to have the whole of the underframe of the vehicle steam-cleaned, engine compartment included, so that a thorough inspection can be carried out to see what minor repairs and renovations are necessary. Steam cleaning is available at many garages, and is necessary for the removal of the accumulation of oily grime, which sometimes is allowed to become thick in certain areas. If steam-cleaning facilities are not available, there are some excellent grease solvents available which can be brush-applied; the dirt can then be simply hosed off. Note that these methods should not be used on vehicles with wax-based underbody protective coating, or the coating will be removed. Such vehicles should be inspected annually, preferably just before Winter, when the underbody should be washed down, and repair any damage to the wax coating. Ideally, a completely fresh coat should be applied. It would also be worth considering the use of such wax-based protection for injection into door panels, sills, box sections, etc, as an additional safeguard against rust damage, where such protection is not provided by the vehicle manufacturer.

4 After washing paintwork, wipe off with a chamois leather to give an unspotted clear finish. A coat of clear protective wax polish will give added protection against chemical pollutants in the air. If the paintwork sheen has dulled or oxidised, use a cleaner/polisher combination to restore the brilliance of the shine. This requires a little effort, but such dulling is usually caused because regular washing has been neglected. Care needs to be taken with metallic paintwork, as special non-abrasive cleaner/polisher is required to avoid damage to the finish. Always check that the door and ventilator opening drain holes and pipes are completely clear, so that water can be drained out. Brightwork should be treated in the same way as paintwork. Windscreens and windows can be kept clear of the smeary film which often appears, by proprietary glass cleaner. Never use any form of wax or other body or chromium polish on glass.

3 Maintenance – upholstery and carpets

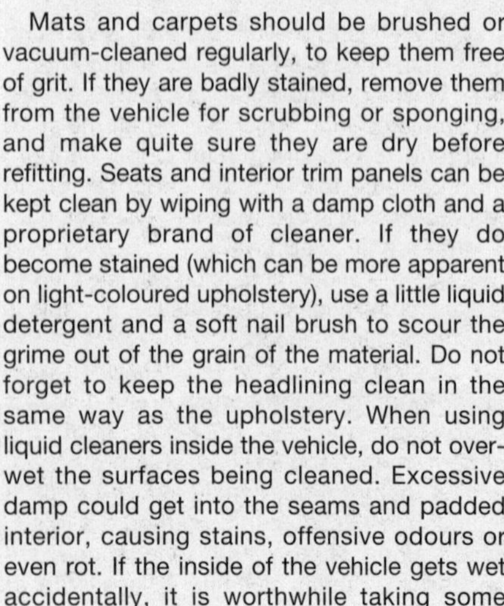

Mats and carpets should be brushed or vacuum-cleaned regularly, to keep them free of grit. If they are badly stained, remove them from the vehicle for scrubbing or sponging, and make quite sure they are dry before refitting. Seats and interior trim panels can be kept clean by wiping with a damp cloth and a proprietary brand of cleaner. If they do become stained (which can be more apparent on light-coloured upholstery), use a little liquid detergent and a soft nail brush to scour the grime out of the grain of the material. Do not forget to keep the headlining clean in the same way as the upholstery. When using liquid cleaners inside the vehicle, do not over-wet the surfaces being cleaned. Excessive damp could get into the seams and padded interior, causing stains, offensive odours or even rot. If the inside of the vehicle gets wet accidentally, it is worthwhile taking some trouble to dry it out properly, particularly where carpets are involved. Do not leave oil or electric heaters inside the vehicle for this purpose.

4 Minor body damage – repair

Minor scratches

1 If the scratch is very superficial, and does not penetrate to the metal of the bodywork, repair is very simple. Lightly rub the area of the scratch with a paintwork renovator or a very fine cutting paste to remove loose paint from the scratch, and to clear the surrounding bodywork of wax polish. Rinse the area with clean water.

2 Apply touch-up paint to the scratch using a fine paint brush; continue to apply fine layers of paint until the surface of the paint in the scratch is level with the surrounding paintwork. Allow the new paint at least two weeks to harden, then blend it into the surrounding paintwork by rubbing the scratch area with a paintwork renovator or a very fine cutting paste. Finally, apply wax polish.

3 Where the scratch has penetrated right through to the metal of the bodywork, causing the metal to rust, a different repair technique is required. Remove any loose rust from the bottom of the scratch with a penknife, then apply rust-inhibiting paint to prevent the formation of rust in the future. Using a rubber or nylon applicator, fill the scratch with bodystopper paste. If required, this paste can be mixed with cellulose thinners to provide a very thin paste which is ideal for filling narrow scratches. Before the stopper-paste in the scratch hardens, wrap a piece of smooth cotton rag around the top of a finger. Dip the finger in cellulose thinners, and quickly sweep it across the surface of the stopper-paste in the scratch; this will ensure that the surface of the stopper-paste is slightly hollowed. The scratch can now be painted over as described earlier in this Section.

Dents

4 When deep denting of the vehicle's bodywork has taken place, the first task is to pull the dent out, until the affected bodywork almost attains its original shape. There is little point in trying to restore the original shape completely, as the metal in the damaged area will have stretched on impact, and cannot be reshaped fully to its original contour. It is better to bring the level of the dent up to a point which is about 3 mm below the level of the surrounding bodywork. In cases where the dent is very shallow anyway, it is not worth trying to pull it out at all. If the underside of the dent is accessible, it can be hammered out gently from behind, using a mallet with a wooden or plastic head. Whilst doing this, hold a suitable block of wood firmly against the outside of the panel, to absorb the impact from the hammer blows and thus prevent a large area of the bodywork from being 'belled-out'.

5 Should the dent be in a section of the bodywork which has a double skin, or some other factor making it inaccessible from behind, a different technique is called for. Drill several small holes through the metal inside the area – particularly in the deeper section. Then screw long self-tapping screws into the holes, just sufficiently for them to gain a good purchase in the metal. Now the dent can be pulled out by pulling on the protruding heads of the screws with a pair of pliers.

6 The next stage of the repair is the removal of the paint from the damaged area, and from an inch or so of the surrounding 'sound' bodywork. This is accomplished most easily by using a wire brush or abrasive pad on a power drill, although it can be done just as effectively by hand, using sheets of abrasive paper. To complete the preparation for filling, score the surface of the bare metal with a screwdriver or the tang of a file, or alternatively, drill small holes in the affected area. This will provide a good 'key' for the filler paste.

7 To complete the repair, see the Section on filling and respraying.

Rust holes or gashes

8 Remove all paint from the affected area, and from an inch or so of the surrounding 'sound' bodywork, using an abrasive pad or a wire brush on a power drill. If these are not available, a few sheets of abrasive paper will do the job most effectively. With the paint removed, you will be able to judge the severity of the corrosion, and therefore decide whether to renew the whole panel (if this is possible) or to repair the affected area. New body panels are not as expensive as most people think, and it is often quicker and more satisfactory to fit a new panel than to attempt to repair large areas of corrosion.

9 Remove all fittings from the affected area, except those which will act as a guide to the original shape of the damaged bodywork (eg headlamp shells etc). Then, using tin snips or a hacksaw blade, remove all loose metal and any other metal badly affected by corrosion. Hammer the edges of the hole inwards, to create a slight depression for the filler paste.

10 Wire-brush the affected area to remove the powdery rust from the surface of the remaining metal. Paint the affected area with rust-inhibiting paint; if the back of the rusted area is accessible, treat this also.

11 Before filling can take place, it will be necessary to block the hole in some way. This can be achieved with aluminium or plastic mesh, or aluminium tape.

12 Aluminium or plastic mesh, or glass-fibre matting, is probably the best material to use for a large hole. Cut a piece to the approximate size and shape of the hole to be filled, then position it in the hole so that its edges are below the level of the surrounding bodywork. It can be retained in position by several blobs of filler paste around its periphery.

13 Aluminium tape should be used for small or very narrow holes. Pull a piece off the roll, trim it to the approximate size and shape required, then pull off the backing paper (if used) and stick the tape over the hole; it can be overlapped if the thickness of one piece is insufficient. Burnish down the edges of the tape with the handle of a screwdriver or similar, to ensure that the tape is securely attached to the metal underneath.

Filling and respraying

14 Before using this Section, see the Sections on dent, deep scratch, rust holes and gash repairs.

15 Many types of bodyfiller are available, but generally speaking, those proprietary kits which contain a tin of filler paste and a tube of resin hardener are best for this type of repair which can be used directly from the tube. A wide, flexible plastic or nylon applicator will be found invaluable for imparting a smooth and well-contoured finish to the surface of the filler.

16 Mix up a little filler on a clean piece of card or board – measure the hardener carefully (follow the maker's instructions on the pack), otherwise the filler will set too rapidly or too slowly. Using the applicator, apply the filler paste to the prepared area; draw the applicator across the surface of the filler to achieve the correct contour and to level the surface. When a contour that approximates to the correct one is achieved, stop working the paste – if you carry on too long, the paste will become sticky and begin to 'pick-up' on the applicator. Continue to add thin layers of filler paste at 20-minute intervals, until the level of the filler is just proud of the surrounding bodywork.

17 Once the filler has hardened, the excess can be removed using a metal plane or file. From then on, progressively-finer grades of abrasive paper should be used, starting with a 40-grade production paper, and finishing with a 400-grade wet-and-dry paper. Always wrap the abrasive paper around a flat rubber, cork, or wooden block – otherwise the surface of the filler will not be completely flat. During the smoothing of the filler surface, the wet-and-dry paper should be periodically rinsed in water. This will ensure that a very smooth finish is imparted to the filler at the final stage.

18 At this stage, the 'dent' should be surrounded by a ring of bare metal, which in turn should be encircled by the finely 'feathered' edge of the good paintwork. Rinse the repair area with clean water, until all the dust produced by the rubbing-down operation has gone.

19 Spray the whole area with a light coat of primer – this will show up any imperfections in the surface of the filler. Repair these imperfections with fresh filler paste or bodystopper, and again smooth the surface with abrasive paper. If bodystopper is used, it can be mixed with cellulose thinners, to form a thin paste which is ideal for filling small holes. Repeat this spray-and-repair procedure until you are satisfied that the surface of the filler, and the feathered edge of the paintwork, are perfect. Clean the repair area with clean water, and allow to dry fully.

20 The repair area is now ready for final spraying. Paint spraying must be carried out in a warm, dry, windless and dust-free atmosphere. This condition can be created artificially if you have access to a large indoor working area, but if you are forced to work in the open, you will have to pick your day very carefully. If you are working indoors, dousing the floor in the work area with water will help to settle the dust which would otherwise be in the atmosphere. If the repair area is confined to one body panel, mask off the surrounding panels; this will help to minimise the effects of a slight mis-match in paint colours. Bodywork fittings (eg chrome strips, door handles etc) will also need to be masked off. Use genuine masking tape, and several thickness of newspaper, for the masking operations.

21 Before starting to spray, agitate the aerosol can thoroughly, then spray a test area (an old tin, or similar) until the technique is mastered. Cover the repair area with a thick coat of primer; the thickness should be built up using several thin layers of paint, rather than one thick one. Using 400 grade wet-and-dry paper, rub down the surface of the primer until it is smooth. While doing this, the work area should be thoroughly doused with water, and the wet-and-dry paper periodically rinsed in water. Allow to dry before spraying on more paint.

22 Spray on the top coat, again building up the thickness by using several thin layers of paint. Start spraying at the top of the repair area, and then, using a side-to-side motion, work downwards until the whole repair area and about 2 inches of the surrounding original paintwork is covered. Remove all masking material 10 to 15 minutes after spraying on the final coat of paint.

23 Allow the new paint at least two weeks to harden, then, using a paintwork renovator or a very fine cutting paste, blend the edges of the paint into the existing paintwork. Finally, apply wax polish.

Plastic components

24 With the use of more and more plastic body components by the vehicle manufacturers (eg bumpers. spoilers, and in some cases major body panels), rectification of more serious damage to such items has become a matter of either entrusting repair work to a specialist in this field, or renewing complete components. Repair of such damage by the DIY owner is not feasible, owing to the cost of the equipment and materials required for effecting such repairs. The basic technique involves making a groove along the line of the crack in the plastic, using a rotary burr in a power drill. The damaged part is then welded back together, using a hot air gun to heat up and fuse a plastic filler rod into the groove. Any excess plastic is then removed, and the area rubbed down to a smooth finish. It is important that a filler rod of the correct plastic is used, as body components can be made of different types (eg polycarbonate, ABS, polypropylene).

25 Damage of a less serious nature (abrasions, minor cracks etc) can be repaired by the DIY owner using a two-part epoxy filler repair material which can be used directly from the tube. Once mixed in equal proportions, this is used in similar fashion to the bodywork filler used on metal panels. The filler is usually cured in twenty to thirty minutes, ready for sanding and painting.

26 If the owner is renewing a complete component himself, or if he has repaired it with epoxy filler, he will be left with the problem of finding a suitable paint for finishing which is compatible with the type of plastic used. At one time, the use of a universal paint was not possible, owing to the complex range of plastics met with in body component applications. Standard paints, generally speaking, will not bond to plastic or rubber satisfactorily, but professional matched paints, to match any plastic or rubber finish, can be obtained from some dealers. However, it is now possible to obtain a plastic body parts finishing kit which consists of a pre-primer treatment, a primer and coloured top coat. Full instructions are normally supplied with a kit, but basically the method of use is to first apply the pre-primer to the component concerned, and allow it to dry for up to 30 minutes. Then the primer is applied, and left to dry for about an hour before finally applying the special-coloured top coat. The result is a correctly coloured component, where the paint will flex with the plastic or rubber, a property that standard paint does not normally posses.

5 Major body damage – repair

Where serious damage has occurred, or large areas need renewal due to neglect, it means that complete new panels will need welding-in, and this is best left to professionals. If the damage is due to impact, it will also be necessary to check completely the alignment of the bodyshell, and this can only be carried out accurately by a BMW dealer using special jigs. If the body is left misaligned, it is primarily dangerous, as the car will not handle properly, and secondly, uneven stresses will be imposed on the steering, suspension and possibly transmission, causing abnormal wear, or complete failure, particularly to such items as the tyres.

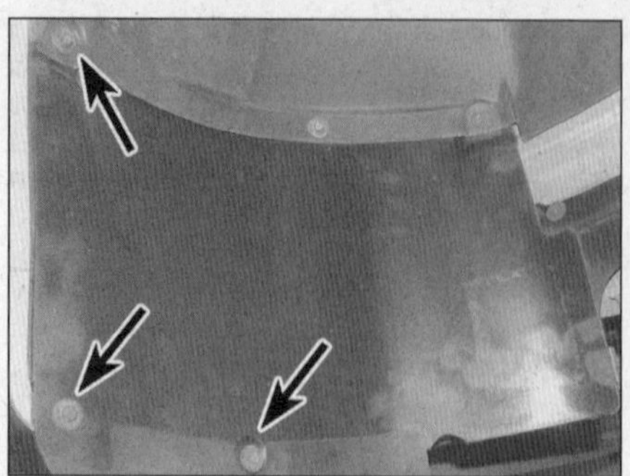

6.1 Undo the three screws (arrowed) securing the bumper to the wheel arch liner

6.2a Lever up the centre pins, then prise out the two plastic rivets (arrowed) . . .

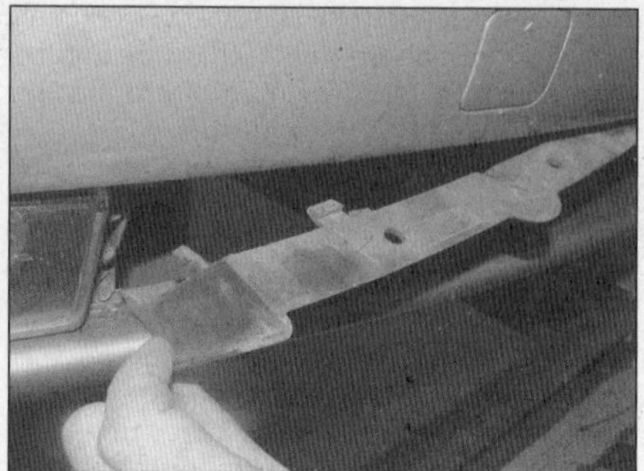

6.2b . . . then remove the plastic grille adjacent to the foglight

6.3 Undo the Torx bolt each side

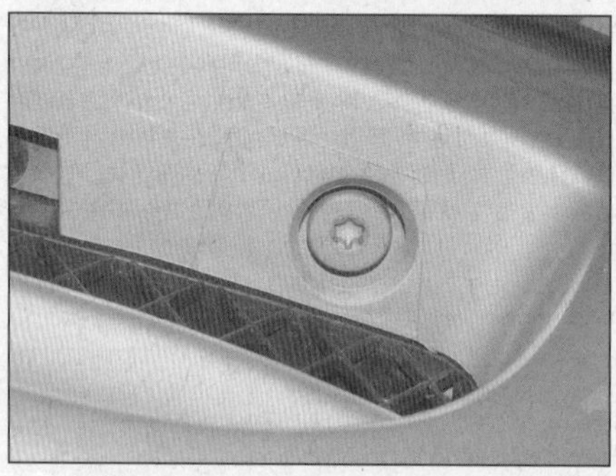

6.8 Bumper Torx bolt – M-sport Aero package models

6 Front bumper – removal and refitting

Removal

Standard models

1 Undo the three screws each side securing the rear edge of the bumper to the wheel arch liner **(see illustration)**.

2 Lever out the centre pins, then prise out the two expansion rivets each side, and remove the plastic grille adjacent to each foglight **(see illustrations)**.

3 Undo the Torx screw each side securing the bumper to the impact absorbers **(see illustration)**.

4 Pull the bumper forward a little, note their fitted locations, and disconnect the various wiring plugs. Where applicable disconnect the headlight washer system hose.

5 Remove the bumper forwards and away from the vehicle.

Models with M-Sport Aero Package

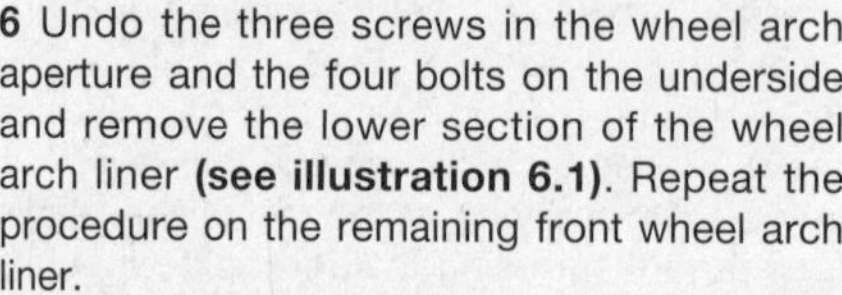

6 Undo the three screws in the wheel arch aperture and the four bolts on the underside and remove the lower section of the wheel arch liner **(see illustration 6.1)**. Repeat the procedure on the remaining front wheel arch liner.

7 Reach up and disconnect the front foglight wiring plugs, and the air temperature sensor (right-hand side liner).

8 Undo the two Torx bolts securing the bumper to the impact absorbers **(see illustration)**.

9 Pull the bumper forward a little, note their fitted locations, and disconnect the parking distance sensor's wiring plugs and headlight washer hoses (where fitted).

10 Pull the bumper forwards and away from the vehicle.

Refitting

11 Refitting is a reverse of the removal procedure, ensuring that the bumper mounting screws are securely tightened. If necessary the height of the bumper can be adjusted by turning the socket head cap screw in the impact absorber mounting.

7 Rear bumper – removal and refitting

Removal

Saloon models

1 Slide out the clips, undo the two screws and remove the mudflaps from both sides **(see illustration)**.

2 Prise out the centre pin and remove the three expanding rivets each side securing the lower edge of the wheel arch liners to the bumper ends **(see illustration)**.

3 On models with Parking Distance Control (PDC), open the luggage compartment right-hand side trim panel, then disconnect the control unit wiring plug, and release the cable from any retaining clips **(see illustration)**.

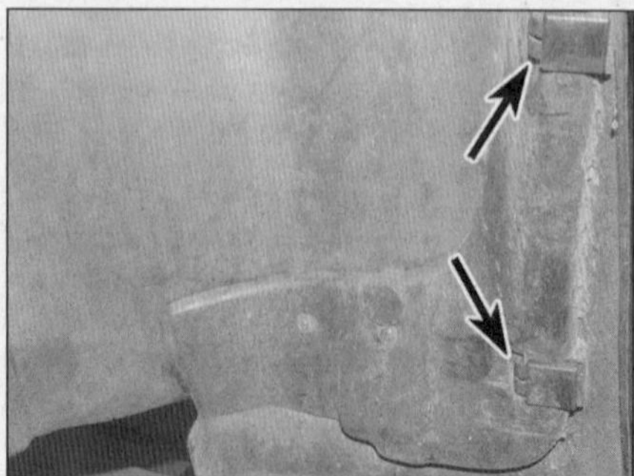

7.1 Slide the metal clips (arrowed) to the centre of the vehicle to release them

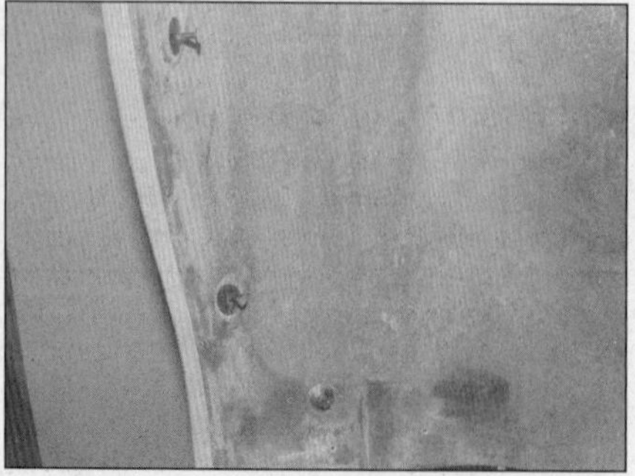

7.2 Prise up the centre pins and remove the three plastic rivets securing the wheel arch liner to the bumper

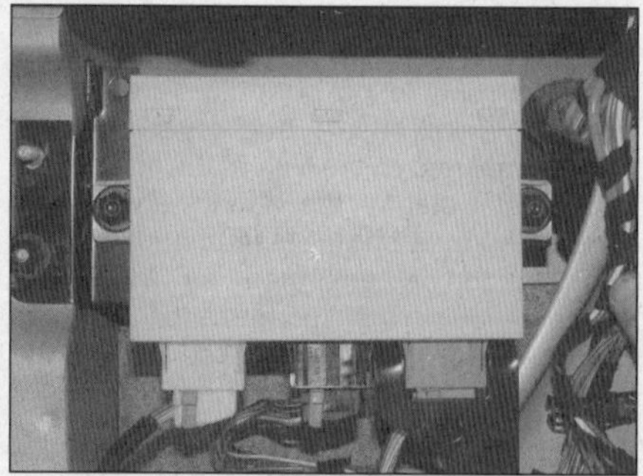

7.3 Disconnect the Parking Distance Control unit wiring plugs – where fitted

7.4 Undo the three nuts each side securing the rear bumper – Saloon models

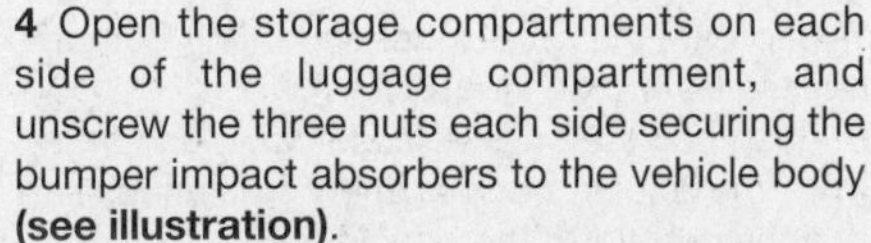

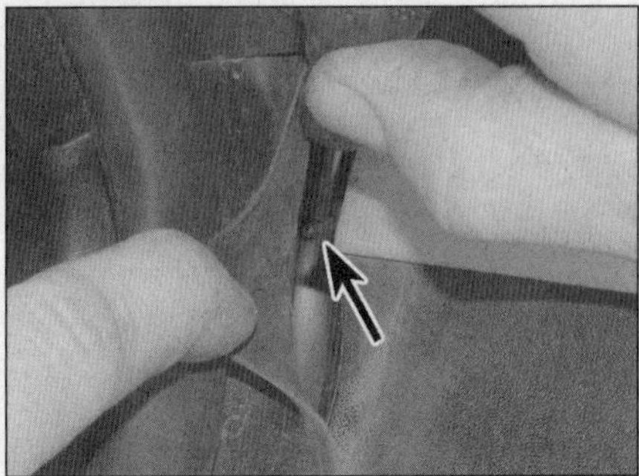

7.6 Pull back the rubber seal, and press down the retaining clip (arrowed) to release the tailgate sill moulding

7.10 Undo the bolt each side securing the bumper to the impact absorber

4 Open the storage compartments on each side of the luggage compartment, and unscrew the three nuts each side securing the bumper impact absorbers to the vehicle body **(see illustration)**.

5 With the help of an assistant, slide the bumper to the rear. On models with PDC, prise out the rubber grommet and pull the cable through the hole as the bumper is removed.

Touring models

6 Open the tailgate, pull back the rubber seal, and press down the two centre section moulding retaining clips using a plastic or wooden tool **(see illustrations)**. Remove the moulding to the rear.

7 Slide out the clips, undo the two screws and remove the mudflaps from both sides **(see illustration 7.1)**.

8 Prise out the centre pin and remove the three expanding rivets each side securing the lower edge of the wheel arch liners to the bumper ends **(see illustration 7.2)**.

9 On models with Parking Distance Control (PDC), open the right-hand luggage compartment trim panel, release the two clips and remove the trim panel, then remove the retaining bolt, and pull the rear edge of the subwoofer speaker (where fitted) in towards the front of the vehicle. Disconnect the PDC control unit wiring plug, and release the cable from any retaining clips **(see illustration 7.3)**.

10 Undo the bolt each side securing the bumper to the impact absorbers **(see illustration)**.

11 With the help of an assistant, slide the bumper to the rear. On models with PDC, prise out the rubber grommet and pull the cable through the hole as the bumper is removed.

Refitting

12 Refitting is a reverse of the removal procedure, ensuring that the front of the bumper engages correctly with the plastic guides, and the mounting bolts/nuts are tightened securely.

8 Bonnet and support struts – removal, refitting and adjustment

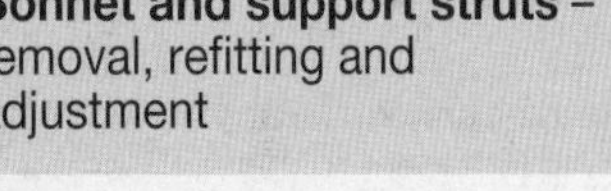

Bonnet

Removal

1 Open the bonnet and have an assistant support it. Using a pencil or felt tip pen, mark the outline of each bonnet hinge relative to the bonnet, to use as a guide on refitting.

2 Lift up the base of the bonnet insulation panel, and disconnect the hose from the washer jets. On models with heated jets also disconnect the wiring connectors **(see illustrations)**. Tie a length of string to the end of the wiring loom and washer hose, then pull the harness/hose from the bonnet channel. Free the harness/hose from any retaining clips. As the harness/hose is pulled from the bonnet channel, untie the string and leave it in place to aid refitment.

3 With the aid of an assistant, support the bonnet in the open position then slacken and remove the left and right-hand hinge-to-bonnet bolts **(see illustration)**. Remove the bonnet.

4 Inspect the bonnet hinges for signs of wear and free play at the pivots, and if necessary renew. Each hinge is secured to the body by two bolts. Mark the position of the hinge on the body then undo the retaining bolts and remove it from the vehicle. On refitting, align the new hinge with the marks and securely tighten the retaining bolts.

Refitting and adjustment

5 With the aid of an assistant, position the bonnet against the hinges. Refit the bolts and tighten them by hand only. Align the hinges with the marks made on removal, then tighten the retaining bolts securely.

6 Close the bonnet, and check for alignment with the adjacent panels. If necessary, slacken the hinge bolts and re-align the bonnet to suit. Once the bonnet is correctly aligned, securely tighten the hinge bolts, and check that the bonnet fastens and releases satisfactorily. Tie the wiring harness/hose to the end of the string and pull them through the bonnet channel to their original positions. Reconnect the hose and wiring.

Support struts

7 Open the bonnet and have an assistant support it. Prise out the retaining clips at the

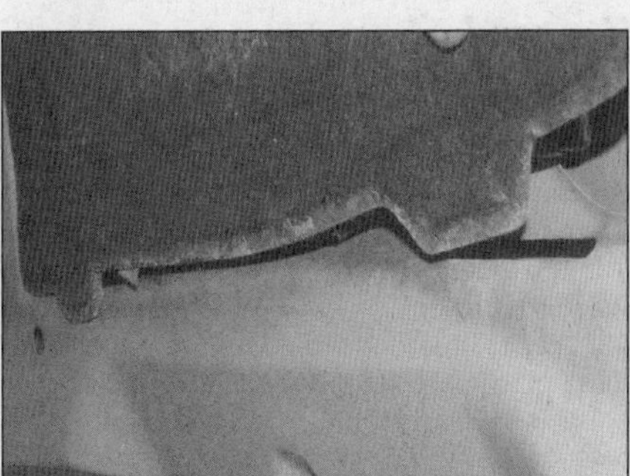

8.2a Lift up the bonnet insulation panel . . .

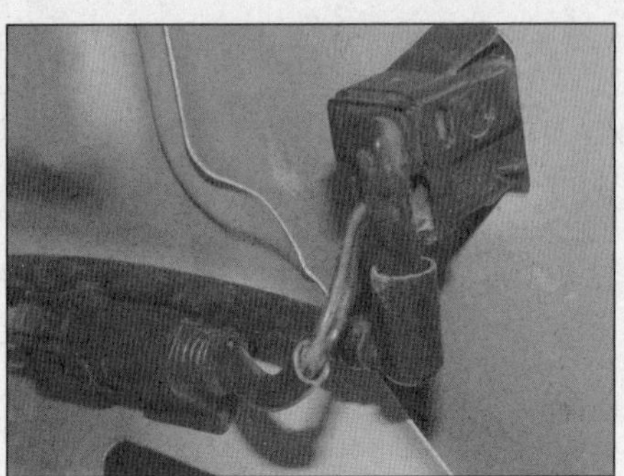

8.2b . . . and disconnect the washer jet hoses and wiring plugs

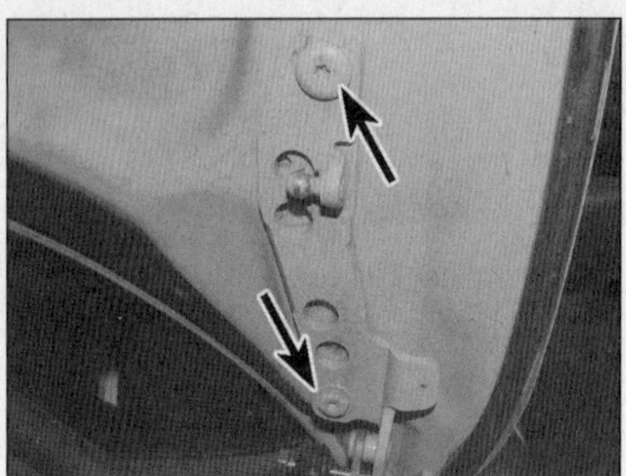

8.3 Undo the bonnet-to-hinge bolts (arrowed)

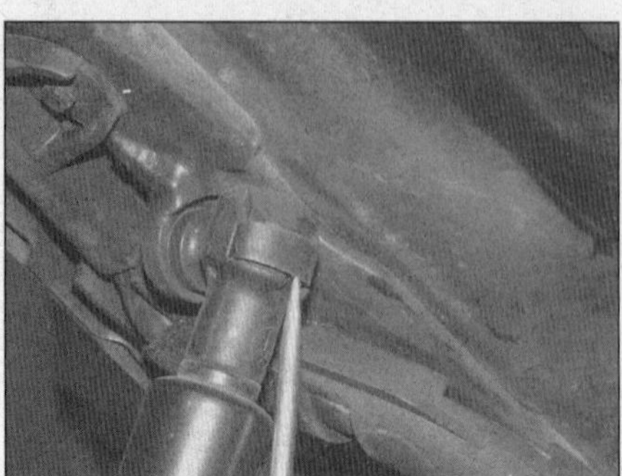
8.7 Prise out the bonnet support strut clip

8.8 Fully open the bonnet and lock it in place using two 8 mm bolts through the hinge linkage

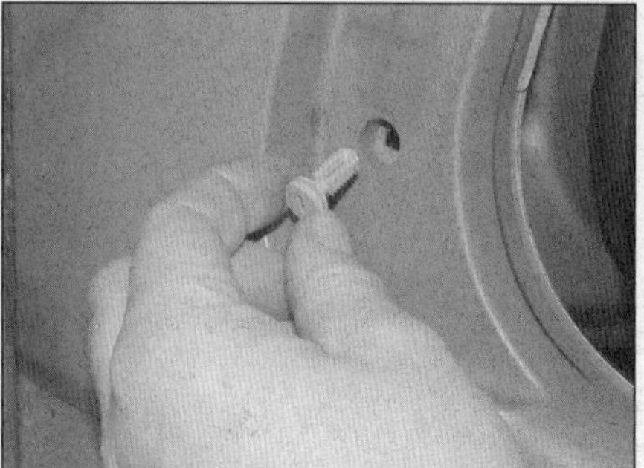
9.6 Undo the screw and remove the footwell kick panel

9.7 Detach the inner cable from the release lever

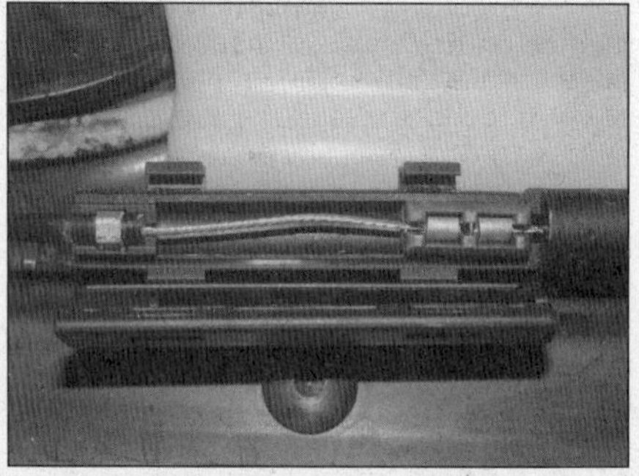
9.9 Disconnect the inner and outer cables from the connection housing

top and bottom of the struts **(see illustration)**.

8 Pull the struts from the mounting balljoints, then either close the bonnet, or raise the bonnet fully, and insert a suitable 8 mm bolt through the hinge each side, to lock it in the 'service position' **(see illustration)**.

9 Refitting is a reversal of removal.

9 Bonnet release cable – removal and refitting

Removal

1 The bonnet release cable is in three sections, the main first cable from the release lever to the connection at the right-hand side inner wing (adjacent to the windscreen washer reservoir), the second from the connection to the right-hand bonnet lock, and one linking the two bonnet locks.

Release lever-to-connection cable

2 Open the driver's door, and carefully pull up the door sill trim panel.

3 Pull up the rubber weatherstrip from the door aperture adjacent to the footwell kick panel.

4 Undo the fasteners and remove the lower facia panel above the pedals. Disconnect any wiring plugs as the panel is withdrawn.

5 Undo the screw and remove the bonnet release lever.

6 Undo the screw and remove the footwell kick panel **(see illustration)**.

7 Separate the cable inner end fitting from the release lever **(see illustration)**.

8 Push/pull the outer release cable end fitting from the engine compartment bulkhead, and pull the cable into the engine compartment.

9 Unclip the connection housing from the inner wing. Prise open the connection housing and disconnect the inner and outer cables **(see illustration)**.

Connection-to-bonnet lock cable

10 Unclip the connection housing from the inner wing. Prise open the housing and disconnect the inner and outer cables **(see illustration 9.9)**

11 Remove the driver's side bonnet lock as described in Section 10.

Lock linking cable

12 The linking cable is removed as part of the bonnet lock removal procedure, as described in Section 10.

Refitting

13 Refitting is the reverse of removal ensuring that the cable is correctly routed, and secured to all the relevant retaining clips. Check that the bonnet locks operate correctly before closing the bonnet.

10 Bonnet lock(s) – removal and refitting

Removal

1 Remove the front bumper as described in Section 6.

2 Remove both front headlights as described in Chapter 12, Section 7.

3 Undo the three bolts and remove the air intake ducting from the plastic front panel **(see illustration)**.

4 Push in the centre pins and prise out the three plastic clips at the top of the plastic front panel **(see illustration)**.

5 Undo the three screws, release the wiring loom from its clips and remove the plastic front panel downwards.

6 The bonnet locks are secured by three Torx

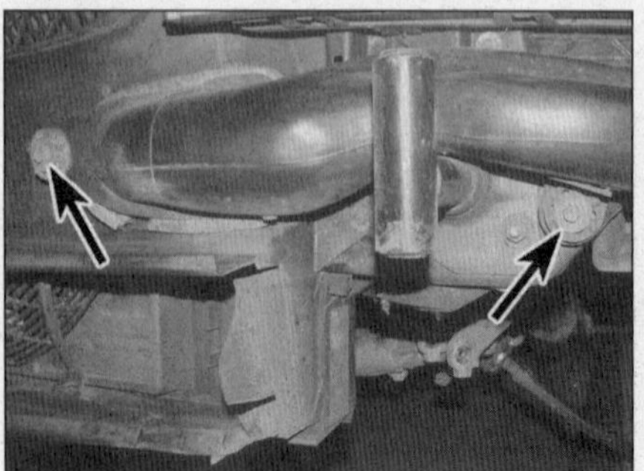
10.3 Undo the three air duct retaining bolts (two inner bolts arrowed)

10.4 Push in the centre pins and prise out the three plastic rivets (arrowed)

10.6 Bonnet lock screws

11.2 Press-in the clip and drive the check strap pin upwards

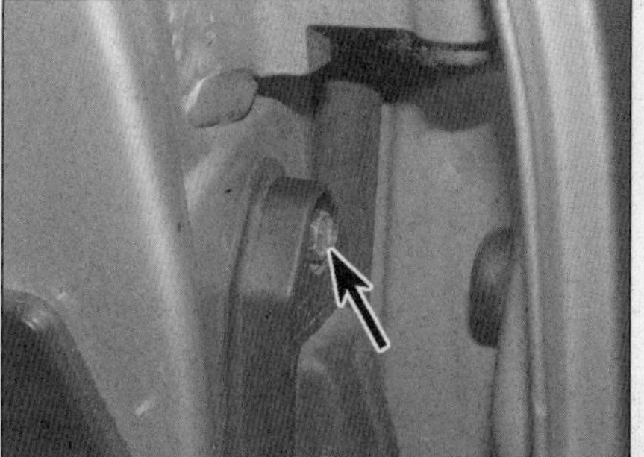

11.3 Undo the bolt (arrowed) and pull the connector from the pillar

screws **(see illustration)**. Undo the three Torx screws, slide the lock(s) to the centre and disconnect the bonnet release cable(s) from the lever.

Refitting

7 Refitting is a reversal of removal.

11 Door – removal, refitting and adjustment

Removal

1 Disconnect the battery negative terminal (see Chapter 5A). This is essential, as all 5-Series models covered by this manual have front door airbags as standard, with rear door side airbags available as an option. Wait at least 1 minute after disconnecting the battery before disconnecting the loom wiring plug (paragraph 4).

2 Peel back the rubber boot, then depress the retaining tang, and drive the check strap pin upwards **(see illustration)**.

3 Undo the bolt securing the door wiring loom connector to the pillar **(see illustration)**.

4 Withdraw the door wiring connector from the pillar, pull out the locking element and unplug the connector **(see illustration)**.

5 Mark the position of the hinge in relation to the door, and undo the retaining nuts **(see illustration)**.

6 Remove the door from the vehicle.

11.4 Slide up the locking catch and disconnect the wiring plug

11.5 Undo the hinge retaining nuts

Refitting

7 Manoeuvre the door into position and reconnect the wiring plug. Push the connector into the pillar and secure it in place with the bolts.

8 Engage the hinges with the studs on the door, and tighten the bolts securely. Note that if necessary, the position of the door can be adjusted by inserting or removing shims between the hinge and the door (available from BMW dealers).

9 Align the check link with the pillar, refit the pin and retaining clip.

Adjustment

10 Always adjust the rear doors first. Close the door and check the door alignment with surrounding body panels. If necessary, slight adjustment of the door position can be made by slackening the hinge retaining nuts and repositioning the hinge/door as necessary. Once the door is correctly positioned, securely tighten the hinge nuts. If the paintwork around the hinges has been damaged, paint the affected area with a suitable touch-in brush to prevent corrosion.

12 Door inner trim panel – removal and refitting

Removal – front door

1 Disconnect the battery negative terminal (see Chapter 5A). This is essential, as all 5-Series models covered by this manual have front door airbags as standard. Wait at least 1 minute after disconnecting the battery before commencing work.

2 Undo the screw in the air duct at the front of the door **(see illustration)**.

3 Prise out the sill light from the case of the trim, and disconnect the wiring plug.

4 On models with memory seats, carefully prise out the switch and disconnect the wiring plug.

5 Using a thick feeler gauge blade or similar, depress the window switch panel retaining clips and the four points shown, as the panel is gently pulled up. Once all four clips are released, remove the panel and disconnect the switch wiring plugs as the switch is withdrawn **(see illustrations)**.

12.2 Undo the screw in the air vent (arrowed)

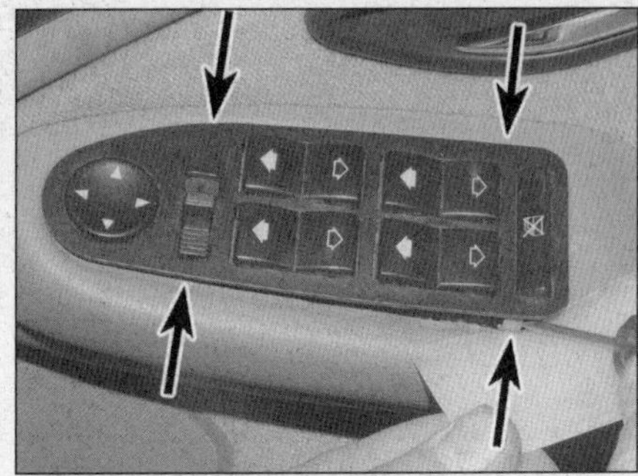

12.5a Press-in the clips at the four points shown

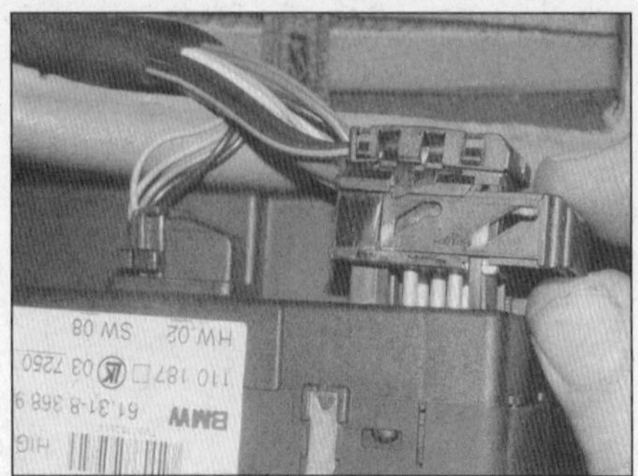

12.5b Slide out the locking catch and disconnect the wiring plug

6 Prise our the cover cap in the interior door handle aperture, and undo the screw **(see illustration)**.

7 Release the door trim panel clips, carefully levering between the panel and door with a flat-bladed screwdriver. Work around the outside of the panel, and when all the studs are released, lift the panel, and slide the interior door handle through the aperture in the panel **(see illustration)**. Note that the clip behind the door grab handle may have to be removed from the door frame and refitted to the trim panel prior to refitment **(see illustration)**.

8 Feed the wiring plugs through as the panel is withdrawn.

9 Remove the door airbag module as described in Chapter 12.

10 On models manufactured up to 03/01, unhook the cable from the interior door handle. On vehicles from 03/01, lever out the locking lever and unclip the cable from the interior handle (see Section 13).

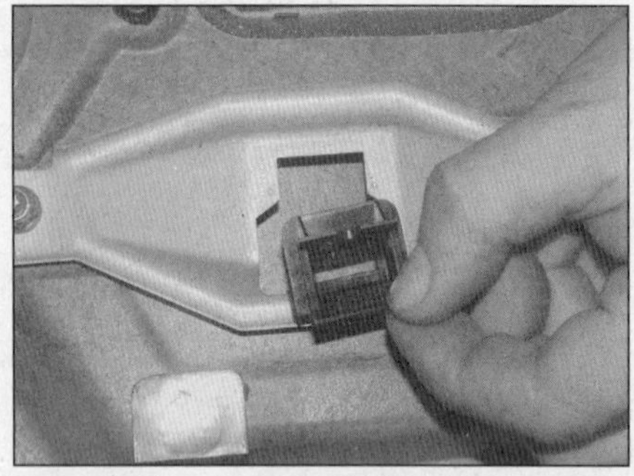

12.7b The clip behind the grab handle may have to be removed from the door frame and fitted to the panel before refitting

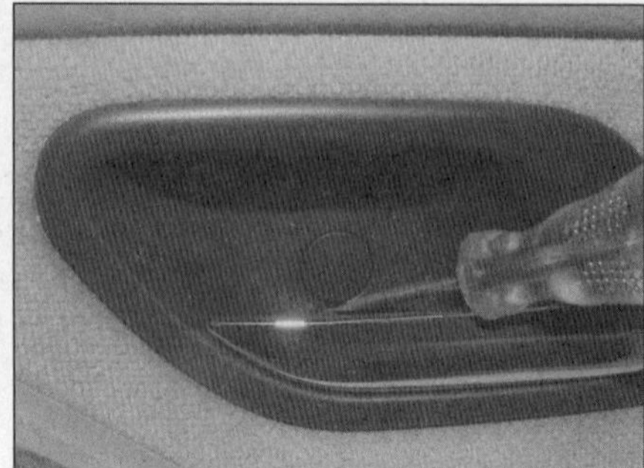

12.6 Prise out the plastic cap and undo the screw

11 Undo the three screws securing the speaker unit, and disconnect the wiring plugs as the unit is withdrawn **(see illustration)**.

12 If required, carefully prise the sound insulation panel away from the door, using a flat-bladed tool to cut through the sealant.

Removal – rear door

13 Disconnect the battery negative terminal then open the door (see Chapter 5A). This is essential on models with rear side door airbags. Wait at least 1 minute after disconnecting the battery before commencing work.

14 Carefully prise out the sill light from the base of the panel, and disconnect the wiring plug.

15 On models with manual windows, carefully prise out the plastic cover from the window winder handle. Undo the retaining screw and remove the handle complete with circular bezel.

16 On models with electric windows, using a small flat-bladed screwdriver, carefully lever out the window switch from the armrest. Use a piece of cardboard under the screwdriver to prevent damage to the armrest. Disconnect the switch wiring plug as it is removed **(see illustration)**.

17 Prise out the cover cap in the interior door handle aperture, and undo the screw **(see illustration 12.6)**.

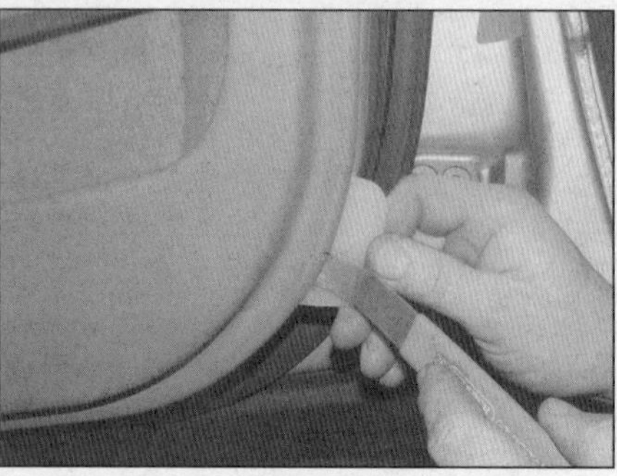

12.7a Carefully lever between the panel and the door to release the clips. Use a piece of plastic or cardboard to protect the paintwork

Models with sun roller blind

18 Unhook the blind at the top, then pull it towards the inside of the cabin, and upwards to remove it.

19 Starting at the rear of the trim, using a trim clip releasing tool or flat-bladed screwdriver, carefully prise the decorative trim from the door panel **(see illustration)**.

20 Undo the two screws securing the panel to the door.

All models

21 Release the door trim panel clips, carefully levering between the panel and door with a flat-bladed screwdriver. Work around the outside of the panel and, when all the studs are released, pull the top of the panel out, lift the panel, and slide the interior door handle through the aperture in the panel **(see illustration 12.7a)**.

22 If fitted, remove the door airbag as described in Chapter 12.

23 Unhook the cable from the interior door handle.

24 If required, carefully prise the sound insulation panel away from the door, using a flat-bladed tool to cut through the sealant.

Refitting

25 Refitting of the trim panel is the reverse of removal. Before refitting, check whether any of the trim panel retaining clips were broken on removal, and renew them as necessary. Ensure that, where removed, the sound

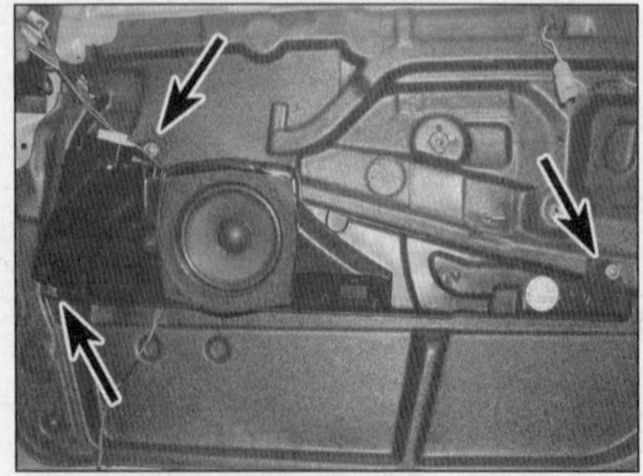

12.11 Undo the three door speaker screws (arrowed)

12.16 Prise the switch from the handle. Use a piece of cardboard or similar to protect the trim surface

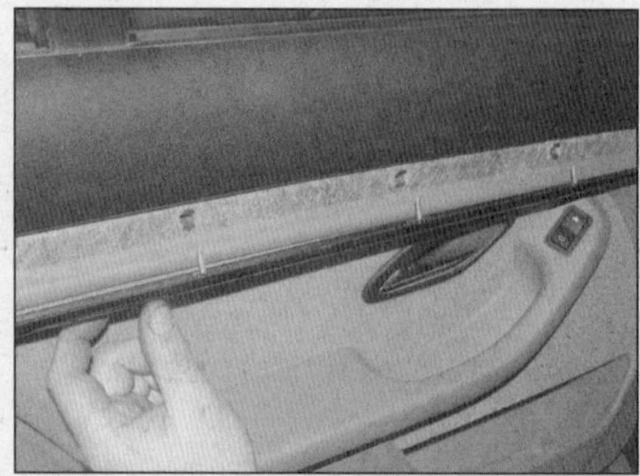

12.19 Prise the decorative trim from the door panel

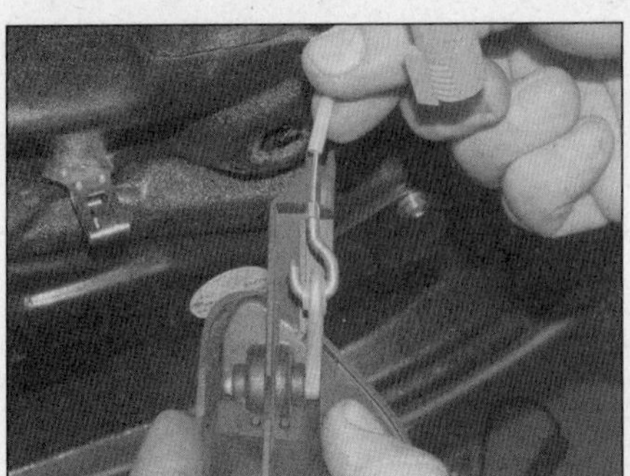
13.2 Pull the outer cable from the guide and unhook it from the lever – models up to 03/01

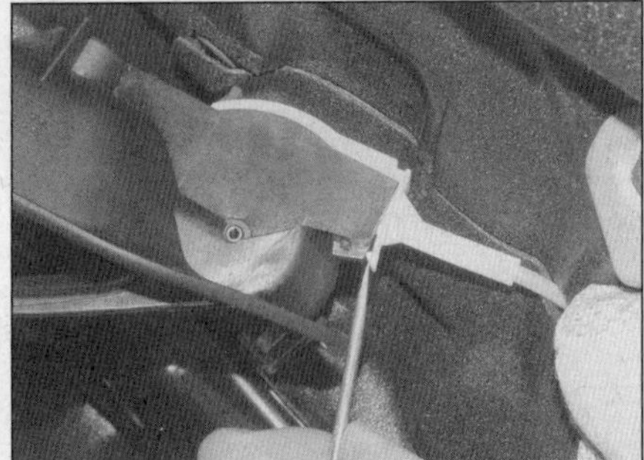
13.3a Prise out the cable 'lock' . . .

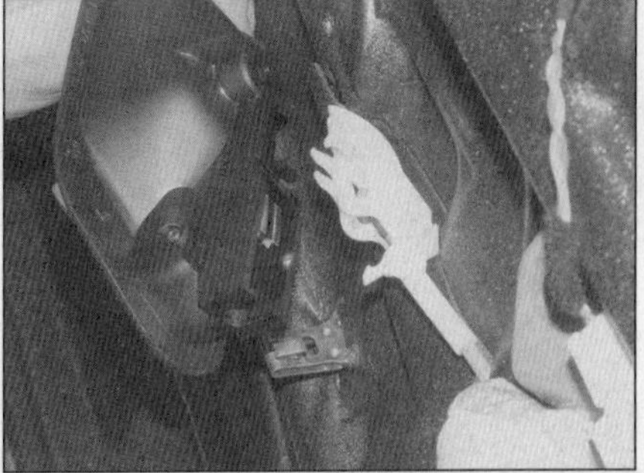
13.3b . . . and detach the cable end fitting from the handle

insulation panel is sealed into its original location. If the sound insulation panel is damaged on removal it must be renewed.

13 Door handle and lock components – removal and refitting

Removal

Interior door handle

1 Remove the door inner trim panel as described in Section 12.

2 On vehicles manufactured up to 03/01, pull the cable from the guide bracket and unhook it from the lever **(see illustration)**.

3 On vehicles manufactured after 03/01, pull the interior door handle to the 'open' position, prise out the cable lock, and detach the cable to the rear of the assembly **(see illustrations)**.

Front door lock assembly

4 Ensure the front door windows are closed, but fully open the rear door windows. Disconnect the battery negative lead as described in Chapter 5A.

5 Remove the door inner trim panel, and sound insulation panel as described in Section 12.

6 Remove the exterior door handle as described in this Section.

7 By pulling downwards and backwards, disconnect the lock wiring plug **(see illustration)**.

8 Disconnect the operating cable from the door lock.

9 Disconnect the micro-switch wiring plug from the door lock **(see illustration)**.

10 Release the operating cable from the retaining clip on the door frame **(see illustration)**.

11 Undo the three Torx screws, and manoeuvre the door lock downwards and out from the door **(see illustration)**.

12 If required, the lock drive unit can be removed by levering out the locking unit and pulling the drive unit from the lock **(see illustration)**.

13 If required, undo the two screws, remove the retaining plate, and lift out the micro-switch **(see illustration)**.

Front door exterior handle

14 Remove the door lock assembly as previously described.

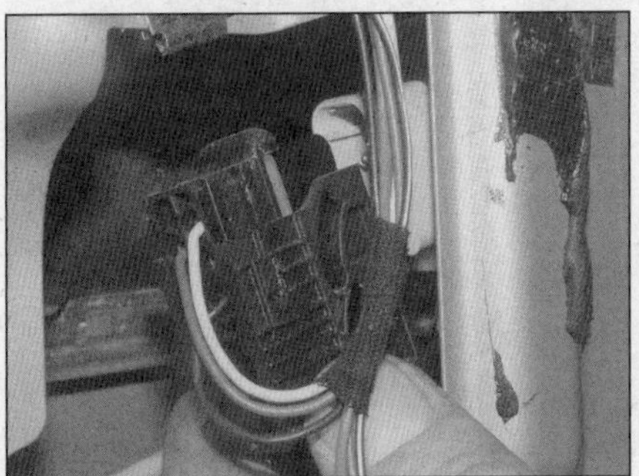
13.7 Disconnect the lock wiring plug

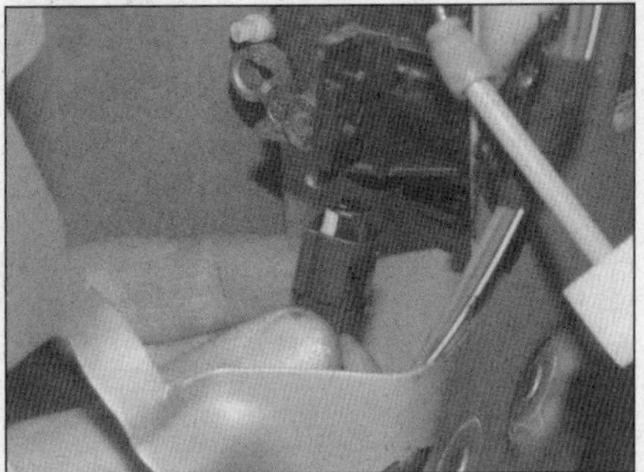
13.9 Disconnect the micro-switch wiring plug

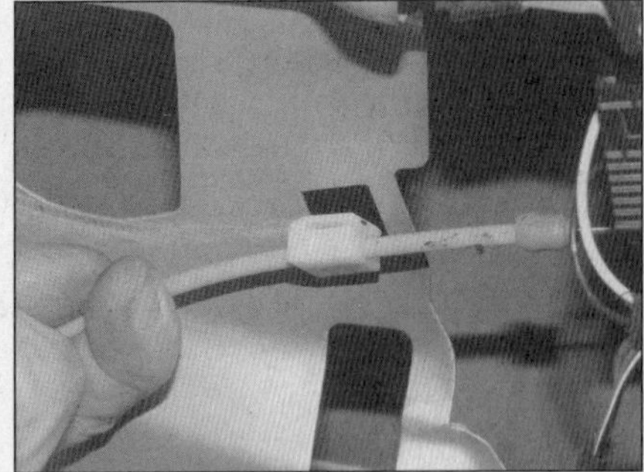
13.10 Release the cable retaining clip from the door frame

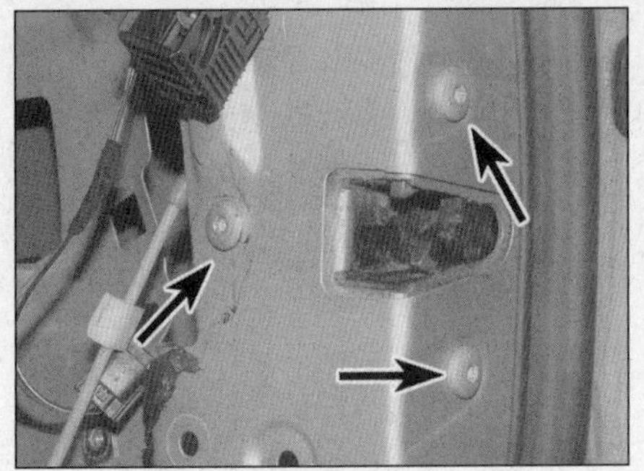
13.11 Undo the three Torx screws (arrowed)

13.12 Lever up the locking clip and pull the drive unit from the lock

13.13 Undo the two screws, remove the plate and lift out the micro-switch

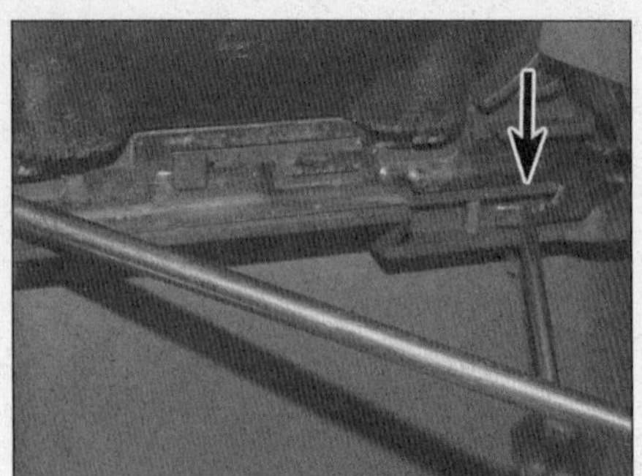
13.15 Lift the retaining tab (arrowed) over the retaining lug and push the plate forwards at the same time

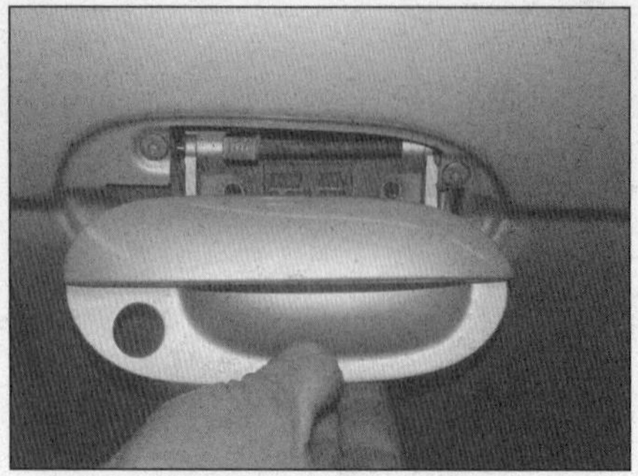
13.16 Pull the lower edge of the handle outwards, then lower it

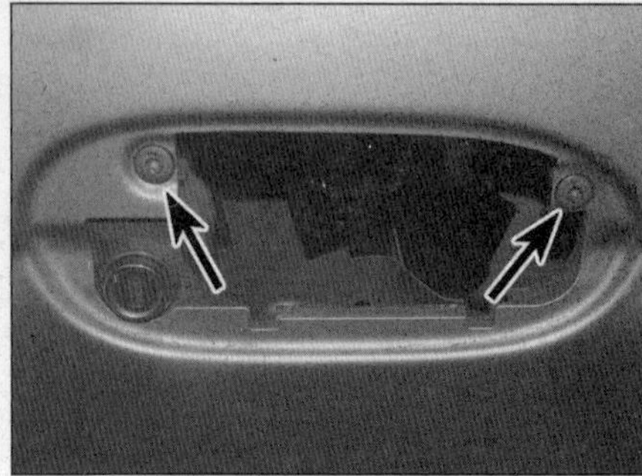
13.18 Undo the two Torx screws (arrowed)

15 Using two small screwdrivers, lever the retaining tab on the locking plate over the retaining lug and push the plate forwards at the same time **(see illustration)**.

16 Pull the lower edge of the exterior handle assembly outwards, and downwards to remove it from the door **(see illustration)**.

Front door lock cylinder

17 Remove the door lock, and exterior handle assembly as described in this Section.

18 Undo the two Torx screws, and manoeuvre the exterior door handle carrier, complete with lock cylinder, from the door **(see illustration)**.

19 Insert a flat-bladed screwdriver into the slot and prise the plastic cover from the lock cylinder **(see illustration)**.

20 No further dismantling is recommended. At the time of writing, the lock cylinder is only available as an assembly with the exterior handle carrier. Check with your local BMW dealer.

Rear door lock

21 Close the rear door windows, and open the front door windows. Disconnect the battery negative lead as described in Chapter 5A.

22 Remove the door inner trim panel and sound insulation material as described in Section 12.

23 Slacken and remove the lock assembly retaining Torx screws **(see illustration)**.

24 Disconnect the two operating cables from the lock assembly **(see illustrations)**.

25 Slide out the locking catch and disconnect the wiring plug from the door lock. Manoeuvre the lock from the door.

26 If required, prise up the locking catch and pull the drive unit from the lock assembly **(see illustration)**.

Rear door exterior handle

27 Prise out the grommet in the door end panel, and using a sharp knife, remove the foam tape (where fitted) visible in the exposed aperture **(see illustration)**.

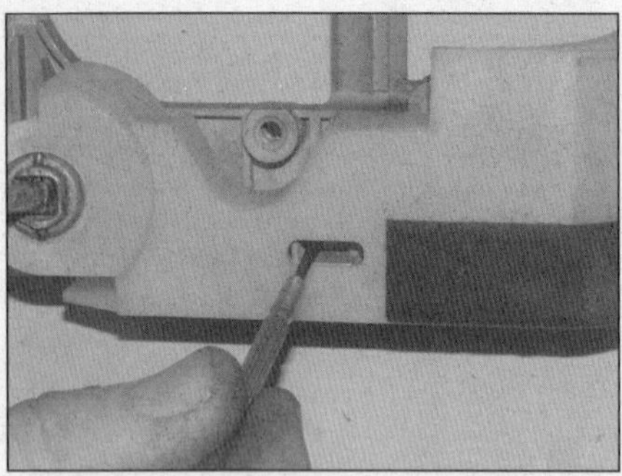
13.19 Insert a flat-bladed screwdriver to release the plastic cover

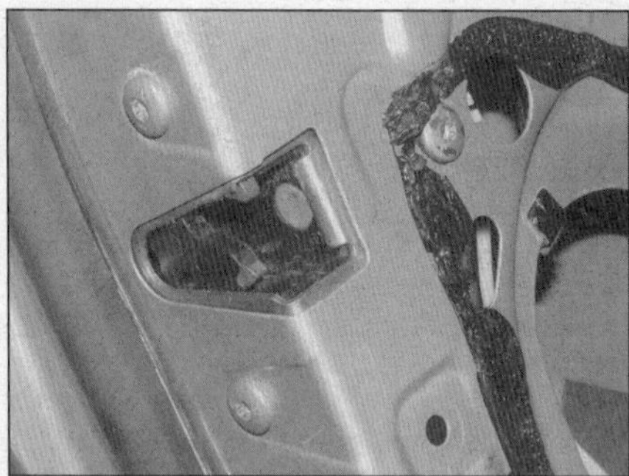
13.23 Undo the three Torx screws

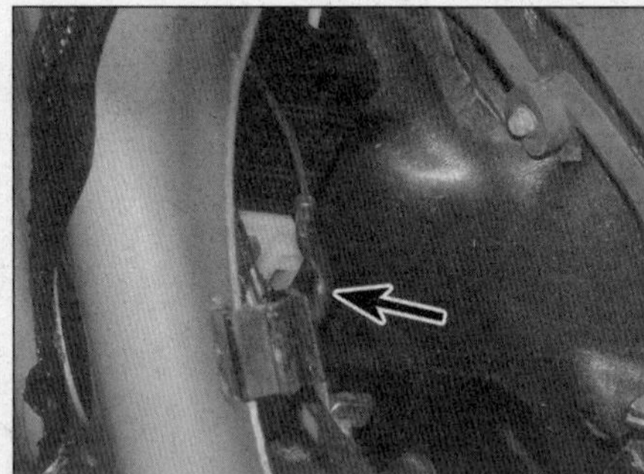
13.24a Disconnect the cable from the interior handle (arrowed) . . .

13.24b . . . and the cable from the exterior handle

13.26 Prise up the catch and remove the drive unit

13.27 Prise out the grommet in the end of the door

13.28 Lift the lock plate retaining clip (arrowed) and push the locking plate forward

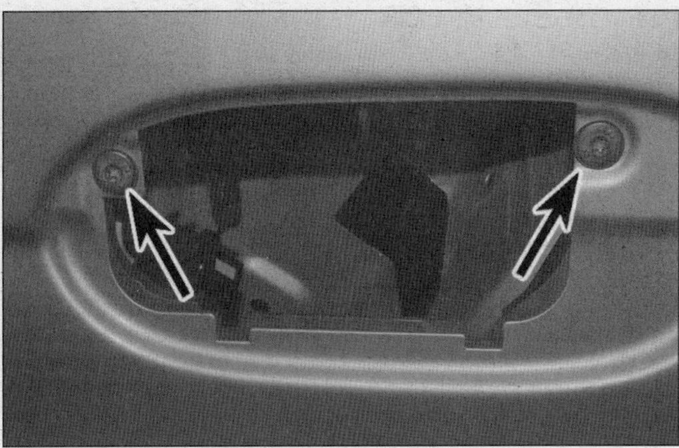

13.32 Undo the two Torx screws (arrowed)

28 Insert a small, flat-bladed screwdriver into the aperture, lift the locking plate retaining clip then, using a second screwdriver, carefully push the locking plate forwards **(see illustration)**. Remove both screwdrivers.

29 Pull the lower edge of the exterior handle assembly outwards, and downwards, and remove it from the door.

Rear door exterior handle carrier/operating cable

30 Remove the door inner trim panel as described in Section 12.

31 Remove the exterior handle as described in this Section.

32 Unscrew the two retaining screws, and remove the exterior handle carrier complete with the operating cable **(see illustration)**.

33 If required, release the retaining clip and disconnect the operating cable from the carrier **(see illustration)**.

Refitting

Interior door handle

34 On vehicles manufactured up to 03/01, hook the inner cable into the handle lever, position the cable into the support bracket groove, and push the outer cable into place.

35 On vehicles manufactured after 03/01, engage the inner cable with the release handle (handle closed), and press the cable lock into place.

Front door lock assembly

36 If removed, refit the micro-switch to the lock assembly, position the retaining plate and tighten the screws securely.

37 If removed, refit the lock drive unit, and secure in place with the locking unit.

38 Prior to refitting the lock, ensure the plastic guide for the lock cylinder shaft is located in the centre at the base of the aperture **(see illustration)**.

39 Manoeuvre the lock into position, ensuring the lock cylinder shaft engages correctly, and tighten the retaining screws securely.

40 Clip the operating cable into place on the door frame.

41 Reconnect the micro-switch wiring plug.

42 Reconnect the operating cable to the door lock.

43 The remainder of refitting is a reversal of removal, but do **not** close the door until you are completely satisfied that the lock is working correctly. If the door is accidentally closed, it may not be possible to open the door without cutting the door outer skin.

Front door exterior handle

44 Manoeuvre the handle assembly into position in the door then, using a screwdriver, slide the locking plate backwards until the retaining clip engages **(see illustration)**.

45 The remainder of refitting is a reversal of removal, but do **not** close the door until you are completely satisfied that the lock is working correctly. If the door is accidentally closed, it may not be possible to open the door without cutting the door outer skin.

Front door lock cylinder

46 If separated, clip the plastic cover back onto the cylinder.

47 Manoeuvre the exterior handle carrier assembly into position, and securely tighten the two retaining screws.

48 The remainder of refitting is a reversal of removal, but do **not** close the door until you are completely satisfied that the lock is working correctly. If the door is accidentally closed, it may not be possible to open the door without cutting the door outer skin.

Rear door lock

49 If removed, refit the drive unit to the lock assembly, ensuring the locking catch engages correctly.

50 Reconnect the lock wiring plug.

51 Reconnect the lock operating cables.

52 Manoeuvre the lock into position, and tighten the Torx screws securely.

53 The remainder of refitting is a reversal of removal, but do **not** close the door until you are completely satisfied that the lock is working correctly. If the door is accidentally closed, it may not be possible to open the door without cutting the door outer skin.

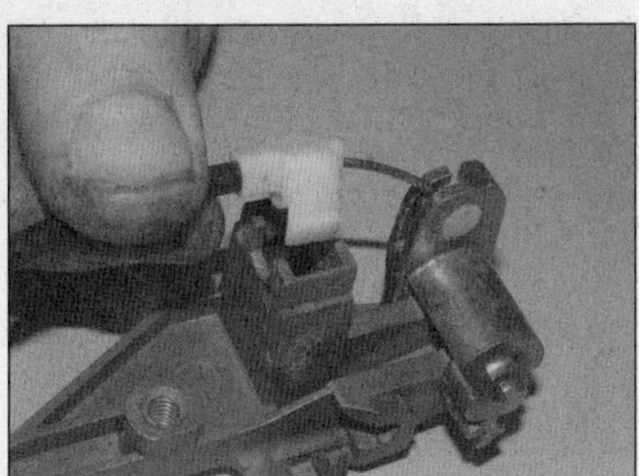

13.33 Disconnect the operating cable from the carrier

13.38 Position the plastic guide for the lock cylinder shaft as shown

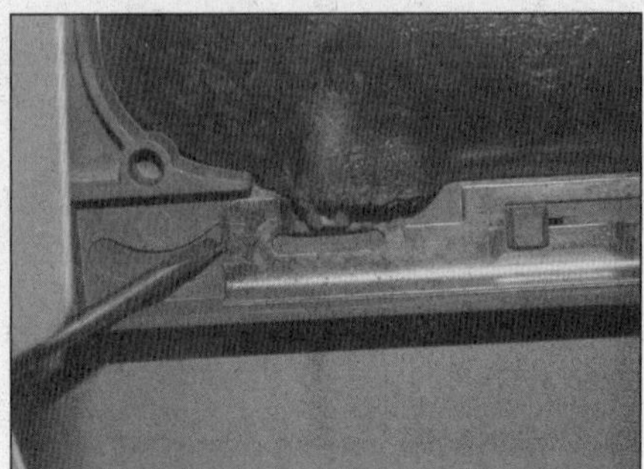

13.44 Use a screwdriver to slide the locking plate backwards

Rear door exterior handle

54 Manoeuvre the handle into position, and using a small flat-bladed screwdriver through the aperture in the rear edge of the door, carefully slide the retaining plate backwards until the retaining clip can be heard to audibly 'click' into place. Refit the rubber grommet.

Rear door exterior handle carrier/operating cable

55 If removed, reconnect the operating cable to the carrier.

56 Manoeuvre the assembly into position, and tighten the retaining screws securely.

57 The remainder of refitting is a reversal of removal, but do **not** close the door until you are completely satisfied that the lock is working correctly. If the door is accidentally closed, it may not be possible to open the door without cutting the door outer skin.

14 Door glass and regulator – removal and refitting

Removal

Front door window

1 Fully lower the window.

2 Remove the door inner trim panel and sound insulation panel as described in Section 12.

3 Apply a length of insulation tape to the top edge of the door outer panel to prevent paintwork damage, then using a plastic or wooden spatula, carefully prise up the door-to-window exterior trim **(see illustration)**.

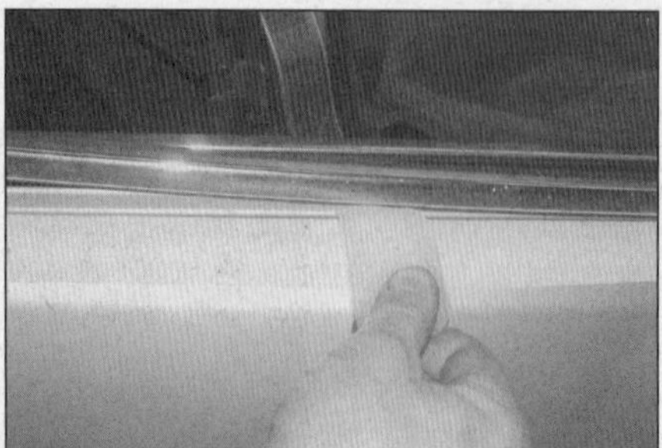

14.3 Carefully prise up the door-to-window exterior trim

4 Slacken the window clamping screws, lift the rear of the window, and manoeuvre it from the door **(see illustration)**.

Front door window regulator

5 Release the door window from the regulator clamps, as described earlier in this Section. Note that there is no need to remove the window from the door, simply use adhesive tape, or rubber wedges, to secure the window in the fully closed position.

6 Disconnect the window regulator wiring plug, and release the plastic guide **(see illustration)**.

7 The regulator is retained by six bolts. Remove the three upper bolts, but only slacken the lower three bolts **(see illustration)**. Manoeuvre the regulator from the door. At the time of writing, it would appear that the electric motor is integral with the regulator, and must be renewd as an assembly. Check with your BMW dealer or specialist.

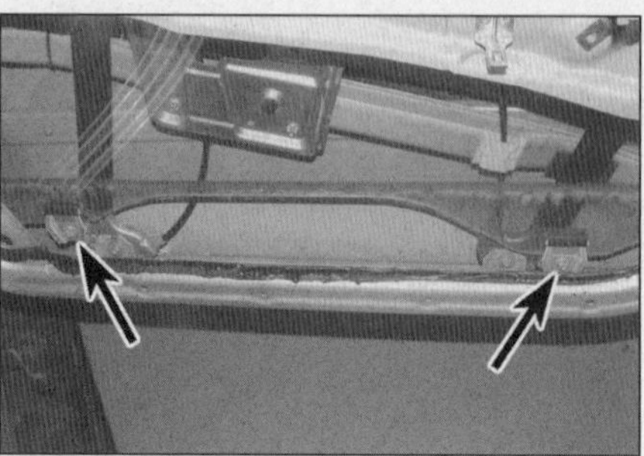

14.4 Slacken the window clamping screws (arrowed)

Rear door window

8 Lower the window completely, then disconnect the battery negative lead as described in Chapter 5A.

9 Apply a length of insulation tape to the top edge of the door outer panel to prevent paintwork damage, then using a plastic or wooden spatula, carefully prise up the door-to-window exterior trim **(see illustration 14.3)**.

10 Remove the door inner trim panel and sound insulation panel as described in Section 12.

11 Using a wide, flat-bladed tool, carefully lever up the window inner sealing strip **(see illustration)**.

12 Carefully lever the fixed-glass cover strip inwards and remove it **(see illustration)**.

13 Prise out the rubber guide, then undo the three screws and remove the fixed-glass guide upwards from the door **(see illustrations)**.

14.6 Release the plastic guide from the door frame

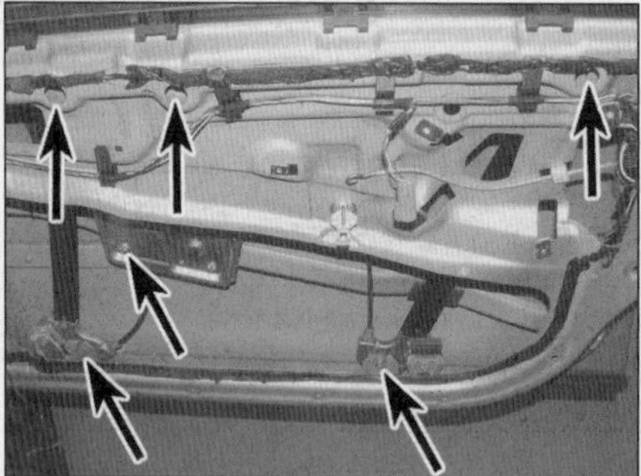

14.7 Window regulator bolts (arrowed)

14.11 Prise up the window inner sealing strip

14.12 Remove the fixed-glass cover strip

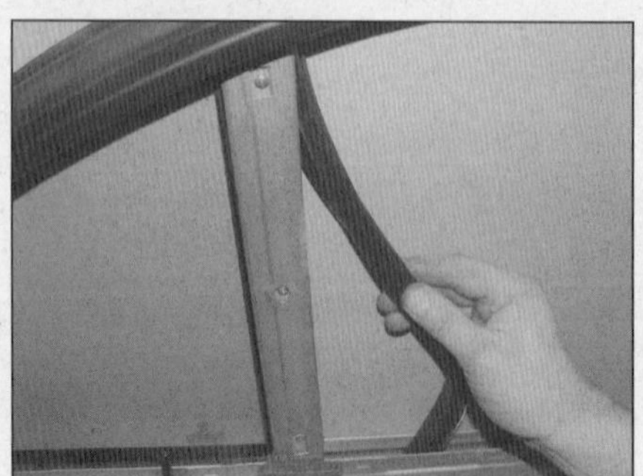

14.13a Prise out the rubber guide . . .

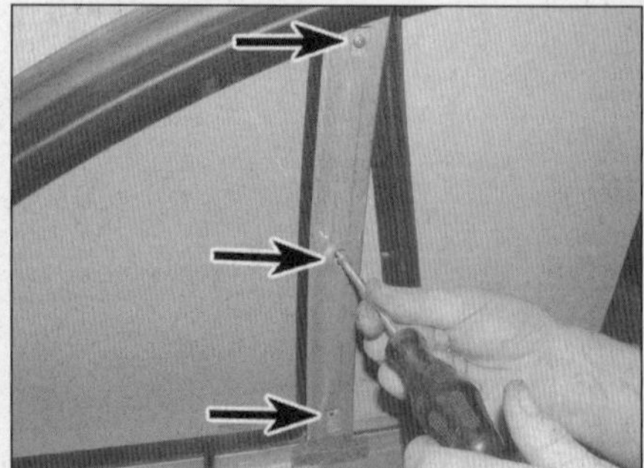

14.13b . . . then undo the three guide retaining screws (arrowed)

14.14a Undo the window clamp screw (arrowed) . . .

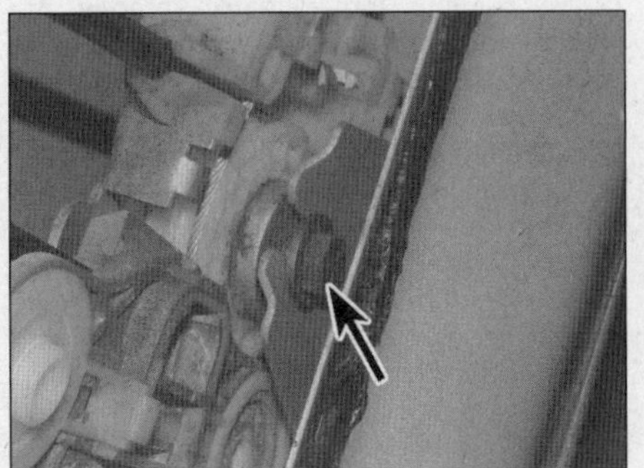

14.18 Slacken the regulator lower mounting screw (arrowed)

14 Remove the retaining screw and washer, the lift the rear window from the door **(see illustrations)**.

Rear door fixed window glass

15 As the rear door fixed window is bonded in place, renewal of the window should be entrusted to a BMW dealer or automotive window specialist.

Rear door window regulator

16 Remove the rear window as described in this Section.

17 Peel back the sealing strip and remove the regulator upper retaining screw **(see illustration)**.

18 Slacken the bolt, and lift the lower end of the regulator from the door **(see illustration)**.

19 Disconnect the electric motor wiring plug.

20 Undo the four retaining screws, and remove the regulator and motor assembly from the door **(see illustration)**.

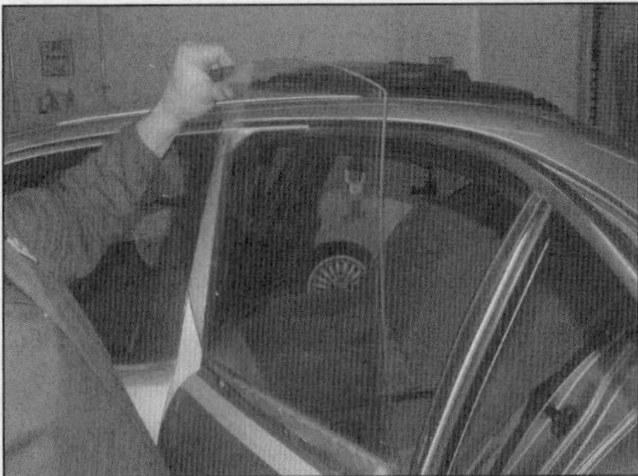

14.14b . . . and remove the window from the door

14.20 Undo the four regulator retaining screws

21 At the time of writing, it would appear that the electric motor is integral with the regulator, and must be renewed as an assembly. Check with your BMW dealer or specialist.

Refitting

Front door window

22 Refitting is the reverse of removal, but prior to tightening the window clamp bolts, reconnect the window switch, and close the window until a gap of 10.0 mm exists between the top edge of the window and the finisher strip **(see illustration).** Adjust the position of the window in the clamps so that a gap of 5.4 mm exists between the front edge of the window and the finisher strip **(see illustration)**. Tighten the window clamp bolts securely. Operate the window and check that it moves easily and squarely in the door frame.

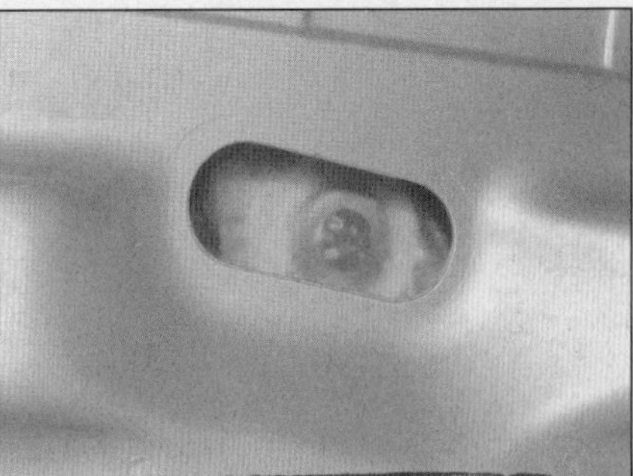

14.17 Peel back the sealing strip and undo the regulator upper mounting screw

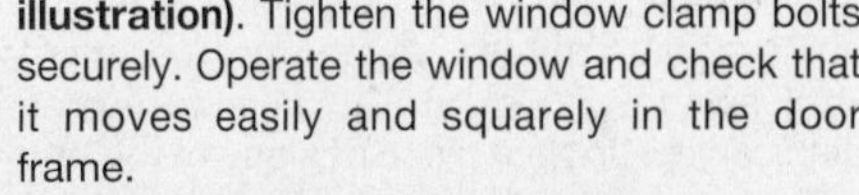

Front door window regulator

23 Refitting is the reverse of removal. Refit the window glass and adjust as described earlier in this Section.

Rear door window

24 Refitting is the reverse of removal. Prior to refitting the door sound insulation panel, check that the window operates smoothly and easily.

Rear door window regulator

25 Refitting is the reverse of removal. Prior to refitting the sound insulation panel, check that the window operates smoothly and easily.

15 Boot lid/tailgate and support struts – removal and refitting

Removal

Boot lid

1 Open the boot, remove the toolbox lid retaining screw, prise off the plastic caps and remove the toolbox hinge screws **(see illustration)**. Remove the toolbox from the boot trim panel.

2 Prise up the centre pins and remove the plastic expanding rivets, then remove the trim panel from the boot lid.

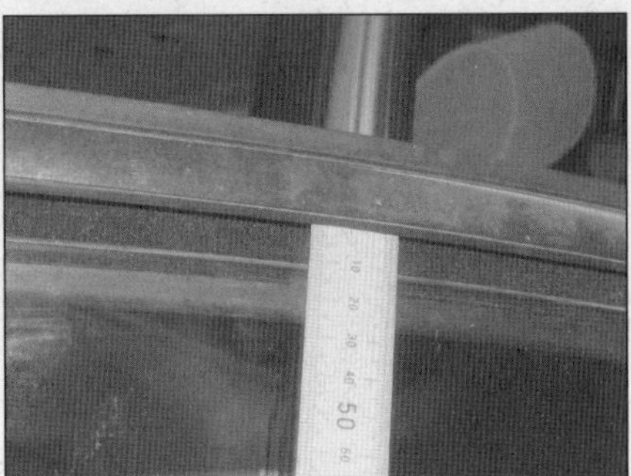

14.22a With a 10 mm gap at the top . . .

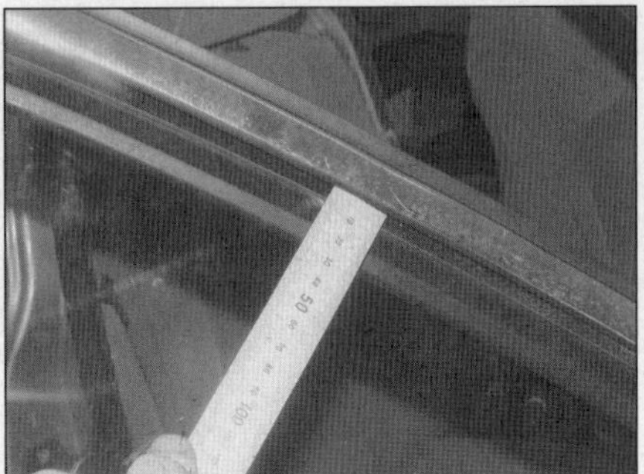

14.22b . . . the gap at the front of the window should be 5.4 mm

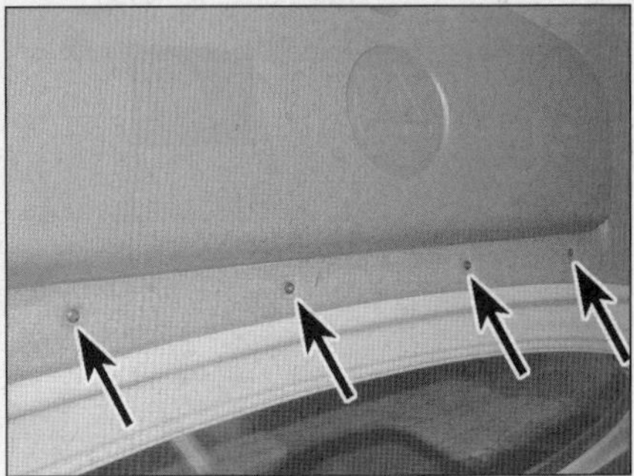

15.1 Prise off the caps and remove the toolbox hinge screws (arrowed)

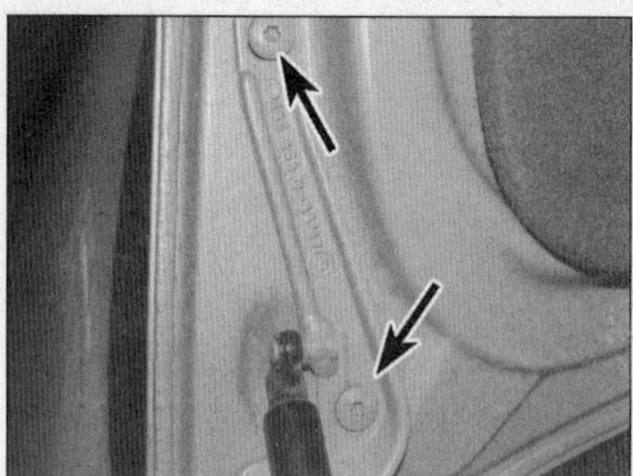
15.4 Boot lid hinge screws (arrowed)

15.8 Unclip the upper trim panel from the tailgate window

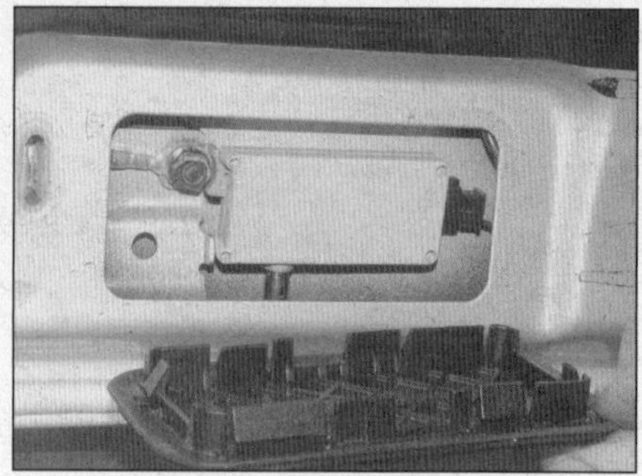
15.9 Unclip the amplifier cover

3 Disconnect the wiring connectors from the number plate lights, luggage compartment light switch and central locking servo (as applicable) and tie a piece of string to the end of the wiring. Noting the correct routing of the wiring harness, release the harness rubber grommets from the boot lid and withdraw the wiring. When the end of the wiring appears, untie the string and leave it in position in the boot lid; it can then be used on refitting to draw the wiring into position.

4 Draw around the outline of each hinge plate with a suitable marker pen then slacken and remove the hinge retaining bolts and remove the boot lid from the vehicle **(see illustration)**.

5 Inspect the hinges for signs of wear or damage and renew if necessary; the hinges are secured to the vehicle by bolts.

Boot lid support struts

6 Support the boot lid in the open position. Using a small flat-bladed screwdriver raise the spring clip, and pull the support strut off its upper mounting. Repeat the procedure on the lower strut mounting and remove the strut from the vehicle.

Tailgate/rear window

7 Open the tailgate, and have an assistant standby ready to support the tailgate.

8 Unclip the upper trim panel from the tailgate window **(see illustration)**,

9 Unclip the aerial amplifier cover **(see illustration)**.

10 Undo the retaining nut, pull out the amplifier, and disconnect the wiring plugs.

11 Prise out the rubber grommets and free the wiring harness from the window frame, then disconnect the rear window washer jet hose **(see illustration)**.

12 Make alignment marks between the window and the hinges, then undo the nuts and remove the window assembly **(see illustration)**.

13 To remove the tailgate, remove the tailgate inner trim panel as described in Section 26. Note their fitted positions, then disconnect the various wiring plugs from the tailgate fittings.

14 Open the tailgate window, then unclip the trim at the top of the tailgate **(see illustration)**.

15 Prise out the three clips each side, remove the rubber bump stops, and remove the left- and right-hand trims from the tailgate to access the hinge nuts **(see illustrations)**.

16 Prise out the rubber grommet and carefully pull the wiring loom from the tailgate.

17 Make alignment marks between the tailgate and the hinges, then undo the nuts and remove the tailgate **(see illustration)**.

Tailgate/rear window support struts

Note: *At the time of writing, no information concerning the automatic tailgate opening/closing system was available. Consult a BMW dealer or specialist.*

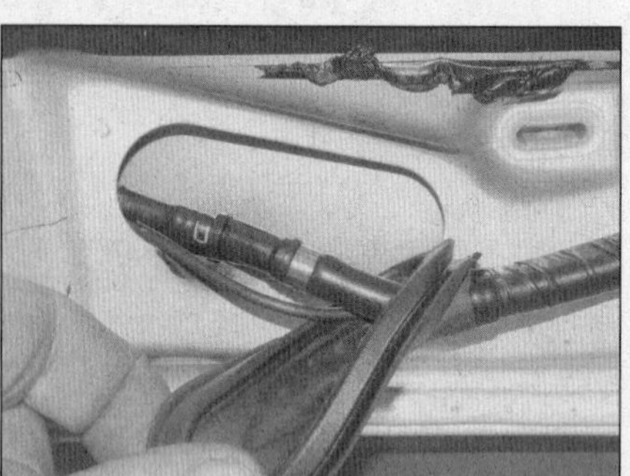
15.11 Pull back the rubber grommet and disconnect the washer jet hose

15.12 Tailgate window hinge nuts

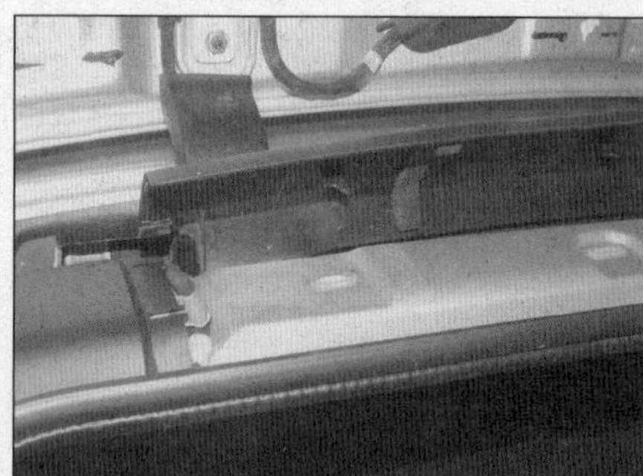
15.14 Unclip the trim at the top of the tailgate

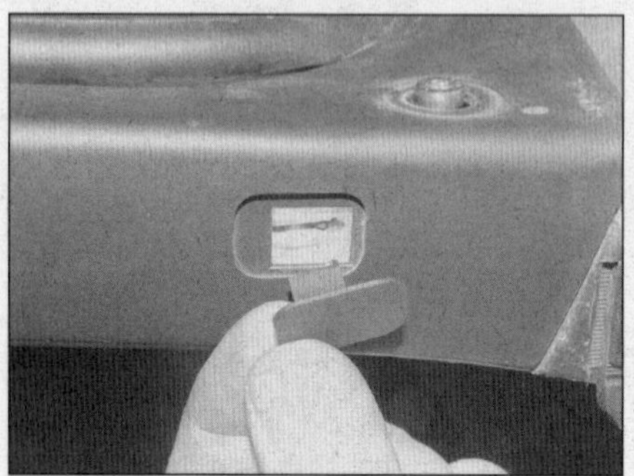
15.15a Prise out the three clips each side . . .

15.15b . . . and remove the bump stops

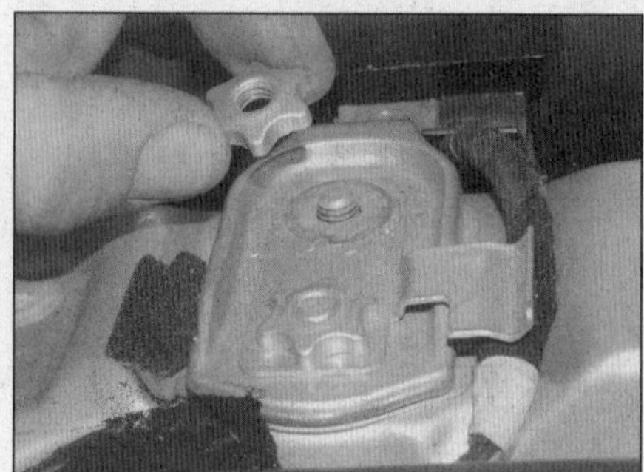
15.17 Undo the tailgate hinge nuts

18 In order to remove the tailgate/rear window support struts, special BMW tools are necessary to disconnect the front of the struts from the vehicle body. Consequently, we recommend this task is entrusted to a BMW dealer or suitably-equipped specialist.

Refitting

Boot lid

19 Refitting is the reverse of removal, aligning the hinges with the marks made before removal.

20 On completion, close the boot lid and check its alignment with the surrounding panels. If necessary slight adjustment can be made by slackening the retaining bolts and repositioning the boot lid on its hinges. If the paint work around the hinges has been damaged, paint the affected area with a suitable touch-in brush to prevent corrosion.

Boot lid support struts

21 Refitting is a reverse of the removal procedure, ensuring that the strut is securely retained by its retaining clips.

Tailgate/rear window

22 Refitting is a reversal of removal, aligning the previously made marks.

16 Boot lid/tailgate lock components – removal and refitting

Removal

Boot lid lock

1 Open the boot, and remove the lower boot lid trim panel (see Section 26). The panel is secured by two plastic expanding rivets (prise up the centre pins, then the complete rivets), and one screw in the handle recess beneath a plastic cover. With these removed, gently pull the trim panel from the four retaining clips.

2 Disconnect the lock button actuating rod.

3 Disconnect the lock wiring plug(s), undo the three bolts and remove the lock assembly **(see illustration)**.

4 If required, undo the two screws and remove the drive unit from the lock.

16.3 Undo the three bolts (arrowed) and remove the boot lid lock

Boot lid lock cylinder

5 Remove the boot lid trim panel as described in Section 26.

6 Disconnect the actuating rod from the lock button assembly, and disconnect the wiring plug.

7 Undo the two nuts and remove the lock button assembly **(see illustration)**.

8 If required, remove the cover, slide out the clip and remove the micro-switch **(see illustrations)**.

9 Release the two clips and remove the black plastic cover from the outside of the lock.

10 Prise off the small circlip and remove the cam and lever **(see illustration)**.

11 Prise out the large circlip and remove the cylinder assembly **(see illustrations)**. Recover the large spring.

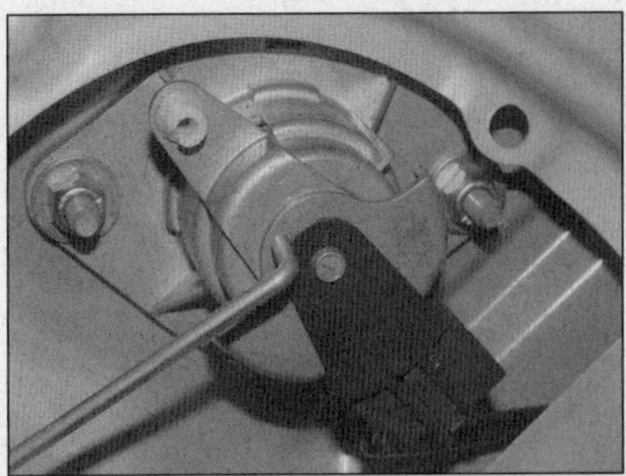

16.7 Undo the two nuts and remove the lock cylinder assembly

12 Slide off the actuating sleeve, remove the small circlip and, using the key, remove the lock cylinder.

Boot lid release button

13 Remove the boot lid trim panel as described in Section 26.

14 Disconnect the button wiring plug.

15 Carefully prise out the upper edge of the button, then lift it from place. If required, slide off the clip and remove the micro-switch.

Tailgate lock

16 Remove the tailgate trim panel as described in Section 26.

17 Lift out the retaining clip, and disconnect the actuating rod from the lock assembly.

18 Using a marker pen, make alignment marks between the lock and the panel. Undo

16.8a Remove the cover . . .

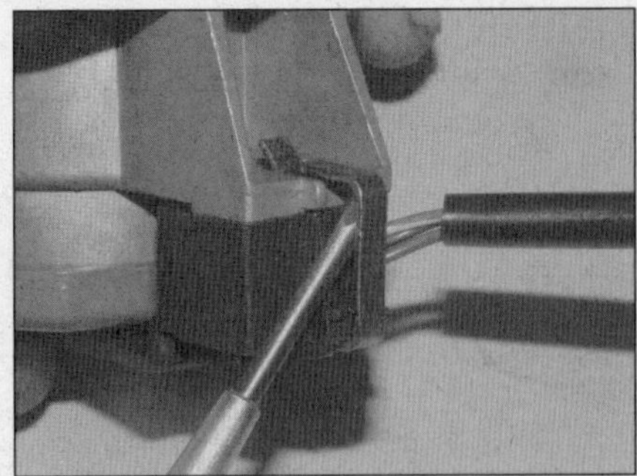

16.8b . . . and slide out the micro-switch retaining clip

16.10 Prise off the circlip

16.11a Remove the large circlip . . .

16.11b . . . and lift out the cylinder assembly

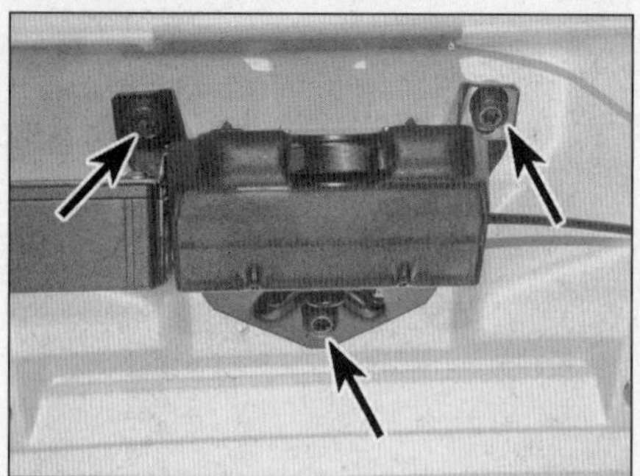

16.18 Undo the three lock securing screws (arrowed)

the three screws and remove the lock **(see illustration)**. Disconnect the wiring plug as the lock is withdrawn.

19 If required, undo the two retaining screws, drive out the pivot pin, and remove the lock actuator from the lock **(see illustration)**.

Refitting

20 Refitting is a reversal of removal, noting the following points:

a) Reconnect all wiring plugs, and secure the wiring harnesses using the retaining clips (where applicable).

b) Match-up any previously made alignment marks.

c) Check the operation of the locks/cylinders before refitting the trim panels.

d) Tighten all fasteners securely.

e) If necessary, the boot lock striker position can be adjusted by removing the plastic cover and slackening the retaining bolts.

17 Central locking components – removal and refitting

***Note:** The central locking system is equipped with a sophisticated self-diagnosis capability. Before removing any of the central locking components, have the system interrogated by a BMW dealer or suitably-equipped specialist to pin-point the fault.*

Removal

Electronic control unit (ECU)

1 The central locking system is controlled by

16.19 The lock actuator is retained by two screws

the central body electronics (ZKE III) control unit, known as the General Module (GM III), which is located behind the passenger side glovebox. To access the control unit, remove the glovebox as described in Section 26.

2 Release the retaining clips and lower the ECU out of position.

3 Release the retaining clip then disconnect the wiring connector(s) and remove the ECU from the vehicle **(see illustration)**. **Note:** *If the control unit is renewed, it will need to be programmed before use. Entrust this task to a BMW dealer or specialist.*

Door lock actuator

4 Remove the door lock as described in Section 13.

5 The lock drive unit can be removed by levering out the locking unit and pulling the drive unit from the lock **(see illustration 13.12)**.

Boot lock actuator

6 Remove the boot lock as described in Section 16.

7 Undo the two screws and remove the drive unit from the lock **(see illustration)**.

Tailgate lock actuator

8 Remove the tailgate lock as described in Section 16.

9 Undo the two retaining screws, lift up the retaining bracket, and remove the actuator from the lock **(see illustration 16.18)**.

Refitting

10 Refitting is the reverse of removal. Prior to refitting any trim panels removed for access thoroughly check the operation of the central locking system.

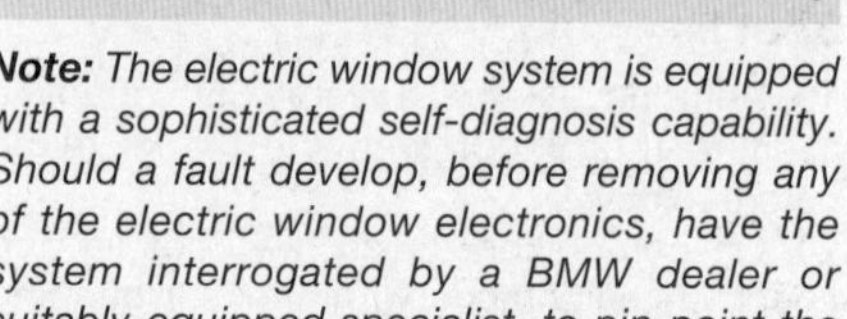

18 Electric window components – removal and refitting

***Note:** The electric window system is equipped with a sophisticated self-diagnosis capability. Should a fault develop, before removing any of the electric window electronics, have the system interrogated by a BMW dealer or suitably-equipped specialist, to pin-point the fault*

Window switches

1 Refer to Chapter 12, Section 4.

Window motors

2 At the time of writing, it would appear that the electric motor is integral with the regulator (see Section 14), and must be renewed as an assembly. Check with your BMW dealer or specialist.

Electronic control unit (ECU)

3 The electric window system is controlled by the central body electronics (ZKE III) control unit, known as the General Module (GM III), which is located behind the passenger side glovebox. To access the control unit, remove the glovebox as described in Section 26.

4 Release the retaining clips and lower the ECU out of position.

5 Release the retaining clip/slide out the locking element, then disconnect the wiring connector(s) and remove the ECU from the vehicle **(see illustration 17.3)**.

19 Mirrors and associated components – removal and refitting

Exterior mirror assembly

1 Remove the door inner trim panel as described in Section 12.

2 Slightly lift and pull the plastic trim away from the front inner edge of the door **(see illustration)**.

17.3 Release the catch and disconnect the wiring plugs

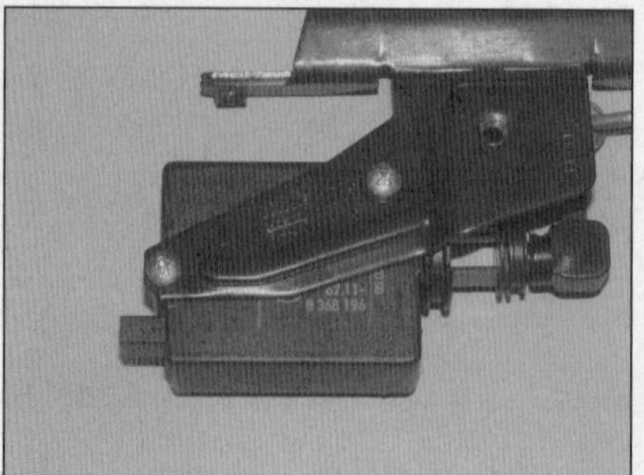

17.7 Undo the two screws and remove the drive unit

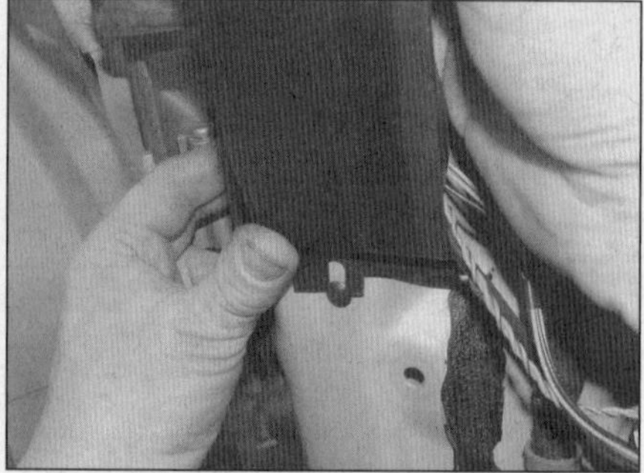

19.2 Lift the trim and pull it from the door

3 Undo the lower retaining Torx bolt and remove the tweeter from the door, then carefully peel the rubber trim at the front edge and undo the front Torx bolt **(see illustrations)**.

4 Undo the remaining Torx bolt and remove the mirror from the door. Recover the rubber seal which is fitted between the door and mirror; if the seal is damaged it must be renewed. Disconnect any wiring plugs as the mirror is withdrawn.

5 Refitting is the reverse of removal, tightening the mirror bolts to the specified torque.

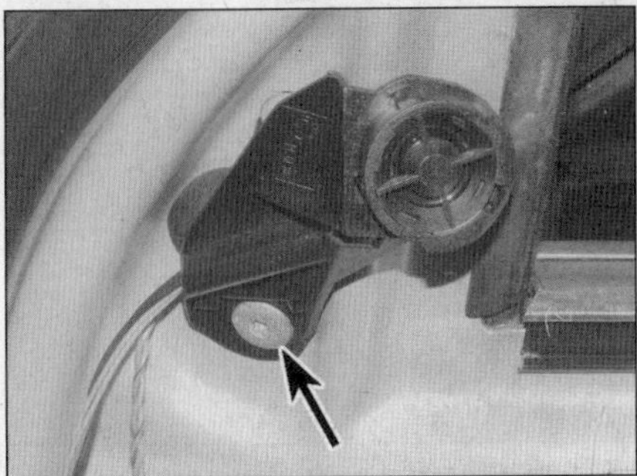

19.3a Undo the tweeter bolt (arrowed) . . .

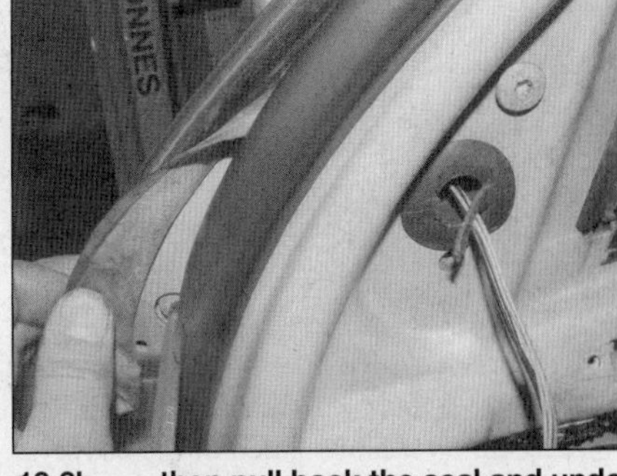

19.3b . . . then pull back the seal and undo the front bolt

Exterior mirror glass

Note: *If the mirror glass is removed when the mirror is cold the glass retaining clips are likely to break.*

Without automatic anti-glare control (no plastic frame)

6 Tilt the mirror glass fully upwards.

7 Insert a wide plastic or wooden wedge in between the base of the mirror glass and mirror housing and carefully prise the glass from the motor **(see illustration)**. Take great care when removing the glass; do not use excessive force as the glass is easily broken.

8 Remove the glass from the mirror and, where necessary, disconnect the wiring connectors from the mirror heating element.

9 On refitting, reconnect the wiring to the glass and clip the glass onto the motor, taking great care not to break it.

With automatic anti-glare control (with plastic frame)

Warning: If the mirror is broken, there is a risk of burns due to the caustic substances used during the manufacture of the mirror. Wear protective gloves.

10 Using a small flat-bladed screwdriver, slide the locking pin to the right, and remove the mirror **(see illustration)**. Disconnect any wiring plugs as the mirror is withdrawn.

11 On refitting, reconnect the wiring plugs, and position the mirror on the mounting. Slide the locking pin left to the vertical position.

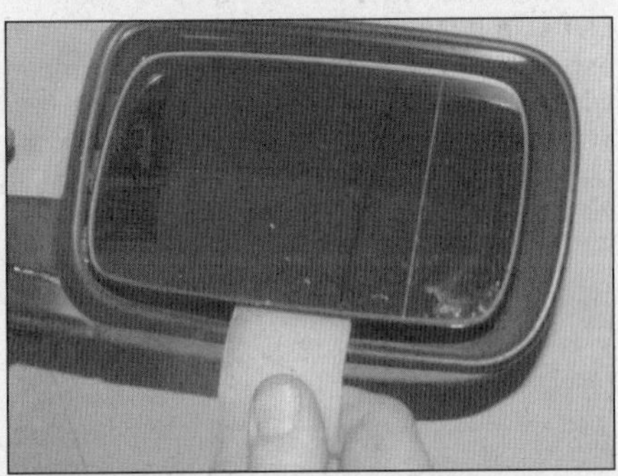

19.7 Carefully prise the bottom of the mirror from the mounting

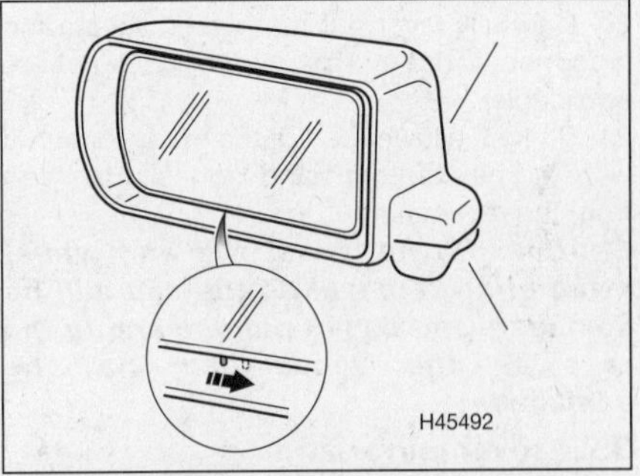

19.10 Slide the locking pin (arrowed) to the right and remove the mirror glass

Exterior mirror switch

12 Refer to Chapter 12.

Exterior mirror cover

13 Remove the mirror glass as described above.

14 Release the four retaining clips and remove the cover.

15 Refitting is the reversal of removal.

Exterior mirror motor

16 Remove the mirror glass as previously described.

17 Undo the three screws, and remove the motor **(see illustration)**. Note that it is necessary to cut the wires to the mirror motor as the plug is too large to pass through the cable guide **(see illustration)**. When refitting the motor, splice the new wires to the plug.

18 Refitting is a reversal of removal.

Interior mirror

19 There are essentially two different types of mirror arms and mountings. One type has a plastic cover over the plug connection, and the other type has a mirror arm which splits in two to reveal the wiring plug.

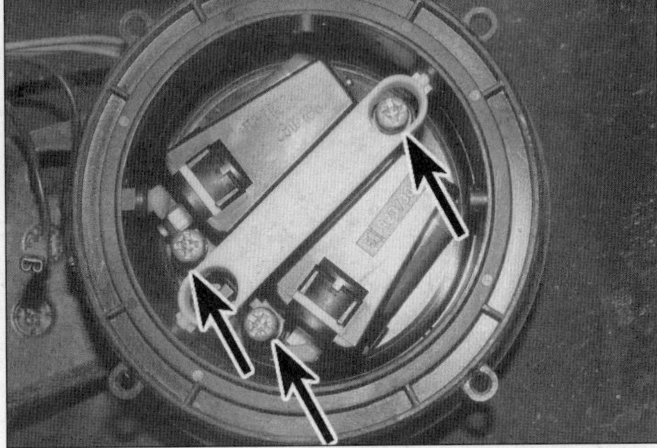

19.17a Undo the three screws (arrowed) and remove the motor assembly

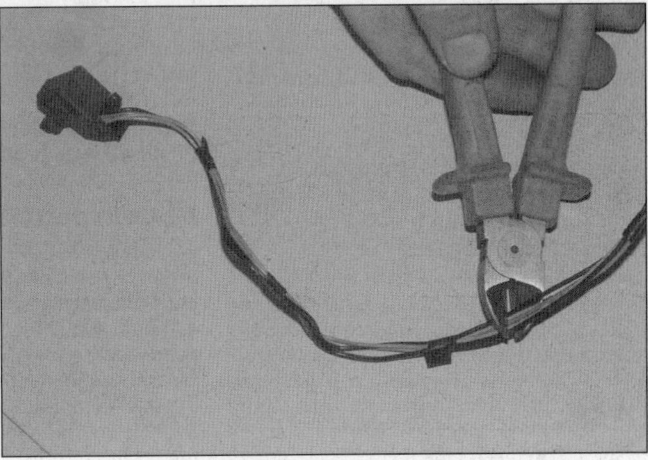

19.17b Cut the wires to the motor, and splice the new wires to the plug

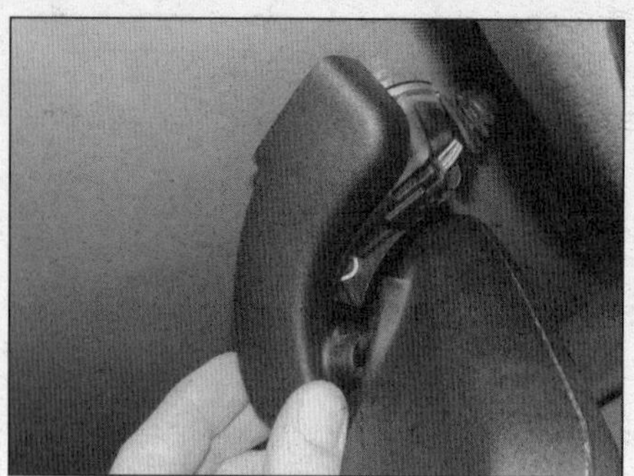
19.22a Pull the two sides of the cover apart

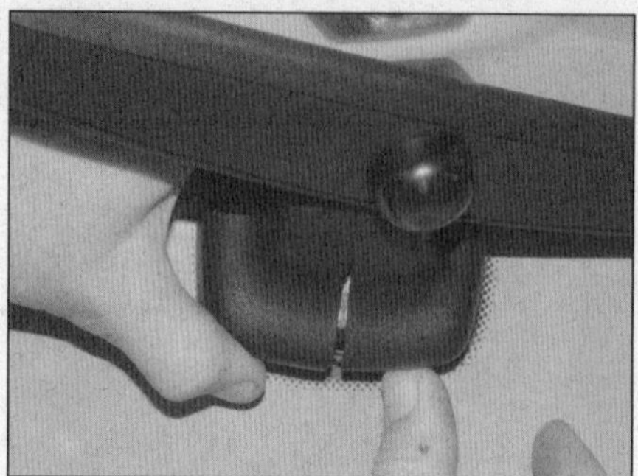
19.22b Press up at the base and pull the two sides apart

19.27 Position the mirror arm over the mounting plate at an angle of 45°

Plastic cover type arm

20 Carefully lever out the plastic cover, and disconnect the mirror wiring plug (where applicable).

21 Strike the lower part of the mirror forwards with the ball of your hand to unclip the arm from the mounting.

Caution: Do not twist the arm whilst attempting removal as the clip will be damaged, and do not pull the arm to the rear as the windscreen may be damaged.

Split cover mirror arm

22 Press the two sides of the arm covers towards the mirror and pull the two sides apart. On mirrors equipped with a rain sensor, press up at the base of the covers and pull the two sides apart **(see illustrations)**.

23 Push the right-hand side of the mirror upwards and towards the front. Swivel the left-hand arm cover to the left and unclip it from the metal part of the arm.

24 Push the left-hand side of the mirror upwards and towards the front. Swivel the right-hand arm cover to the right and unclip it from the arm.

25 Disconnect the mirror wiring plug.

26 Rotate the mirror mounting arm 45° and lift the arm off its mounting spigot.

All types

27 To refit the mirrors, position the mirror arm over the mounting at an angle of 45° to the vertical on the driver's side. Push the arm to the vertical and check that it engaged correctly **(see illustration)**. Where applicable, refit the covers and reconnect the wiring plug.

20 Windscreen and rear screen/tailgate glass - general information

1 These areas of glass are secured by the tight fit of the weatherstrip in the body aperture, and are bonded in position with a special adhesive. Renewal of such fixed glass is a difficult, messy and time-consuming task, which is beyond the scope of the home mechanic. It is difficult, unless one has plenty of practice, to obtain a secure, waterproof fit. Furthermore, the task carries a high risk of breakage; this applies especially to the laminated glass windscreen. In view of this, owners are strongly advised to have this sort of work carried out by one of the many specialist windscreen fitters.

21 Sunroof - general information, motor renewal and initialisation

General information

1 Due to the complexity of the sunroof mechanism, considerable expertise is needed to repair, renew or adjust the sunroof components successfully. Removal of the roof first requires the headlining to be removed, which is a complex and tedious operation, and not a task to be undertaken lightly. Therefore, any problems with the sunroof (except sunroof motor renewal) should be referred to a BMW dealer or specialist.

2 On models with an electric sunroof, if the sunroof motor fails to operate, first check the relevant fuse. If the fault cannot be traced and rectified, the sunroof can be opened and closed manually using an Allen key to turn the motor spindle (a suitable key is supplied with the vehicle tool kit). To gain access to the motor, unclip the cover from the headlining. Remove the Allen key from the tool kit, remove the plastic cover and insert the Allen key into the motor spindle. Disconnect the motor wiring connector and rotate the key to move the sunroof to the required position.

Motor renewal

3 Carefully prise the interior light unit from the headlining between the sunvisors. Disconnect the wiring plug(s) as the unit is withdrawn.

4 Carefully pull the front edge of the motor panel down and remove it complete with the switch. Disconnect the wiring plug as the panel is withdrawn.

5 Undo the three retaining screws, and pull the motor from its location. Disconnect the wiring plug as the motor is removed.

6 Refitting is a reversal of removal, but carry out the initialisation procedure as described next.

Initialisation

7 With the battery reconnected, and the ignition on, press the sunroof operating switch into the 'tilt' position and hold it there.

8 Once the sunroof has reached the 'fully-tilted' position, hold the switch in that position for approximately 20 seconds. Initialisation is complete when the sunroof briefly lifts at the rear again.

9 On vehicles manufactured after 03/98, the 'Learning characteristic curve' procedure must also be carried out as follows.

10 Release the switch after initialisation for a maximum of 5 seconds, then press and hold the switch in the tilt position until the sunroof returns to the closed position after a complete opening cycle has been completed.

22 Body exterior fittings - removal and refitting

Wheel arch liners and body underpanels

1 The various plastic covers fitted to the underside of the vehicle are secured in position by a mixture of screws, nuts and retaining clips, and removal will be fairly obvious on inspection. Work methodically around, removing its retaining screws and releasing its retaining clips until the panel is

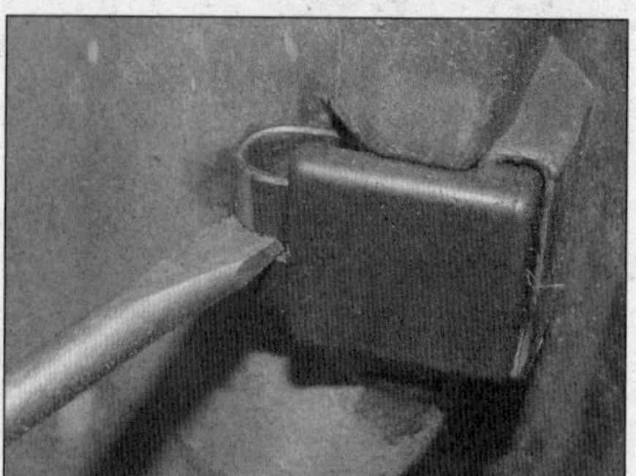
22.1a Spread the metal part of the mudflap clip apart . . .

22.1b . . . then slide it out

23.2 Disconnect the seat belt anchorage bracket from the seat

23.3 Pull down the locking catch, and pull out the pin (arrowed)

free and can be removed from the underside of the vehicle. Most clips used on the vehicle are simply prised out of position. Other clips can be released by unscrewing/prising out the centre pins and then removing the clip. Note that the rear mudflaps are secured by two clips – use a screwdriver to spread the two sides of the locking element apart, then prise out the locking element and remove the clips **(see illustrations)**.

2 On refitting, renew any retaining clips that may have been broken on removal, and ensure that the panel is securely retained by all the relevant clips and screws.

Body trim strips and badges

3 The various body trim strips and badges are held in position with a special adhesive tape. Removal requires the trim/badge to be heated, to soften the adhesive, and then cut away from the surface. Due to the high risk of damage to the vehicle's paintwork during this operation, it is recommended that this task should be entrusted to a BMW dealer or suitably-equipped specialist.

23 Seats and positioning motors – removal and refitting

Front seat

1 Slide the seat fully forwards and raise the seat cushion fully.

2 Undo the bolt and disconnect the seat belt anchorage bracket from the seat **(see illustration)**.

3 Unlock the retaining clip, then remove the pin securing the seat belt height adjustment cable **(see illustration)**.

4 Lift the front edge of the seat rail trim (where fitted), unclip the sides, and pull the trim to the rear.

5 Slacken and remove the bolts and washers securing the rear of the seat rails to the floor.

6 Slide the seat fully backwards and remove the trim caps (where fitted) from the seat front mounting bolts, then slacken and remove the bolts and washers.

7 Disconnect the battery negative lead. Due to pyrotechnic pretensioners being fitted, wait at least 1 minute before proceeding.

8 On models with manual seats, reach under the front of the seat, disconnect the wiring plug(s) and release the harness cable ties. On models with electric seats, unlock and fold forward the cover under the front of the seat, then disconnect the wiring plugs **(see illustration)**.

9 Lift the seat out from the vehicle.

10 Refitting is the reverse of removal, noting the following points.

a) *On manually-adjusted seats, fit the seat retaining bolts and tighten them by hand only. Slide the seat fully forwards and then slide it back by two stops of the seat locking mechanism. Rock the seat to ensure that the seat locking mechanism is correctly engaged then tighten the mounting bolts securely.*
b) *On electrically-adjusted seats, ensure that the wiring is connected and correctly routed then tighten the seat mounting bolts securely.*
c) *Tighten the seat belt mounting bolt to the specified torque.*
d) *tighten the seat mounting bolts to the specified torque in the following sequence: Front inner, front outer, rear inner, followed by the rear outer.*

Folding rear seat

Saloon

11 Pull up on the front of the seat cushion to release the left- and right-hand retaining clips, and remove it forwards and out from the vehicle. Disconnect the seat heating wiring connectors (where applicable) as the seat is withdrawn.

12 If required, pull down the rear seat armrest (where fitted) and unbolt it from the seat back.

13 Slacken and remove the bolts securing the seat belt lower mountings to the body.

14 Fold the seat backs forward, undo the centre mounting bolt, and remove the seats.

15 Refitting is the reverse of removal ensuring that the seat outer pivots engage correctly with the corresponding locating holes in the vehicle body. Tighten the seat belt lower mounting bolts to the specified torque setting.

Touring

16 Carefully prise the plastic cover from the brackets at the front on the seat cushion on each side, then undo the Allen bolts and remove the brackets **(see illustrations)**.

23.8 Disconnect the seat wiring plugs, and release the loom cable ties – manual seat

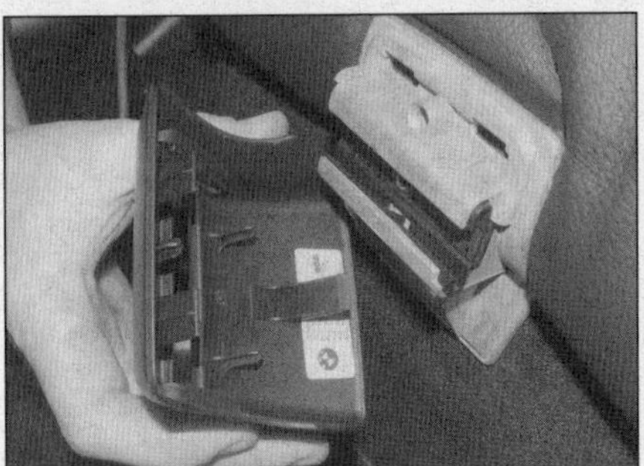
23.16a Prise the plastic cover from the seat bracket . . .

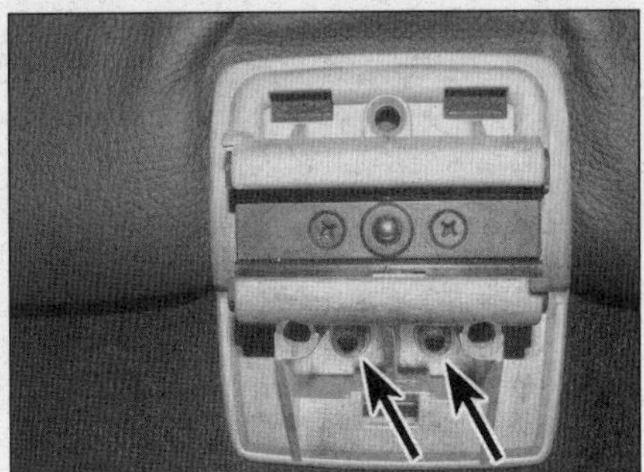
23.16b . . . then undo the two Allen screws (arrowed)

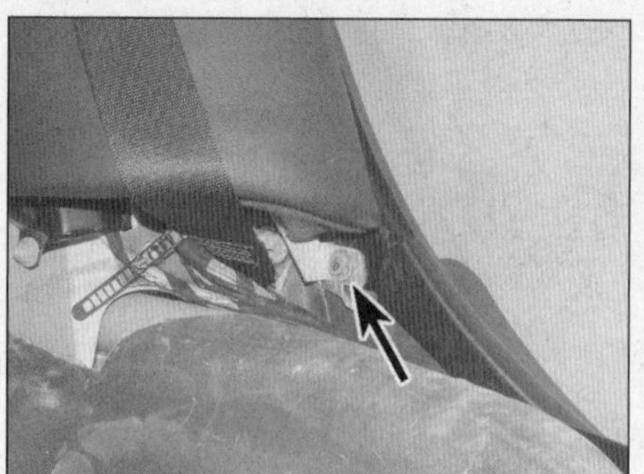

23.18 Unscrew the bolt (arrowed) at the base of the side cushion

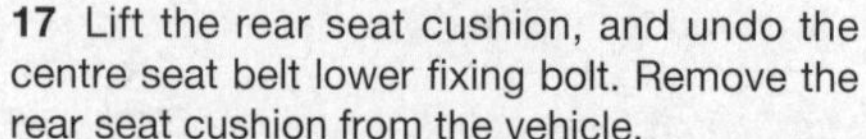

23.20a Undo the Allen screw (arrowed) and remove the centre hinge cover . . .

23.20b . . . followed by the side hinge cover

17 Lift the rear seat cushion, and undo the centre seat belt lower fixing bolt. Remove the rear seat cushion from the vehicle.

18 Undo the bolt at the base of the side cushion, pull the top of the cushion forward, and then pull the whole cushion upwards to release it **(see illustration)**. Repeat the procedure on the remaining side cushion.

19 Release the rear seat backrest, and fold it forward.

20 Undo the Allen screw securing the cover over the centre hinge, and the screw securing the cover of the side hinge each side **(see illustrations)**. Remove the rear seat backrests from the vehicle.

21 Refitting is a reversal of removal.

Fixed rear seat

22 Pull up on the seat base cushion to release the left- and right-hand retaining clips and remove it from the vehicle. Pull the centre headrest from place.

23 Undo the screw each side at the lower, outer edge of the seat back, then unclip the top of the seat back then slide it upwards to release its lower retaining pins. Remove it from the vehicle.

24 Refitting is the reverse of removal, making sure the seat back lower locating pegs are correctly engaged with the body, and the seat belt buckles and lap belt are fed through the intended openings.

Front seat positioning motors

25 Remove the front seat as described previously in this Section.

26 Disconnect the wiring plug and remove it from the support bracket.

27 Undo the two Torx screws and remove the motor from the drive gearbox.

28 Refitting is a reversal of removal. Tighten the motor mounting screws securely.

24 Front seat belt tensioning mechanism – general information

1 Most models are fitted with a front seat belt tensioner system. The system is designed to instantaneously take up any slack in the seat belt in the case of a sudden frontal impact, therefore reducing the possibility of injury to the front seat occupants. Each front seat is fitted with its own system, the tensioner being situated on the inboard seat rail.

2 The seat belt tensioner is triggered by a frontal impact above a predetermined force. Lesser impacts, including impacts from behind, will not trigger the system.

3 When the system is triggered, a large spring in the anchorage bracket retracts and locks the seat belt. This prevents the seat belt moving and keeps the occupant in position in the seat. Once the tensioner has been triggered, the seat belt will be permanently locked and the assembly must be renewed.

4 There is a risk of injury if the system is triggered inadvertently when working on the vehicle. If any work is to be carried out on the seat/seat belt disable the tensioner by disconnecting the battery negative lead (see Chapter 5A), and waiting at least 1 minute before proceeding.

5 Also note the following warnings before contemplating any work on the front seat.

Warning: If the tensioner mechanism is dropped, it must be renewed, even it has suffered no apparent damage.

- ***Do not allow any solvents to come into contact with the tensioner mechanism.***
- ***Do not subject the seat to any form of shock as this could accidentally trigger the seat belt tensioner.***
- ***Check for any deformation of the seat belt stalk tensioner, and anchorage brackets. Renew any that are damaged.***

25 Seat belt components – removal and refitting

Warning: Read Section 24 before proceeding.

Front seat belt

1 Remove the front seat as described in Section 23.

2 Disconnect the pretensioner wiring plug, and release the cable tie **(see illustration)**.

3 Undo the bolt and remove the pretensioner.

4 Remove the B-pillar trim panel as described in Section 26.

5 Undo the screws and remove the seat belt guide from the pillar.

6 Undo the screw securing the upper seat belt mounting **(see illustration)**.

7 Unscrew the inertia reel retaining bolt and remove the seat belt from the door pillar.

8 If necessary, undo the retaining bolts and remove the height adjustment mechanism from the door pillar.

9 Refitting is a reversal of the removal procedure, ensuring that all the seat belt mounting bolts are securely tightened, and all disturbed trim panels are securely retained by all the relevant retaining clips.

Automatic height adjuster cable

10 On the BMW 5-Series, as the position of the seat is adjusted, the height adjuster is automatically repositioned. This is achieved

25.2 Cut the cable tie and disconnect the wiring plug (arrowed)

25.6 Undo the seat belt upper mounting nut

25.13 Disconnect the cable end fittings (arrowed) from the height adjuster

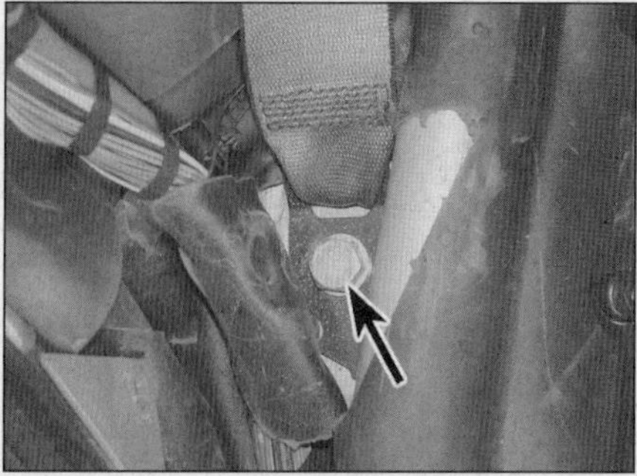
25.17a Rear-outer seat belt lower fixing bolt (arrowed)

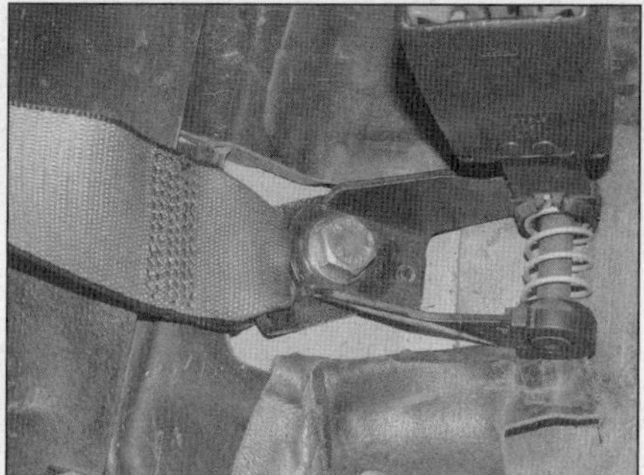
25.17b Centre belt and buckle

by a cable attached to the seat base and the height adjuster in the B-pillar.

11 Remove the relevant front seat as described in Section 23.

12 Remove the B-pillar trim as described in Section 26.

13 Disconnect the cable end fittings from the height adjuster, and the cable reel, release the cable from its retaining clips, note how the cable is routed, then manoeuvre it from the vehicle **(see illustration)**.

14 Refitting is the reverse of removal.

Fixed rear seat belts

15 Remove the rear seat as described in Section 23.

16 Remove the parcel shelf as described in Section 26.

17 Slacken and remove the bolts and washers securing the rear seat belts to the vehicle body and remove the centre belt and buckle **(see illustrations)**.

18 Unscrew the inertia reel retaining nut and remove the seat belt(s) **(see illustration)**.

19 Refitting is the reverse of removal, ensuring that all seat belt mountings are tighten to the specified torque and all trim panels are clipped securely in position.

Folding rear seat side belts

Saloon

20 Remove the rear parcel shelf trim as described in Section 26.

21 Slacken and remove the Torx bolt securing the lower end of the belt to the body. Feed the belt through the slot in the shelf trim.

22 The inertia reel is secured by one Torx bolt. Slacken and remove the bolt and washer.

23 Manoeuvre the assembly from the mounting bracket and withdraw it from the vehicle.

24 Refitting is the reverse of removal, making sure the inertia reel is clipped securely in position and all seat belt mounting bolts are tightened to the torque.

Touring

25 Remove the C-pillar trim as described in Section 26.

26 Undo the screw, then pull the front edge of the inertia reel cover upwards and forwards to remove it **(see illustration)**.

27 Undo the bolt securing the inertia reel **(see illustration)**.

28 Refitting is the reverse of removal, making sure the inertia reel is clipped securely in position and all seat belt mounting bolts are tightened to the torque.

Rear centre inertia reel

Touring models

29 Removal of the centre inertia reel involves removal of the seat cover. This is an involved procedure, which requires some patience to accomplish successfully.

30 Remove the rear seat backrest as described in Section 23, then pull the headrests from place.

31 Carefully prise the catch surround trim from place **(see illustration)**.

32 Undo the two screws securing the headrest trim **(see illustration)**.

25.18 Rear seat belt inertia reel

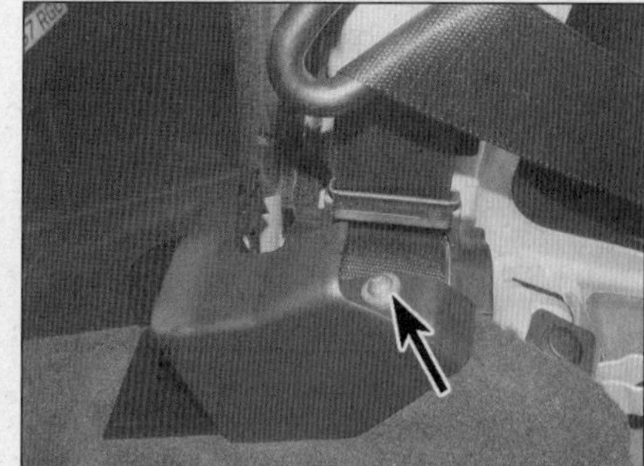
25.26 Undo the screw (arrowed) and remove the seat belt inertia reel cover

25.27 Undo the inertia reel bolt (arrowed)

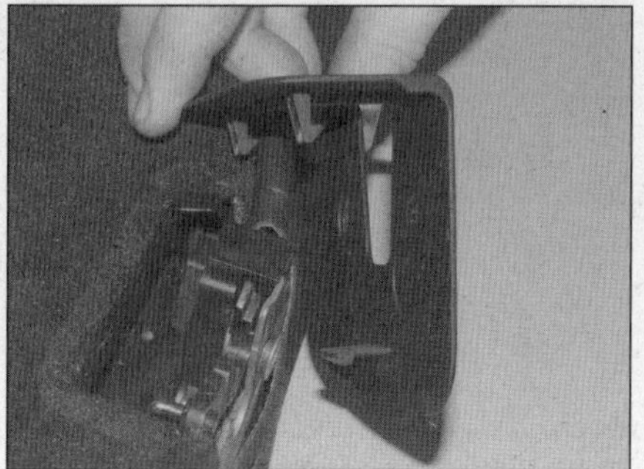
25.31 Prise off the catch surround

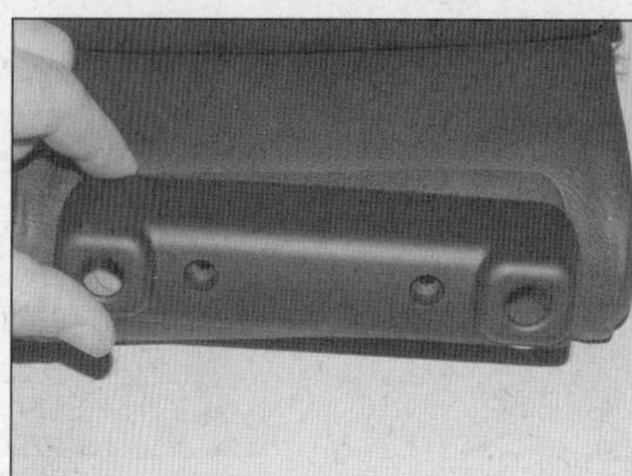
25.32 Undo the two screws and remove the headrest trim

25.33 Remove the seat-back button surround

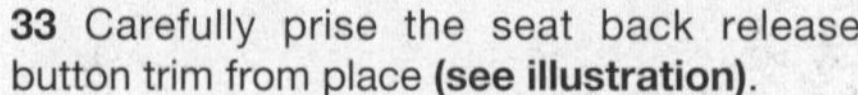

33 Carefully prise the seat back release button trim from place **(see illustration)**.

34 Fold down the armrest and pull the trim panel behind it from its Velcro fasteners. Release the trim at the edge of the armrest aperture **(see illustration)**.

35 Undo the two screws and remove the trim from around the seat belt webbing **(see illustration)**.

36 Using a small screwdriver (or similar), carefully work around the top and left-hand side of the seat, release the fabric from the seat back channels **(see illustration)**.

37 The rear panel is secured by three clips along its lower edge, two clips on the left-hand side, and two along the top edge. To release these clips, press down on the panel and use a tool to lever the clips away from the panel centre. With the outer clips released,

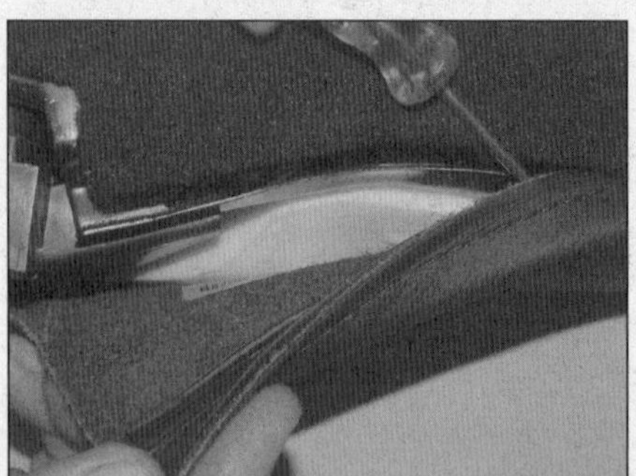

25.36 Release the fabric from the seat back channels

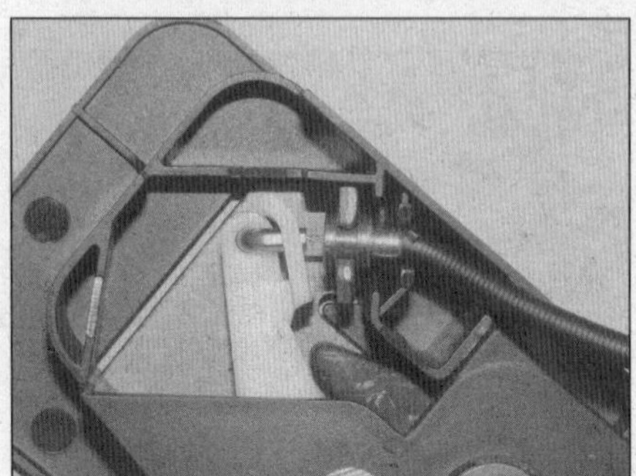

25.39 Pull the outer cable from the bracket, and disengage the cable from the lever

25.34 Pull the panel from its Velco fasteners

press down in the centre of the panel and slide the panel to the right-hand side of the backrest to release the four central clips **(see illustration)**.

38 Undo the two Allen screws securing the catch to the backrest, and slide the catch from place.

39 Pull the cable from its bracket, and disengage it from the lever **(see illustration)**.

40 Undo the inertia reel retaining bolt and manoeuvre the assembly from position **(see illustration)**.

41 Refitting is a reversal of removal, but refit the seat cover fabric to the seat frame prior to refitting the rear panel.

Rear seat stalk

42 Remove the rear seat cushion as described in Section 23.

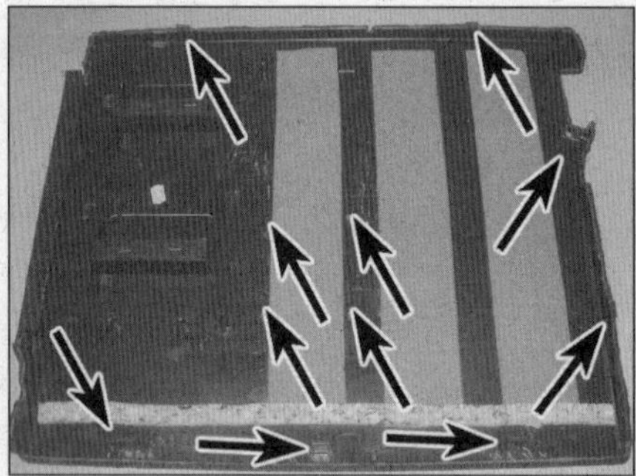

25.37 The rear panel is secured by 11 clips (arrowed)

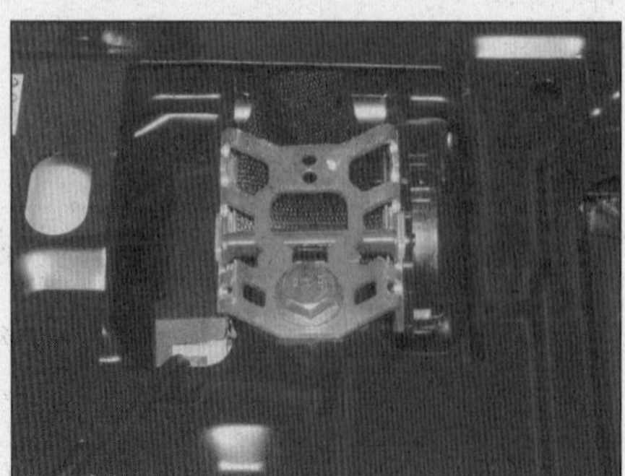

25.40 Undo the bolt and remove the inertia reel

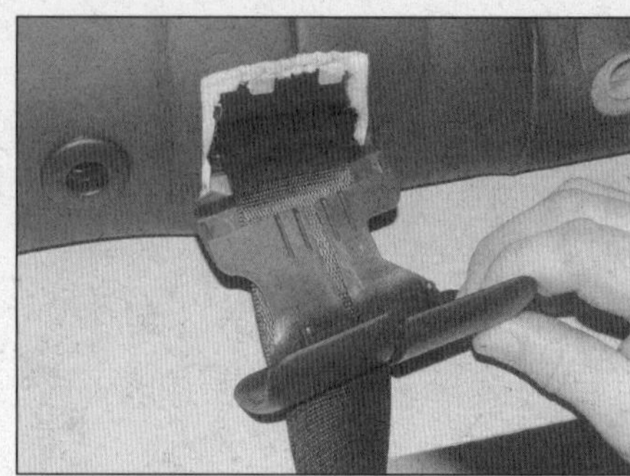

25.35 Remove the seat belt trim

43 Slacken and remove the bolt and washer and remove the stalk from the vehicle.

44 Refitting is the reverse of removal, tightening the mounting bolt to the specified torque.

Rear seat centre belt/buckle

Saloon models

45 Remove the rear seat cushion as described in Section 23.

46 Slacken and remove the bolt securing the centre belt/buckle to the body and remove it from the vehicle.

47 Refitting is the reverse of removal, tightening the mounting bolts to the specified torque.

26 Interior trim – removal and refitting

Interior trim panels

1 The interior trim panels are secured using either screws or various types of trim fasteners, usually studs or clips.

2 Check that there are no other panels overlapping the one to be removed; usually there is a sequence that has to be followed that will become obvious on close inspection.

3 Remove all obvious fasteners, such as screws. If the panel will not come free, it is held by hidden clips or fasteners. These are usually situated around the edge of the panel and can be prised up to release them; note, however that they can break quite easily so new ones should be available. The best way of releasing such clips, without the correct type of tool, is to use a large flat-bladed screwdriver. Note that some panels are secured by plastic expanding rivets, where the centre pin must be prised up before the rivet can be removed. Note in many cases that the adjacent sealing strip must be prised back to release a panel.

4 When removing a panel, never use excessive force or the panel may be damaged; always check carefully that all fasteners have been removed or released before attempting to withdraw a panel.

5 Refitting is the reverse of the removal

26.7 Prise out the emblem and undo the Torx bolt

26.8 Starting at the top, pull the trim from the pillar

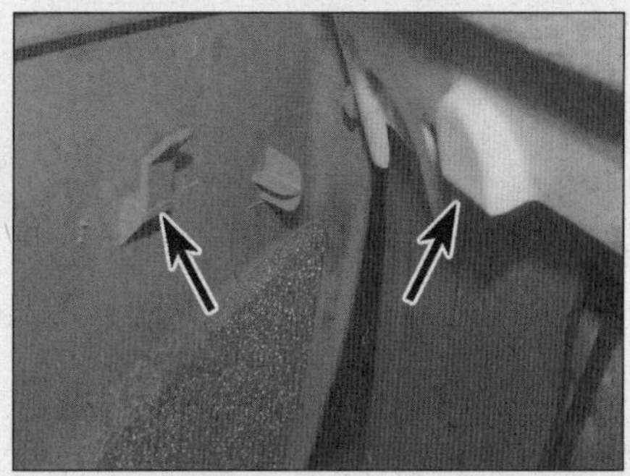

26.12 The lug (arrowed) on the lower trim fits behind the recess (arrowed) in the upper trim

procedure; secure the fasteners by pressing them firmly into place and ensure that all disturbed components are correctly secured to prevent rattles.

A-pillar trim

6 Due to the head-impact airbag fitted in the area, disconnect the battery as described in Chapter 5A.

7 Using a wooden or plastic flat-bladed lever, carefully prise out the trim insert (where fitted) from the A-pillar trim **(see illustration)**. Undo the Torx retaining bolt. **Note:** *Not all models are fitted with the insert and bolt.*

8 Pull the trim to the rear, starting at the top **(see illustration)**.

9 Refitting is the reverse of the removal procedure; secure the fasteners by pressing them firmly into place and ensure that all disturbed components are correctly secured to prevent rattles.

B-pillar trim

10 Begin by carefully prising up the front door sill trim panel with its retaining clips.

11 Pull the rubber weatherstrip away from the door apertures, adjacent to the B-pillar.

12 Pull the bottom edge of the lower trim in towards the centre of the vehicle, then pull the trim downwards to release it from the retaining clips. Note how the lower part of the trim engages with the upper section of trim **(see illustration)**.

13 Undo the bolt securing the seat belt anchorage to the seat.

14 Pull the top edge and lower edge of the upper trim in towards the centre of the vehicle, then pull it up to release it from the retaining clips **(see illustration)**

15 Refitting is the reverse of the removal procedure; secure the fasteners by pressing them firmly into place and ensure that all disturbed components are correctly secured to prevent rattles.

C-pillar trim – Saloon

16 Prise out the outer edge of the courtesy light, and remove it from the pillar trim. Disconnect the wiring plug as the unit is withdrawn.

17 Pull the door weatherstrip away from the area adjacent to the pillar trim. Pull the top edge of the pillar trim away, releasing the two retaining clips, and then lift the trim away **(see illustration)**.

18 Refitting is the reverse of the removal procedure; secure the fasteners by pressing them firmly into place and ensure that all disturbed components are correctly secured to prevent rattles.

C-pillar trim – Touring

19 Remove the rear seat cushion as described in Section 23.

20 Undo the retaining screw at the lower edge of the seat side cushion **(see illustration 23.18)**.

21 Pull the top edge of the seat side cushion forwards and lift it upwards from place. Note how it engages with the retaining clips.

22 Pull the top of the pillar trim towards the centre of the cabin to release the top push-on clip.

23 With the top released, pull up the lower edge of the trim and remove it.

24 If required, undo the bolt from the seat belt anchorage, and feed the belt through the slot in the trim.

25 Refitting is a reversal of removal.

D-pillar trim – Touring

26 Open the tailgate, and remove the luggage compartment floor panel.

27 Prise out the plastic cover, and undo the two Allen screws each side securing the luggage lashing brackets to the floor **(see illustration)**.

28 Prise up the covers each side of the tailgate lock striker, and remove the two Torx bolts securing the tailgate sill trim panel **(see illustration)**.

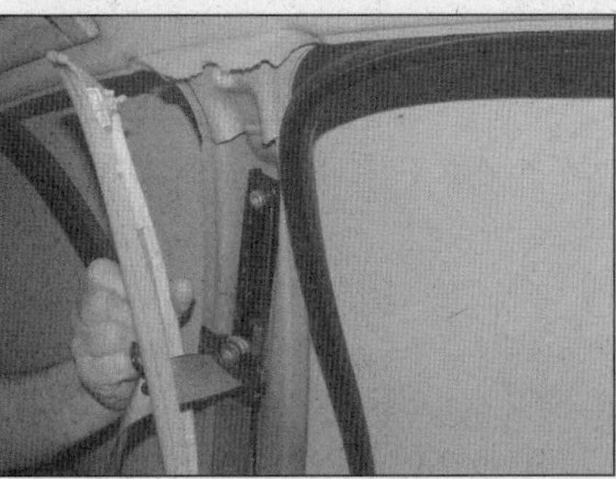

26.14 Unclip the upper B-pillar trim

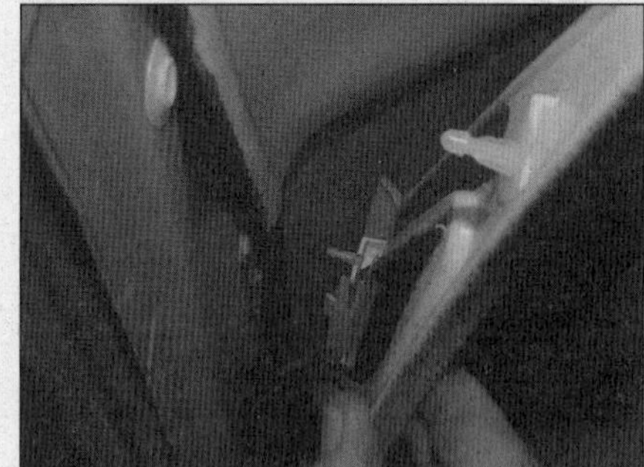

26.17 Pull the top edge of the C-pillar trim from the push-in clips

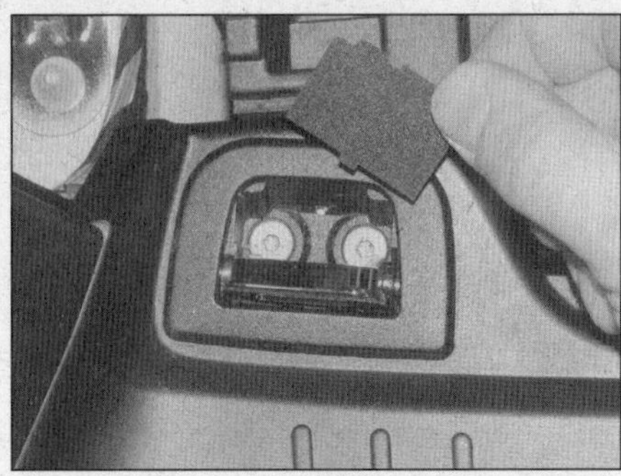

26.27 Undo the Allen screws and remove the luggage lashing brackets

26.28 Undo the Torx bolts (arrowed) either side of the lock striker

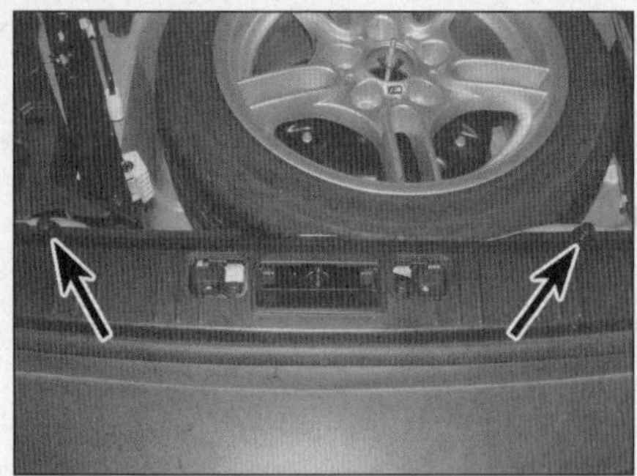
26.30 Remove the two expansion rivets (arrowed)

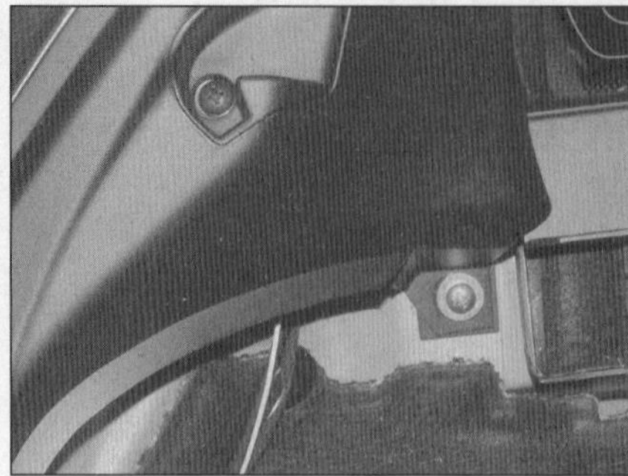
26.31 D-pillar trim retaining screws

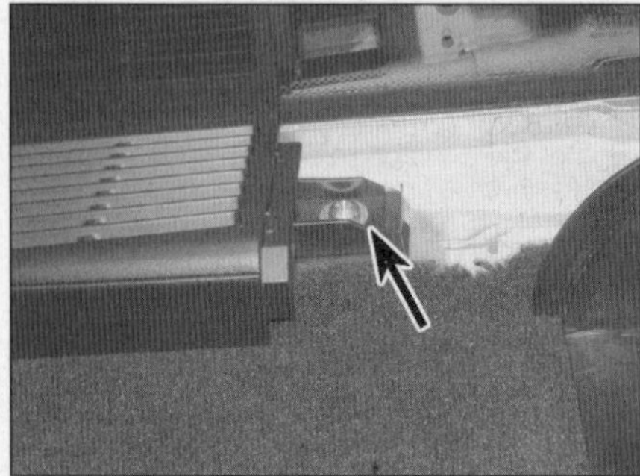
26.37a Luggage area side trim panel front screw (arrowed) . . .

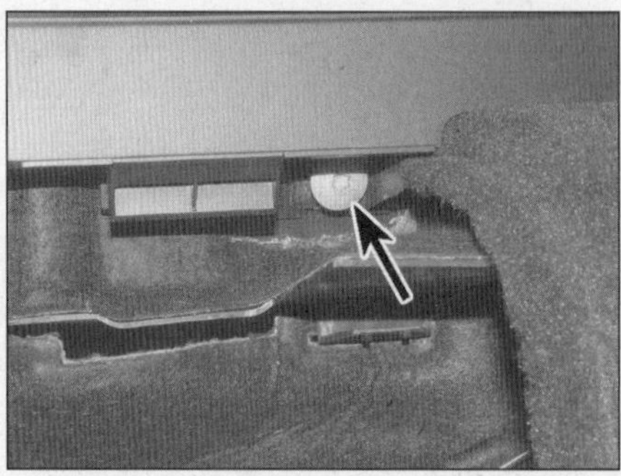
26.37b . . . and rear screw (arrowed)

29 Open the luggage compartment storage compartment lids each side, and remove them.

30 Remove the two expansion rivets, pull the sill trim panel upwards and remove it **(see illustration)**.

31 The pillar trim is secured by two screws in the centre, and three push-on clips **(see illustration)**. Undo the screws, pull away the tailgate rubber weatherstrip from the aperture, then pull the pillar trim from place.

32 Refitting is a reversal of removal.

Luggage area trim panel – Touring

33 Release the catch and lift out the luggage compartment floor panel.

34 Remove the rear seat as described in Section 23.

35 Remove the C- and D-pillar trims as described earlier in this Section.

36 Undo the screw, and pull the front of the seat belt inertia reel cover trim upwards, then slide the trim forwards to unclip it.

37 The rear side window cavity cover trim is secured by one screw at the front and one at the rear **(see illustrations)**. Undo the screws and remove the trim upwards.

38 Prise out the plastic covers, undo the two Allen screws each side and remove the two forward luggage lashing brackets. Undo the central bolt and lift out the front section of the luggage compartment floor panel.

39 Lever out the centre pins and prise out the expanding plastic rivets – two at the front edge, and one at the rear lower edge of the luggage area trim panel. Remove the panel from the vehicle.

40 Refitting is a reversal of removal.

Tailgate trim panel

41 Open the tailgate, and carefully prise out the luggage compartment light from the tailgate panel. Disconnect the wiring plug as the light is withdrawn.

42 Undo the rotary fastener, and open the toolbox.

43 Prise out the cover from the emergency tailgate release, and push it back through the hole in the panel **(see illustration)**.

44 Detach the tool box straps, and lift the toolbox from the tailgate, complete with hinges **(see illustration)**.

45 Open the tailgate window, and pull up the trim panel around the wiper drive mechanism in the centre of the window aperture **(see illustration)**.

46 Undo the two screws in the exposed aperture **(see illustration)**.

47 Carefully unclip the trim around the tailgate lock **(see illustration)**.

48 The tailgate trim panel is now secured by

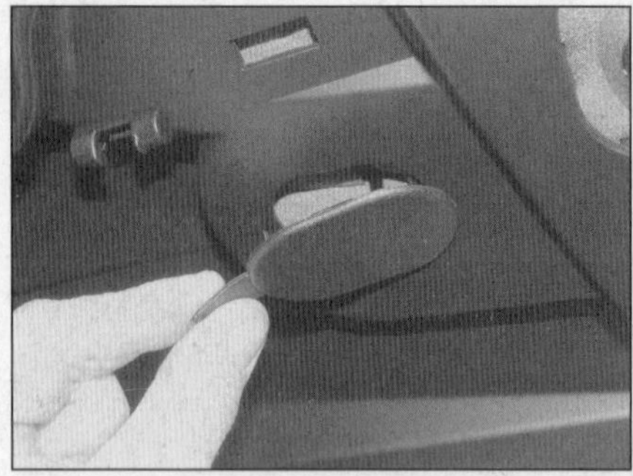
26.43 Push the emergency tailgate release though the hole in the panel

26.44 Remove the toolbox along with its hinges

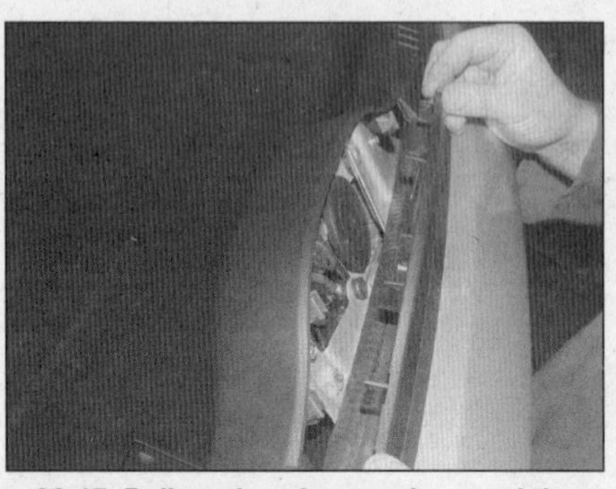
26.45 Pull up the trim panel around the wiper drive mechanism

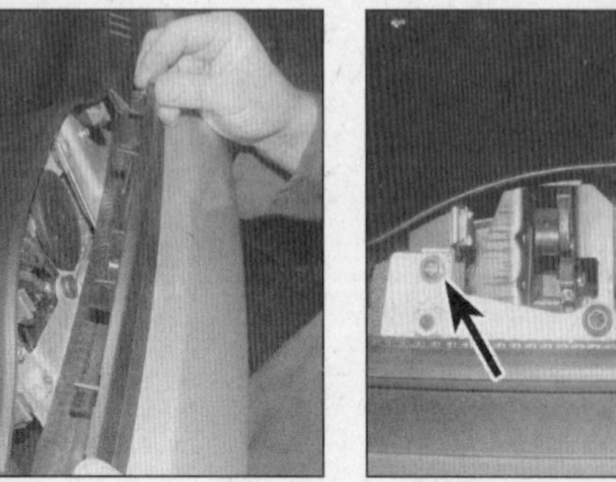
26.46 Undo the two screws (arrowed)

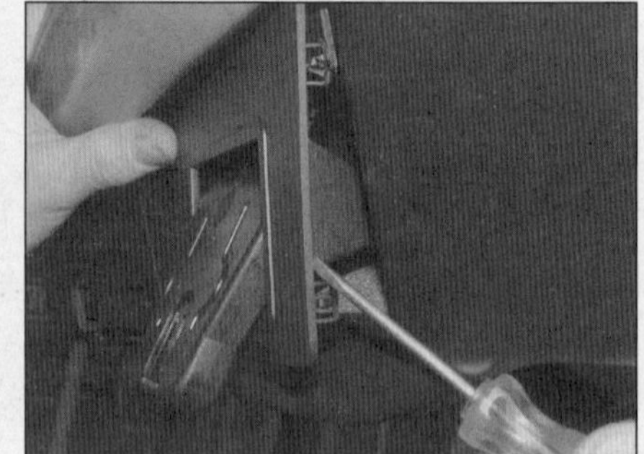
26.47 Unclip the tailgate lock trim

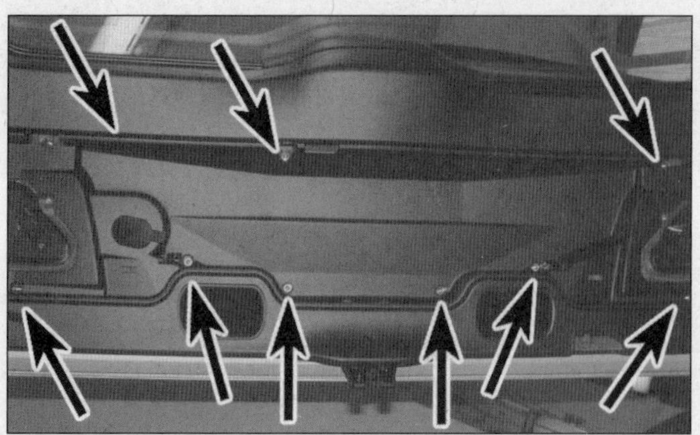

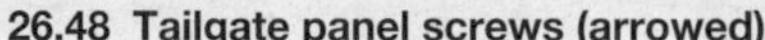

26.48 Tailgate panel screws (arrowed)

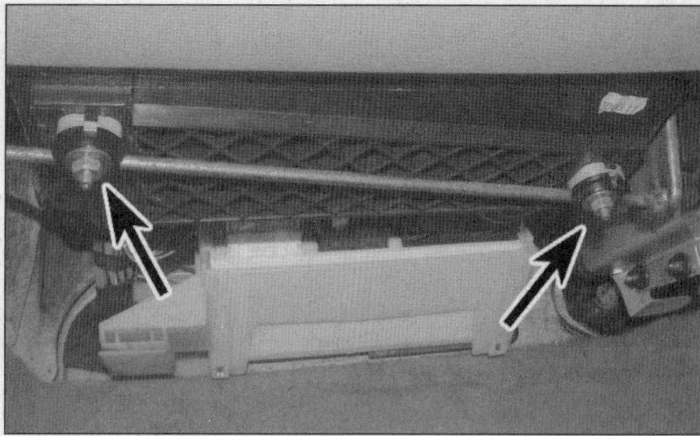

26.51 Undo the two nuts (arrowed) securing the glovebox

three screws in the centre, and six at its lower edge. Undo the screws, unclip the trim from each side of the window, and pull the trim downwards to release it **(see illustration)**.

49 Refitting is a reversal of removal, ensuring any damaged clips are renewed.

Glovebox

50 Pull the trim panel beneath the glovebox to the rear and remove it.

51 Slacken the two retaining nuts under the glovebox **(see illustration)**.

52 Open the glovebox, prise off the clips securing shock absorber strut and check strap, then pull the glovebox to the rear **(see illustration)**. Disconnect the glovebox light wiring plug as it's withdrawn.

Glovebox lock

53 Open the glovebox lid, undo the two retaining screws and remove the lock **(see illustration)**.

Carpets

54 The passenger compartment floor carpet is in one piece, secured at its edges by screws or clips, usually the same fasteners used to secure the various adjoining trim panels.

55 Carpet removal and refitting is reasonably straightforward but very time-consuming because all adjoining trim panels must be removed first, as must components such as the seats, the centre console and seat belt lower anchorages.

Headlining

56 The headlining is clipped to the roof and can be withdrawn only once all fittings such as the grab handles, sun visors, sunroof (if fitted), windscreen, rear quarter windows and related trim panels have been removed, and the door, tailgate and sunroof aperture sealing strips have been prised clear.

57 Note that headlining removal requires considerable skill and experience if it is to be carried out without damage and is therefore best entrusted to an expert.

Cup holders

Front cup holders

58 Open both cup holders a little, and remove the two retaining screws **(see illustration)**. Remove both cup holders.

59 Refitting is a reversal of removal.

Rear cup holders

60 Using a flat, plastic or wooden tool carefully prise the rear cup holder assembly from the centre console. Take great care not to damage the centre console trim – use a piece of cardboard or similar between the tool and the trim surface.

61 Push cup holder assembly into place.

Rear headrests

62 Pull the headrests from place with a sharp tug.

63 Refitting is a reversal of removal.

Parcel shelf – Saloon

64 Remove both C-pillar trims and rear headrests as described previously in this Section.

65 Remove the rear seat as described in Section 23.

66 Undo the bolts, and remove all lower rear seat belt fixings (not the seat belt stalks) – see Section 25.

67 On models with folding rear seats, remove the seat side cushion. The cushion is secured with a screw at its base, then pull the top of the cushion away at the top to release the clip, then lift it upwards and remove it **(see illustration 23.18)**.

68 Release the four clips at each front edge, then lift the front edge and pull the grilles from the parcel shelf **(see illustration)**.

26.52 Depress the clip and slide it from the groove in the pin

26.53 Undo the two screws and remove the lock

26.58 Undo the cup holder screws

26.68 Prise the grilles up at the front edge

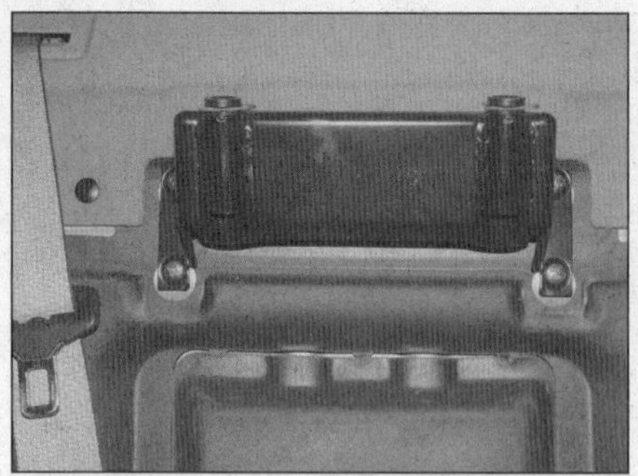
26.69 Undo the four bolts securing the headrest bracket

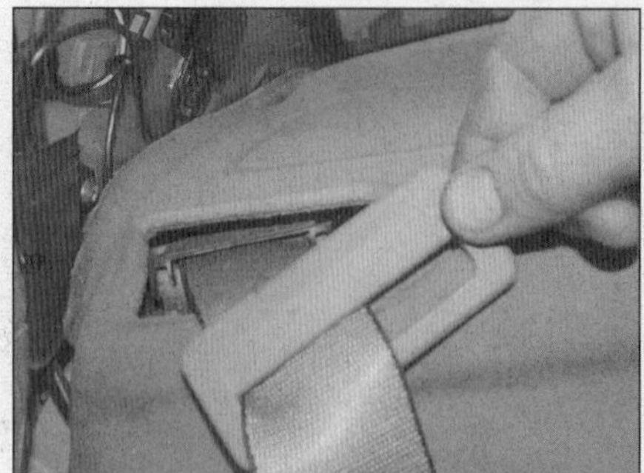
26.70 Prise out the seat belt trims

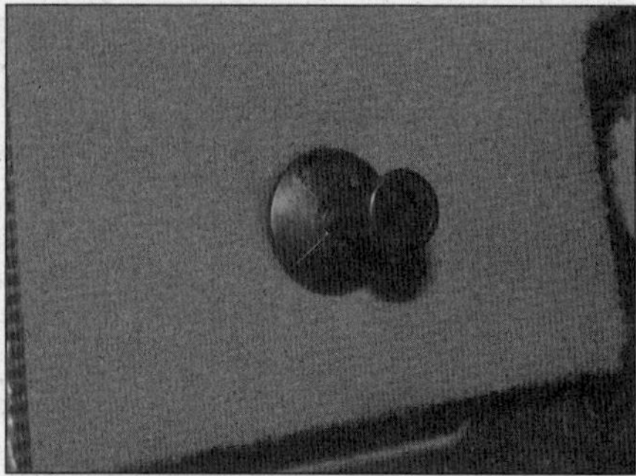
26.71 Prise up the centre pin then prise out the complete plastic expanding rivet

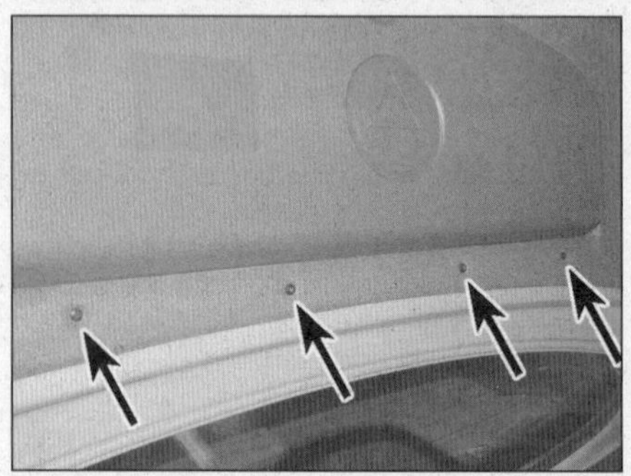
26.76 Prise off the plastic caps, undo the screws (arrowed) and remove the tool kit

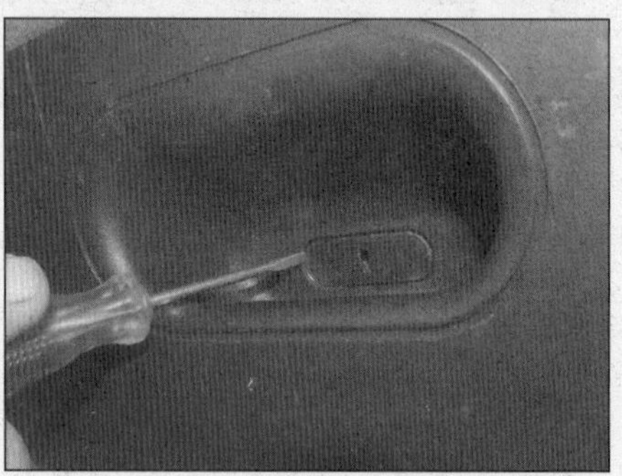
26.79 Prise out the cap and undo the screw

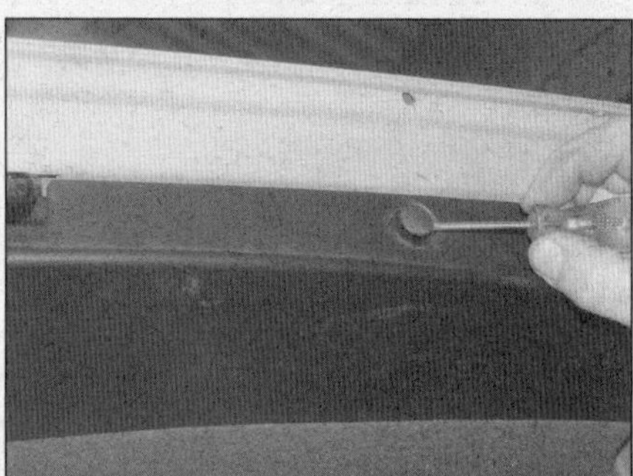
26.80 Remove the plastic expanding rivets

Models without folding rear seats

69 Undo the four bolts securing the centre headrest bracket, and remove it **(see illustration)**.

70 Carefully prise out the seat belt slot trims from the parcel shelf **(see illustration)**.

71 Pull the centre pins out, and prise out the plastic rivets, and remove the parcel shelf to the front **(see illustration)**. Disconnect any wiring plugs as the shelf is withdrawn. Note how the parcel shelf pins locate into the guides at the rear.

Models with folding rear seats

72 Pull the centre pins out, and prise out the plastic rivets, then remove the plastic trim from the front edge of the parcel shelf.

73 Carefully prise out the seat belt slot trims from the parcel shelf

74 Remove the parcel shelf to the front, disconnecting any wiring plugs as the shelf is withdrawn. Note how the parcel shelf pins locate into the guides at the rear.

All models

75 Refitting is a reversal of removal.

Boot lid trim panel

76 Prise off the plastic caps and remove the four tool kit retaining screws **(see illustration)**.

77 Open the tool kit lid, release the check strap and lift the tool kit from the boot lid.

78 Prise out the boot lid light and disconnect the wiring plug.

79 Prise out the plastic cap and undo the retaining screw in the handle recess **(see illustration)**.

80 Lever up the centre pins and prise out the two plastic rivets **(see illustration)**.

81 Carefully release the four push-on clips and remove the plastic trim from the lower section of the boot lid **(see illustration)**.

82 Carefully release the three push-clips each side using a flat-bladed tool, and remove the trim panel from the boot lid **(see illustration)**.

83 Refitting is a reversal of removal.

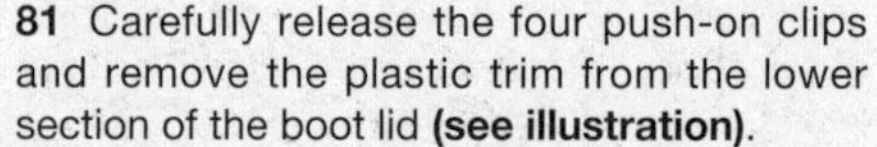

27 Centre console – removal and refitting

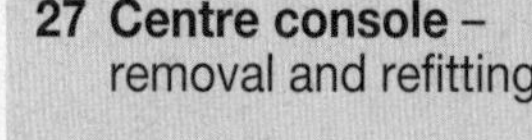

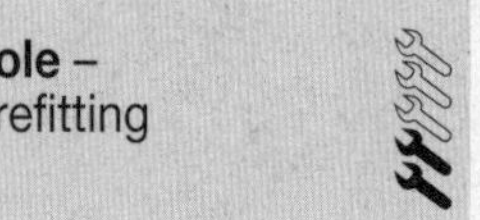

Removal

1 Remove the rear cup holders as described in Section 26. On models without rear cup holders, carefully prise the rear storage tray from place **(see illustration)**.

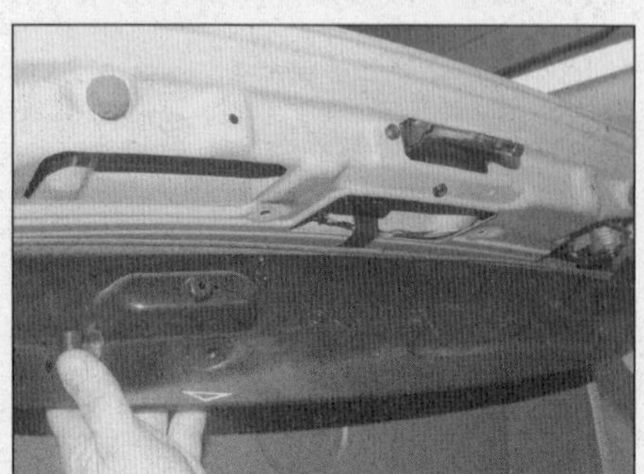
26.81 Pull the lower boot panel from its retaining clips

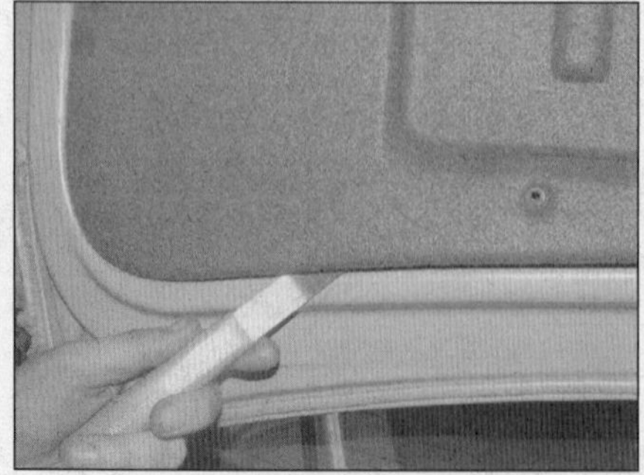
26.82 Use a flat-bladed tool to release the panel clips

27.1 Carefully prise the rear storage tray from place

27.2 Slide the rear air vents down, then pull them from the console

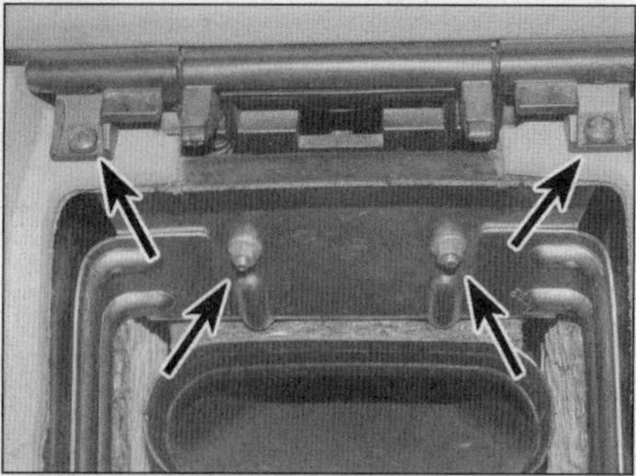

27.3 Two screws (arrowed) retain the armrest, whilst two nuts (arrowed) secure the storage tray

27.4a Pull the gear knob straight up from the lever . . .

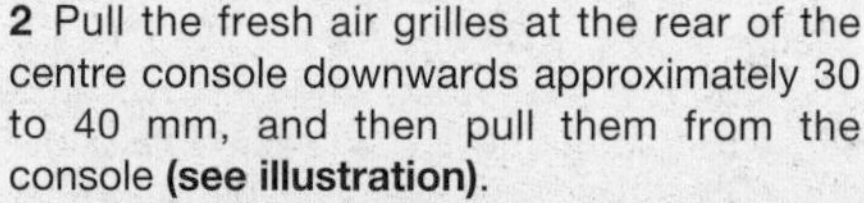

2 Pull the fresh air grilles at the rear of the centre console downwards approximately 30 to 40 mm, and then pull them from the console **(see illustration)**.

3 Undo the two screws securing the armrest hinge, and the two nuts securing the storage tray **(see illustration)**. Pull the armrest from place along with the storage tray.

4 Pull the gear lever knob sharply straight upwards and remove it, followed by the gaiter (where fitted). Release the wiring plug from its retaining bracket **(see illustrations)**.

5 Undo the two screws at the front of the gear/selector lever aperture, prise out the hazard switch and remove the screw beneath it **(see illustration)**.

6 Undo the two screws at the rear of the trim, then carefully prise it from place **(see illustration)**. Disconnect the wiring plugs as the trim is removed.

7 Prise up the rear edge, and unclip the handbrake lever gaiter from the console **(see illustration)**.

8 Undo the three screws and remove the handbrake lever surround trim **(see illustration)**.

9 Remove the heater control panel as described in Chapter 3.

10 Remove the stability control, traction control, heated seats, electronic damper control, and rear window roller blind switches (as applicable) from the centre console, as described in Chapter 12.

11 Undo the screw each side securing the carpet trim at the front of the console, then pull the carpet trim backwards from its clips **(see illustration)**.

12 Undo the two screws each side securing the centre console **(see illustration)**.

13 The rear of the console is secured by one

27.5a . . . and prise the gaiter from the panel

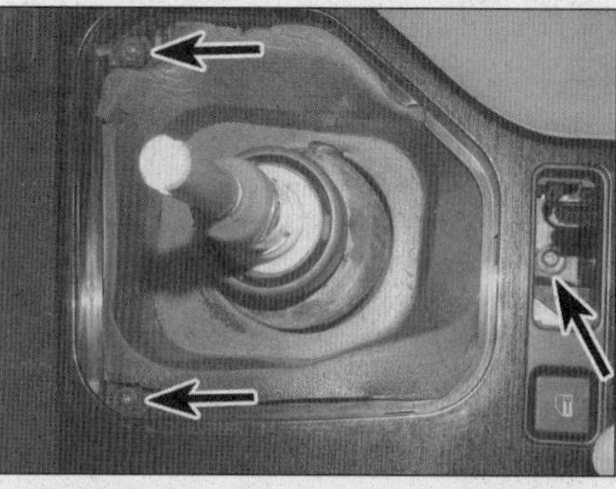

27.5b Two screws at the front (arrowed) and one at the rear (arrowed), under the hazard warning switch

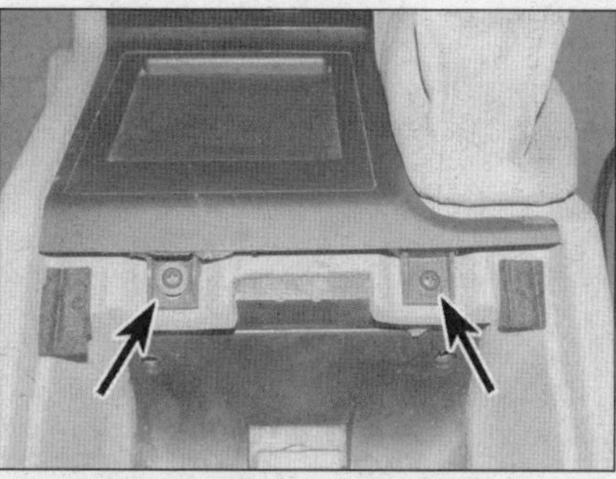

27.6 Undo the two screws (arrowed) in the storage compartment aperture

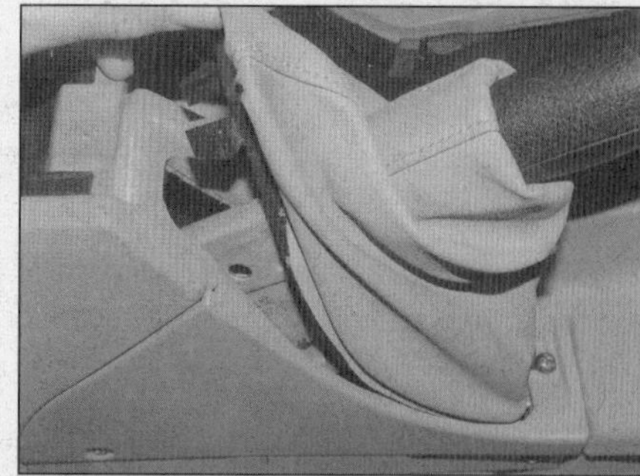

27.7 Unclip the handbrake lever gaiter . . .

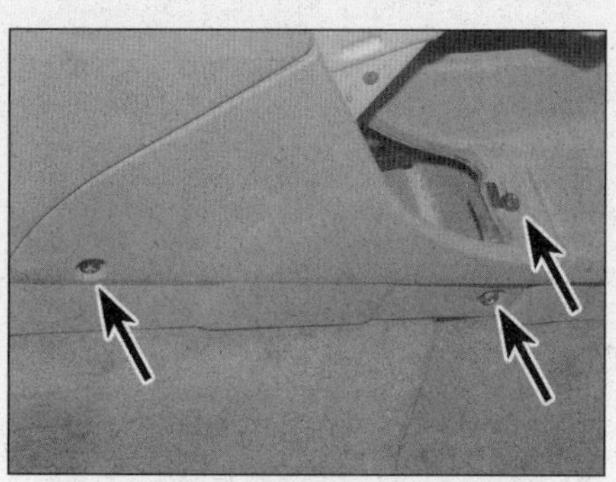

27.8 . . . then undo the three screws (arrowed) and remove the handbrake lever trim

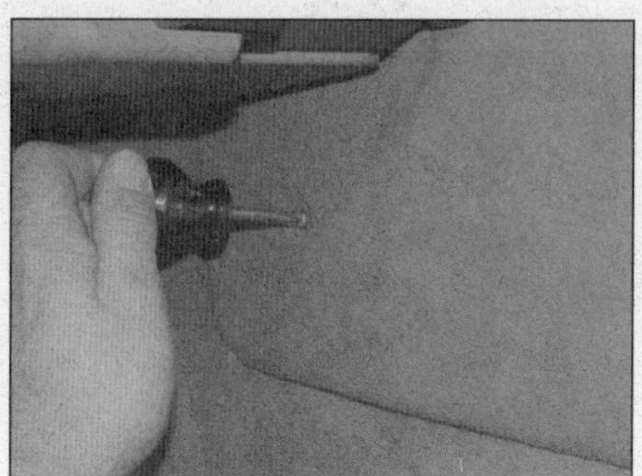

27.11 Undo the carpet trim screws

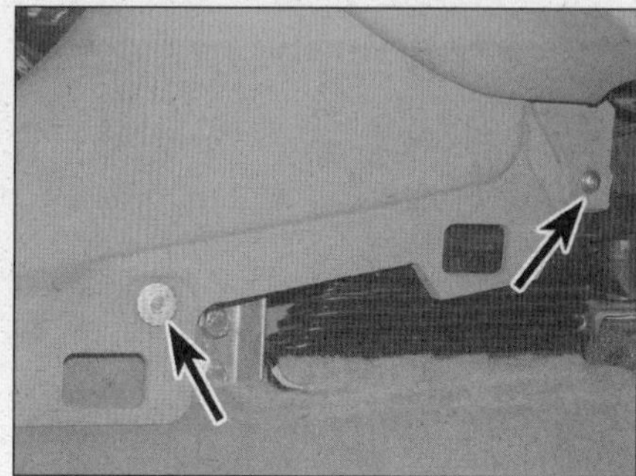

27.12 Undo the two screws at the front each side (arrowed)

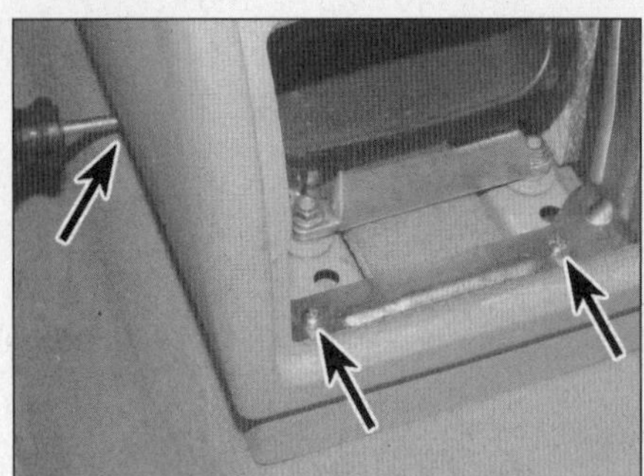
27.13 The console is secured by two screws at the rear (arrowed) and one each side (left-hand side arrowed)

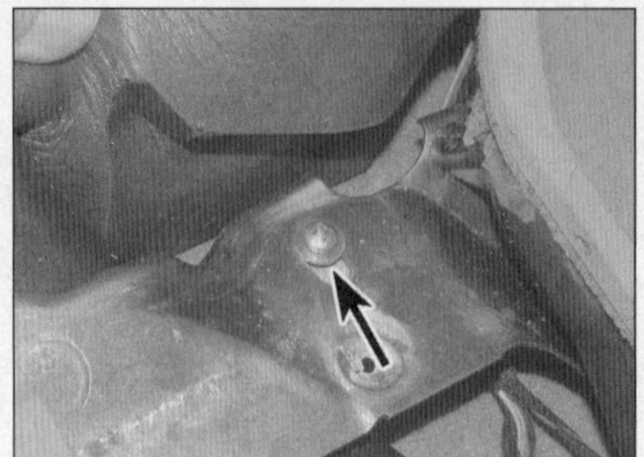
27.14 Undo the screw behind the gear lever (arrowed)

27.16 Lift up the rear of the console and manoeuvre it from the vehicle

screw each side, and two at the rear **(see illustration)**. Remove the screws.

14 Remove the screw at the rear of the gear lever aperture **(see illustration)**.

15 Lift the rear of the console and disconnect the cigarette lighter wiring plug (where fitted).

16 With both seats and backrests in their rearmost positions, lift up the rear of the console and manoeuvre it from place, over the gear and handbrake levers, and remove it on the passenger side **(see illustration)**. Note their fitted locations, then disconnect any wiring plugs as the console is withdrawn.

Refitting

17 Refitting is the reverse of removal, making sure all fasteners are securely tightened.

28 Facia panel assembly – removal and refitting

Label each wiring connector as it is disconnected from its relevant component. The labels will prove useful on refitting, when routing the wiring and feeding the wiring through the facia apertures.

Removal

Lower facia assembly

1 Disconnect the battery negative lead as described in Chapter 5A.

2 Remove the centre console as described in Section 27.

3 Undo the screws, rotate the fasteners anti-clockwise and remove the lower facia panel above the driver's pedals **(see illustration)**.

4 Remove the instrument cluster and audio unit as described in Chapter 12.

5 Remove the glovebox as described in Section 26.

6 Using a wooden or plastic tool, carefully prise the decorative trim from the passenger side, and undo the five screws exposed **(see illustrations)**.

7 Prise out the cap and remove the screw from the passenger's end of the facia **(see illustration)**.

8 Undo the 5 screws in the passenger glovebox aperture, and remove the trim strip **(see illustrations)**.

9 Undo the retaining screw, located on the

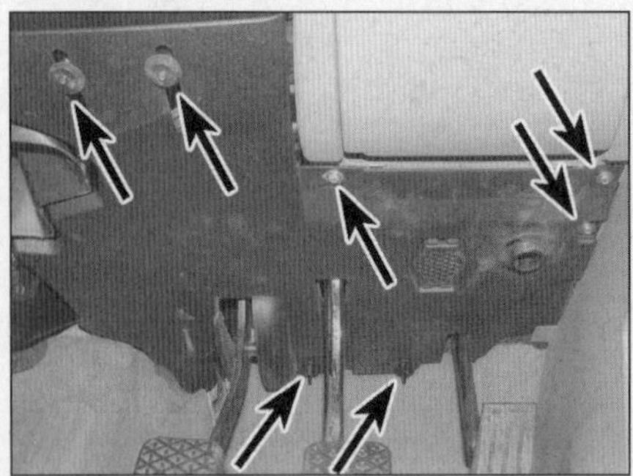
28.3 Undo the screws and fasteners (arrowed), then pull the panel to the rear

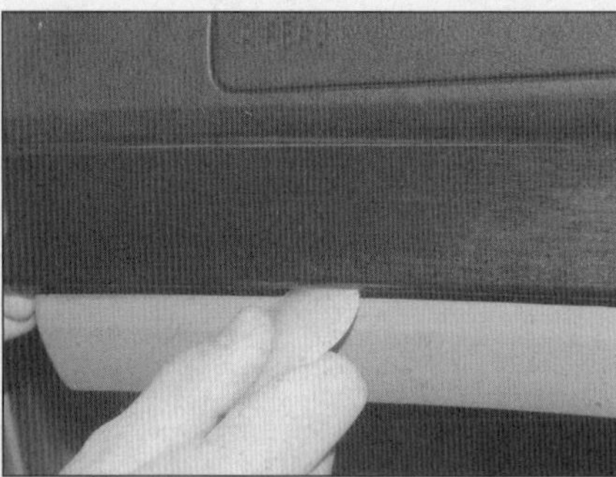
28.6a Carefully prise the trim off . . .

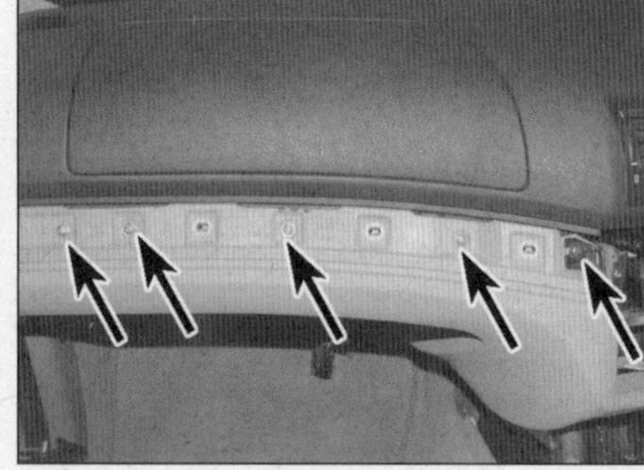
28.6b . . . then undo the 5 screws (arrowed)

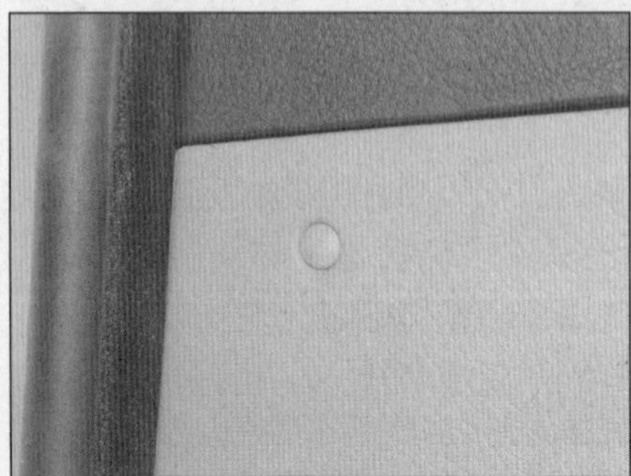
28.7 Prise off the plastic cap and undo the screw

28.8 Undo the five screws (arrowed)

28.9 Undo the screw on the driver's side (arrowed)

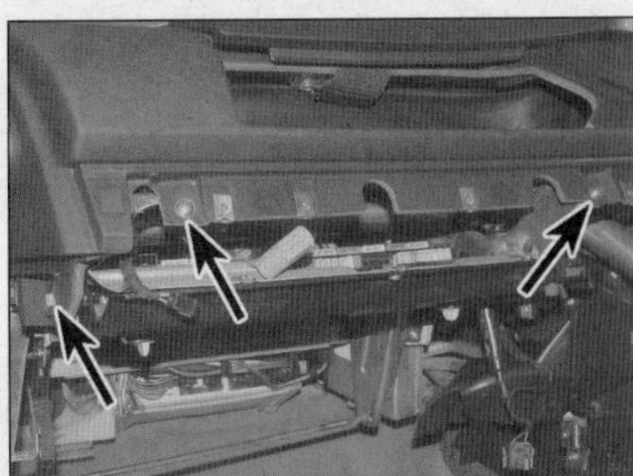
28.14 Upper facia panel screws (arrowed) – passenger's side

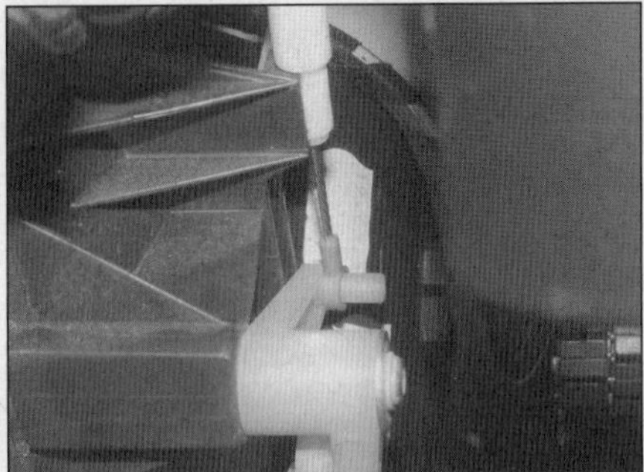
28.15 Disconnect the temperature control ventilation cable from the driver's side of the heater housing

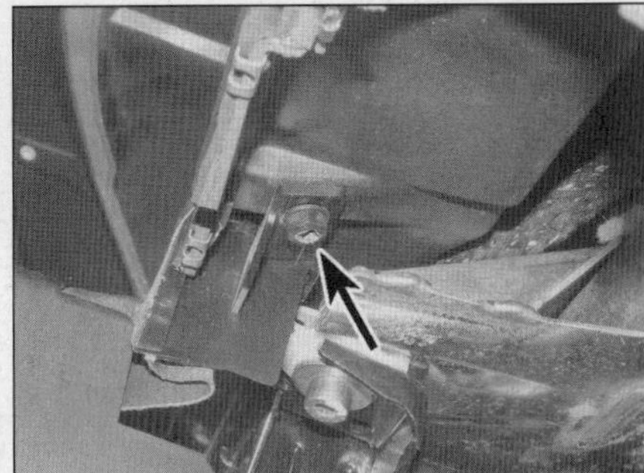
28.16 Undo the plastic bolt each side (right-hand side arrowed) and remove the steering column gaiter from the facia

driver's side of the MID/on-board computer aperture **(see illustration)**.

10 Manoeuvre the lower facia assembly from position.

Upper facia panel

11 Remove the lower facia panel as previously described.

12 Remove both A-pillar trims as described in Section 26.

13 Remove the passenger's airbag as described in Chapter 12.

14 Undo the 3 screws securing the upper facia panel on the passenger's side **(see illustration)**.

15 Note its fitted position, then disconnect the temperature control ventilation cable **(see illustration)**.

16 Undo the plastic bolt either side and detach the steering column rubber gaiter from the facia **(see illustration)**.

17 Undo the 3 facia retaining screws on the driver's side, pull the facia slightly to the rear, lift it up and manoeuvre it through the passenger's door opening **(see illustrations)**.

Refitting

18 Refitting is a reversal of the removal procedure, noting the following points:

a) *Manoeuvre the facia into position and, using the labels stuck on during removal, ensure that the wiring is correctly routed and securely retained by its facia clips.*
b) *Clip the facia back into position, ensure the centre locating lug at the front edge of the facia engages correctly, making sure all the wiring connectors are fed through their respective apertures, then refit all the facia fasteners, and tighten them securely.*
c) *On completion, reconnect the battery and check that all the electrical components and switches function correctly.*

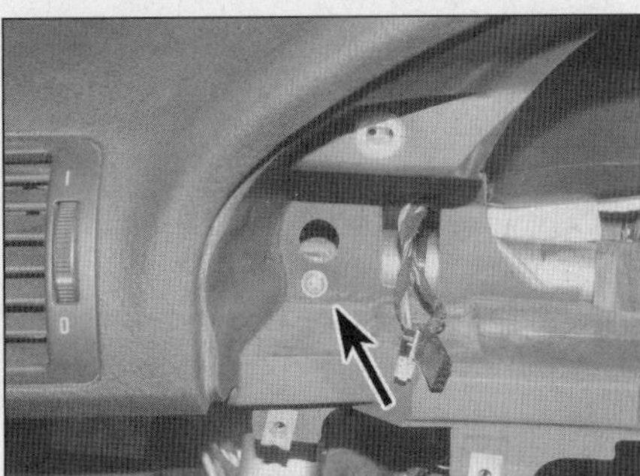
28.17a Undo the screw in the corner of the instrument cluster aperture (arrowed) . . .

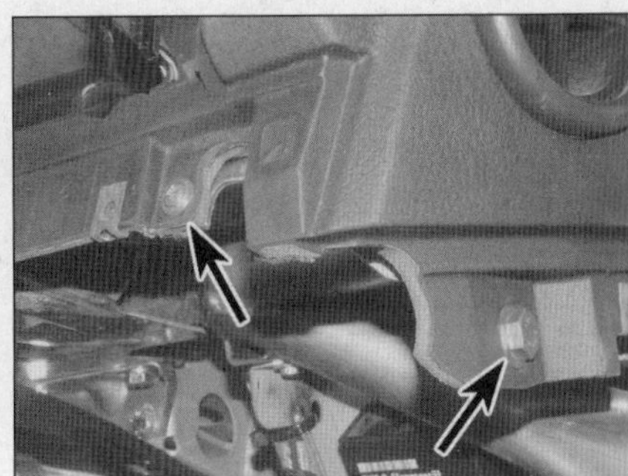
28.17b . . . and two (arrowed) at the driver's side end

Chapter 12
Body electrical system

Contents

Degrees of difficulty

Easy, suitable for novice with little experience 	**Fairly easy,** suitable for beginner with some experience 	**Fairly difficult,** suitable for competent DIY mechanic	**Difficult,** suitable for experienced DIY mechanic	**Very difficult,** suitable for expert DIY or professional

Specifications

System type	12 volt negative earth
Fuses	See inside fusebox
Bulbs	**Wattage**
Exterior lights	
Direction indicator side repeater	5
Direction indicator	21
Front foglight:	
Models up to 09/2000	55 (H7 type)
Models from 09/2000	55 (H8 type)
M-Sport Aerodynamic models	55 (HB4 type)
Headlight:	
Dipped beam:	
Models up to 09/2000	55 (HB4 type)
Models from 09/2000	55 (H7 type)
Main beam:	
Models up to 09/2000	60 (HB3 type)
Models from 09/2000	55 (H7 type)
High-level stop-light	21
Number plate light	5
Rear foglight	21
Reversing light	21
Sidelight:	
Models up to 09/2000	5
Models from 09/2000	10
Stop-light	21
Taillight	5

Bulbs (continued)

Interior lights	Wattage
Front courtesy lights	10
Glovebox light	5
Instrument panel:	
Illumination bulbs	3
Warning light bulbs	1.5
Luggage compartment light	10
Rear courtesy lights	5

Component location

Air conditioning blower relay	Behind passenger's glovebox
Airbag control module	Beneath centre console
Airbag crash sensor	Front seat crossmember under carpet
Alarm control module	Under facia on the driver's side
Automatic transmission control module	E-box in engine compartment
Engine management ECM	E-box in engine compartment
Engine management main relay	E-box in engine compartment
Fuel injector relay	Behind storage tray, right side of luggage compartment
Fuel pump relay	Behind passenger's glovebox
General module (GM III)	Behind passenger's glovebox
Heated rear window relay	Right-hand side of luggage compartment
Horn relay	Behind passenger's glovebox
Ignition relay	E-box in engine compartment
Instrument cluster control unit	Instrument cluster
Light control module	Behind driver's side footwell kick panel
Parking distance control module	Right-hand side of luggage compartment
Seat control module	Base of seat cushion
Tyre pressure control module	Behind passenger's glovebox
Windscreen wiper relay	E-box in engine compartment

Note that not all models are equipped with the components listed.

Torque wrench settings

	Nm	lbf ft
Airbag system fixings:		
Door airbag retaining screws	8	6
Driver's airbag retaining screws	8	6
Impact sensor mounting bolts	10	7
Passenger's airbag cover straps screws	8	6
Passenger's airbag retaining nuts	10	7
Tyre pressure transmitter Torx screw	3.5	2.6
Wiper arm-to-wiper spindle nut:		
Passenger side	25	18
Driver's side	40	30
Rear wiper	30	22

1 General information and precautions

Warning: Before carrying out any work on the electrical system, read through the precautions given in 'Safety First!' at the beginning of this manual and Chapter 5A.

The electrical system is of the 12 volt negative earth type. Power for the lights and all electrical accessories is supplied by a lead-acid type battery which is charged by the alternator.

This Chapter covers repair and service procedures for the various electrical components not associated with engine. Information on the battery, alternator and starter motor can be found in Chapter 5A.

It should be noted that prior to working on any component in the electrical system, the battery negative terminal should first be disconnected to prevent the possibility of electrical short circuits and/or fires (see Chapter 5A).

2 Electrical fault finding – general information

Note: *Refer to the precautions given in 'Safety first!' and in Section 1 of this Chapter before starting work. The following tests relate to testing of the main electrical circuits, and should not be used to test delicate electronic circuits (such as anti-lock braking systems), particularly where an electronic control module/unit (ECM/ECU) is used.*

Caution: The BMW 5-Series electrical system is extremely complex. Many of the ECMs are connected via a 'Databus' system, where they are able to share information from the various sensors, and communicate with each other. For instance, as the automatic gearbox approaches a gear ratio shift point, it signals the engine management ECM via the Databus. As the gearchange is made by the transmission ECM, the engine management ECM retards the ignition timing, momentarily reducing engine output, to ensure a smoother transition from one gear ratio to the next. Due to the design of the Databus system, it is not advisable to backprobe the ECMs with a multimeter in the traditional manner. Instead, the electrical systems are equipped with a sophisticated self-

diagnosis system, which can interrogate the various ECMs to reveal stored fault codes, and help pin-point faults. In order to access the self-diagnosis system, specialist test equipment (fault code reader/scanner) is required.

General

1 A typical electrical circuit consists of an electrical component, any switches, relays, motors, fuses, fusible links or circuit breakers related to that component, and the wiring and connectors which link the component to both the battery and the chassis. To help to pin-point a problem in an electrical circuit, wiring diagrams are included at the end of this Chapter.

2 Before attempting to diagnose an electrical fault, first study the appropriate wiring diagram to obtain a complete understanding of the components included in the particular circuit concerned. The possible sources of a fault can be narrowed down by noting if other components related to the circuit are operating properly. If several components or circuits fail at one time, the problem is likely to be related to a shared fuse or earth connection.

3 Electrical problems usually stem from simple causes, such as loose or corroded connections, a faulty earth connection, a blown fuse, a melted fusible link, or a faulty relay (refer to Section 3 for details of testing relays). Visually inspect the condition of all fuses, wires and connections in a problem circuit before testing the components. Use the wiring diagrams to determine which terminal connections will need to be checked in order to pin-point the trouble spot.

4 The basic tools required for electrical fault finding include a circuit tester or voltmeter (a 12 volt bulb with a set of test leads can also be used for certain tests); a self-powered test light (sometimes known as a continuity tester); an ohmmeter (to measure resistance); a battery and set of test leads; and a jumper wire, preferably with a circuit breaker or fuse incorporated, which can be used to bypass suspect wires or electrical components. Before attempting to locate a problem with test instruments, use the wiring diagram to determine where to make the connections.

5 To find the source of an intermittent wiring fault (usually due to a poor or dirty connection, or damaged wiring insulation), a 'wiggle' test can be performed on the wiring. This involves wiggling the wiring by hand to see if the fault occurs as the wiring is moved. It should be possible to narrow down the source of the fault to a particular section of wiring. This method of testing can be used in conjunction with any of the tests described in the following sub-Sections.

6 Apart from problems due to poor connections, two basic types of fault can occur in an electrical circuit – open circuit, or short circuit.

7 Open circuit faults are caused by a break somewhere in the circuit, which prevents current from flowing. An open circuit fault will prevent a component from working, but will not cause the relevant circuit fuse to blow.

8 Short circuit faults are caused by a 'short' somewhere in the circuit, which allows the current flowing in the circuit to 'escape' along an alternative route, usually to earth. Short circuit faults are normally caused by a breakdown in wiring insulation, which allows a feed wire to touch either another wire, or an earthed component such as the bodyshell. A short circuit fault will normally cause the relevant circuit fuse to blow.

Finding an open circuit

9 To check for an open circuit, connect one lead of a circuit tester or voltmeter to either the negative battery terminal or a known good earth.

10 Connect the other lead to a connector in the circuit being tested, preferably nearest to the battery or fuse.

11 Switch on the circuit, bearing in mind that some circuits are live only when the ignition switch is moved to a particular position.

12 If voltage is present (indicated either by the tester bulb lighting or a voltmeter reading, as applicable), this means that the section of the circuit between the relevant connector and the battery is problem-free.

13 Continue to check the remainder of the circuit in the same fashion.

14 When a point is reached at which no voltage is present, the problem must lie between that point and the previous test point with voltage. Most problems can be traced to a broken, corroded or loose connection.

Finding a short circuit

15 To check for a short circuit, first disconnect the load(s) from the circuit (loads are the components which draw current from a circuit, such as bulbs, motors, heating elements, etc).

16 Remove the relevant fuse from the circuit, and connect a circuit tester or voltmeter to the fuse connections.

17 Switch on the circuit, bearing in mind that some circuits are live only when the ignition switch is moved to a particular position.

18 If voltage is present (indicated either by the tester bulb lighting or a voltmeter reading, as applicable), this means that there is a short circuit.

19 If no voltage is present, but the fuse still blows with the load(s) connected, this indicates an internal fault in the load(s).

Finding an earth fault

20 The battery negative terminal is connected to 'earth' – the metal of the engine/transmission and the car body – and most systems are wired so that they only receive a positive feed, the current returning through the metal of the car body **(see illustrations)**. This means that the component mounting and the body form part of that circuit. Loose or corroded mountings can therefore cause a range of electrical faults, ranging from total failure of a circuit, to a puzzling partial fault. In particular, lights may shine dimly (especially when another circuit sharing the same earth point is in operation), motors (eg, wiper motors or the radiator cooling fan motor) may run slowly, and the operation of one circuit may have an apparently unrelated effect on another. Note that on many vehicles, earth straps are used between certain components, such as the engine/transmission and the body, usually where there is no metal-to-metal contact between components due to flexible rubber mountings, etc.

21 To check whether a component is properly earthed, disconnect the battery and connect one lead of an ohmmeter to a known good earth point. Connect the other lead to the wire or earth connection being tested. The resistance reading should be zero; if not, check the connection as follows.

22 If an earth connection is thought to be faulty, dismantle the connection and clean back to bare metal both the bodyshell and the wire terminal or the component earth connection mating surface. Be careful to remove all traces of dirt and corrosion, then use a knife to trim away any paint, so that a clean metal-to-metal joint is made. On reassembly, tighten the joint fasteners securely; if a wire terminal is being refitted, use serrated washers between the terminal

2.20a An earth strap (arrowed) is bolted from the vehicle body to the right-hand engine mounting bracket . . .

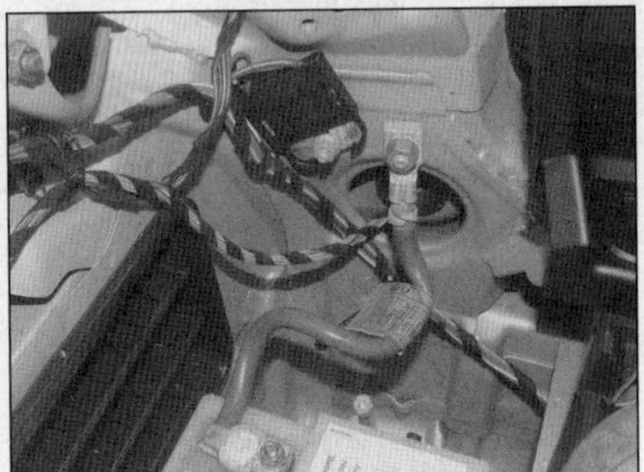

2.20b . . . and from the vehicle body to the battery negative terminal

3.2 Undo the two fasteners (arrowed), and lower the fusebox cover

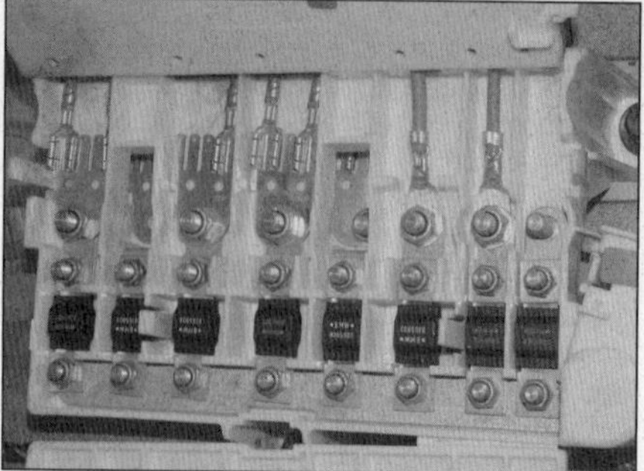

3.3 High amperage fusible inks

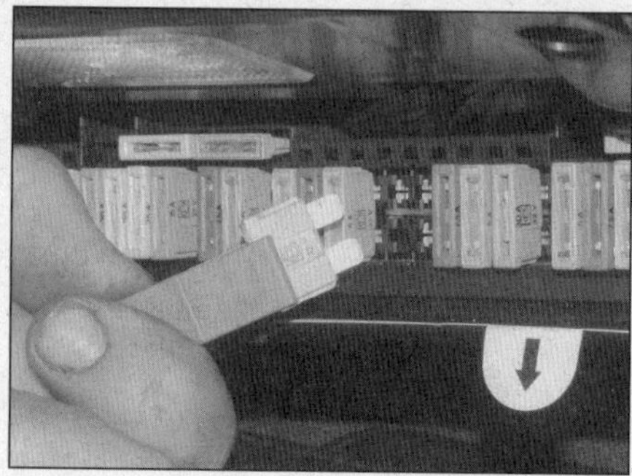

3.4 Use the tweezers provided to pull the fuse from its terminals

and the bodyshell to ensure a clean and secure connection. When the connection is remade, prevent the onset of corrosion in the future by applying a coat of petroleum jelly or silicone-based grease, or by spraying on (at regular intervals) a proprietary ignition sealer or a water dispersant lubricant.

3 Fuses and relays – general information

Main fuses

1 The majority of the fuses are located behind passenger's side glovebox, whilst some others are located in the 'E-box' located in the left-hand corner of the engine compartment, and behind the right-hand storage tray in the luggage compartment.

2 To remove the main fusebox cover, open the glovebox, turn the two white quick-release fasteners and pull down the cover **(see illustration)**. The fuses in the 'E-box' are accessed once the cover retaining screws have been removed.

3 A list of the circuits each fuse protects is given on the label attached to the inside of the main fusebox cover. A pair of tweezers for removing the fuses is also clipped to the fusebox. Note that the vertical fuses are active, and the horizontal fuses are spare. High amperage 'fusible links' are located adjacent to the battery in the luggage compartment and under the carpet beneath the driver's seat **(see illustration)**.

4 To remove a fuse, first switch off the circuit concerned (or the ignition), then pull the fuse out of its terminals using the tweezers which are clipped to the inside of the fusebox cover **(see illustration)**. The wire within the fuse should be visible; if the fuse is blown it will be broken or melted.

5 Always renew a fuse with one of an identical rating; never use a fuse with a different rating from the original or substitute anything else. Never renew a fuse more than once without tracing the source of the trouble. The fuse rating is stamped on top of the fuse; note that the fuses are also colour-coded for easy recognition.

6 If a new fuse blows immediately, find the cause before renewing it again; a short to earth as a result of faulty insulation is most likely. Where a fuse protects more than one circuit, try to isolate the defect by switching on each circuit in turn (if possible) until the fuse blows again. Always carry a supply of spare fuses of each relevant rating on the vehicle, a spare of each rating should be clipped into the base of the fusebox.

Relays

7 The majority of relays are located behind the passenger's side glovebox, whilst other relays are located above the battery in the luggage compartment **(see illustration)** and in the 'E-box' in the left-hand corner of the engine compartment.

8 If a circuit or system controlled by a relay develops a fault and the relay is suspect, operate the system; if the relay is functioning it should be possible to hear it click as it is energised. If this is the case the fault lies with the components or wiring of the system. If the relay is not being energised then either the relay is not receiving a main supply or a switching voltage or the relay itself is faulty. Testing is by the substitution of a known good unit but be careful; while some relays are identical in appearance and in operation, others look similar but perform different functions.

9 To renew a relay first ensure that the ignition switch is off. The relay can then simply be pulled out from the socket and the new relay pressed in.

4 Switches – removal and refitting

Note: *Disconnect the battery negative lead (see Chapter 5A) before removing any switch, and reconnect the lead after refitting the switch.*

Ignition switch/ steering column lock

1 Refer to Chapter 10.

Steering column switches

2 Fully extend the steering column and set it in its lowest position, then remove the driver's side facia lower trim panel as described in Chapter 11.

3 Undo the screw, and prise out the rivet securing the upper column shroud, then squeeze together the sides of the shroud and

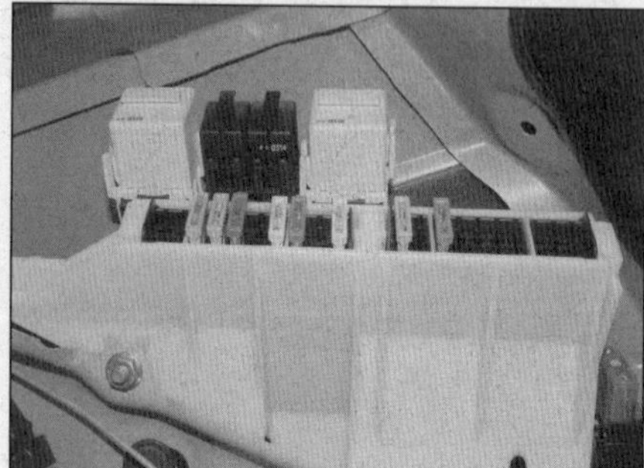

3.7 Relays mounted above the battery in the luggage compartment

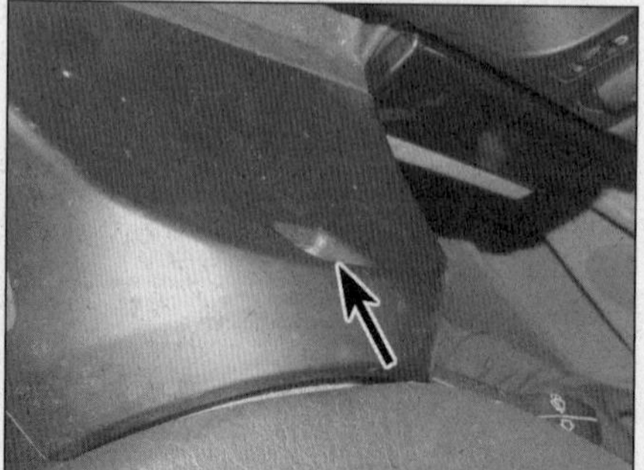

4.3a Undo the shroud retaining screw (arrowed)

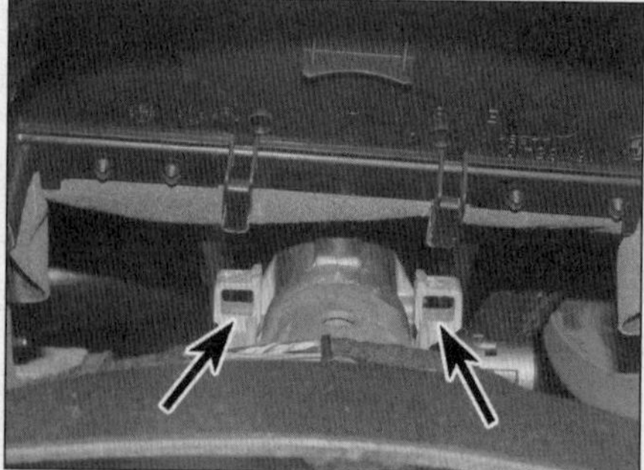

4.3b Note how the hooks at the front of the shroud engage with the slots (arrowed)

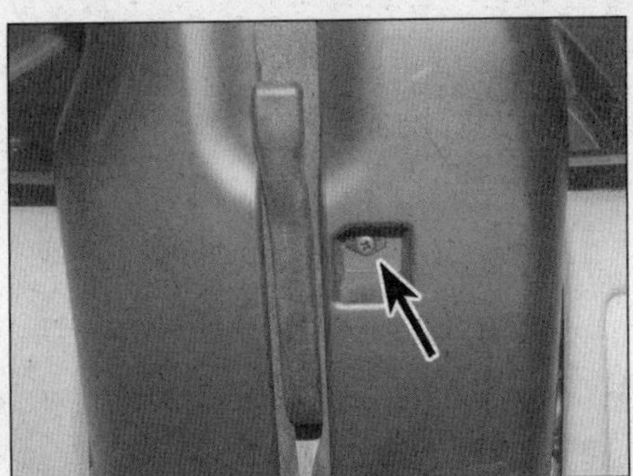

4.4 Undo the screw (arrowed) and remove the steering column lower shroud

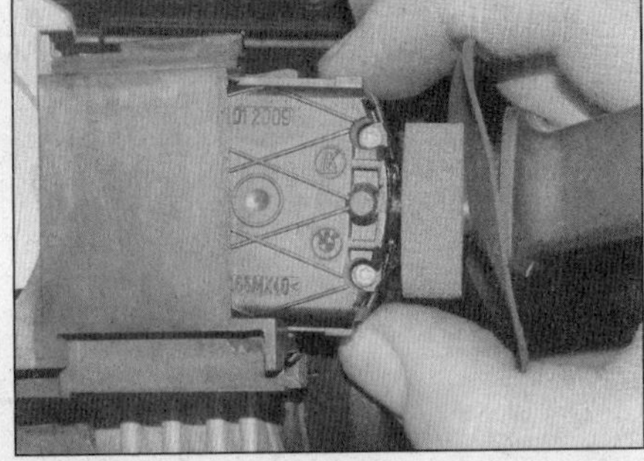

4.5 Squeeze together the retaining clips and slide the switch from the holder

4.6 Undo the two Torx screws (arrowed) and slide the switch holder from the column

lift it upwards, disengaging the hooks at the front **(see illustrations)**.

4 Undo the screw, prise out the plastic rivet and remove the lower steering column shroud **(see illustration)**.

5 Disconnect the relevant switch wiring plug, then squeeze together the retaining clips and slide the switch from the holder **(see illustration)**.

6 If it's necessary to remove the switch holder, remove the steering wheel (Chapter 10), undo the two retaining Torx screws, release the cable ties and the upper retaining clips, and slide the switch holder down from the column **(see illustration)**.

7 Refitting is a reversal of the removal procedure, ensuring that the wiring is correctly routed.

Lighting switch and foglight switch

8 Using a wooden or plastic tool, carefully prise the decorative strip from the driver's side of the facia, either side of the steering column **(see illustration)**. Take care not to damage the facia panels.

9 Undo the screws and remove the instrument panel surround **(see illustrations 9.4a and 9.4b)**.

10 Carefully pull the central knob from the light switch **(see illustration)**.

11 Undo the retaining nut, and manoeuvre the light switch from the surround, disconnecting the wiring plug as it is withdrawn **(see illustration)**.

12 Refitting is the reverse of removal.

Hazard warning switch and central locking switch

13 On manual transmission models, carefully unclip the gearchange lever gaiter from the centre console and fold it back over the lever.

14 On models with automatic transmission carefully prise up the selector lever gaiter complete with plastic surrounding trim.

15 Push the switch(es) from place. Disconnect the wiring plugs as the switch(es) are removed **(see illustration)**.

16 Refitting is the reverse of removal.

Electric window and exterior mirror switches

17 Using a flat-bladed screwdriver, carefully lever the switch out from the armrest **(see illustration)**. Use a piece of cardboard or similar to protect the trim fabric.

18 Disconnect the wiring connector and remove the switch.

19 Refitting is the reverse of removal.

Cruise control clutch switch

20 Undo the driver's side lower facia panel retaining screws then unclip the panel and remove it from the vehicle. Note their fitted positions and disconnect any wiring plugs as the panel is withdrawn.

21 Disconnect the wiring plug from the switch.

22 Depress the clutch pedal, and pull the switch plunger out to its fully extended position.

23 Depress the retaining clips and slide the switch out of position.

24 Refitting is the reverse of removal. With the switch fitted, and the plunger fully

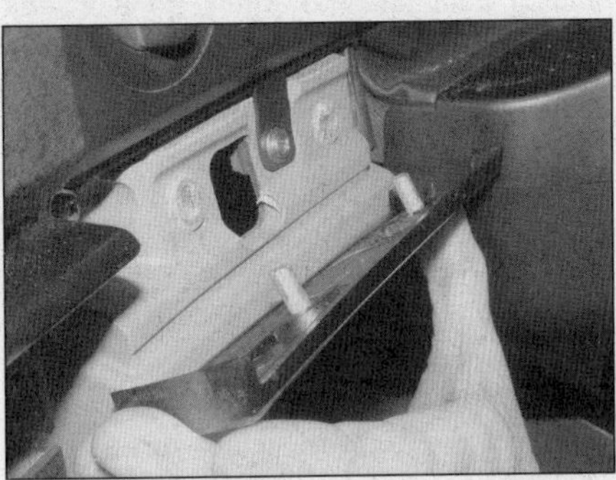

4.8 Carefully prise away the facia decorative trim from either side of the steering column

4.10 Pull the knob from the light switch

4.11 Undo the nut and pull the switch from the surround

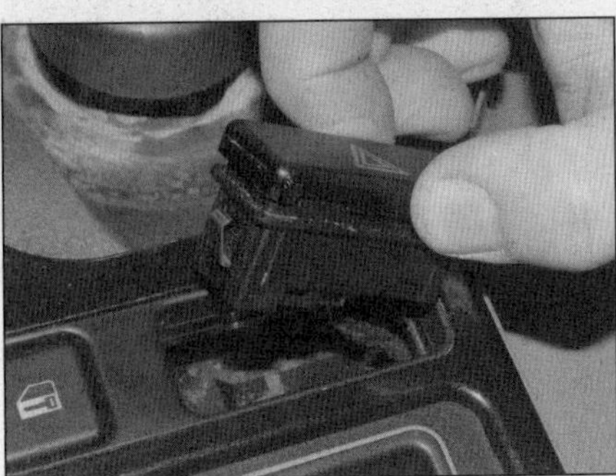

4.15 Remove the hazard switch from the centre console

4.17 Carefully prise the switch from the armrest

4.32 Prise the switch from the centre console

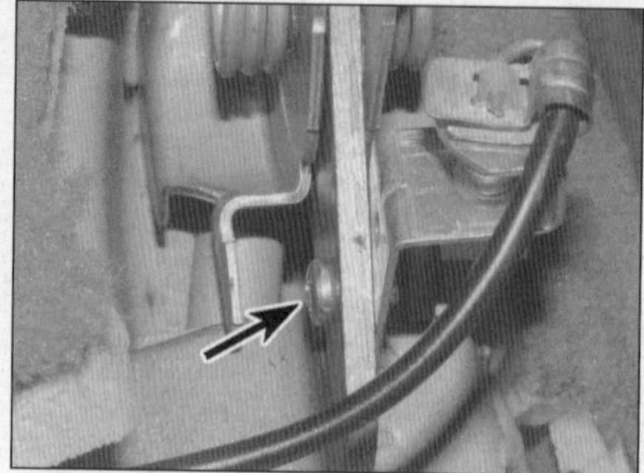
4.36 Handbrake switch retaining screw (arrowed)

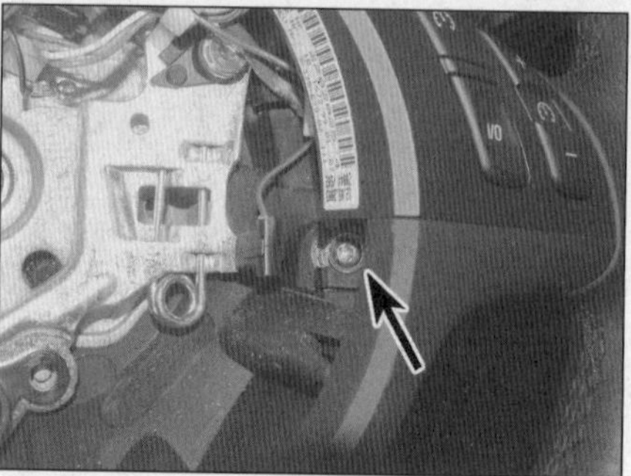
4.42 Steering wheel switch panel retaining screw (arrowed)

extended, allow the pedal to slowly return to its 'at rest' position.

Heated rear window switch

With automatic air conditioning

25 On these models the switch is an integral part of the control unit and cannot be renewed. If the switch is faulty seek the advice of a BMW dealer.

Without automatic air conditioning

26 On these models the switch is an integral part of the heater control panel printed circuit.
27 Remove the heater control panel as described in Chapter 3.
28 Disconnect the switch wiring plug, release the retaining clips and pull the switch from the panel.
29 Refitting is the reverse of removal. Check the operation of the switch before refitting the control panel to the facia.

Heater blower motor switch

30 The switch is an integral part of the control unit and cannot be renewed. If the switch is faulty seek the advice of a BMW dealer.

Air conditioning system switches

31 The switch is an integral part of the control unit and cannot be renewed. If the switch is faulty seek the advice of a BMW dealer.

Heated seat, rear sun blind, electronic damper control and traction control switches

32 Using a flat-bladed wooden or plastic tool, carefully prise the switch from the centre console **(see illustration)**. Use a piece of cardboard (or similar) positioned under the tool to prevent damage to any trim surface.
33 Disconnect the wiring connector as the switch is withdrawn.
34 Refitting is the reverse of removal.

Handbrake warning switch

35 Remove the centre console as described in Chapter 11 to gain access to the handbrake lever.
36 Disconnect the wiring connector from the warning light switch then undo the screw and remove the switch **(see illustration)**.
37 Refitting is the reverse of removal. Check the operation of the switch before refitting the centre console, the warning light should illuminate between the first and second clicks of the ratchet mechanism.

Stop-light switch

38 Refer to Chapter 9.

Interior light switches

39 The function of the courtesy light switches is incorporated into the door/boot lid/tailgate lock assembly. To remove the relevant lock refer to Chapter 11.

Steering wheel switches

40 Two different types of steering wheels are fitted to the 5-Series range. Either a Multifunction steering wheel, or a Sports steering wheel. To remove the switches, remove the driver's airbag as described in Section 25, then proceed under the relevant heading.

Multifunction steering wheel

41 Carefully prise the switch from the steering wheel, and disconnect the switch wiring plugs. Note that the horn switch is integral with the airbag unit.

Sports steering wheel

42 Undo the four retaining screws (two securing the upper section and two securing the lower section), and unclip the switch carrier panel from the steering wheel **(see illustration)**. Disconnect the wiring plug as the panel with withdrawn.

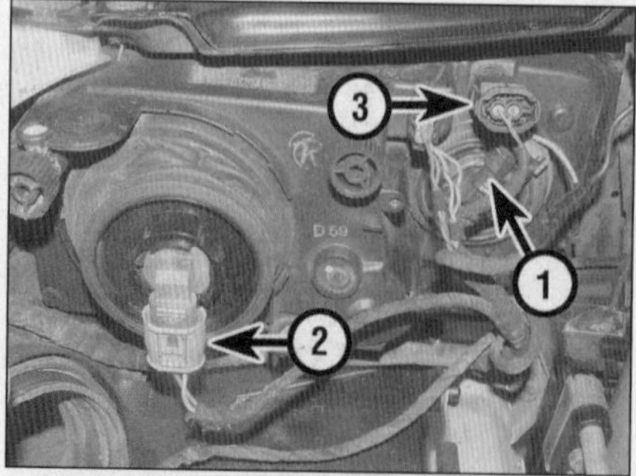

5.2 Main beam headlight wiring plug (1), dipped beam (2), and sidelight (3) – models up to 09/2000

Electric sunroof switch

43 Depress the clip at the rear of the switch, and pull the switch from the panel.
44 Disconnect the switch wiring connector and remove the switch.
45 Refitting is the reverse of removal.

Headlight levelling and instrument illumination control

46 Using a wooden or plastic spatula, carefully prise the decorative strip from the driver's side of the facia, either side of the steering column **(see illustration 4.8)**. Take care not to damage the facia panels.
47 Undo the screws and remove the instrument panel surround **(see illustrations 9.4a and 9.4b)**.
48 Disconnect the switch wiring plugs, then carefully push the switch from the panel.
49 Refitting is a reversal of removal.

5 Bulbs (exterior lights) – renewal

General

1 Whenever a bulb is renewed, note the following points.

a) Remember that if the light has just been in use the bulb may be extremely hot.
b) Always check the bulb contacts and holder, ensuring that there is clean metal-to-metal contact between the bulb and its live(s) and earth. Clean off any corrosion or dirt before fitting a new bulb.
c) Wherever bayonet-type bulbs are fitted ensure that the live contact(s) bear firmly against the bulb contact.
d) Always ensure that the new bulb is of the correct rating and that it is completely clean before fitting it; this applies particularly to headlight/foglight bulbs (see below).

Halogen headlight bulbs

Models up to 09/2000

2 Disconnect the wiring connector from the rear of the bulbholder **(see illustration)**.

5.3 Rotate the bulbholder anti-clockwise and remove it

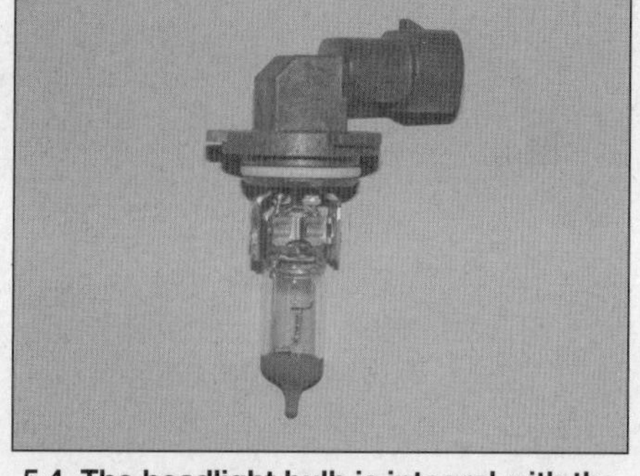

5.4 The headlight bulb is integral with the bulbholder

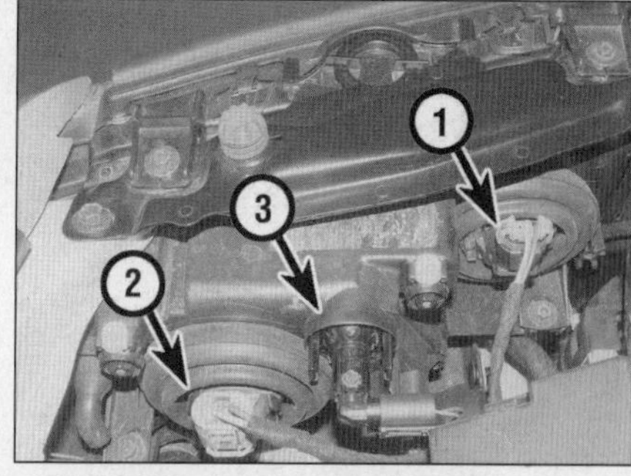

5.7 Main beam headlight wiring plug (1), dipped beam (2), and sidelight (3) – models from 09/2000

3 Turn the bulbholder assembly anti-clockwise and remove it from the rear of the headlight **(see illustration)**. To improve access to the left-hand headlight, remove the air cleaner housing as described in Chapter 4A. The main beam is the inner of the two bulbs.

4 The bulb is integral with the bulbholder, and is supplied as an assembly **(see illustration)**.

5 When handling the new bulb, use a tissue or clean cloth to avoid touching the glass with the fingers; moisture and grease from the skin can cause blackening and rapid failure of this type of bulb. If the glass is accidentally touched, wipe it clean using methylated spirit.

6 Refit the bulbholder to the rear of the headlight, rotating it clockwise until the retaining clips lock. Reconnect the wiring plug.

Models from 09/2000

7 Disconnect the wiring connector from the rear of the bulbholder **(see illustration)**.

8 Turn the bulbholder assembly anti-clockwise and remove it from the headlight **(see illustration)**.

9 Carefully pull the bulb from the bulbholder **(see illustration)**.

10 When handling the new bulb, use a tissue or clean cloth to avoid touching the glass with the fingers; moisture and grease from the skin can cause blackening and rapid failure of this type of bulb. If the glass is accidentally touched, wipe it clean using methylated spirit.

11 Refit the bulb to the bulbholder, and then refit the bulbholder to the rear of the headlight, rotating it clockwise until the retaining clips lock. Reconnect the wiring plug.

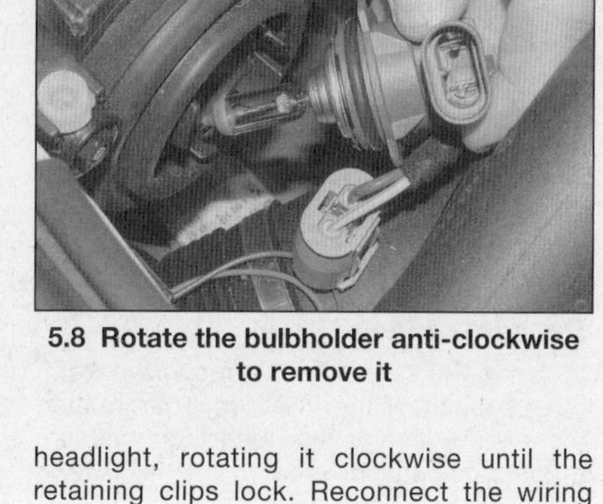

5.8 Rotate the bulbholder anti-clockwise to remove it

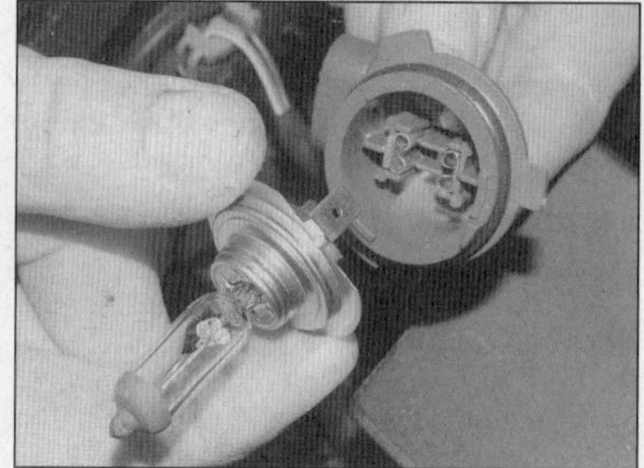

5.9 Pull the bulb from the holder

Xenon headlight bulbs

12 On models equipped with Xenon high-intensity dip-beam bulbs, due to the potential high voltages involved, disconnect the battery negative lead as described in Chapter 5A. To improve access to the left-hand headlight, remove the air cleaner housing as described in Chapter 4A.

Models up to 09/2000

13 Undo the three screws and pull the igniter from the rear of the bulb.

14 Pull the bulb from the rear of the headlight. Note how the lugs of the bulb engage with the corresponding slots in the bulbholder.

15 Fit the new bulb into the headlight, refit the igniter and tighten the retaining screws securely.

Models from 09/2000

16 Rotate the bulb igniter unit on the rear of the bulb anti-clockwise and disconnect it.

17 Detach the plastic cover from the rear of the headlight.

18 Twist the bulb retaining ring anti-clockwise and remove it, with the bulb, from the headlight.

19 Fit the new bulb to the headlight, and secure it in place with the retaining ring.

20 Refit the igniter to the rear of the bulb, turning it clockwise to secure it.

21 Where necessary, refit the air cleaner housing.

22 Reconnect the battery negative lead as described in Chapter 5A.

Sidelight

23 To improve access to the left-hand headlight, remove the air cleaner housing as described in Chapter 4A.

Models up to 09/2000

24 Rotate the bulbholder anti-clockwise and withdraw it from the headlight unit. The bulb is of the capless type and is a push-fit in the holder **(see illustrations)**.

5.24a Rotate the sidelight bulbholder anti-clockwise . . .

5.24b . . . and pull the capless bulb from the holder – models up to 09/2000

5.25 Rotate the bulbholder anti-clockwise to remove it – models from 09/2000

5.27 Pull the rubber O-ring from the clip mechanism

5.28 Squeeze together the clips and pull the bulbholder from the headlight

Models from 09/2000

25 Rotate the bulbholder anti-clockwise and withdraw it from the headlight unit. The bulb is integral with the bulbholder **(see illustration)**.

26 Refitting is the reverse of removal.

Front direction indicator

27 Disconnect the wiring plug, and pull the rubber O-ring from the clip mechanism **(see illustration)**.

28 Squeeze together the retaining clips and pull the bulbholder to remove it from the headlight **(see illustration)**.

29 The bulb is a bayonet fitting in the holder. Push the bulb in slightly, then rotate it anti-clockwise and pull it from the holder.

30 Refitting is a reverse of the removal procedure.

Side repeater

31 Using finger pressure, push the side repeater lens gently forwards. Pull out the rear edge of the lens and withdraw it from the wing **(see illustration)**.

32 Rotate the bulbholder anti-clockwise and pull it from the lens, pull the capless bulb it from the holder **(see illustration)**.

33 Refitting is a reverse of the removal procedure.

Front foglight

Standard models

34 Undo the screws and remove the front, lower section of the front wheel arch liner. There is no need to disconnect the ambient temperature sensor located in the driver's side panel, but take care not to strain the wiring.

35 Disconnect the wiring plug and release the cover retaining clip **(see illustration)**.

36 Disconnect the wiring from the bulb, squeeze together the ends of the retaining clip, and remove the bulb **(see illustrations)**.

37 When handling the new bulb, use a tissue or clean cloth to avoid touching the glass with the fingers; moisture and grease from the skin can cause blackening and rapid failure of this type of bulb. If the glass is accidentally touched, wipe it clean using methylated spirit.

38 Refitting is a reversal of removal. If necessary, adjust the aim of the light by rotating the adjusting screw adjacent to the lens.

M Sport Aerodynamic models

39 Remove the foglight as described in Section 7.

40 Rotate the bulbholder anti-clockwise, and remove it from the light. The bulb is integral with the bulbholder.

41 Refitting is a reversal of removal.

Saloon rear light cluster

42 Open the luggage compartment storage compartment on the relevant side.

Models up to 09/2000

43 Rotate the fastener 90° anti-clockwise and remove the bulbholder **(see illustration)**.

44 Press the relevant bulb in slightly, twist it anti-clockwise, and remove it from the

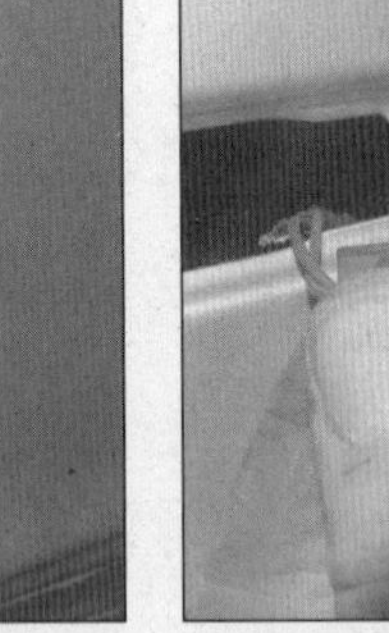

5.31 Push the lens forward, and pull out the rear edge

5.32 The side repeater bulb is capless, and simply pulls from the bulbholder

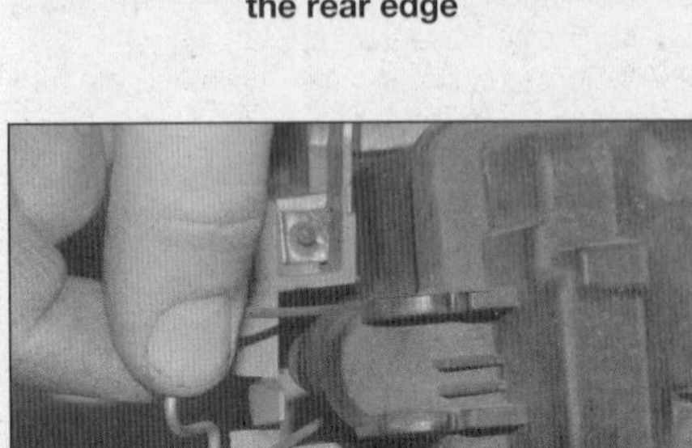

5.35 Release the foglight cover retaining clip

5.36a Squeeze together the ends of the retaining clip . . .

5.36b . . . then remove the bulb

5.43 Rotate the fastener (arrowed) anti-clockwise and remove the bulbholder assembly – models up to 09/2000

5.44 Press the bulb in slightly, twist it anti-clockwise, and remove it

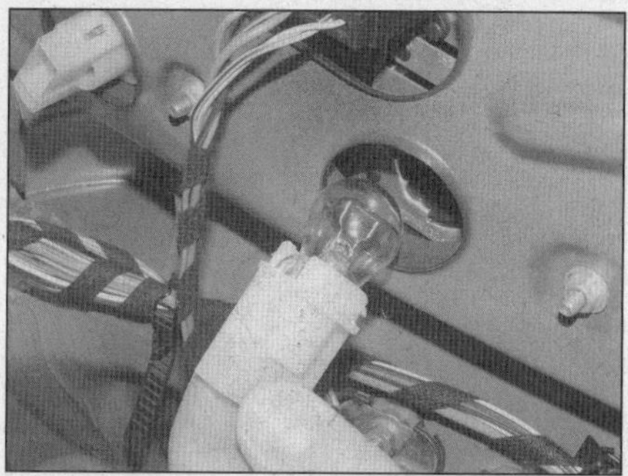
5.45 Rotate the bulbholder anti-clockwise to remove it – models from 09/2000

bulbholder **(see illustration)**. **Note:** *If renewing the double element stop/tail bulb, the bayonet fitting pins are offset, and the bulb will only fit one way around.*

Models from 09/2000

45 Rotate the relevant bulbholder anti-clockwise and remove it from the rear light cluster **(see illustration)**.

46 Press the relevant bulb in slightly, twist it anti-clockwise, and remove it from the bulbholder. **Note:** *If renewing the double element stop/tail bulb, the bayonet fitting pins are offset, and the bulb will only fit one way around.*

All models

47 Refitting is a reversal of removal.

Touring rear light cluster

Body-mounted lights

48 Depress the clip and remove the relevant storage compartment from the corner of the luggage compartment. Rotate the fastener anti-clockwise and remove the cover.

49 Rotate the fastener anti-clockwise and remove the bulbholder assembly **(see illustration)**.

50 Press the relevant bulb in slightly, twist it anti-clockwise, and remove it from the bulbholder.

51 Refitting is a reversal of removal.

Tailgate-mounted lights

52 Undo the two rotary fasteners and open the toolbox.

53 Rotate the fastener anti-clockwise and remove the bulbholder assembly **(see illustration)**.

54 Press the relevant bulb in slightly, twist it anti-clockwise, and remove it from the bulbholder.

55 Refitting is a reversal of removal.

High-level stop-light

Saloon models

56 Working in the luggage compartment, prise open the plastic cover under the light unit **(see illustration)**.

57 Rotate the bulbholder anti-clockwise and remove it from the unit **(see illustration)**.

58 The bulb is a bayonet fitting. Push-in, rotate it anti-clockwise and remove the bulb from the holder.

59 Refitting is a reversal of removal.

Touring models

60 The Tourer models are equipped LEDs in the high-level stop-light. If defective the complete light unit must be renewed.

Number plate light

61 Carefully push the light unit away from the end with the slot to compress the retaining spring, then lever the lens unit from place **(see illustration)**.

62 The bulb is of the 'festoon' type, and can be prised from the contacts.

63 Refitting is the reverse of removal, making sure the bulb is securely held in position by the contacts.

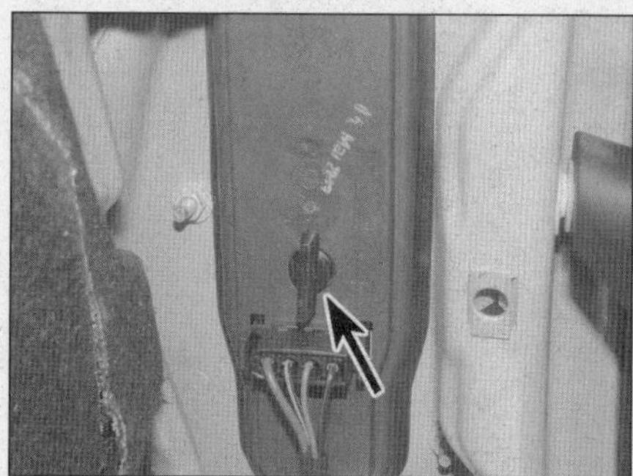
5.49 Rotate the fastener (arrowed) anti-clockwise

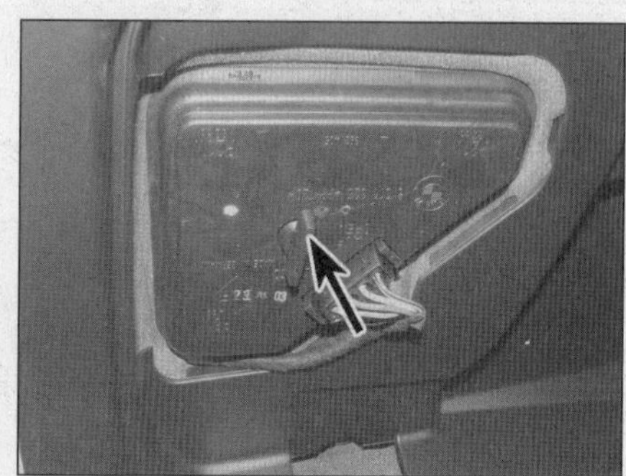
5.53 Rotate the fastener (arrowed) anti-clockwise

5.56 Prise upon the high-level stop-light cover (arrowed)

5.57 Rotate the bulbholder anti-clockwise and pull it from the high-level stop-light

5.61 Insert a screwdriver into the slot and push the light unit towards the other end, then lever the unit from place

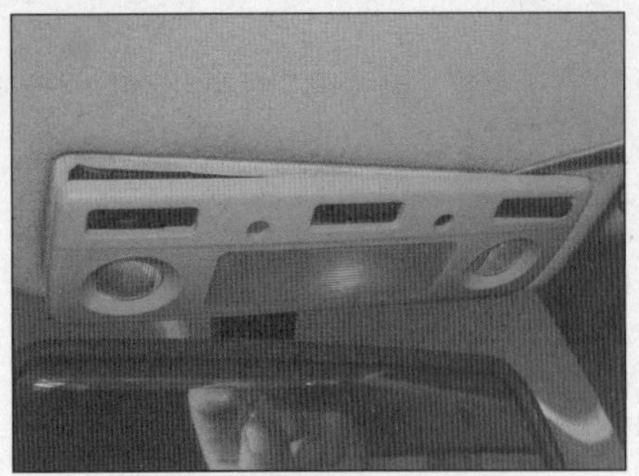
6.2 Prise the lens from the light

6.3 Remove the relevant bulb from the interior light unit

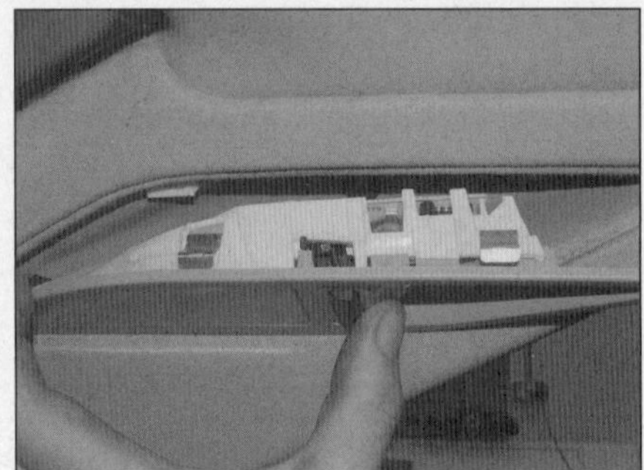
6.4 Starting at the top edge, prise the light unit from place

6 Bulbs (interior lights) – renewal

General

1 Refer to Section 5, paragraph 1.

Central interior lights

2 Using a flat-bladed screwdriver, carefully prise the lens from the light **(see illustration)**.
3 Remove the relevant bulb from the unit **(see illustration)**.

Side courtesy lights

4 Using a small, flat-bladed screwdriver, starting at the top edge carefully prise light unit out of position **(see illustration)**. Disconnect the wiring plug as the unit is withdrawn.

Saloon models

5 Depress the retaining clip and remove the baseplate from the light unit **(see illustration)**.
6 Remove the relevant bulb from the holder **(see illustration)**.
7 Push the new bulb(s) into the holder(s), and refit the baseplate to the light unit. Refit the light unit.

Touring models

8 Depress the two retaining clips and remove the lens.
9 Remove the relevant bulb from the holder.
10 Push the new bulb(s) into the holder(s), and refit the light unit.

Footwell light

11 Carefully lever the light lens out from the panel.
12 Prise the festoon bulb from the contacts **(see illustration)**.
13 Fit the new bulb into position and refit the lens to the light unit.

Luggage compartment light

14 Carefully prise the light unit from place. Disconnect the wiring plug as the unit is withdrawn.
15 Remove the metal cover from the light unit, and prise out the festoon bulb. Note that Saloon models have a metal cover which must be slid from place, and on Touring models the cover must be opened to expose the bulb **(see illustrations)**.

Instrument illumination/ warning lights

16 Instrument illumination is provided by integral LEDs. If faulty the instrument cluster may have to be renewed. Consult you BMW dealer or specialist.

Glovebox illumination bulb

17 Open up the glovebox. Using a small flat-bladed screwdriver carefully prise the light assembly from place and withdraw it. Release the bulb from its contacts.
18 Install the new bulb, ensuring it is securely held in position by the contacts, and clip the light unit back into position.

Heater control illumination

With automatic air conditioning

19 The heater control panel is illuminated by LEDs which are not serviceable. If a fault develops, have the system checked by a BMW dealer or suitably-equipped specialist.

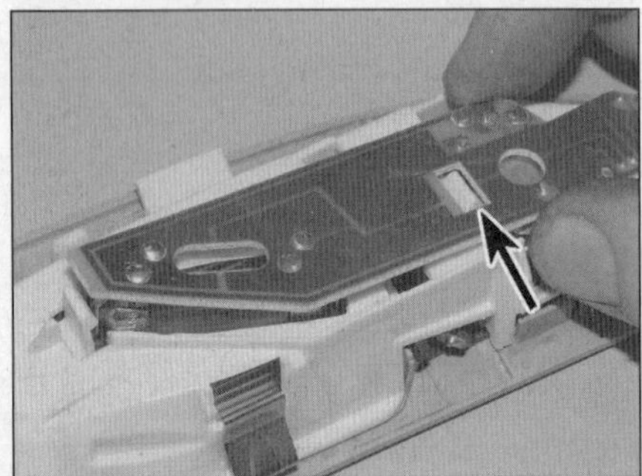
6.5 Release the clip (arrowed) and lift off the baseplate . . .

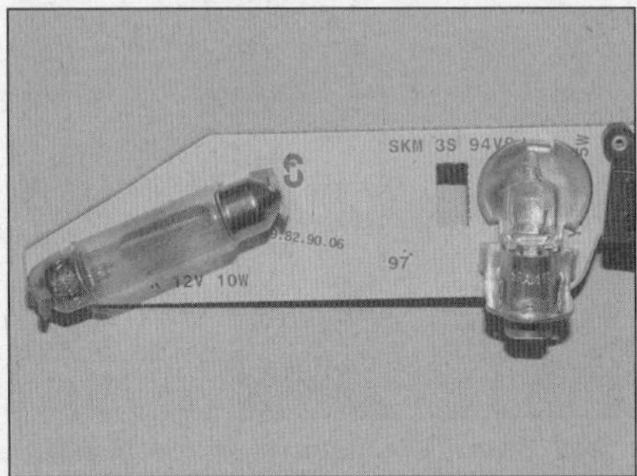

6.6 . . . then remove the relevant light bulb

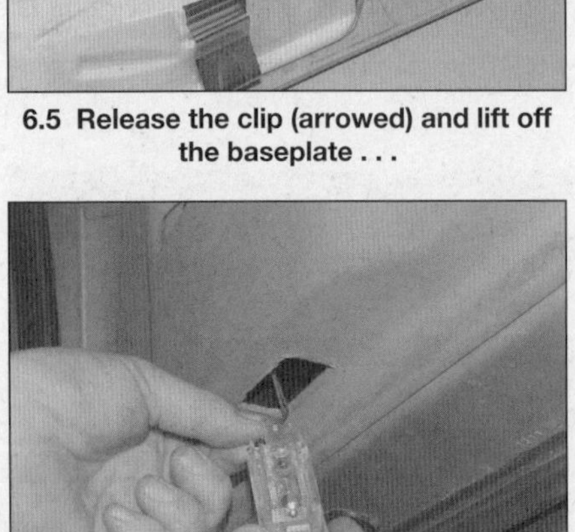
6.12 Prise the festoon bulb from its contacts

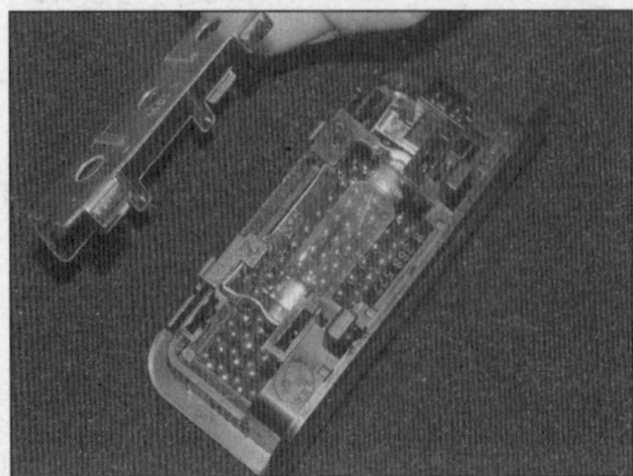
6.15a On Touring models, the metal cover must be opened . . .

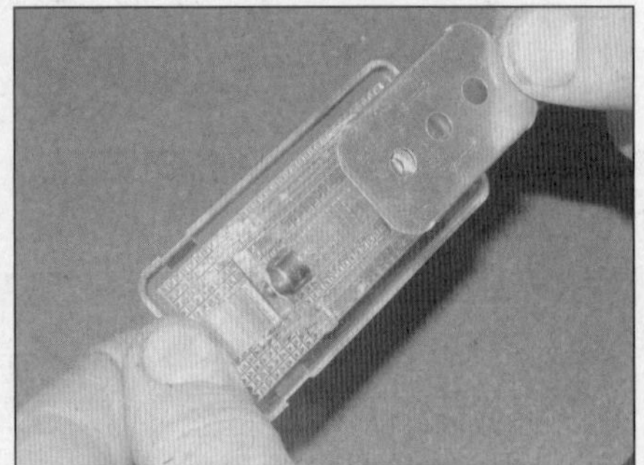
6.15b . . . on Saloon models, slide the metal cover from place

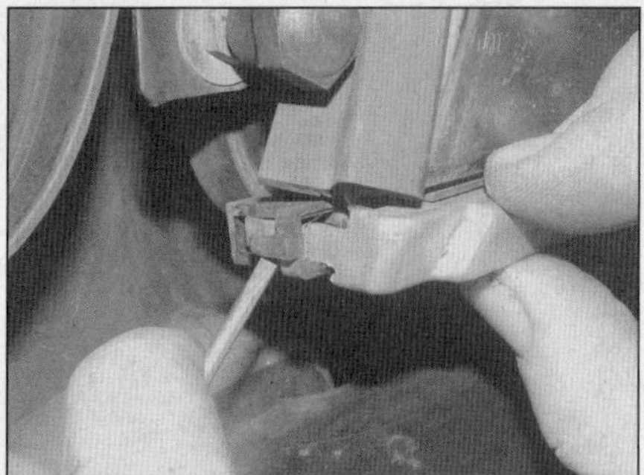
7.2a Depress the clip and release the inner end the trim . . .

7.2b . . . then lever down in the centre of the trim to release it from the clips under the headlight . . .

7.2c . . . and disengage the outer end of the trim

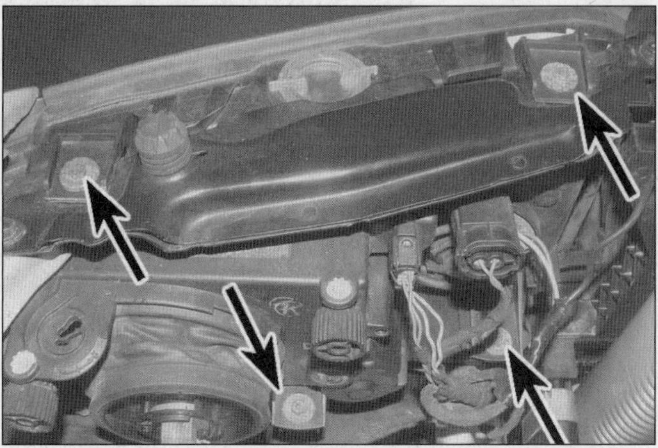
7.3a Headlight screws (arrowed) – models before 09/2000 . . .

7.3b . . . and after 09/2000

Without automatic air conditioning

20 Pull off the heater control panel knobs then undo the retaining screws and unclip the faceplate from the front of the control unit.

21 Using a pair of pointed-nose pliers, rotate the bulbholder anti-clockwise and remove it from the vehicle. On some models the panel is illuminated by LEDs which are not serviceable.

22 Refitting is the reverse of removal.

Switch illumination bulbs

23 All of the switches are fitted with illuminating bulbs/LEDs; some are also fitted with a bulb/LED to show when the circuit concerned is operating. On all switches, these bulbs/LEDs are an integral part of the switch assembly and cannot be obtained separately. Bulb/LED renewal will therefore require the renewal of the complete switch assembly.

7 Exterior light units – removal and refitting

Headlight

1 Disconnect the wiring plugs from the rear of the headlight **(see illustration 5.2 or 5.7)**.

2 Depress the clip, then pull the inboard end of the trim below the headlight forward, carefully lever down the centre of the trim to release it from the lugs under the headlight, then disengage it from the front edge of the wing **(see illustrations)**.

3 Each headlight is retained by four screws. Slacken and remove the headlight retaining screws **(see illustrations)**.

4 Remove the headlight unit from the vehicle. If required, unclip the lens unit from the headlamp **(see illustration)**.

5 Refitting is a direct reversal of the removal procedure. Lightly tighten the retaining screws and check the alignment of the headlight with the bumper and bonnet. Once the light unit is correctly positioned, securely tighten the retaining screws and check the headlight beam alignment using the information given in Section 8

7.4 Release the clips to remove the headlight lens

Xenon headlight control unit

Models up to 09/2000

6 Remove the relevant headlight as described earlier in this Section.

7 Undo the two retaining screws, slide the control unit to the rear of the headlight remove it.

8 If required, the control unit can be separated from the mounting bracket by removing the two securing screws.

9 Refitting is a reversal of removal.

Models from 09/2000

10 Remove the relevant headlight as described earlier in this Section.

11 Disconnect the unit wiring plug, undo the clamp screw and remove the control unit.

Front direction indicator

12 The indicator is integral with the headlight unit.

Side repeater

13 Using finger pressure, push the side repeater lens gently forwards. Pull out the rear edge of the lens and withdraw it from the wing

7.15 Prise up the centre pins, and lever out the plastic rivets (arrowed)

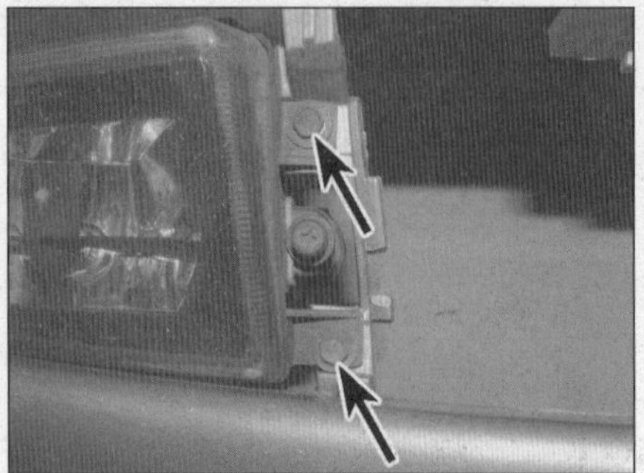

7.16 Undo the two bolts (arrowed) and remove the foglight

7.17 To adjust the foglight aim, rotate the adjusting screw (arrowed)

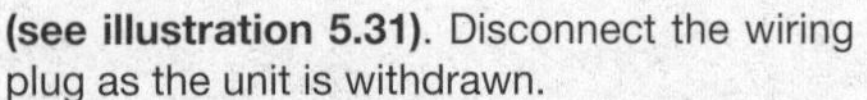

(see illustration 5.31). Disconnect the wiring plug as the unit is withdrawn.

14 Refitting is a reverse of the removal procedure.

Front foglight

Standard models

15 Prise up the centre pins, then lever out the complete plastic rivets, and remove the plastic trim adjacent to the fog light **(see illustration)**.

16 Undo the two mounting bolts, and remove the foglight. Disconnect the wiring plug as the light is withdrawn **(see illustration)**.

17 Refitting is a reversal of removal. If required, the foglight aim can be adjusted by rotating the adjuster screw adjacent to the foglight **(see illustration)**.

M-Sport Aerodynamic models

18 Using a plastic or wooden flat-bladed

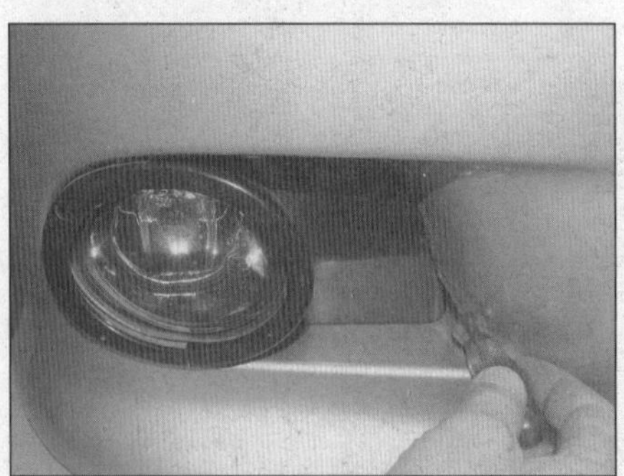

7.18 Carefully prise out the foglight trim

tool, carefully prise out the foglight trim surround **(see illustration)**.

19 Undo the retaining screw, and manoeuvre the foglight from place **(see illustration)**. Disconnect the wiring plug as the unit is withdrawn.

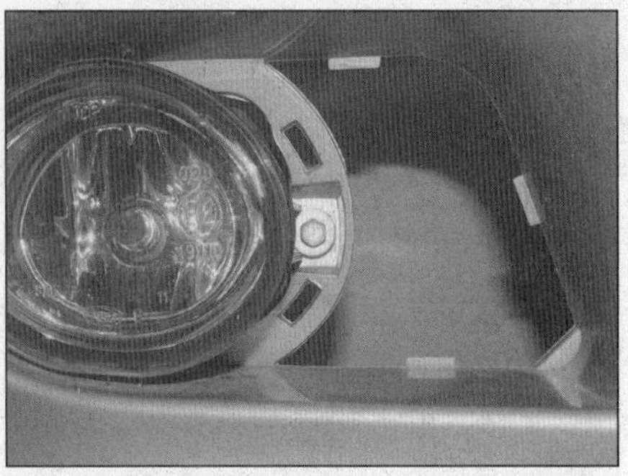

7.19 Undo the foglight retaining screw

20 Refitting is a reversal of removal.

Saloon rear light cluster

21 Open the luggage compartment storage compartment to access the rear of the light unit.

22 On models up to 09/2000, rotate the fastener 90° anti-clockwise and remove the bulbholder assembly **(see illustration 5.43)**.

23 On models from 09/2000, disconnect the rear light cluster wiring plug.

24 On all models, undo the retaining nuts and remove the cluster from the wing **(see illustrations)**.

25 Refitting is a reversal of removal.

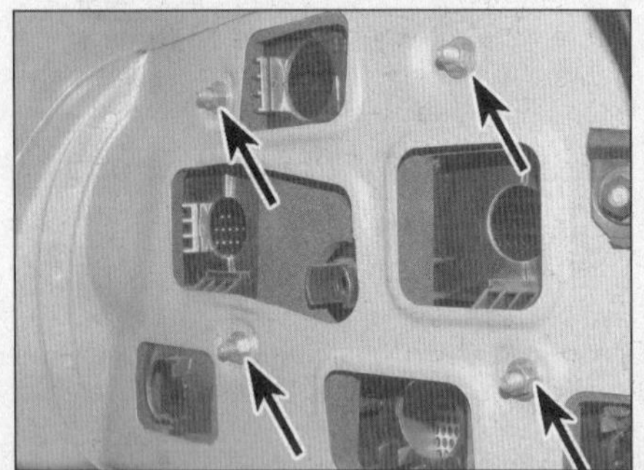

7.24a Rear light cluster retaining nuts (arrowed) – models up to 09/2000 . . .

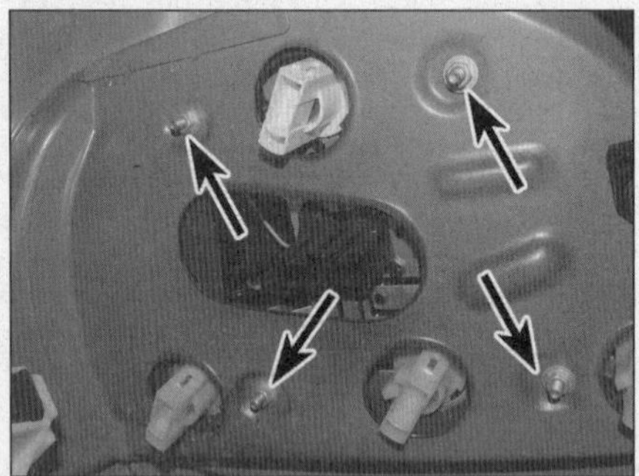

7.24b . . . and models from 09/2000

Touring rear light cluster

Body-mounted lights

26 Fold back the flap in the luggage compartment to expose the bulbholder cover. Rotate the fastener anti-clockwise and remove the cover.

27 Rotate the fastener anti-clockwise and remove the bulbholder assembly **(see illustration 5.49)**.

28 Undo the three retaining nuts, and remove the light cluster **(see illustration)**.

29 Refitting is a reversal of removal.

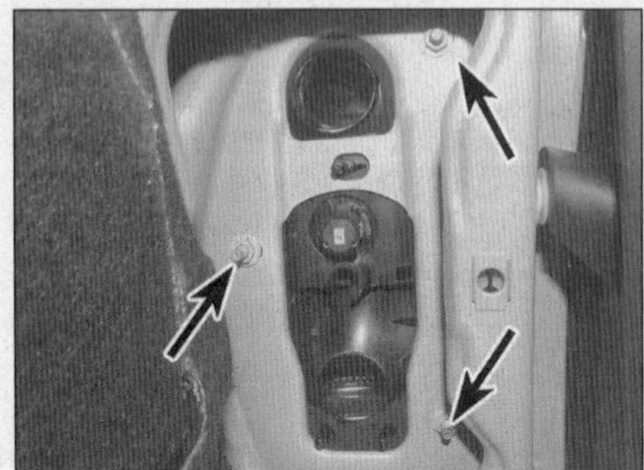

7.28 Undo the three nuts (arrowed) and remove the light cluster

Tailgate-mounted lights

30 Remove the tailgate trim panel as described in Chapter 11, Section 26.

31 Rotate the fastener anti-clockwise and remove the bulbholder from the rear of the light unit.

32 Undo the three nuts and remove the light unit **(see illustration)**.

33 Refitting is a reversal of removal.

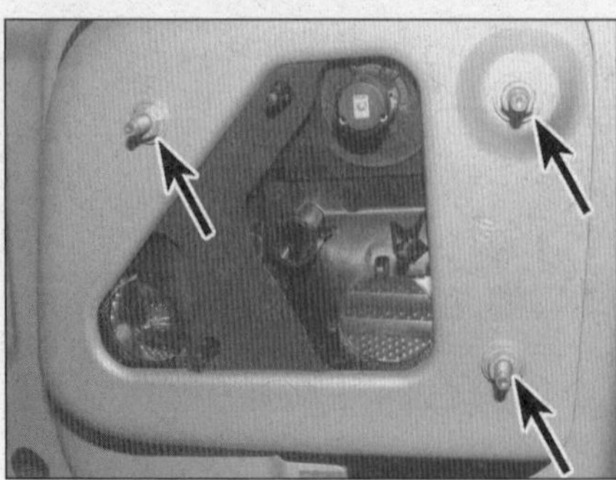

7.32 The tailgate-mounted light cluster is secured by three nuts (arrowed)

7.41 Undo the high-level stop-light retaining bolt (arrowed) – Saloon models

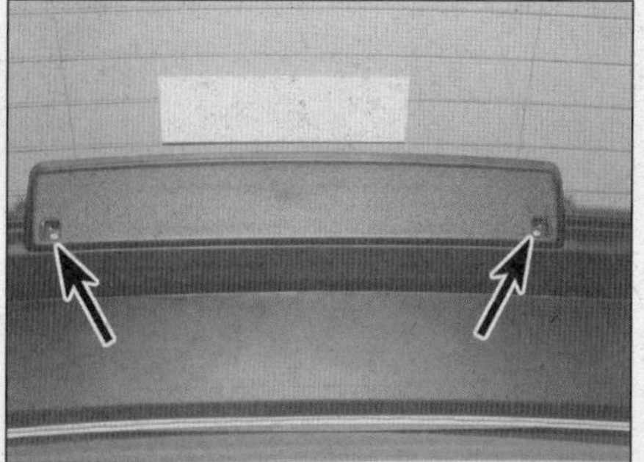

7.43 Undo the screws (arrowed) and remove the high-level stop-light – Touring models

7.49 Undo the bonnet release handle screw

Number plate light

Saloon models

34 Carefully push the light unit away from the end with the slot to compress the retaining spring, then lever the light unit from place **(see illustration 5.61)**. Disconnect the wiring plug as the unit is withdrawn.

35 Refitting is the reverse of removal.

Touring models

36 Undo the tailgate lower trim panel as described in Chapter 11, Section 26.

37 Disconnect the wiring plug, then undo the four nuts and remove the number plate light panel from the tailgate. The light units are integral with the panel.

38 Refitting is a reversal of removal.

Headlight range control motors

39 At the time of writing, the range control motors do not appear to be available separately. If defective, the complete headlight may need to be renewed. Check with your BMW dealer or parts specialist.

High-level stop-light

Saloon models

40 Remove the rear parcel shelf as described in Chapter 11, Section 26.

41 Working in the luggage compartment, undo the retaining bolt and remove the light unit. Disconnect the wiring plug as the unit is withdrawn **(see illustration)**.

42 Refitting is a reversal of removal.

Touring models

43 Open the tailgate window, unclip the cover caps, and undo the two retaining screws **(see illustration)**.

44 Carefully pull away the tailgate window upper trim panel, releasing the five retaining clips.

45 Prise out the rubber grommet in the tailgate, and disconnect the brake light wiring plug.

46 Remove the brake light.

47 Refitting is a reversal of removal.

Light Control Module (LCM)

48 The LCM controls and monitors all external light units, as well as buttons/switches, and the function of dimming the instrument cluster illumination and courtesy lights. Should a fault occur with any of these components/bulbs, the LCM will illuminate a warning light in the instrument cluster, and in some cases, storage a fault code for later retrieval. The LCM is in constant communication with the vehicle's other ECMs via BMW's databus system. By monitoring the output of various sensors, the LCM is responsible for illuminating the instrument cluster warning lights, and headlight range control. The sensors monitored are the oil temperature/level, brake fluid level, coolant level and the windscreen washer level.

49 The LCM is located behind the driver's side footwell kick panel. Undo the bonnet release handle screw and remove the handle. Release the retaining clips and remove panel **(see illustration)**.

50 Undo the two retaining screws and move the bonnet release mechanism to one side.

51 Slacken and remove the retaining bolt, release the LCM from its retaining clips and disconnect the wiring plug as the panel is withdrawn **(see illustration)**.

52 Refitting is a reversal of removal. **Note:** *If the LCM has been renewed, it must be programmed prior to use. This can only be carried out by a BMW dealer or suitably-equipped specialist.*

8 Headlight beam alignment – general information

1 Accurate adjustment of the headlight beam is only possible using optical beam setting equipment and this work should therefore be carried out by a BMW dealer or suitably-equipped workshop.

2 For reference, the headlights can be adjusted by rotating the adjuster screws on the top of the headlight unit **(see illustration)**. The outer adjuster alters the horizontal position of the beam whilst the inner adjuster alters the vertical aim of the beam.

3 Some models have an electrically-operated headlight beam adjustment system which is controlled through the switch in the facia. On these models ensure that the switch is set to the off position before adjusting the headlight aim.

4 On all models, it is possible to set the headlight beams for driving on the left- or right-hand side of the road by moving a lever within the headlight housing. Remove the plastic cap by rotating it anti-clockwise, and move the lever to the centre of the vehicle for driving on the left, and move the lever to the outside for driving on the right **(see illustration)**.

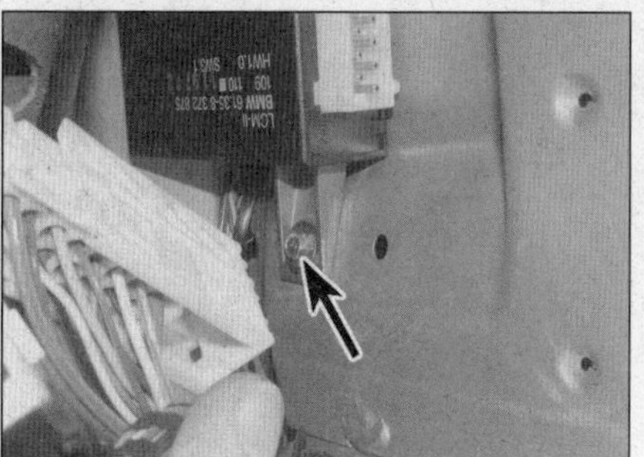

7.51 Undo the bolt (arrowed) securing the LCM (Light Control Module)

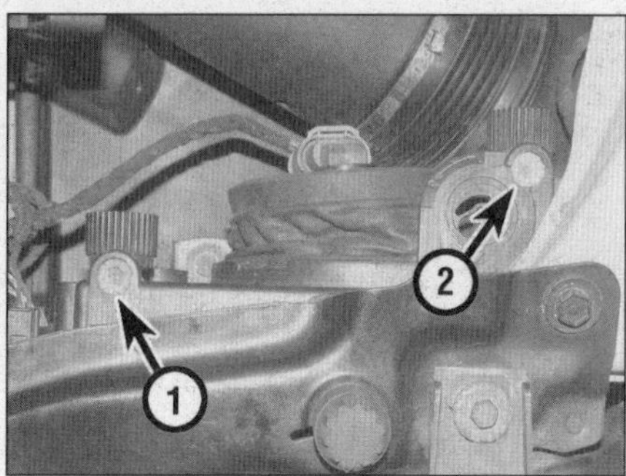

8.2 Vertical headlight adjustment (1) and horizontal adjustment (2)

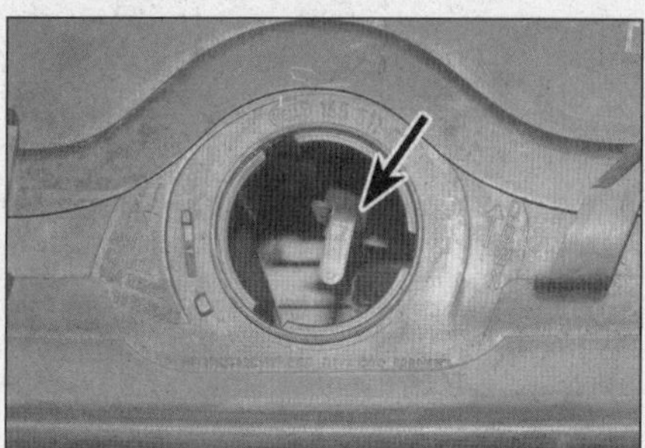

8.4 By moving the lever (arrowed) the headlight aim can be set for driving on the left- or right-hand side of the road

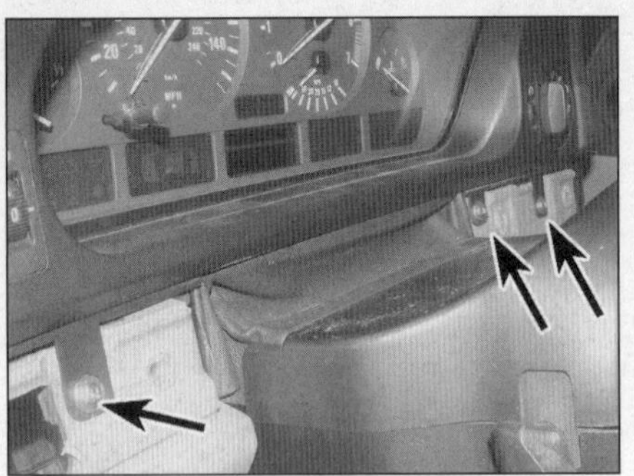

9.4a Undo the three screws at the lower edge of the cluster surround (arrowed) . . .

9.4b . . . and the three upper screws (arrowed)

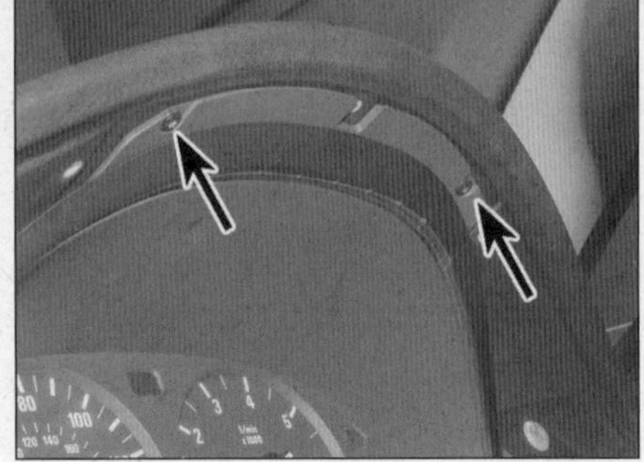

9.5a Undo the two screws at the top of the cluster (arrowed)

9 Instrument panel – removal and refitting

Removal

1 Disconnect the battery negative terminal (see Chapter 5A).

2 Move the steering column down as far as it will go, and extend it completely.

3 Carefully prise the decorative strips from either side of the steering column under the instrument panel.

4 Slacken and remove the three retaining Torx screws from the top of the instrument panel surround, and the three cross-head screws at the base, then carefully pull the surround from the panel **(see illustrations)**. Make a note of their fitted positions, and disconnect the wiring plugs as the panel is withdrawn.

5 Undo the two screws at the top of the instrument panel, and pull the top edge back and remove it from the facia. Lift up the retaining clips then disconnect the wiring connectors and remove the instrument panel from the vehicle **(see illustrations)**.

Refitting

6 Refitting is the reverse of removal, making sure the instrument panel wiring is correctly reconnected and securely held in position by any retaining clips. On completion reconnect the battery and check the operation of the panel warning lights to ensure that they are functioning correctly. **Note:** *If the instrument cluster has been renewed, the new unit must be coded to match the vehicle. This can only be carried out by a BMW dealer or suitably-equipped specialist.*

10 Instrument panel components – removal and refitting

Through its connections, via 'bus' networks with most of the systems and sensors within the vehicle, the instrument cluster is the control and information centre for the BMW 5-Series models. The 'K-bus' is connected to the supplementary restraint system, exterior and interior lights, rain sensor, heating/air conditioning, and the central body electrical system. The 'CAN-bus' (Controlled Area Network) is connected to the engine management, transmission management, and the ABS/traction control/dynamic stability control systems. The 'D-bus' is connected to the diagnostic link connector and EOBD (European On-Board Diagnostics) connector (where applicable).

The speedometer displays the vehicle's roadspeed from information supplied by the ABS ECM, generated from the left-hand rear wheel speed sensor.

At the time of writing, no individual components are available for the instrument panel and therefore the panel must be treated as a sealed unit. If there is a fault with one of the instruments, remove the panel as described in Section 9 and take it to your BMW dealer or specialist for testing. They have access to a special diagnostic tester which will be able to locate the fault and will then be able to advise you on the best course of action.

11 Rain/light sensor – removal and refitting

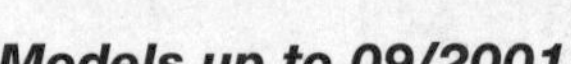

Models up to 09/2001

1 The rain sensor is incorporated into the front face of the interior mirror mounting base. Remove the interior mirror as described in Chapter 11.

2 Squeeze together the sides of the sensor cover, then pull the cover upwards and to the rear **(see illustration)**.

3 Unclip the cable cover and disconnect the wiring plug.

4 Pull out the two sensor retaining clips, and pull the sensor to the rear **(see illustration)**.

5 Refitting is a reversal of removal. **Note:** *If the rain sensor has been renewed, the new unit must be initialised. This can only be carried out by a BMW dealer or suitably-equipped specialist.*

Models from 09/2001

6 On models from 09/2001, the rain sensor also incorporates a light sensor for automatic headlight operation.

7 The sensor is incorporated into the front face of the interior mirror mounting base. Press up on the lower end of the mounting trim, and press the two halves of the mounting trim apart at the base, and release the trim retaining clips.

8 With the trim removed, disconnect the wiring plug.

9 Depress the locking catches, and remove the sensor.

9.5b Lever over the catch and disconnect the cluster wiring plugs

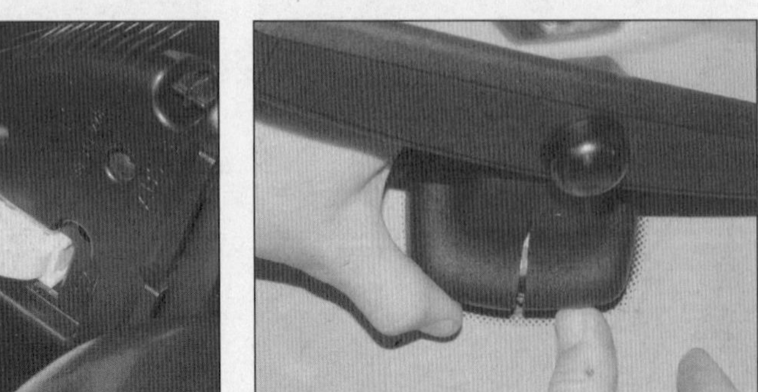

11.2 Press the two halves of the trim apart

11.4 Pull out the clip each side (arrowed) and remove the sensor

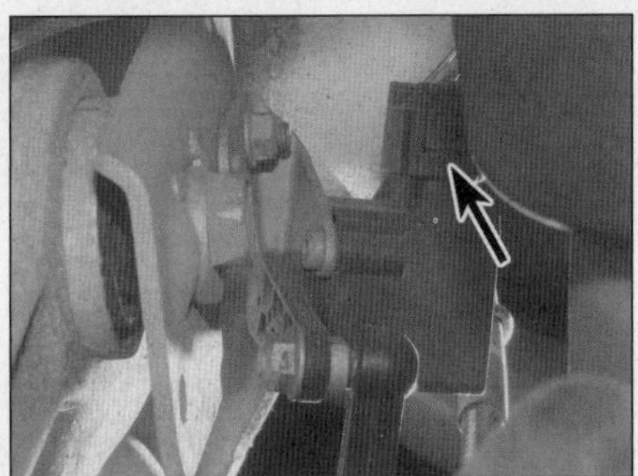

12.3 Disconnect the height sensor wiring plug (arrowed)

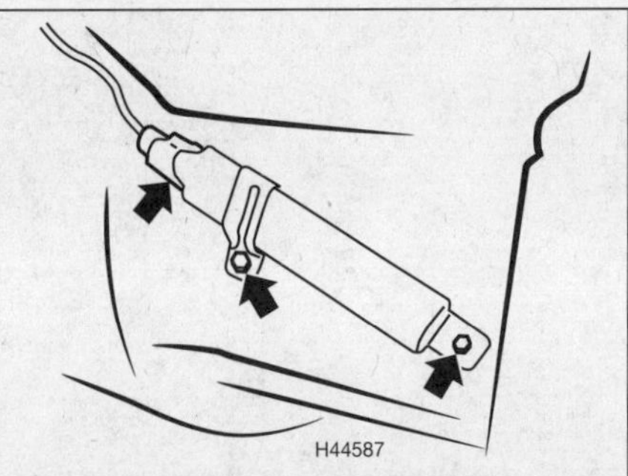

13.8 Disconnect the wiring plug, undo the two screws, and remove the receiver

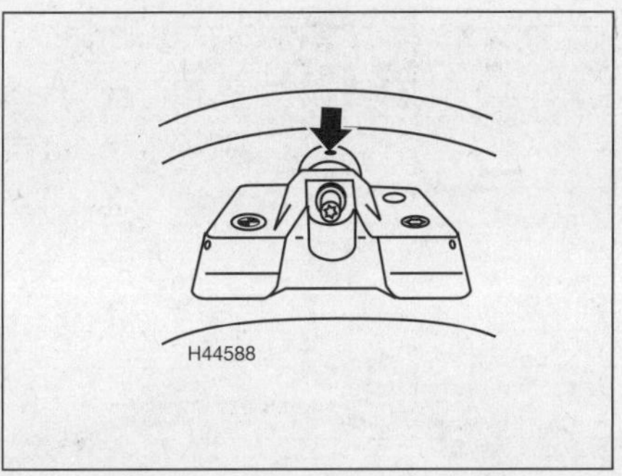

13.14 Ensure the hole in the retaining collar (arrowed) faces outwards

10 Refitting is a reversal of removal. **Note:** *If the rain sensor has been renewed, the new unit must be initialised. This can only be carried out by a BMW dealer or suitably-equipped specialist.*

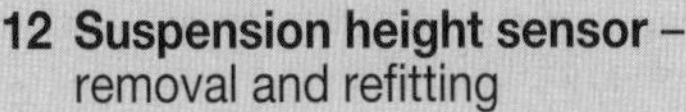

12 Suspension height sensor – removal and refitting

Removal

1 Vehicles equipped with Xenon headlights or air suspension are also equipped with suspension height sensors. Ride sensors fitted to the front and rear suspension provide information on the suspension ride height, whilst the headlight range control motors alter the headlight beam angle as necessary (Xenon headlights), or the suspension control unit maintains the ride height. The sensors are fitted between the suspension subframes and control arms. To access the sensors, jack the relevant end of the vehicle, and support securely on axle stands (see *Jacking and vehicle support*). Where applicable remove the engine undershield, or the triangular trim panel in front of the rear lower swinging arm.

2 Undo the nut securing the control rod to the sensor arm, and disconnect the rod.

3 Undo the two mounting nuts and remove the sensor. Disconnect the wiring plug as the sensor is withdrawn **(see illustration)**.

Refitting

4 Refitting is a reversal of the removal procedure, ensuring all the wiring connectors are securely reconnected.

13 Tyre pressure control system (RDC) – information and component renewal

Information

1 A tyre pressure monitoring system (RDC) is available as an option on most of the 5-Series range. The system consists of a transmitter in each wheel, attached to the base of the inflation valve, a receiver behind the wheel arch liner adjacent to each wheel, and a control module behind the passenger side glovebox. A warning light in the instrument cluster alerts the driver should the tyre pressure deviate from the set pressure. Note that due to the weight of the wheel-mounted transmitter unit, it is essential that any new tyres are balanced correctly before use.

Component renewal

Control module

2 Disconnect the battery negative lead as described in Chapter 5A.

3 Remove the passenger side glovebox as described in Chapter 11, Section 26.

4 Unlock the wiring plug catch, and disconnect it. Depress the retaining clip and slide the control unit from the carrier.

5 Refitting is a reversal of removal. Reprogram the system's reference pressure settings as described in the Owner's Handbook.

Receiver

6 Jack up the relevant roadwheel, and support the vehicle securely on axle stands (see *Jacking and vehicle support*).

7 Release the retaining clips/screws and remove the wheel arch liner.

8 Disconnect the receiver wiring plug, undo the two retaining nuts, and withdrawn the unit **(see illustration)**. Note that the right-hand side front, and the rear receivers, are mounted on the inside of the front section of the wheel arch liner.

9 Refitting is a reversal of removal.

Transmitter

10 A transmitter is fitted to the base of each inflation valve. Have the relevant tyre removed by a suitably-equipped specialist.

11 Undo the Torx screw and slide the transmitter from the base of the valve. Note the following precautions:

a) Do not clean the transmitter with compressed air.

b) Do not clean the wheel rim (tyre removed) with high-pressure cleaning equipment.

c) Do not use solvent to clean the transmitter.

d) If tyre sealing fluid has been used, the transmitter and valve must be renewed.

e) It is not possible to use the valve with the transmitter removed.

12 Insert a rod into the hole in the valve body retaining collar, unscrew the body and remove the valve.

13 Fit the new valve body (with collar) into the transmitter, only finger-tighten the Torx screw at this stage.

14 Insert the assembly into the hole in the wheel, ensuring that the hole in the valve body retaining collar faces outwards. Tighten the valve body nut, using a rod in the hole in the collar to counterhold the nut **(see illustration)**.

15 Tighten the transmitter Torx screw to the specified torque.

16 Have the tyre refitted.

14 Horn(s) – removal and refitting

Removal

1 The horn(s) is/are located behind the left-hand end of the front bumper.

2 To gain access to the horn(s) from below, apply the handbrake then jack up the front of the vehicle and support it on axle stands (see *Jacking and vehicle support*). Remove the roadwheel.

3 Undo the retaining screws and remove the lower front section of the wheel arch liner.

4 Undo the retaining nuts and remove the horns, disconnecting their wiring connectors as they become accessible **(see illustration)**.

Refitting

5 Refitting is the reverse of removal.

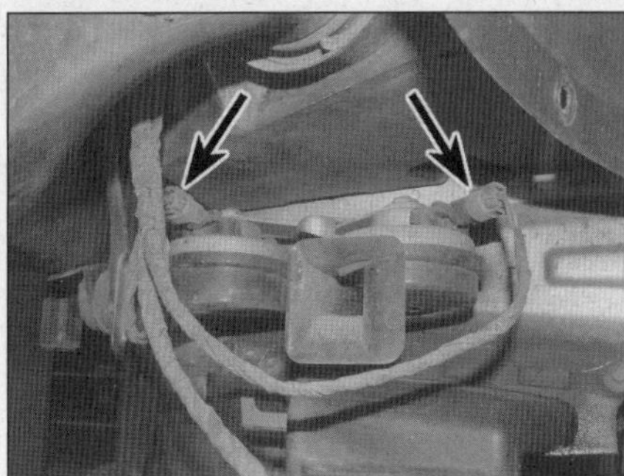

14.4 Disconnect the horn's wiring plugs (arrowed)

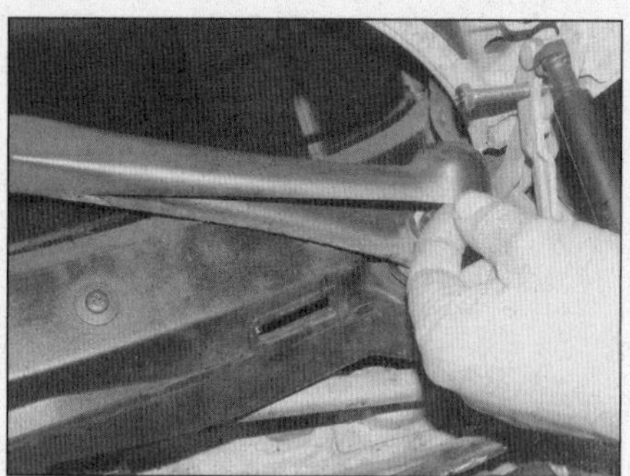

15.3a Prise off the wiper arm nut cover

15.3b If necessary, use a puller to detach the wiper arm from the spindle

15.3c Make alignment marks on the driver's side arm to ensure the arm is refitted at the same angle in relation to the screen

15 Wiper arm – removal and refitting

Removal

Front wiper arm

1 Operate the wiper motor, then switch it off so that the wiper arm returns to the 'at rest' position. Open the bonnet

2 Stick a piece of masking tape along the edge of the wiper blade to use as an alignment aid on refitting.

3 Prise off the wiper arm spindle nut cover(s) then slacken and remove the spindle nut(s). Lift the blade off the glass and pull the wiper arm off its spindle. If necessary the arm can be levered off the spindle using a suitable flat-bladed screwdriver or suitable puller **(see illustrations). Note:** *On the driver's side wiper arm (RHD models) it is possible to adjust the angle of the blade in relation to the windscreen, but the procedure requires a special tool from BMW. In order to refit the arm to its existing position mark the centre of the spindle in relation to the arm* ***(see illustration).***

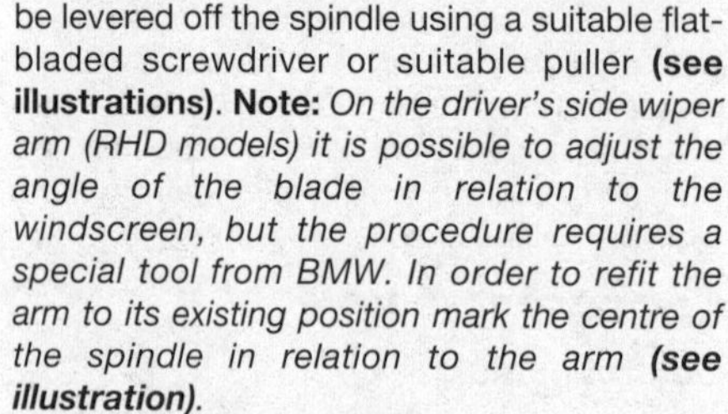

Rear wiper arm

4 Undo the Torx screw on the underside of the spindle housing, then prise the outer cover from position **(see illustration)**.

5 Open the rear window, position the wiper arm vertically (in-line with the washer jet), then prise off the rubber cap, undo the nut and remove the wiper arm **(see illustration)**.

Refitting

6 Ensure that the wiper arm and spindle splines are clean and dry then refit the arm to the spindle, aligning the wiper blade with the tape fitted on removal. Refit the spindle nut, tightening it to the specified torque setting, and clip the nut cover back in position.

16 Windscreen wiper motor and linkage – removal and refitting

Removal

Front windscreen wiper motor

1 Remove the wiper arms as described in the previous Section, then use a puller to remove the serrated spacer from the driver's side spindle **(see illustration)**.

2 Remove the scuttle cover as follows **(see illustrations)**:

a) Pull up the rubber weatherstrip from the bulkhead partition.

b) Release the clips and remove the pollen filter covers.

c) Release the clips and remove the air ducting from the pollen filter housings.

d) Release the clips and remove both pollen filter housings.

e) Remove the screws and prise up the plastic expansion rivets, then remove the scuttle cover.

15.4 Undo the Torx screw on the underside of the spindle housing

15.5 Prise off the rubber cap to access the spindle nut

16.1 Use a puller to remove the serrated washer

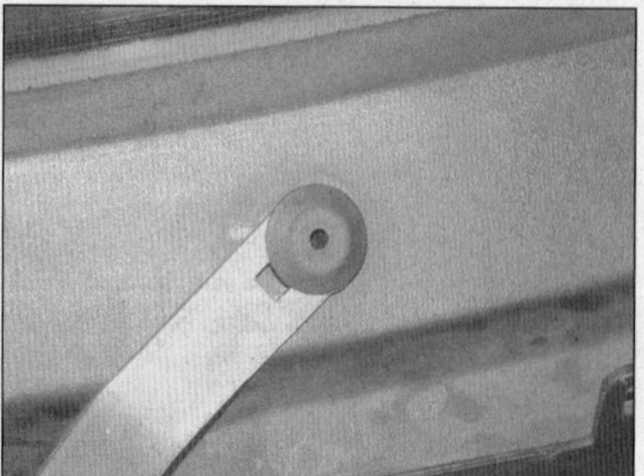

16.2a Prise out the rivets securing the scuttle cover

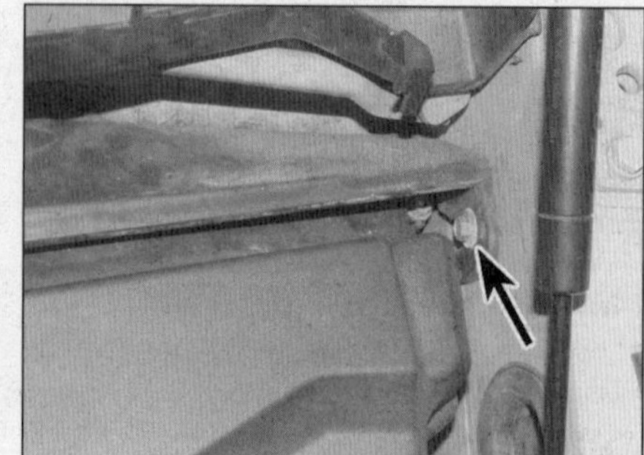

16.2b Undo the bolt (arrowed) and remove the rain deflector

16.4 Disconnect the wiper motor wiring plug

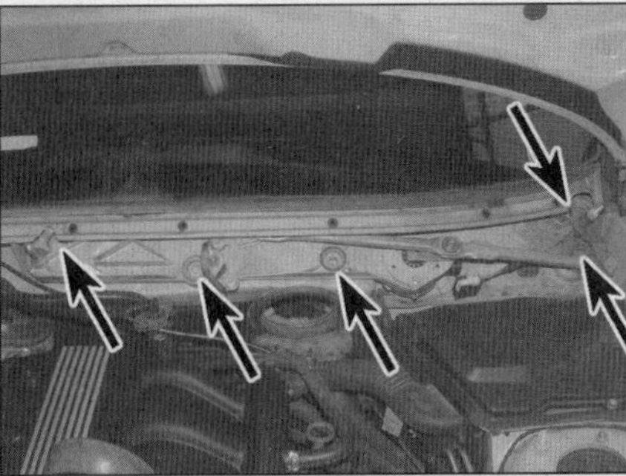
16.5 Undo the screws (arrowed) and manoeuvre the motor/linkage assembly from the vehicle

16.6 Prise the linkage from the motor crank

f) Undo the screw and remove the rain deflector from the rear of the electrical box in the left-hand corner of the engine compartment.

3 Rotate the four fasteners 90° anti-clockwise, and remove the cable cover from the centre of the engine compartment bulkhead.

4 Disconnect the wiper motor wiring plug **(see illustration)**.

5 Undo the screws securing the motor/linkage assembly and manoeuvre it from the vehicle **(see illustration)**.

6 If necessary, mark the relative positions of the motor shaft and crank then prise the wiper linkage from the motor balljoint. Unscrew the retaining nut and free the crank from the motor spindle. Unscrew the motor retaining bolts and separate the motor and linkage **(see illustration)**.

Rear windscreen wiper motor

7 Remove the tailgate lower trim panel as described in Chapter 11, Section 26.

8 Disconnect the motor wiring plug.

9 Make alignment marks where the motor and bracket touch the tailgate, to aid refitting. Undo the screws, and remove the wiper motor **(see illustration)**.

Rear wiper arm spindle and housing

10 Remove the rear wiper arm as described in the previous Section.

11 On the outside of the windscreen, slacken and remove the wiper arm spindle nut. Recover any washers **(see illustration)**.

12 Open the tailgate window, prise out the plastic caps and undo the two screws and remove the cover **(see illustration)**.

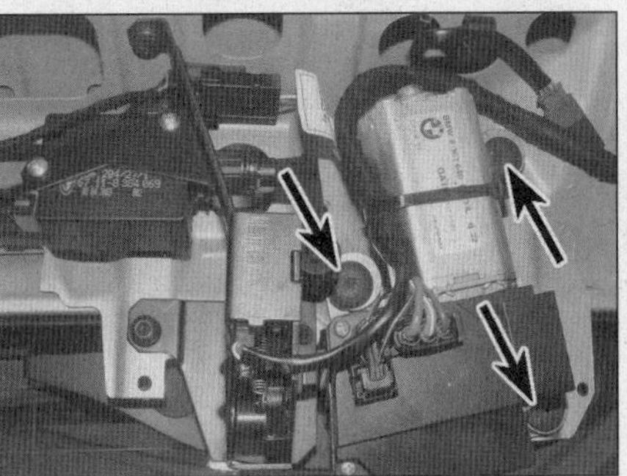
16.9 Undo the screws (arrowed) and remove the rear wiper motor

16.11 Slacken and remove the spindle nut

13 Make alignment marks between the tailgate catch lock nut and the spindle housing to aid refitting, then slacken the locknut and unscrew the catch **(see illustration)**. Count the number of turns required to unscrew the catch, so that it can be refitted to the same position.

14 Mark the position of the spindle housing relative to the tailgate to aid refitting, then undo the Torx bolt and remove the housing **(see illustration)**. When refitting the housing, it is essential that the centre of the wiper drive gear is exactly in-line with the centre of the spindle.

Refitting

15 Refitting is the reverse of removal. On completion refit the wiper arms as described in Section 15.

17 Windscreen/headlight washer system components – removal and refitting

Washer system reservoir

1 The windscreen washer reservoir is situated in the engine compartment. On models equipped with headlight washers the reservoir also supplies the headlight washer jets via an additional pump.

2 Empty the contents of the reservoir or be prepared for fluid spillage.

3 Jack up the front of the vehicle, and support it securely on axle stands (see *Jacking and vehicle support*). Remove the front right-hand roadwheel.

4 Undo the screws and remove the wheel arch liner.

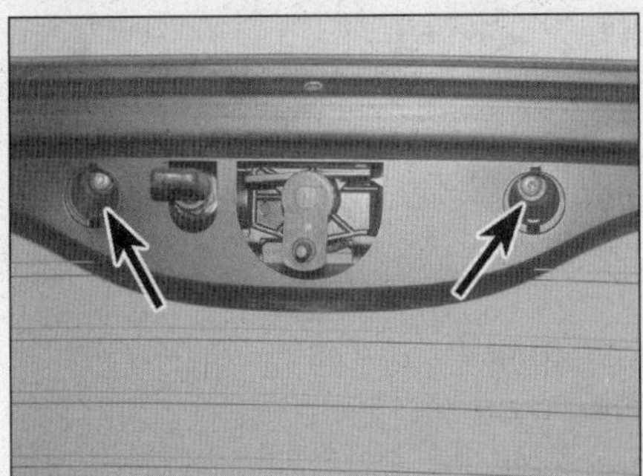
16.12 Prise out the plastic caps and undo the two screws (arrowed)

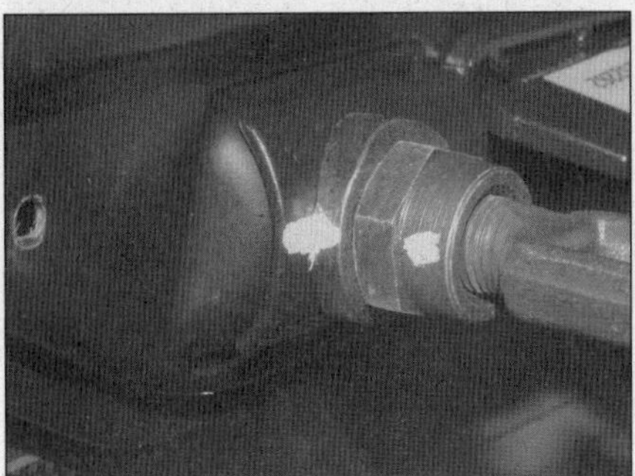
16.13 Make alignment marks between the catch locknut and the spindle housing

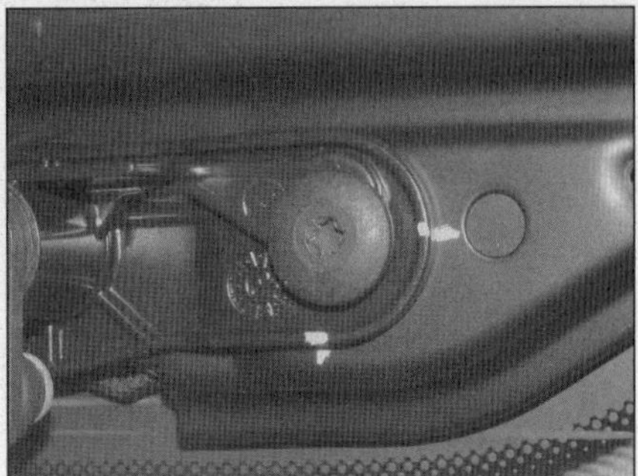
16.14 Make alignment marks between the spindle housing and the tailgate

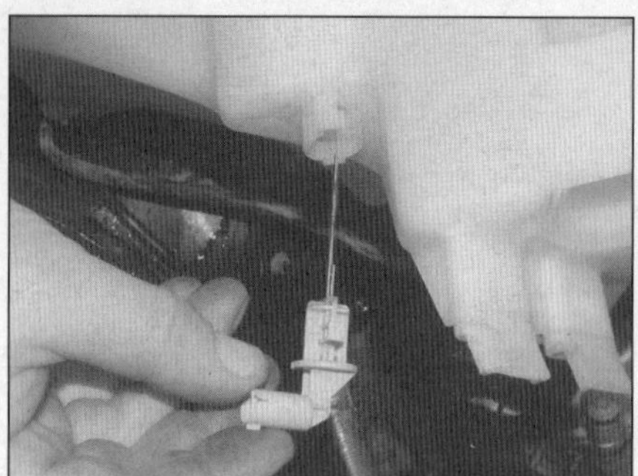
17.12 Rotate the level switch anti-clockwise and remove it from the reservoir

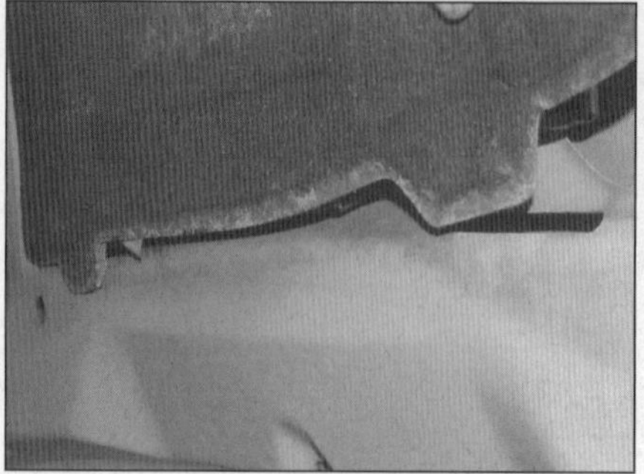
17.14 Detach the bonnet insulation panel at the base

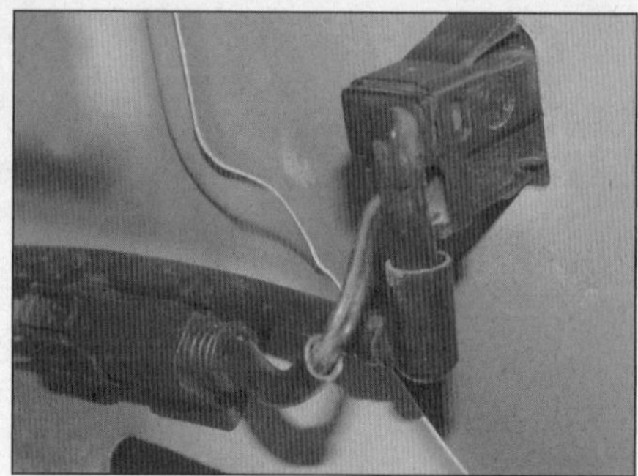
17.15 Disconnect the hose and wiring plug from the jet

5 Disconnect the wiring connector(s) from the reservoir level switch, then note their fitted locations, and disconnect the various hoses from the reservoir.

6 Slacken and remove the reservoir retaining nuts and lift the reservoir upwards and out of position. Wash off any spilt fluid with cold water.

7 Refitting is a reversal of removal. Ensure the locating lugs on the base of the reservoir engage correctly with the corresponding slots in the inner wing. Refill the reservoir and check for leakage.

Washer pumps

8 Remove the right-hand front wheel arch liner as described in Paragraphs 3 and 4.

9 Disconnect the wiring connector(s) and hose(s) from the washer pump(s). Carefully rotate the pump(s) clockwise, and pull them up from the reservoir. Be prepared for fluid spillage. Inspect the pump sealing grommet(s) for signs of damage or deterioration and renew if necessary. **Note:** *Take care when removing the pump(s) not to dislodge the strainer on the pump inlet. If the strainer falls into the reservoir, it will be necessary to remove reservoir to retrieve the strainer.*

10 Refitting is the reverse of removal, using a new sealing grommet if the original one shows signs of damage or deterioration. Refill the reservoir and check the pump grommet for leaks.

Washer reservoir level switch

11 Remove the reservoir as described earlier in this Section.

12 Rotate the level switch anti-clockwise and remove it from the reservoir **(see illustration)**.

13 Refitting is the reverse of removal, using a new sealing grommet if the original one shows signs of damage or deterioration. Refill the reservoir and check for leaks.

Windscreen washer jets

14 Open the bonnet and detach the bonnet sound insulation panel at the base of the bonnet **(see illustration)**.

15 Disconnect the washer hose(s) from the base of the jet. Where necessary, also disconnect the wiring connector from the jet **(see illustration)**.

16 Depress the clip at the top of the jet and manoeuvre it out the top of the bonnet.

17 On refitting, push the jet back into position in the bonnet, and securely connect the jet to the hose. Where necessary also reconnect the wiring connector. If necessary adjust the nozzles using a pin, aiming one nozzle to a point slightly above the centre of the swept area and the other to slightly below the centre point to ensure complete coverage.

Headlight washer jets

18 Remove the front bumper as described in Chapter 11.

19 Release the retaining clip and disconnect the hose from the jet.

20 Where applicable disconnect the jet heater wiring plug.

21 Squeeze together the two clips, and slide the jet upwards from place.

22 Refitting is a reversal of removal. Adjustment of the jets requires a special tool.

Wash/wipe control module

23 The wash/wipe system is controlled by the central body electronics (ZKE III) control module, known as the General Module (GM III), which is located behind the passenger side glovebox. To access the control unit, remove the glovebox as described in Chapter 11, Section 26.

24 Disconnect the module wiring plugs. Some plugs have locking levers, and some have sliding locking elements.

25 Release the retaining clip then remove the ECM from the vehicle **(see illustration)**.

26 Refitting is the reverse of removal.

Rear screen washer jet

27 The washer jet is a push-fit into the end of the washer tube fitting. Using a plastic or wooden lever, carefully prise the washer jet from the rubber fitting at the top of the window.

28 Refitting is a reversal of removal. Aim the jet to an area 100 mm from the top, and 320 mm from the edge of the window.

Intensive wash reservoir

29 The intensive wash reservoir is located on the right-hand inner wing in the engine compartment **(see illustration)**. To remove the reservoir, disconnect the washer hose and wiring plug from the pump.

30 Undo the plastic nut, release the clip and remove the reservoir. If required, release the pump from its retaining clip and ease the pump out from the sealing grommet.

31 Refitting is a reversal of removal.

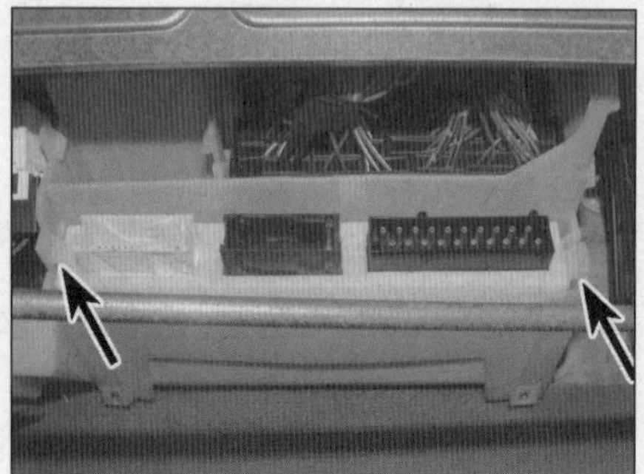
17.25 Release the clips (arrowed) and slide the ECM to the rear

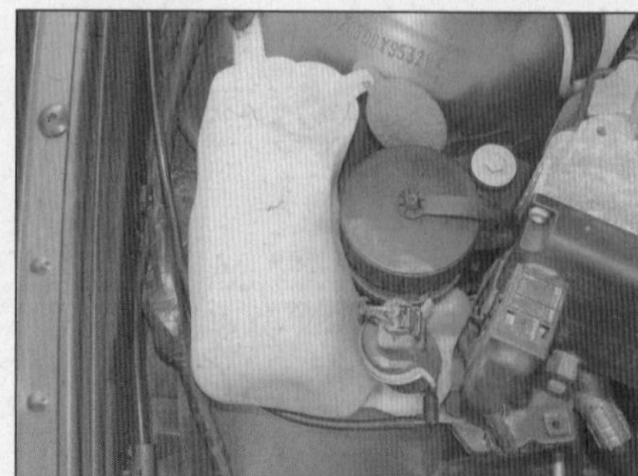
17.29 Intensive wash reservoir

18 Audio unit – removal and refitting

Note: *The following removal and refitting procedure is for the range of radio/cassette/CD units which BMW fit as standard equipment. Removal and refitting procedures of non-standard will differ slightly.*

Removal

IRIS unit

1 Pull the volume control knob from its spindle, insert a screwdriver into the slot to the right of the spindle and twist to release the catch mechanism, then pull the unit from place **(see illustration)**. Disconnect the wiring plugs as the unit is withdrawn.

MID unit

2 Pull the volume control knob from its spindle, insert an Allen key into the screw below the volume control spindle. Rotate the Allen key 90° anti-clockwise and pull the unit from the facia **(see illustration)**. Disconnect the wiring plugs as the unit is withdrawn.

Top facia-mounted unit

3 Remove the IRIS or MID as applicable, then slacken the two Allen screws sufficiently to release the retaining tabs, and remove the cassette player **(see illustrations)**.

4 Note their fitted positions, and disconnect the wiring plugs from the rear of the unit (slide out the locking element on the main plug) **(see illustration)**.

CD autochanger

5 Open the left-hand side luggage compartment storage tray.

6 Undo the three screws securing the mounting bracket to the vehicle body **(see illustration)**.

7 Slacken the four mounting screws, and lift

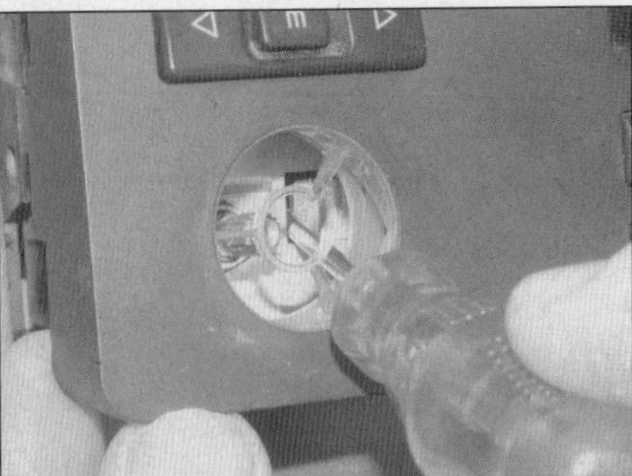

18.1 Insert a flat-bladed screwdriver into the slot, and twist it to release the catch mechanism

the unit from position **(see illustration)**. Disconnect the wiring plugs as the unit is withdrawn.

Amplifier

8 The amplifier (where fitted) is located behind the left-hand side luggage compartment trim panel. Press the button, and remove the first aid kit trim panel.

9 Remove the storage/tool kit tray.

10 Disconnect the amplifier wiring plugs, undo the retaining bolts and remove the unit.

18.2 Insert an Allen key into the hole, and rotate it 90° anti-clockwise to release the MID unit

Refitting

11 Refitting is a reversal of removal.

19 Loudspeakers – removal and refitting

Door main loudspeaker

1 Remove the door inner trim panel as described in Chapter 11.

18.3a To remove the cassette/cd player in the facia, slacken the Allen screws at the lower edge (arrowed)

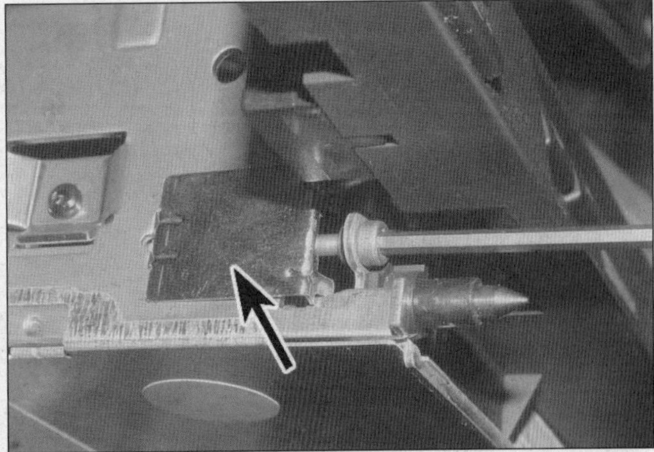

18.3b When the Allen screws are slackened, the metal catches (arrowed) retract – shown with the unit removed

18.4 Slide the locking element out, then disconnect the main plug

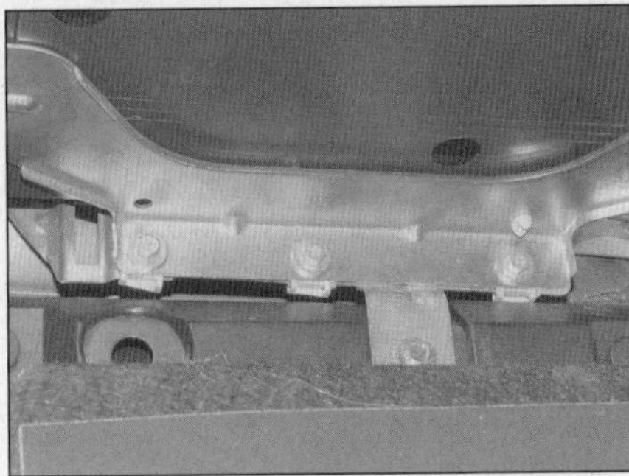

18.6 Undo the three screws securing the CD autochanger to the vehicle body

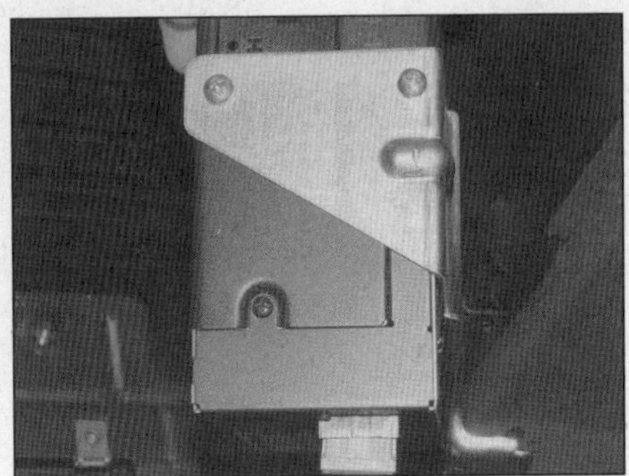

18.7 The bracket is secured to the autochanger by two screws at each end

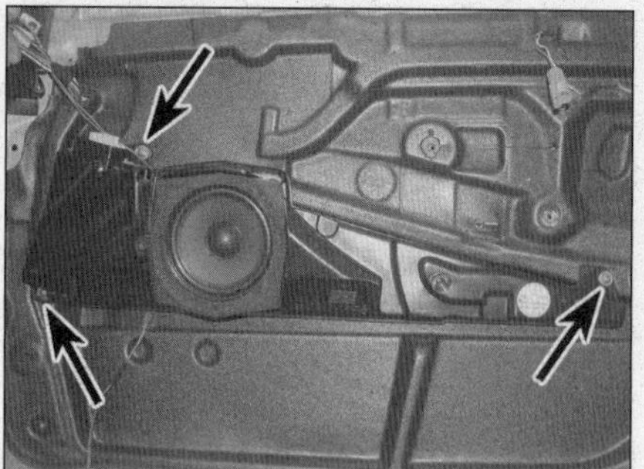

19.2 Undo the three screws (arrowed) and remove the speaker

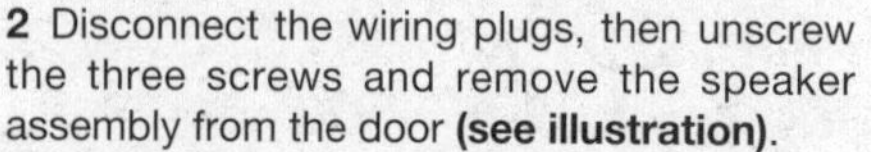

2 Disconnect the wiring plugs, then unscrew the three screws and remove the speaker assembly from the door **(see illustration)**.
3 Where fitted, unscrew the large retaining collar and remove the small speaker from the trim panel.
4 Refitting is the reverse of removal.

Door upper loudspeaker

5 Remove the door inner trim as described in Chapter 11.
6 Slightly lift and pull the plastic trim away from the front inner edge of the door.
7 Undo the lower retaining Torx bolt and remove the speaker from the door **(see illustration)**. Disconnect the wiring plug as the speaker is withdrawn.
8 Refitting is a reversal of removal.

19.10 Undo the four speaker screws

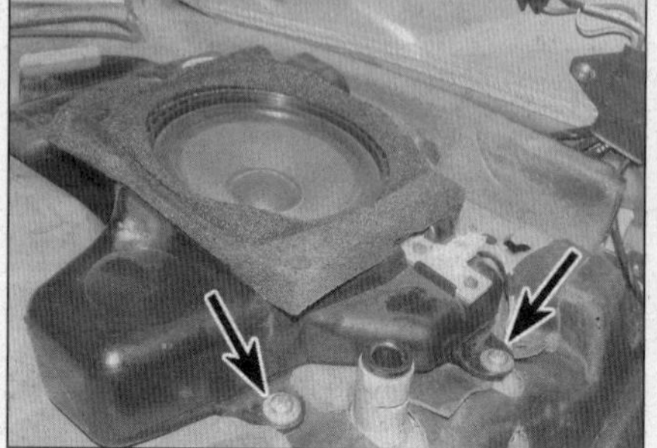

19.13 Undo the two speaker retaining screws (arrowed)

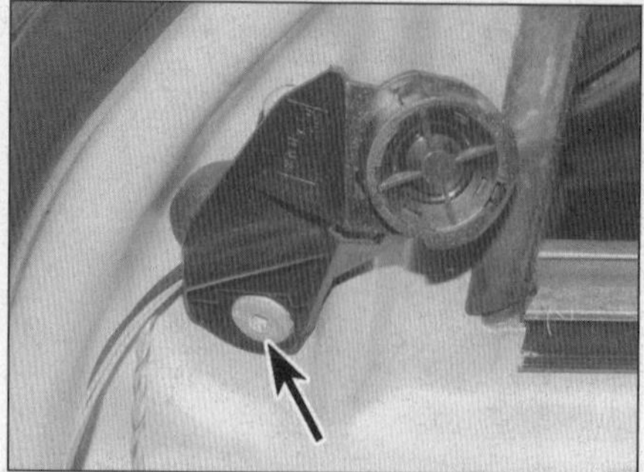

19.7 The upper speaker is secure by one screw (arrowed)

Luggage area loudspeaker

Touring models

9 Unclip the sides of the speaker trim, and pull it rearwards to remove it **(see illustration)**.
10 Undo the retaining screws and remove the speaker, disconnect its wiring connectors as they become accessible **(see illustration)**.
11 Refitting is the reverse of removal making sure the speaker is correctly located. Fit the steel clips into the speaker surround prior to refitting the trim **(see illustration)**.

Rear loudspeaker

Saloon models

12 Remove the parcel shelf as described in Chapter 11, Section 26.

19.11 Fit the steel clips to the speaker surround before refitting the grille

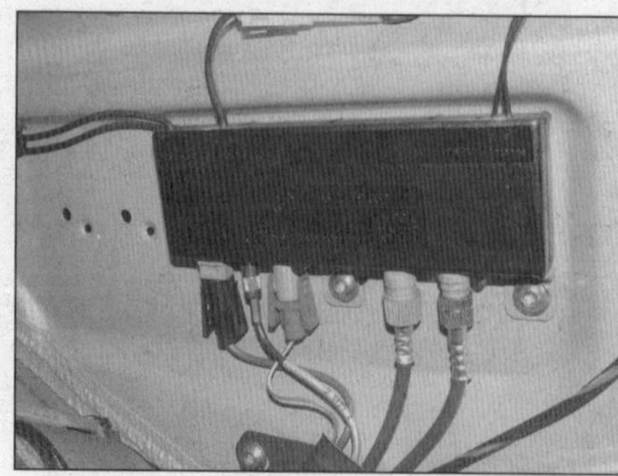

20.2 Radio signal amplifier – Saloon models

19.9 Unclip the side of the speaker grille

13 Undo the two retaining screws, lift the front edge of the rear speaker up and disengage it from the lug at the rear **(see illustration)**. Disconnect the speaker wiring plug as it is withdrawn.
14 Refitting is the reverse of removal.

20 Radio aerial – general information

The radio aerial is built into the rear screen. In order to improve reception an amplifier is fitted to boost the signal to the radio/cassette unit.

Saloon models

1 Remove the left-hand C-pillar trim panel as described in Chapter 11, Section 26.
2 Undo the retaining nuts/screws, and remove the amplifier **(see illustration)**. Disconnect the wiring plugs as the unit is withdrawn.
3 Refitting is a reversal of removal.

Touring models

4 Open the tailgate, and carefully pull the tailgate upper trim panel from its retaining clips **(see illustration)**.
5 Unclip the cover over the amplifier, undo the retaining nuts and manoeuvre the amplifier

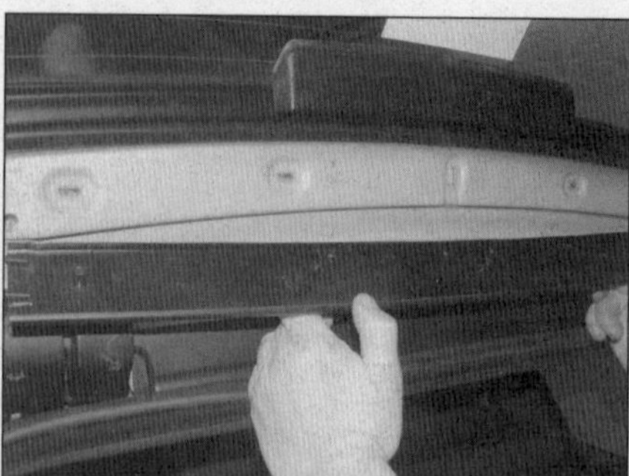

20.4 Remove the tailgate upper trim panel

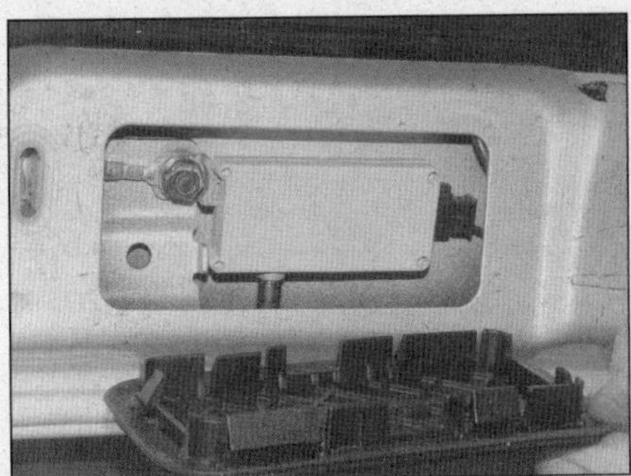

20.5 Unclip the cover to access the amplifier

from place **(see illustration)**. Disconnect the wiring plugs as the amplifier is withdrawn.

6 Refitting is a reversal of removal.

21 Cruise control/traction control systems – information and component renewal

Information

1 The cruise control function is incorporated into the engine management ECM. The only renewable external components are the clutch pedal switch, and the throttle actuator (M52 engines only). The traction control system incorporates elements of the ABS braking system (see Chapter 9), as well as an engine power reduction system.

Component renewal

Clutch pedal switch

2 See Section 4.

Cruise control throttle actuator

3 The actuator is located on the left-hand side inner wing. Ensure the ignition is switched off, disconnect the wiring plug, undo the nuts, then remove the actuator from the inner wing. Squeeze together the sides of the grommet and separate the throttle cable from the throttle quadrant on the underside of the inner throttle body **(see illustration)**.

Traction control throttle actuator

4 The actuator is located on the left-hand side inner wing in the engine compartment. Ensure the ignition is switched off, disconnect the wiring plug, undo the nut/bolt, then remove the actuator from the inner wing. Squeeze together the sides of the grommet and separate the throttle cable from the throttle lever **(see illustrations)**.

22 Anti-theft alarm system – general information

The 5-Series models are equipped with a sophisticated anti-theft alarm and immobiliser system. Should a fault develop, the system's self-diagnosis facility should be interrogated using dedicated test equipment. Consult your BMW dealer or suitably-equipped specialist.

23 Heated front seat components – removal and refitting

Heater mats

On models equipped with heated front seats, a heater pad is fitted to the both the seat back and seat cushion. Renewal of either heater mat involves peeling back the upholstery, removing the old mat, sticking the new mat in position and then refitting the upholstery. Note that upholstery removal and refitting requires considerable skill and experience if it is to be carried out successfully and is therefore best entrusted to your BMW dealer or specialist. In practice, it will be very difficult for the home mechanic to carry out the job without ruining the upholstery.

Heated seat switches

Refer to Section 4.

24 Airbag system – general information and precautions

The models covered by this manual are equipped with a driver's airbag mounted in the centre of the steering wheel, a passenger's airbag located behind the facia, two head airbags located in each A-pillar/headlining, two airbags located in each front door trim panel and, on some models, behind each rear door trim. The airbag system comprises of the airbag unit(s) (complete with gas generators), impact sensors, the control unit and a warning light in the instrument panel.

The airbag system is triggered in the event of a heavy frontal or side impact above a predetermined force; depending on the point of impact. The airbag(s) is inflated within milliseconds and forms a safety cushion between the cabin occupants and the cabin interior, and therefore greatly reduces the risk of injury. The airbag then deflates almost immediately.

Every time the ignition is switched on, the airbag control unit performs a self-test. The self-test takes approximately 2 to 6 seconds and during this time the airbag warning light on the facia is illuminated. After the self-test has been completed the warning light should go out. If the warning light fails to come on, remains illuminated after the initial period, or comes on at any time when the vehicle is being driven, there is a fault in the airbag system. The vehicle be taken to a BMW dealer for examination at the earliest possible opportunity.

Warning: Before carrying out any operations on the airbag system, disconnect the battery negative terminal, and wait for at least 1 minute. This will allow the capacitors in the system to discharge. When operations are complete, make sure no one is inside the vehicle when the battery is reconnected.

- ***Note that the airbag(s) must not be subjected to temperatures in excess of 90°C (194°F). When the airbag is removed, ensure that it is stored the correct way up to prevent possible inflation (padded surface uppermost).***
- ***Do not allow any solvents or cleaning agents to contact the airbag assemblies. They must be cleaned using only a damp cloth.***
- ***The airbags and control unit are both sensitive to impact. If either is dropped or damaged they should be renewed.***
- ***Disconnect the airbag control unit wiring plug prior to using arc-welding equipment on the vehicle.***

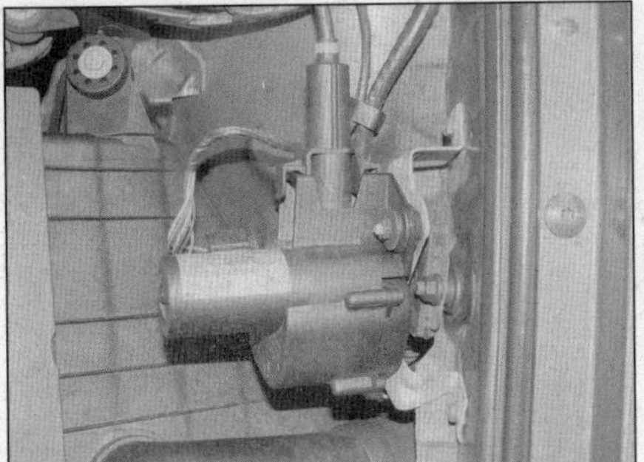

21.3 Cruise control throttle actuator

21.4a Disengage the cable from the throttle valve lever

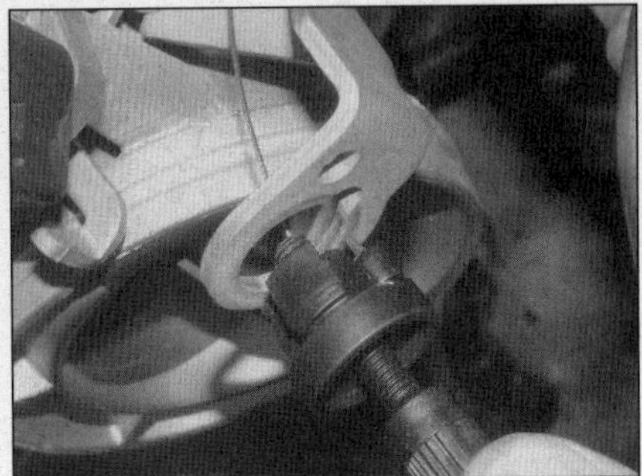

21.4b Squeeze together the sides of the grommet and pull it from the bracket

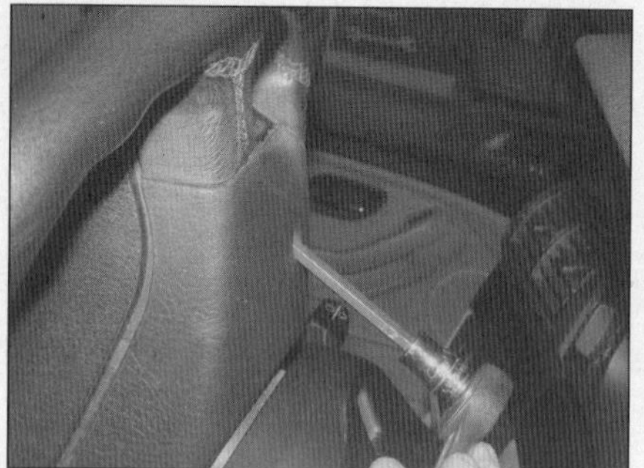
25.2 Two Torx screws secure the airbag to the steering wheel – models up to 03/2002

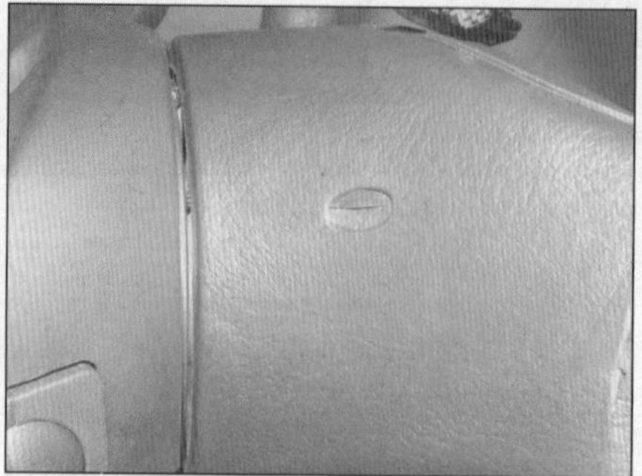
25.3a Insert a screwdriver through one of the holes in the back of the steering wheel . . .

25.3b . . . and release the airbag retaining clip (arrowed)

25 Airbag system components – removal and refitting

Note: *Refer to the warnings in Section 24 before carrying out the following operations.*

1 Disconnect the battery negative terminal (see Chapter 5A), then continue as described under the relevant heading.

Driver's airbag

Models up to 03/2002

2 Slacken and remove the two airbag retaining Torx T30 screws from the rear of the steering wheel, rotating the wheel as necessary to gain access to the screws **(see illustration)**.

Models from 03/2002

3 Insert a flat-bladed screwdriver through the hole in the back of the steering wheel and release the airbag retaining clip. Turn the wheel half a turn and release the clip on the other side **(see illustrations)**.

4 If required, remove the steering wheel and column shrouds (Chapter 10), disconnect the contact unit wiring plug, then undo the four Torx screws and remove the contact unit **(see illustration)**.

All models

5 Return the steering wheel to the straight-ahead position then carefully lift the airbag assembly away from the steering wheel. Note their fitted positions and disconnect the wiring plugs from the airbag unit **(see illustrations)**. Note that the airbag must not be knocked or dropped and should be stored with its padded surface uppermost.

6 On refitting reconnect the wiring connector(s) and seat the airbag unit in the steering wheel, making sure the wire does not become trapped. On models from 03/2002, fit the retaining screws and tighten them to the specified torque setting. On models from 03/2002, push the airbag into the steering wheel to re-engage the retaining clips. Reconnect the battery.

Passenger airbag

7 Insert two wooden or plastic flat-bladed tools either side of the airbag cover, and carefully prise the airbag cover from place **(see illustration)**.

8 Undo the four retaining nuts and lift the airbag unit from place. Make a note of the position of any washers – they must be refitted to their original positions. Disconnect the airbag wiring plug as the unit is withdrawn **(see illustrations)**.

9 Refitting is a reversal of removal. Tighten the

25.4 Undo the four screws (arrowed) and remove the airbag contact unit

25.5a Driver's airbag plug – models up to 03/2002

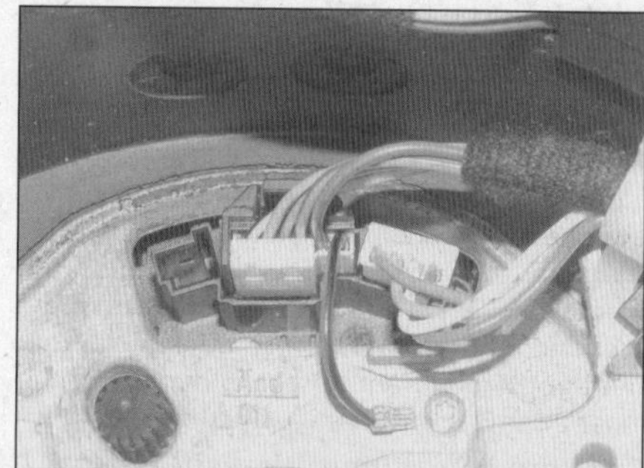
25.5b Driver's airbag plugs – models from 03/2002

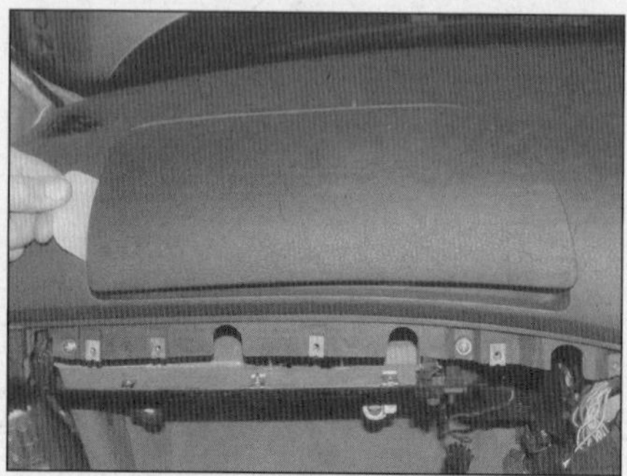
25.7 Carefully prise the passenger airbag cover from the facia

25.8a The airbag is secured by two nuts at each end

25.8b Disconnect the airbag wiring plug as the unit is withdrawn

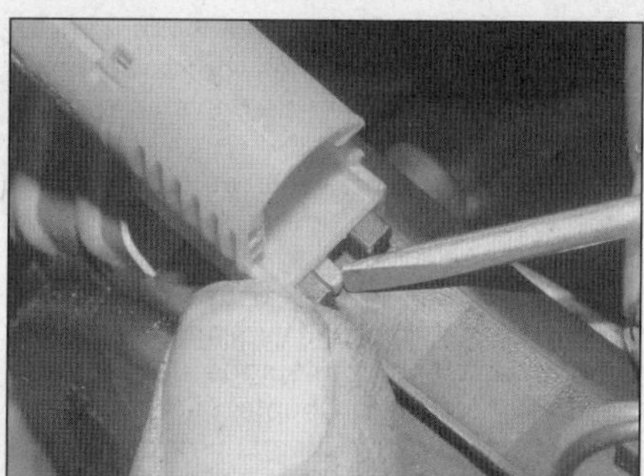
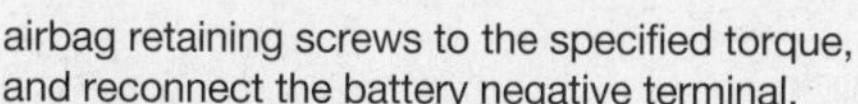

25.11 With the wiring plug release from its bracket, release the locking clip and disconnect the plug

25.12 Undo the four screws and remove the door airbag

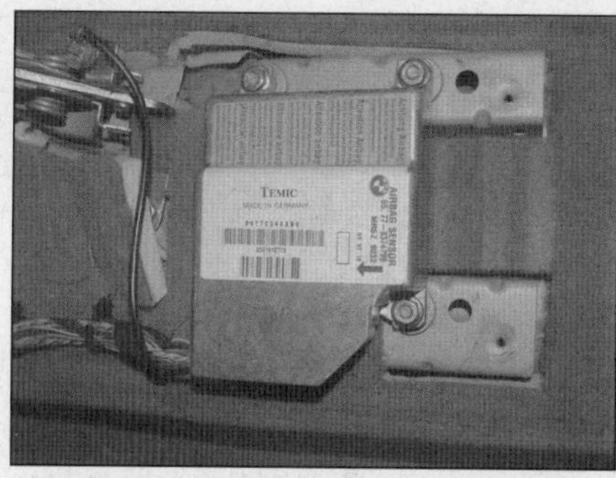

25.17 Undo the nuts and remove the airbag control unit

airbag retaining screws to the specified torque, and reconnect the battery negative terminal.

Door airbags

10 Remove the door inner trim panel as described in Chapter 11.

11 Release the wiring plug from its bracket, then release the locking clip and disconnect the airbag wiring plug **(see illustration)**.

12 Undo the retaining screws and lift the airbag from position **(see illustration)**.

13 Refitting is a reversal of removal. Tighten the airbag retaining screws to the specified torque, and reconnect the battery negative terminal.

Head airbags

14 On each side of the passenger cabin, a Head Protection Airbag (HPS) is fitted. The airbag runs from the lower part of the windscreen pillar to above the rear door and, on some models, down to the rear parcel shelf. The airbag is approximately 1.5 metres in length, and 130 mm in diameter when inflated. To remove the airbag, the entire facia and headlining must be removed. This task is outside the scope of the DIYer, and therefore we recommend that the task be entrusted to a BMW dealer or specialist.

Airbag control unit

15 Remove the centre console as described in Chapter 11.

16 Prise out the plastic rivet and remove the centre rear air duct.

17 Undo the retaining nuts and lift the module. Disconnect the wiring plug as the unit is withdrawn **(see illustration)**.

18 Refitting is the reverse of removal. Note that the control unit must be installed with the arrow pointing towards the front of the vehicle, and that the earth strap is fitted under one of the module mounting nuts.

Impact sensor

19 There are two impact sensors, one on each side of the passenger cabin. Remove the seats as described in Chapter 11.

20 Unclip the door sill trim panel, and fold the carpet away from the side. To improve access if required, remove the floor level heater duct.

21 Undo the two retaining screws, and remove the sensor. Disconnect the wiring plug as the sensor is withdrawn.

22 Refitting is a reversal of removal, noting that the arrow on the sensor must point towards the door sill **(see illustration)**.

26 Parking distance control (PDC) – information and component renewal

General information

1 In order to aid parking, a models in the 5-Series range can be equipped with a system that informs the driver of the distance between the rear of the vehicle, and any vehicle/obstacle behind whilst reversing. The system consists of several ultrasonic sensors mounted in the rear bumper which measure the distance between themselves and the nearest object. The distance is indicated by an audible signal in the passenger cabin. The closer the object, the more frequent the signals, until at less than 30 cm, the signal becomes continuous.

PDC electronic control module

Removal

2 Release the clip and remove the storage compartment from the right-hand side of the luggage compartment, then undo the rotary fastener and lift out the battery cover.

3 Prise out the two plastic rivets, and remove the trim panel from the right-hand side of the luggage compartment. Feed the fuel filler cap emergency release cable through the panel as it is removed **(see illustration)**.

4 Note their fitted positions, and disconnect the unit's wiring plugs. Undo the mounting screws and remove the control unit **(see illustration)**.

Refitting

5 Refitting is a reversal of removal.

Ultrasonic sensors

Removal

6 Remove the rear bumper as described in Chapter 11.

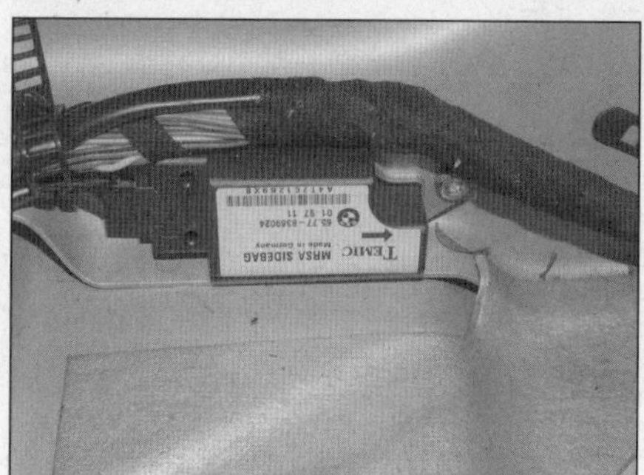

25.22 The impact sensor must be installed with the arrow towards the door sill

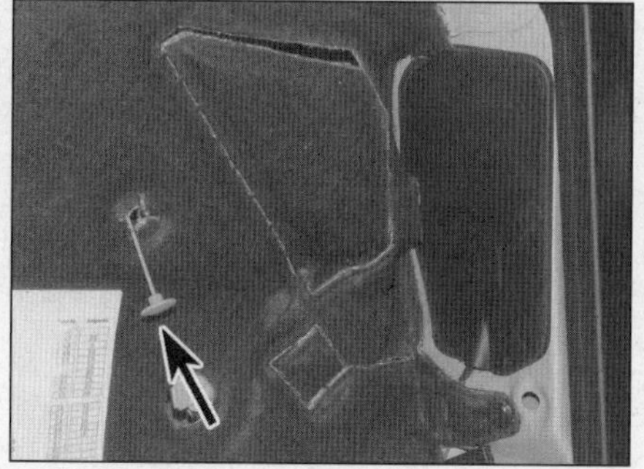

26.3 Feed the emergency fuel cap release cable (arrowed) through the panel as it is removed

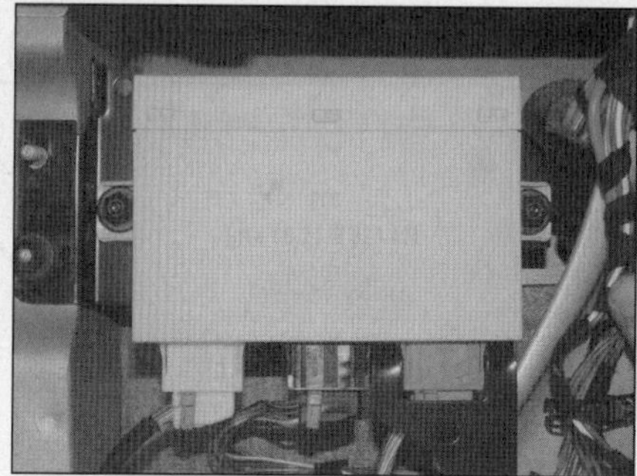

26.4 Disconnect the PDC control module wiring plugs

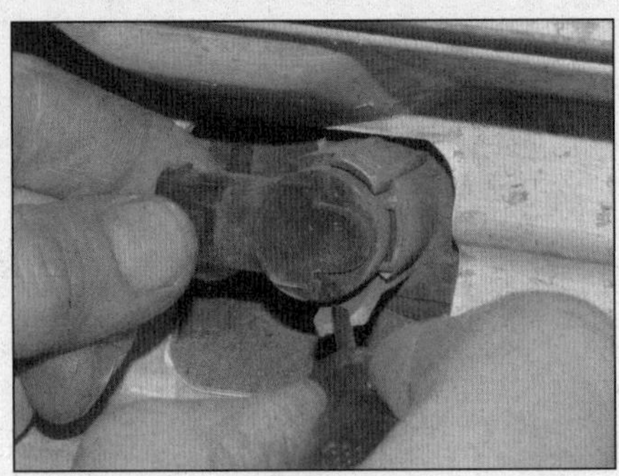

26.7 Release the clips and pull the sensor from the bumper

7 Disconnect the sensor wiring plugs, release the retaining clips and remove the sensors from the bumper **(see illustration)**.

Refitting

8 Refitting is the reverse of removal.

27 Wiring diagrams – general information

1 The wiring diagrams which follow only offer limited coverage of the electrical systems fitted to the BMW 5-Series.

2 Due to the sheer volume of wiring circuits applicable to the 5-Series, comprehensive coverage of all the vehicle's systems is not possible.

3 Bear in mind that, while wiring diagrams offer a useful quick-reference guide to the vehicle electrical systems, it is still possible to trace faults, and to check for supplies and earths, using a simple multimeter. Refer to the general fault finding methods described in Section 2 of this Chapter (ignoring the references to wiring diagrams if one is not provided for the system concerned).

BMW 5 Series wiring diagrams

Diagram 1

Key to symbols

Bulb

Flashing bulb

Switch

Multiple contact switch (ganged)

Fuse/fusible link F5

Resistor

Variable resistor

Variable resistor

Wire splice, unspecified connector or soldered joint

Connecting wires

Item no. 2

Single speed pump/motor M

Twin speed motor M

Gauge/meter

Earth point

Diode

Light emitting diode (LED)

Solenoid actuator

Heating element

Plug and socket connection

Wire colour (green with yellow tracer) Gn/Ge

Screened cable

Dashed outline denotes part of a larger item, containing in this case an electronic or solid state device.

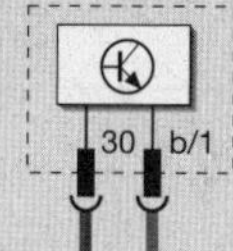

30 DIN standard termination
b/1 connector B, pin 1

Typical luggage compartment fusebox

Fuse	Rating	Circuit protected
F46	15A	Independent ventilation/heater
F47	15A	Independent heater
F48	5A	Alarm
F49	30A	Air suspension
F50	7.5A	Air suspension
F51	-	Not fitted
F52	30A	Cigar lighter
F53	7.5A	Central locking
F54	15A	Fuel pump
F55	20A	Rear wash/wipe
F56	30A	Rear wash/wipe, CD changer, navigation system, on-board monitor, radio
F57	10A	Telephone
F58	10A	Navigation system, on-board monitor, radio, telephone
F59	-	Not fitted
F60	15A	Electronic damper control
F61	-	Not fitted
F62	-	Not fitted
F63	-	Not fitted
F64	-	Not fitted
F65	-	Not fitted
F66	40A	Heated rear window

46 47 48 49 50 51 52 53 54 55 | 56 57 58 59 60 61 62 63 64 65 | 66

Typical passenger compartment fusebox

Fuse	Rating	Circuit protected
F1	30A	Windscreen wiper
F2	30A	Windscreen washer, headlight washer
F3	15A	Horn
F4	20A	Passenger compartment lighting, luggage compartment lighting, windscreen washer
F5	20A	Sunroof
F6	30A	Electric windows, central locking, electric mirrors
F7	20A	Engine cooling fan
F8	25A	Automatic stability control
F9	15A	Air conditioning, heated washer jets
F10	30A	Passenger seat adjustment
F11	7.5A	Steptronic
F12	5A	Immobilizer
F13	30A	Steering column adjustment, driver's seat adjustment
F14	5A	Engine control
F15	7.5A	Engine control, diagnostic connector
F16	5A	Lighting module
F17	10A	Fuel pump, ABS, automatic stability control
F18	5A	Instrument cluster
F19	-	Not fitted
F20	7.5A	Heated rear window, heater, air conditioning, engine cooling fan, tyre pressure control
F21	5A	Anti-glare interior mirror, driver's seat adjustment, garage door opener, thermal sensor, parking distance control
F22	30A	Engine cooling fan
F23	10A	Heater, independent heater
F24	5A	Instrument cluster, shift gate illumination, tyre pressure control
F25	7.5A	Radio, multi-information display
F26	5A	Windscreen wiper
F27	30A	Central locking, electric windows
F28	30A	Air conditioning, heater blower
F29	30A	Electric mirrors, electric windows, central locking
F30	25A	ABS
F31	10A	ABS automatic stability control, fuel pump
F32	15A	Heated seats
F33	-	Not fitted
F34	10A	Heated steering wheel
F35	-	Not fitted
F36	-	Not fitted
F37	5A	Immobilizer
F38	5A	Horn, shift gate illumination, diagnostic connector
F39	7.5A	Charging socket, courtesy mirror illumination
F40	5A	Airbag, instrument cluster
F41	5A	Stop light, lighting module, speed control
F42	5A	Airbag
F43	5A	Radio, telephone, on board monitor
F44	5A	Multifunction steering wheel, multi-information display, radio, telephone
F45	7.5A	Roller sun blind
F75	50A	Engine cooling fan
F76	40A	Heater blower

1 2 3 4 5 6 7 8 9 10 11 12 13 14 15 16 17 18 19 20 | 75 76

21 22 23 24 25 26 27 28 29 30 31 32 33 34 35 36 37 38 39 40 41 42 43 44 45

H33053

Diagram 2

Wire colours

Bl	Blue	**Vi**	Violet
Br	Brown	**Ws**	White
Ge	Yellow	**Or**	Orange
Gr	Grey	**Rt**	Red
Gn	Green	**Sw**	Black

Key to items

1 Battery
2 Ignition switch
3 Starter motor
4 Alternator
5 Passenger compartment fusebox
6 Engine cooling fan stage 1 relay
7 Engine cooling fan stage 2 relay
8 Engine cooling fan stage 3 relay
9 Engine cooling fan motor
10 Dual temperature switch
11 Fusible link
12 Horn relay
13 LH horn
14 RH horn
15 Horn switch
16 Steering wheel clock spring
17 Heater blower relay
18 Output amplifier
19 Heater blower motor

H33054

Typical starting and charging

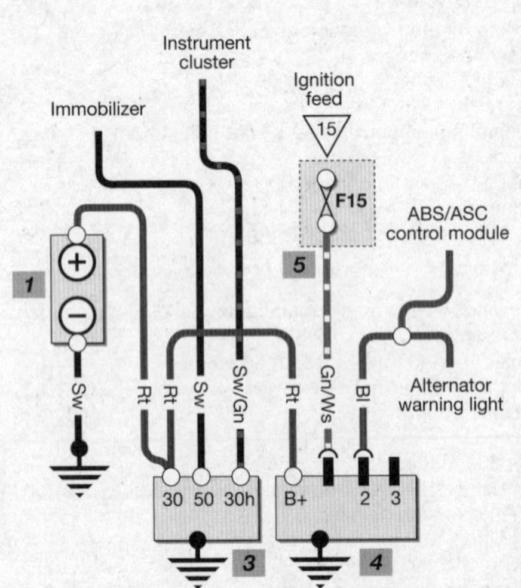

Typical engine cooling fan

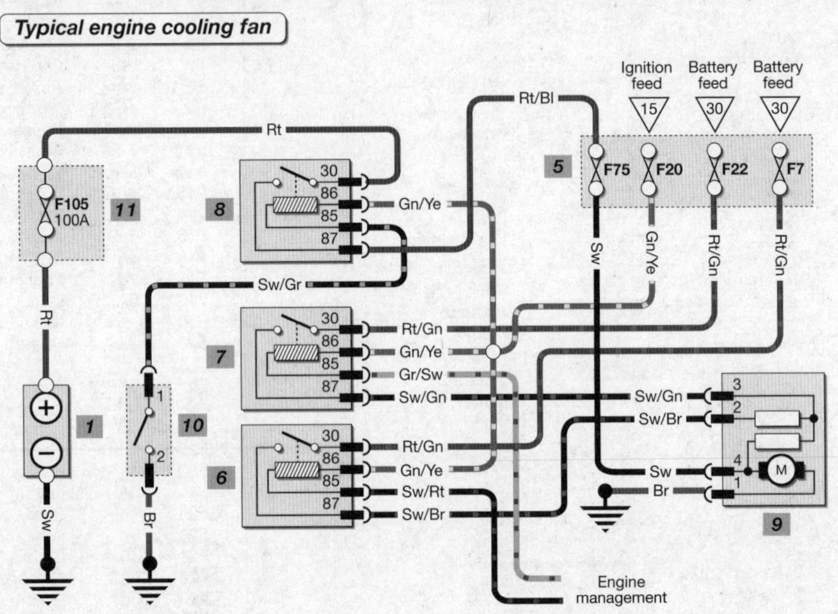

Typical horn

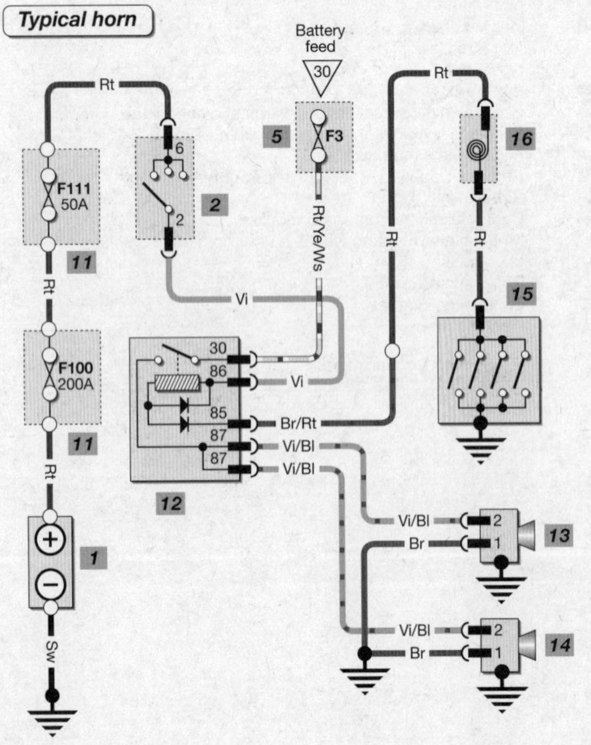

Typical heater blower

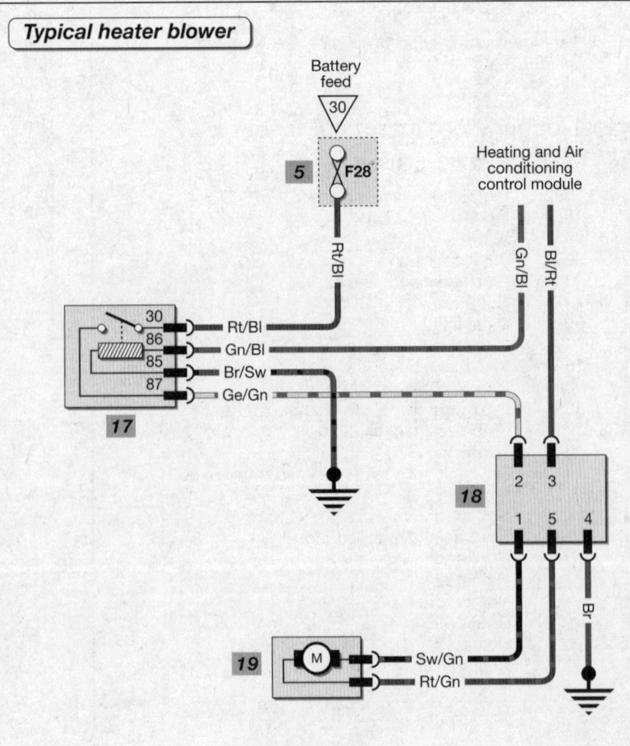

Wire colours

Bl	Blue	**Vi**	Violet
Br	Brown	**Ws**	White
Ge	Yellow	**Or**	Orange
Gr	Grey	**Rt**	Red
Gn	Green	**Sw**	Black

Key to items

1 Battery
2 Ignition switch
5 Passenger compartment fusebox
11 Fusible link
22 Headlight washer module
23 Headlight washer pump
24 Windscreen washer jet heater
25 Luggage compartment fusebox
26 Front cigar lighter
27 Charging socket
28 Cigar lighter relay
29 General control module
30 Wiper relay 1
31 Wiper relay 2
32 Front wiper motor
33 Wash/wipe switch
34 Washer pump

Diagram 3

H33055

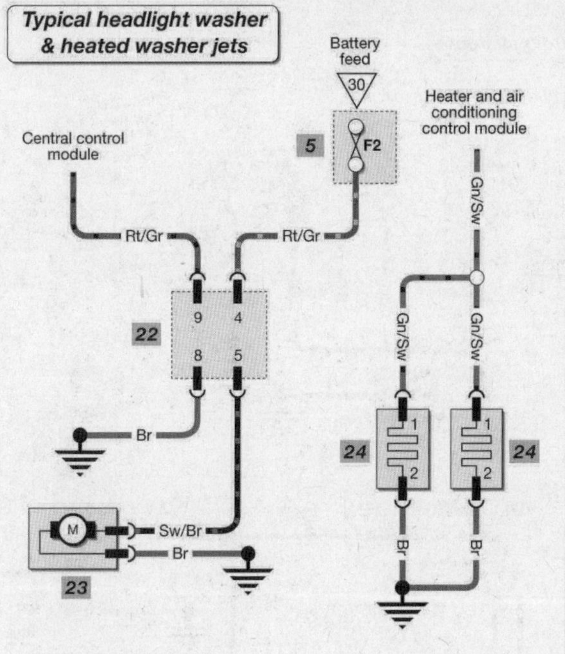
Typical headlight washer & heated washer jets
Battery feed
30
F2
5
Central control module
Heater and air conditioning control module
Rt/Gr
Gn/Sw
22
9
4
8
5
Br
24
Sw/Br
M
23

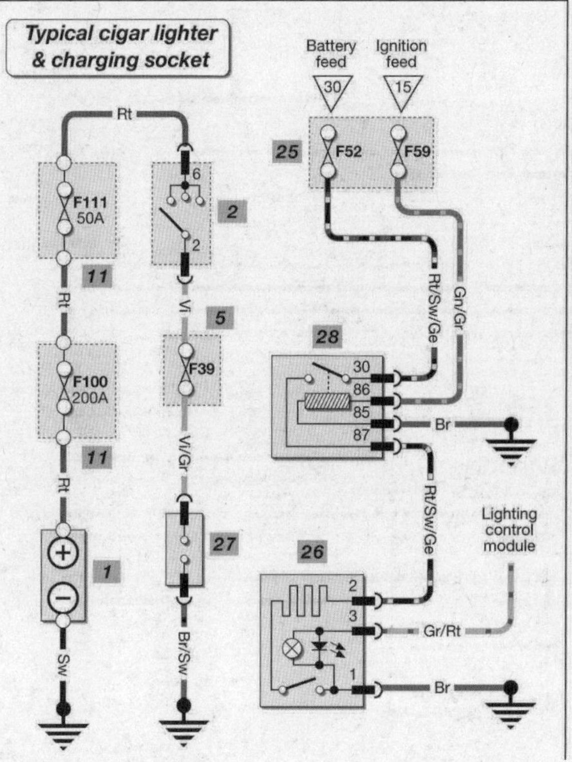
Typical cigar lighter & charging socket
Battery feed
Ignition feed
30
15
Rt
F111 50A
F100 200A
11
2
5
F39
25
F52
F59
Rt/Sw/Ge
Gn/Gr
28
30
86
85
87
Br
Vi
Vi/Gr
Br/Sw
27
1
Sw
26
Lighting control module
Gr/Rt

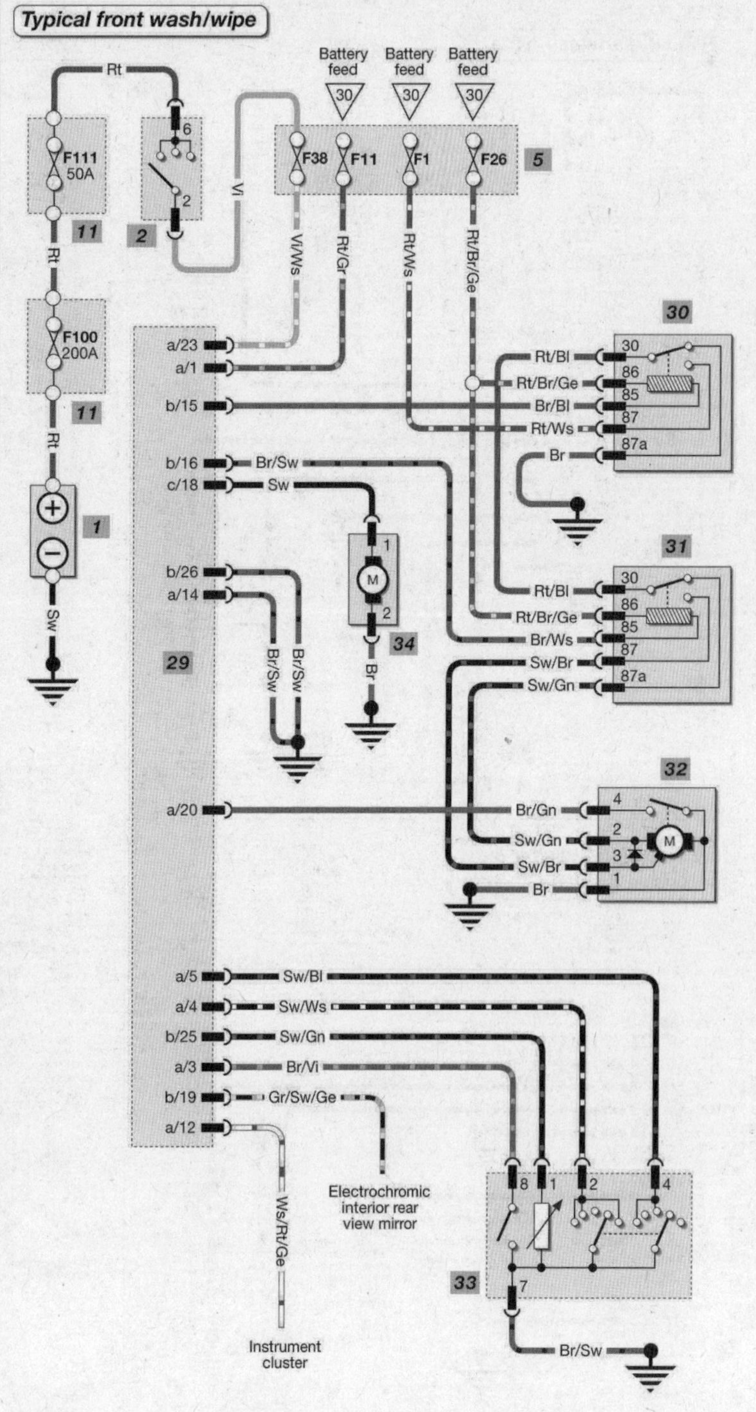
Typical front wash/wipe
Rt
Battery feed
Battery feed
Battery feed
30
F111 50A
F100 200A
11
2
Vi
F38
F11
F1
F26
5
Vi/Ws
Rt/Gr
Rt/Ws
Rt/Br/Ge
1
Sw
29
a/23
a/1
b/15
b/16
c/18
b/26
a/14
a/20
a/5
a/4
b/25
a/3
b/19
a/12
Br/Sw
Sw
M
34
Br
30
Rt/Bl
Rt/Br/Ge
Br/Bl
Rt/Ws
86
85
87
87a
31
Br/Ws
Sw/Br
Sw/Gn
32
Br/Gn
Sw/Bl
Sw/Ws
Br/Vi
Gr/Sw/Ge
Electrochromic interior rear view mirror
Ws/Rt/Ge
Instrument cluster
33

Diagram 4

Wire colours

Bl	Blue	**Vi**	Violet
Br	Brown	**Ws**	White
Ge	Yellow	**Or**	Orange
Gr	Grey	**Rt**	Red
Gn	Green	**Sw**	Black

Key to items

1 Battery
2 Ignition switch
5 Passenger compartment fusebox
11 Fusible link
25 Luggage compartment fusebox
33 Wash/wipe switch
38 Rear wash/wipe control unit
39 Tailgate/boot open switch
40 Rear washer pump
41 Headlight washer module
42 Headlight washer pump
43 Intensive washer pump
44 Unload relay
45 Antenna module
46 CD changer
47 Audio unit
48 LH tweeter
49 LH front speaker
50 LH rear speaker
51 RH front tweeter
52 RH front speaker
53 RH rear speaker

H33056

Typical rear wash/wipe

Battery feed
30
General control module
Lighting control module
F111 50A
F100 200A
F43
F55
Rt
Vi
Vi/Rt
Rt/Ws
Sw
a/3
b/2 Rt/Ws
a/5 Sw/Gr
a/6 Bl/Ge
a/4 Br/Ge
b/3 Sw/Rt
b/1 Br
a/2
a/1
Sw/Ws
Sw/Bl
Br/Sw
Br
10 5 7
1 2 6
1 2 5 11 25 38 40 39 33

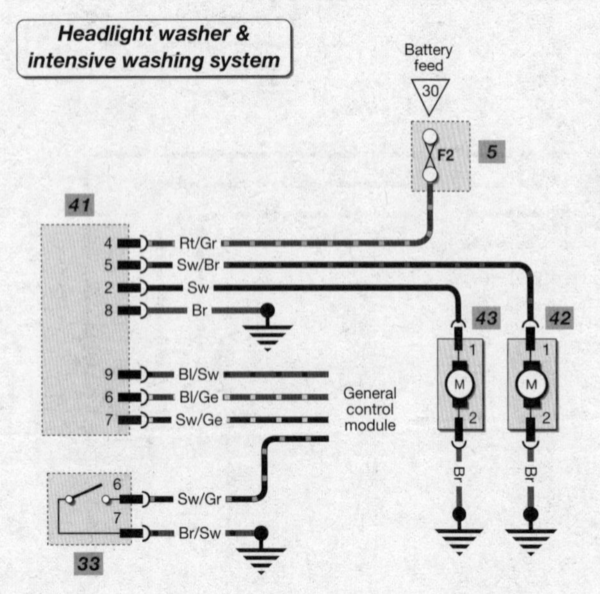

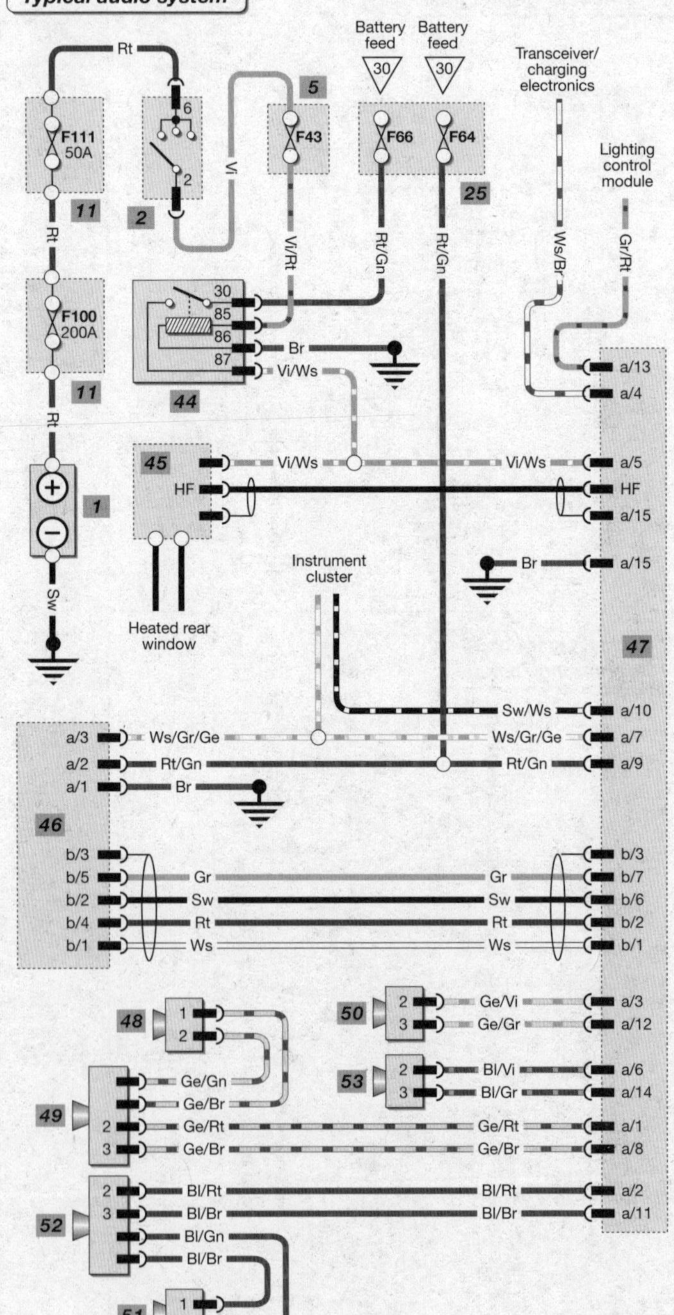

Wire colours

Bl	Blue	**Vi**	Violet
Br	Brown	**Ws**	White
Ge	Yellow	**Or**	Orange
Gr	Grey	**Rt**	Red
Gn	Green	**Sw**	Black

Key to items

Diagram 5

1 Battery
2 Ignition switch
5 Passenger compartment fusebox
11 Fusible link
29 General control module
45 Antenna module
57 Heated rear window relay
58 FM amplifier lockout circuit
59 Heated rear window
60 Driver's mirror assembly
61 Passenger's mirror assembly
62 Driver's door module
63 Driver's window motor
64 Driver's jamming switch
65 Passenger's door module
66 Passenger's window motor
67 Passenger's jammingswitch
68 Passenger's door window switch
69 LH rear window motor
70 LH rear jamming switch
71 LH rear door window switch
72 RH rear window motor
73 RH rear jamming switch
74 RH rear door window switch

H33057

Typical heated rear window

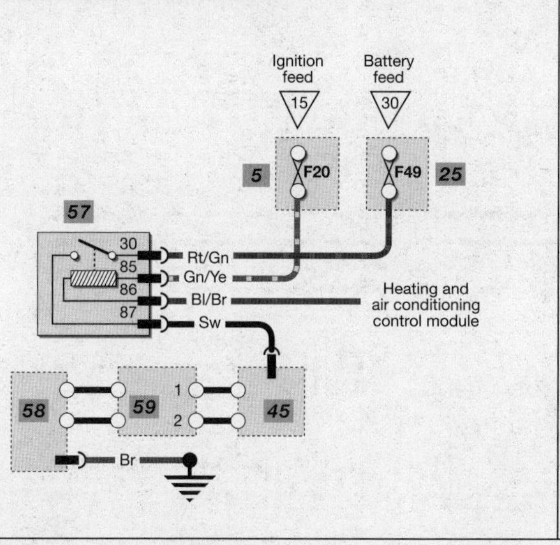

Typical electric mirrors

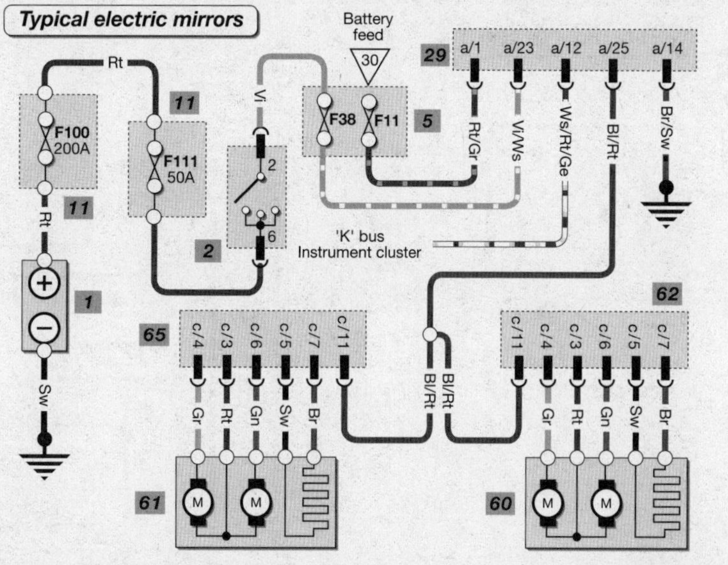

Typical electric windows

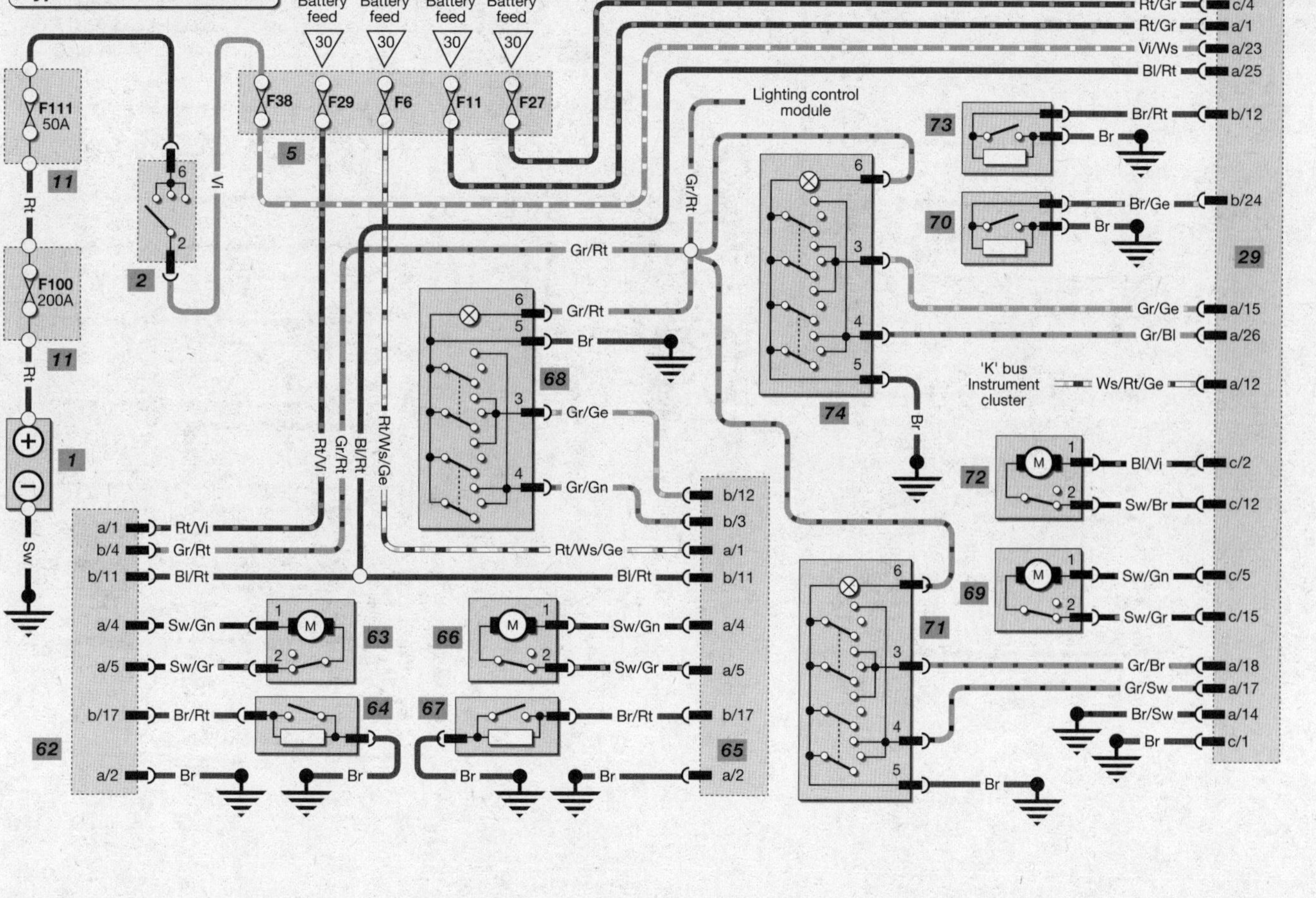

Wire colours

Bl	Blue	**Vi**	Violet
Br	Brown	**Ws**	White
Ge	Yellow	**Or**	Orange
Gr	Grey	**Rt**	Red
Gn	Green	**Sw**	Black

Key to items

Diagram 6

1 Battery
2 Ignition switch
5 Passenger compartment fusebox
11 Fusible link
25 Luggage compartment fusebox
29 General control module
62 Driver's door module
65 Passenger's door module
78 Driver's door lock switch
79 Driver's door lock motor
80 Passenger's door lock switch
81 Passenger's door lock motor
82 Tailgate/boot release switch
83 LH rear door lock
84 RH rear door lock
85 Central locking master switch
86 Tailgate/boot lock motor
87 Fuel filler flap lock motor
88 Tailgate/boot lock switch
89 Driver's door contact switch
90 Passenger's door contact switch
91 LH rear door contact switch
92 RH rear door contact switch
93 Tailgate/boot unlocking switch
94 Inertia switch

H33058

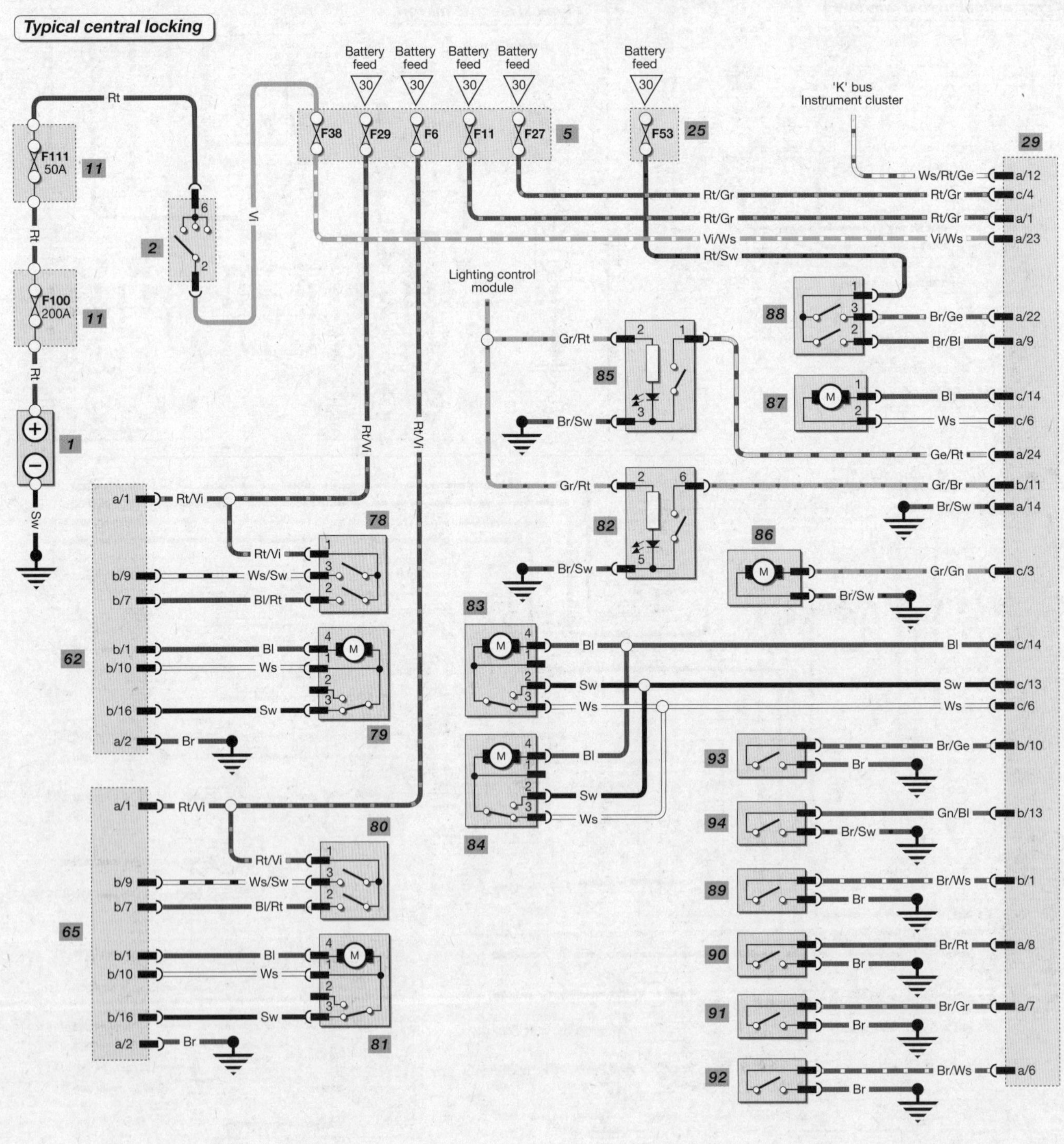

Wire colours

Bl	Blue	**Vi**	Violet
Br	Brown	**Ws**	White
Ge	Yellow	**Or**	Orange
Gr	Grey	**Rt**	Red
Gn	Green	**Sw**	Black

Key to items

1 Battery
2 Ignition switch
5 Passenger compartment fusebox
11 Fusible link
96 Stop light switch
97 Lighting control module
98 LH stop light
99 RH stop light
100 High level stop light
101 LH reversing light
102 RH reversing light
103 Reversing light switch
104 Light switch
a = side/headlights
b = flasher/dip
105 RH headlight high beam
106 RH headlight low beam
107 RH parking light
108 LH headlight high beam
109 LH headlight high beam
110 LH parking light
111 RH number plate light
112 LH number plate light
113 LH tail light
114 LH tailgate tail light
115 RH tail light
116 RH tailgate tail light

Diagram 7

H33059

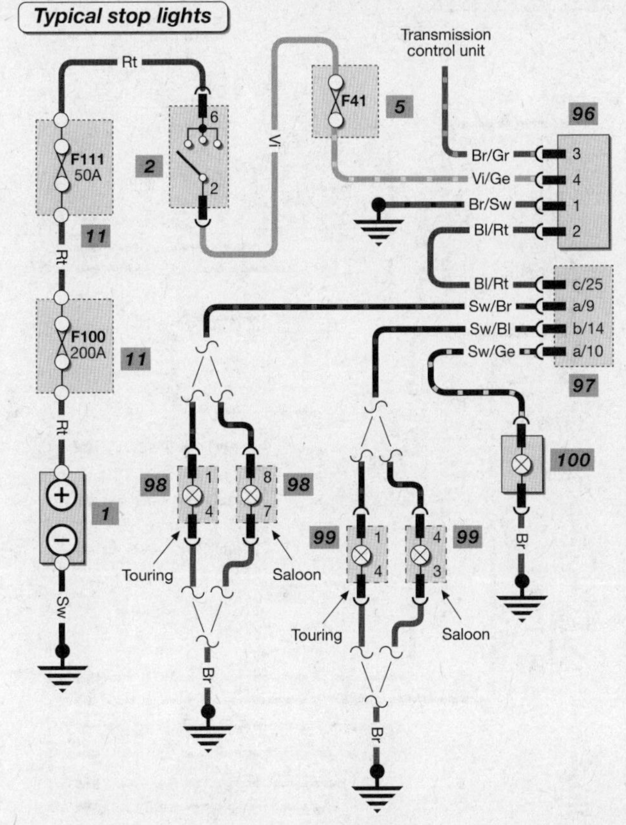

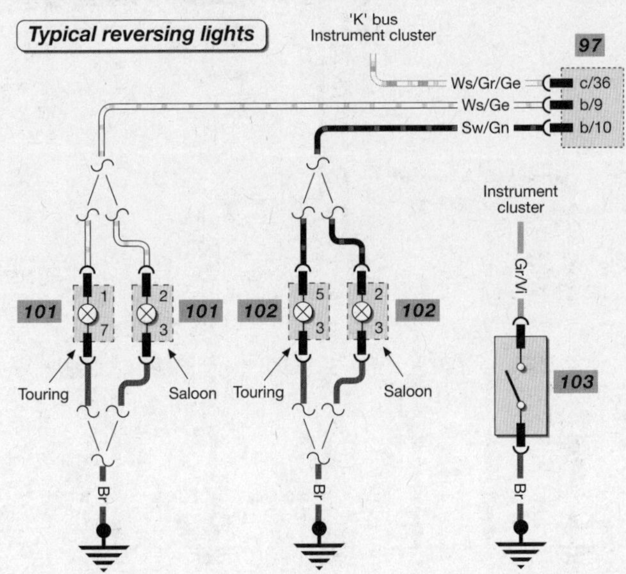

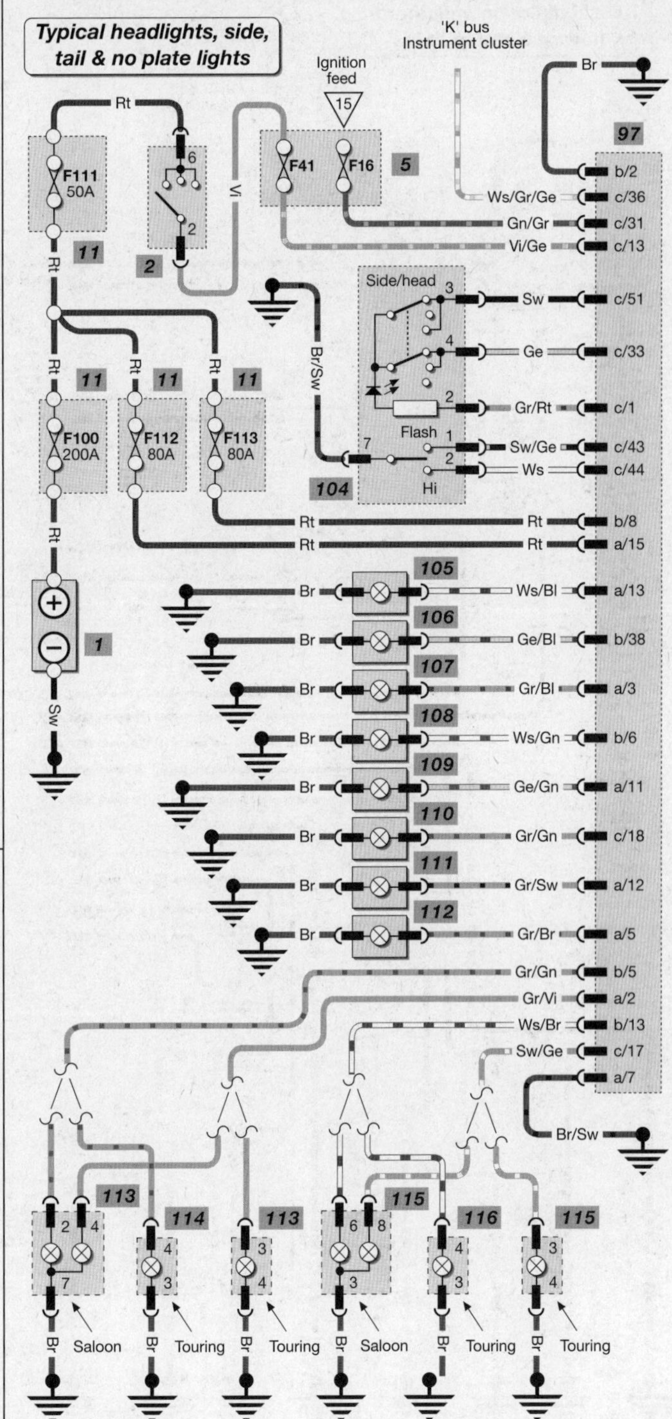

Wire colours

Bl	Blue	**Vi**	Violet
Br	Brown	**Ws**	White
Ge	Yellow	**Or**	Orange
Gr	Grey	**Rt**	Red
Gn	Green	**Sw**	Black

Key to items

Diagram 8

1 Battery
2 Ignition switch
5 Passenger compartment fusebox
11 Fusible link
97 Lighting control module
104 Light switch
c = direction indicator switch
120 LH front direction indicator
121 LH direction indicator side repeater
122 LH rear direction indicator
123 RH front direction indicator
124 RH direction indicator side repeater
125 RH rear direction indicator
126 Hazard warning switch
127 Foglight switch
128 LH front foglight
129 RH front foglight
130 LH rear foglight
131 LH tailgate foglight
132 RH rear foglight
133 RH tailgate foglight

H33060

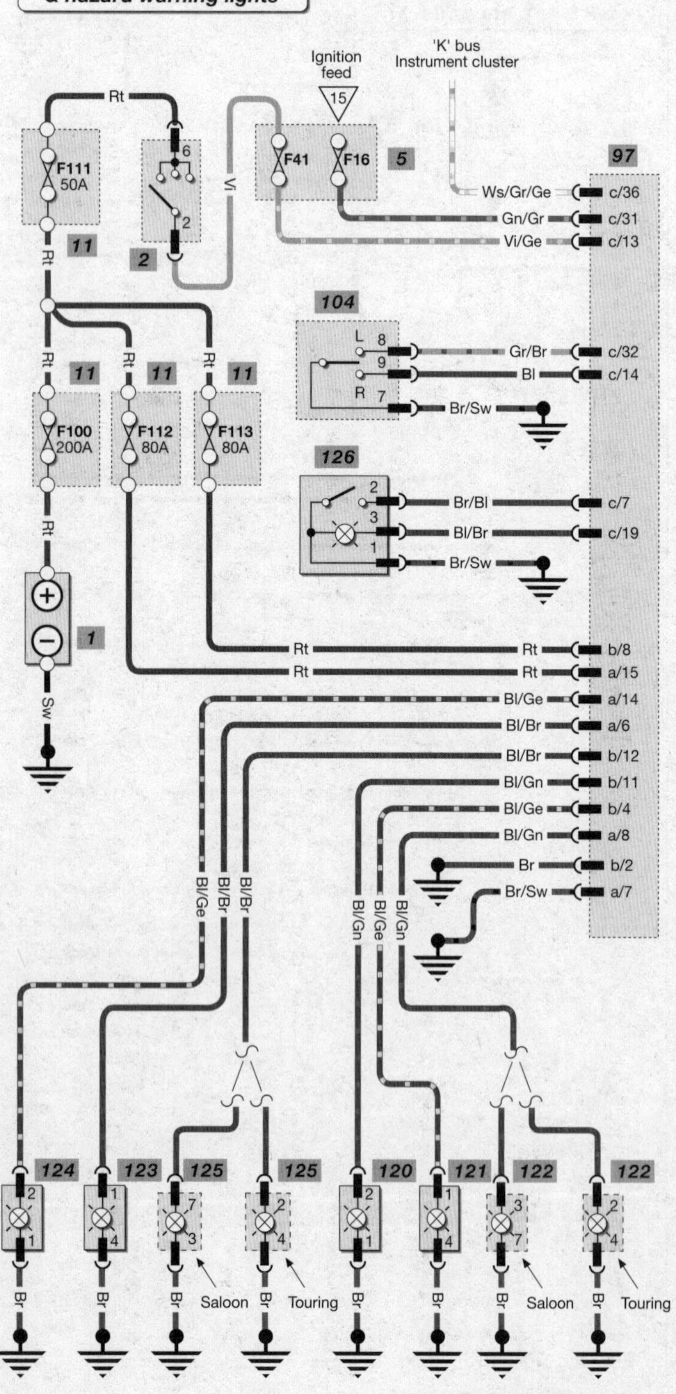

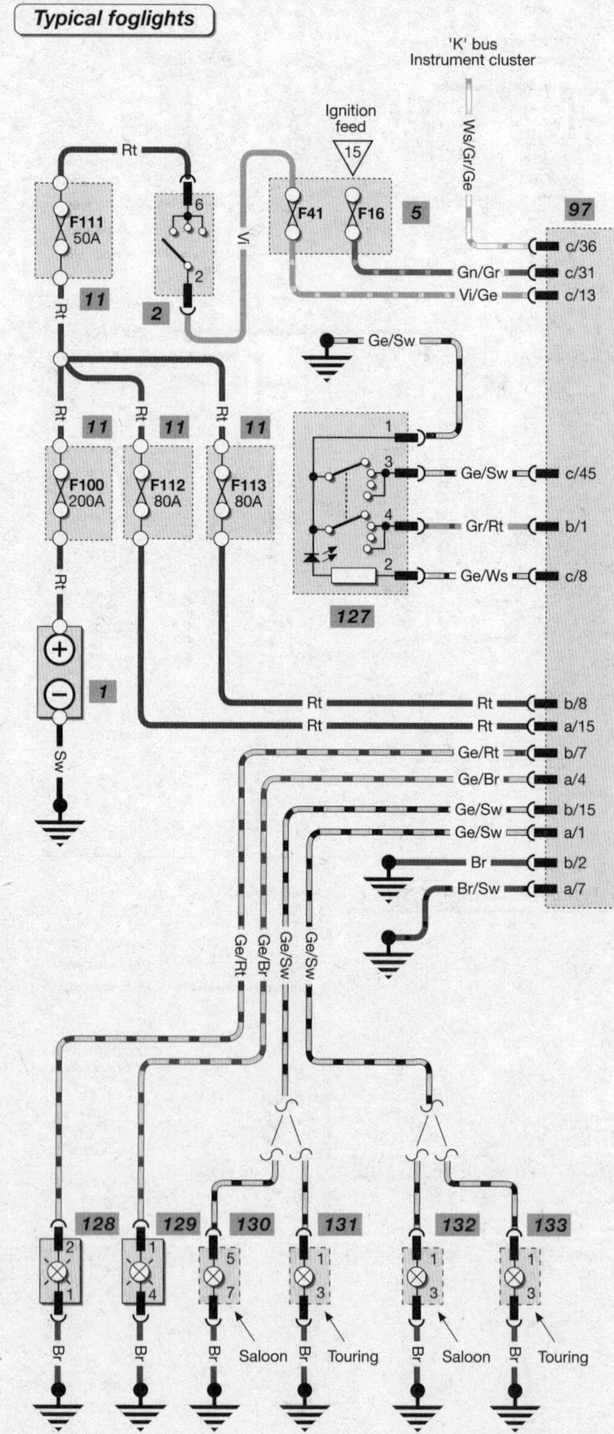

Diagram 9

Wire colours

Bl	Blue	**Vi**	Violet
Br	Brown	**Ws**	White
Ge	Yellow	**Or**	Orange
Gr	Grey	**Rt**	Red
Gn	Green	**Sw**	Black

Key to items

1	Battery
2	Ignition switch
5	Passenger compartment fusebox
11	Fusible link
29	General control module
86	Tailgate/boot lock motor
89	Driver's door contact switch
90	Passenger's door contact switch
91	LH rear door contact switch
92	RH rear door contact switch
97	Lighting control module
135	Headlight levelling adjuster
136	LH headlight levelling actuator
137	RH headlight levelling actuator
138	Driver's door courtesy light
139	Passenger's door courtesy light
140	LH rear door courtesy light
141	RH rear door courtesy light
142	Driver's vanity mirror light
143	Driver's vanity mirror light switch
144	Passenger's vanity mirror light
145	Passenger's vanity mirror light switch
146	Front interior light
147	Rear interior light (touring)
148	LH rear interior light (saloon)
149	RH rear interior light (saloon)
150	Luggage compartment light
151	Glove box light
152	Glove box light switch

H33061

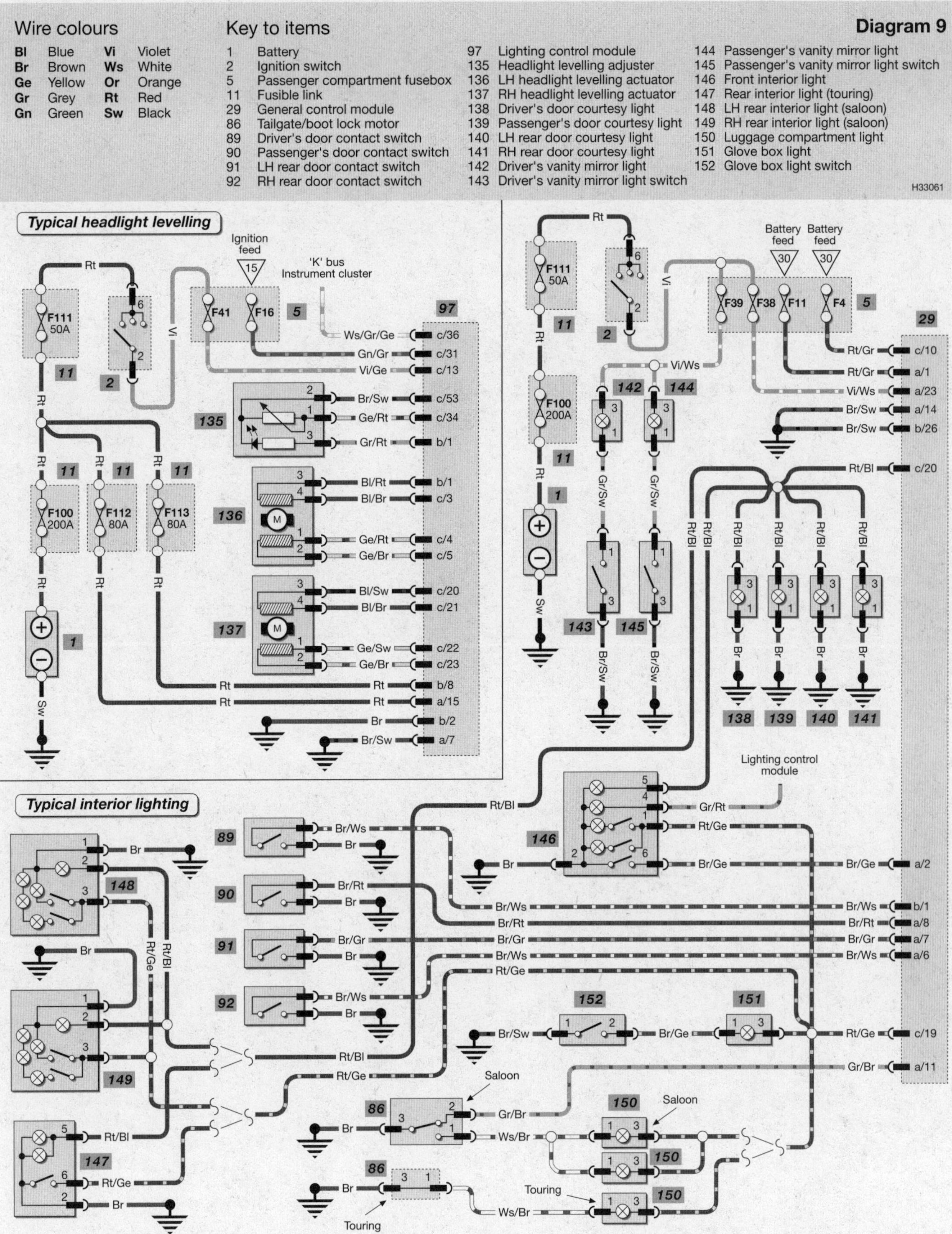

Dimensions and Weights

Note: *All figures are approximate, and may vary according to model. Refer to manufacturer's data for exact figures.*

Dimensions

Overall length:	
Saloon	4775 mm
Touring	4805 mm
Overall width*	1800 mm
Overall height (unladen):	
Saloon	1435 mm
Touring	1440 to 1445 mm
Wheelbase	2830 mm

** Excluding wing mirrors*

Weights

Kerb weight*:	
Saloon	1570 to 1730 kg
Touring	1670 to 1785 kg
Maximum gross vehicle weight*:	
Saloon	1945 to 2085 kg
Touring	1905 to 2300 kg
Maximum roof rack load	100 kg
Maximum towing weight**:	
Unbraked trailer	740 to 750 kg
Braked trailer	1500 to 2000 kg

** Depending on model and specification*
*** Refer to BMW dealer for exact recommendation*

Conversion factors

Length (distance)

Inches (in)	x 25.4 =	Millimetres (mm)	x 0.0394 =	Inches (in)
Feet (ft)	x 0.305 =	Metres (m)	x 3.281 =	Feet (ft)
Miles	x 1.609 =	Kilometres (km)	x 0.621 =	Miles

Volume (capacity)

Cubic inches (cu in; in^3)	x 16.387 =	Cubic centimetres (cc; cm^3)	x 0.061 =	Cubic inches (cu in; in^3)
Imperial pints (Imp pt)	x 0.568 =	Litres (l)	x 1.76 =	Imperial pints (Imp pt)
Imperial quarts (Imp qt)	x 1.137 =	Litres (l)	x 0.88 =	Imperial quarts (Imp qt)
Imperial quarts (Imp qt)	x 1.201 =	US quarts (US qt)	x 0.833 =	Imperial quarts (Imp qt)
US quarts (US qt)	x 0.946 =	Litres (l)	x 1.057 =	US quarts (US qt)
Imperial gallons (Imp gal)	x 4.546 =	Litres (l)	x 0.22 =	Imperial gallons (Imp gal)
Imperial gallons (Imp gal)	x 1.201 =	US gallons (US gal)	x 0.833 =	Imperial gallons (Imp gal)
US gallons (US gal)	x 3.785 =	Litres (l)	x 0.264 =	US gallons (US gal)

Mass (weight)

Ounces (oz)	x 28.35 =	Grams (g)	x 0.035 =	Ounces (oz)
Pounds (lb)	x 0.454 =	Kilograms (kg)	x 2.205 =	Pounds (lb)

Force

Ounces-force (ozf; oz)	x 0.278 =	Newtons (N)	x 3.6 =	Ounces-force (ozf; oz)
Pounds-force (lbf; lb)	x 4.448 =	Newtons (N)	x 0.225 =	Pounds-force (lbf; lb)
Newtons (N)	x 0.1 =	Kilograms-force (kgf; kg)	x 9.81 =	Newtons (N)

Pressure

Pounds-force per square inch (psi; lbf/in^2; lb/in^2)	x 0.070 =	Kilograms-force per square centimetre (kgf/cm^2; kg/cm^2)	x 14.223 =	Pounds-force per square inch (psi; lbf/in^2; lb/in^2)
Pounds-force per square inch (psi; lbf/in^2; lb/in^2)	x 0.068 =	Atmospheres (atm)	x 14.696 =	Pounds-force per square inch (psi; lbf/in^2; lb/in^2)
Pounds-force per square inch (psi; lbf/in^2; lb/in^2)	x 0.069 =	Bars	x 14.5 =	Pounds-force per square inch (psi; lbf/in^2; lb/in^2)
Pounds-force per square inch (psi; lbf/in^2; lb/in^2)	x 6.895 =	Kilopascals (kPa)	x 0.145 =	Pounds-force per square inch (psi; lbf/in^2; lb/in^2)
Kilopascals (kPa)	x 0.01 =	Kilograms-force per square centimetre (kgf/cm^2; kg/cm^2)	x 98.1 =	Kilopascals (kPa)
Millibar (mbar)	x 100 =	Pascals (Pa)	x 0.01 =	Millibar (mbar)
Millibar (mbar)	x 0.0145 =	Pounds-force per square inch (psi; lbf/in^2; lb/in^2)	x 68.947 =	Millibar (mbar)
Millibar (mbar)	x 0.75 =	Millimetres of mercury (mmHg)	x 1.333 =	Millibar (mbar)
Millibar (mbar)	x 0.401 =	Inches of water (inH_2O)	x 2.491 =	Millibar (mbar)
Millimetres of mercury (mmHg)	x 0.535 =	Inches of water (inH_2O)	x 1.868 =	Millimetres of mercury (mmHg)
Inches of water (inH_2O)	x 0.036 =	Pounds-force per square inch (psi; lbf/in^2; lb/in^2)	x 27.68 =	Inches of water (inH_2O)

Torque (moment of force)

Pounds-force inches (lbf in; lb in)	x 1.152 =	Kilograms-force centimetre (kgf cm; kg cm)	x 0.868 =	Pounds-force inches (lbf in; lb in)
Pounds-force inches (lbf in; lb in)	x 0.113 =	Newton metres (Nm)	x 8.85 =	Pounds-force inches (lbf in; lb in)
Pounds-force inches (lbf in; lb in)	x 0.083 =	Pounds-force feet (lbf ft; lb ft)	x 12 =	Pounds-force inches (lbf in; lb in)
Pounds-force feet (lbf ft; lb ft)	x 0.138 =	Kilograms-force metres (kgf m; kg m)	x 7.233 =	Pounds-force feet (lbf ft; lb ft)
Pounds-force feet (lbf ft; lb ft)	x 1.356 =	Newton metres (Nm)	x 0.738 =	Pounds-force feet (lbf ft; lb ft)
Newton metres (Nm)	x 0.102 =	Kilograms-force metres (kgf m; kg m)	x 9.804 =	Newton metres (Nm)

Power

Horsepower (hp)	x 745.7 =	Watts (W)	x 0.0013 =	Horsepower (hp)

Velocity (speed)

Miles per hour (miles/hr; mph)	x 1.609 =	Kilometres per hour (km/hr; kph)	x 0.621 =	Miles per hour (miles/hr; mph)

Fuel consumption*

Miles per gallon, Imperial (mpg)	x 0.354 =	Kilometres per litre (km/l)	x 2.825 =	Miles per gallon, Imperial (mpg)
Miles per gallon, US (mpg)	x 0.425 =	Kilometres per litre (km/l)	x 2.352 =	Miles per gallon, US (mpg)

Temperature

Degrees Fahrenheit = (°C x 1.8) + 32

Degrees Celsius (Degrees Centigrade; °C) = (°F - 32) x 0.56

** It is common practice to convert from miles per gallon (mpg) to litres/100 kilometres (l/100km), where mpg x l/100 km = 282*

Spare parts are available from many sources, including maker's appointed garages, accessory shops, and motor factors. To be sure of obtaining the correct parts, it will sometimes be necessary to quote the vehicle identification number. If possible, it can also be useful to take the old parts along for positive identification. Items such as starter motors and alternators may be available under a service exchange scheme – any parts returned should be clean.

Our advice regarding spare parts is as follows.

Officially appointed garages

This is the best source of parts which are peculiar to your car, and which are not otherwise generally available (eg, badges, interior trim, certain body panels, etc). It is also the only place at which you should buy parts if the vehicle is still under warranty.

Accessory shops

These are very good places to buy materials and components needed for the maintenance of your car (oil, air and fuel filters, light bulbs, drivebelts, greases, brake pads, touch-up paint, etc). Components of this nature sold by a reputable shop are usually of the same standard as those used by the car manufacturer.

Besides components, these shops also sell tools and general accessories, usually have convenient opening hours, charge lower prices, and can often be found close to home. Some accessory shops have parts counters where components needed for almost any repair job can be purchased or ordered.

Motor factors

Good factors will stock all the more important components which wear out comparatively quickly, and can sometimes supply individual components needed for the overhaul of a larger assembly (eg, brake seals and hydraulic parts, bearing shells, pistons, valves). They may also handle work such as cylinder block reboring, crankshaft regrinding, etc.

Tyre and exhaust specialists

These outlets may be independent, or members of a local or national chain. They frequently offer competitive prices when compared with a main dealer or local garage, but it will pay to obtain several quotes before making a decision. When researching prices, also ask what 'extras' may be added – for instance fitting a new valve and balancing the wheel are both commonly charged on top of the price of a new tyre.

Other sources

Beware of parts or materials obtained from market stalls, car boot sales or similar outlets. Such items are not invariably sub-standard, but there is little chance of compensation if they do prove unsatisfactory. in the case of safety-critical components such as brake pads, there is the risk not only of financial loss, but also of an accident causing injury or death.

Second-hand components or assemblies obtained from a car breaker can be a good buy in some circumstances, but this sort of purchase is best made by the experienced DIY mechanic.

Vehicle identification

Modifications are a continuing and unpublicised process in vehicle manufacture, quite apart from major model changes. Spare parts manuals and lists are compiled upon a numerical basis, the individual vehicle identification numbers being essential to correct identification of the component concerned.

When ordering spare parts, always give as much information as possible. Quote the car model, year of manufacture and registration, chassis and engine numbers as appropriate.

The *Vehicle Identification Number (VIN)* plate is stamped onto the right-hand suspension turret in the front corner of the engine compartment, stamped onto a plate on the left-hand side of the engine compartment, and on later models, visible through the passenger side of the windscreen **(see illustrations)**.

The *engine number* is stamped on the left-hand face of the cylinder block near the base of the oil level dipstick.

The VIN plate is stamped onto the right-hand suspension turret in the engine compartment

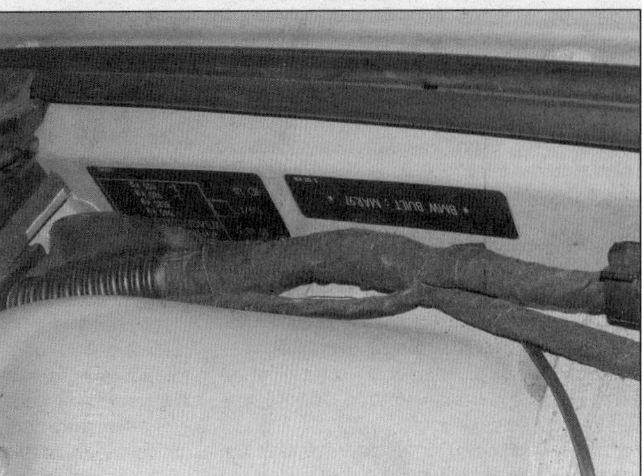

The VIN is riveted to the body panel in the left-hand front section of the engine compartment

Whenever servicing, repair or overhaul work is carried out on the car or its components, observe the following procedures and instructions. This will assist in carrying out the operation efficiently and to a professional standard of workmanship.

Joint mating faces and gaskets

When separating components at their mating faces, never insert screwdrivers or similar implements into the joint between the faces in order to prise them apart. This can cause severe damage which results in oil leaks, coolant leaks, etc upon reassembly. Separation is usually achieved by tapping along the joint with a soft-faced hammer in order to break the seal. However, note that this method may not be suitable where dowels are used for component location.

Where a gasket is used between the mating faces of two components, a new one must be fitted on reassembly; fit it dry unless otherwise stated in the repair procedure. Make sure that the mating faces are clean and dry, with all traces of old gasket removed. When cleaning a joint face, use a tool which is unlikely to score or damage the face, and remove any burrs or nicks with an oilstone or fine file.

Make sure that tapped holes are cleaned with a pipe cleaner, and keep them free of jointing compound, if this is being used, unless specifically instructed otherwise.

Ensure that all orifices, channels or pipes are clear, and blow through them, preferably using compressed air.

Oil seals

Oil seals can be removed by levering them out with a wide flat-bladed screwdriver or similar implement. Alternatively, a number of self-tapping screws may be screwed into the seal, and these used as a purchase for pliers or some similar device in order to pull the seal free.

Whenever an oil seal is removed from its working location, either individually or as part of an assembly, it should be renewed.

The very fine sealing lip of the seal is easily damaged, and will not seal if the surface it contacts is not completely clean and free from scratches, nicks or grooves. If the original sealing surface of the component cannot be restored, and the manufacturer has not made provision for slight relocation of the seal relative to the sealing surface, the component should be renewed.

Protect the lips of the seal from any surface which may damage them in the course of fitting. Use tape or a conical sleeve where possible. Lubricate the seal lips with oil before fitting and, on dual-lipped seals, fill the space between the lips with grease.

Unless otherwise stated, oil seals must be fitted with their sealing lips toward the lubricant to be sealed.

Use a tubular drift or block of wood of the appropriate size to install the seal and, if the seal housing is shouldered, drive the seal down to the shoulder. If the seal housing is unshouldered, the seal should be fitted with its face flush with the housing top face (unless otherwise instructed).

Screw threads and fastenings

Seized nuts, bolts and screws are quite a common occurrence where corrosion has set in, and the use of penetrating oil or releasing fluid will often overcome this problem if the offending item is soaked for a while before attempting to release it. The use of an impact driver may also provide a means of releasing such stubborn fastening devices, when used in conjunction with the appropriate screwdriver bit or socket. If none of these methods works, it may be necessary to resort to the careful application of heat, or the use of a hacksaw or nut splitter device.

Studs are usually removed by locking two nuts together on the threaded part, and then using a spanner on the lower nut to unscrew the stud. Studs or bolts which have broken off below the surface of the component in which they are mounted can sometimes be removed using a stud extractor. Always ensure that a blind tapped hole is completely free from oil, grease, water or other fluid before installing the bolt or stud. Failure to do this could cause the housing to crack due to the hydraulic action of the bolt or stud as it is screwed in.

When tightening a castellated nut to accept a split pin, tighten the nut to the specified torque, where applicable, and then tighten further to the next split pin hole. Never slacken the nut to align the split pin hole, unless stated in the repair procedure.

When checking or retightening a nut or bolt to a specified torque setting, slacken the nut or bolt by a quarter of a turn, and then retighten to the specified setting. However, this should not be attempted where angular tightening has been used.

For some screw fastenings, notably cylinder head bolts or nuts, torque wrench settings are no longer specified for the latter stages of tightening, "angle-tightening" being called up instead. Typically, a fairly low torque wrench setting will be applied to the bolts/nuts in the correct sequence, followed by one or more stages of tightening through specified angles.

Locknuts, locktabs and washers

Any fastening which will rotate against a component or housing during tightening should always have a washer between it and the relevant component or housing.

Spring or split washers should always be renewed when they are used to lock a critical component such as a big-end bearing retaining bolt or nut. Locktabs which are folded over to retain a nut or bolt should always be renewed.

Self-locking nuts can be re-used in non-critical areas, providing resistance can be felt when the locking portion passes over the bolt or stud thread. However, it should be noted that self-locking stiffnuts tend to lose their effectiveness after long periods of use, and should then be renewed as a matter of course.

Split pins must always be replaced with new ones of the correct size for the hole.

When thread-locking compound is found on the threads of a fastener which is to be re-used, it should be cleaned off with a wire brush and solvent, and fresh compound applied on reassembly.

Special tools

Some repair procedures in this manual entail the use of special tools such as a press, two or three-legged pullers, spring compressors, etc. Wherever possible, suitable readily-available alternatives to the manufacturer's special tools are described, and are shown in use. In some instances, where no alternative is possible, it has been necessary to resort to the use of a manufacturer's tool, and this has been done for reasons of safety as well as the efficient completion of the repair operation. Unless you are highly-skilled and have a thorough understanding of the procedures described, never attempt to bypass the use of any special tool when the procedure described specifies its use. Not only is there a very great risk of personal injury, but expensive damage could be caused to the components involved.

Environmental considerations

When disposing of used engine oil, brake fluid, antifreeze, etc, give due consideration to any detrimental environmental effects. Do not, for instance, pour any of the above liquids down drains into the general sewage system, or onto the ground to soak away. Many local council refuse tips provide a facility for waste oil disposal, as do some garages. If none of these facilities are available, consult your local Environmental Health Department, or the National Rivers Authority, for further advice.

With the universal tightening-up of legislation regarding the emission of environmentally-harmful substances from motor vehicles, most vehicles have tamperproof devices fitted to the main adjustment points of the fuel system. These devices are primarily designed to prevent unqualified persons from adjusting the fuel/air mixture, with the chance of a consequent increase in toxic emissions. If such devices are found during servicing or overhaul, they should, wherever possible, be renewed or refitted in accordance with the manufacturer's requirements or current legislation.

Note: It is antisocial and illegal to dump oil down the drain. To find the location of your local oil recycling bank, call this number free.

The jack supplied with the vehicle tool kit should only be used for changing the roadwheels – see *Wheel changing* at the front of this manual. When carrying out any other kind of work, raise the vehicle using a hydraulic (or 'trolley') jack, and always supplement the jack with axle stands positioned under the vehicle jacking points.

When using a hydraulic jack or axle stands, always position the jack head or axle stand head under the relevant rubber lifting blocks. These are situated directly underneath the vehicle jack location holes in the sill **(see illustration)**.

The jack supplied with the vehicle locates in the holes provided in the sill. Ensure that the jack head is correctly engaged before attempting to raise the vehicle.

Never work under, around, or near a raised vehicle, unless it is adequately supported in at least two places.

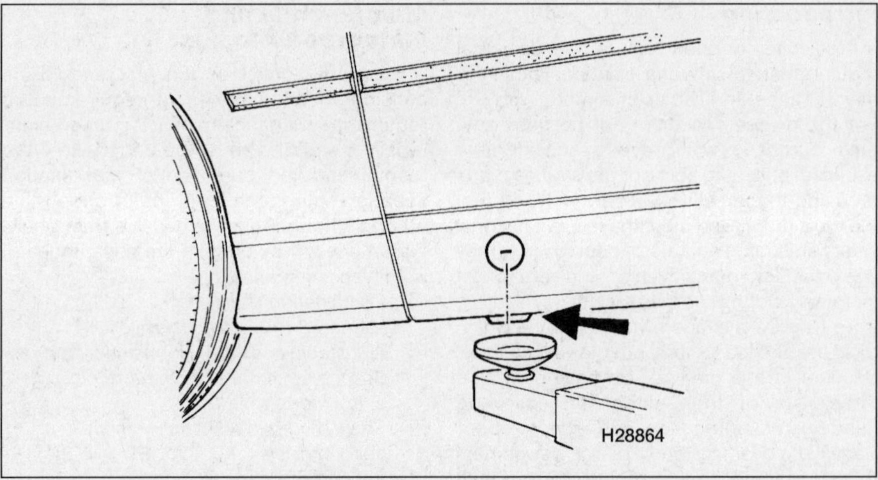

Then raising the vehicle, locate the jack/ramp arm underneath the rubber lifting block (arrowed) located under the sill

Audio unit Anti-Theft System

The radio/cassette/CD player/autochanger unit fitted as standard equipment by BMW is equipped with a built-in security code, to deter thieves. If the power source to the unit is cut, the anti-theft system will activate. Even if the power source is immediately reconnected, the radio/cassette unit will not function until the correct security code has been entered. Therefore if you do not know the correct security code for the unit, **do not** disconnect the battery negative lead, or remove the radio/cassette unit from the vehicle.

The procedure for reprogramming a unit that has been disconnected from its power supply varies from model to model – consult the handbook supplied with the unit for specific details or refer to your BMW dealer.

Tools and working facilities

Introduction

A selection of good tools is a fundamental requirement for anyone contemplating the maintenance and repair of a motor vehicle. For the owner who does not possess any, their purchase will prove a considerable expense, offsetting some of the savings made by doing-it-yourself. However, provided that the tools purchased meet the relevant national safety standards and are of good quality, they will last for many years and prove an extremely worthwhile investment.

To help the average owner to decide which tools are needed to carry out the various tasks detailed in this manual, we have compiled three lists of tools under the following headings: *Maintenance and minor repair*, *Repair and overhaul*, and *Special*. Newcomers to practical mechanics should start off with the *Maintenance and minor repair* tool kit, and confine themselves to the simpler jobs around the vehicle. Then, as confidence and experience grow, more difficult tasks can be undertaken, with extra tools being purchased as, and when, they are needed. In this way, a *Maintenance and minor repair* tool kit can be built up into a *Repair and overhaul* tool kit over a considerable period of time, without any major cash outlays. The experienced do-it-yourselfer will have a tool kit good enough for most repair and overhaul procedures, and will add tools from the *Special* category when it is felt that the expense is justified by the amount of use to which these tools will be put.

Maintenance and minor repair tool kit

The tools given in this list should be considered as a minimum requirement if routine maintenance, servicing and minor repair operations are to be undertaken. We recommend the purchase of combination spanners (ring one end, open-ended the other); although more expensive than open-ended ones, they do give the advantages of both types of spanner.

- ☐ *Combination spanners:*
  Metric - 8 to 19 mm inclusive
- ☐ *Adjustable spanner - 35 mm jaw (approx.)*
- ☐ *Spark plug spanner (with rubber insert) - petrol models*
- ☐ *Spark plug gap adjustment tool - petrol models*
- ☐ *Set of feeler gauges*
- ☐ *Brake bleed nipple spanner*
- ☐ *Screwdrivers:*
  Flat blade - 100 mm long x 6 mm dia
  Cross blade - 100 mm long x 6 mm dia
  Torx - various sizes (not all vehicles)
- ☐ *Combination pliers*
- ☐ *Hacksaw (junior)*
- ☐ *Tyre pump*
- ☐ *Tyre pressure gauge*
- ☐ *Oil can*
- ☐ *Oil filter removal tool*
- ☐ *Fine emery cloth*
- ☐ *Wire brush (small)*
- ☐ *Funnel (medium size)*
- ☐ *Sump drain plug key (not all vehicles)*

Repair and overhaul tool kit

These tools are virtually essential for anyone undertaking any major repairs to a motor vehicle, and are additional to those given in the *Maintenance and minor repair* list. Included in this list is a comprehensive set of sockets. Although these are expensive, they will be found invaluable as they are so versatile - particularly if various drives are included in the set. We recommend the half-inch square-drive type, as this can be used with most proprietary torque wrenches.

The tools in this list will sometimes need to be supplemented by tools from the *Special* list:

- ☐ *Sockets (or box spanners) to cover range in previous list (including Torx sockets)*
- ☐ *Reversible ratchet drive (for use with sockets)*
- ☐ *Extension piece, 250 mm (for use with sockets)*
- ☐ *Universal joint (for use with sockets)*
- ☐ *Flexible handle or sliding T "breaker bar" (for use with sockets)*
- ☐ *Torque wrench (for use with sockets)*
- ☐ *Self-locking grips*
- ☐ *Ball pein hammer*
- ☐ *Soft-faced mallet (plastic or rubber)*
- ☐ *Screwdrivers:*
  Flat blade - long & sturdy, short (chubby), and narrow (electrician's) types
  Cross blade – long & sturdy, and short (chubby) types
- ☐ *Pliers:*
  Long-nosed
  Side cutters (electrician's)
  Circlip (internal and external)
- ☐ *Cold chisel - 25 mm*
- ☐ *Scriber*
- ☐ *Scraper*
- ☐ *Centre-punch*
- ☐ *Pin punch*
- ☐ *Hacksaw*
- ☐ *Brake hose clamp*
- ☐ *Brake/clutch bleeding kit*
- ☐ *Selection of twist drills*
- ☐ *Steel rule/straight-edge*
- ☐ *Allen keys (inc. splined/Torx type)*
- ☐ *Selection of files*
- ☐ *Wire brush*
- ☐ *Axle stands*
- ☐ *Jack (strong trolley or hydraulic type)*

- ☐ *Light with extension lead*
- ☐ *Universal electrical multi-meter*

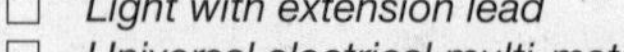

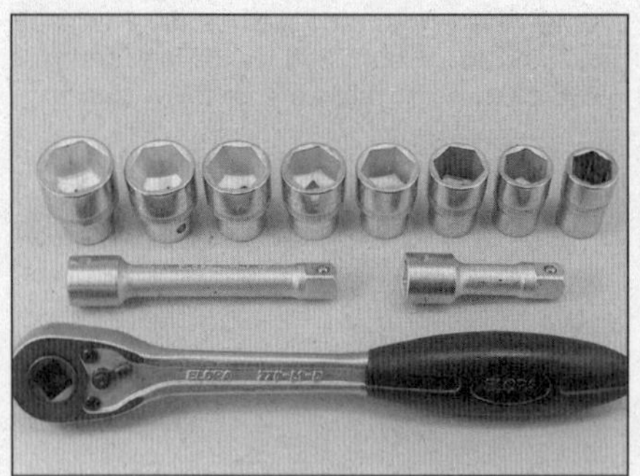

Sockets and reversible ratchet drive

Brake bleeding kit

Torx key, socket and bit

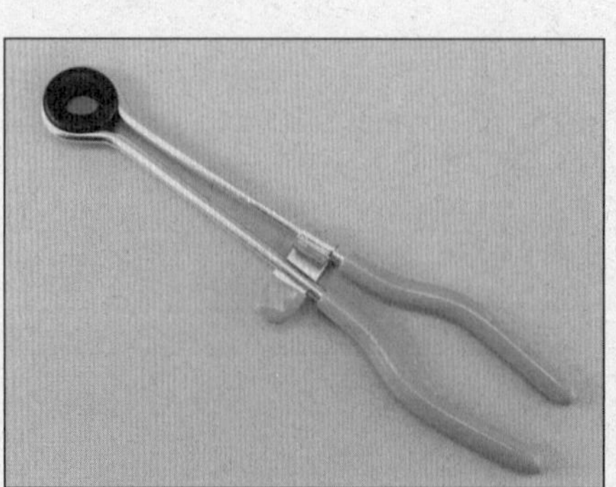

Hose clamp

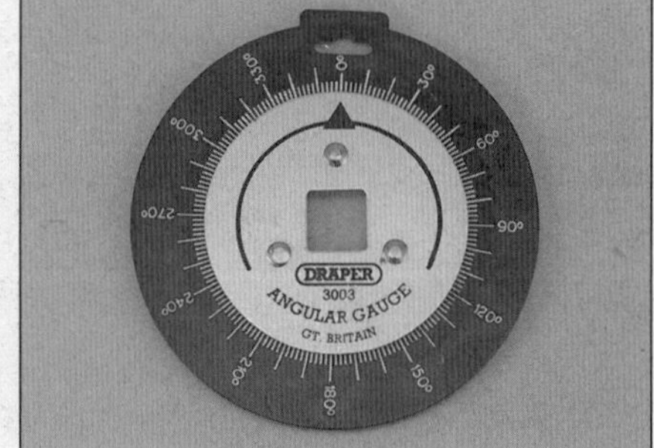

Angular-tightening gauge

Special tools

The tools in this list are those which are not used regularly, are expensive to buy, or which need to be used in accordance with their manufacturers' instructions. Unless relatively difficult mechanical jobs are undertaken frequently, it will not be economic to buy many of these tools. Where this is the case, you could consider clubbing together with friends (or joining a motorists' club) to make a joint purchase, or borrowing the tools against a deposit from a local garage or tool hire specialist. It is worth noting that many of the larger DIY superstores now carry a large range of special tools for hire at modest rates.

The following list contains only those tools and instruments freely available to the public, and not those special tools produced by the vehicle manufacturer specifically for its dealer network. You will find occasional references to these manufacturers' special tools in the text of this manual. Generally, an alternative method of doing the job without the vehicle manufacturers' special tool is given. However, sometimes there is no alternative to using them. Where this is the case and the relevant tool cannot be bought or borrowed, you will have to entrust the work to a dealer.

- ☐ *Angular-tightening gauge*
- ☐ *Valve spring compressor*
- ☐ *Valve grinding tool*
- ☐ *Piston ring compressor*
- ☐ *Piston ring removal/installation tool*
- ☐ *Cylinder bore hone*
- ☐ *Balljoint separator*
- ☐ *Coil spring compressors (where applicable)*
- ☐ *Two/three-legged hub and bearing puller*
- ☐ *Impact screwdriver*
- ☐ *Micrometer and/or vernier calipers*
- ☐ *Dial gauge*
- ☐ *Stroboscopic timing light*
- ☐ *Dwell angle meter/tachometer*
- ☐ *Fault code reader*
- ☐ *Cylinder compression gauge*
- ☐ *Hand-operated vacuum pump and gauge*
- ☐ *Clutch plate alignment set*
- ☐ *Brake shoe steady spring cup removal tool*
- ☐ *Bush and bearing removal/installation set*
- ☐ *Stud extractors*
- ☐ *Tap and die set*
- ☐ *Lifting tackle*
- ☐ *Trolley jack*

Buying tools

Reputable motor accessory shops and superstores often offer excellent quality tools at discount prices, so it pays to shop around.

Remember, you don't have to buy the most expensive items on the shelf, but it is always advisable to steer clear of the very cheap tools. Beware of 'bargains' offered on market stalls or at car boot sales. There are plenty of good tools around at reasonable prices, but always aim to purchase items which meet the relevant national safety standards. If in doubt, ask the proprietor or manager of the shop for advice before making a purchase.

Care and maintenance of tools

Having purchased a reasonable tool kit, it is necessary to keep the tools in a clean and serviceable condition. After use, always wipe off any dirt, grease and metal particles using a clean, dry cloth, before putting the tools away. Never leave them lying around after they have been used. A simple tool rack on the garage or workshop wall for items such as screwdrivers and pliers is a good idea. Store all normal spanners and sockets in a metal box. Any measuring instruments, gauges, meters, etc, must be carefully stored where they cannot be damaged or become rusty.

Take a little care when tools are used. Hammer heads inevitably become marked, and screwdrivers lose the keen edge on their blades from time to time. A little timely attention with emery cloth or a file will soon restore items like this to a good finish.

Working facilities

Not to be forgotten when discussing tools is the workshop itself. If anything more than routine maintenance is to be carried out, a suitable working area becomes essential.

It is appreciated that many an owner-mechanic is forced by circumstances to remove an engine or similar item without the benefit of a garage or workshop. Having done this, any repairs should always be done under the cover of a roof.

Wherever possible, any dismantling should be done on a clean, flat workbench or table at a suitable working height.

Any workbench needs a vice; one with a jaw opening of 100 mm is suitable for most jobs. As mentioned previously, some clean dry storage space is also required for tools, as well as for any lubricants, cleaning fluids, touch-up paints etc, which become necessary.

Another item which may be required, and which has a much more general usage, is an electric drill with a chuck capacity of at least 8 mm. This, together with a good range of twist drills, is virtually essential for fitting accessories.

Last, but not least, always keep a supply of old newspapers and clean, lint-free rags available, and try to keep any working area as clean as possible.

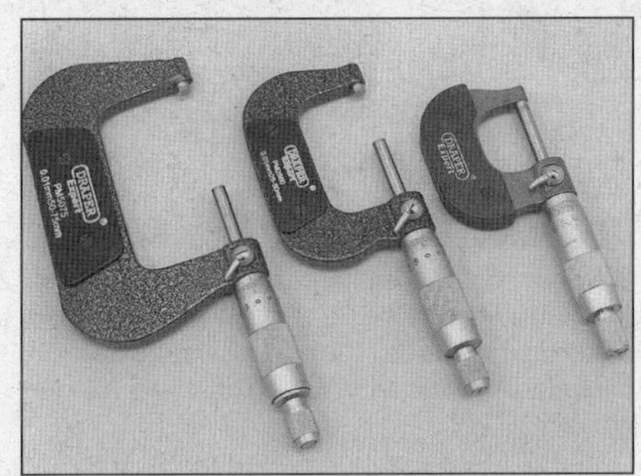

Micrometers

Dial test indicator ("dial gauge")

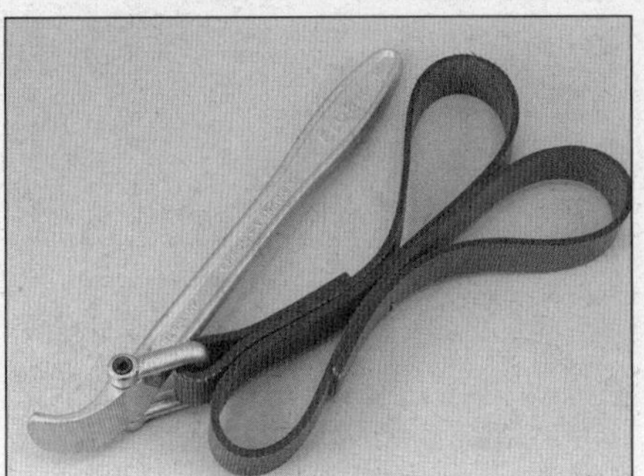

Strap wrench

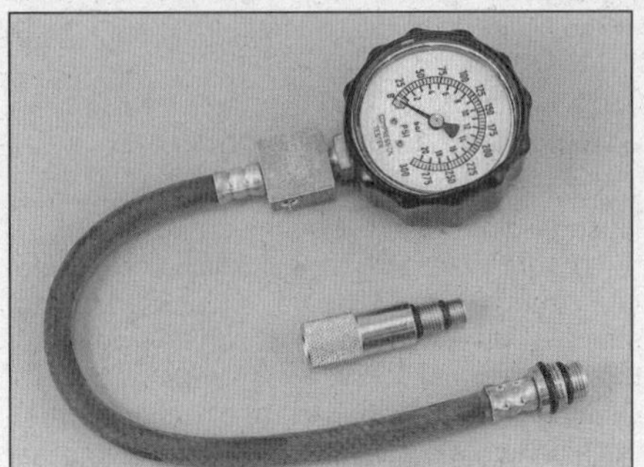

Compression tester

Fault code reader

This is a guide to getting your vehicle through the MOT test. Obviously it will not be possible to examine the vehicle to the same standard as the professional MOT tester. However, working through the following checks will enable you to identify any problem areas before submitting the vehicle for the test.

Where a testable component is in borderline condition, the tester has discretion in deciding whether to pass or fail it. The basis of such discretion is whether the tester would be happy for a close relative or friend to use the vehicle with the component in that condition. If the vehicle presented is clean and evidently well cared for, the tester may be more inclined to pass a borderline component than if the vehicle is scruffy and apparently neglected.

It has only been possible to summarise the test requirements here, based on the regulations in force at the time of printing. Test standards are becoming increasingly stringent, although there are some exemptions for older vehicles.

An assistant will be needed to help carry out some of these checks.

The checks have been sub-divided into four categories, as follows:

1 Checks carried out **FROM THE DRIVER'S SEAT**

2 Checks carried out **WITH THE VEHICLE ON THE GROUND**

3 Checks carried out **WITH THE VEHICLE RAISED AND THE WHEELS FREE TO TURN**

4 Checks carried out on **YOUR VEHICLE'S EXHAUST EMISSION SYSTEM**

1 Checks carried out FROM THE DRIVER'S SEAT

Handbrake

☐ Test the operation of the handbrake. Excessive travel (too many clicks) indicates incorrect brake or cable adjustment.

☐ Check that the handbrake cannot be released by tapping the lever sideways. Check the security of the lever mountings.

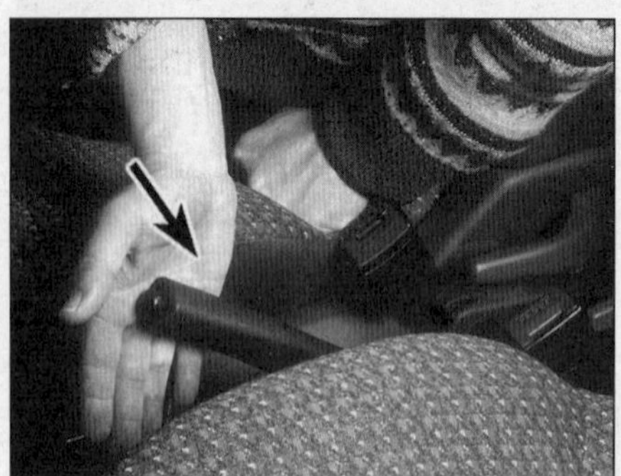

Footbrake

☐ Depress the brake pedal and check that it does not creep down to the floor, indicating a master cylinder fault. Release the pedal, wait a few seconds, then depress it again. If the pedal travels nearly to the floor before firm resistance is felt, brake adjustment or repair is necessary. If the pedal feels spongy, there is air in the hydraulic system which must be removed by bleeding.

☐ Check that the brake pedal is secure and in good condition. Check also for signs of fluid leaks on the pedal, floor or carpets, which would indicate failed seals in the brake master cylinder.

☐ Check the servo unit (when applicable) by operating the brake pedal several times, then keeping the pedal depressed and starting the engine. As the engine starts, the pedal will move down slightly. If not, the vacuum hose or the servo itself may be faulty.

Steering wheel and column

☐ Examine the steering wheel for fractures or looseness of the hub, spokes or rim.

☐ Move the steering wheel from side to side and then up and down. Check that the steering wheel is not loose on the column, indicating wear or a loose retaining nut. Continue moving the steering wheel as before, but also turn it slightly from left to right.

☐ Check that the steering wheel is not loose on the column, and that there is no abnormal

movement of the steering wheel, indicating wear in the column support bearings or couplings.

Windscreen, mirrors and sunvisor

☐ The windscreen must be free of cracks or other significant damage within the driver's field of view. (Small stone chips are acceptable.) Rear view mirrors must be secure, intact, and capable of being adjusted.

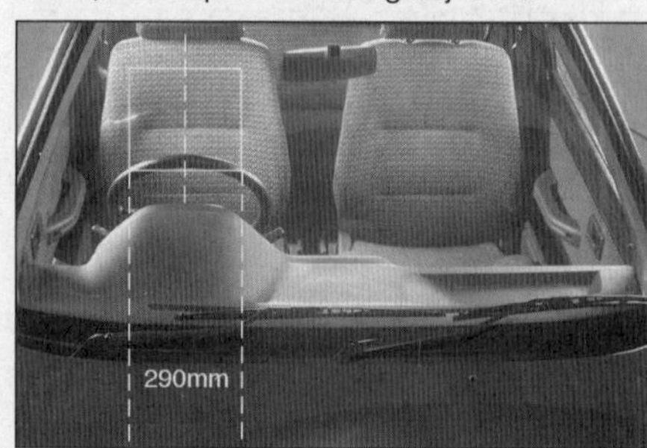

☐ The driver's sunvisor must be capable of being stored in the "up" position.

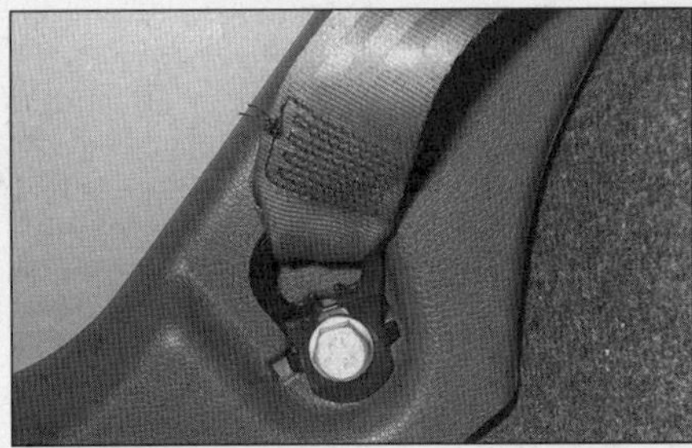

Seat belts and seats

Note: *The following checks are applicable to all seat belts, front and rear.*

☐ Examine the webbing of all the belts (including rear belts if fitted) for cuts, serious fraying or deterioration. Fasten and unfasten each belt to check the buckles. If applicable, check the retracting mechanism. Check the security of all seat belt mountings accessible from inside the vehicle.

☐ Seat belts with pre-tensioners, once activated, have a "flag" or similar showing on the seat belt stalk. This, in itself, is not a reason for test failure.

☐ The front seats themselves must be securely attached and the backrests must lock in the upright position.

Doors

☐ Both front doors must be able to be opened and closed from outside and inside, and must latch securely when closed.

2 Checks carried out WITH THE VEHICLE ON THE GROUND

Vehicle identification

☐ Number plates must be in good condition, secure and legible, with letters and numbers correctly spaced – spacing at (A) should be at least twice that at (B).

☐ The VIN plate and/or homologation plate must be legible.

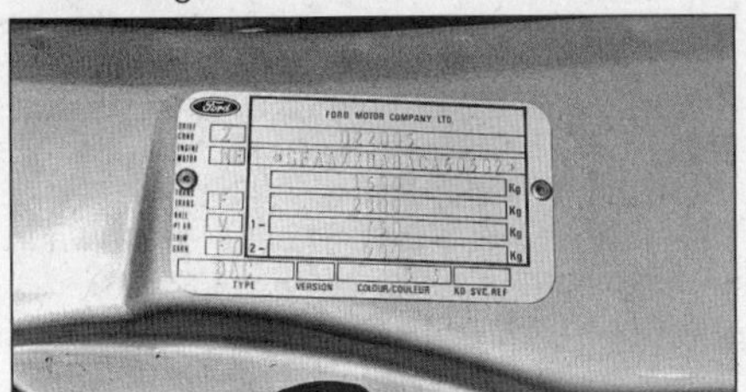

Electrical equipment

☐ Switch on the ignition and check the operation of the horn.

☐ Check the windscreen washers and wipers, examining the wiper blades; renew damaged or perished blades. Also check the operation of the stop-lights.

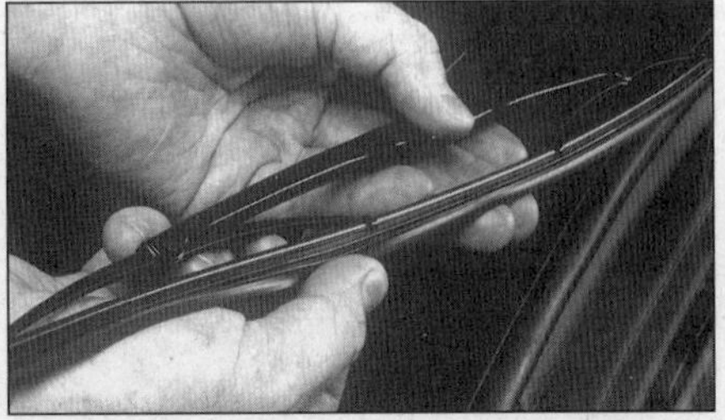

☐ Check the operation of the sidelights and number plate lights. The lenses and reflectors must be secure, clean and undamaged.

☐ Check the operation and alignment of the headlights. The headlight reflectors must not be tarnished and the lenses must be undamaged.

☐ Switch on the ignition and check the operation of the direction indicators (including the instrument panel tell-tale) and the hazard warning lights. Operation of the sidelights and stop-lights must not affect the indicators - if it does, the cause is usually a bad earth at the rear light cluster.

☐ Check the operation of the rear foglight(s), including the warning light on the instrument panel or in the switch.

☐ The ABS warning light must illuminate in accordance with the manufacturers' design. For most vehicles, the ABS warning light should illuminate when the ignition is switched on, and (if the system is operating properly) extinguish after a few seconds. Refer to the owner's handbook.

Footbrake

☐ Examine the master cylinder, brake pipes and servo unit for leaks, loose mountings, corrosion or other damage.

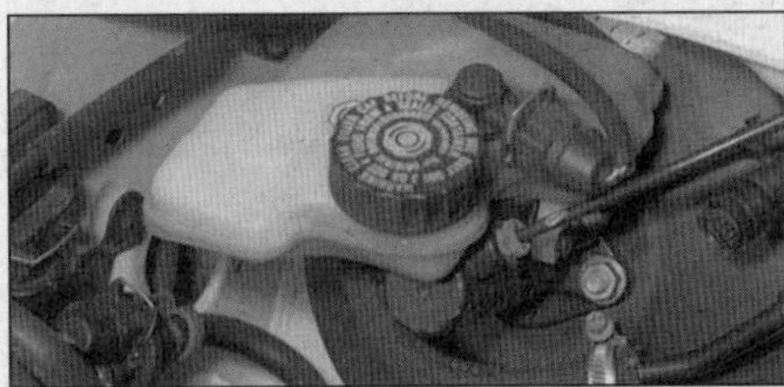

☐ The fluid reservoir must be secure and the fluid level must be between the upper (**A**) and lower (**B**) markings.

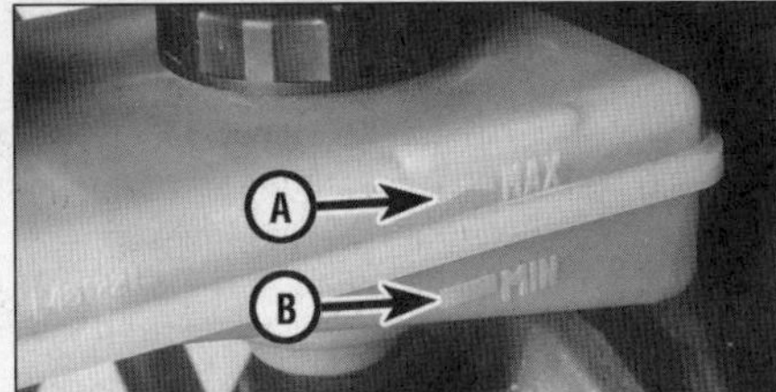

☐ Inspect both front brake flexible hoses for cracks or deterioration of the rubber. Turn the steering from lock to lock, and ensure that the hoses do not contact the wheel, tyre, or any part of the steering or suspension mechanism. With the brake pedal firmly depressed, check the hoses for bulges or leaks under pressure.

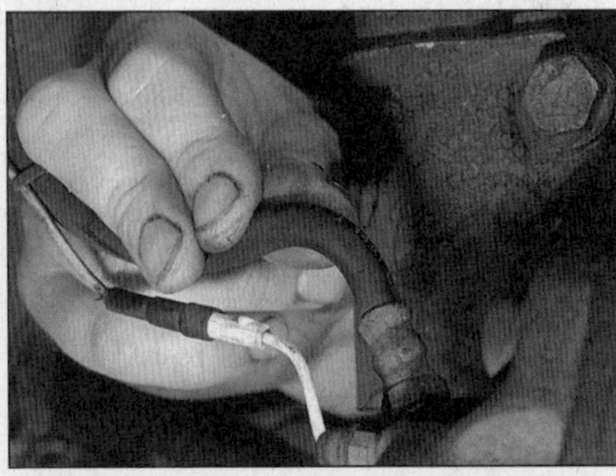

Steering and suspension

☐ Have your assistant turn the steering wheel from side to side slightly, up to the point where the steering gear just begins to transmit this movement to the roadwheels. Check for excessive free play between the steering wheel and the steering gear, indicating wear or insecurity of the steering column joints, the column-to-steering gear coupling, or the steering gear itself.

☐ Have your assistant turn the steering wheel more vigorously in each direction, so that the roadwheels just begin to turn. As this is done, examine all the steering joints, linkages, fittings and attachments. Renew any component that shows signs of wear or damage. On vehicles with power steering, check the security and condition of the steering pump, drivebelt and hoses.

☐ Check that the vehicle is standing level, and at approximately the correct ride height.

Shock absorbers

☐ Depress each corner of the vehicle in turn, then release it. The vehicle should rise and then settle in its normal position. If the vehicle continues to rise and fall, the shock absorber is defective. A shock absorber which has seized will also cause the vehicle to fail.

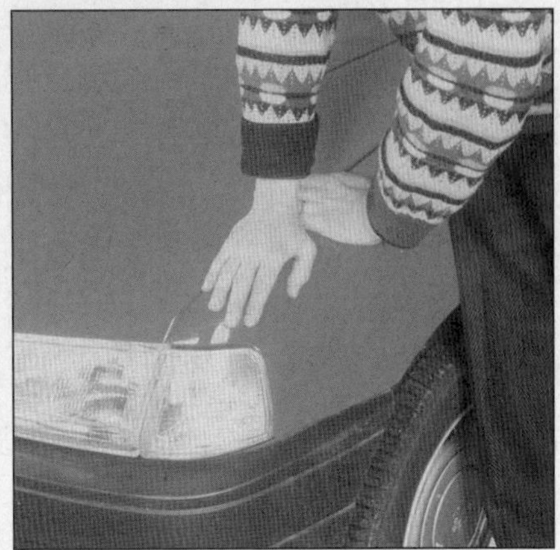

Exhaust system

☐ Start the engine. With your assistant holding a rag over the tailpipe, check the entire system for leaks. Repair or renew leaking sections.

3 Checks carried out WITH THE VEHICLE RAISED AND THE WHEELS FREE TO TURN

Jack up the front and rear of the vehicle, and securely support it on axle stands. Position the stands clear of the suspension assemblies. Ensure that the wheels are clear of the ground and that the steering can be turned from lock to lock.

Steering mechanism

☐ Have your assistant turn the steering from lock to lock. Check that the steering turns smoothly, and that no part of the steering mechanism, including a wheel or tyre, fouls any brake hose or pipe or any part of the body structure.

☐ Examine the steering rack rubber gaiters for damage or insecurity of the retaining clips. If power steering is fitted, check for signs of damage or leakage of the fluid hoses, pipes or connections. Also check for excessive stiffness or binding of the steering, a missing split pin or locking device, or severe corrosion of the body structure within 30 cm of any steering component attachment point.

Front and rear suspension and wheel bearings

☐ Starting at the front right-hand side, grasp the roadwheel at the 3 o'clock and 9 o'clock positions and rock gently but firmly. Check for free play or insecurity at the wheel bearings, suspension balljoints, or suspension mountings, pivots and attachments.

☐ Now grasp the wheel at the 12 o'clock and 6 o'clock positions and repeat the previous inspection. Spin the wheel, and check for roughness or tightness of the front wheel bearing.

☐ If excess free play is suspected at a component pivot point, this can be confirmed by using a large screwdriver or similar tool and levering between the mounting and the component attachment. This will confirm whether the wear is in the pivot bush, its retaining bolt, or in the mounting itself (the bolt holes can often become elongated).

☐ Carry out all the above checks at the other front wheel, and then at both rear wheels.

Springs and shock absorbers

☐ Examine the suspension struts (when applicable) for serious fluid leakage, corrosion, or damage to the casing. Also check the security of the mounting points.

☐ If coil springs are fitted, check that the spring ends locate in their seats, and that the spring is not corroded, cracked or broken.

☐ If leaf springs are fitted, check that all leaves are intact, that the axle is securely attached to each spring, and that there is no deterioration of the spring eye mountings, bushes, and shackles.

☐ The same general checks apply to vehicles fitted with other suspension types, such as torsion bars, hydraulic displacer units, etc. Ensure that all mountings and attachments are secure, that there are no signs of excessive wear, corrosion or damage, and (on hydraulic types) that there are no fluid leaks or damaged pipes.

☐ Inspect the shock absorbers for signs of serious fluid leakage. Check for wear of the mounting bushes or attachments, or damage to the body of the unit.

Driveshafts (fwd vehicles only)

☐ Rotate each front wheel in turn and inspect the constant velocity joint gaiters for splits or damage. Also check that each driveshaft is straight and undamaged.

Braking system

☐ If possible without dismantling, check brake pad wear and disc condition. Ensure that the friction lining material has not worn excessively, (A) and that the discs are not fractured, pitted, scored or badly worn (B).

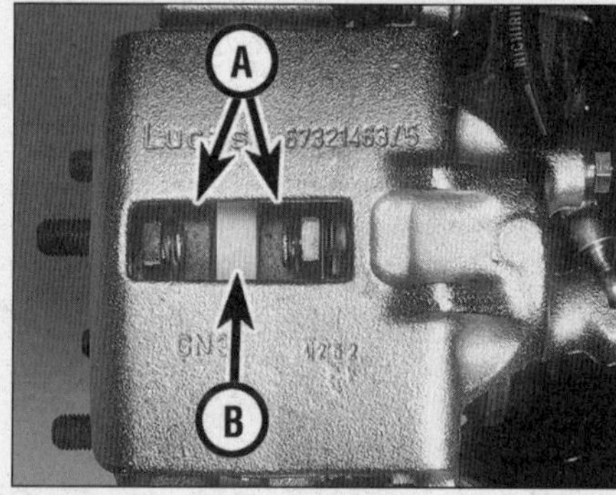

☐ Examine all the rigid brake pipes underneath the vehicle, and the flexible hose(s) at the rear. Look for corrosion, chafing or insecurity of the pipes, and for signs of bulging under pressure, chafing, splits or deterioration of the flexible hoses.

☐ Look for signs of fluid leaks at the brake calipers or on the brake backplates. Repair or renew leaking components.

☐ Slowly spin each wheel, while your assistant depresses and releases the footbrake. Ensure that each brake is operating and does not bind when the pedal is released.

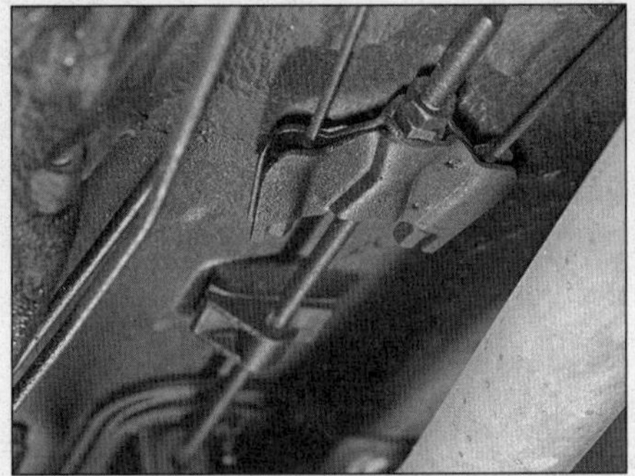

☐ Examine the handbrake mechanism, checking for frayed or broken cables, excessive corrosion, or wear or insecurity of the linkage. Check that the mechanism works on each relevant wheel, and releases fully, without binding.

☐ It is not possible to test brake efficiency without special equipment, but a road test can be carried out later to check that the vehicle pulls up in a straight line.

Fuel and exhaust systems

☐ Inspect the fuel tank (including the filler cap), fuel pipes, hoses and unions. All components must be secure and free from leaks.

☐ Examine the exhaust system over its entire length, checking for any damaged, broken or missing mountings, security of the retaining clamps and rust or corrosion.

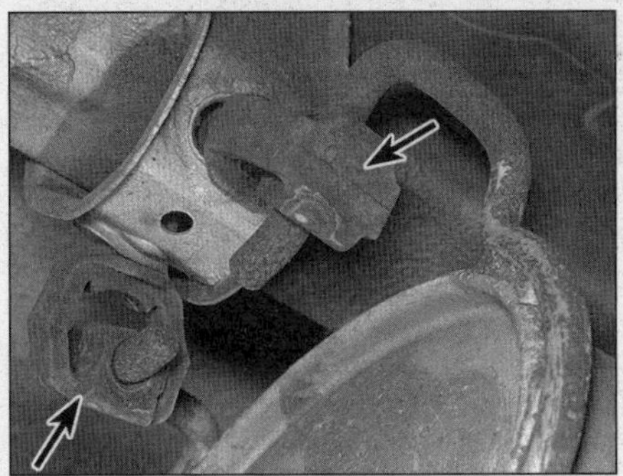

Wheels and tyres

☐ Examine the sidewalls and tread area of each tyre in turn. Check for cuts, tears, lumps, bulges, separation of the tread, and exposure of the ply or cord due to wear or damage. Check that the tyre bead is correctly seated on the wheel rim, that the valve is sound and properly seated, and that the wheel is not distorted or damaged.

☐ Check that the tyres are of the correct size for the vehicle, that they are of the same size and type on each axle, and that the pressures are correct.

☐ Check the tyre tread depth. The legal minimum at the time of writing is 1.6 mm over at least three-quarters of the tread width. Abnormal tread wear may indicate incorrect front wheel alignment.

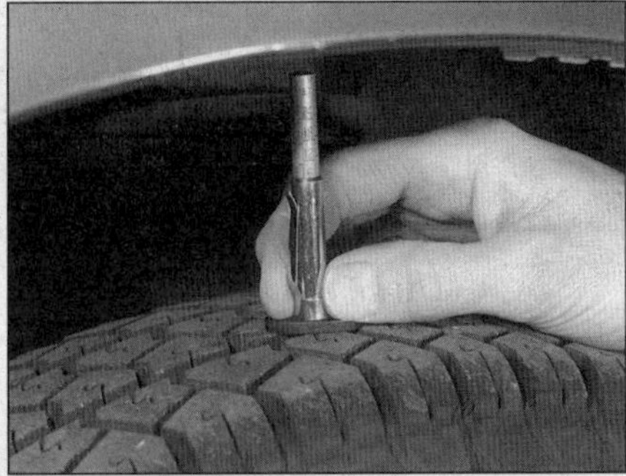

Body corrosion

☐ Check the condition of the entire vehicle structure for signs of corrosion in load-bearing areas. (These include chassis box sections, side sills, cross-members, pillars, and all suspension, steering, braking system and seat belt mountings and anchorages.) Any corrosion which has seriously reduced the thickness of a load-bearing area is likely to cause the vehicle to fail. In this case professional repairs are likely to be needed.

☐ Damage or corrosion which causes sharp or otherwise dangerous edges to be exposed will also cause the vehicle to fail.

4 Checks carried out on **YOUR VEHICLE'S EXHAUST EMISSION SYSTEM**

Petrol models

☐ Have the engine at normal operating temperature, and make sure that it is in good tune (ignition system in good order, air filter element clean, etc).

☐ Before any measurements are carried out, raise the engine speed to around 2500 rpm, and hold it at this speed for 20 seconds. Allow the engine speed to return to idle, and watch for smoke emissions from the exhaust tailpipe. If the idle speed is obviously much too high, or if dense blue or clearly-visible black smoke comes from the tailpipe for more than 5 seconds, the vehicle will fail. As a rule of thumb, blue smoke signifies oil being burnt (engine wear) while black smoke signifies unburnt fuel (dirty air cleaner element, or other carburettor or fuel system fault).

☐ An exhaust gas analyser capable of measuring carbon monoxide (CO) and hydrocarbons (HC) is now needed. If such an instrument cannot be hired or borrowed, a local garage may agree to perform the check for a small fee.

CO emissions (mixture)

☐ At the time of writing, for vehicles first used between 1st August 1975 and 31st July 1986 (P to C registration), the CO level must not exceed 4.5% by volume. For vehicles first used between 1st August 1986 and 31st July 1992 (D to J registration), the CO level must not exceed 3.5% by volume. Vehicles first used after 1st August 1992 (K registration) must conform to the manufacturer's specification. The MOT tester has access to a DOT database or emissions handbook, which lists the CO and HC limits for each make and model of vehicle. The CO level is measured with the engine at idle speed, and at "fast idle". The following limits are given as a general guide:

At idle speed -
CO level no more than 0.5%
At "fast idle" (2500 to 3000 rpm) -
CO level no more than 0.3%
(Minimum oil temperature 60°C)

☐ If the CO level cannot be reduced far enough to pass the test (and the fuel and ignition systems are otherwise in good condition) then the carburettor is badly worn, or there is some problem in the fuel injection system or catalytic converter (as applicable).

HC emissions

☐ With the CO within limits, HC emissions for vehicles first used between 1st August 1975 and 31st July 1992 (P to J registration) must not exceed 1200 ppm. Vehicles first used after 1st August 1992 (K registration) must conform to the manufacturer's specification. The MOT tester has access to a DOT database or emissions handbook, which lists the CO and HC limits for each make and model of vehicle. The HC level is measured with the engine at "fast idle". The following is given as a general guide:

At "fast idle" (2500 to 3000 rpm) -
HC level no more than 200 ppm
(Minimum oil temperature 60°C)

☐ Excessive HC emissions are caused by incomplete combustion, the causes of which can include oil being burnt, mechanical wear and ignition/fuel system malfunction.

Diesel models

☐ The only emission test applicable to Diesel engines is the measuring of exhaust smoke density. The test involves accelerating the engine several times to its maximum unloaded speed.

Note: *It is of the utmost importance that the engine timing belt is in good condition before the test is carried out.*

☐ The limits for Diesel engine exhaust smoke, introduced in September 1995 are:

Vehicles first used before 1st August 1979:
Exempt from metered smoke testing, but must not emit "dense blue or clearly visible black smoke for a period of more than 5 seconds at idle" or "dense blue or clearly visible black smoke during acceleration which would obscure the view of other road users".

Non-turbocharged vehicles first used after 1st August 1979: $2.5m^{-1}$

Turbocharged vehicles first used after 1st August 1979: $3.0m^{-1}$

☐ Excessive smoke can be caused by a dirty air cleaner element. Otherwise, professional advice may be needed to find the cause.

Engine

- ☐ Engine fails to rotate when attempting to start
- ☐ Engine rotates, but will not start
- ☐ Engine difficult to start when cold
- ☐ Engine difficult to start when hot
- ☐ Starter motor noisy or rough in engagement
- ☐ Starter motor turns engine slowly
- ☐ Engine starts, but stops immediately
- ☐ Engine idles erratically
- ☐ Engine misfires at idle speed
- ☐ Engine misfires throughout the driving speed range
- ☐ Engine stalls
- ☐ Engine lacks power
- ☐ Engine backfires
- ☐ Oil pressure warning light illuminated with engine running
- ☐ Engine runs-on after switching off
- ☐ Engine noises

Cooling system

- ☐ Overheating
- ☐ Overcooling
- ☐ External coolant leakage
- ☐ Internal coolant leakage
- ☐ Corrosion

Fuel and exhaust systems

- ☐ Excessive fuel consumption
- ☐ Fuel leakage and/or fuel odour
- ☐ Excessive noise or fumes from exhaust system

Clutch

- ☐ Pedal travels to floor – no pressure or very little resistance
- ☐ Clutch fails to disengage (unable to select gears)
- ☐ Clutch slips (engine speed increases, with no increase in vehicle speed)
- ☐ Judder as clutch is engaged
- ☐ Noise when depressing or releasing clutch pedal

Manual transmission

- ☐ Noisy in neutral with engine running
- ☐ Noisy in one particular gear
- ☐ Difficulty engaging gears
- ☐ Jumps out of gear
- ☐ Vibration
- ☐ Lubricant leaks

Automatic transmission

- ☐ Fluid leakage
- ☐ Transmission fluid brown, or has burned smell
- ☐ General gear selection problems
- ☐ Transmission will not downshift (kickdown) with accelerator fully depressed
- ☐ Engine will not start in any gear, or starts in gears other than Park or Neutral
- ☐ Transmission slips, shifts roughly, is noisy, or has no drive in forward or reverse gears

Differential and propeller shaft

- ☐ Vibration when accelerating and decelerating
- ☐ Low-pitched whining, increasing with road speed

Braking system

- ☐ Vehicle pulls to one side under braking
- ☐ Noise (grinding or high-pitched squeal) when brakes applied
- ☐ Excessive brake pedal travel
- ☐ Brake pedal feels spongy when depressed
- ☐ Excessive brake pedal effort required to stop vehicle
- ☐ Judder felt through brake pedal or steering wheel when braking
- ☐ Brakes binding

Suspension and steering systems

- ☐ Vehicle pulls to one side
- ☐ Wheel wobble and vibration
- ☐ Excessive pitching and/or rolling around corners, or during braking
- ☐ Wandering or general instability
- ☐ Excessively-stiff steering
- ☐ Excessive play in steering
- ☐ Lack of power assistance
- ☐ Tyre wear excessive

Electrical system

- ☐ Battery will only hold a charge for a few days
- ☐ Ignition/no-charge warning light remains illuminated with engine running
- ☐ Ignition/no-charge warning light fails to come on
- ☐ Lights inoperative
- ☐ Instrument readings inaccurate or erratic
- ☐ Horn inoperative, or unsatisfactory in operation
- ☐ Wipers inoperative, or unsatisfactory in operation
- ☐ Washers inoperative, or unsatisfactory in operation
- ☐ Electric windows inoperative, or unsatisfactory in operation
- ☐ Central locking system inoperative, or unsatisfactory in operation

Introduction

The vehicle owner who does his or her own maintenance according to the recommended service schedules should not have to use this section of the manual very often. Modern component reliability is such that, provided those items subject to wear or deterioration are inspected or renewed at the specified intervals, sudden failure is comparatively rare. Faults do not usually just happen as a result of sudden failure, but develop over a period of time. Major mechanical failures in particular are usually preceded by characteristic symptoms over hundreds or even thousands of miles. Those components which do occasionally fail without warning are often small and easily carried in the vehicle.

With any fault-finding, the first step is to decide where to begin investigations. Sometimes this is obvious, but on other occasions, a little detective work will be necessary. The owner who makes half a dozen haphazard adjustments or replacements may be successful in curing a fault (or its symptoms), but will be none the wiser if the fault recurs, and ultimately may have spent more time and money than was necessary. A calm and logical approach will be found to be more satisfactory in the long run. Always take into account any warning signs or abnormalities that may have been noticed in the period preceding the fault – power loss, high or low gauge readings, unusual smells, etc – and remember that failure of components such as fuses or spark plugs may only be pointers to some underlying fault.

The pages which follow provide an easy-reference guide to the more common problems which may occur during the operation of the vehicle. These problems and their possible causes are grouped under headings denoting various components or systems, such as Engine, Cooling system, etc. The general Chapter which deals with the problem is also shown in brackets; refer to the relevant part of that Chapter for system-specific information. Whatever the fault, certain basic principles apply. These are as follows:

Verify the fault. This is simply a matter of being sure that you know what the symptoms are before starting work. This is particularly important if you are investigating a fault for someone else, who may not have described it very accurately.

Don't overlook the obvious. For example, if the vehicle won't start, is there fuel in the tank? (Don't take anyone else's word on this particular point, and don't trust the fuel gauge either!) If an electrical fault is indicated, look for loose or broken wires before using the test gear.

Cure the disease, not the symptom. Substituting a flat battery with a fully-charged one will get you off the hard shoulder, but if the underlying cause is not attended to, the new battery will go the same way. Similarly, changing oil-fouled spark plugs for a new set will get you moving again, but remember that the reason for the fouling (if it wasn't simply an incorrect grade of plug) will have to be established and corrected.

Don't take anything for granted. Particularly, don't forget that a 'new' component may itself be defective (especially if it's been rattling around in the boot for months), and don't leave components out of a fault diagnosis sequence just because they are new or recently-fitted. When you do finally diagnose a difficult fault, you'll probably realise that all the evidence was there from the start.

Engine

Engine fails to rotate when attempting to start

- ☐ Battery terminal connections loose or corroded (*Weekly checks*)
- ☐ Battery discharged or faulty (Chapter 5A)
- ☐ Broken, loose or disconnected wiring in the starting circuit (Chapter 5A)
- ☐ Defective starter solenoid or switch (Chapter 5A)
- ☐ Defective starter motor (Chapter 5A)
- ☐ Starter pinion or flywheel ring gear teeth loose or broken (Chapter 2 or 5A)
- ☐ Engine earth strap broken or disconnected (Chapter 5A)

Engine rotates, but will not start

- ☐ Fuel tank empty
- ☐ Battery discharged (engine rotates slowly) (Chapter 5A)
- ☐ Battery terminal connections loose or corroded (*Weekly checks*)
- ☐ Air filter element dirty or clogged (Chapter 1)
- ☐ Low cylinder compressions (Chapter 2)
- ☐ Major mechanical failure (eg, broken timing chain) (Chapter 2)
- ☐ Ignition components damp or damaged (Chapter 5B)
- ☐ Fuel injection system fault (Chapter 4)
- ☐ Worn, faulty or incorrectly-gapped spark plugs (Chapter 1)
- ☐ Broken, loose or disconnected wiring in ignition circuit (Chapter 5B)

Engine difficult to start when cold

- ☐ Battery discharged (Chapter 5A)
- ☐ Battery terminal connections loose or corroded (*Weekly checks*)
- ☐ Air filter element dirty or clogged (Chapter 1)
- ☐ Worn, faulty or incorrectly-gapped spark plugs (Chapter 1)
- ☐ Low cylinder compressions (Chapter 2)
- ☐ Fuel injection system fault (Chapter 4)
- ☐ Ignition system fault (Chapter 5B)

Engine difficult to start when hot

- ☐ Battery discharged (Chapter 5A)
- ☐ Battery terminal connections loose or corroded (*Weekly checks*)
- ☐ Air filter element dirty or clogged (Chapter 1)
- ☐ Fuel injection system fault (Chapter 4)

Starter motor noisy or excessively-rough in engagement

- ☐ Starter pinion or flywheel ring gear teeth loose or broken (Chapter 2 or 5A)
- ☐ Starter motor mounting bolts loose or missing (Chapter 5A)
- ☐ Starter motor internal components worn or damaged (Chapter 5A)

Starter motor turns engine slowly

- ☐ Battery discharged (Chapter 5A)
- ☐ Battery terminal connections loose or corroded (*Weekly checks*)
- ☐ Earth strap broken or disconnected (Chapter 5A)
- ☐ Starter motor wiring loose (Chapter 5A)
- ☐ Starter motor internal fault (Chapter 5A)

Engine starts, but stops immediately

- ☐ Loose ignition system wiring (Chapter 5B)
- ☐ Dirt in fuel system (Chapter 4)
- ☐ Fuel injector fault (Chapter 4)
- ☐ Fuel pump or pressure regulator fault (Chapter 4)
- ☐ Vacuum leak at throttle body, inlet manifold or hoses (Chapters 2 and 4)

Engine (continued)

Engine idles erratically

- ☐ Air filter element clogged (Chapter 1)
- ☐ Air in fuel system (Chapter 4)
- ☐ Worn, faulty or incorrectly-gapped spark plugs (Chapter 1)
- ☐ Vacuum leak at throttle body, inlet manifold or hoses (Chapters 2 and 4)
- ☐ Uneven or low cylinder compressions (Chapter 2)
- ☐ Timing chain incorrectly fitted or tensioned (Chapter 2)
- ☐ Camshaft lobes worn (Chapter 2)
- ☐ Faulty fuel injector(s) (Chapter 4)

Engine misfires at idle speed

- ☐ Faulty fuel injector(s) (Chapter 4)
- ☐ Uneven or low cylinder compressions (Chapter 2)
- ☐ Disconnected, leaking, or perished crankcase ventilation hoses (Chapter 4)
- ☐ Vacuum leak at the throttle body, inlet manifold or associated hoses (Chapter 4)

Engine misfires throughout the driving speed range

- ☐ Fuel filter choked (Chapter 1)
- ☐ Fuel pump faulty, or delivery pressure low (Chapter 4)
- ☐ Fuel tank vent blocked, or fuel pipes restricted (Chapter 4)
- ☐ Uneven or low cylinder compressions (Chapter 2)
- ☐ Worn, faulty or incorrectly-gapped spark plugs (Chapter 1)
- ☐ Faulty ignition coils (Chapter 5B)

Engine stalls

- ☐ Fuel filter choked (Chapter 1)
- ☐ Blocked injector/fuel injection system fault (Chapter 4)
- ☐ Fuel pump faulty, or delivery pressure low (Chapter 4)
- ☐ Vacuum leak at the throttle body, inlet manifold or associated hoses (Chapter 4)
- ☐ Fuel tank vent blocked, or fuel pipes restricted (Chapter 4)

Engine lacks power

- ☐ Fuel filter choked (Chapter 1)
- ☐ Timing chain incorrectly fitted or tensioned (Chapter 2)
- ☐ Fuel pump faulty, or delivery pressure low (Chapter 4)
- ☐ Worn, faulty or incorrectly-gapped spark plugs (Chapter 1)
- ☐ Vacuum leak at the throttle body, inlet manifold or associated hoses (Chapter 4)
- ☐ Uneven or low cylinder compressions (Chapter 2)
- ☐ Brakes binding (Chapters 1 and 9)
- ☐ Clutch slipping (Chapter 6)
- ☐ Blocked injector/fuel injection system fault (Chapter 4)

Engine backfires

- ☐ Timing chain incorrectly fitted (Chapter 2)
- ☐ Faulty injector/fuel injection system fault (Chapter 4).

Oil pressure warning light illuminated with engine running

- ☐ Low oil level, or incorrect oil grade (*Weekly checks*)
- ☐ Faulty oil pressure sensor (Chapter 2)
- ☐ Worn engine bearings and/or oil pump (Chapter 2)
- ☐ Excessively high engine operating temperature (Chapter 3)
- ☐ Oil pressure relief valve defective (Chapter 2)
- ☐ Oil pick-up strainer clogged (Chapter 2)

Note: *Low oil pressure in a high-mileage engine at tickover is not necessarily a cause for concern. Sudden pressure loss at speed is far more significant. In any event, check the gauge or pressure sensor before condemning the engine.*

Engine runs-on after switching off

- ☐ Excessive carbon build-up in engine (Chapter 2)
- ☐ Excessively high engine operating temperature (Chapter 3)

Engine noises

Pre-ignition (pinking) or knocking during acceleration or under load

- ☐ Excessive carbon build-up in engine (Chapter 2)
- ☐ Faulty fuel injector(s) (Chapter 4)
- ☐ Ignition system fault (Chapter 5B)

Whistling or wheezing noises

- ☐ Leaking exhaust manifold gasket (Chapter 4)
- ☐ Leaking vacuum hose (Chapter 4 or 9)
- ☐ Blowing cylinder head gasket (Chapter 2)

Tapping or rattling noises

- ☐ Worn valve gear or camshaft (Chapter 2)
- ☐ Ancillary component fault (coolant pump, alternator, etc) (Chapters 3, 5, etc)

Knocking or thumping noises

- ☐ Worn big-end bearings (regular heavy knocking, perhaps less under load) (Chapter 2)
- ☐ Worn main bearings (rumbling and knocking, perhaps worsening under load) (Chapter 2)
- ☐ Piston slap (most noticeable when cold) (Chapter 2)
- ☐ Ancillary component fault (coolant pump, alternator, etc) (Chapters 3, 5, etc)

Cooling system

Overheating

- ☐ Insufficient coolant in system (*Weekly checks*)
- ☐ Thermostat faulty (Chapter 3)
- ☐ Radiator core blocked, or grille restricted (Chapter 3)
- ☐ Cooling fan or viscous coupling faulty (Chapter 3)
- ☐ Inaccurate temperature gauge sender unit (Chapter 3)
- ☐ Airlock in cooling system (Chapter 3)
- ☐ Expansion tank pressure cap faulty (Chapter 3)

Overcooling

- ☐ Thermostat faulty (Chapter 3)
- ☐ Inaccurate temperature gauge sender unit (Chapter 3)
- ☐ Viscous coupling faulty (Chapter 3)

External coolant leakage

- ☐ Deteriorated or damaged hoses or hose clips (Chapter 1)
- ☐ Radiator core or heater matrix leaking (Chapter 3)
- ☐ Pressure cap faulty (Chapter 3)
- ☐ Coolant pump internal seal leaking (Chapter 3)
- ☐ Coolant pump-to-block seal leaking (Chapter 3)
- ☐ Boiling due to overheating (Chapter 3)
- ☐ Core plug leaking (Chapter 2)

Internal coolant leakage

- ☐ Leaking cylinder head gasket (Chapter 2)
- ☐ Cracked cylinder head or cylinder block (Chapter 2)

Corrosion

- ☐ Infrequent draining and flushing (Chapter 1)
- ☐ Incorrect coolant mixture or inappropriate coolant type (Chapter 1)

Fuel and exhaust systems

Excessive fuel consumption

- ☐ Air filter element dirty or clogged (Chapter 1)
- ☐ Fuel injection system fault (Chapter 4)
- ☐ Ignition timing incorrect/ignition system fault (Chapters 1 and 5)
- ☐ Tyres under-inflated (*Weekly checks*)

Fuel leakage and/or fuel odour

- ☐ Damaged or corroded fuel tank, pipes or connections (Chapter 4)

Excessive noise or fumes from exhaust system

- ☐ Leaking exhaust system or manifold joints (Chapters 1 and 4)
- ☐ Leaking, corroded or damaged silencers or pipe (Chapters 1 and 4)
- ☐ Broken mountings causing body or suspension contact (Chapter 1)

Clutch

Pedal travels to floor – no pressure or very little resistance

- ☐ Hydraulic fluid level low/air in the hydraulic system (Chapter 6)
- ☐ Broken clutch release bearing or fork (Chapter 6)
- ☐ Broken diaphragm spring in clutch pressure plate (Chapter 6)

Clutch fails to disengage (unable to select gears)

- ☐ Clutch disc sticking on gearbox input shaft splines (Chapter 6)
- ☐ Clutch disc sticking to flywheel or pressure plate (Chapter 6)
- ☐ Faulty pressure plate assembly (Chapter 6)
- ☐ Clutch release mechanism worn or poorly assembled (Chapter 6)

Clutch slips (engine speed increases, with no increase in vehicle speed)

- ☐ Clutch disc linings excessively worn (Chapter 6)
- ☐ Clutch disc linings contaminated with oil or grease (Chapter 6)
- ☐ Faulty pressure plate or weak diaphragm spring (Chapter 6)

Judder as clutch is engaged

- ☐ Clutch disc linings contaminated with oil or grease (Chapter 6)
- ☐ Clutch disc linings excessively worn (Chapter 6)
- ☐ Faulty or distorted pressure plate or diaphragm spring (Chapter 6)
- ☐ Worn or loose engine or gearbox mountings (Chapter 2A or 2B)
- ☐ Clutch disc hub or gearbox input shaft splines worn (Chapter 6)

Noise when depressing or releasing clutch pedal

- ☐ Worn clutch release bearing (Chapter 6)
- ☐ Worn or dry clutch pedal bushes (Chapter 6)
- ☐ Faulty pressure plate assembly (Chapter 6)
- ☐ Pressure plate diaphragm spring broken (Chapter 6)
- ☐ Broken clutch disc cushioning springs (Chapter 6)

Manual transmission

Noisy in neutral with engine running

- ☐ Input shaft bearings worn (noise apparent with clutch pedal released, but not when depressed) (Chapter 7A)*
- ☐ Clutch release bearing worn (noise apparent with clutch pedal depressed, possibly less when released) (Chapter 6)

Noisy in one particular gear

- ☐ Worn, damaged or chipped gear teeth (Chapter 7A)*

Difficulty engaging gears

- ☐ Clutch fault (Chapter 6)
- ☐ Worn or damaged gearchange linkage (Chapter 7A)
- ☐ Incorrectly-adjusted gearchange linkage (Chapter 7A)
- ☐ Worn synchroniser units (Chapter 7A)*

Jumps out of gear

- ☐ Worn or damaged gearchange linkage (Chapter 7A)
- ☐ Worn synchroniser units (Chapter 7A)*
- ☐ Worn selector forks (Chapter 7A)*

Vibration

- ☐ Lack of oil (Chapter 1)
- ☐ Worn bearings (Chapter 7A)*

Lubricant leaks

- ☐ Leaking differential output oil seal (Chapter 7A)
- ☐ Leaking housing joint (Chapter 7A)*
- ☐ Leaking input shaft oil seal (Chapter 7A)*

**Although the corrective action necessary to remedy the symptoms described is beyond the scope of the home mechanic, the above information should be helpful in isolating the cause of the condition, so that the owner can communicate clearly with a professional mechanic.*

Automatic transmission

Note: *Due to the complexity of the automatic transmission, it is difficult for the home mechanic to properly diagnose and service this unit. For problems other than the following, the vehicle should be taken to a dealer service department or automatic transmission specialist. Do not be too hasty in removing the transmission if a fault is suspected, as most of the testing is carried out with the unit still fitted.*

Fluid leakage

- ☐ Automatic transmission fluid is usually dark in colour. Fluid leaks should not be confused with engine oil, which can easily be blown onto the transmission by airflow
- ☐ To determine the source of a leak, first remove all built-up dirt and grime from the transmission housing and surrounding areas using a degreasing agent, or by steam-cleaning. Drive the vehicle at low speed, so airflow will not blow the leak far from its source. Raise and support the vehicle, and determine where the leak is coming from. The following are common areas of leakage:

a) *Oil pan (Chapter 1 and 7B).*
b) *Dipstick tube (Chapter 1 and 7B)*
c) *Transmission-to-fluid cooler pipes/unions (Chapter 7B)*

Transmission fluid brown, or has burned smell

- ☐ Transmission fluid level low, or fluid in need of renewal (Chapter 1)

General gear selection problems

- ☐ Chapter 7B deals with checking and adjusting the selector cable on automatic transmissions. The following are common problems which may be caused by a poorly-adjusted cable:

a) *Engine starting in gears other than Park or Neutral*
b) *Indicator panel indicating a gear other than the one actually being used*
c) *Vehicle moves when in Park or Neutral*
d) *Poor gear shift quality or erratic gear changes*

- ☐ Refer to Chapter 7B for the selector cable adjustment procedure

Transmission will not downshift (kickdown) with accelerator pedal fully depressed

- ☐ Low transmission fluid level (Chapter 1)
- ☐ Incorrect selector cable adjustment (Chapter 7B)
- ☐ Throttle position sensor fault (Chapter 4)

Engine will not start in any gear, or starts in gears other than Park or Neutral

- ☐ Incorrect selector cable adjustment (Chapter 7B)

Transmission slips, shifts roughly, is noisy, or has no drive in forward or reverse gears

- ☐ There are many probable causes for the above problems, but the home mechanic should be concerned with only one possibility – fluid level. Before taking the vehicle to a dealer or transmission specialist, check the fluid level and condition of the fluid as described in Chapter 1. Correct the fluid level as necessary, or change the fluid and filter if needed. If the problem persists, professional help will be necessary

Differential and propshaft

Vibration when accelerating or decelerating

- ☐ Worn universal joint (Chapter 8)
- ☐ Bent or distorted propeller shaft (Chapter 8)

Low-pitched whining; increasing with road speed

- ☐ Worn differential (Chapter 8)

Braking system

Note: *Before assuming that a brake problem exists, make sure that the tyres are in good condition and correctly inflated, that the front wheel alignment is correct, and that the vehicle is not loaded with weight in an unequal manner. Apart from checking the condition of all pipe and hose connections, any faults occurring on the anti-lock braking system should be referred to a BMW dealer or specialist for diagnosis.*

Vehicle pulls to one side under braking

- ☐ Worn, defective, damaged or contaminated brake pads/shoes on one side (Chapters 1 and 9)
- ☐ Seized or partially-seized brake caliper (Chapters 1 and 9)
- ☐ A mixture of brake pad lining materials fitted between sides (Chapters 1 and 9)
- ☐ Brake caliper mounting bolts loose (Chapter 9)
- ☐ Worn or damaged steering or suspension components (Chapters 1 and 10)

Noise (grinding or high-pitched squeal) when brakes applied

- ☐ Brake pad friction lining material worn down to metal backing (Chapters 1 and 9)
- ☐ Excessive corrosion of brake disc. (May be apparent after the vehicle has been standing for some time (Chapters 1 and 9)
- ☐ Foreign object (stone chipping, etc) trapped between brake disc and shield (Chapters 1 and 9)

Excessive brake pedal travel

- ☐ Faulty master cylinder (Chapter 9)
- ☐ Air in hydraulic system (Chapters 1 and 9)
- ☐ Faulty vacuum servo unit (Chapter 9)

Brake pedal feels spongy when depressed

- ☐ Air in hydraulic system (Chapters 1 and 9)
- ☐ Deteriorated flexible rubber brake hoses (Chapters 1 and 9)
- ☐ Master cylinder mounting nuts loose (Chapter 9)
- ☐ Faulty master cylinder (Chapter 9)

Excessive brake pedal effort required to stop vehicle

- ☐ Faulty vacuum servo unit (Chapter 9)
- ☐ Disconnected, damaged or insecure brake servo vacuum hose (Chapter 9)
- ☐ Primary or secondary hydraulic circuit failure (Chapter 9)
- ☐ Seized brake caliper (Chapter 9)
- ☐ Brake pads incorrectly fitted (Chapters 1 and 9)
- ☐ Incorrect grade of brake pads fitted (Chapters 1 and 9)
- ☐ Brake pads contaminated (Chapters 1 and 9)

Judder felt through brake pedal or steering wheel when braking

- ☐ Excessive run-out or distortion of discs (Chapters 1 and 9)
- ☐ Brake pad linings worn (Chapters 1 and 9)
- ☐ Brake caliper mounting bolts loose (Chapter 9)
- ☐ Wear in suspension or steering components or mountings (Chapters 1 and 10)

Brakes binding

- ☐ Seized brake caliper (Chapter 9)
- ☐ Incorrectly-adjusted handbrake mechanism (Chapter 9)
- ☐ Faulty master cylinder (Chapter 9)

Suspension and steering

Note: *Before diagnosing suspension or steering faults, be sure that the trouble is not due to incorrect tyre pressures, mixtures of tyre types, or binding brakes.*

Vehicle pulls to one side

- ☐ Defective tyre (*Weekly checks*)
- ☐ Excessive wear in suspension or steering components (Chapters 1 and 10)
- ☐ Incorrect front wheel alignment (Chapter 10)
- ☐ Accident damage to steering or suspension components (Chapter 1)

Wheel wobble and vibration

- ☐ Front roadwheels out of balance (vibration felt mainly through the steering wheel) (Chapters 1 and 10)
- ☐ Rear roadwheels out of balance (vibration felt throughout the vehicle) (Chapters 1 and 10)
- ☐ Roadwheels damaged or distorted (Chapters 1 and 10)
- ☐ Faulty or damaged tyre (*Weekly checks*)
- ☐ Worn steering or suspension joints, bushes or components (Chapters 1 and 10)
- ☐ Wheel bolts loose (Chapters 1 and 10)

Excessive pitching and/or rolling around corners, or during braking

- ☐ Defective shock absorbers (Chapters 1 and 10)
- ☐ Broken or weak spring and/or suspension component (Chapters 1 and 10)
- ☐ Worn or damaged anti-roll bar or mountings (Chapter 10)

Wandering or general instability

- ☐ Incorrect front wheel alignment (Chapter 10)
- ☐ Worn steering or suspension joints, bushes or components (Chapters 1 and 10)
- ☐ Roadwheels out of balance (Chapters 1 and 10)
- ☐ Faulty or damaged tyre (*Weekly checks*)
- ☐ Wheel bolts loose (Chapters 1 and 10)
- ☐ Defective shock absorbers (Chapters 1 and 10)
- ☐ Dynamic stability system fault (Chapter 10)

Excessively-stiff steering

- ☐ Lack of steering gear lubricant (Chapter 10)
- ☐ Seized track rod end balljoint or suspension balljoint (Chapters 1 and 10)
- ☐ Broken or incorrectly-adjusted drivebelt – power steering (Chapter 1)
- ☐ Incorrect front wheel alignment (Chapter 10)
- ☐ Steering rack or column bent or damaged (Chapter 10)

Excessive play in steering

- ☐ Worn steering column intermediate shaft universal joint (Chapter 10)
- ☐ Worn steering track rod end balljoints (Chapters 1 and 10)
- ☐ Worn rack-and-pinion steering gear (Chapter 10)
- ☐ Worn steering or suspension joints, bushes or components (Chapters 1 and 10)

Suspension and steering (continued)

Lack of power assistance

- ☐ Broken or incorrectly-adjusted auxiliary drivebelt (Chapter 1)
- ☐ Incorrect power steering fluid level (*Weekly checks*)
- ☐ Restriction in power steering fluid hoses (Chapter 1)
- ☐ Faulty power steering pump (Chapter 10)
- ☐ Faulty rack-and-pinion steering gear (Chapter 10)

Tyre wear excessive

Tyres worn on inside or outside edges

- ☐ Tyres under-inflated (wear on both edges) (*Weekly checks*)
- ☐ Incorrect camber or castor angles (wear on one edge only) (Chapter 10)
- ☐ Worn steering or suspension joints, bushes or components (Chapters 1 and 10)
- ☐ Excessively-hard cornering.
- ☐ Accident damage.

Tyre treads exhibit feathered edges

- ☐ Incorrect toe setting (Chapter 10)

Tyres worn in centre of tread

- ☐ Tyres over-inflated (*Weekly checks*)

Tyres worn on inside and outside edges

- ☐ Tyres under-inflated (*Weekly checks*)

Tyres worn unevenly

- ☐ Tyres/wheels out of balance (Chapter 1)
- ☐ Excessive wheel or tyre run-out (Chapter 1)
- ☐ Worn shock absorbers (Chapters 1 and 10)
- ☐ Faulty tyre (*Weekly checks*)

Electrical system

Note: *For problems associated with the starting system, refer to the faults listed under 'Engine' earlier in this Section.*

Battery will only hold a charge for a few days

- ☐ Battery defective internally (Chapter 5A)
- ☐ Battery terminal connections loose or corroded (*Weekly checks*)
- ☐ Auxiliary drivebelt worn or incorrectly adjusted (Chapter 1)
- ☐ Alternator not charging at correct output (Chapter 5A)
- ☐ Alternator or voltage regulator faulty (Chapter 5A)
- ☐ Short-circuit causing continual battery drain (Chapters 5A and 12)

Ignition/no-charge warning light remains illuminated with engine running

- ☐ Auxiliary drivebelt broken, worn, or incorrectly adjusted (Chapter 1)
- ☐ Alternator brushes worn, sticking, or dirty (Chapter 5A)
- ☐ Alternator brush springs weak or broken (Chapter 5A)
- ☐ Internal fault in alternator or voltage regulator (Chapter 5A)
- ☐ Broken, disconnected, or loose wiring in charging circuit (Chapter 5A)

Ignition/no-charge warning light fails to come on

- ☐ Warning light bulb blown (Chapter 12)
- ☐ Broken, disconnected, or loose wiring in warning light circuit (Chapter 12)
- ☐ Alternator faulty (Chapter 5A)

Lights inoperative

- ☐ Bulb blown (Chapter 12)
- ☐ Corrosion of bulb or bulbholder contacts (Chapter 12)
- ☐ Blown fuse (Chapter 12)
- ☐ Faulty relay (Chapter 12)
- ☐ Broken, loose, or disconnected wiring (Chapter 12)
- ☐ Faulty switch (Chapter 12)

Instrument readings inaccurate or erratic

Instrument readings increase with engine speed

- ☐ Faulty voltage regulator (Chapter 12)

Fuel or temperature gauges give no reading

- ☐ Faulty gauge sender unit (Chapters 3 and 4)
- ☐ Wiring open-circuit (Chapter 12)
- ☐ Faulty gauge (Chapter 12)

Fuel or temperature gauges give continuous maximum reading

- ☐ Faulty gauge sender unit (Chapters 3 and 4)
- ☐ Wiring short-circuit (Chapter 12)
- ☐ Faulty gauge (Chapter 12)

Horn inoperative, or unsatisfactory in operation

Horn operates all the time

- ☐ Horn push either earthed or stuck down (Chapter 12)
- ☐ Horn cable-to-horn push earthed (Chapter 12)

Horn fails to operate

- ☐ Blown fuse (Chapter 12)
- ☐ Cable or cable connections loose, broken or disconnected (Chapter 12)
- ☐ Faulty horn (Chapter 12)

Horn emits intermittent or unsatisfactory sound

- ☐ Cable connections loose (Chapter 12)
- ☐ Horn mountings loose (Chapter 12)
- ☐ Faulty horn (Chapter 12)

Windscreen wipers inoperative, or unsatisfactory in operation

Wipers fail to operate, or operate very slowly

- ☐ Wiper blades stuck to screen, or linkage seized or binding (Chapters 1 and 12)
- ☐ Blown fuse (Chapter 12)
- ☐ Cable or cable connections loose, broken or disconnected (Chapter 12)
- ☐ Faulty wiper motor (Chapter 12)

Wiper blades sweep over too large or too small an area of the glass

- ☐ Wiper arms incorrectly positioned on spindles (Chapter 1)
- ☐ Excessive wear of wiper linkage (Chapter 12)
- ☐ Wiper motor or linkage mountings loose or insecure (Chapter 12)

Wiper blades fail to clean the glass effectively

- ☐ Wiper blade rubbers worn or perished (*Weekly checks*)
- ☐ Wiper arm tension springs broken, or arm pivots seized (Chapter 12)
- ☐ Insufficient windscreen washer additive to adequately remove road film (*Weekly checks*)

Electrical system (continued)

Windscreen washers inoperative, or unsatisfactory in operation

One or more washer jets inoperative

- ☐ Blocked washer jet (Chapter 1)
- ☐ Disconnected, kinked or restricted fluid hose (Chapter 12)
- ☐ Insufficient fluid in washer reservoir (*Weekly checks*)

Washer pump fails to operate

- ☐ Broken or disconnected wiring or connections (Chapter 12)
- ☐ Blown fuse (Chapter 12)
- ☐ Faulty washer switch (Chapter 12)
- ☐ Faulty washer pump (Chapter 12)

Washer pump runs for some time before fluid is emitted from jets

- ☐ Faulty one-way valve in fluid supply hose (Chapter 12)

Electric windows inoperative, or unsatisfactory in operation

Window glass will only move in one direction

- ☐ Faulty switch (Chapter 12)

Window glass slow to move

- ☐ Regulator seized or damaged, or in need of lubrication (Chapter 11)
- ☐ Door internal components or trim fouling regulator (Chapter 11)
- ☐ Faulty motor (Chapter 11)

Window glass fails to move

- ☐ Blown fuse (Chapter 12)
- ☐ Faulty relay (Chapter 12)
- ☐ Broken or disconnected wiring or connections (Chapter 12)
- ☐ Faulty motor (Chapter 11)

Central locking system inoperative, or unsatisfactory in operation

Complete system failure

- ☐ Blown fuse (Chapter 12)
- ☐ Faulty control unit (Chapter 12)
- ☐ Broken or disconnected wiring or connections (Chapter 12)
- ☐ Faulty motor (Chapter 11)

Latch locks but will not unlock, or unlocks but will not lock

- ☐ Faulty master switch (Chapter 12)
- ☐ Broken or disconnected latch operating rods or levers (Chapter 11)
- ☐ Faulty control unit (Chapter 12)
- ☐ Faulty motor (Chapter 11)

One solenoid/motor fails to operate

- ☐ Broken or disconnected wiring or connections (Chapter 12)
- ☐ Faulty operating assembly (Chapter 11)
- ☐ Broken, binding or disconnected latch operating rods or levers (Chapter 11)
- ☐ Fault in door latch (Chapter 11)

Note: *References throughout this index are in the form - "Chapter number" • "Page number"*

M

N

O

P

R

S

T

U

V

W

Preserving Our Motoring Heritage

<
The Model J Duesenberg Derham Tourster. Only eight of these magnificent cars were ever built – this is the only example to be found outside the United States of America

Almost every car you've ever loved, loathed or desired is gathered under one roof at the Haynes Motor Museum. Over 300 immaculately presented cars and motorbikes represent every aspect of our motoring heritage, from elegant reminders of bygone days, such as the superb Model J Duesenberg to curiosities like the bug-eyed BMW Isetta. There are also many old friends and flames. Perhaps you remember the 1959 Ford Popular that you did your courting in? The magnificent 'Red Collection' is a spectacle of classic sports cars including AC, Alfa Romeo, Austin Healey, Ferrari, Lamborghini, Maserati, MG, Riley, Porsche and Triumph.

A Perfect Day Out

Each and every vehicle at the Haynes Motor Museum has played its part in the history and culture of Motoring. Today, they make a wonderful spectacle and a great day out for all the family. Bring the kids, bring Mum and Dad, but above all bring your camera to capture those golden memories for ever. You will also find an impressive array of motoring memorabilia, a comfortable 70 seat video cinema and one of the most extensive transport book shops in Britain. The Pit Stop Cafe serves everything from a cup of tea to wholesome, home-made meals or, if you prefer, you can enjoy the large picnic area nestled in the beautiful rural surroundings of Somerset.

>
John Haynes O.B.E., Founder and Chairman of the museum at the wheel of a Haynes Light 12.

<
Graham Hill's Lola Cosworth Formula 1 car next to a 1934 Riley Sports.

MOTOR MUSEUM
A359 CASTLE CARY
A303 ANDOVER
A303 EXETER TO M5 J 25 TAUNTON
SPARKFORD
A359 YEOVIL
HAYNES PUBLISHING
OLD A303
NOT TO SCALE

The Museum is situated on the A359 Yeovil to Frome road at Sparkford, just off the A303 in Somerset. It is about 40 miles south of Bristol, and 25 minutes drive from the M5 intersection at Taunton.

Open 9.30am - 5.30pm (10.00am - 4.00pm Winter) 7 days a week, *except Christmas Day, Boxing Day and New Years Day*

Special rates available for schools, coach parties and outings Charitable Trust No. 292048